Berthas

For WANT of a

Martine ~~Re~~
Renault
Animals plus Car

AF326883

licis

ram 720

Alfred Jason

Time Cannon ? Ball

500 Loose Ret

Relic a skeletal
here's been a death
Old soldiers never die
Friends.
Worn out people

a Whorehead.

A LIFE IN INK

Ralph STEADman

CHRONICLE CHROMA

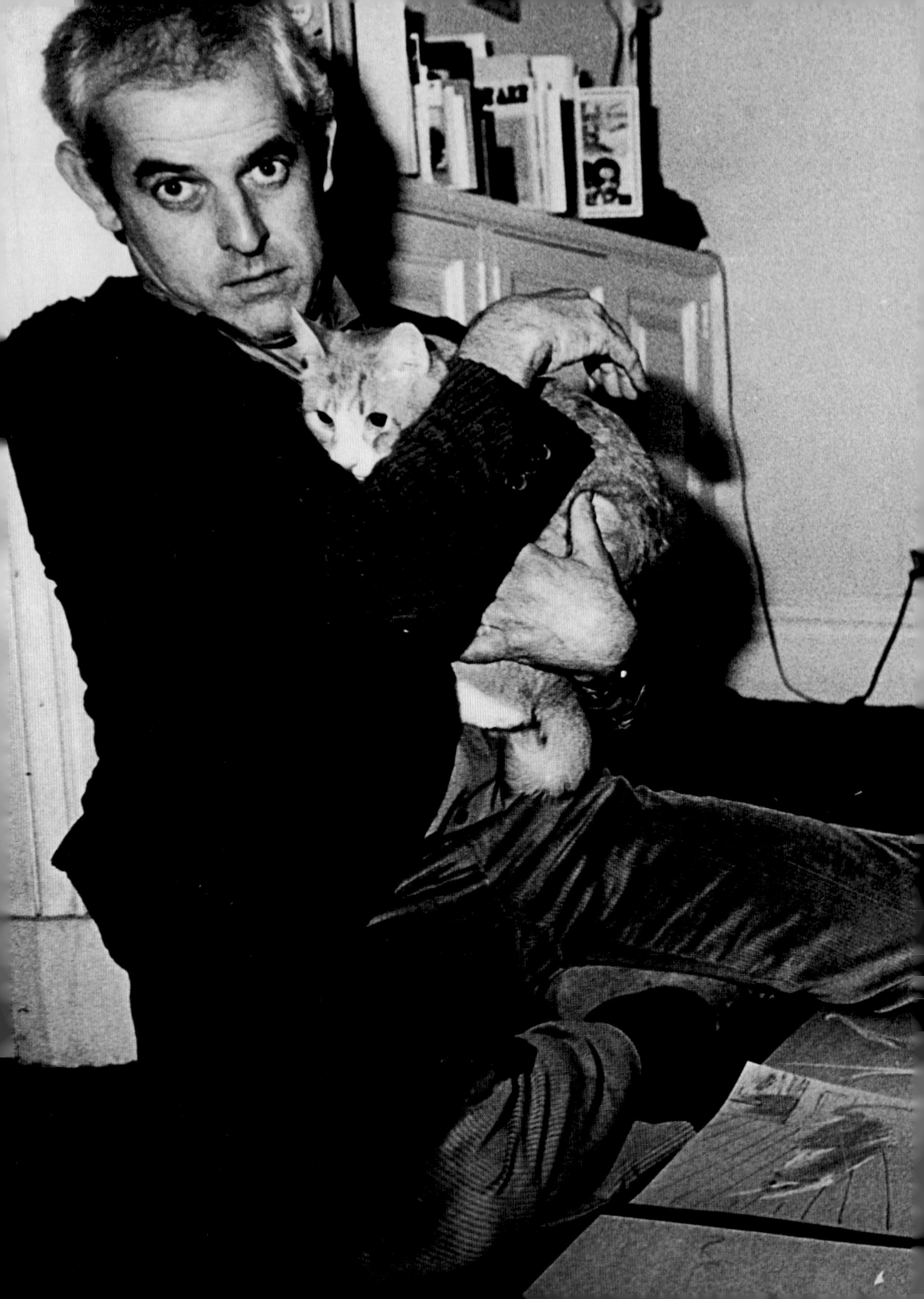

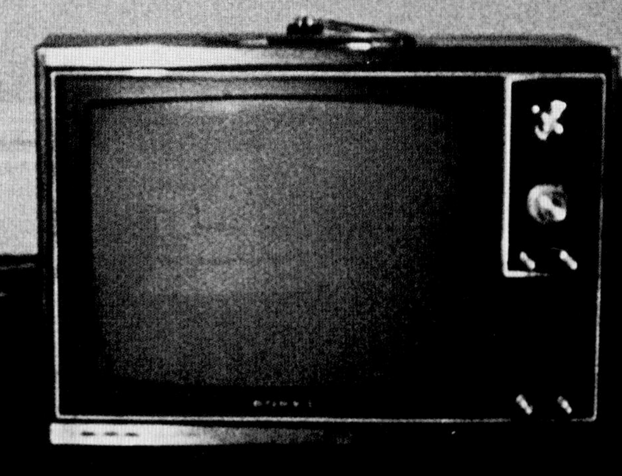

L'AURORE
LITTÉRAIRE·ARTISTIQUE·SOCIALE
JOURNAL QUOTIDIEN A 5 CENTIMES

Ralph Steadman's Life In Ink

Maniacal, twisted, insane.

Many adjectives have been used to describe the art of the artist Ralph Idris Steadman. However, words such as these barely scratch the surface and often fail to characterize the work on a deeper level. Across a career now spanning more than six decades, Ralph's work has sought to both expose the depravity of our society and fight the powers that be. To be sure, Ralph has never shied away from controversy or provocation. In fact, it has been his life's calling to attempt to change our world for the better, using his mighty pen and brush as his weapons of choice.

The images featured in this book cover a broad range of Steadman's prolific work—from some of his earliest sketches, to his legendary *Gonzo* collaborations with the writer Hunter S. Thompson, to his acerbic contemporary portraits that continue to satirize and skewer deserving pundits and politicians of our day. No one is spared here, and if you find yourself on the receiving end of Ralph's pen, you will be revealed to all, just as Ralph sees you.

His drawings can indeed seem angry. They frequently combine aggressively bold strokes and dramatic signature ink splatter. And yet, to the seasoned Steadman observer, they are always in favor of humanity, whether ironic or sincere, and often implore faint traces of sweetness. The intensity is palpable when you are in front of an original Steadman, and it's a rare treat to view the work in person.

Many assume these types of drawings must come from some sort of madman. On the contrary, Ralph embodies the courteous manner of an English gentleman. In contrast to his fearless, audacious, and sometimes disturbing work, Ralph is the epitome of sensitivity, and it's with that sensitivity that he honed a great ability to observe and respond via his drawings. Somehow, he managed to retain a great sense of humor and an abundance of kindness.

His home and studio lie in the countryside of Kent in South East England. This idyllic setting includes gentle hills and valleys less than a two-hour drive from busy London. Maidstone is the town Ralph has called home since 1980, well after his career as an internationally recognized artist flourished. Ralph and his wife, Anna, restored their historic British home. Together, they have built a life with their daughter, Sadie, and her family. The serenity of this green location is interrupted often by wild animals wandering at random throughout the large garden, two growing grandsons, and the occasional guest. Old friends, new friends, random journalists writing stories about Ralph, other creative types seeking counsel, and the occasional Hollywood actor or celebrity are all part of a stream of visitors that arrive for their appointments.

In addition to a thriving career and recognition any artist would dare to hope for, Ralph has enjoyed a more quiet life at the same time. Unlike a few of his out-of-control, up-all-night counterparts, Ralph's schedule is surprisingly quite normal. He puts serious effort down on paper by day, and then sets it aside in the evenings, unless he is on a deadline for an assignment.

In an outbuilding dating back hundreds of years, Ralph created his studio within a structure of stone and rough-hewn timber. The vintage wood floors cover a mechanical pit that used to service the previous owner's grand motorcar. One might agree Ralph's studio still feels

Previous Spread: Ralph and Tishy, the cat, at home, ca. 1963.
*Opposite: Press shot for **Alice in Wonderland**, ca. 1967. The representation of Alice is based on Ralph's eldest daughter, Suzannah.*

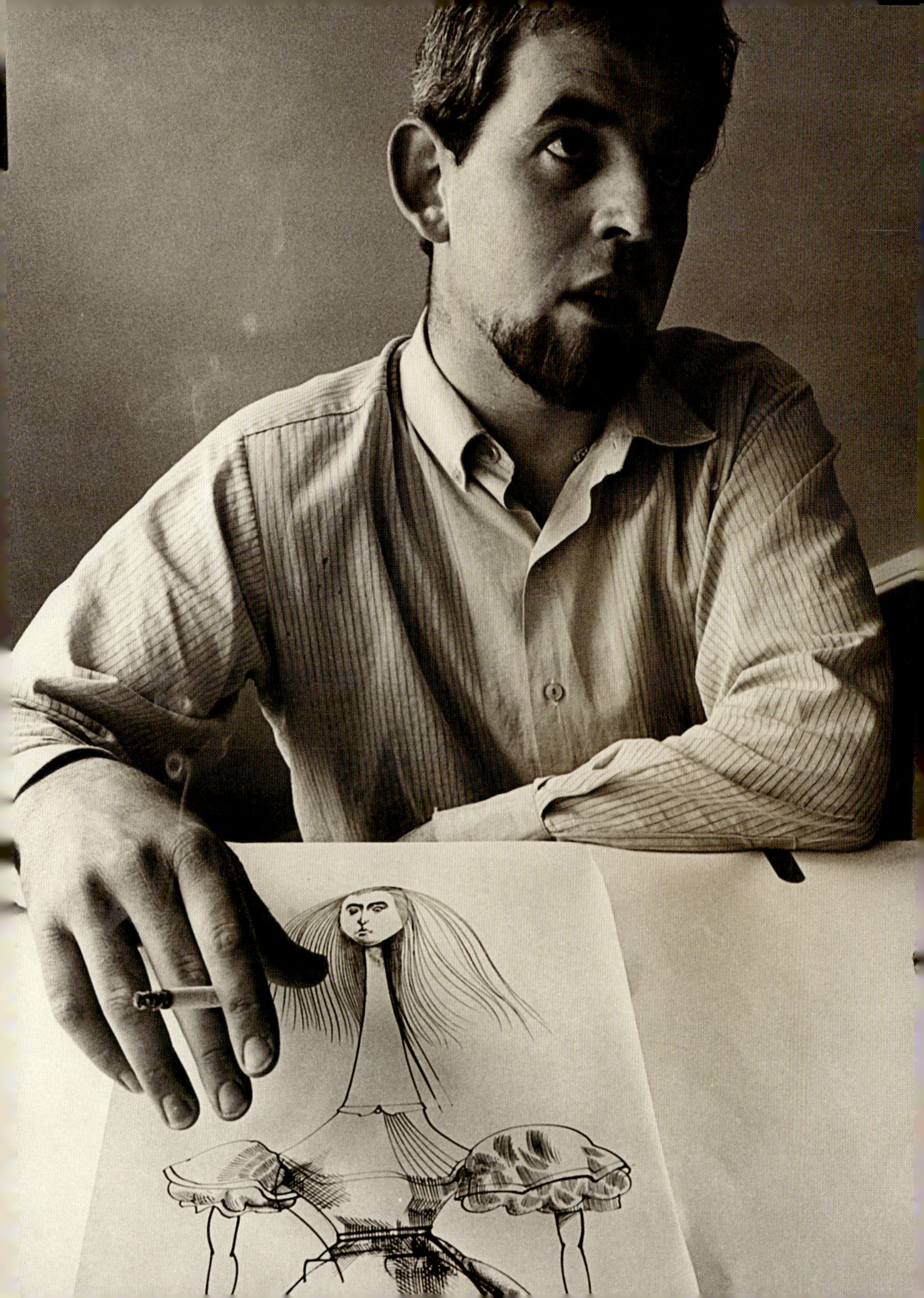

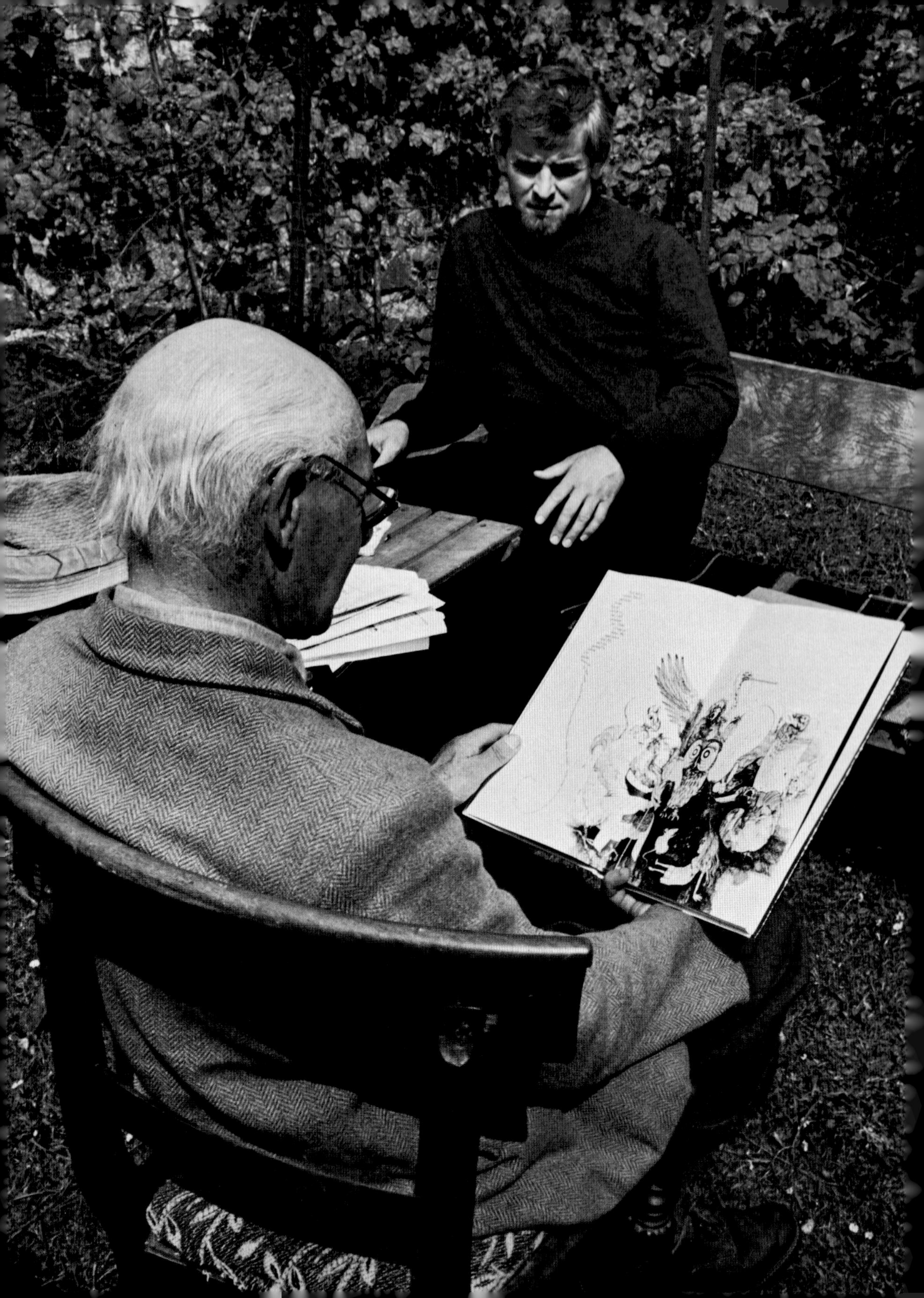

a bit like a mechanic's workshop. It is now a quiet place for Ralph to both tinker and invent. Most new creations take place on paper, but scattered throughout the studio are tables filled with decades of his sculptures, rescued wooden typefaces, model wooden airplanes built by hand, shelves of books for reference and inspiration, and the various tools necessary for his creations.

Ralph's drawing table greets visitors upon entry. Most weekdays, one can find Ralph working away, while the animals can be seen out the window romping in the garden. From this creative command post, Ralph developed a workman-like routine that allows him to create without interruption. The heavy drawing table is covered with the tools of a working artist. His loyal inkpots stand at the ready on his desktop. Ink has always been Ralph's favorite medium; its many colors splatter the edges of the walls and floors. Decades of layers of dried ink seem to create their own topography. The occasional bright color, recently added and still quite vibrant, is found on the "blotter sheets" that lie below, absorbing any unused droplets.

Starting a day with a blank sheet of paper often strikes the worst of anguish and fear into many a writer and artist. Ralph bravely takes this step just as consistently as he swims in his pool on brisk Kent mornings. He begins. He pushes forth, and, after decades, this consistency has paid great dividends. Ralph's razor-sharp wit and intellect emerge on a drawing board daily.

At age eighty-four, Ralph is at the top of his craft. He can play his brushes, pens, and atomizer much like a virtuoso orchestral musician plays an instrument. His hands glide across every fresh sheet of paper with great expertise. Not yet knowing where he's going or where he'll end up, he takes a leap into the unknown with each new drawing, always eager to venture forth—and jump in. We, his legion of fans, await patiently: the lucky recipients of his next creation.

Steve Crist
Los Angeles, California
July 22, 2020

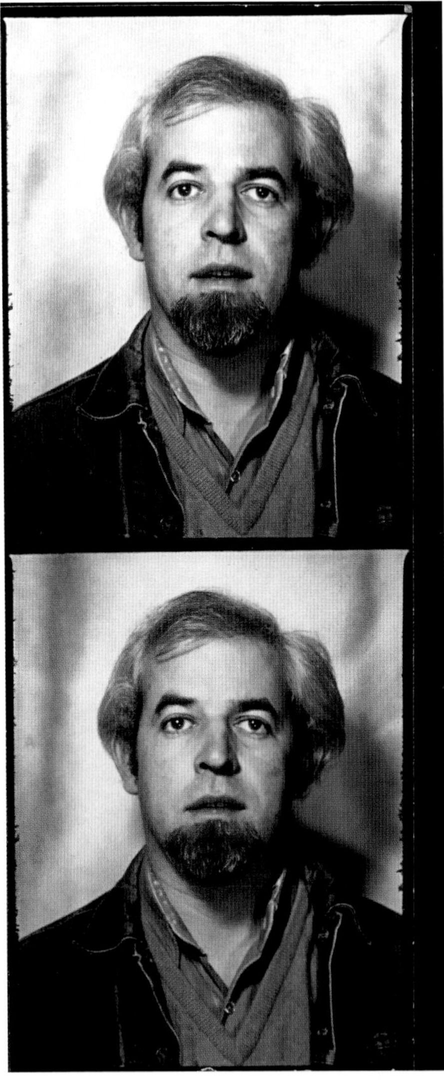

*Opposite: Ralph travelled to H.M. Bateman's home in the West Country to show him his **Alice in Wonderland**. It was a very proud moment for Ralph. Bateman enjoyed the interpretation immensely. **Above**: Photo booth shots of Ralph.*

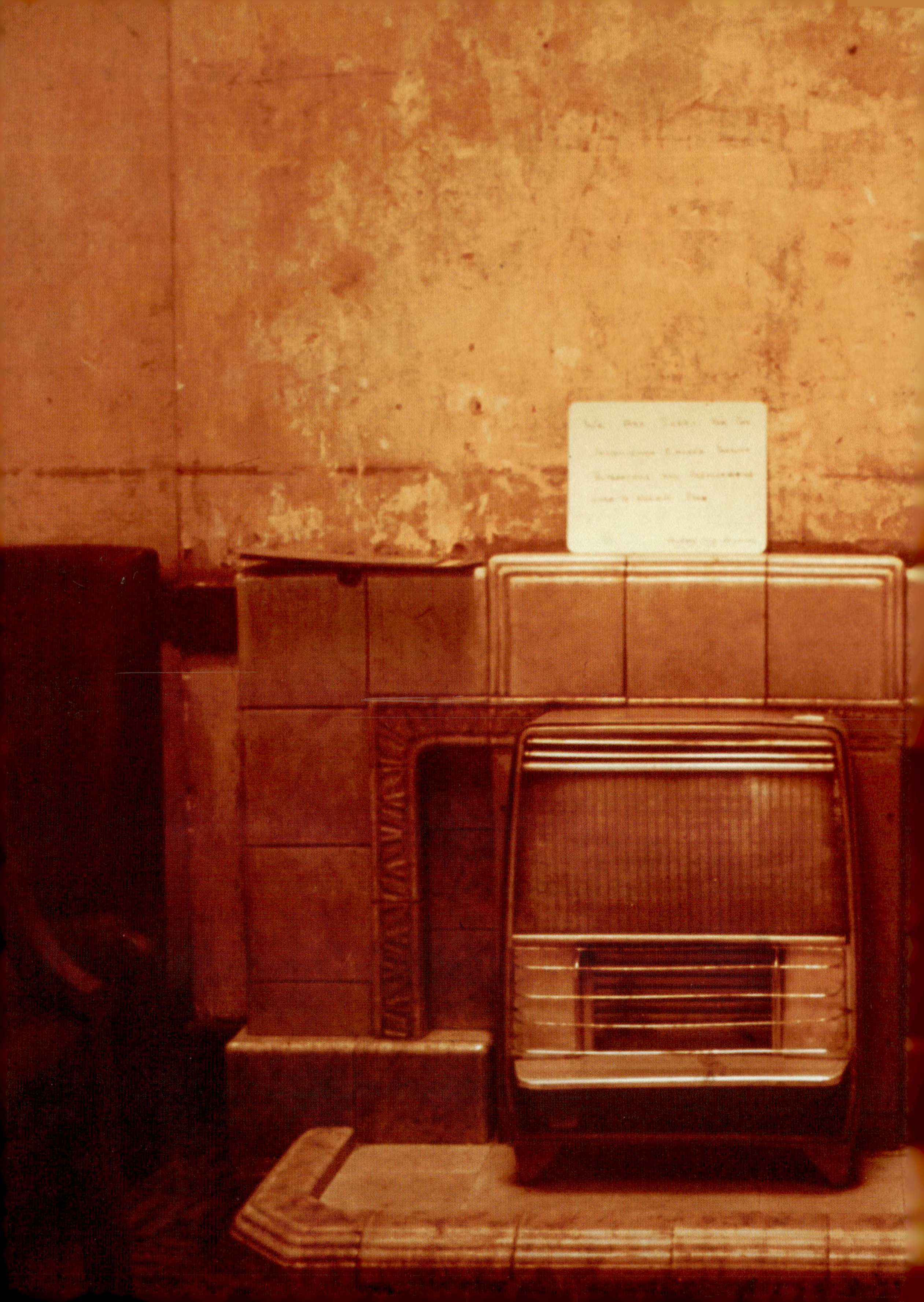

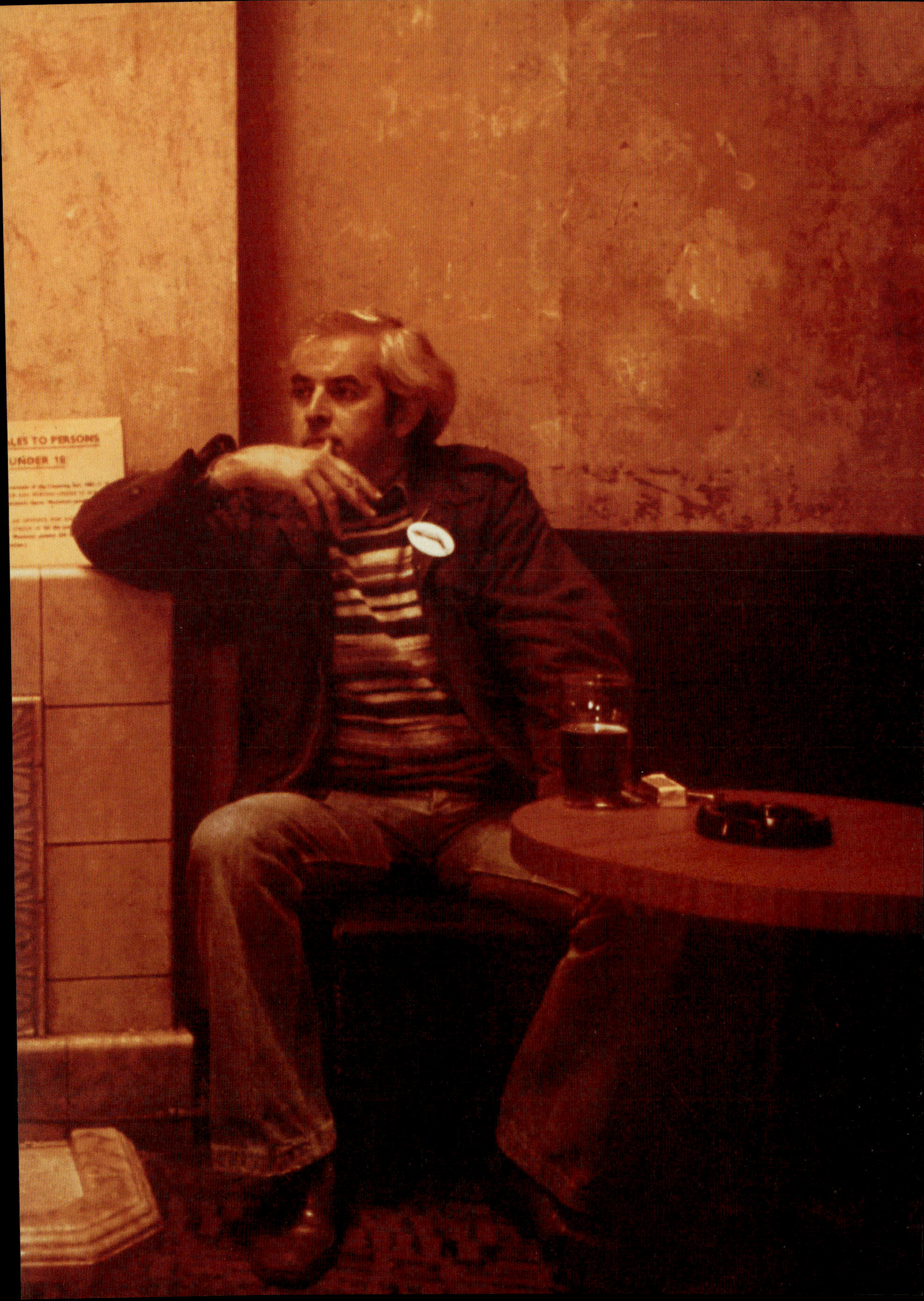

...LES TO PERSONS
UNDER 18

I was born in Wallasey, Liverpool, in 1936. My mother, Gwendoline, was a homemaker of Welsh descent. My father, Lionel, was what they call a commercial traveler. He traveled by car and sold women's coats and costumes, and ladies knickers, to shops and stores. My father loved tinkering and making things, and I surely inherited many of those traits from him.

One of my earliest memories as a child in Liverpool was hearing the air-raid sirens and being carried by my mother into what they called an Anderson shelter during the war with Germany. At night the sirens would begin to wail, and everyone would go into hiding. The war was terrible, and it affected everyone we knew. Like many other families, the bombings during the war caused my family to flee, and we relocated to Abergele, North Wales.

We had moved to Wales, and the headmaster at my grammar school in Abergele was a hideous monster of a man that carried a cane. He surely shouldn't have been working with children. From him I quickly learned to loathe authority figures, especially because I was brought up to believe there was good in this world.

Generally speaking, as a child I was in constant mortal fear of authority. I tended to my studies, of course, but I really preferred to spend much of my time building things, such as model airplanes. I didn't realize it then, but I preferred to work with my hands and create things instead of doing schoolwork.

In 1952, I left school at age sixteen and started to look for work, and went through a series of odd jobs. Because I had always loved airplanes, I first found a job as an apprentice aircraft engineer for the de Havilland Aircraft Company that was based in Broughton, Chester. However, after a few months, I quickly came to hate the drudgery of factory life and quit. This was a disappointment in some ways because having such a "good job" after the war was considered valuable. Luckily, I picked up some mechanical

drawing skills in the process, but I left de Havilland and had to take a new job as a stock boy at a Woolworths store in Colwyn Bay.

Finally, in 1954 I started as a "tea boy" working for the McConnells advertising agency. That job was more hopeful and allowed me to help out on some advertising jobs. It was quickly interrupted as I was required to start my National Service. All of those steps were leading me to where I was headed, but I sure didn't know it at the time!

Yes, my compulsory military service began in late 1954, and I was assigned to the RAF—Royal Air Force—in Hope Cove, Devon. My training was for the role of a radar operator. I wouldn't say I was perfectly fit for military life, but everyone was required to help protect us from the great fear of communism. The RAF experience was serious business in terms of discipline and rules. The authority figures I so loathed were everywhere. Still, I managed to get along well with my mates, and I was allowed further training in technical drawing and drafting work, which I really enjoyed.

Indeed, it did. At that point I really took to the drawing part of things, and one day I noticed an advertisement in a newspaper that read, "You too can learn to draw and earn pounds!" That one advertisement managed to change my life, and I quickly enrolled in Percy V. Bradshaw's Press Art School via correspondence. Each week, a new lesson would arrive in the post for me to finish. While I was doing my National Service, I could take this type of class on my own time at night. That is when I started practicing all types of drawing, including life drawing and studies of people. That was a big advance for me, and it kept me busy drawing my mates in the RAF.

Also, I started to cartoon and submit my work to newspapers, such as the **Sheffield Telegraph, Leicester Mercury**, and the **Manchester Evening Chronicle**. Most of my submissions were rejected, but finally I was published in July 1956 in the **Manchester Evening Chronicle**, and that really helped me realize I could have a career in drawing.

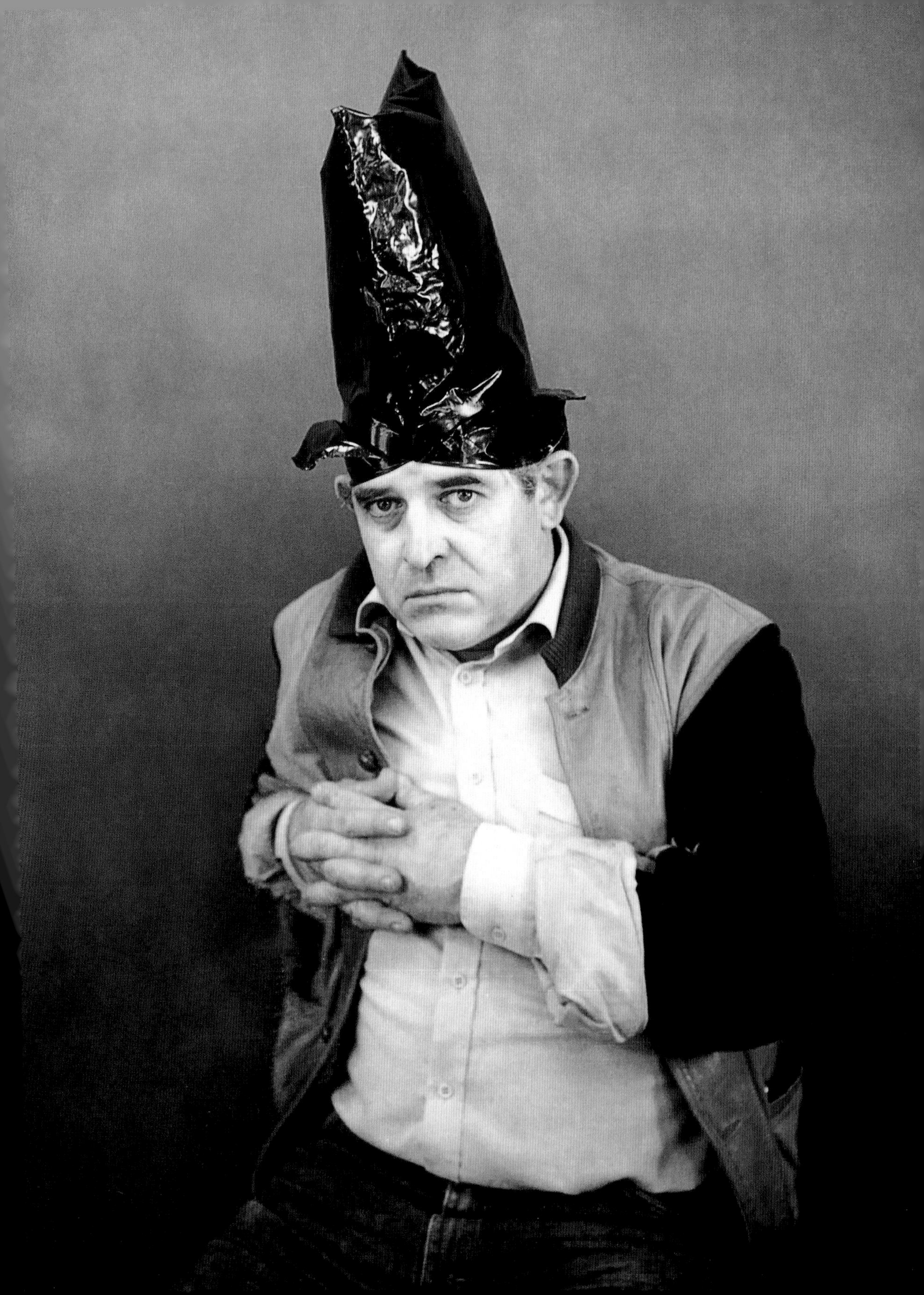

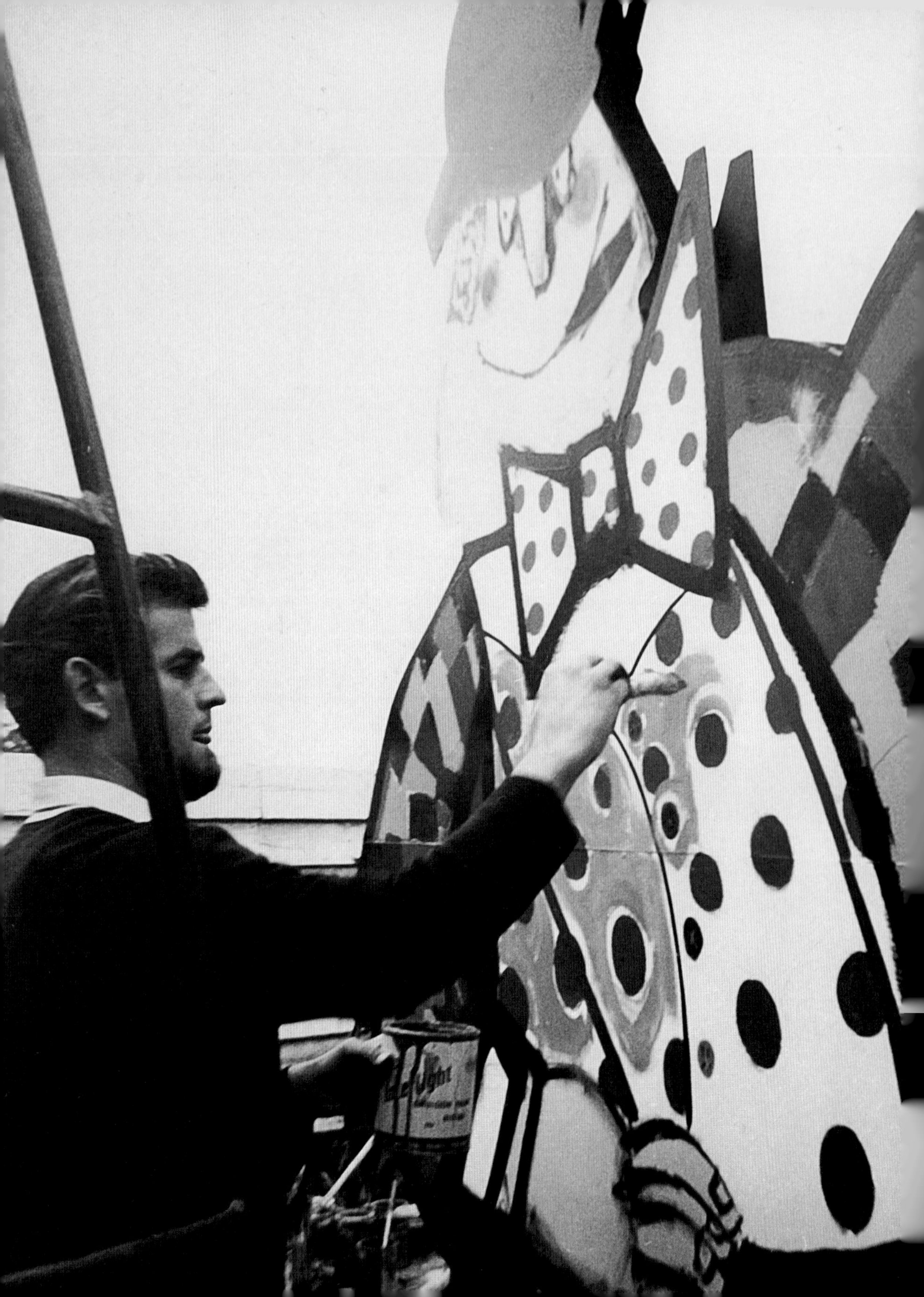

In 1956, I decided to move to London after the RAF days and look for work.

What were your early days as a working artist in London like?

I got on a job working for the Kemsley Newspapers. Kemsley owned many papers across the country, and I drew cartoons for them in the London office. Every day I was required to come up with ten ideas for jokes or cartoons that could be considered at meetings. At that point, even though I was employed as a cartoonist and things were going well, I became a bit frustrated and really wanted to do more serious and different types of drawings. It seemed like the assignments were merely to fill up the paper and much less about art.

In 1959, I enrolled as an art student at East Ham Technical College in London. I would continue to take—and eventually teach—classes there. I met a man named Leslie Richardson that became my mentor. He really encouraged my work and became a lifelong friend. I was encouraged by Leslie to study different media—literature and philosophy, art history and photography, and that really changed things for me.

During those years, I would work hard during the day at my job of cartooning; then, in the afternoons, I would take art classes or go to galleries. I became friends with the illustrator Gerald Scarfe and joined the Cartoon Club. Leslie encouraged me to take classes at the London School of Printing and Graphic Arts. This allowed me to start to work with typography and movable type, something I still use in my studio to this day.

In 1961, I had the great fortune of meeting Leslie Illingworth, who was a great cartoonist at the *Daily Mail*. When I asked him for career advice he smartly suggested that I "get the sack!" from my company job. That was the day I started to work for myself, and I haven't looked back.

*Let's move forward some years. **Still Life With Raspberry** was published back in 1969. How did that book change things for you?*

It was my first collection of works, but *Jelly Book*, a book for children, was published in 1967, as was *Alice in Wonderland*. Well, like any artist, I was proud to have my first book of collected works published, and I used it as a calling card to get more assignments. Ultimately, I took the book to America and tried to get jobs in New York. Carrying that book to New York was an important moment for me and led me to meet several people who would be instrumental in what I guess was my "big break." Although, you never know at the time it's your big break, you are just in the moment of it all being swept along and reacting to things and people as they come into your life.

But having that book under my arm gave me confidence probably, and I could say to people, "Hey look at this! This is what I think and how I say it!" It gave people something tangible to see. Wittgenstein said, "The only thing of value is the thing you cannot say." I could not have described my artwork to people, not effectively anyway, but I could show them.

As it turns out, your first trip to America was a pivotal moment in your career and life. What did you think of New York and America when you arrived?

Well, when I arrived, I really didn't know what might happen. It's very isolating to be in another country, looking for work. I went walking down Skid Row in New York City with a small Minox camera around my neck and a pocket full of dimes, so that as the homeless—god,

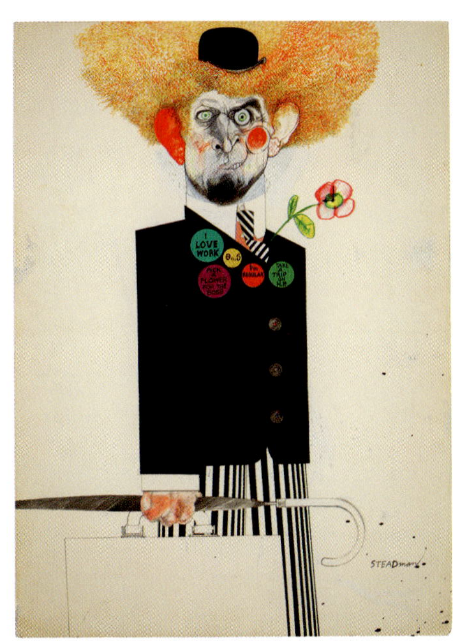

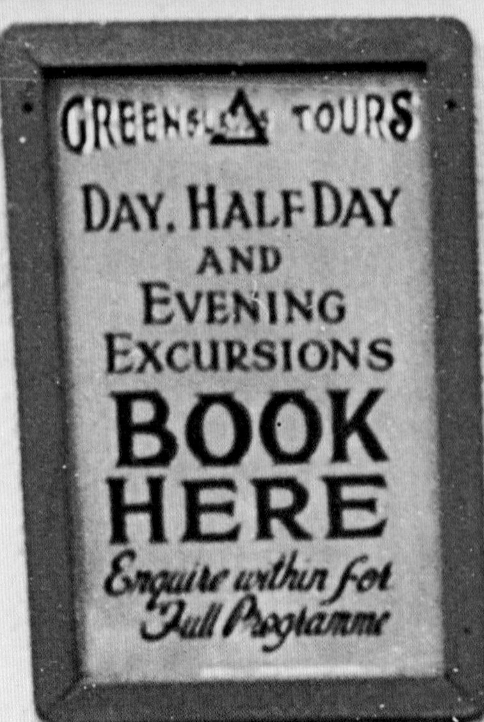

GREENSLADES TOURS
DAY, HALF DAY
AND
EVENING
EXCURSIONS
BOOK
HERE
Enquire within for
Full Programme

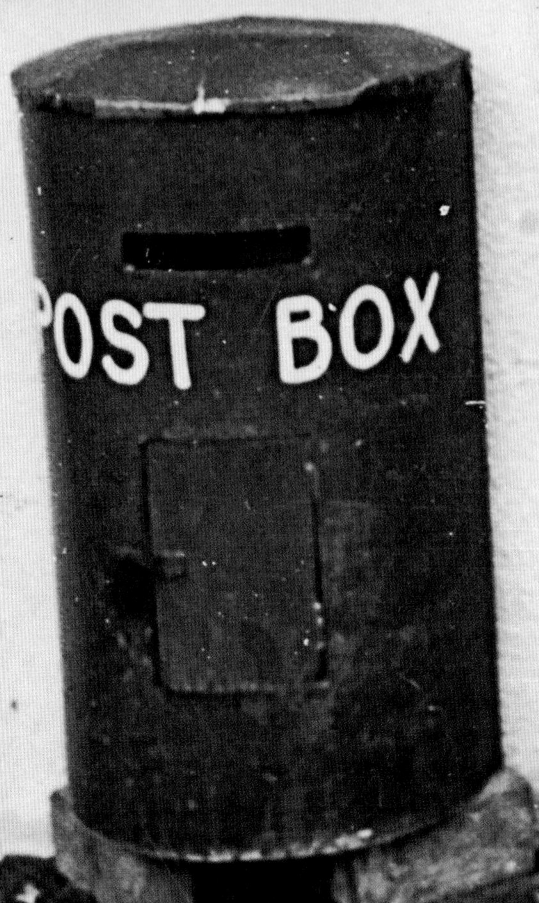

POST BOX

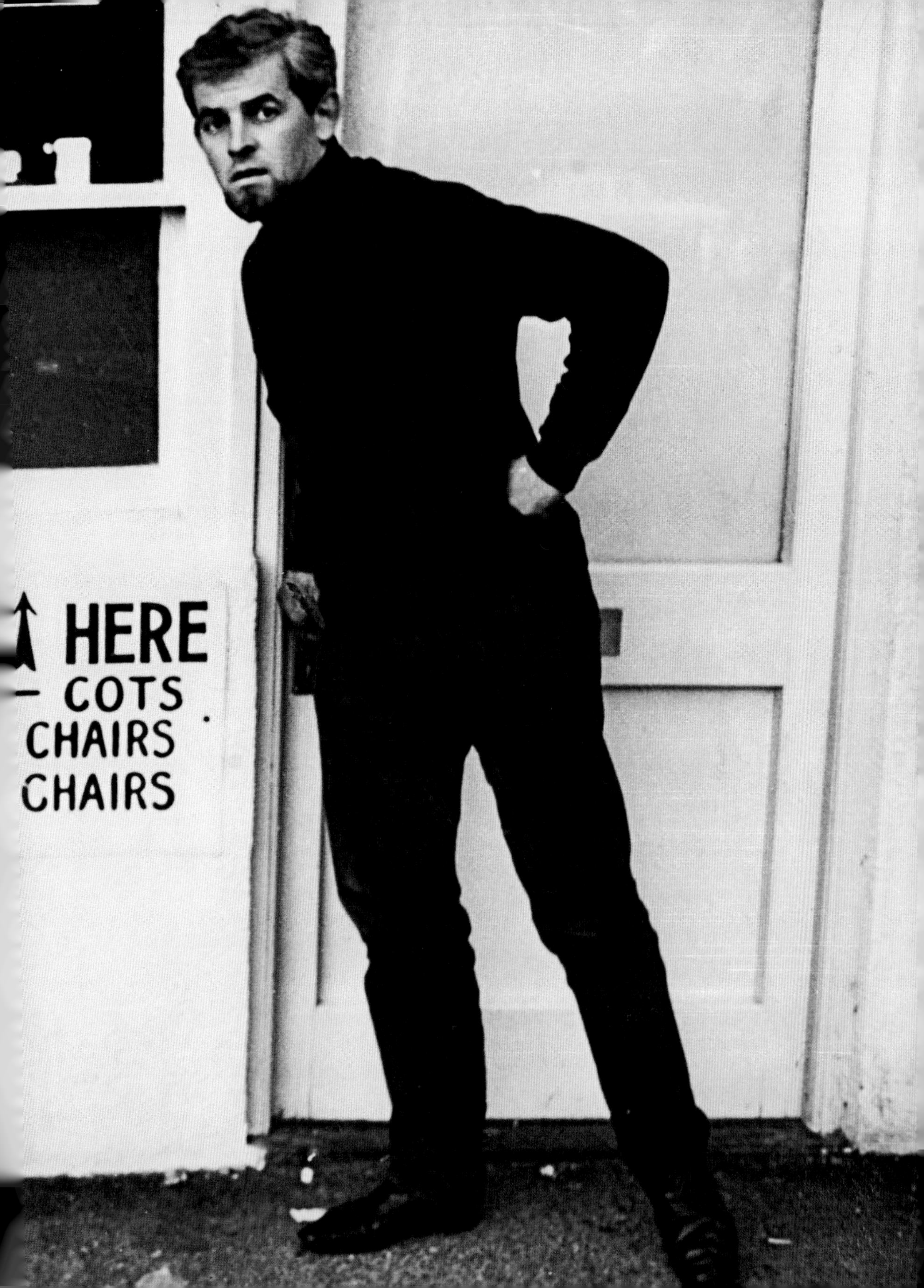

↑ HERE
— COTS
CHAIRS
CHAIRS

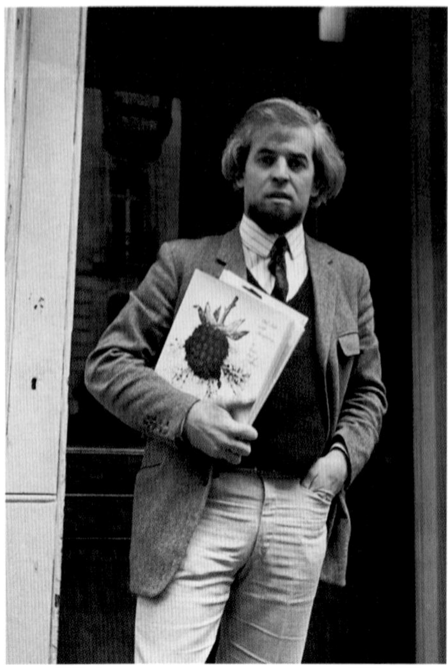

some of them were in terrible shape—approached, I could snap photos and then drop some change into their hands. One poor sod was hanging off a fire hydrant in a dreadful state, and a very prim, well-dressed lady was berating him in a shrill twang, saying, "Why don't you get up and get a jooooob?" He was just trying to stay upright, saying, "Oh leave me alone, lady!" It was very sad, and I later incorporated those photos into drawings.

Did you meet Hunter S. Thompson on that trip?

It was early 1970, when I was asked to travel on assignment to illustrate the Kentucky Derby for an article for **Scanlan's Monthly,** which was run by Warren Hinckle. It was named after a little-known Nottingham pig farmer. The magazine's goal was to get Nixon impeached and clean up the dirty kitchen of NY. A guy called JC Suarez asked me *[Ralph affects a thick New Jersey accent],* "How'd you like to go ta' Kentucky and meet a Hell's Angel who's just shaved his head?" And that was how I met the one person in all of the USA I was supposed to meet, and it nearly didn't happen. Hunter had asked for an American artist who had oddly just travelled to England to attend a cartoon conference or something, so I was a substitute. When he first saw me, he said I looked like a matted-

haired geek with string warts. I had a small goatee at the time, and that was unusual in Kentucky back then. He said *[Ralph's slips into Hunter's gruff drawl],* "They said you were weird, but not that weird."

*Did you enjoy the work for **Rolling Stone?***

Yes, Nixon especially had a great face for caricature, and I could really go to town on him. He was at least a real politician, even if he was a crooked one. I went directly in and did the drawings—I have never done "roughs." Hunter would say, "Holy God, Ralph!"

He said he had never seen anything like them, and he was as thrilled as he would ever let on, not wanting to seem too enthusiastic. I would usually have done the drawings for a project before Hunter had even started his writing. I would often send him the finished art to write from.

It was exciting because we felt like we were making a difference and trying to challenge the way things were, and the **Rolling Stone** offices were exciting to be around. We went back in about 2016 to publicize the film **For No Good Reason**, and went to see Jann Wenner at the new **Rolling Stone** offices. They seemed cleaner than I remembered.

*Your grand collaboration with Hunter, **Fear and Loathing in Las Vegas,** is considered a legendary book by many. What was the reaction to the publication back in 1971?*

Definitely the phone rang more, and I received many more assignments. But I decided early on never to expect a weekly wage, so it's always been up down, up down; it's been fairly consistent. I seem to have managed to do what I wanted to do, particularly when attempting characters like Sigmund Freud and Leonardo da Vinci. But the only way I could approach Leonardo da Vinci (because so many people have done him) was to become Leonardo da Vinci, to do some of the things he did, like paint the **Last Supper** on the bedroom wall. And I built a flying machine with a bamboo frame and tent nylon—which he wouldn't have had in his time, but he would always have had some cloth. He tried to make a pair of wings; he tried to think of it like he was going to be a bird. The notion hadn't occurred to him; although he thought that man would fly one day, he never imagined a machine like the Blériot that flew the channel—or the Wright brothers, who flew together.

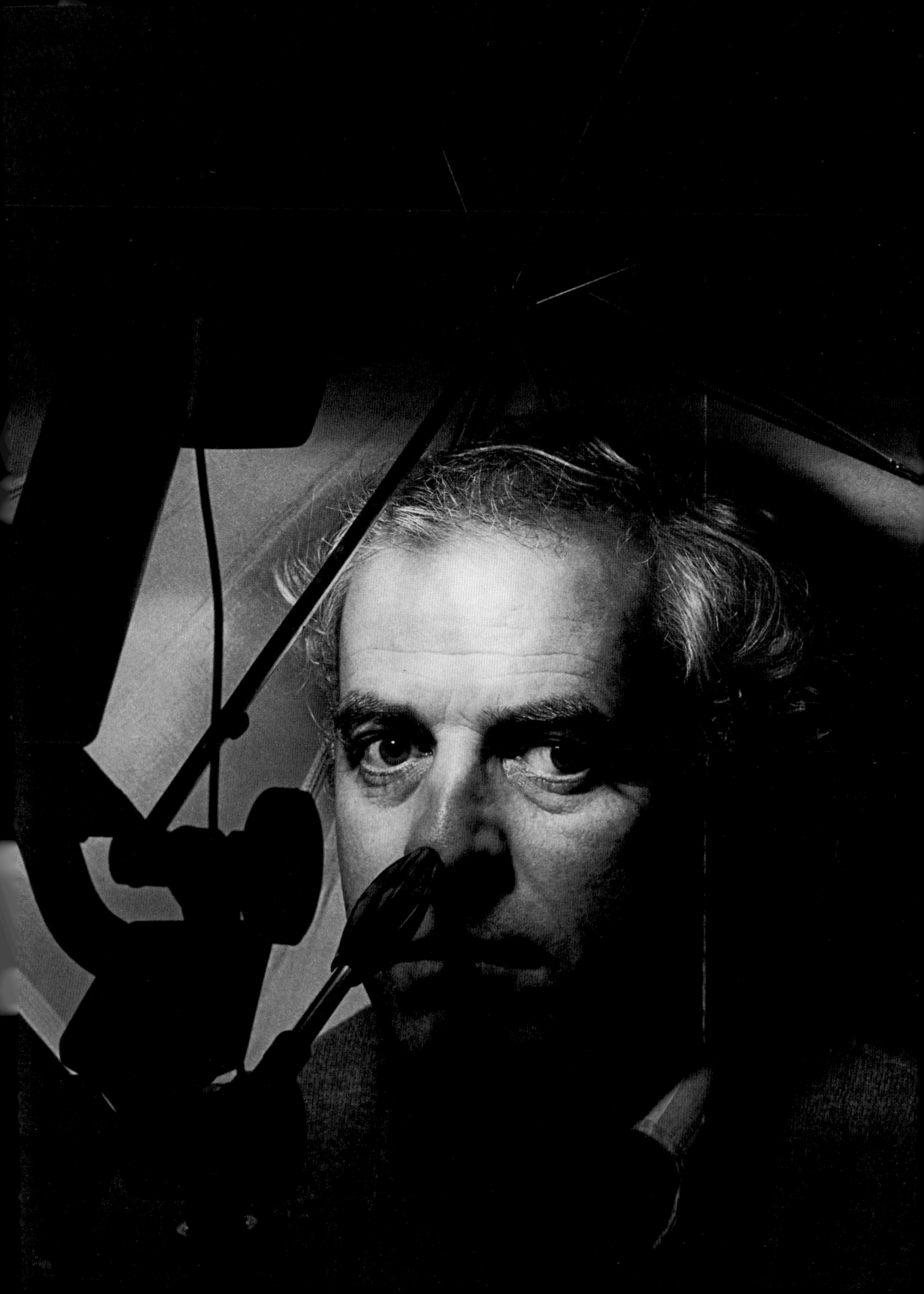

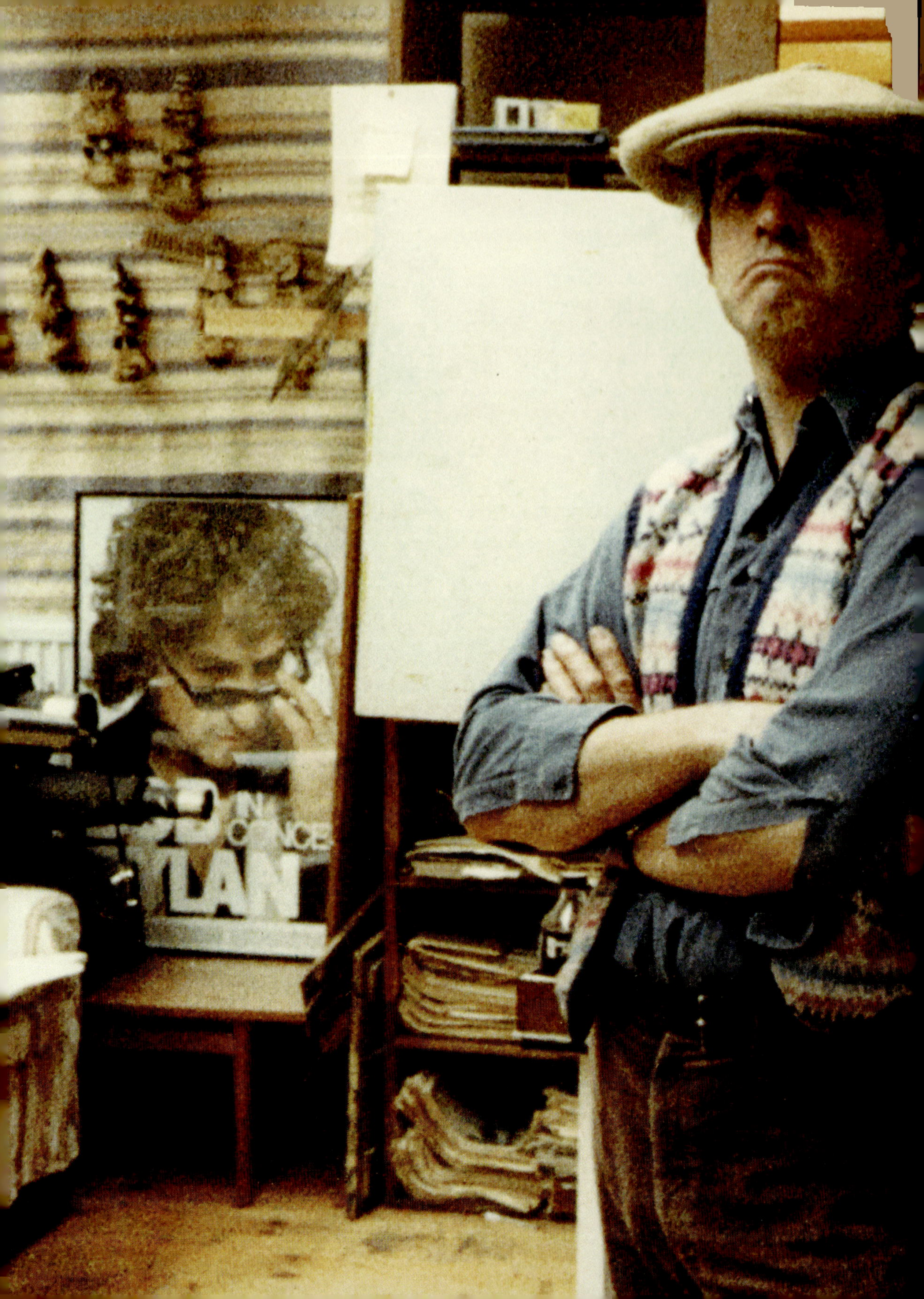
CANCE
YLAN

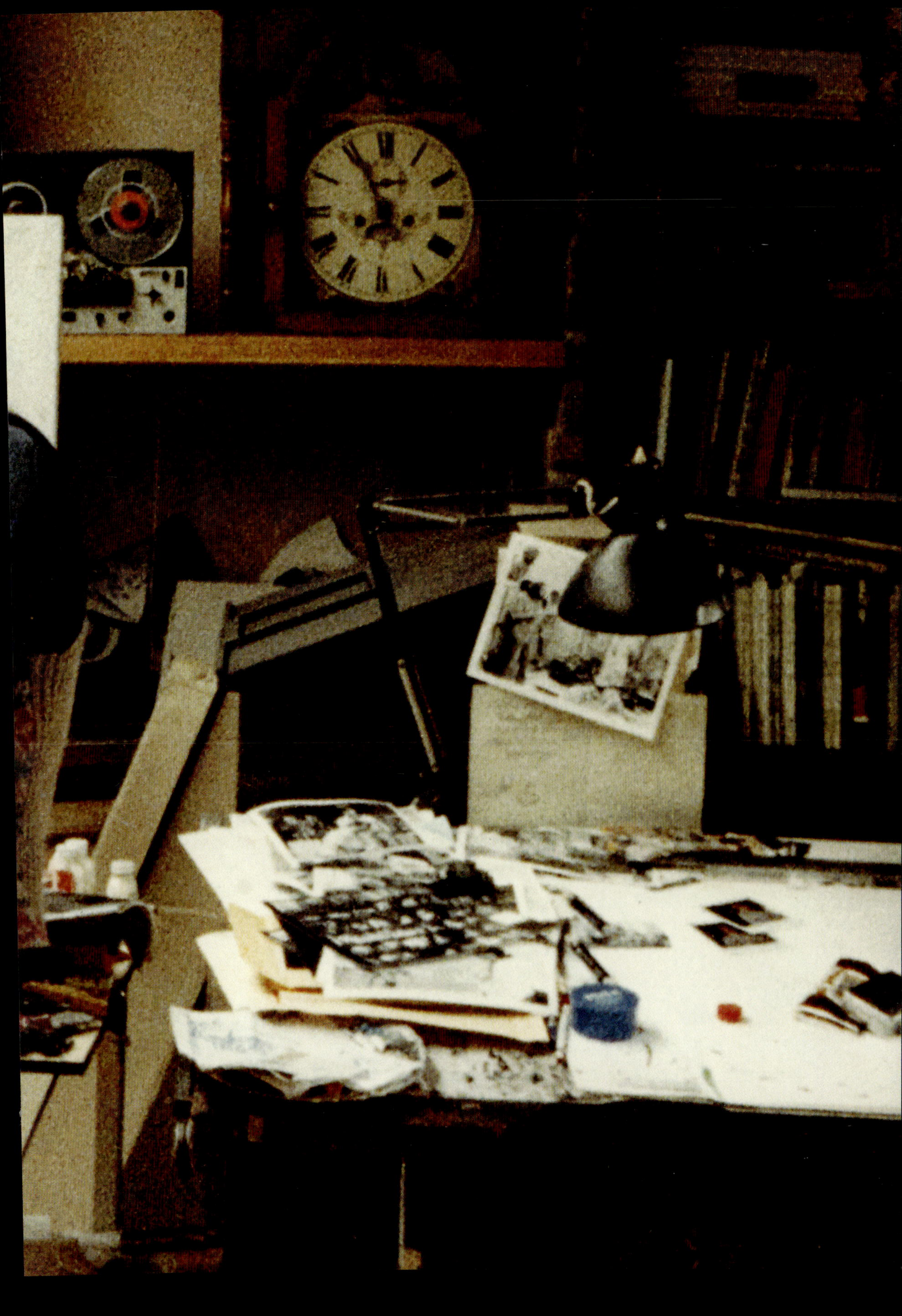

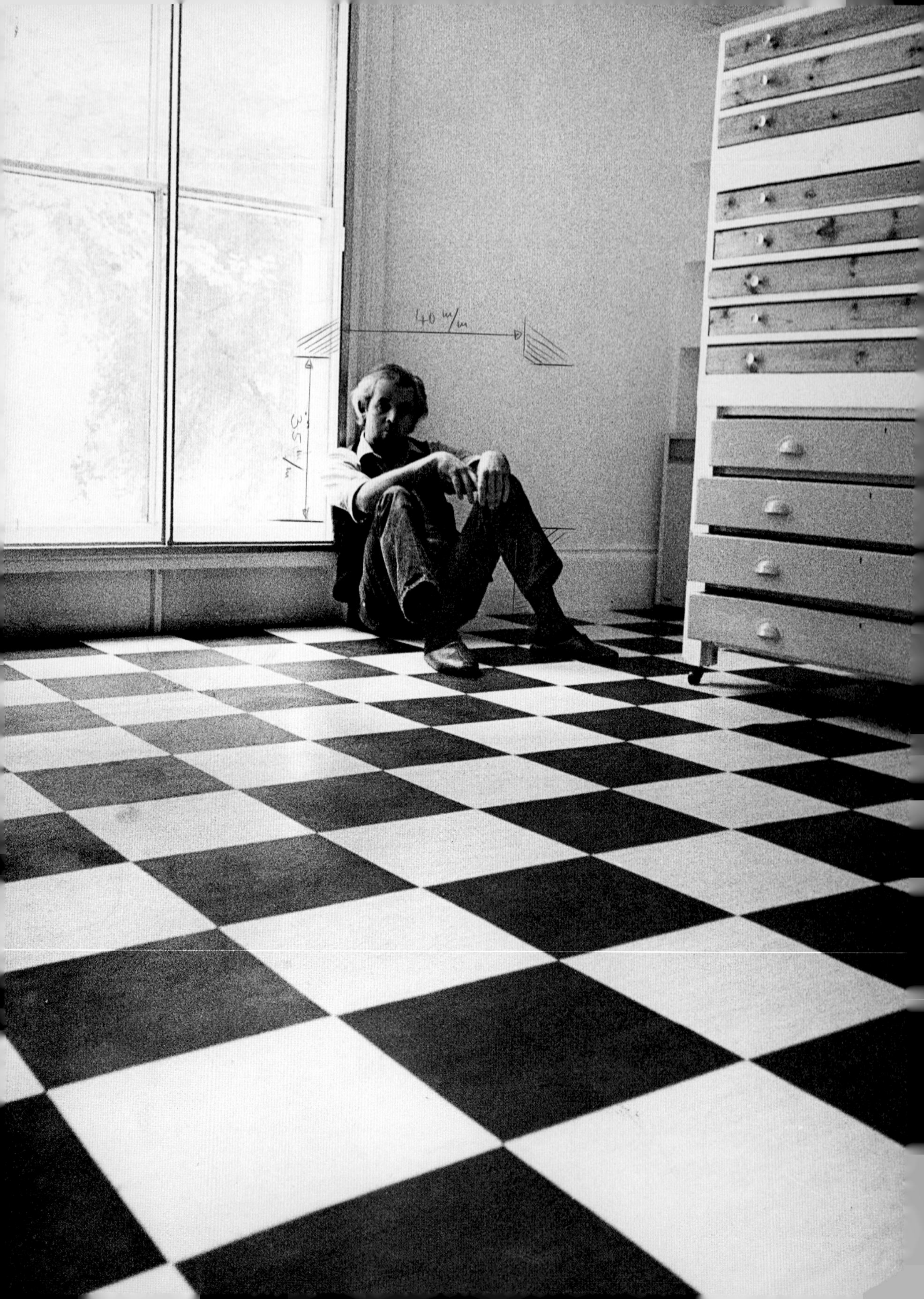

140 m/m
35 m/m

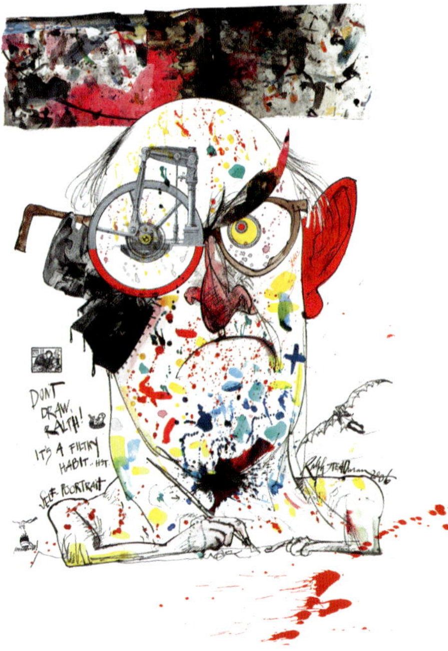

It became central to everything I did really. Of all the people in America, he was the one I should meet, had to meet. That's how important he was. And I still miss him.

But, Hunter could be very difficult, we were chalk and cheese, which I think worked in our favour. I think he wanted to write like F. Scott Fitzgerald and Ernest Hemingway; those were the people he wanted to be. But his own style was quite different, and he had a turn of phrase, which he seemed to invent all on his own, that seemed to encapsulate the very thing he was trying to describe. He was definitely intellectual with it; there was no pretension. He called a spade a spade.

He made me laugh. Life was fun. It was supposed to be fun; you were supposed to enjoy it. And yet, when he introduced me to his friends at the Pendennis Club in Kentucky, I started drawing, and they were horrified. They took my drawings of themselves and their wives

to be insults. Hunter had to step in and explain, "They're nothing; they're filthy scribblings!" The wife of one of them said, "That ain't purrty; I'm purrty, ain't I? Here, let me." And she took my pen and paper off me and started tearing into the paper. She was so angry at me. Hunter explained they don't see caricature as friendly drawings; they take it as a kind of insult.

He would sleep all day and work all night, so when I went over there, I had to work to his hours. But then, if it felt 9 to 5ish, he didn't want to know!

One of the things he said when he came here was—he a wrote postcard—and he said, "Postcard from a wrong vacation," And he said, "Don't bother us with your piffle. We'll get up when we want, thank you." He was a difficult guest, but a very funny guest. He got on remarkably well with the publican Martin Loch at our local pub, The Chequers Inn. He called him "a good man; he offered me his daughter and his gun!"

It's much more volatile, politics in the USA. It allows you to really explore the viciousness and the duplicity of the people because they are so committed to their "cause." Maybe because the Wild West is really not such distant past, and in the UK our history and politics have been shaped by hundreds or even thousands of years of struggle and chaos. American politics seem born out of the barrel of a gun.

I never pre-imagine; I just start drawing and things emerge from the approach. Forget style and learn to draw; that is really most important. Learn to draw; go to life drawing—dressed people as well, dressing up too with a big hat on or something, and that kind of costume. The "Creative Process" begins with a mark on a white sheet of Cartridge Paper (350 grams), pure white. Then the image takes over and leads me to God knows where—but THAT is Creation!

My art teacher, Leslie Richardson, and even Percy V. Bradshaw really believed in learning to draw, old school. After I went to America and met Hunter, I think I got braver, and that freed me up to not be afraid to lose some control, to embrace the accidental.

When I started working with Ceri Levy, I started using my dirty water technique. I throw dirty water—from the water I wash my brushes in—down onto pure white paper (300gsm) and wait three days, at least, for it dry. Probably when the drawing, or painting, is nearing completion, then I do something spontaneous, and I either succeed, or it's buggered! The surprising result, effects, encourage me to use my inventive aptitude, and it challenges me to draw something that simply would not be there before. There is nothing more challenging than a white sheet of paper.

When the Internet started to become popular in the 1990s, people could learn more about art and artists. Has the Internet made the world better or worse for visual artists?

I think it stops people getting their hands dirty. The technology is so clever, but it loses something. You cannot totally imitate the human element and the accidents that can bring.

People ask me, "Don't you ever make a mistake?" I say, "There is no such thing as a mistake. A mistake is an opportunity to do something else."

I wonder if the young generation are just bored—and not motivated by their own creative possibilities. It is ALL on a plate, and they wait for some other gizmo to appear that they can stuff up their apps and be "inspired" yet again! I think that the electronic revolution has robbed them of all their own personal struggle.

It's amazing that you have been covering many of the same issues for decades. Sometimes, it feels like the faces and names have changed, but the issues haven't.

In the past few decades, you became known for more political drawings, social issues, and portraits. What brought you toward that type of drawing?

The 1990s were particularly busy years for me. I drew assignments for many publications and often tackled things that were in the news and relevant. The election of George W. Bush and the Bush years and Iraq were difficult, and that unfortunately gave me a lot of subject matter to work with. I never really set out to cover politics, but the events of the day kept pulling me in. The injustice found in previous decades still continues, and is worse in many ways. People need a voice, and the events of today are not surprising.

This book will be published during a moment of global chaos. At this writing, we are in the middle of the 2020 coronavirus pandemic and months away from a major US election. This November we will find out if America will have a new president—or we will have four more years of Donald Trump. Do you have any predictions?

I don't think anyone can predict what might happen with this crazy man. I live in the UK, and if I could guess, I would like to think that America might just throw Trump out on his arse! Europeans find Trump crazy and scary. Hunter always said no one could be crazier than George W. Bush! Trump has taken it to another level!

Ralph, after so many years of drawing, it's an enormous task to gather a view of your work into any one type of volume. We have included hundreds but unfortunately had to leave out many thousands of drawings. How do you see your work evolving in 2020 and beyond?

Almost every day I draw, but I never know where it will take me. Even today, I drew something new. I start with a fresh sheet of paper and just take it from there. Few people believe that I work every day with regularity like some folks might at any office. I show up on time and put in my workday as much as any other worker. Still, drawing has been an incredible journey for me, and I am grateful to be able to push the limits each day. We have a complex and challenging world, and I feel it's my duty to Confront The Menace—whether that be your local constable or the President of the United States. People can make change happen, and the governments can be made to do the right thing—if we step up and demand it.

*Opposite: Close-up, ca. 1975. **Following Spread:** Ralph in his London Studio, 103 New King's Road. When the roof had to be replaced, Ralph decided to convert the attic into a studio space at the same time.*

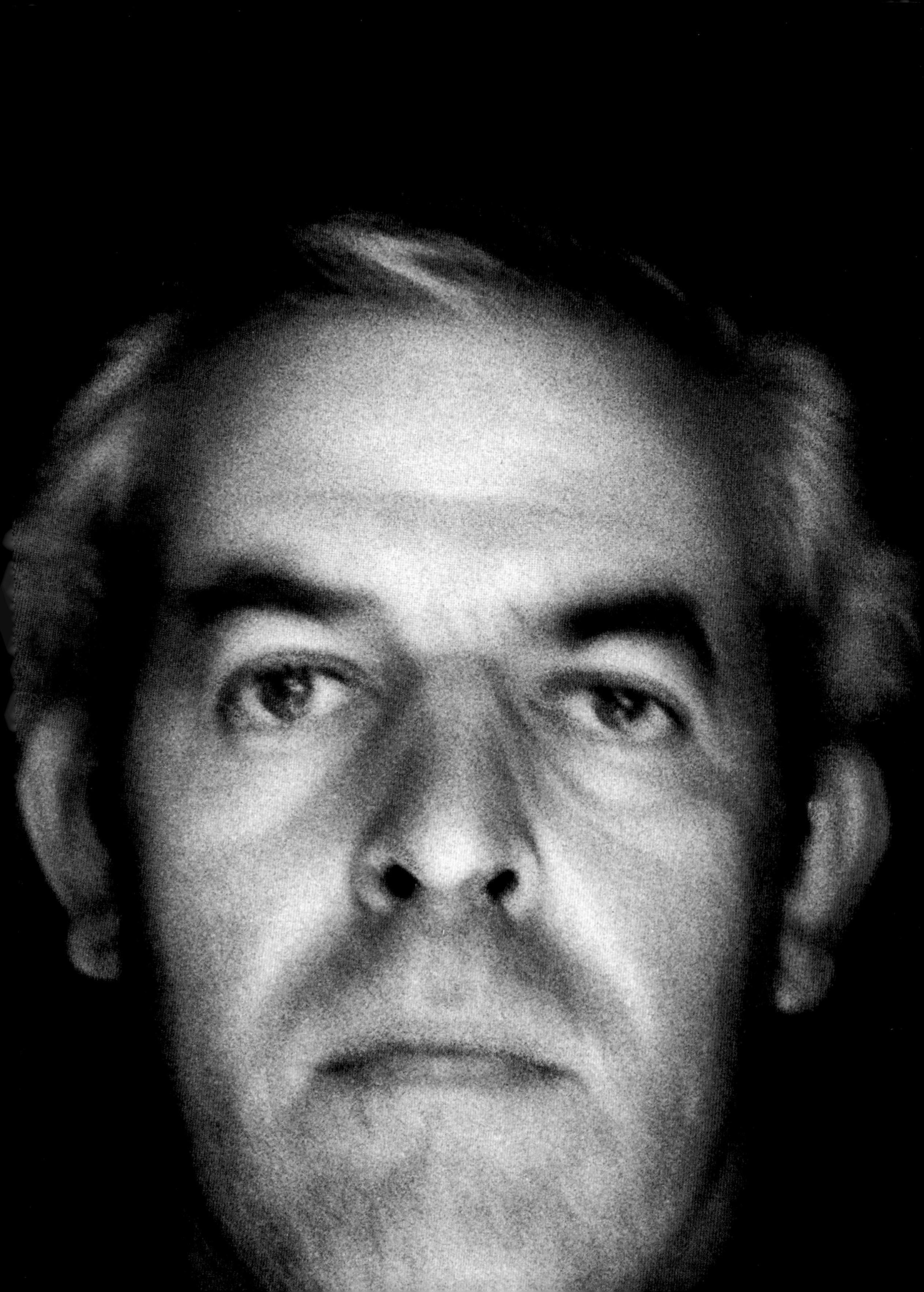

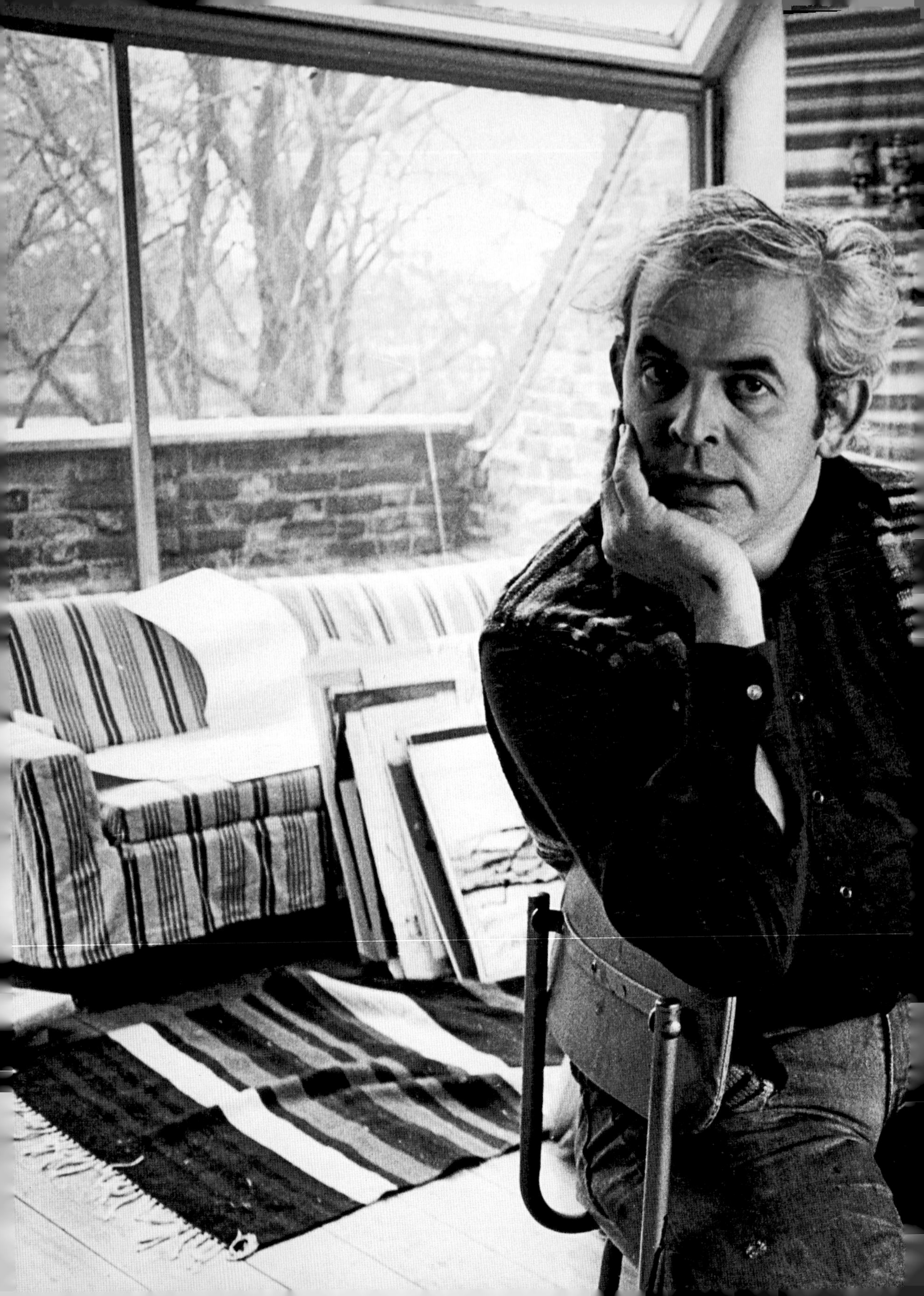

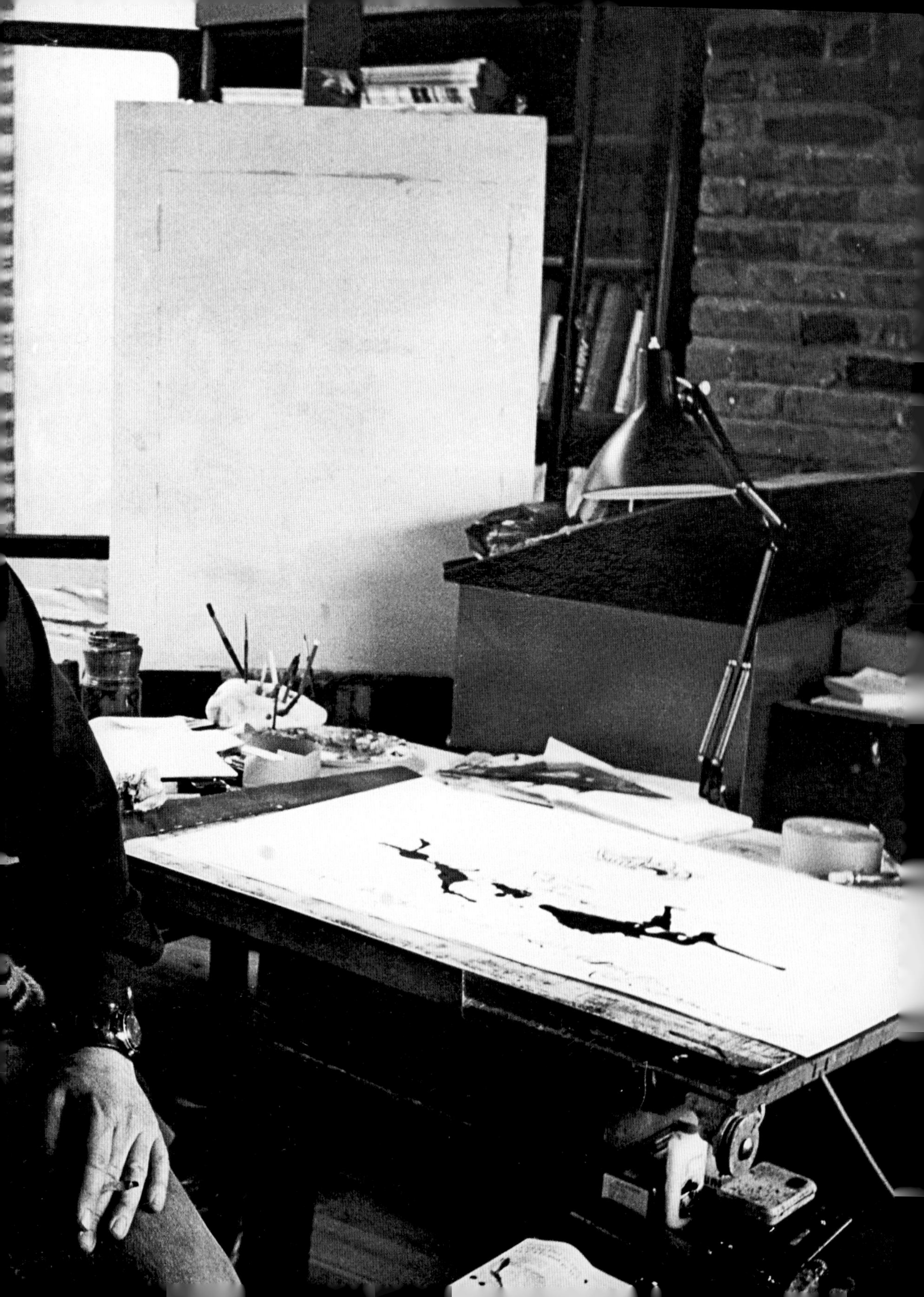

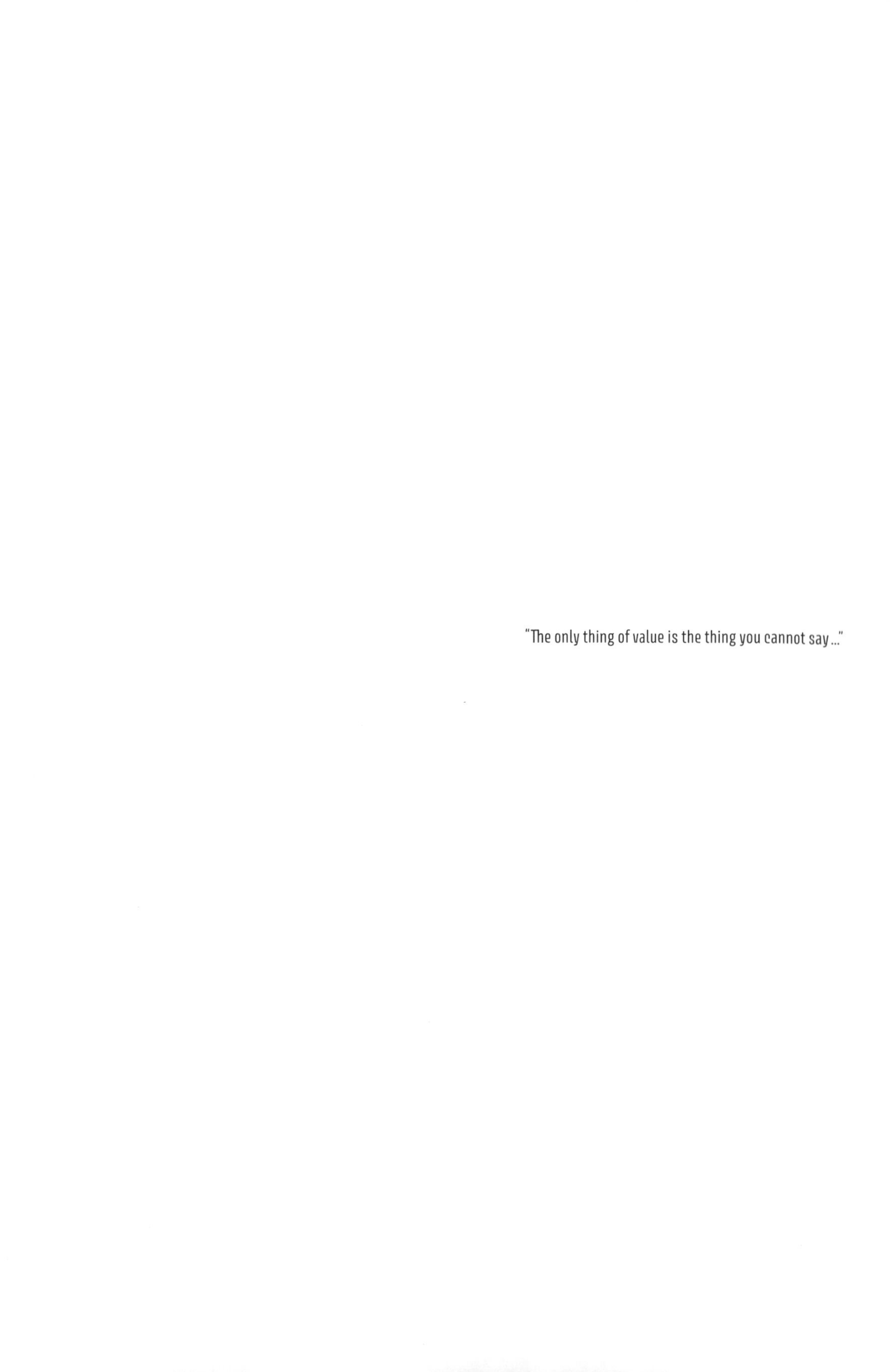
"The only thing of value is the thing you cannot say…"

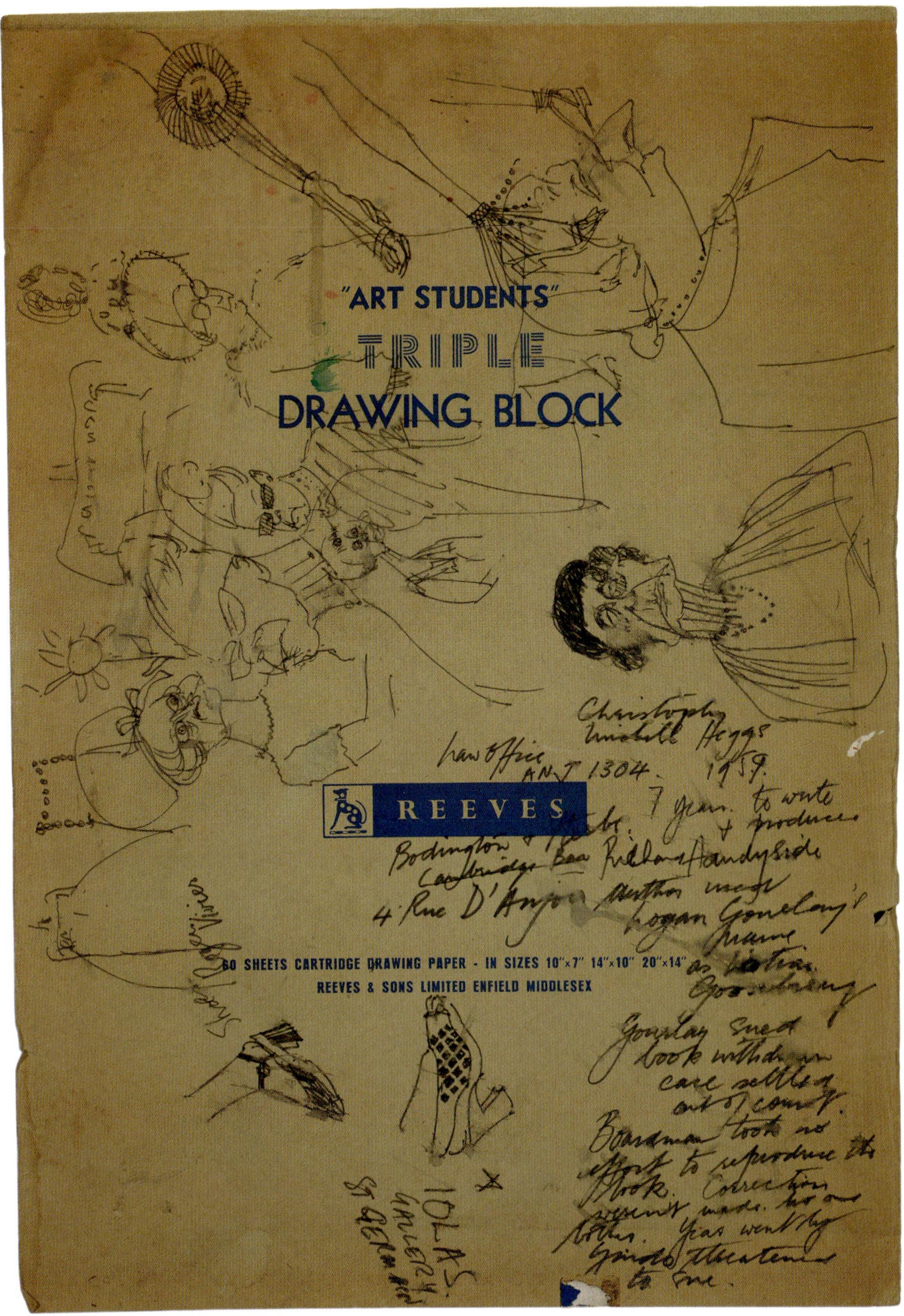

Student Sketchbook, 1959

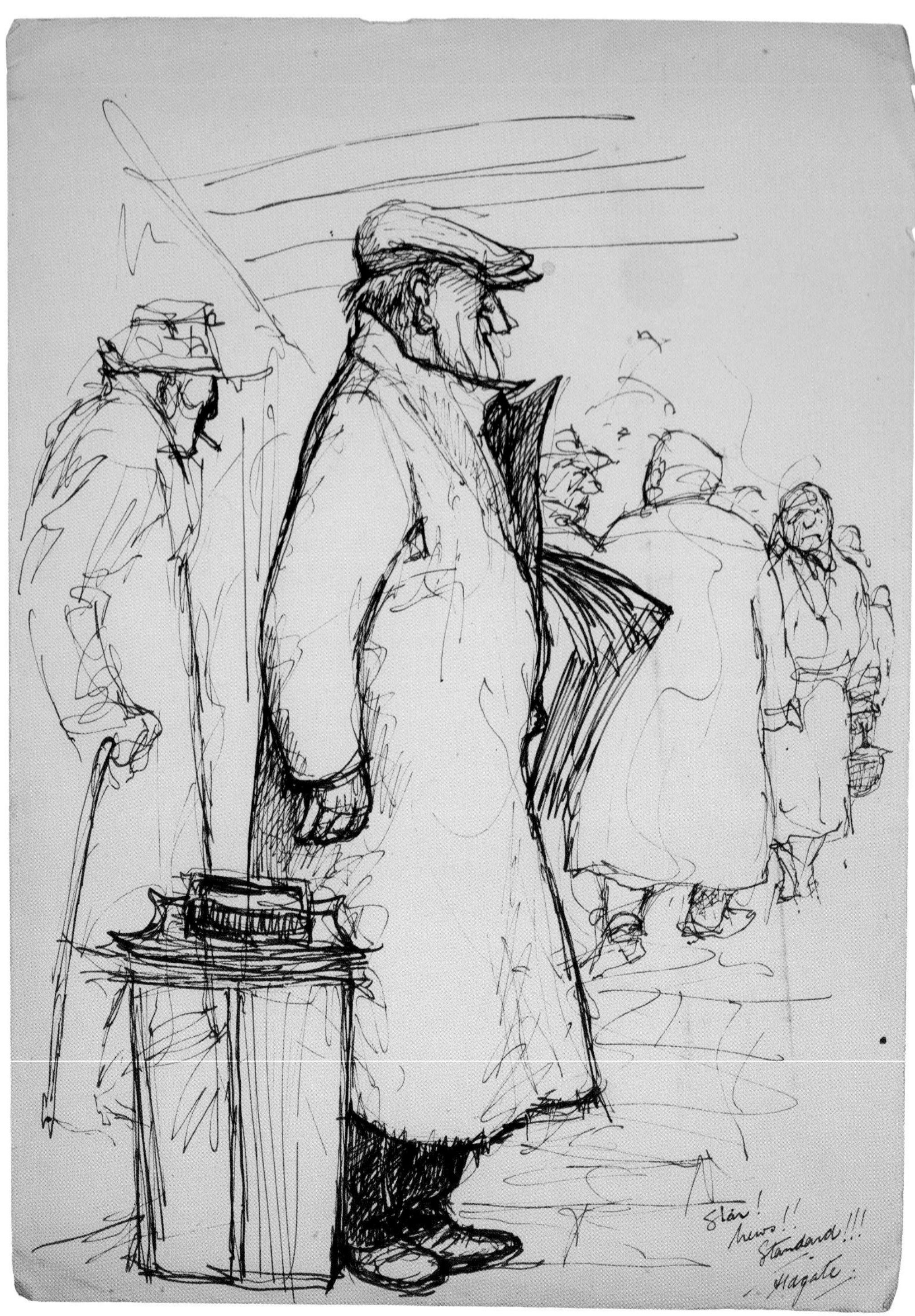

Figures on a London Street, 1956

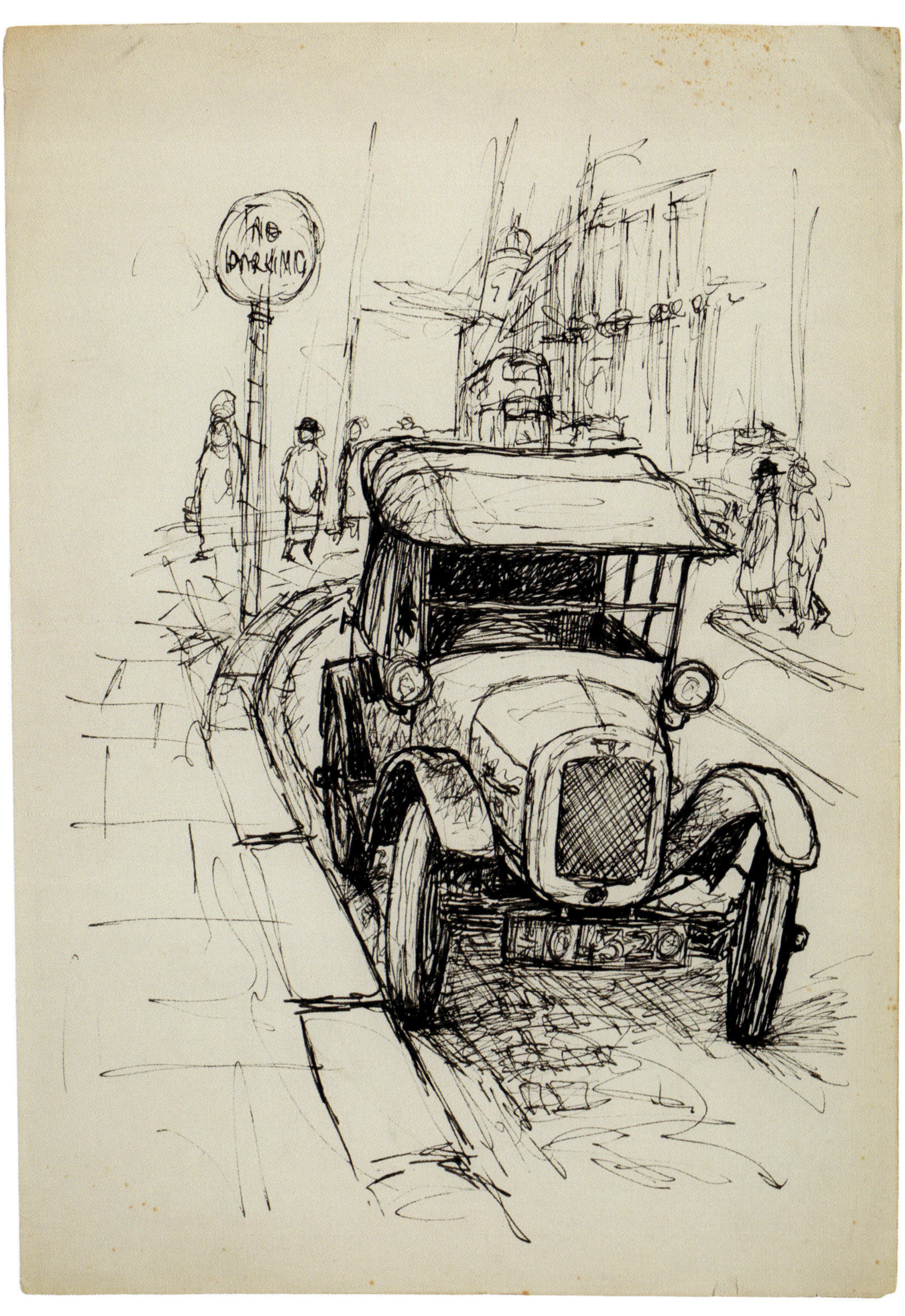

"Really I used to draw all the time: in the street, in the pub, waiting for the bus. My pen was like a sixth finger." *Car in a No Parking Zone, ca. 1956*

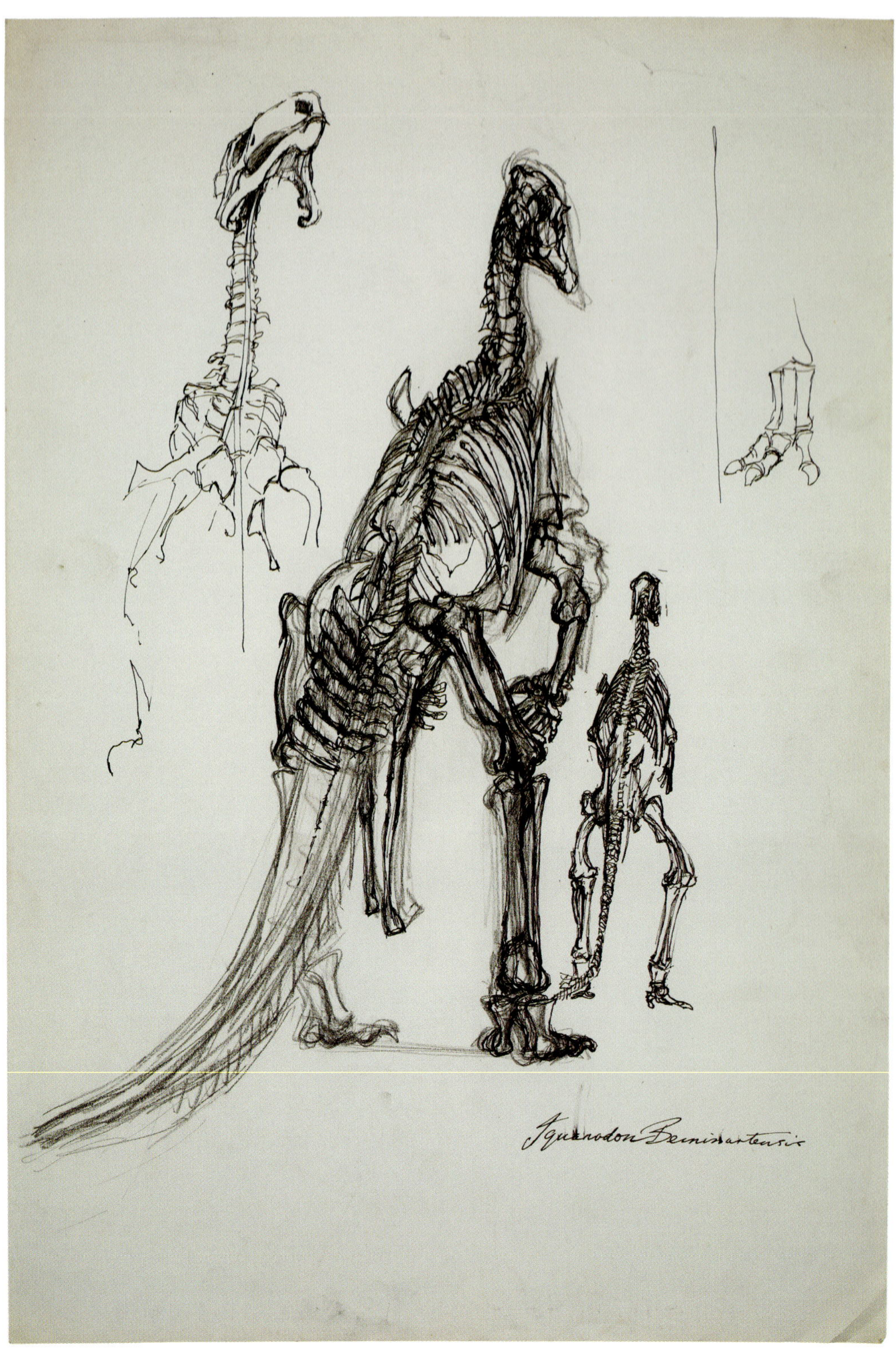

Dinosaur Skeleton at the Natural History Museum, ca. 1958

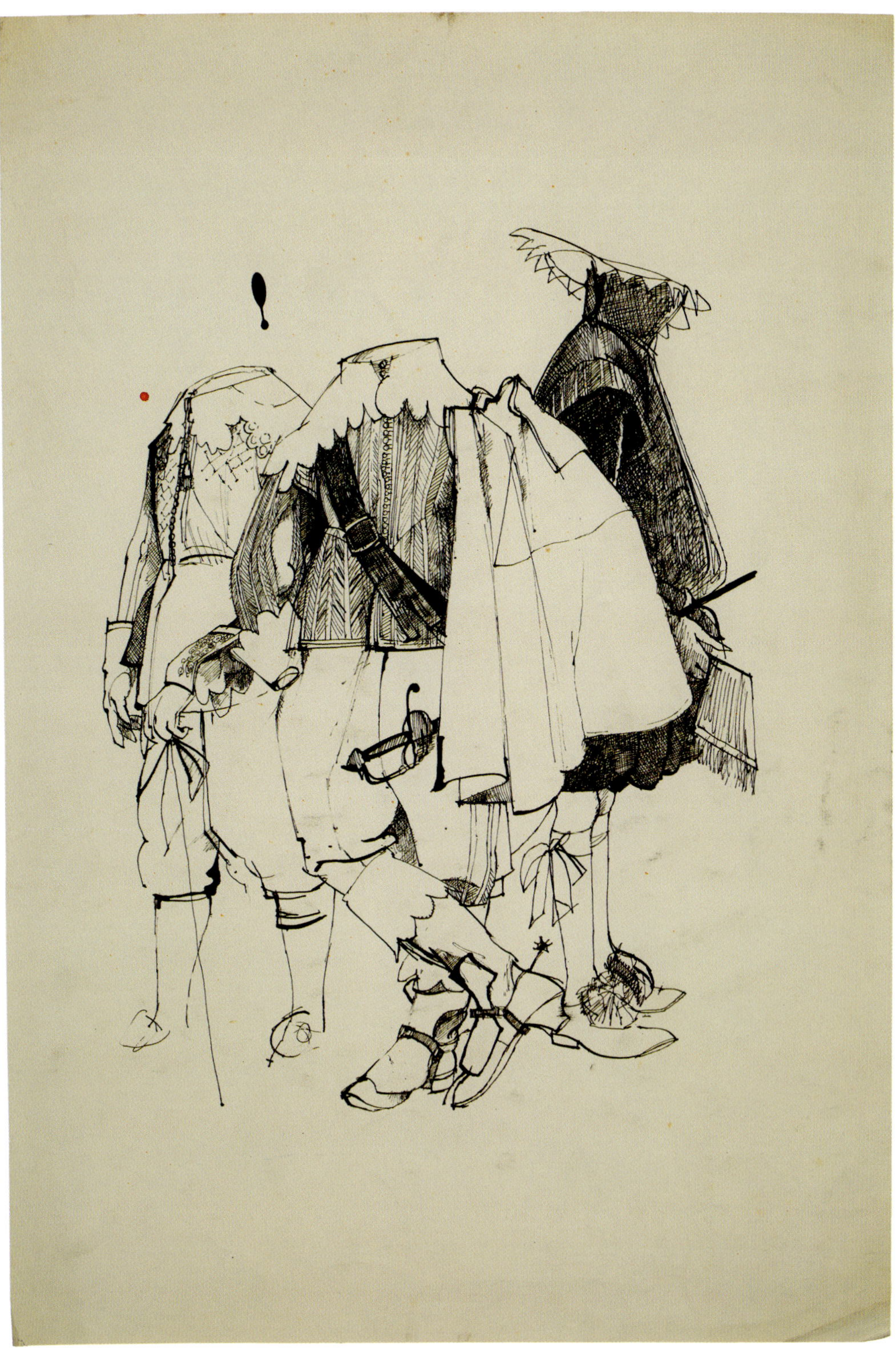

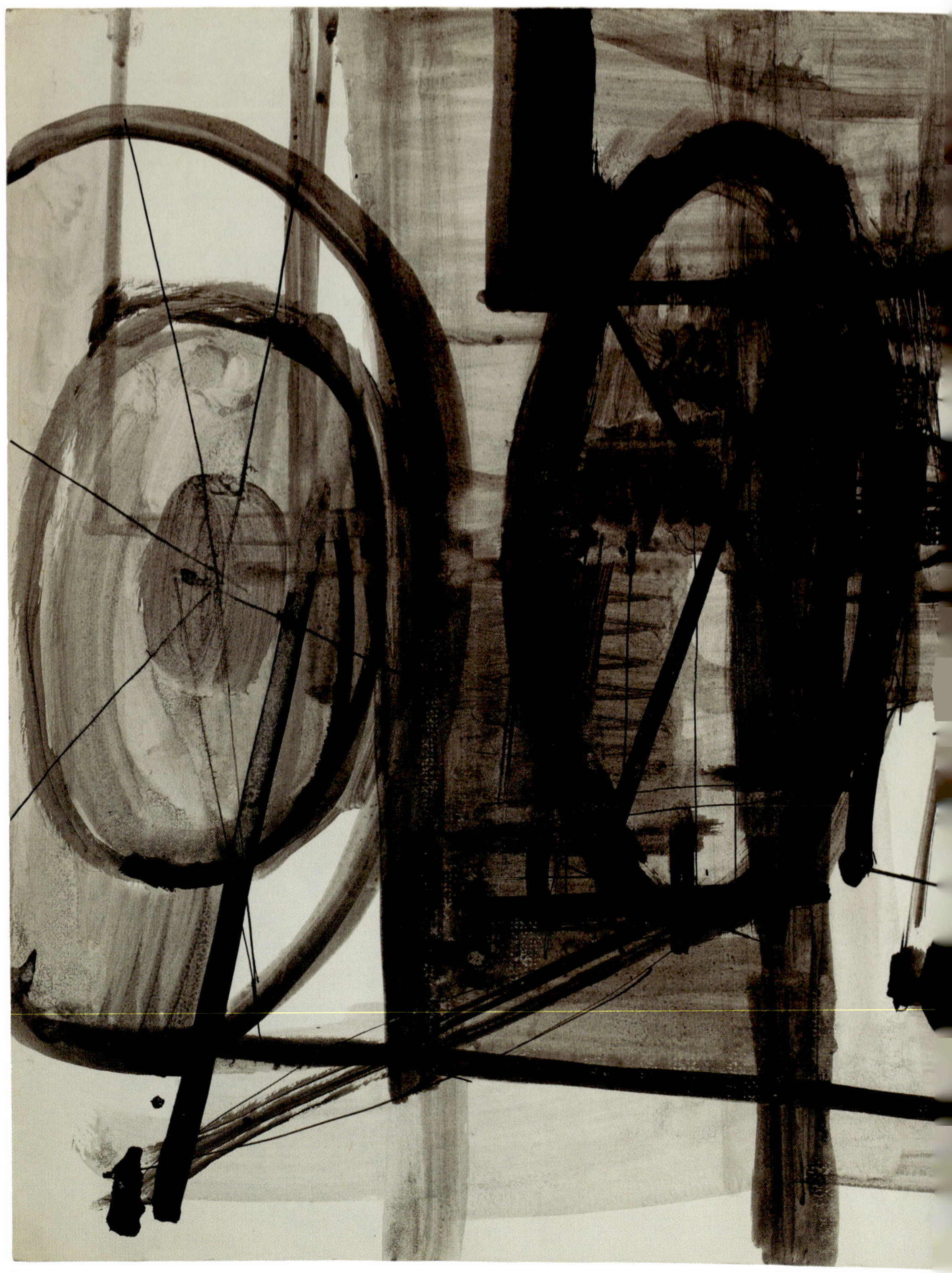

Sketch from the Science Museum, London, ca. 1954

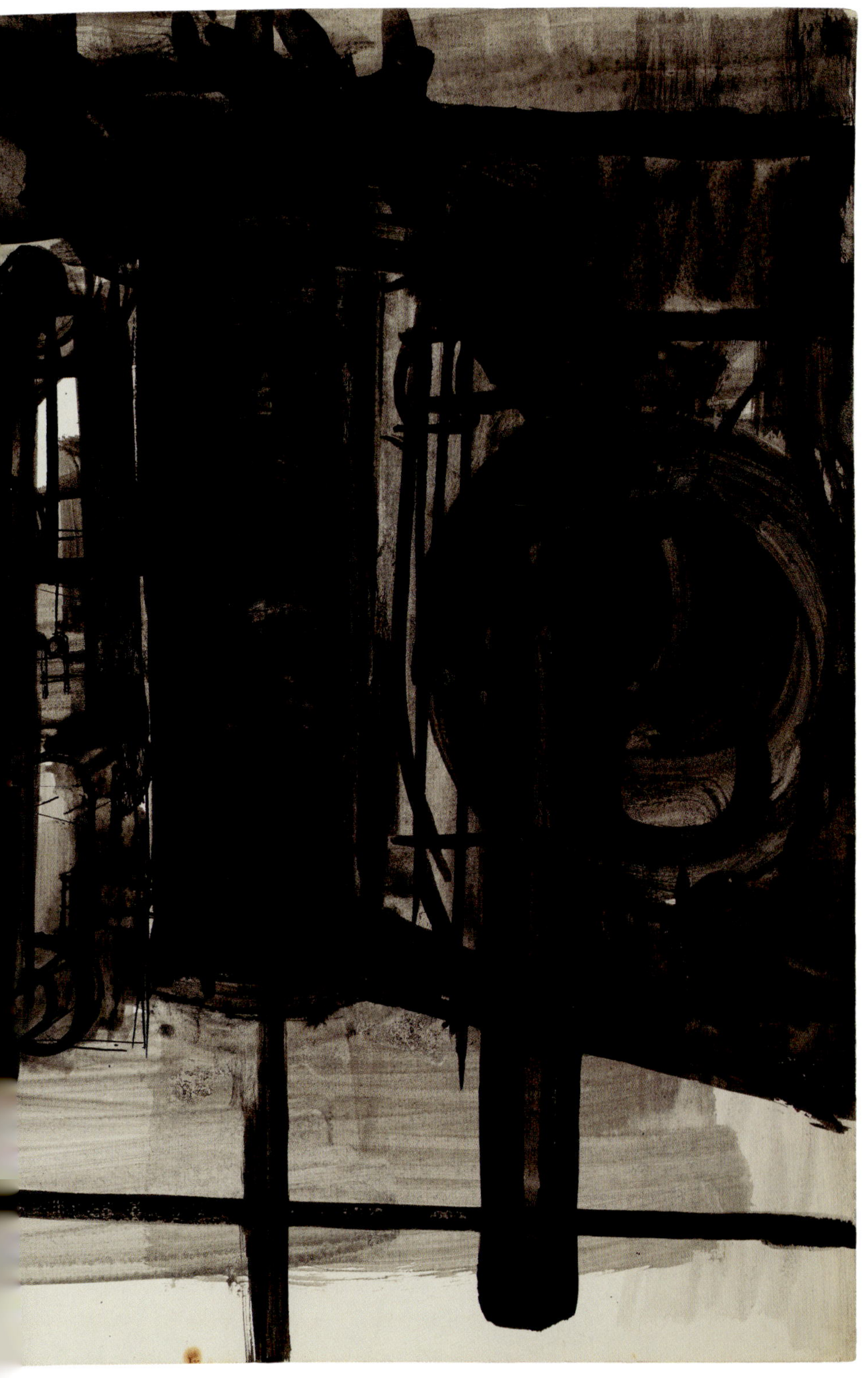

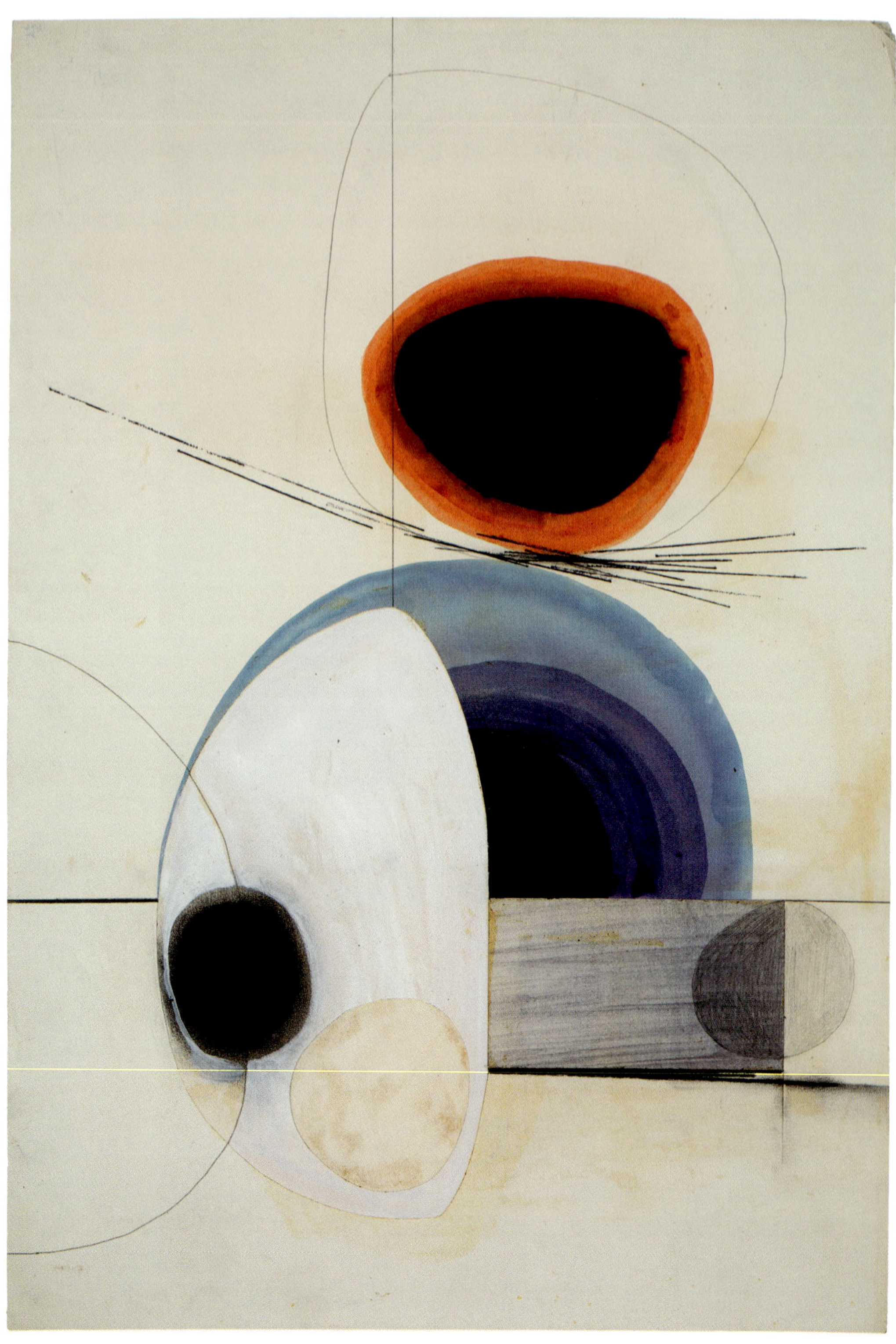

Abstract Paintings, 1958 "From my time at East Ham Technical College. It's where I met my mentor and friend, Leslie Richardson."

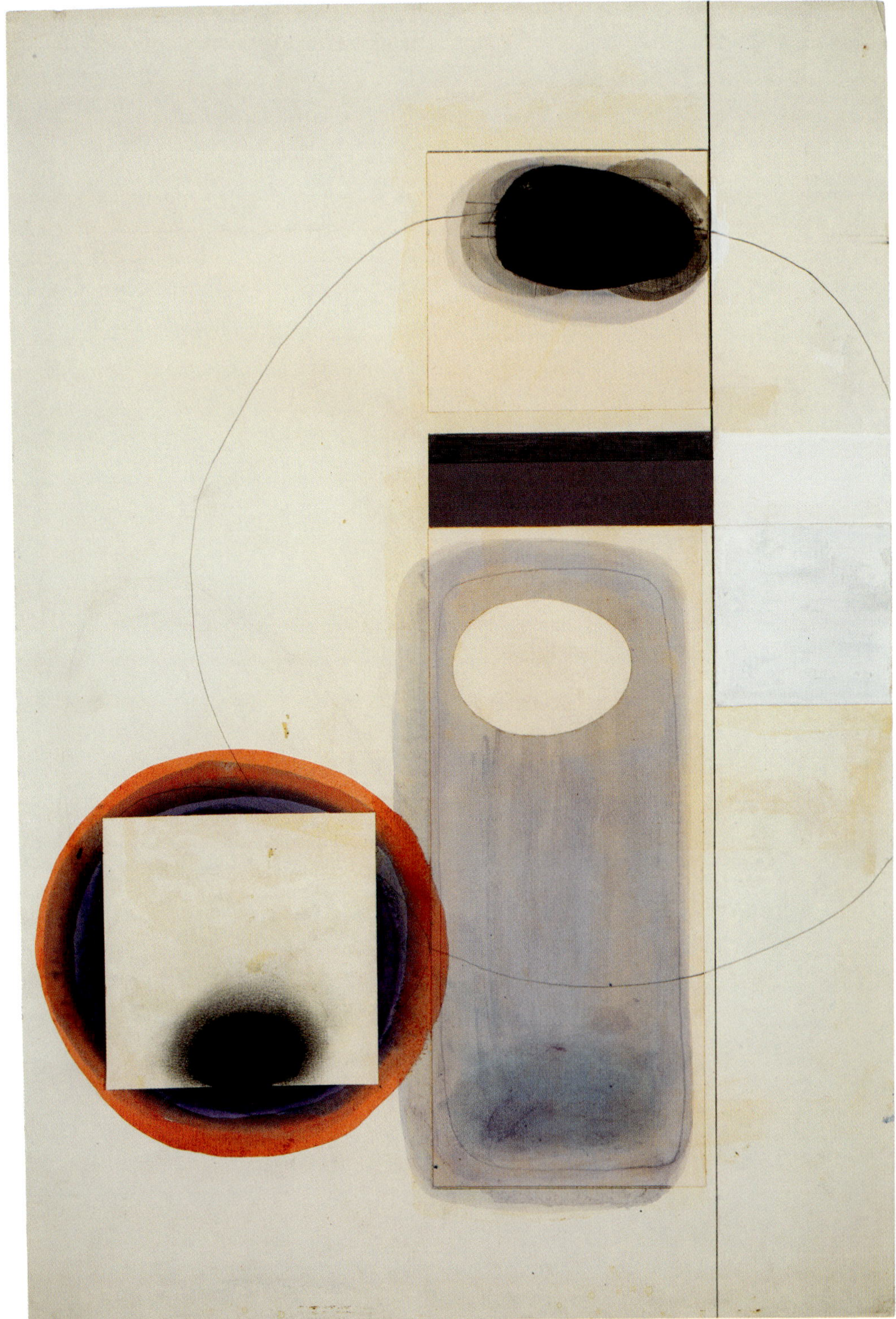

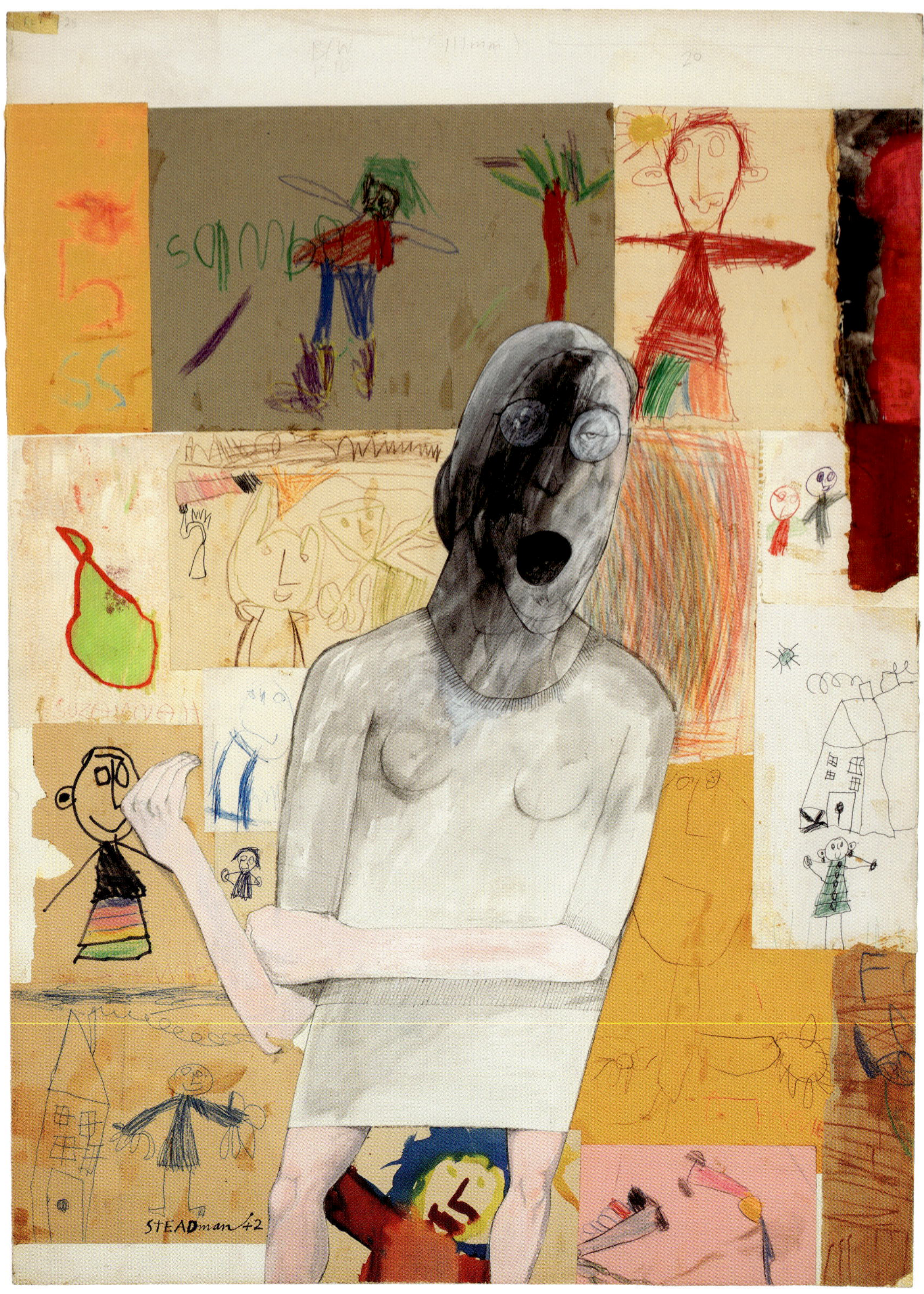

The English Teacher, ca. 1960

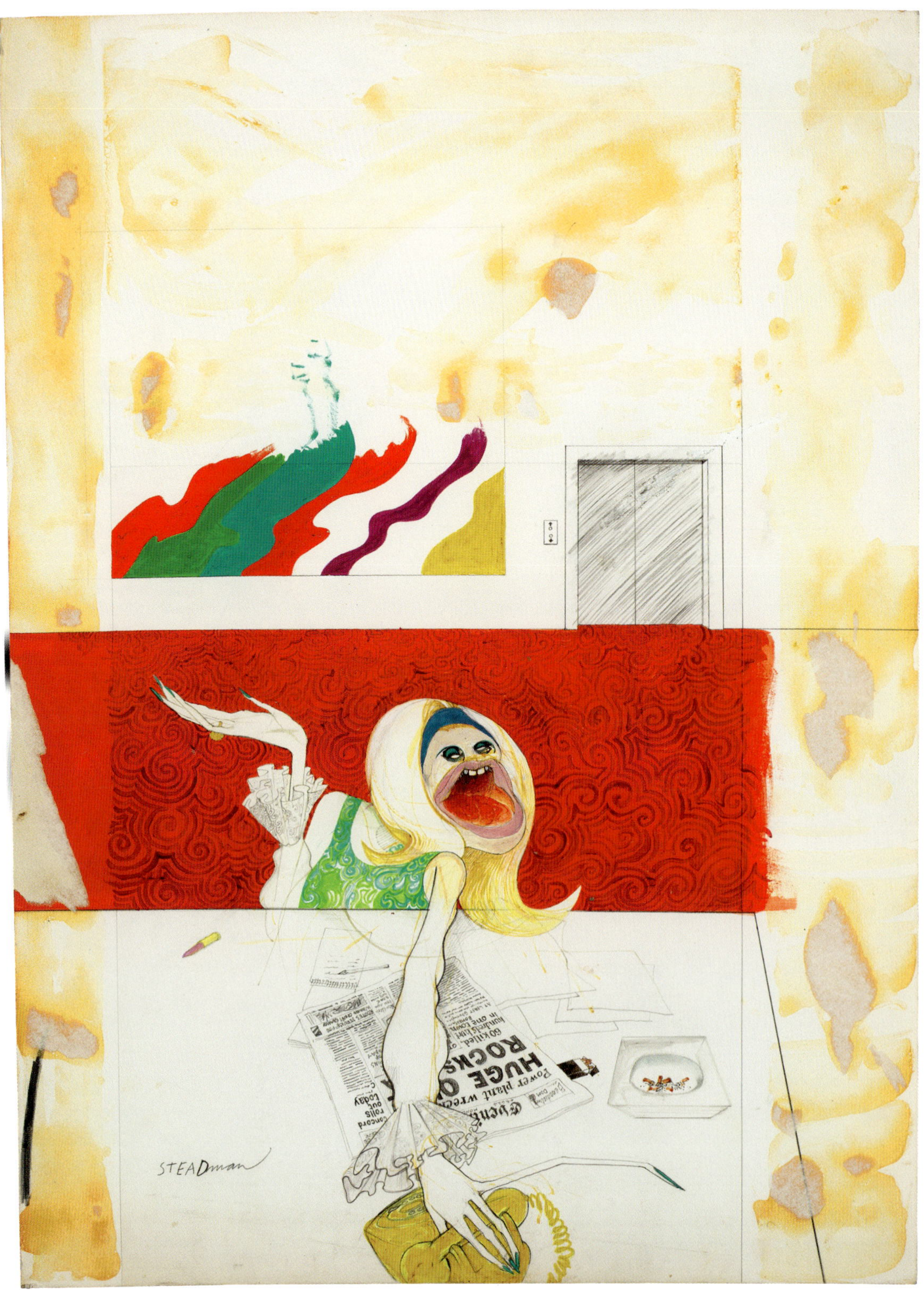

STEADman
HUGE O
ROCKS
Power plant wrec
Event
60 killed or
hundreds kil
in one coun
Concord
rolls
out
today

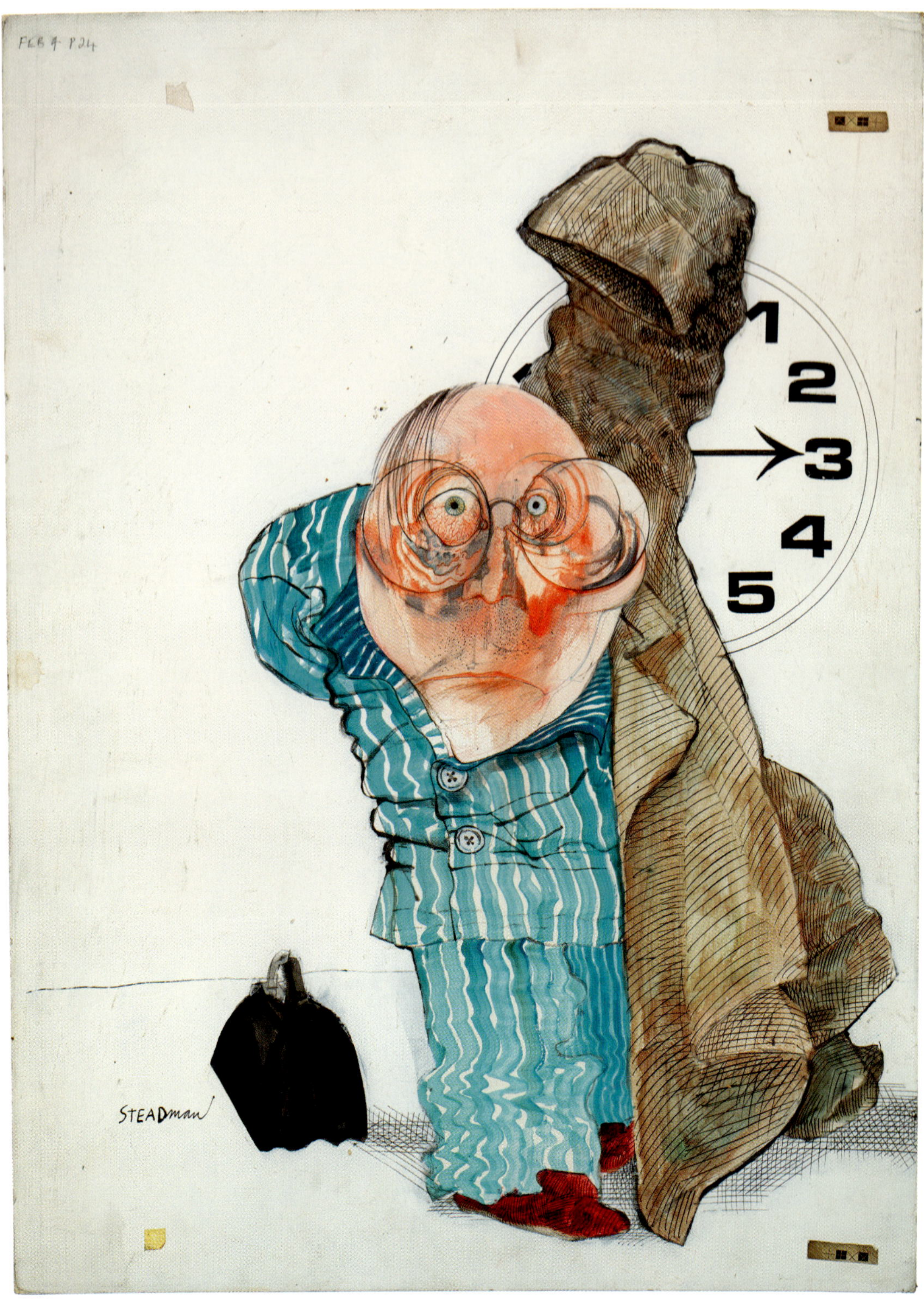

The Doctor's Call Out, ca. 1960

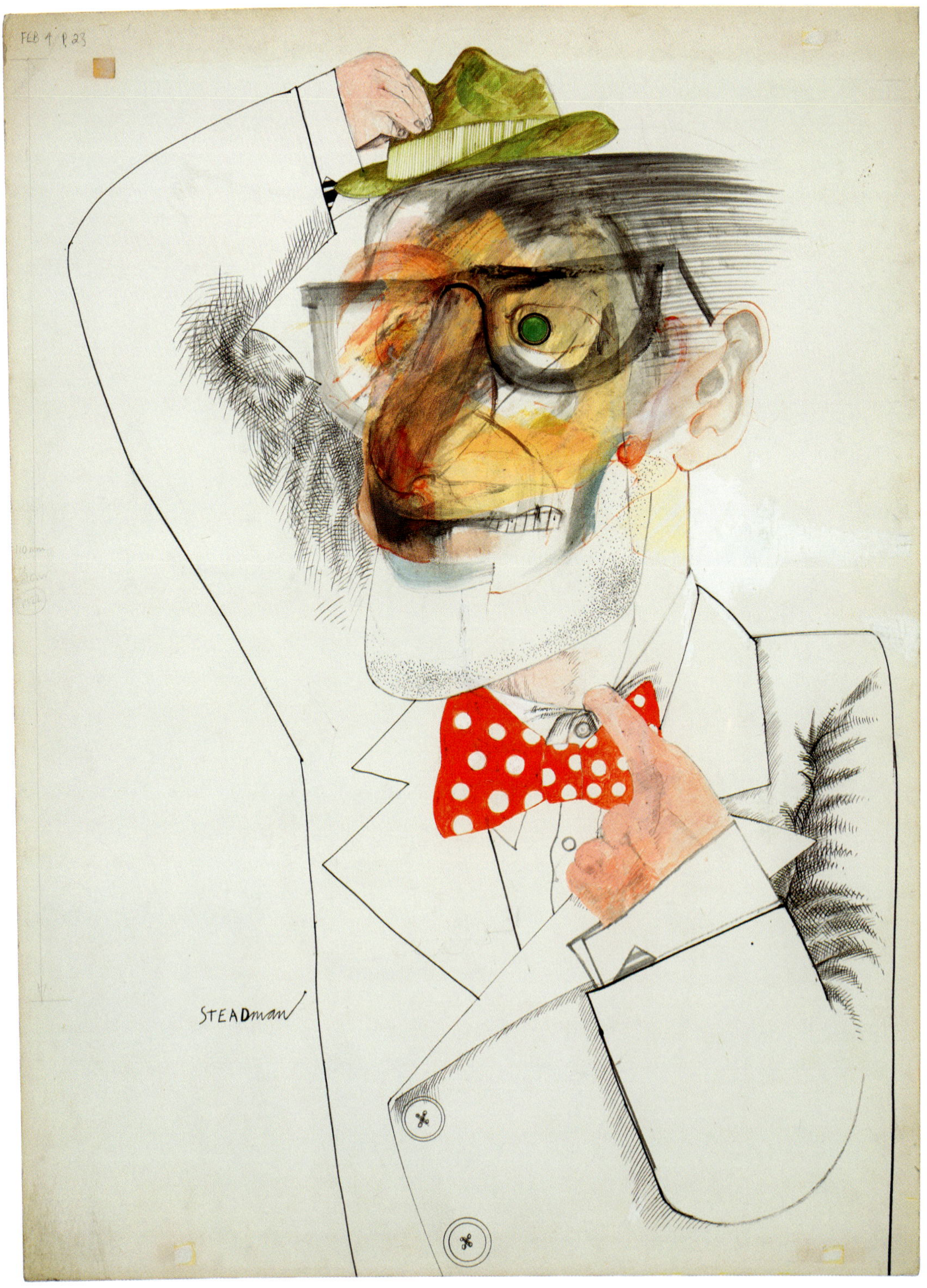

Door-to-Door Salesman, ca. 1960

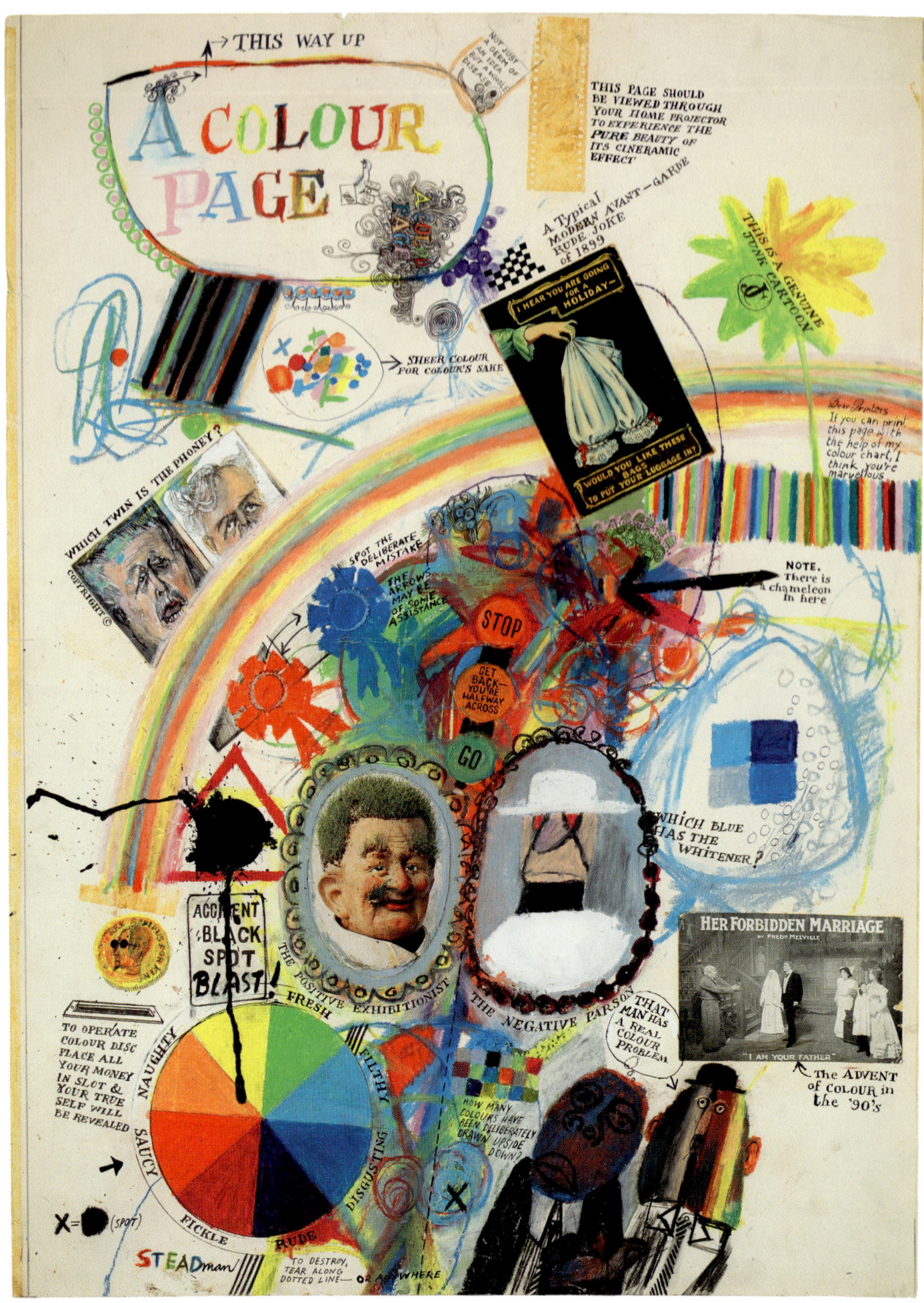

The Genesis of Colour, ca. 1960

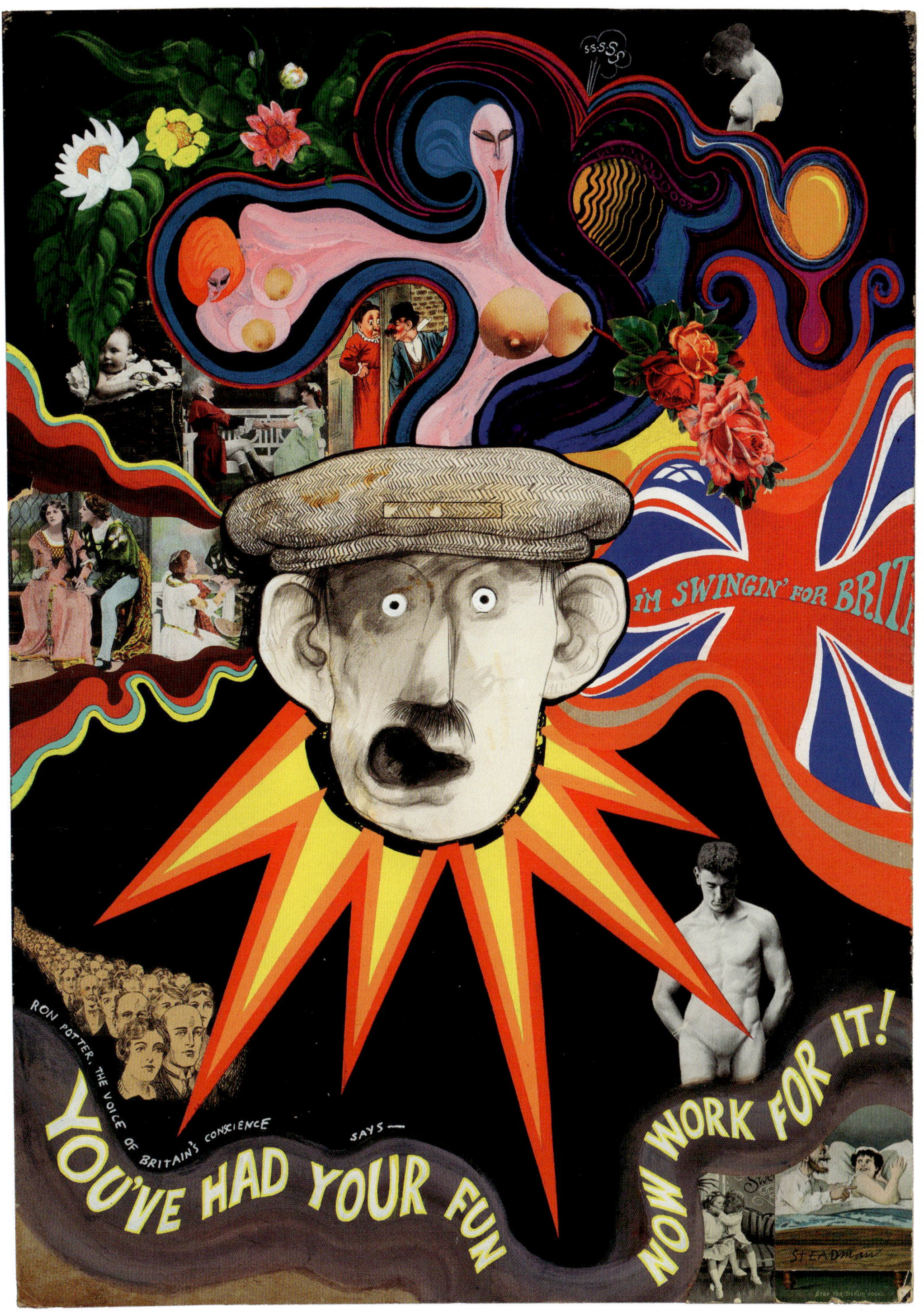

You've Had Your Fun—Now Work For It! ca. 1960

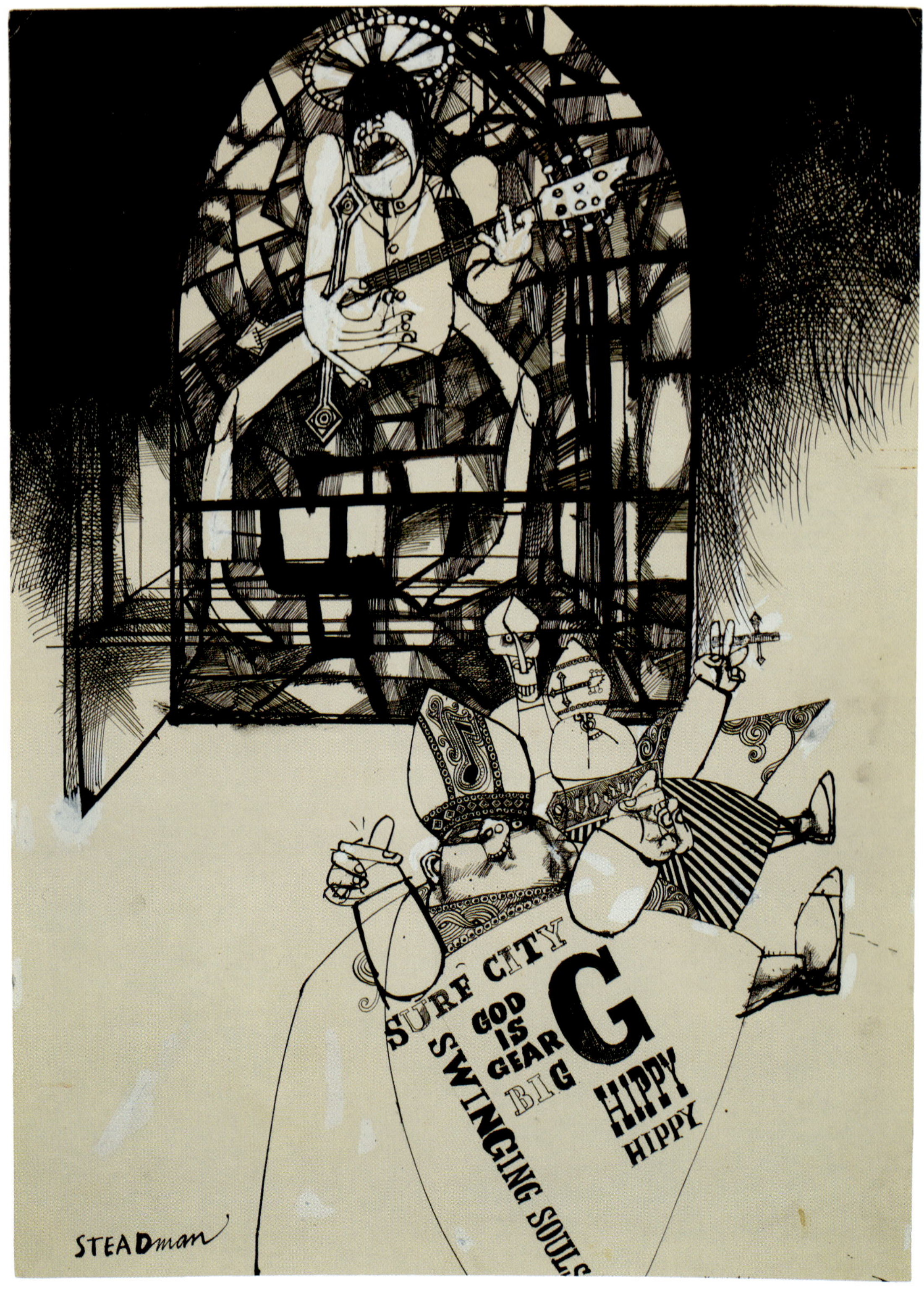

Swingin' '60s, ca. 1960 "Can you see the signatures? I used to sign myself STEAD like Giles or Searle—cartoonists had short names...

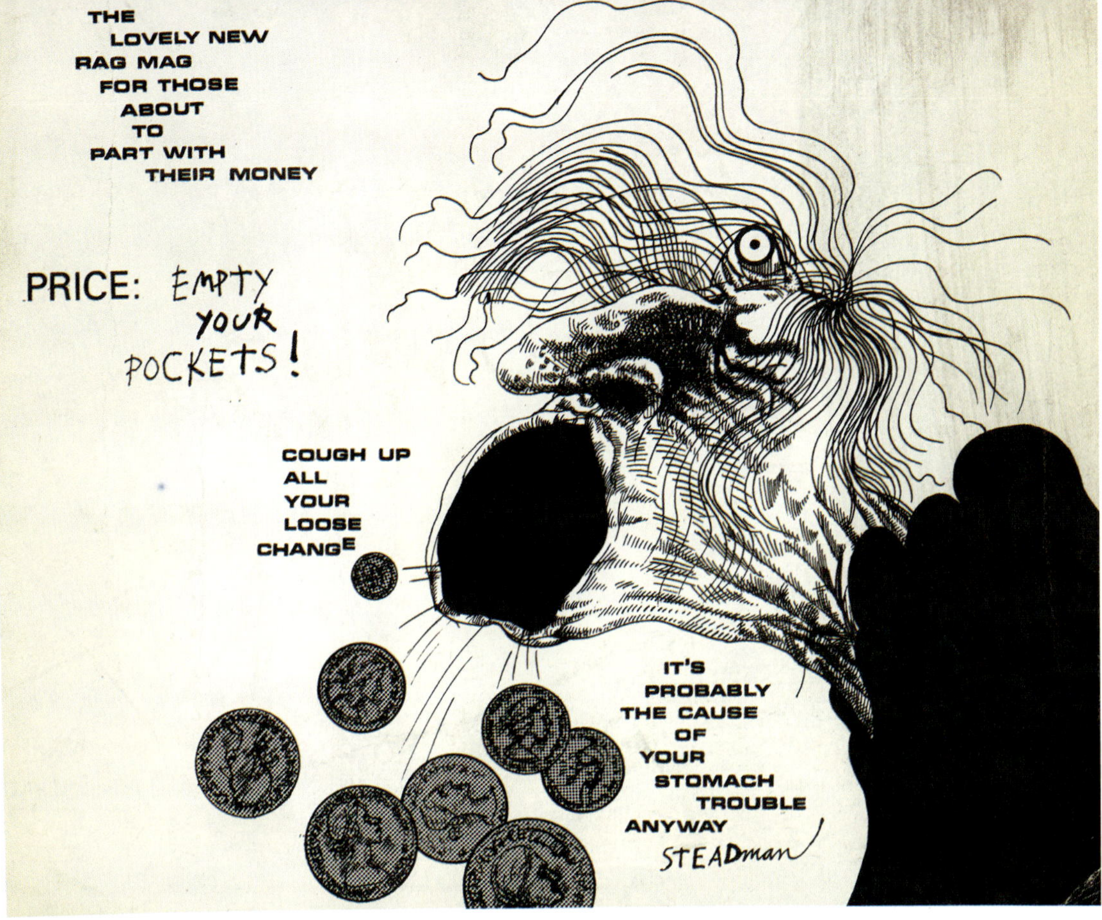

...My mum asked me if I was ashamed of my name, so I half-heartedly added the 'man' on the end." *Cough It Up! Empty Your Pockets! ca. 1960*

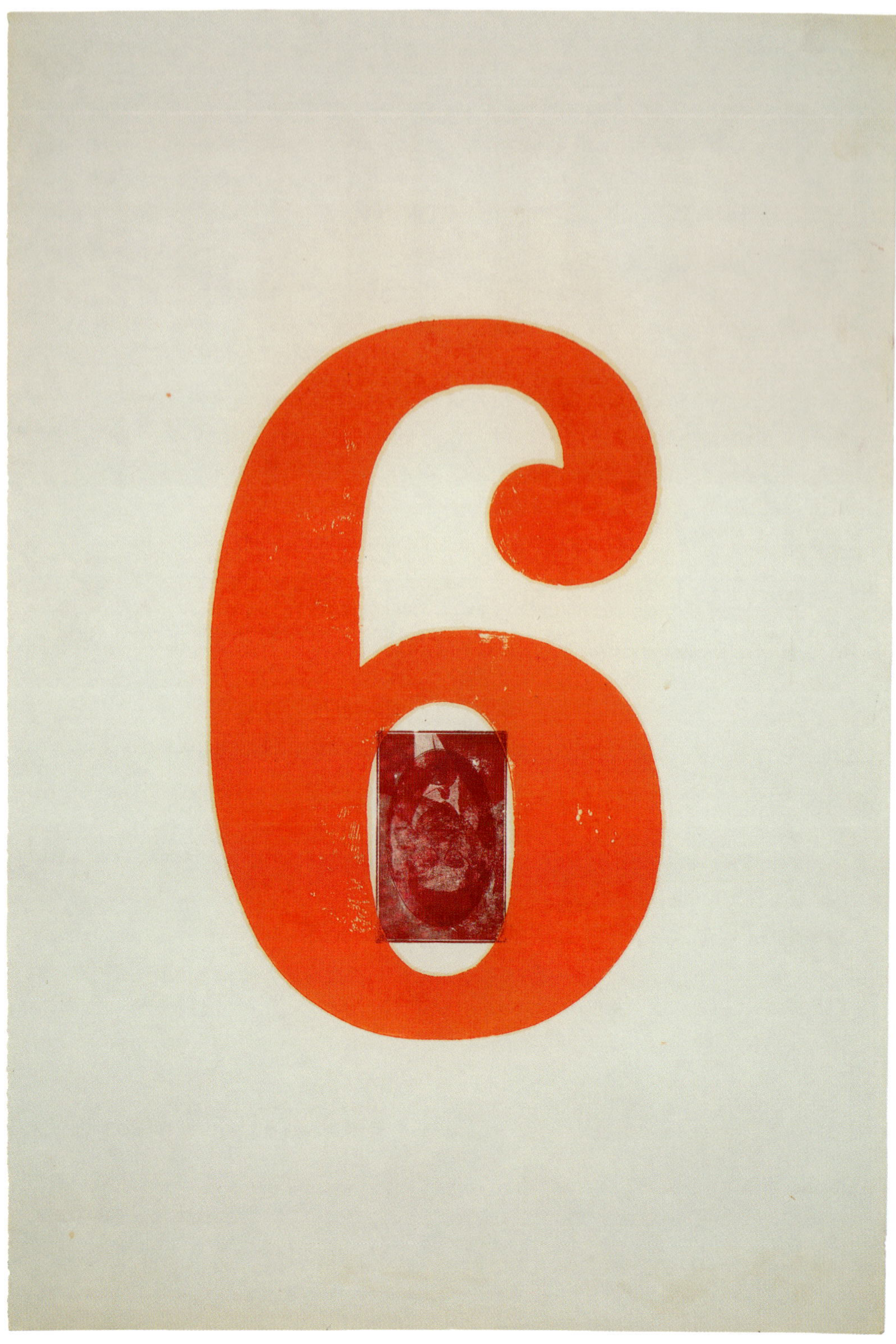

Wood Type Printing, ca. 1954

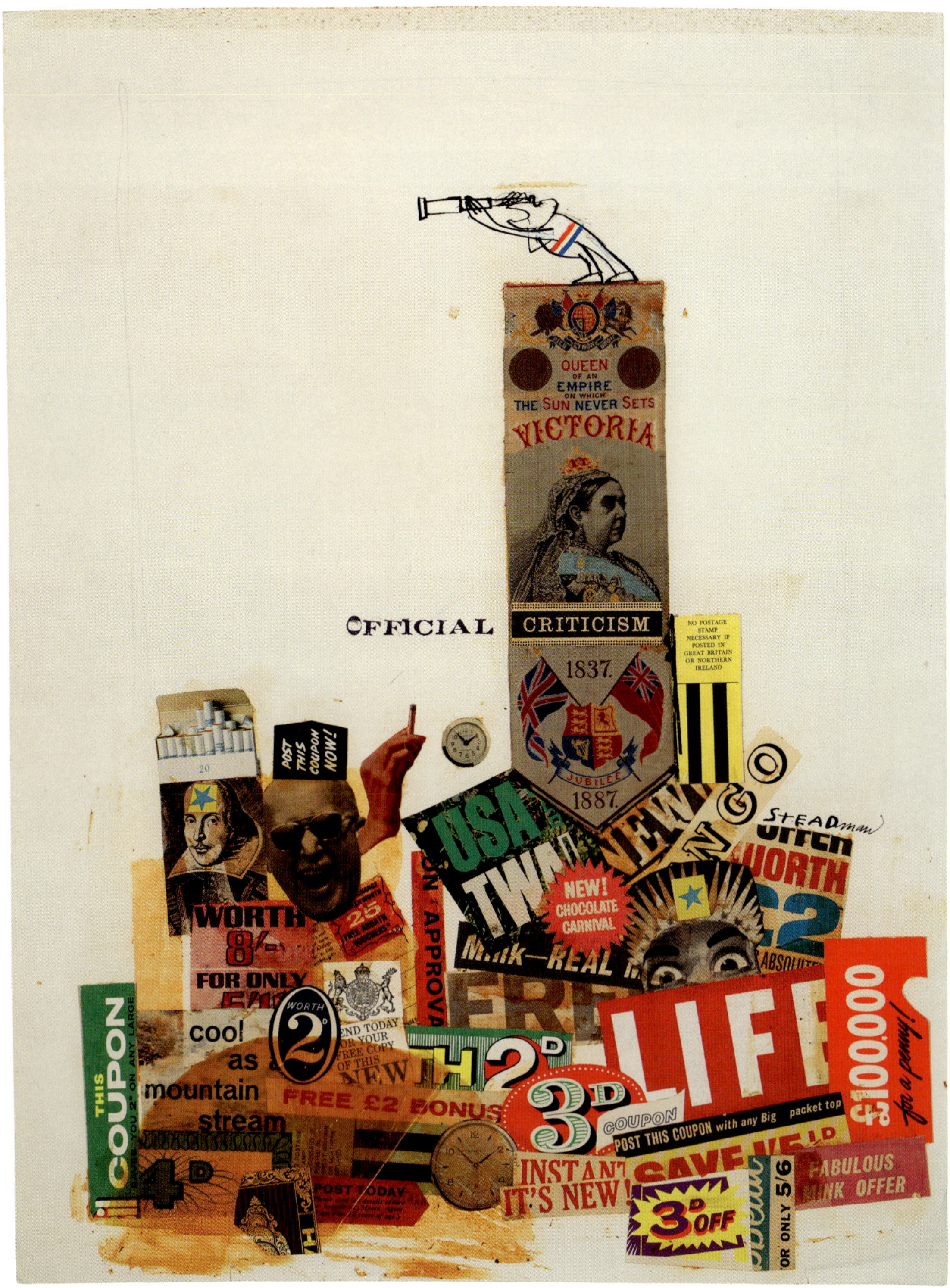

Official Criticism, ca. 1954

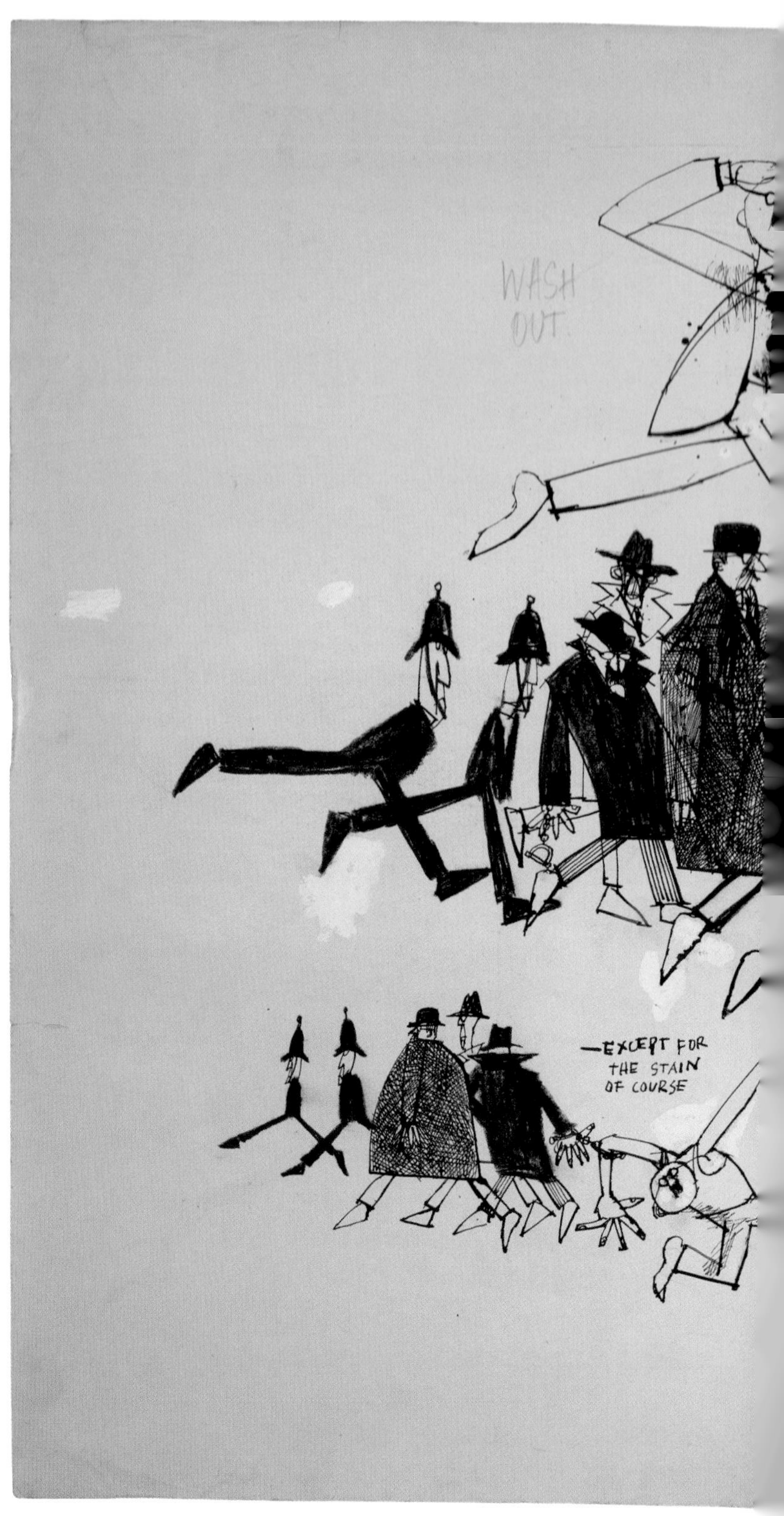

Advertising Heydays, ca. 1960

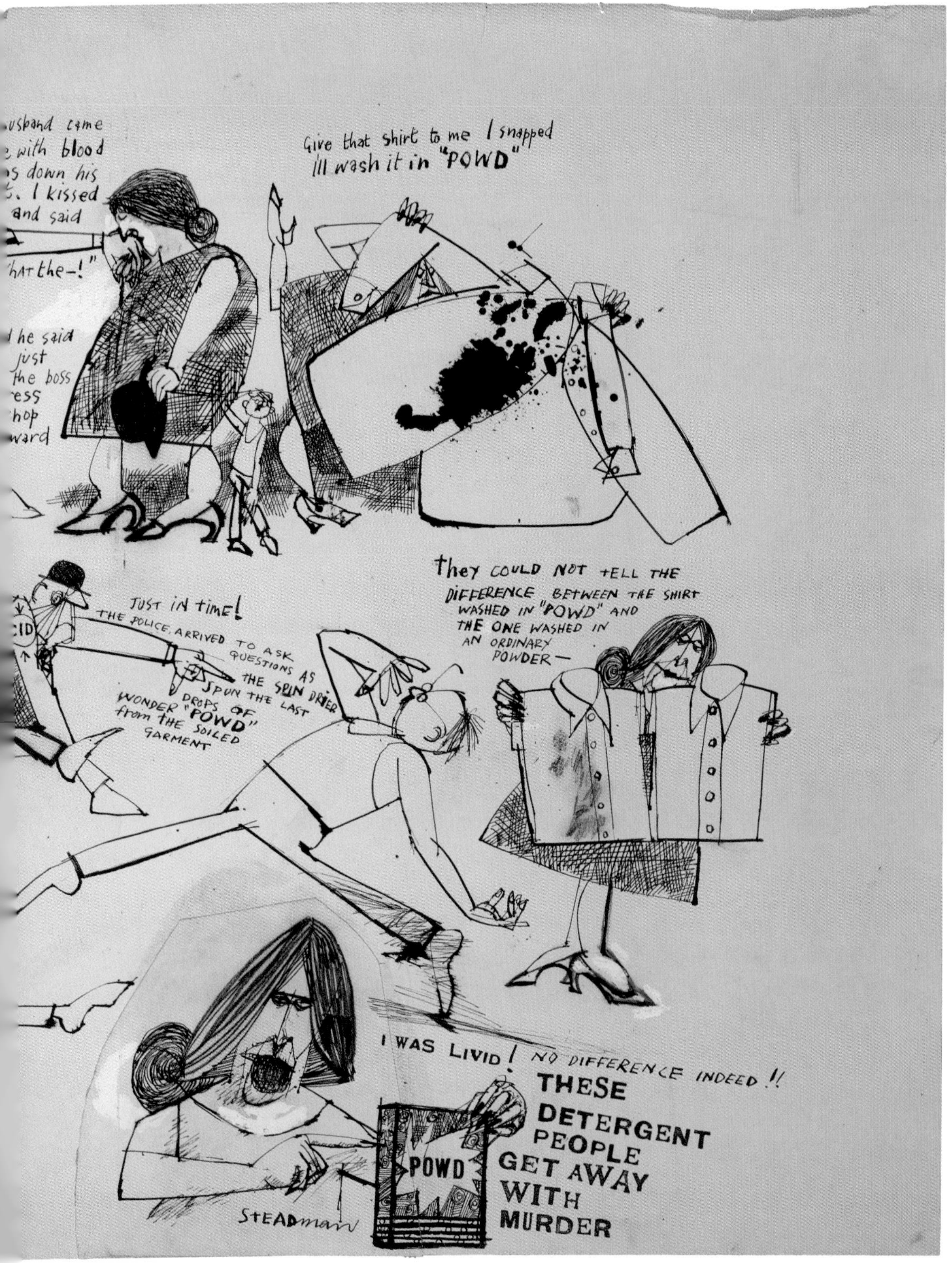
usband came
with blood
s down his
. I kissed
and said
hat the—!"
he said
just
he boss
ress
hop
ward
Give that shirt to me I snapped
I'll wash it in "POWD"
JUST IN TIME!
THE POLICE, ARRIVED TO ASK
QUESTIONS AS
THE SPIN DRIER
SPUN THE LAST
WONDER "POWD"
DROPS OF
from the SOILED
GARMENT
CID
they COULD NOT tELL THE
DIFFERENCE BETWEEN THE SHIRT
WASHED IN "POWD" AND
THE ONE WASHED IN
AN ORDINARY
POWDER—
I WAS LIVID! NO DIFFERENCE INDEED!!
THESE
DETERGENT
PEOPLE
GET AWAY
WITH
MURDER
POWD
STEADman

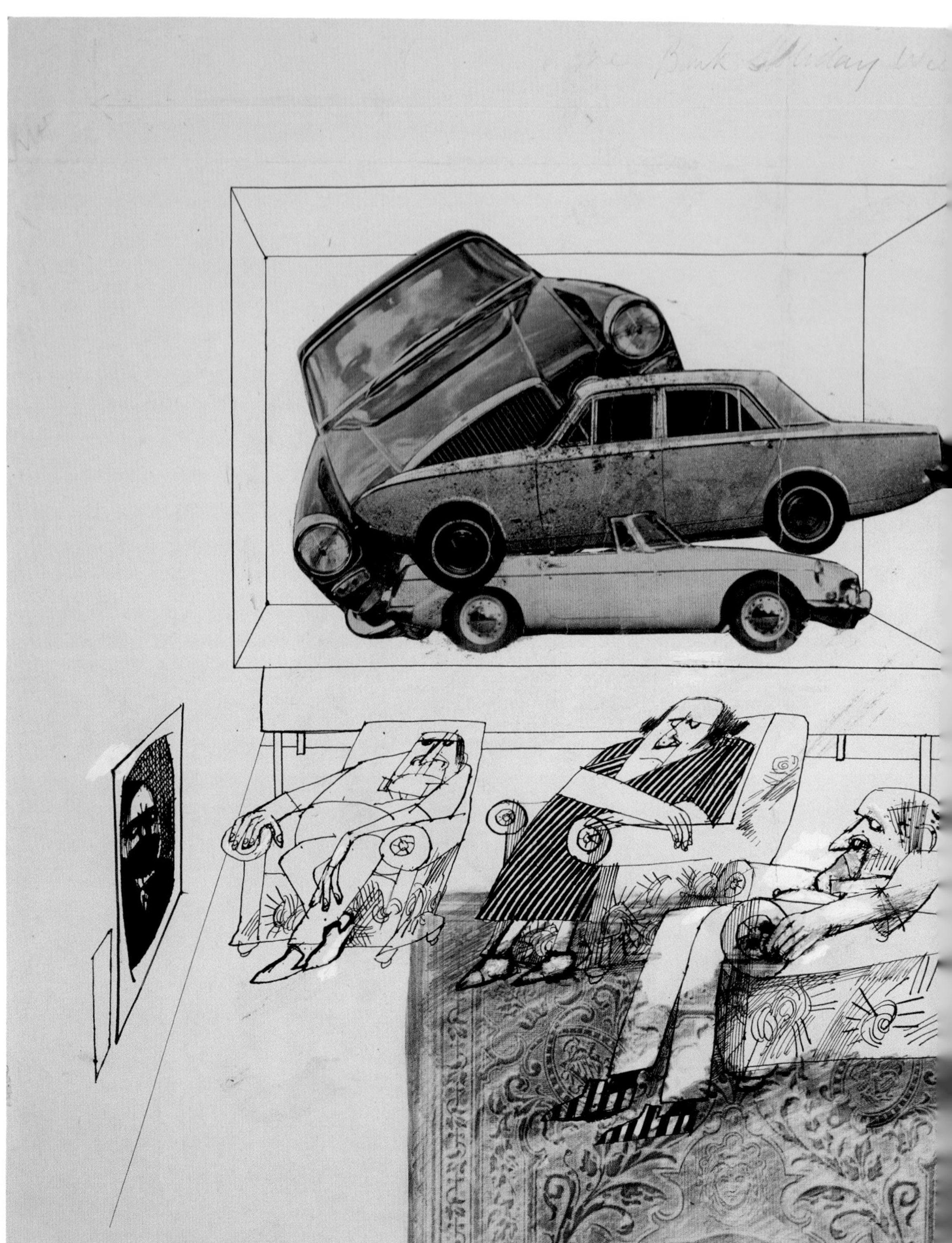

Interior Design, ca. 1962

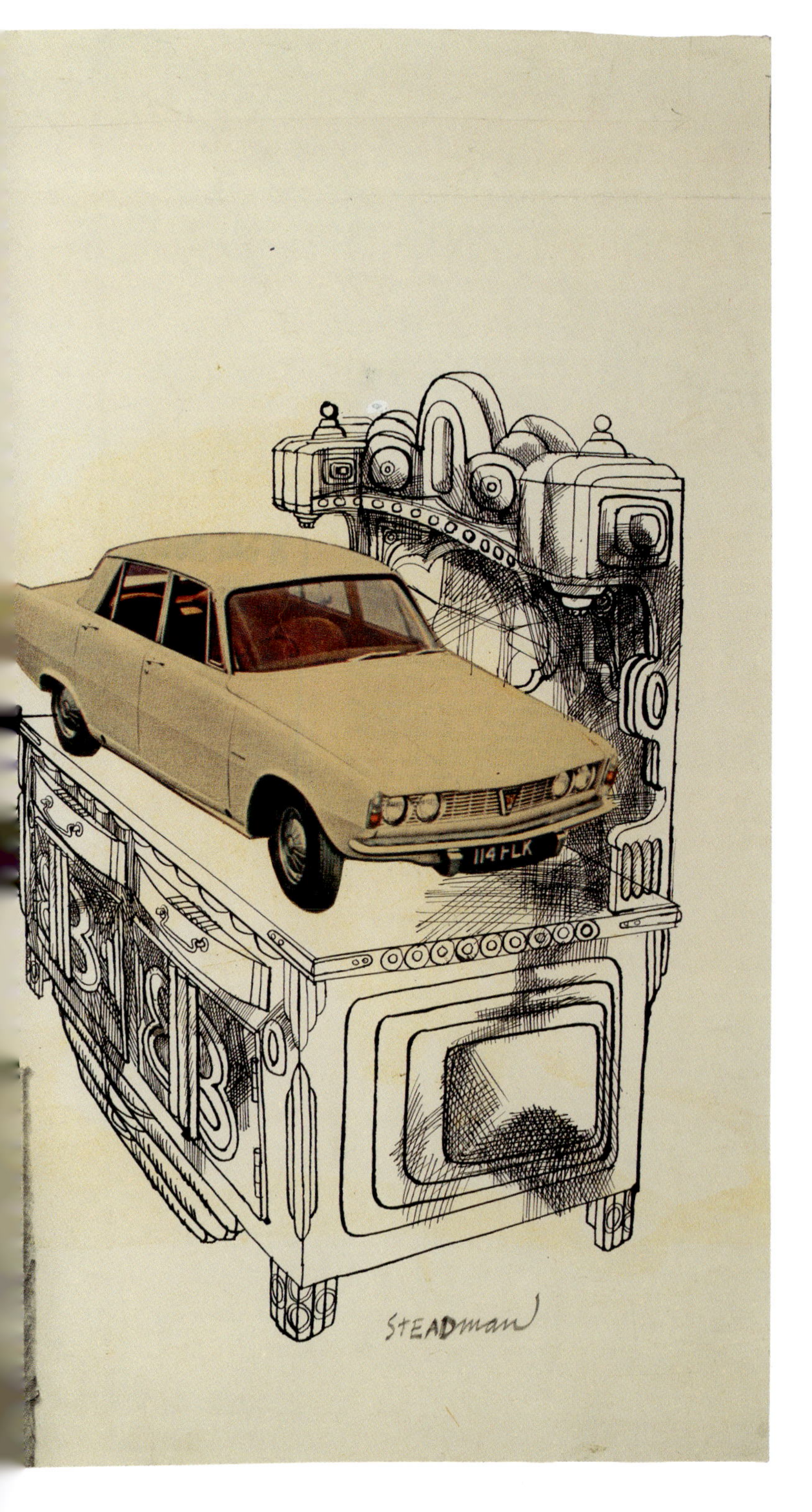

114 FLK
STEADman

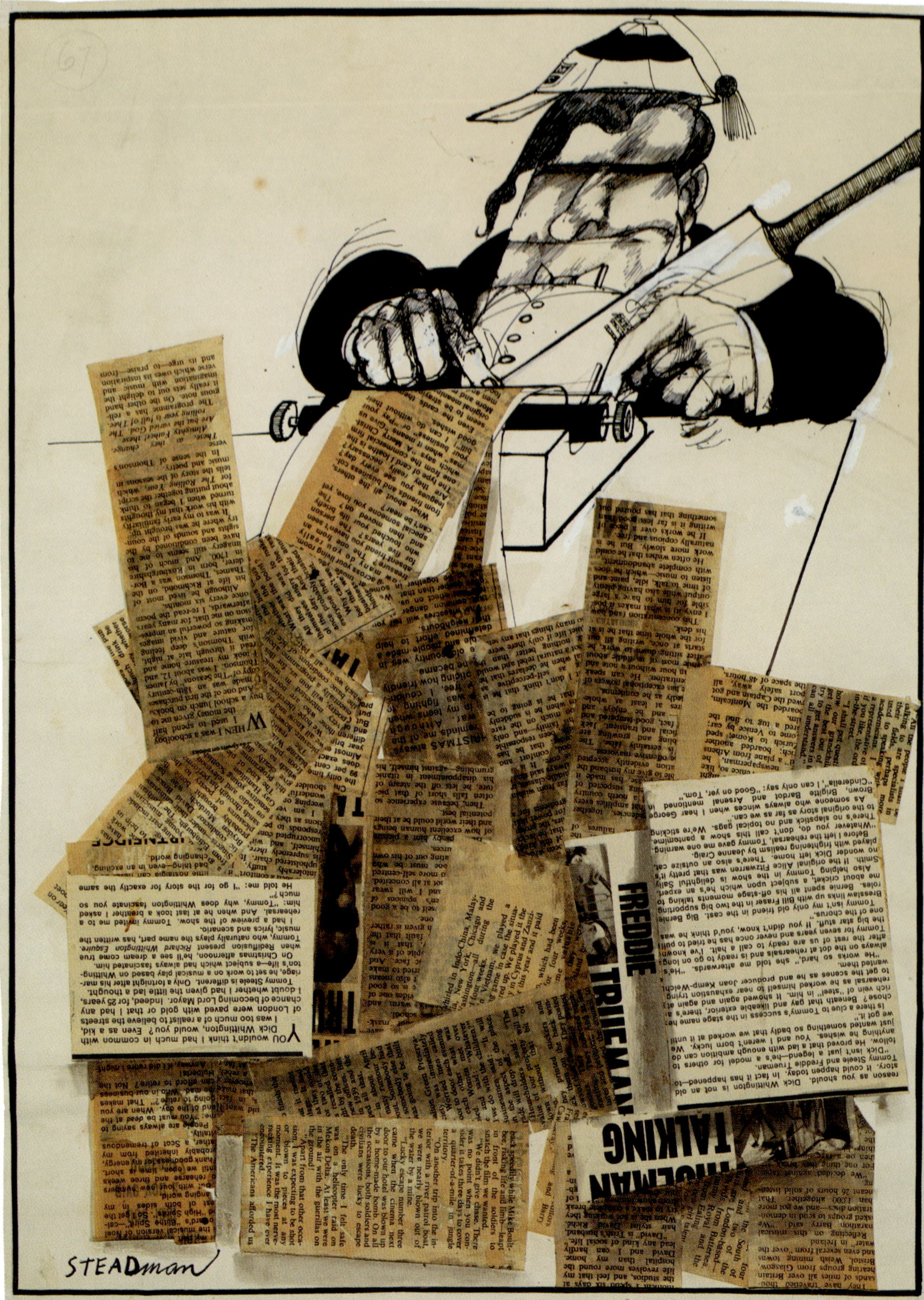

Sporting Memoirs, ca. 1967

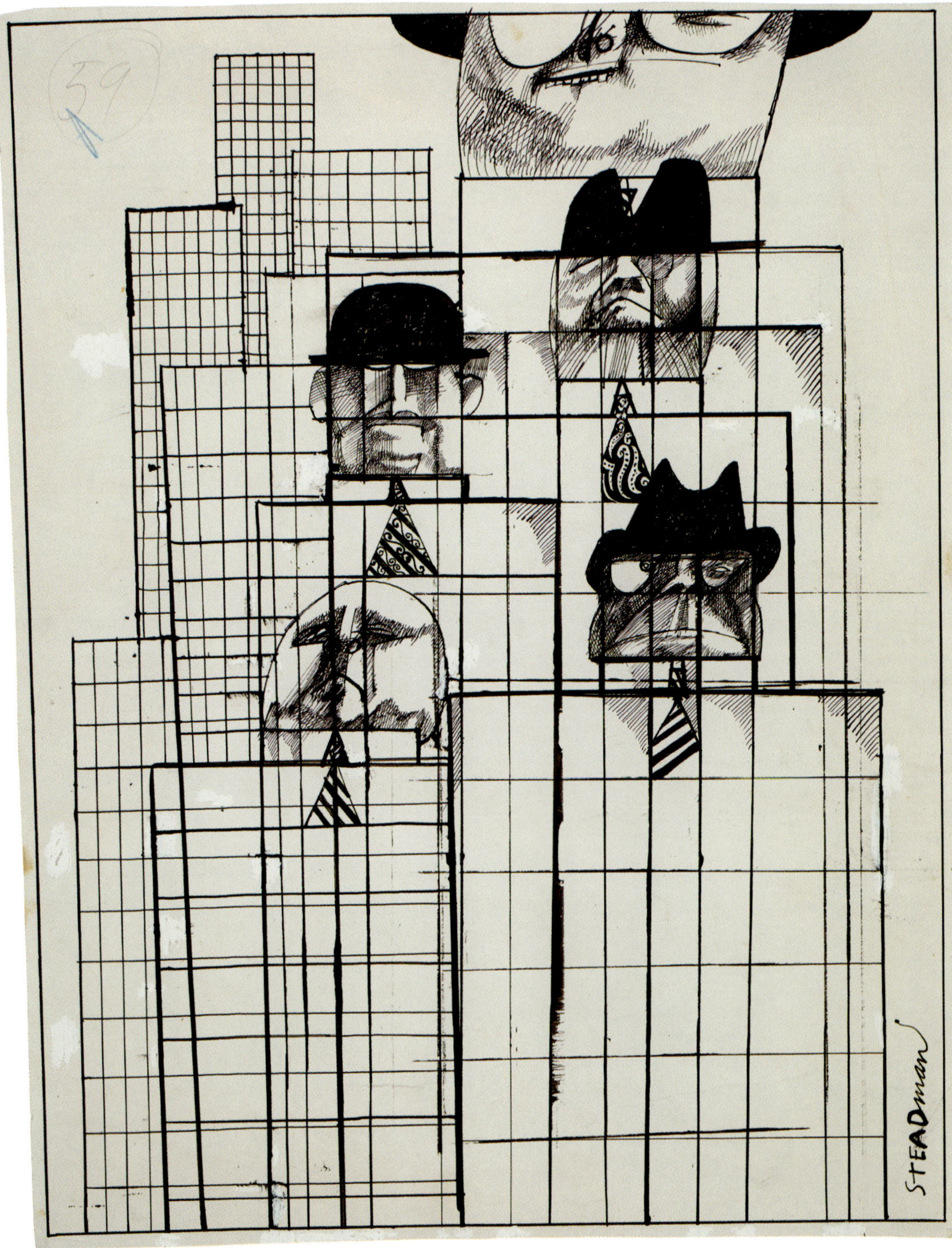

Beginning of High Rise... ca. 1967

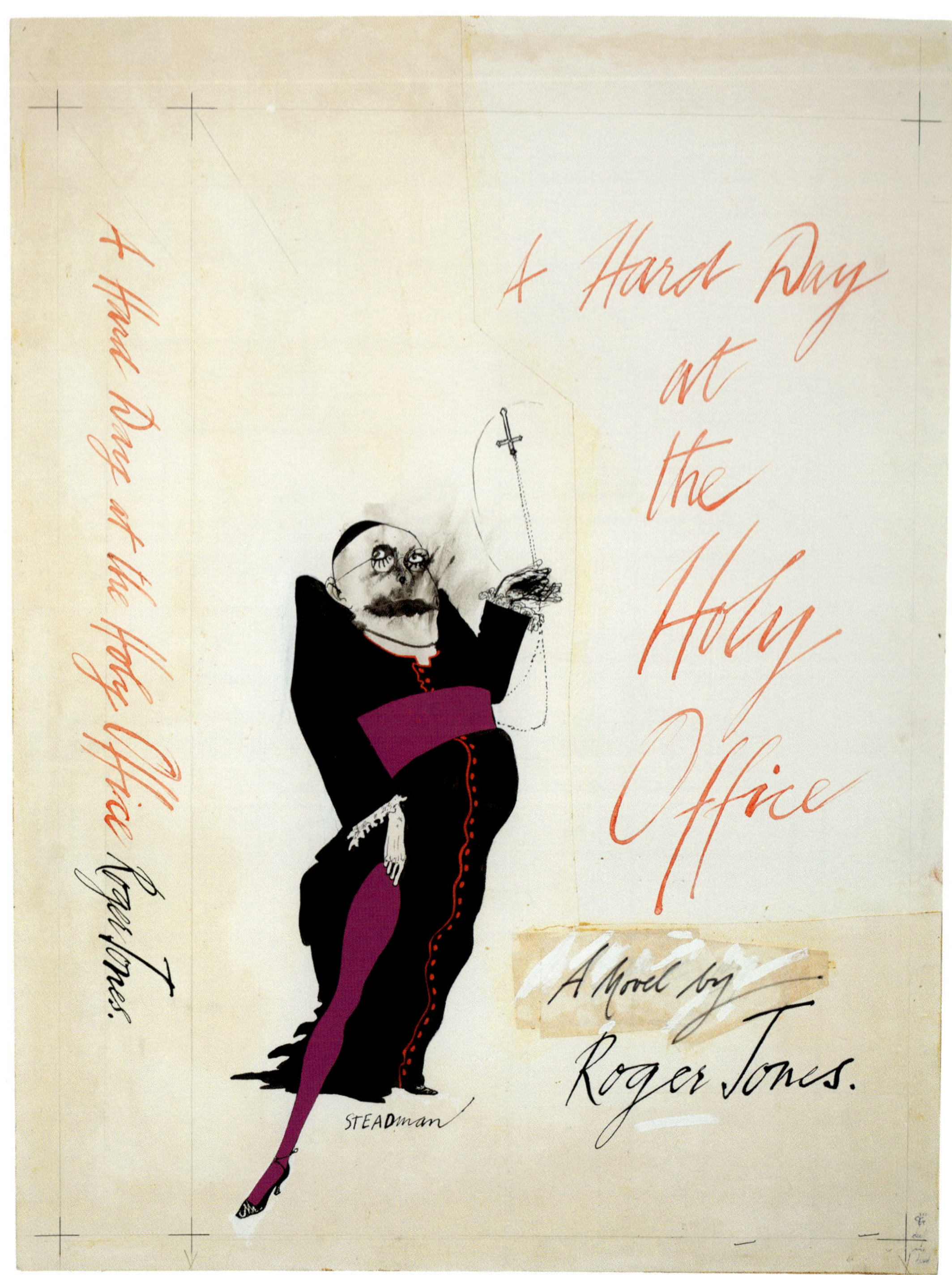

Hard Day at the Holy Office, *Cover Artwork, ca. 1967*

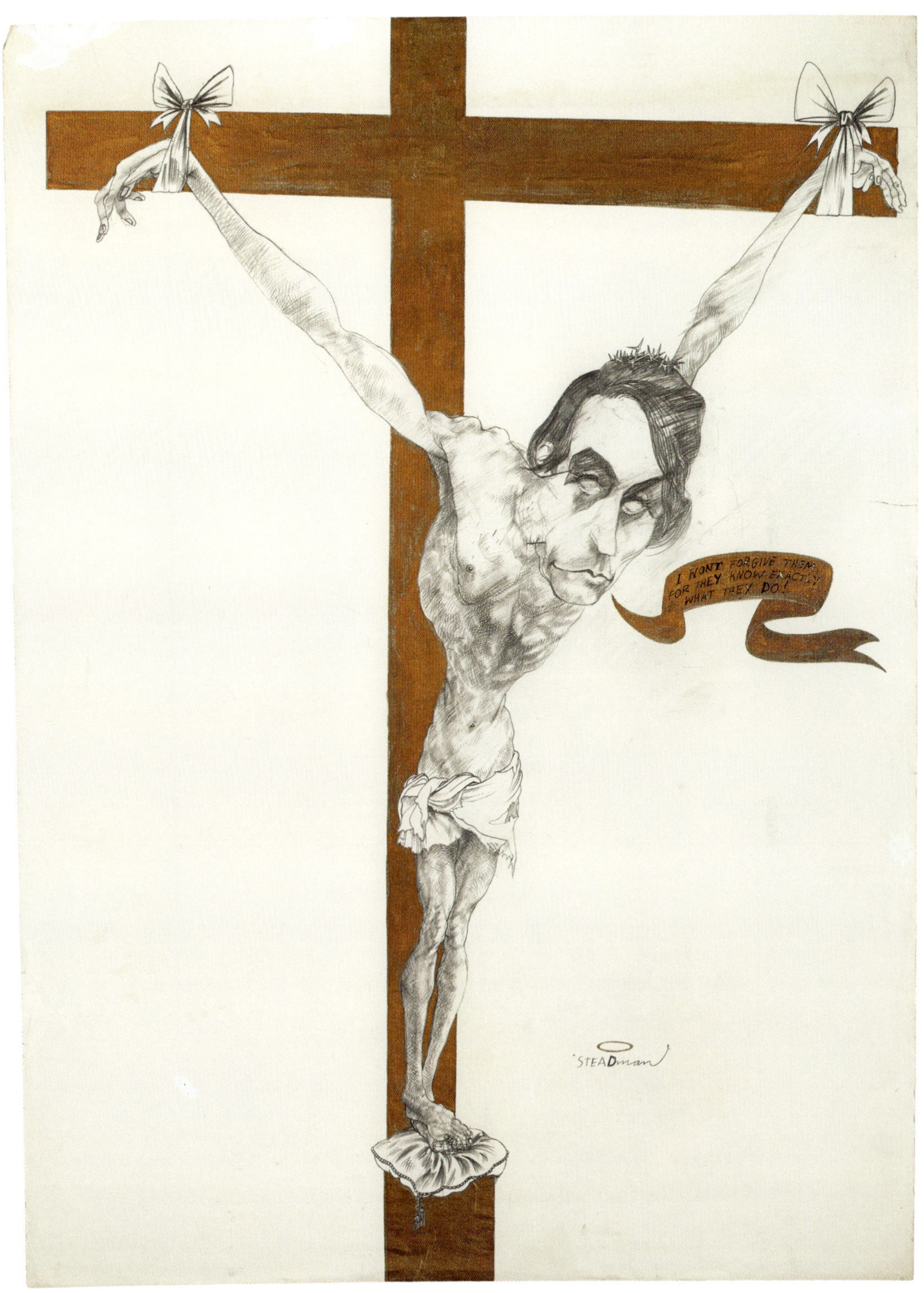

"I was a choir boy in Abergele, in fact, and used to sing every Sunday." *I Won't Forgive Them for They Know What They Do, ca. 1967*

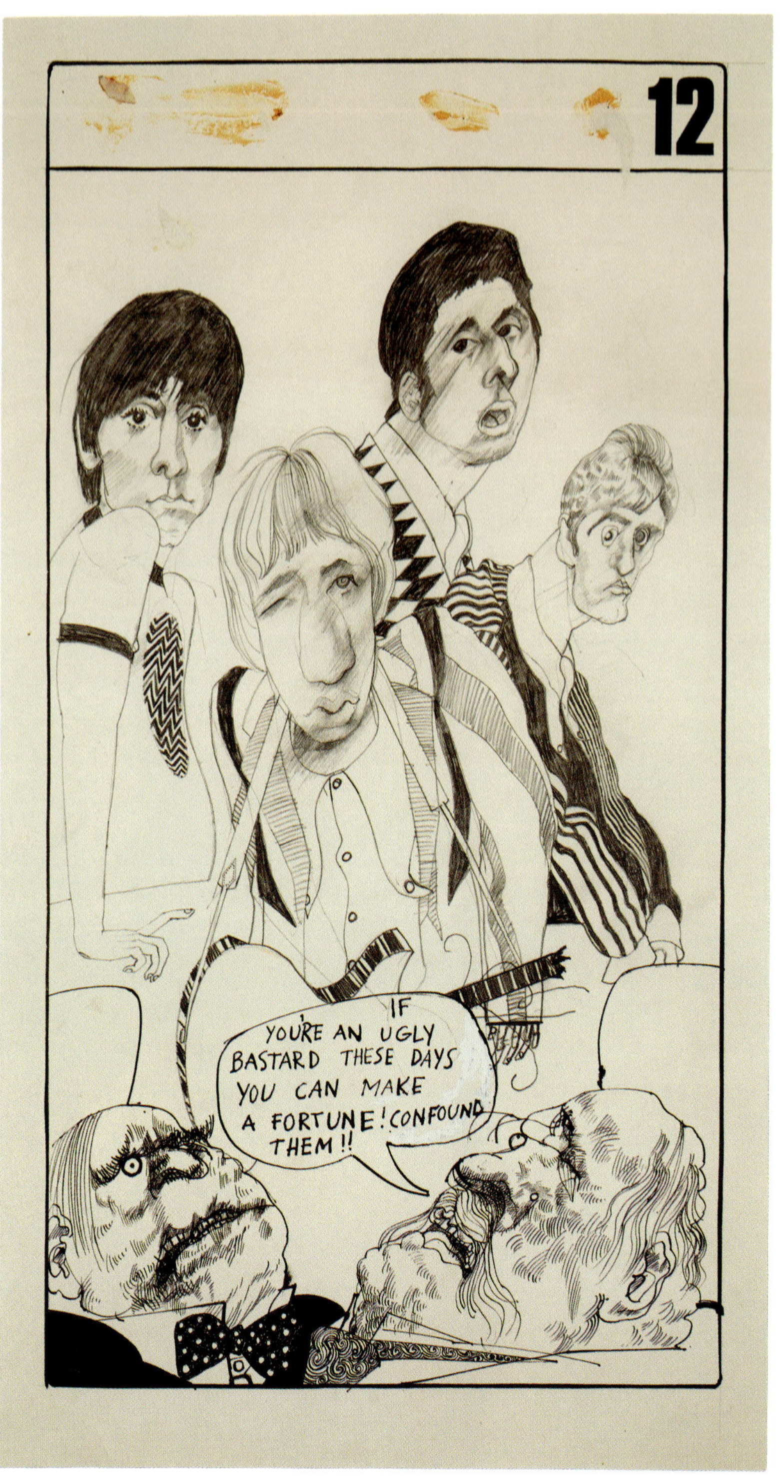

New London Cries 12, The Who, ca. 1967

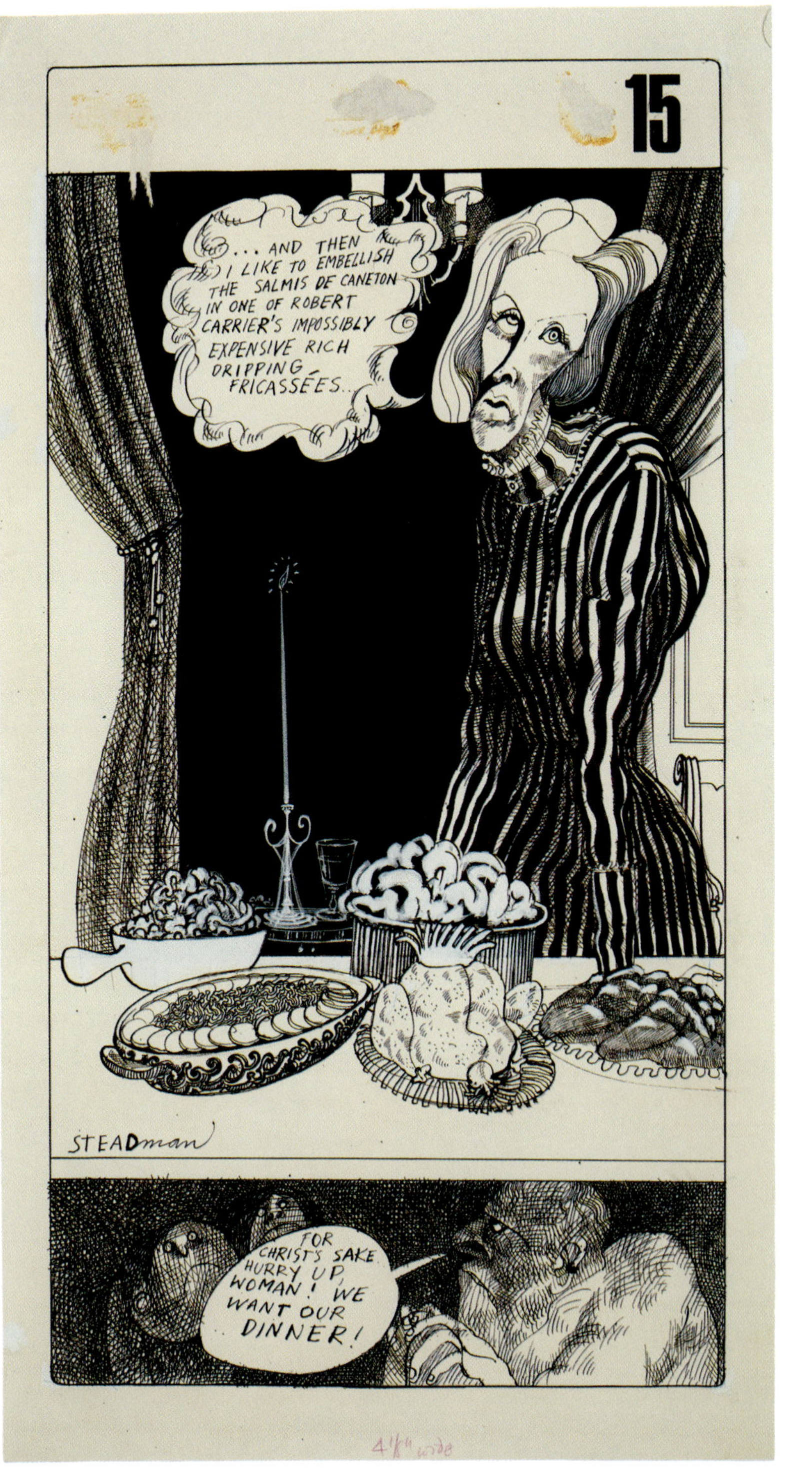

"Fanny Craddock, an early TV chef. The forerunner for the likes of Gordon Ramsay and Anthony Bourdain."
***New London Cries 15**, Cooking on TV, ca. 1967*

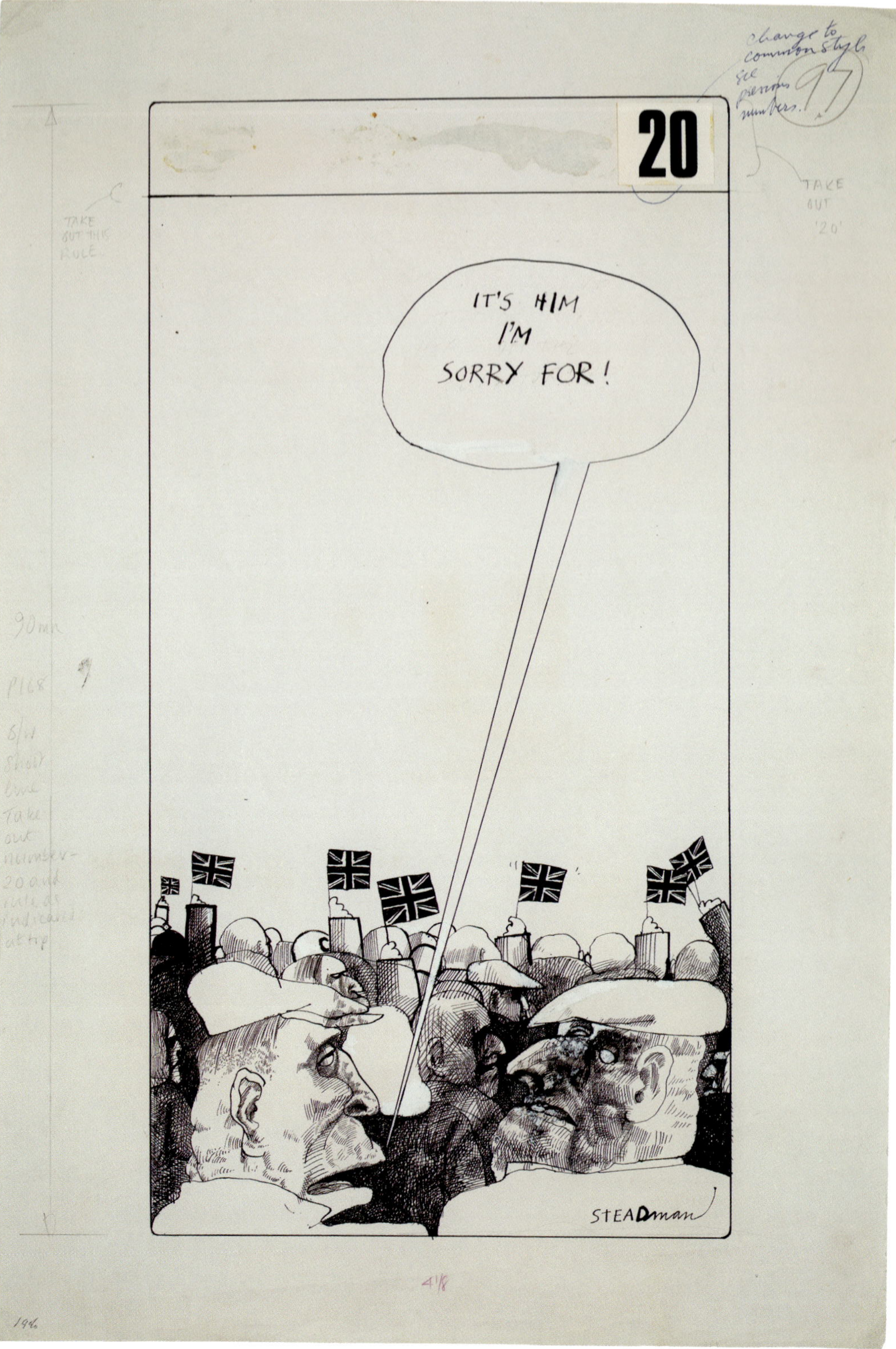

New London Cries 20, *It's Him I'm Sorry For!* 1967

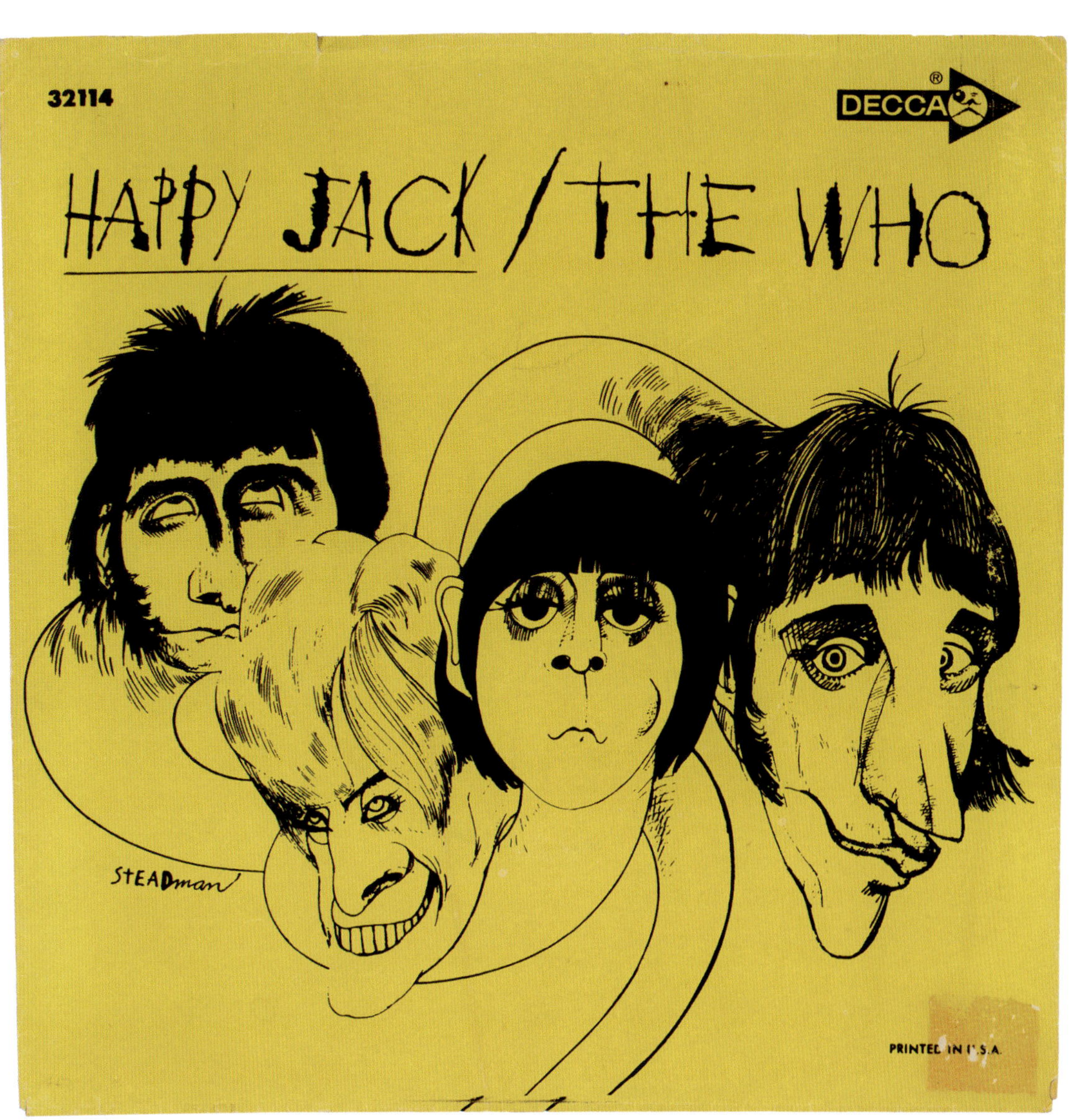

Happy Jack/The Who, *Record Sleeve, 1967*

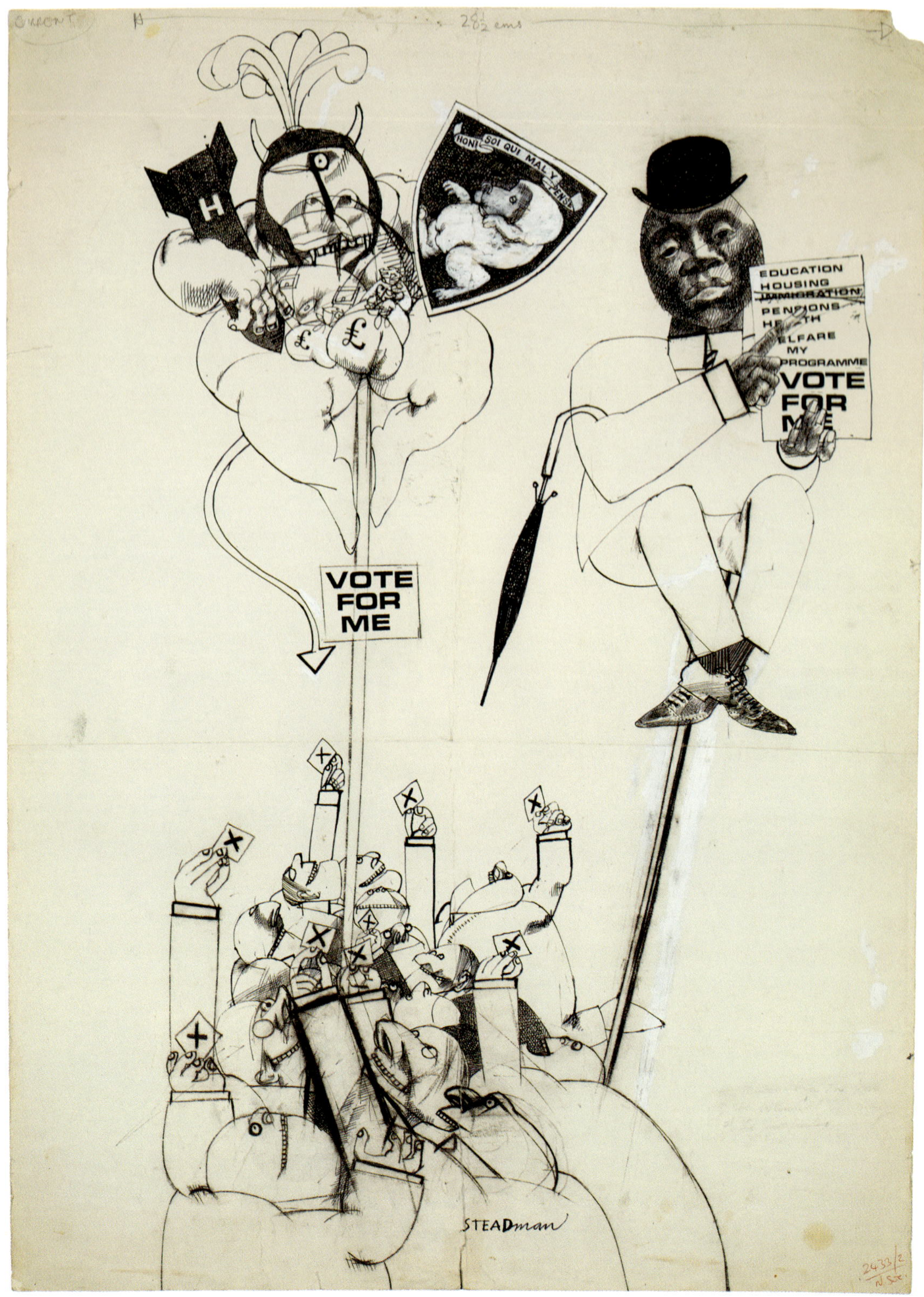

Vote For Me! ca. 1968

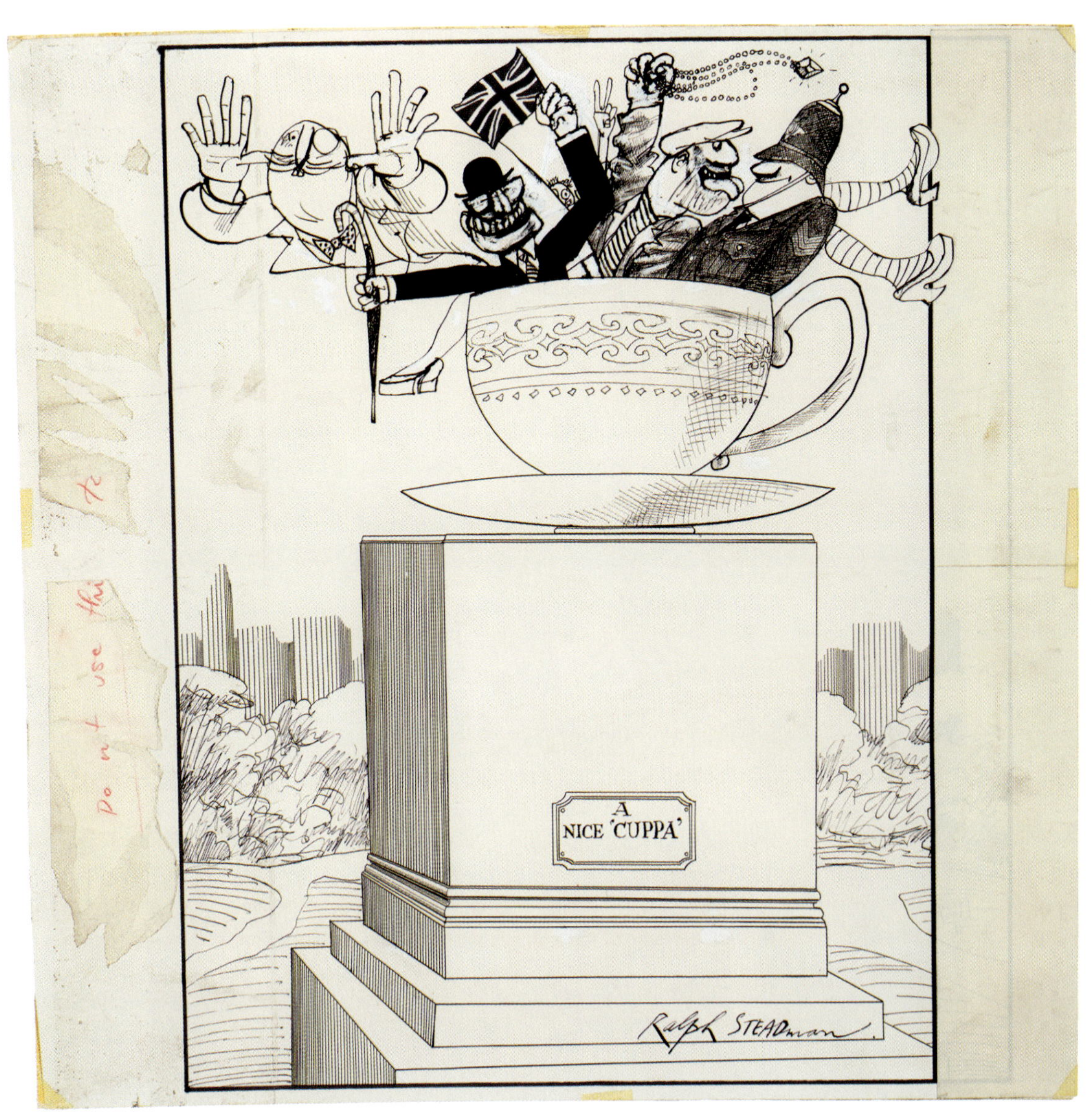

"Really, insert Trump's face, and it's a message for today!" *New Public Art, ca. 1968*

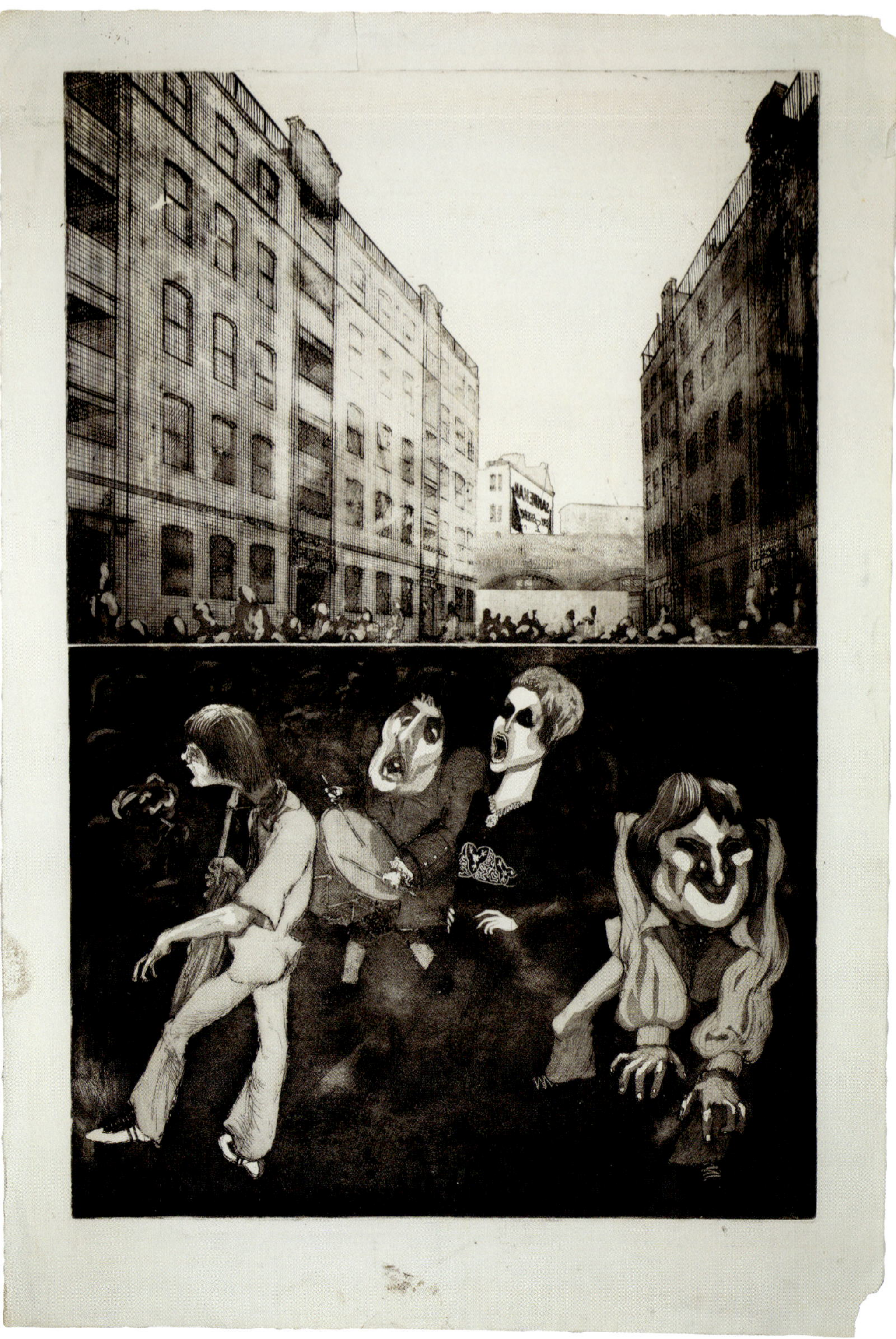

Julie Driscoll and Brian Auger & the Trinity, ca. 1968

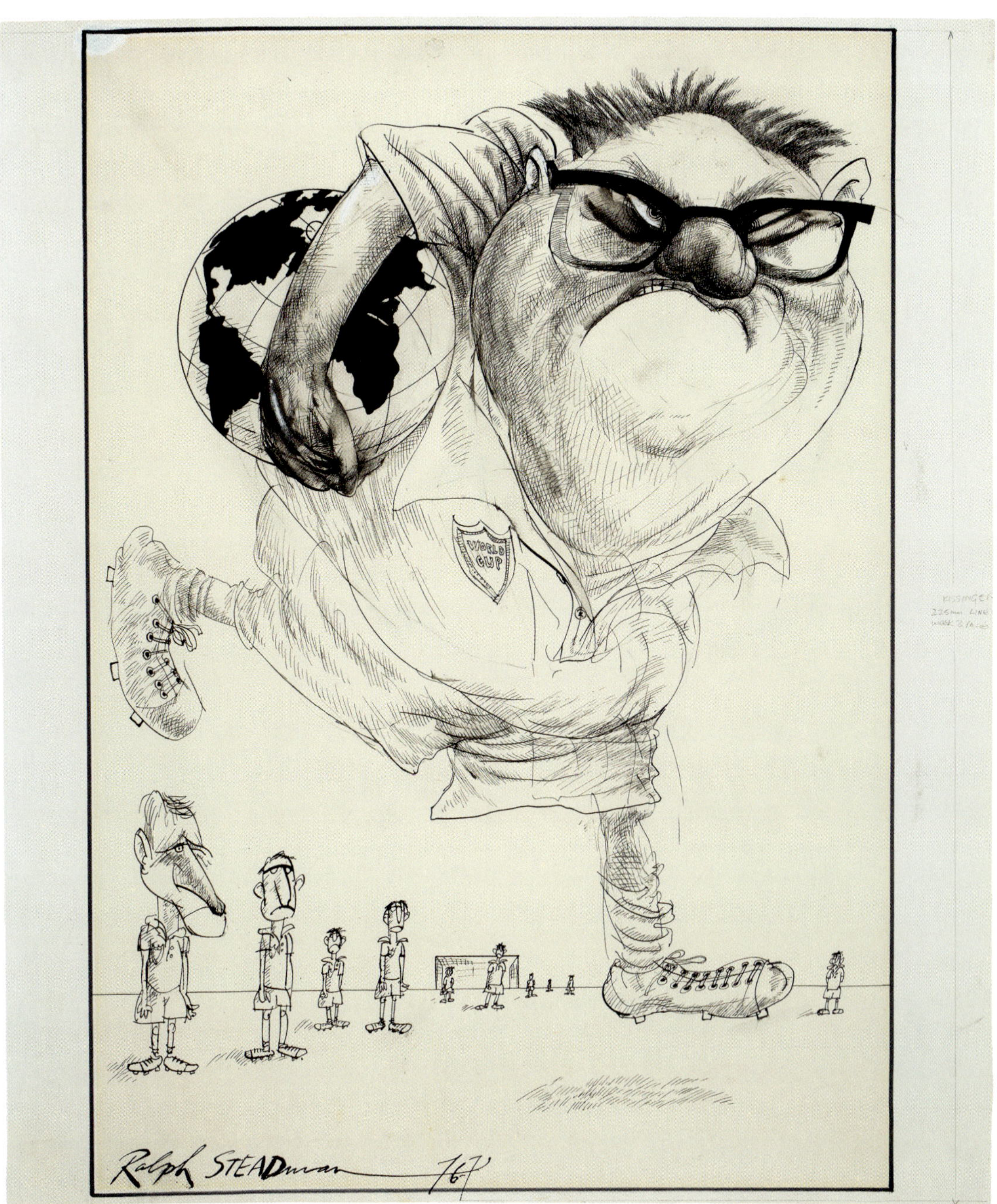

Ralph STEADman 76

Henry Kissinger, 1976

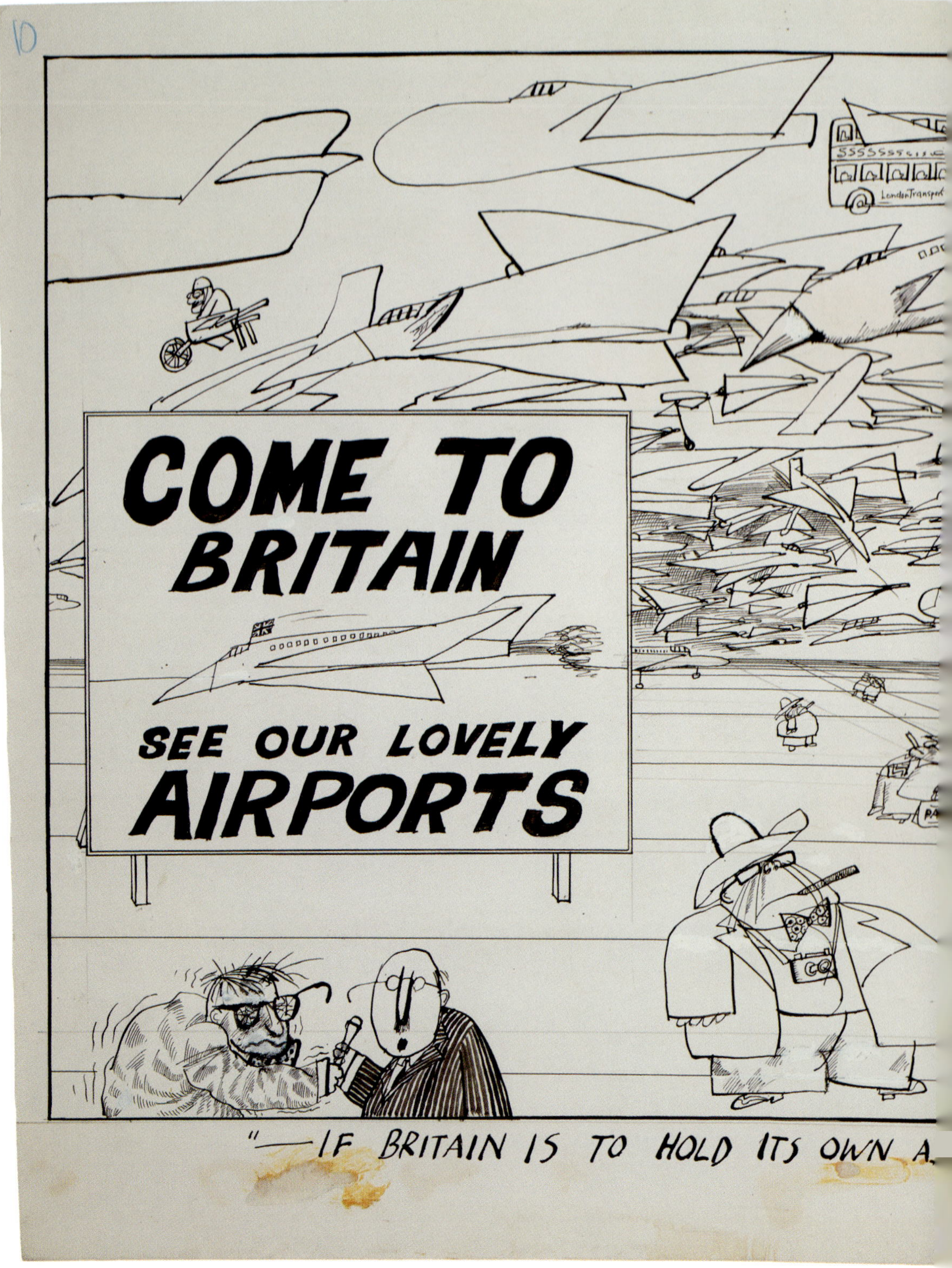

"It's so strange not hearing planes in the sky for the last few months."

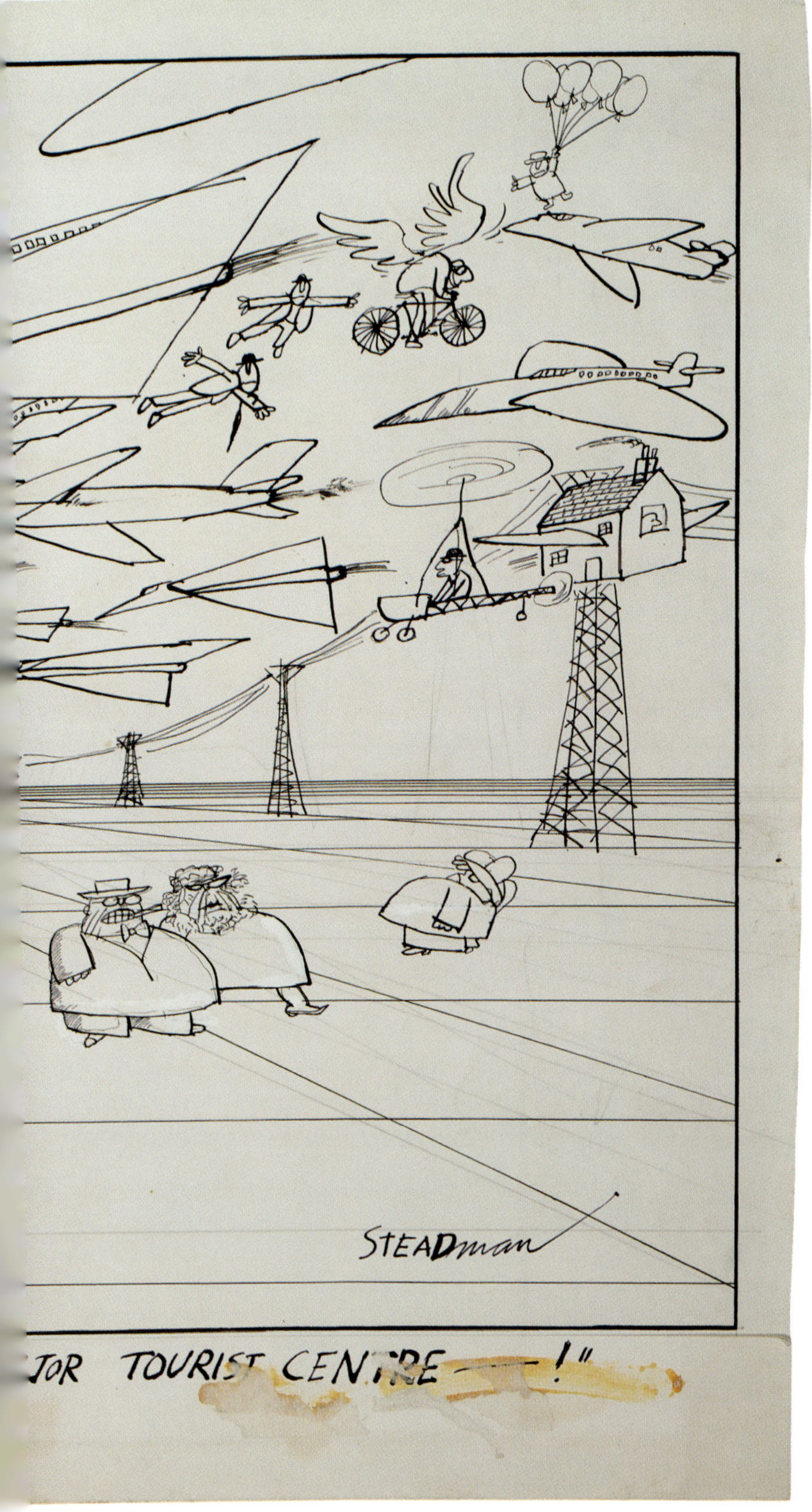

Pride in Our Airports, ca. 1968

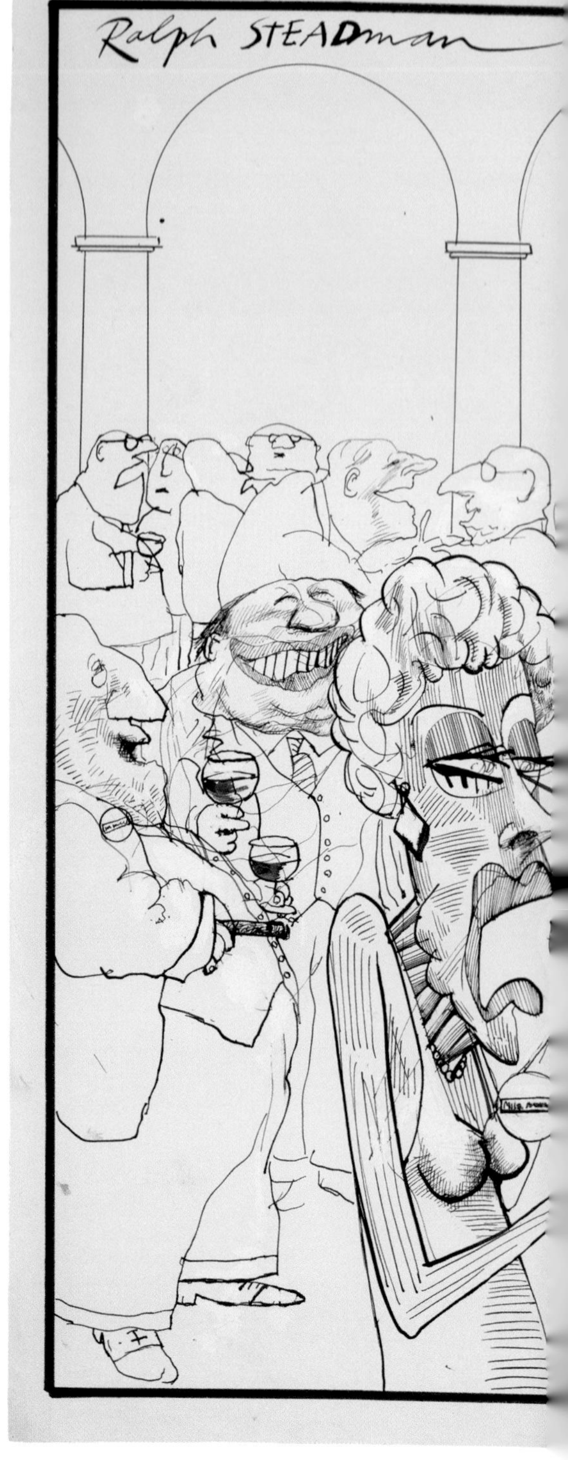
Ralph STEADman

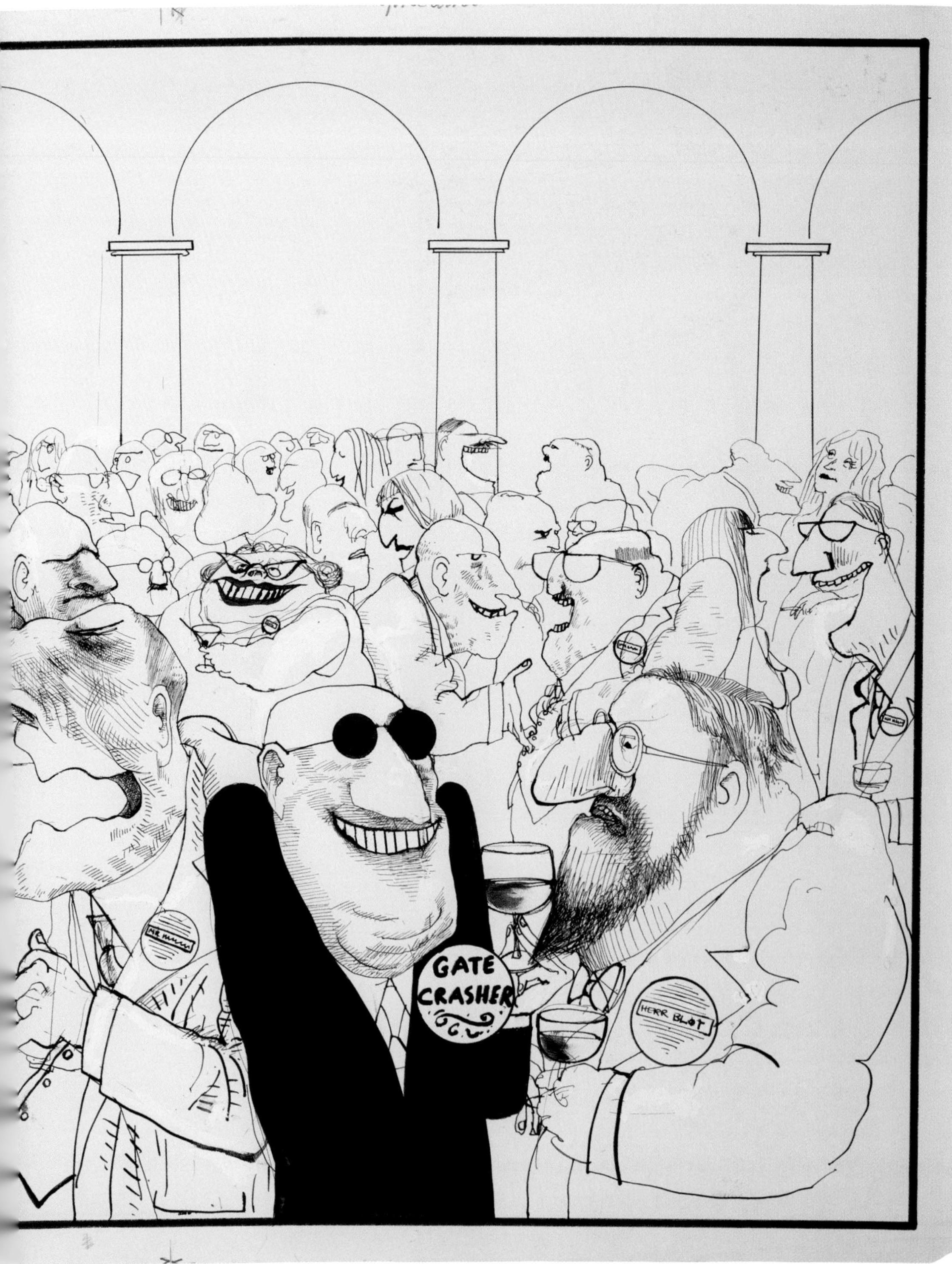

The Gate Crasher, ca. 1972

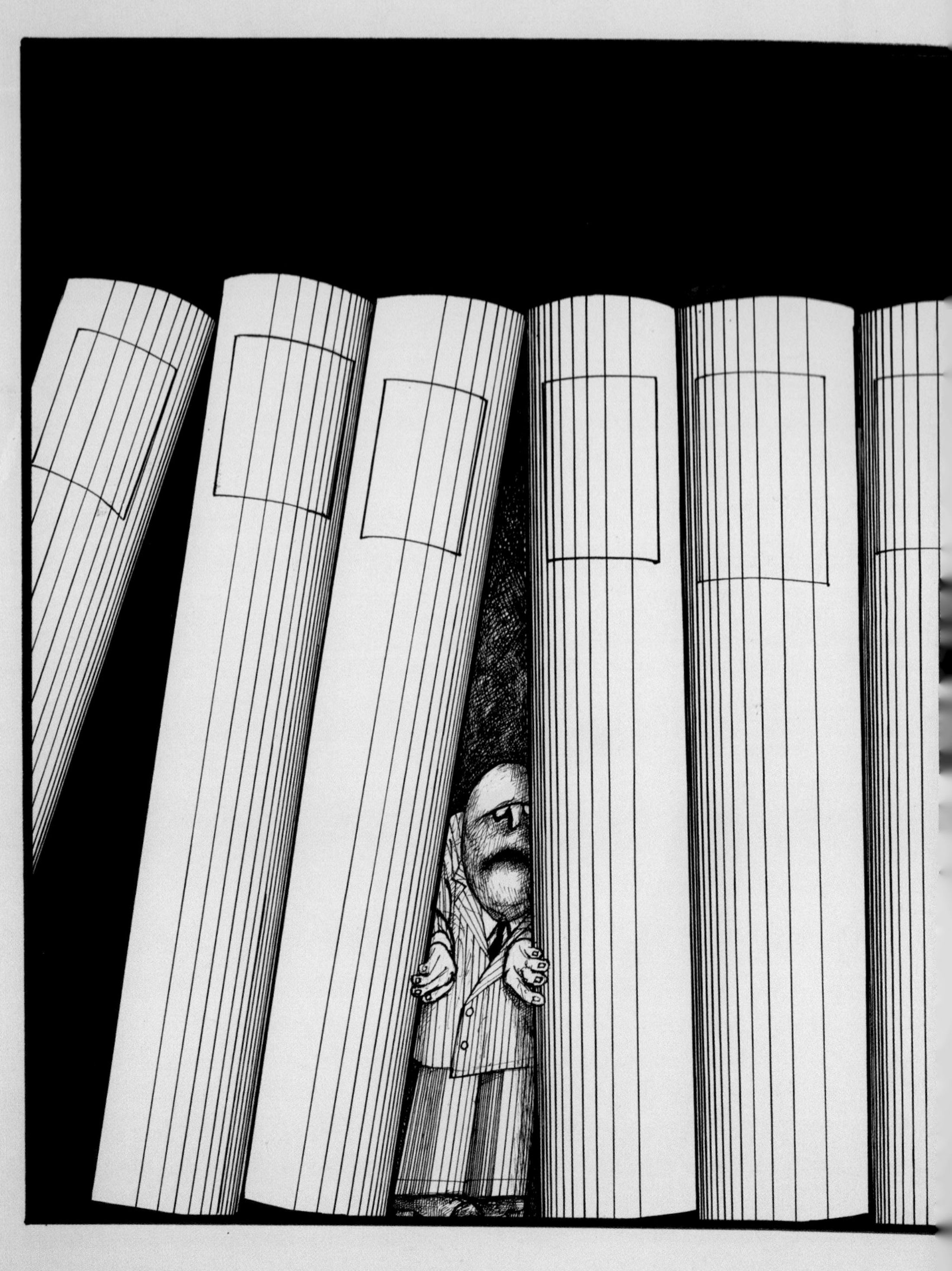

Frankfurt Book Fair, ca. 1969

Ralph STEADman

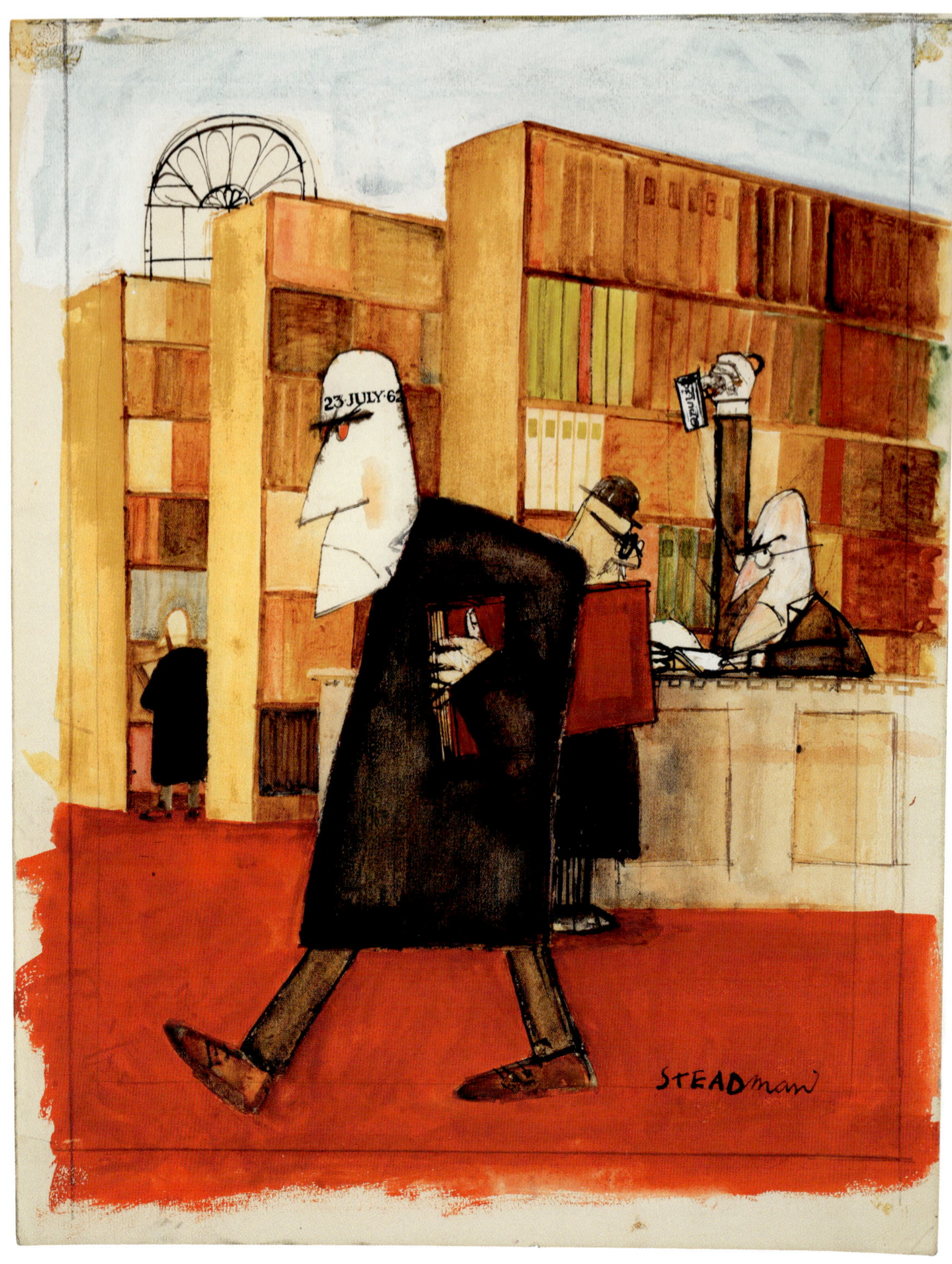

Punch *Magazine Cover, ca. 1968* "It was all about getting a *Punch* cover back then. I am not even sure if these made it."

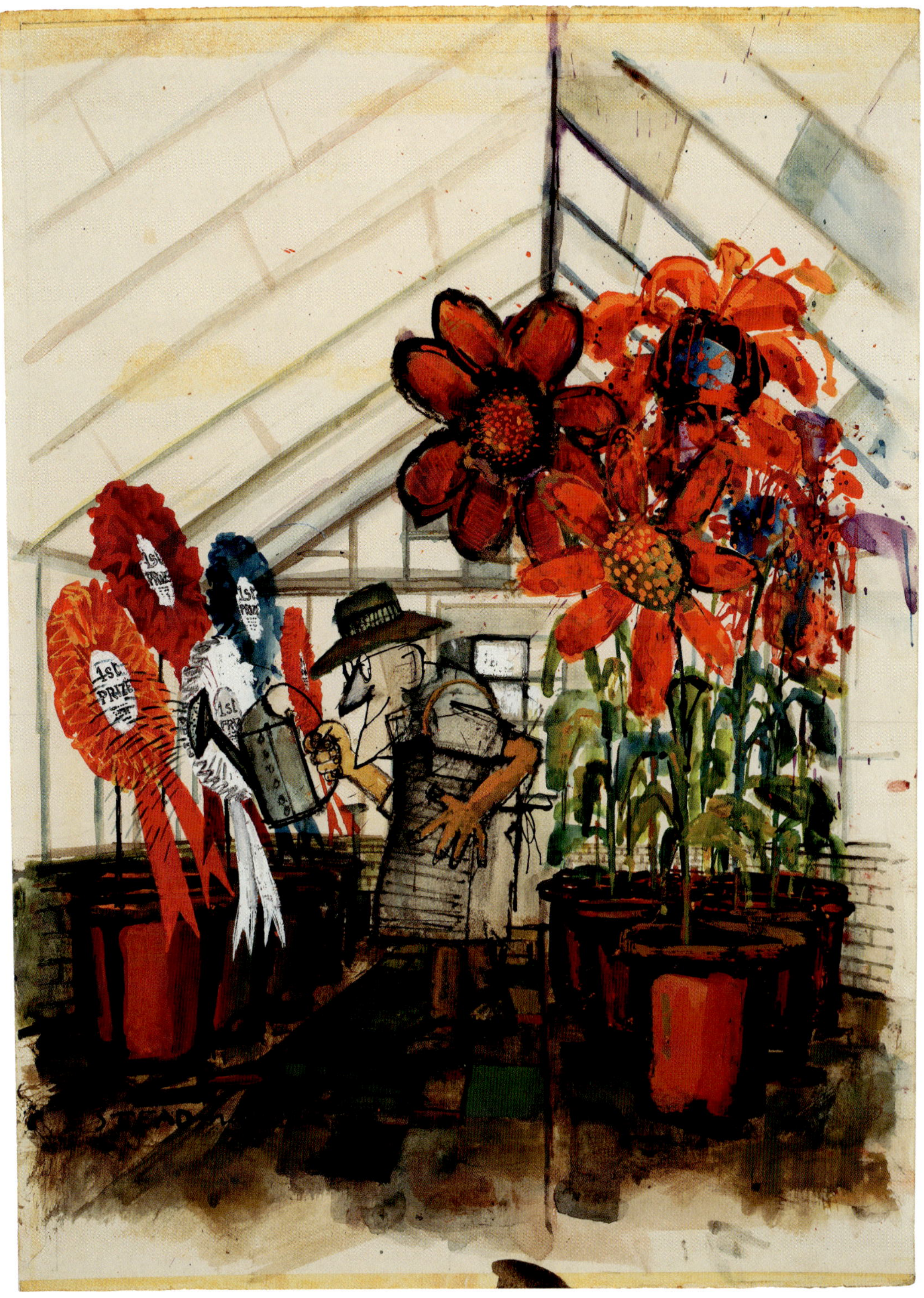

Punch Cover, ca. 1968

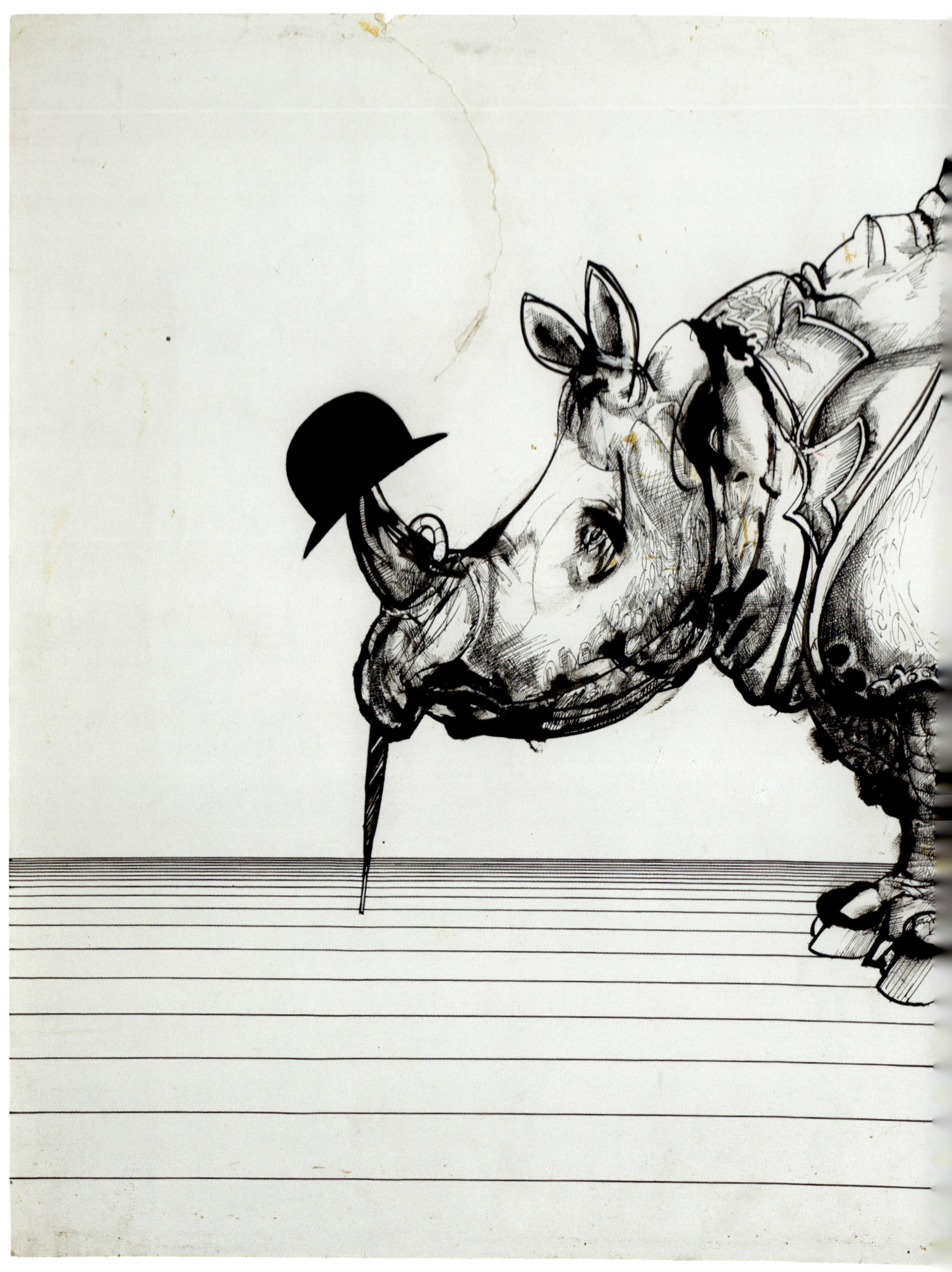

"I think all that time spent at the Natural History Museum, drawing the skeletons, must have really helped me understand what was going on underneath the skin."

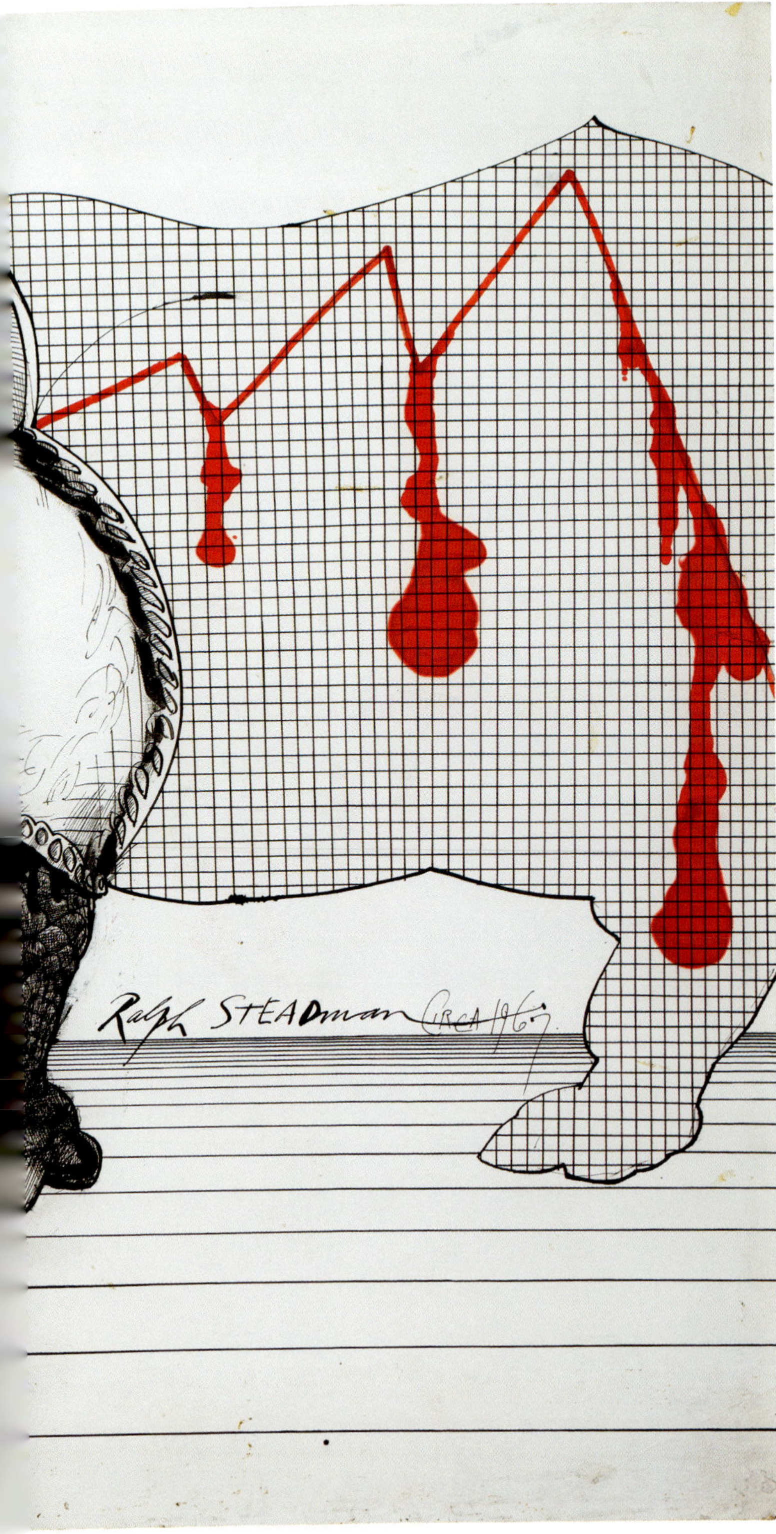

City Finance, ca. 1967

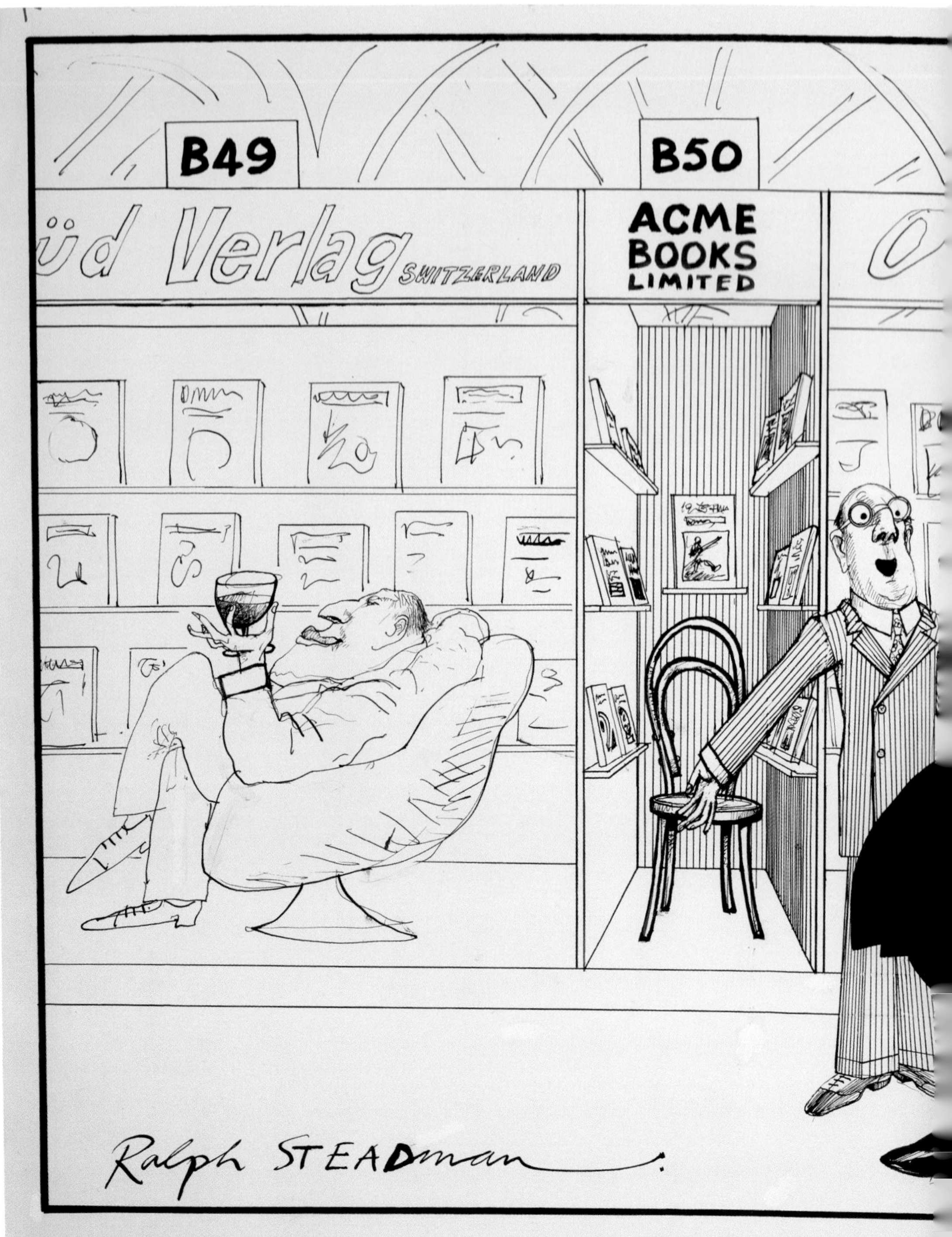

Ralph STEADman

At the Frankfurt Book Fair, ca. 1969

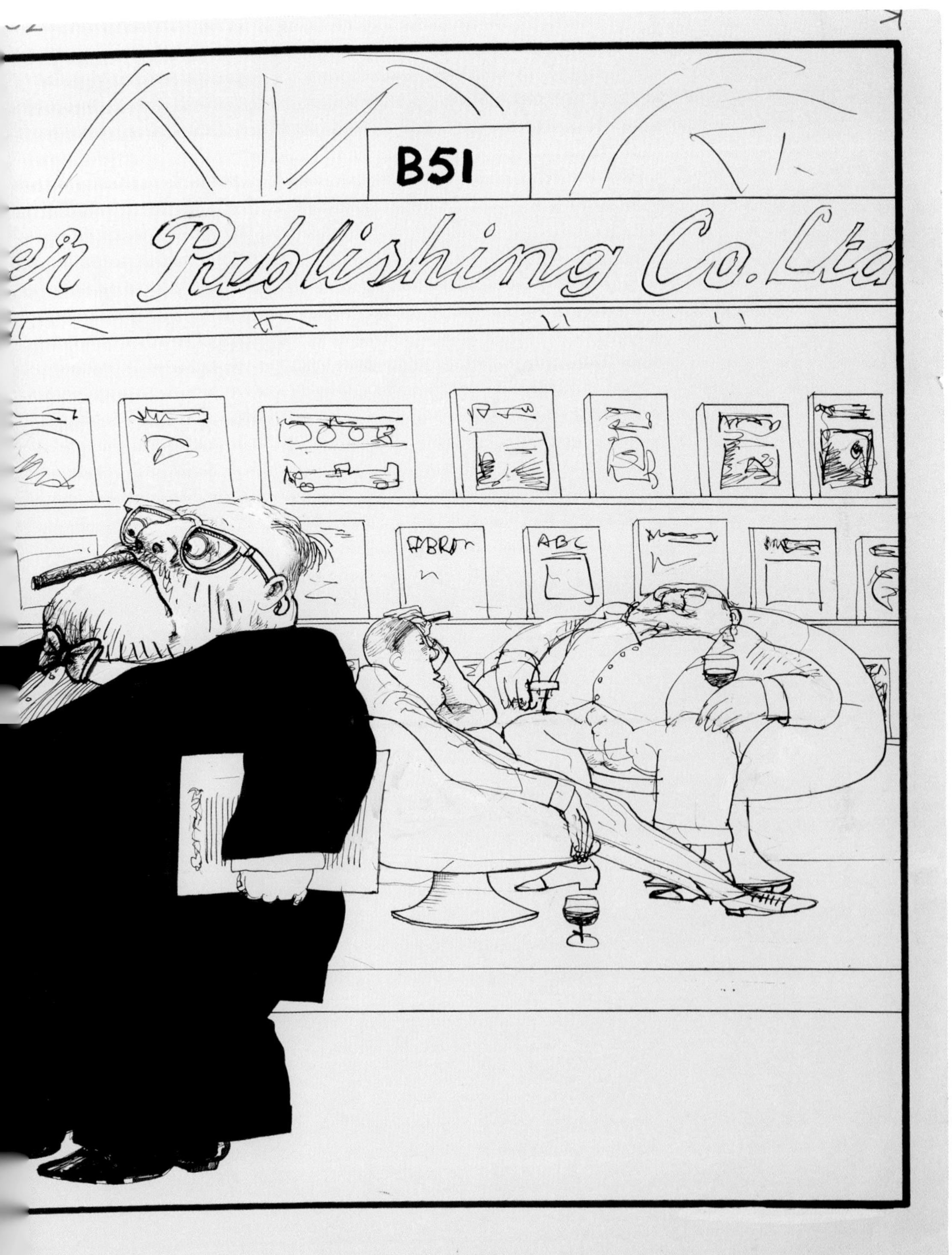

"The hope and enthusiasm of the new, young publisher amidst all the fat cats really stood out."

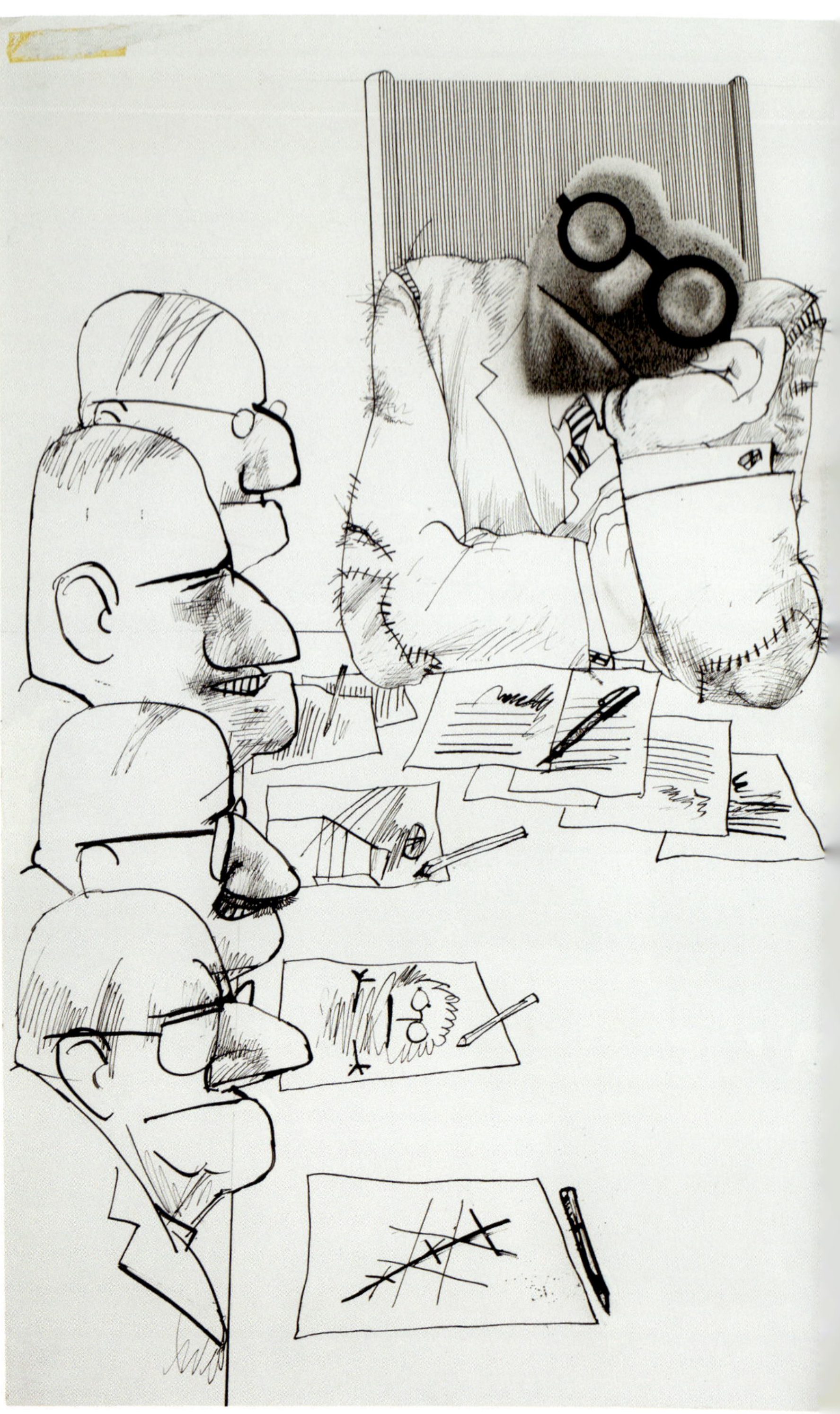

Bored Meeting, ca. 1967

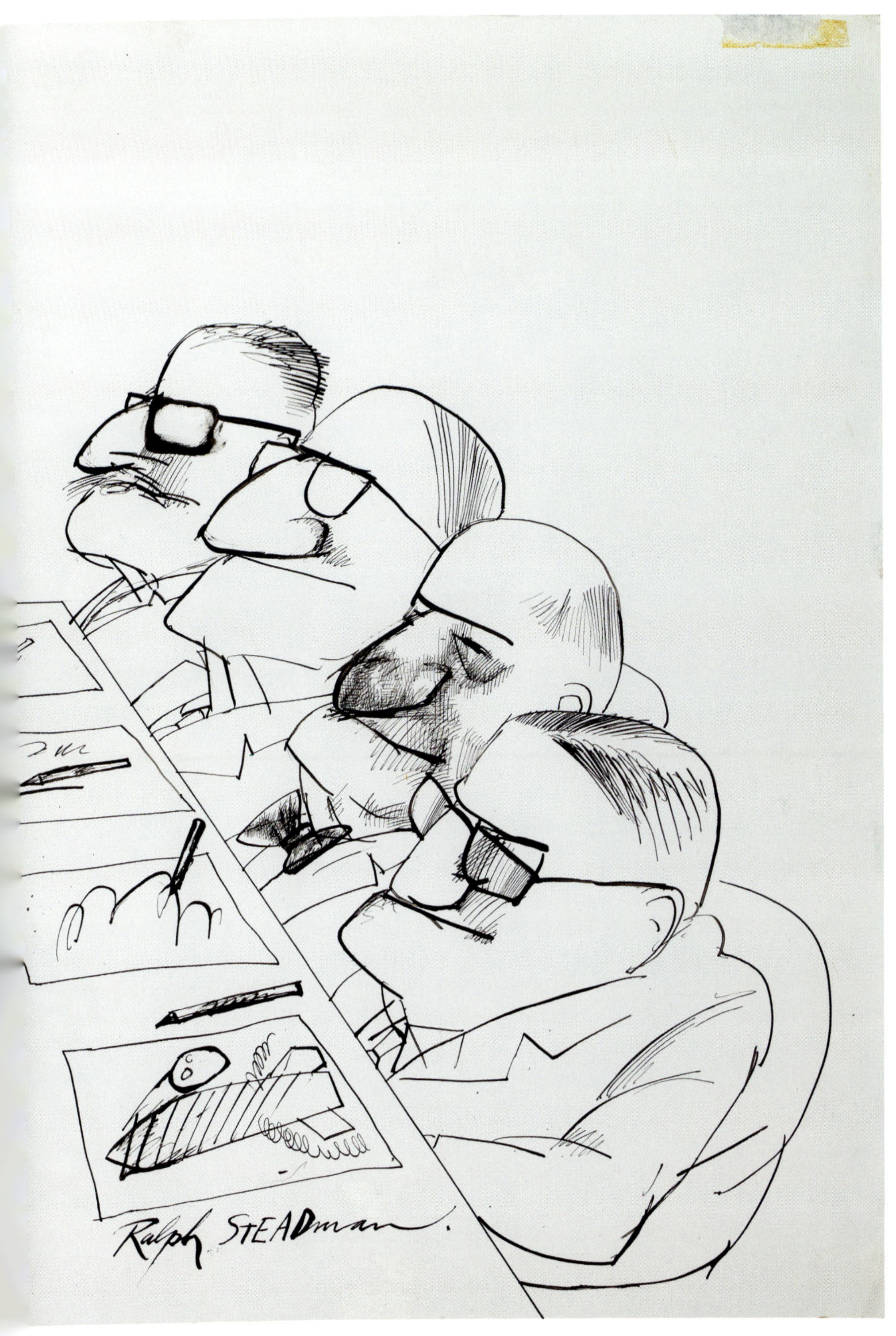

"I never wanted to work in an office. I decided after I got fired from Woolworths simply never to expect a weekly paycheck, and I just explored projects that interested me after that."

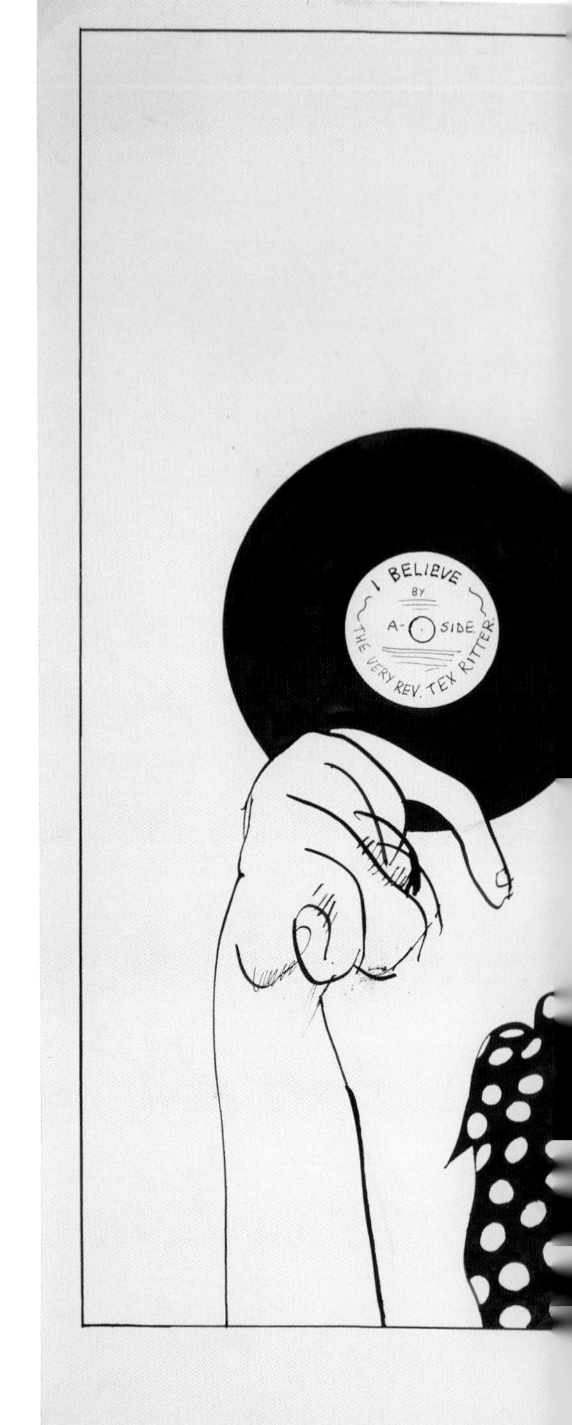

I BELIEVE
BY
A- SIDE.
THE VERY REV. TEX RITTER.

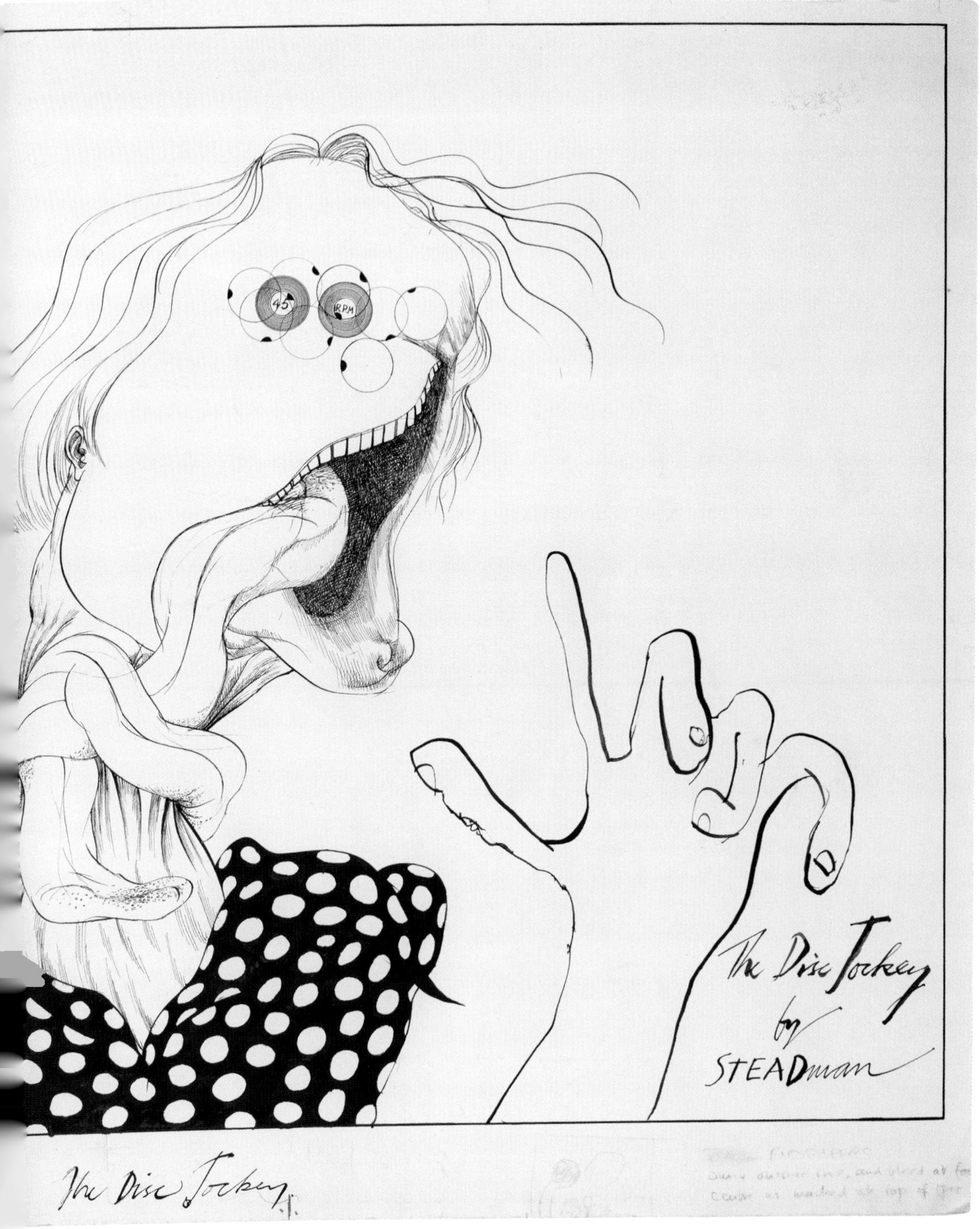

The Disc Jockey, **Born Under a Bad Sign**, *ca. 1969*

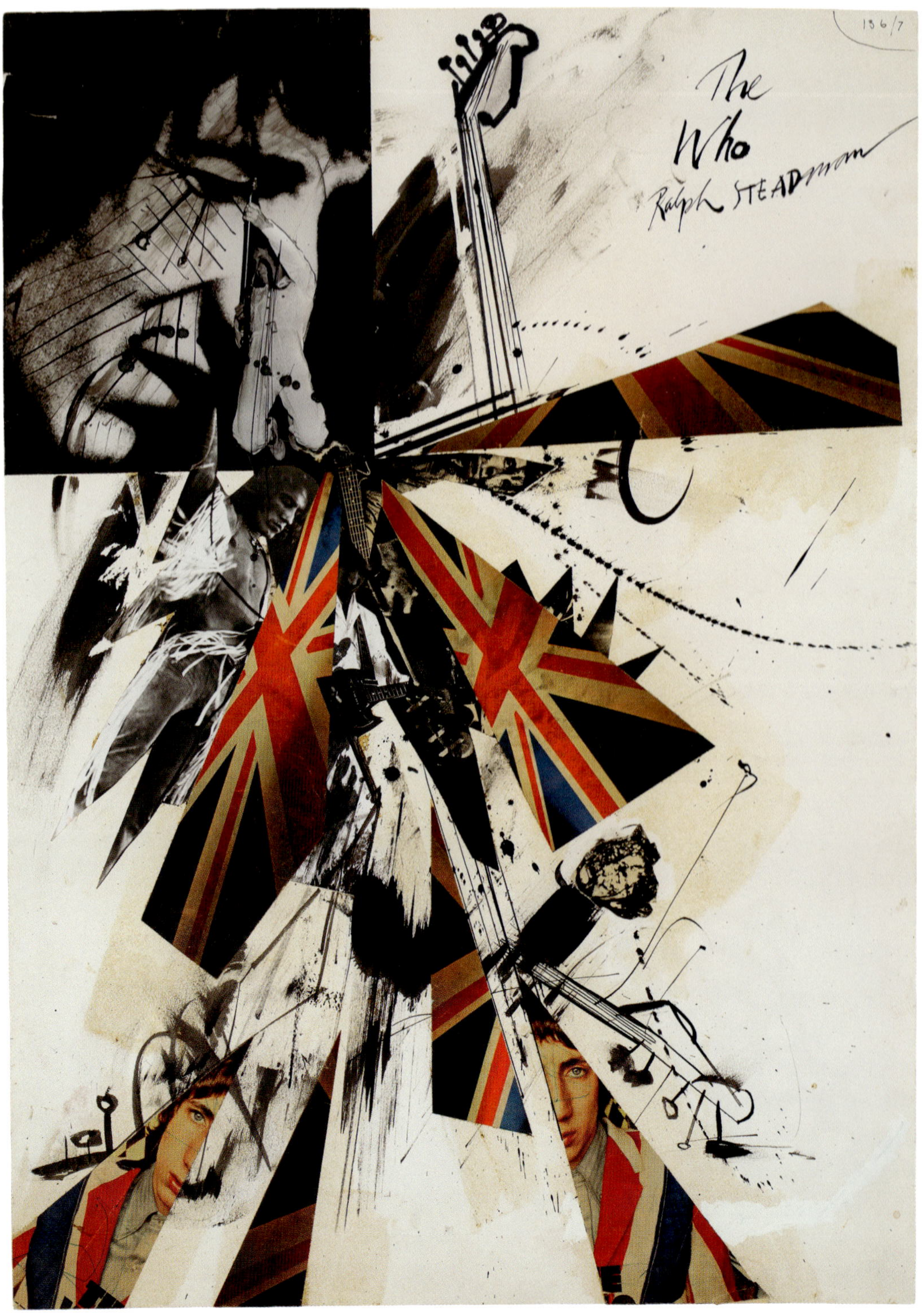

The Who, **Born Under a Bad Sign**, ca. 1969

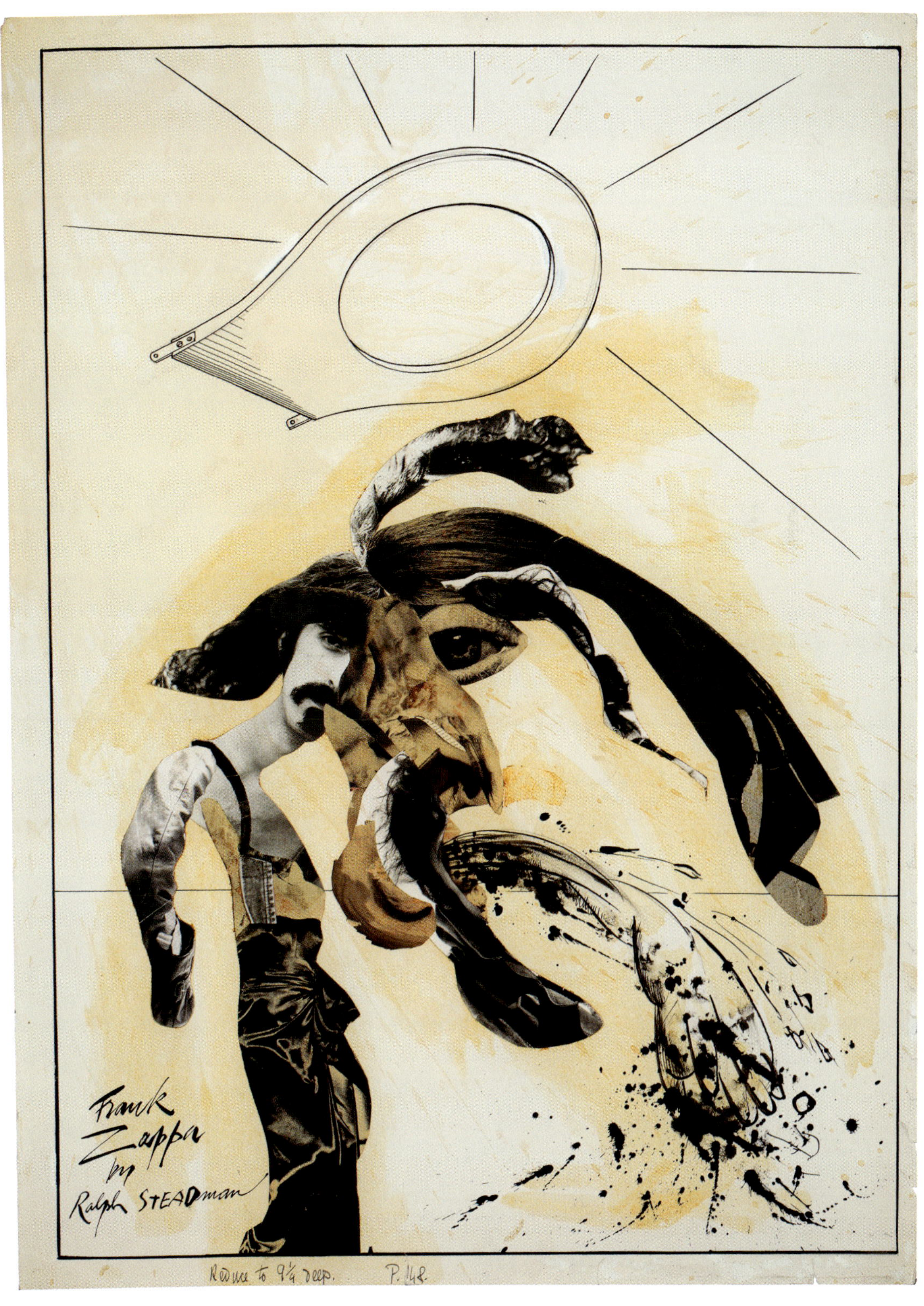

"Cow gum was the glue I used back in the 1970s. It has coloured the paper yellow over the years." *Frank Zappa*, **Born Under a Bad Sign**, *ca. 1969*

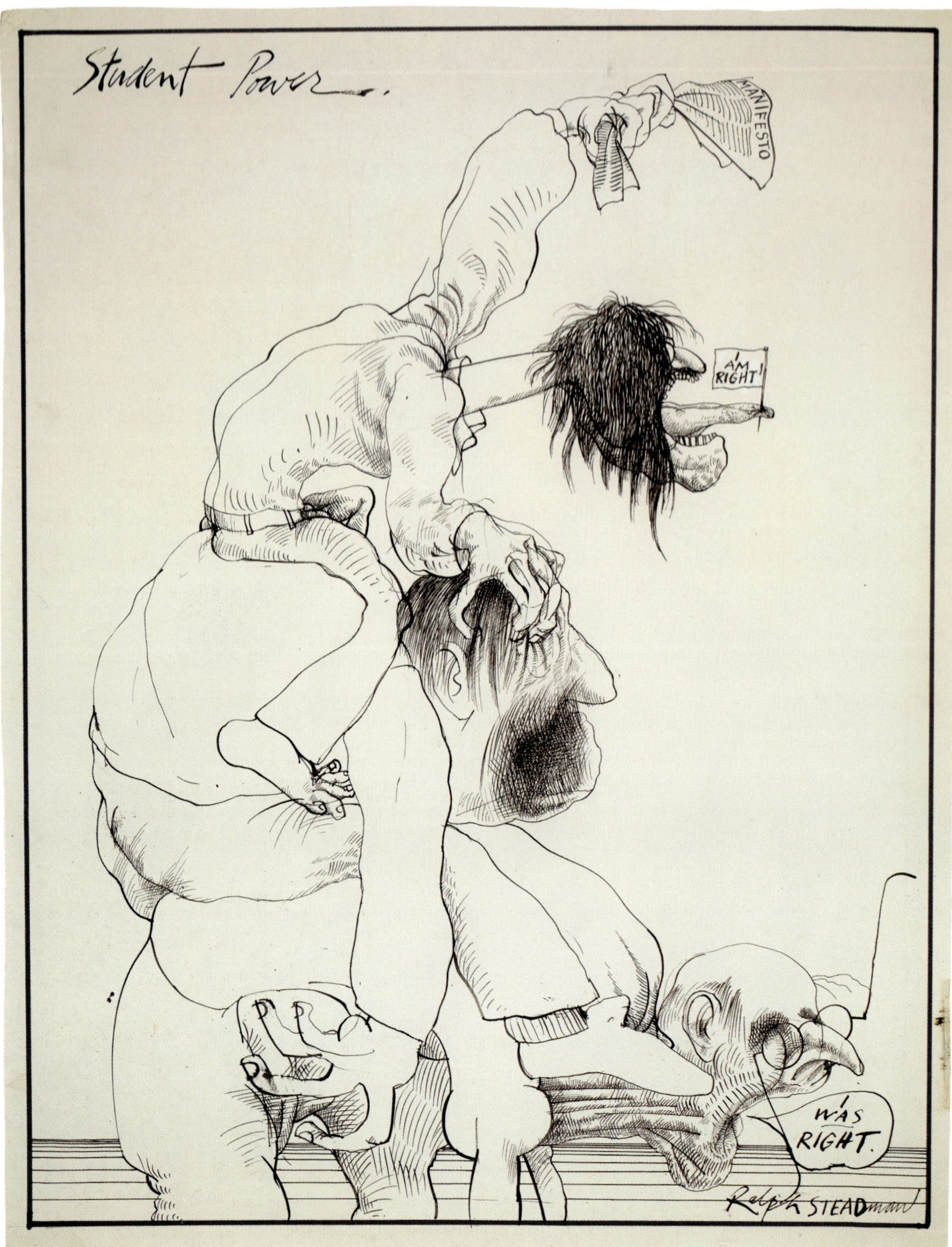

Student Power, ca. 1969

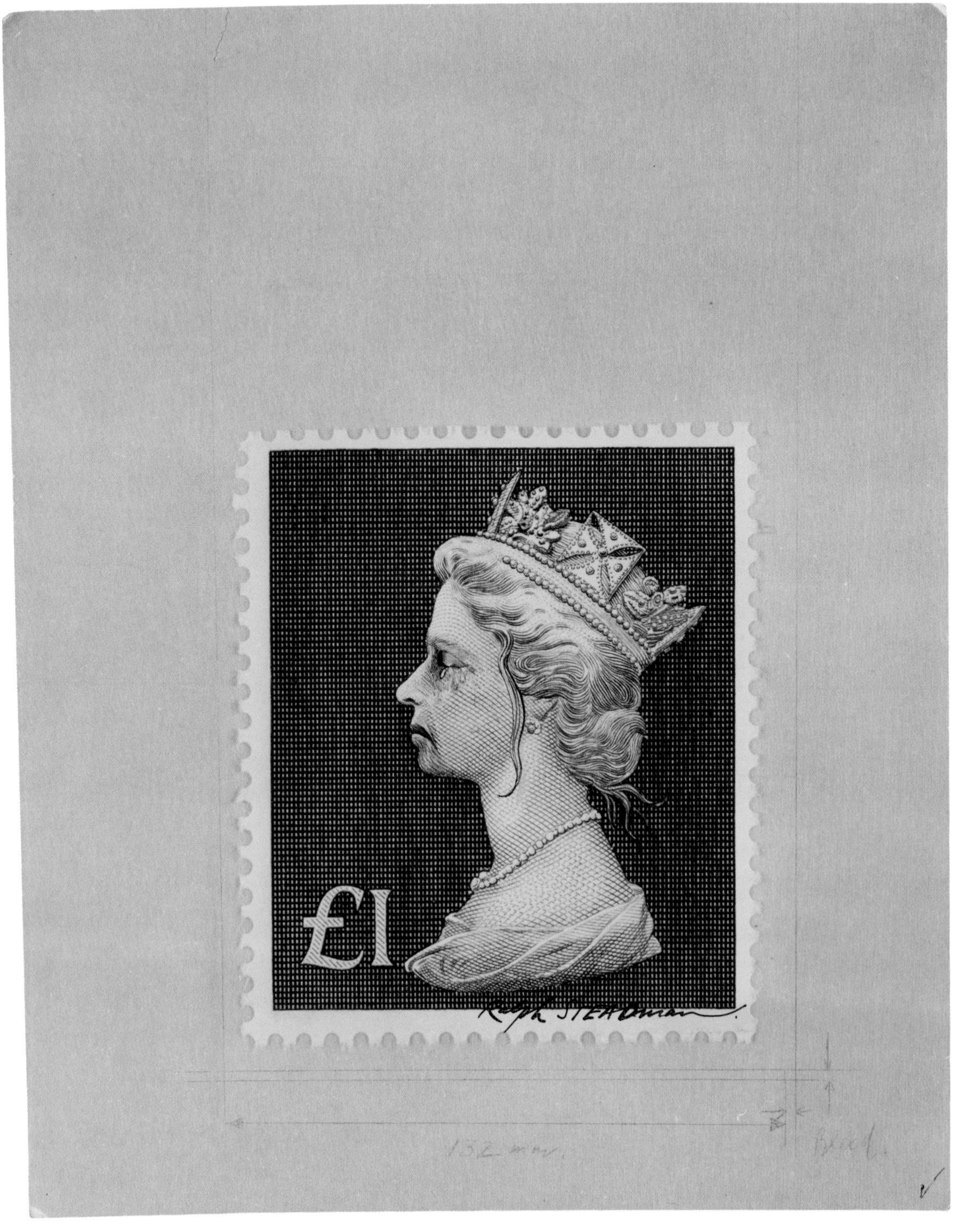

"I have a real soft spot for the Queen. She seems like a lovely lady." *Crying Queen, ca. 1970*

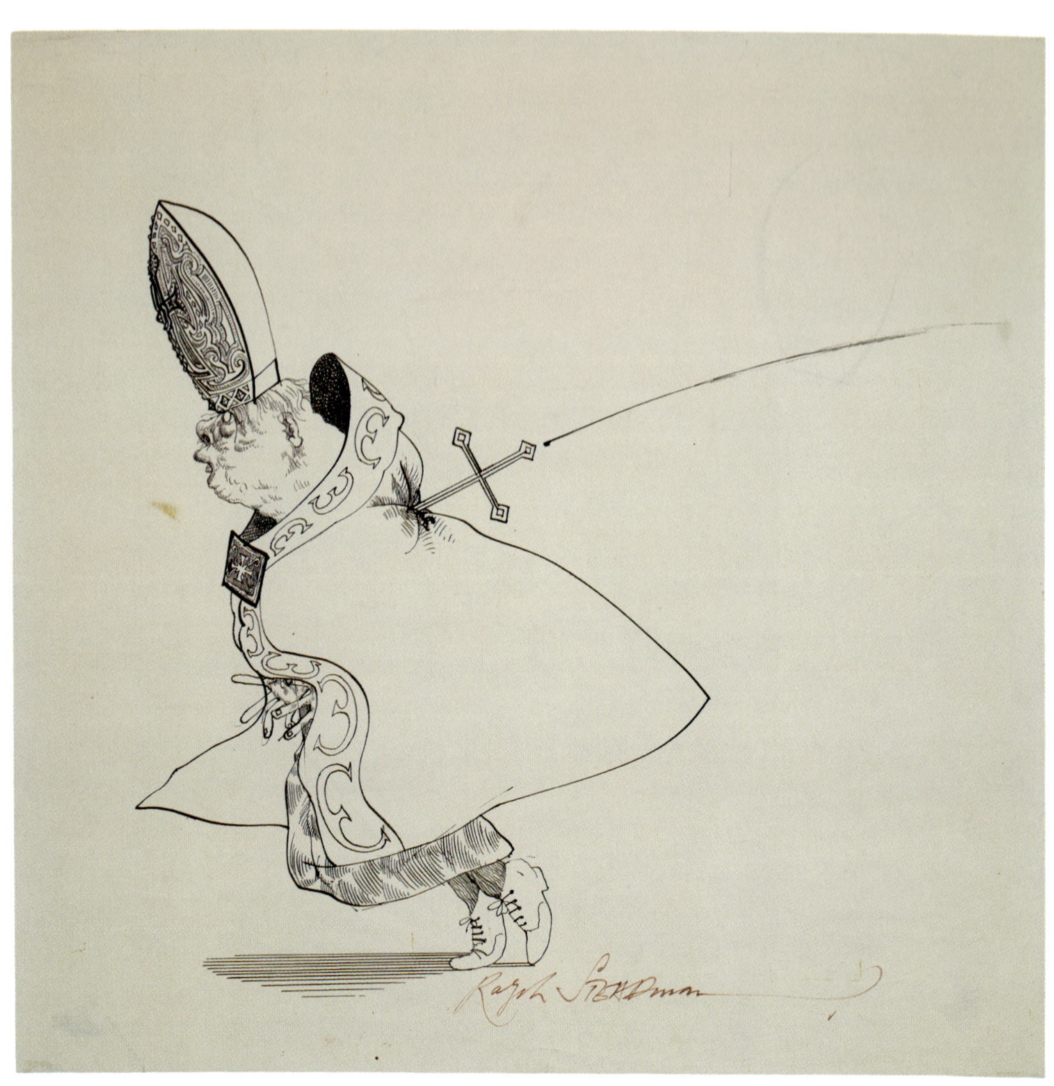

Contempt for the Church, ca. 1967

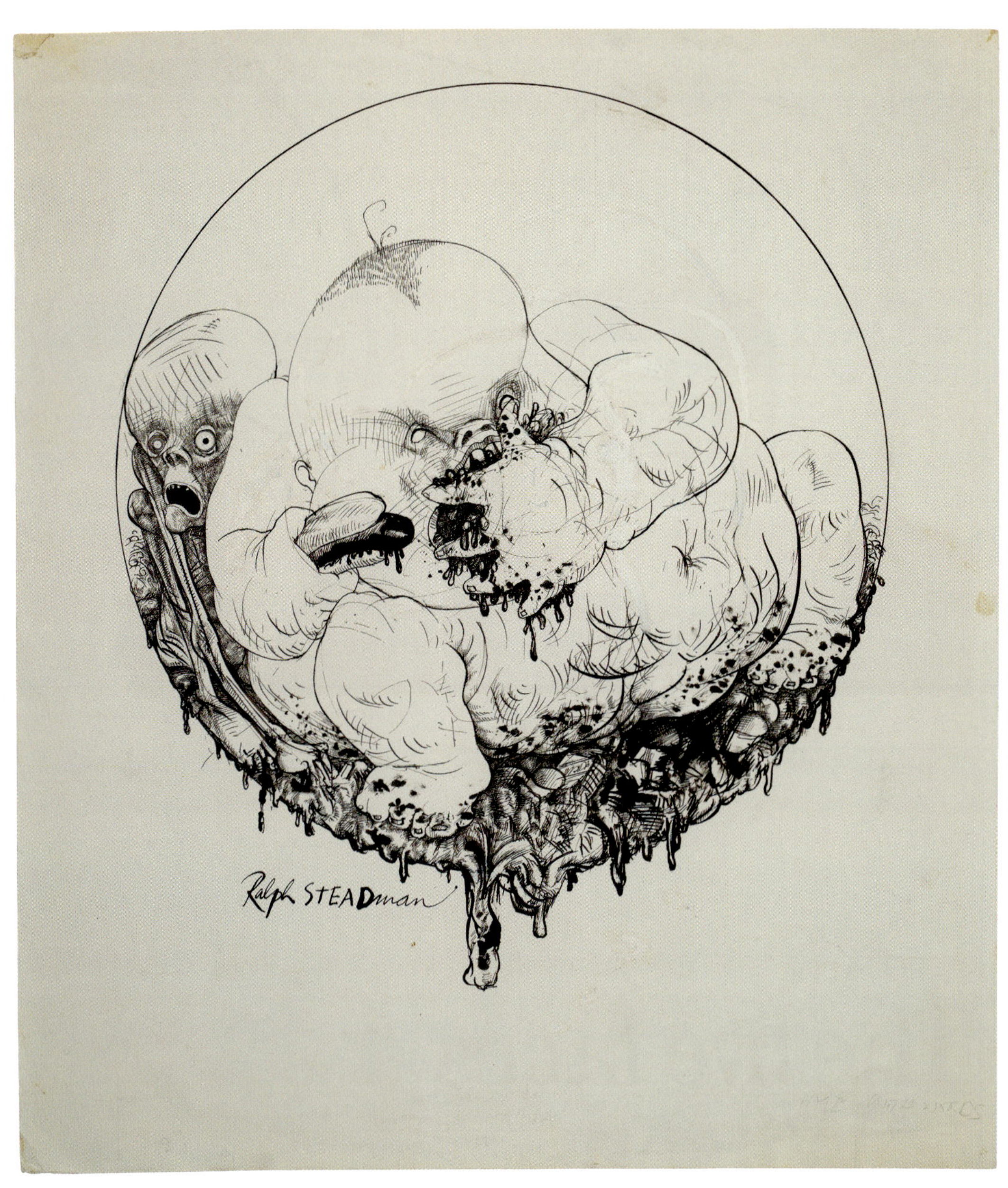

Hunger and Greed Nations, ca. 1967

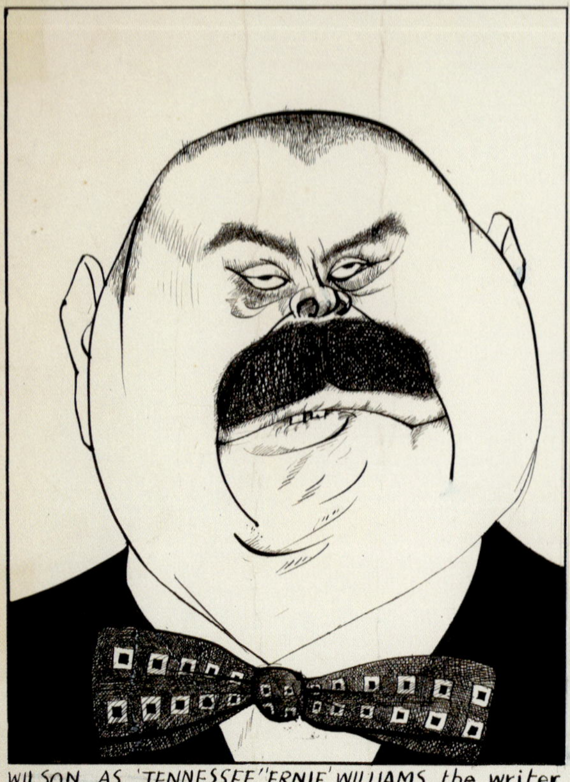

WILSON AS 'TENNESSEE' 'ERNIE' WILLIAMS, the writer.   WILSON AS WILLIAMS, the technology rep.

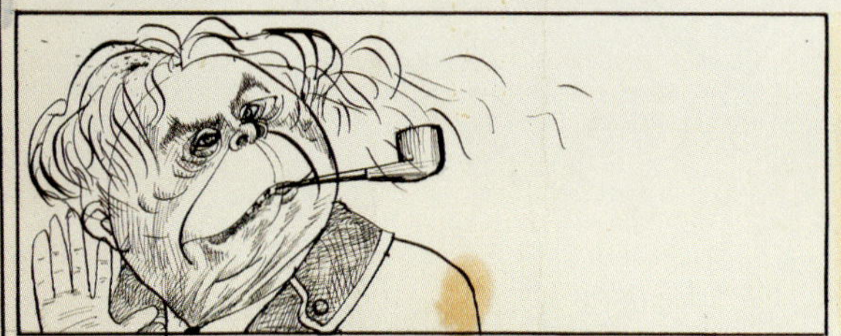

WILSON AS WILSON AS WE ALL KNOW AND LOVE HIM.

The five faces of Wilson

STEADman

HAROLD WILSON, hunted ringleader of the Great Train Robbery, booked into a smart hotel in Mexico City in March 1967 and signed the register K. Miller. He had a passport in the name of Keith Miller and he told people he was a sales representative for Alfred Dunhill, the London tobacco firm.

This alias was one of Reynolds's favourites. He loved to be a crook with a gilt front. He smoked only cigars and talked knowledgably of tobacco blends and pipe-making craftsmanship as the agent for the famous St James's firm. This gave him an entree to company in bars and clubs.

But a fantastic coincidence, which illustrates the combination of skill and chance which kept Reynolds free for five and a half years, suddenly brought the tobacco salesman front to an end and nearly caught him out.

Dunhill decided to send their chief sales representative Mr Kenneth Miller, on a Latin American sales drive. When he arrived in Mexico City he signed in as K. Miller at the same hotel as Reynolds.

An observant Englishman, also resident, spotted that two K. Millers, both representing the same firm, had signed the register. He wrote to Scotland Yard about this oddity and gave Det. Chief Supt. Tom Butler, head of the Flying Squad, the lead to one of the aliases Reynolds was using.

By 1958 when he went to prison for three and a half years for maliciously wounding a policeman he had totted up 11 convictions.

In his youth Reynolds fell in with another youngster with anti-social tendencies, Ernie Watts, who, had he lived, would have been an even more intelligent and formidable criminal than Reynolds. The chip on Watts's shoulder was that he had won a scholarship to Christ's Hospital but his family would not let him take it up and he was eager to plunder the society that had denied him an education.

Watts took crime seriously. He admired American efficiency and studied the technique of the bank robber, Von Lamm, who would leave half a strongroom's contents, if necessary, rather than imperil the split-second timing which ensured a safe getaway. (This type of timing showed up at Sears Crossing when £40,000 was left behind.)

A different man

Watts also impressed on Reynolds and his friends the need to get in advance from people, often innocent, the information which ensures success in crime. This was the origin of the South Western Gang, although Watts died in a diabetic coma before it began its more notorious jobs.

The beautiful simplicity of many of them had the world admiring London's criminals while deploring their motives.

When Reynolds came out of ... ham Common where they would meet Mrs Reynolds.

After the reunion, Mrs Reynolds, Mrs Manson and Nicholas travelled for a month in Ireland and the French Riviera but were closely shadowed by the police who expected to be led to Reynolds.

The trio returned to London where the police supervision seems to have slackened off. It remains one of the big mysteries of the affair that the wives of Reynolds, Buster Edwards and Charlie Wilson were all able to join their husbands abroad. Despite police supervision, they were able to buy hot weather outfits, get injections, secure false passports and arrange visas, and slip away.

The Edwards family at one time lived close to the Reynolds in Mexico City and Nicholas and their daughter, Nicolette, went to the same school.

The surrender in September of 1966 of Buster Edwards signalled the end of real safety for Reynolds and Wilson. Why Edwards alone chose to give himself up is another major mystery. Unbelievably, he received only a 15-year sentence which may have led Reynolds to consider risking a return to England.

After Edwards's surrender, Reynolds wandered in the USA and Canada but family problems and dwindling money finally got on top of him. His premonition of doom is illustrated by the fact that, through friends, he offered his story to the highest bidder two years ago.

For a time Reynolds rented a pop singer's cottage in a remote spot near Gatwick Airport and then moved to the villa in Torquay where he was arrested last November. (Wilson had been captured in Canada in January 1968.)

Reynolds often visited London to drop in the Markham and the Revolution in Chelsea. This led ... that Reynolds ... with a friend ... The pub w ... detectives.

But only n ... nolds was du ... a brawl sta ... dialled 999. ... up from the ... and the Yar ... had wasted th ... in fact watch ... dent from a ...

A shock

But Mr Bu ... precaution of ... to take the ... car parked ... were discreetl ... remained, Mr ... quay. The Yar ... alias and had ... in Torquay ... convinced he ... is taking a fat ... the betrayal.

When Reyn ... 25-year sente ... absolutely co ... but when he ... under Aylesb ... he broke down ... a lighter sente ... received 15 ... White 18 year ... Thompson he ... five years of h ... people's mone ... leniency.

Reynolds re ... less than Wils ... Welch, Hussey, ...

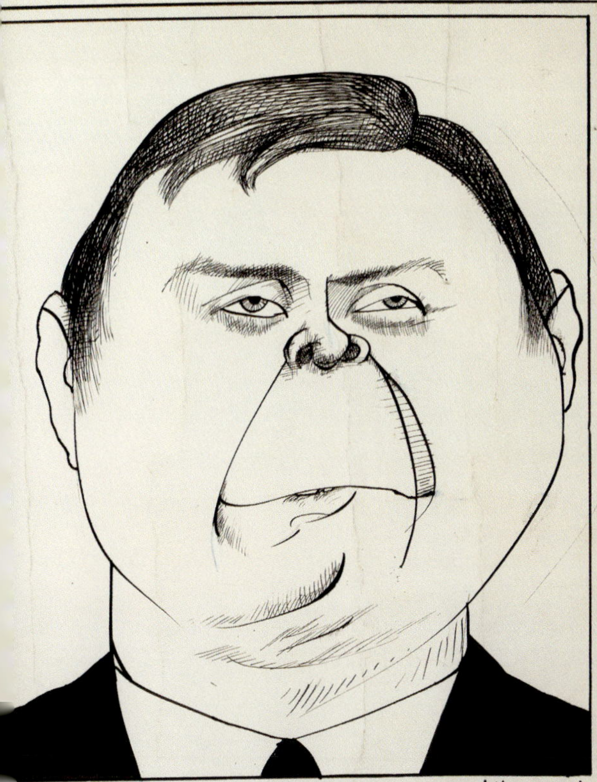

N AS HAROLD ASPEL, the T.V. personality and
al Englishman.

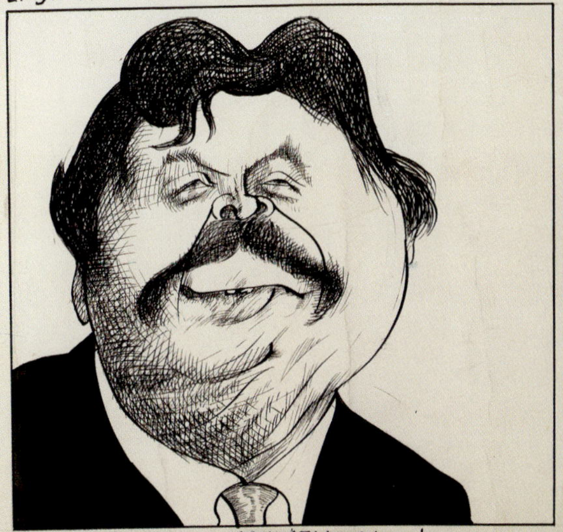

WILSON AS HAROLD MAXWELL, the tycoon.

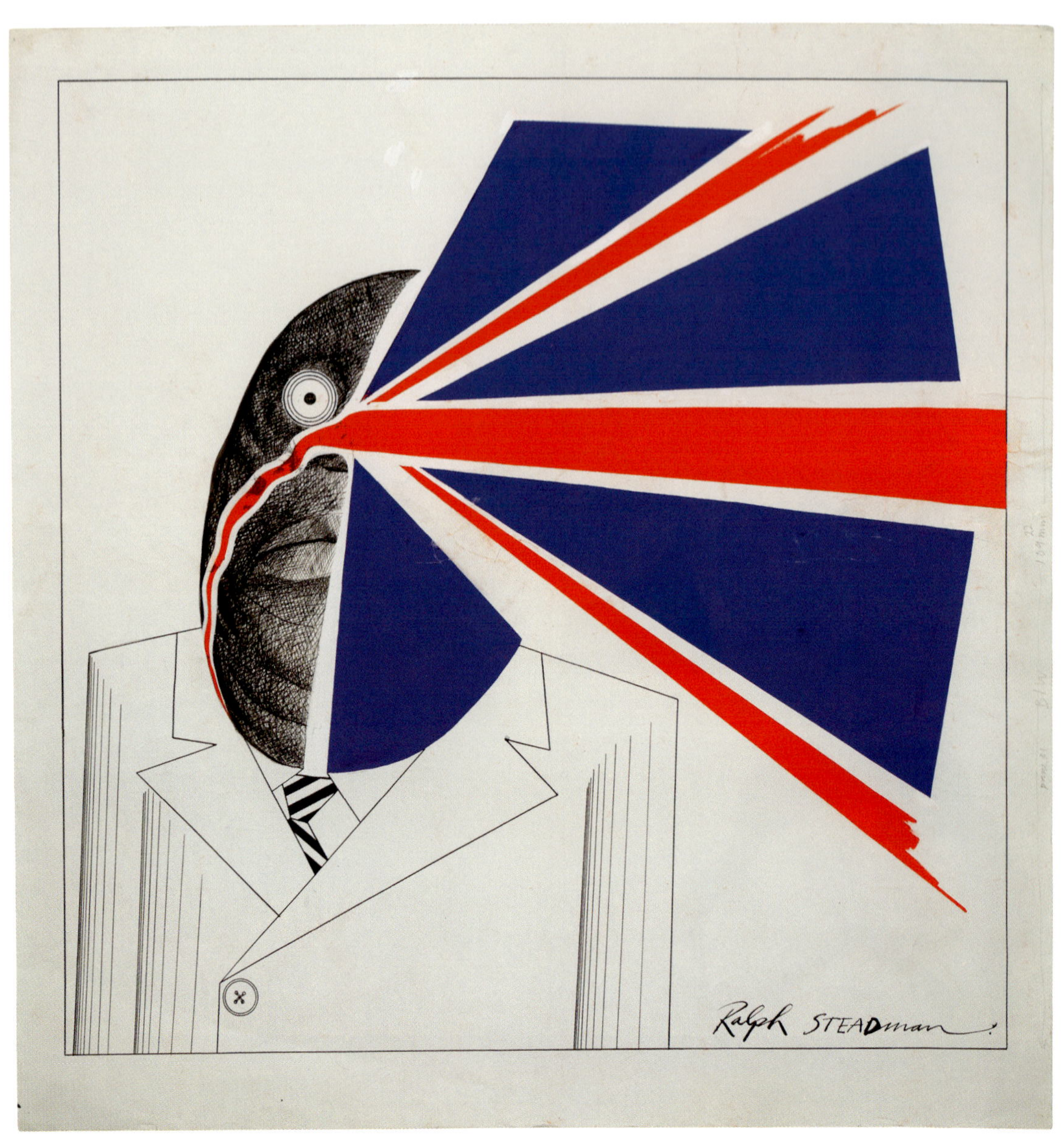

The "Windrush Generation" Getting Naturalised, ca. 1970

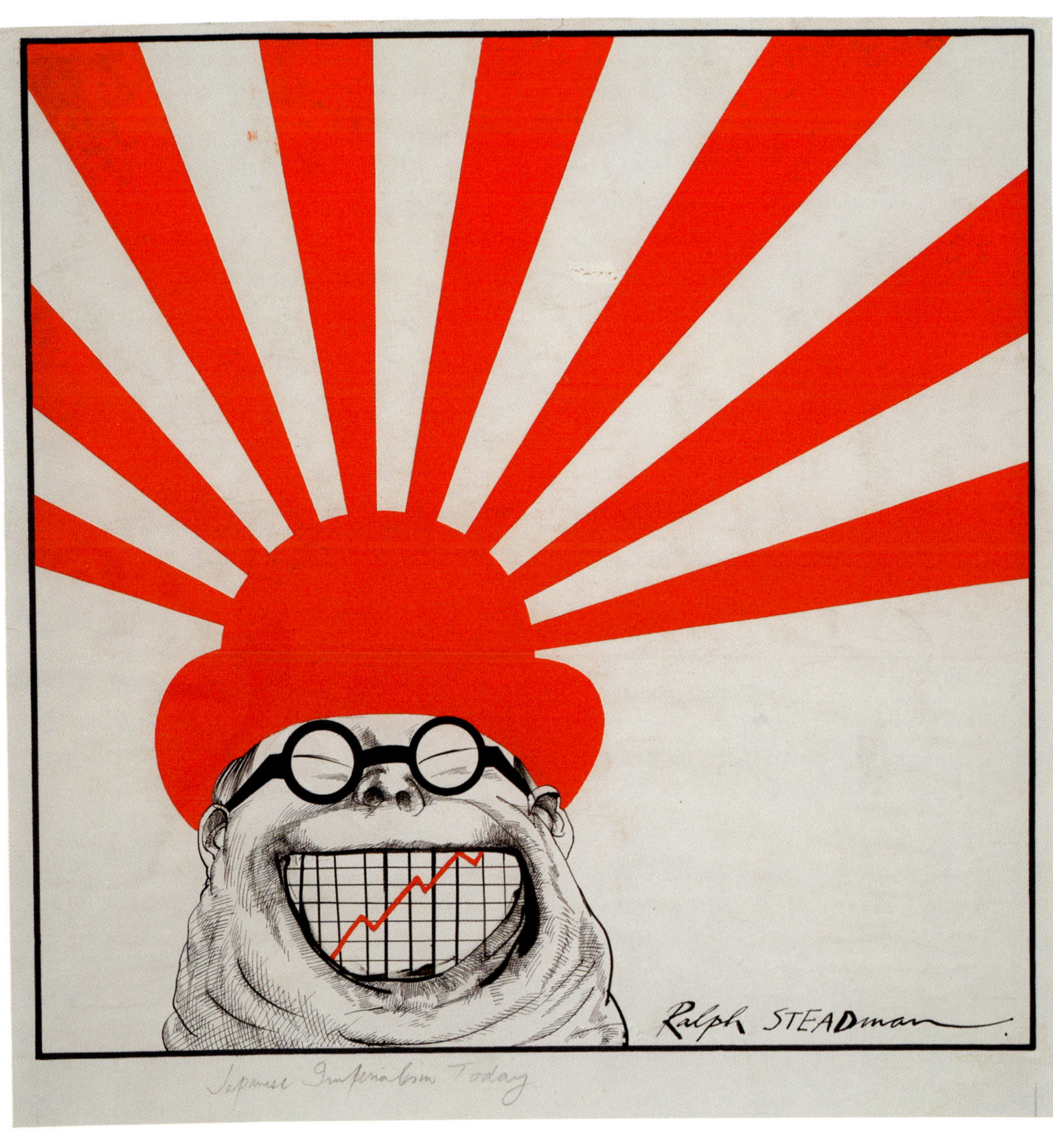

Business is Good in Japan, ca. 1970

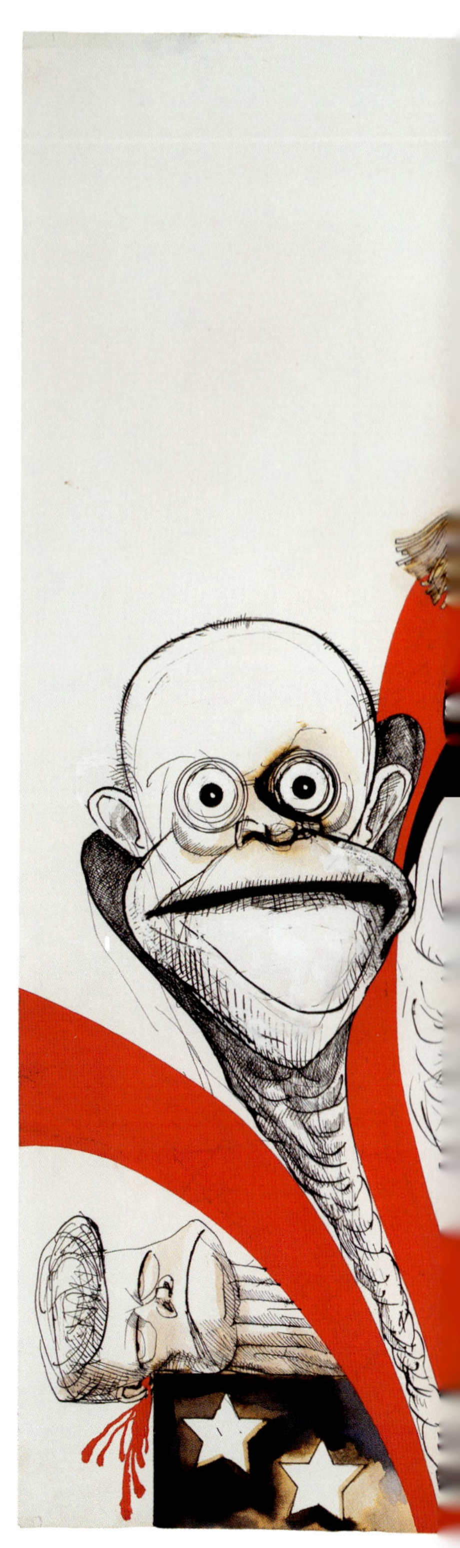

American Presidents, ca. 1973

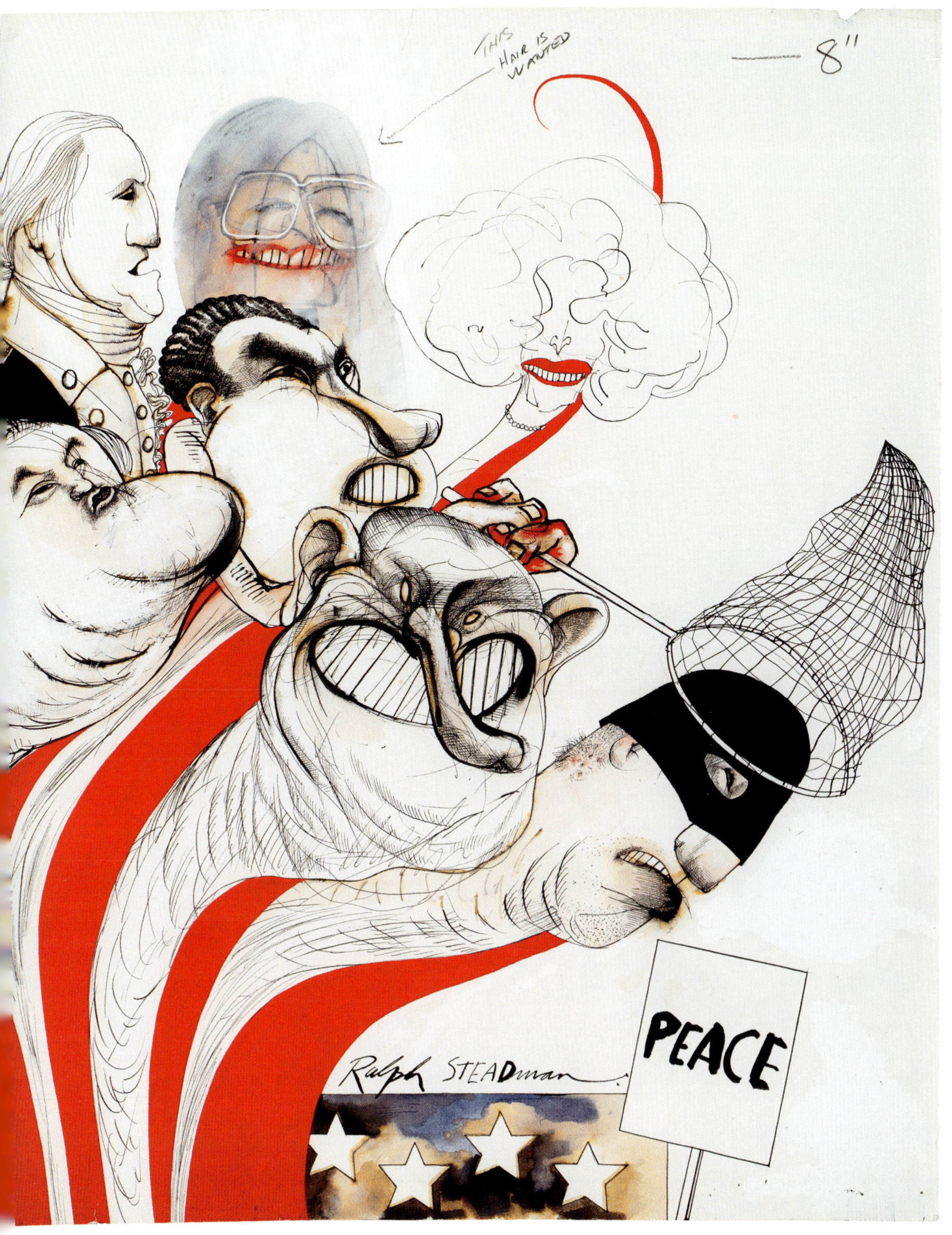

"Looking at some of these older pieces, it's incredible how the message still holds, but the landscape really should have changed."

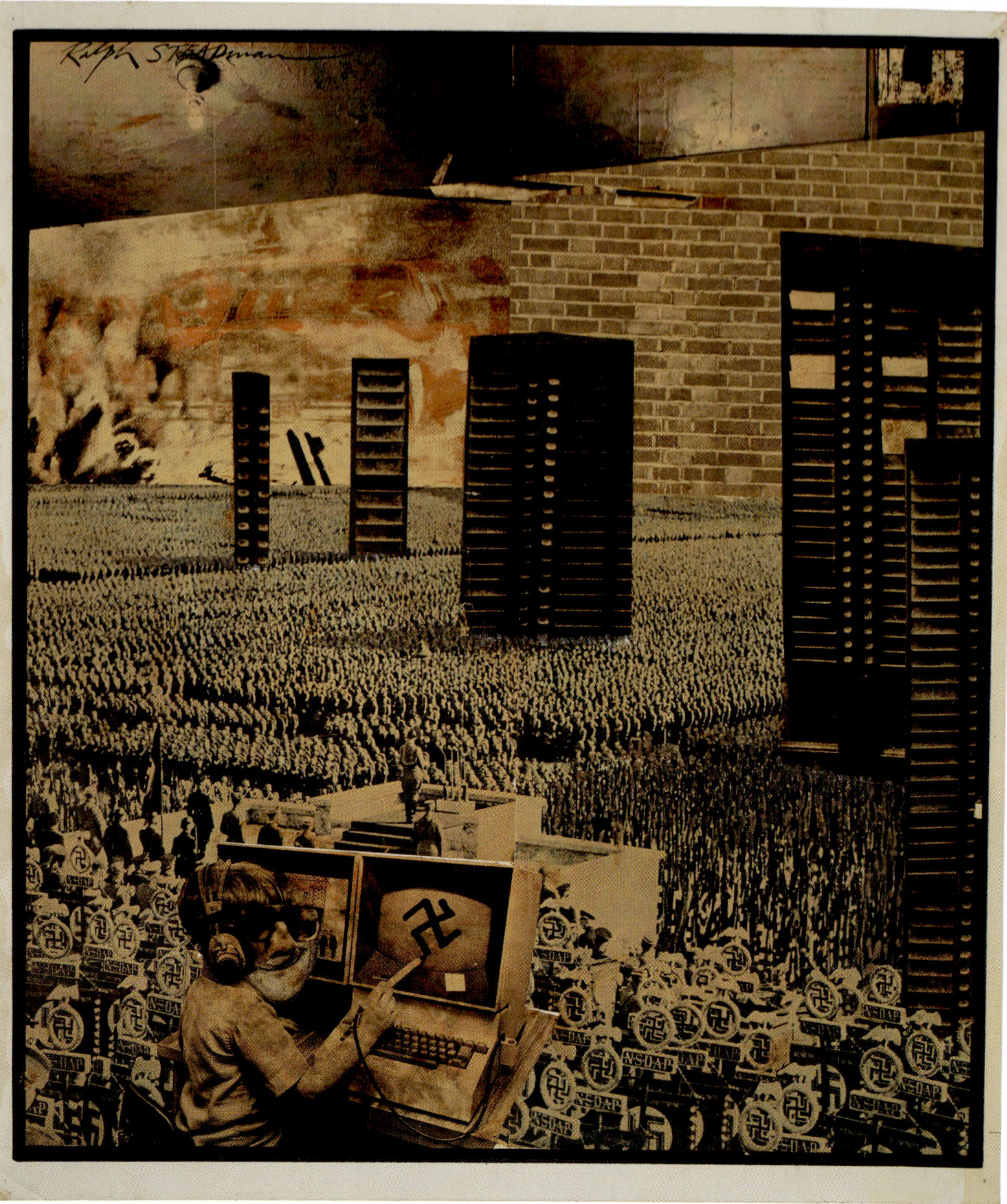

Population Hysteria, 1977

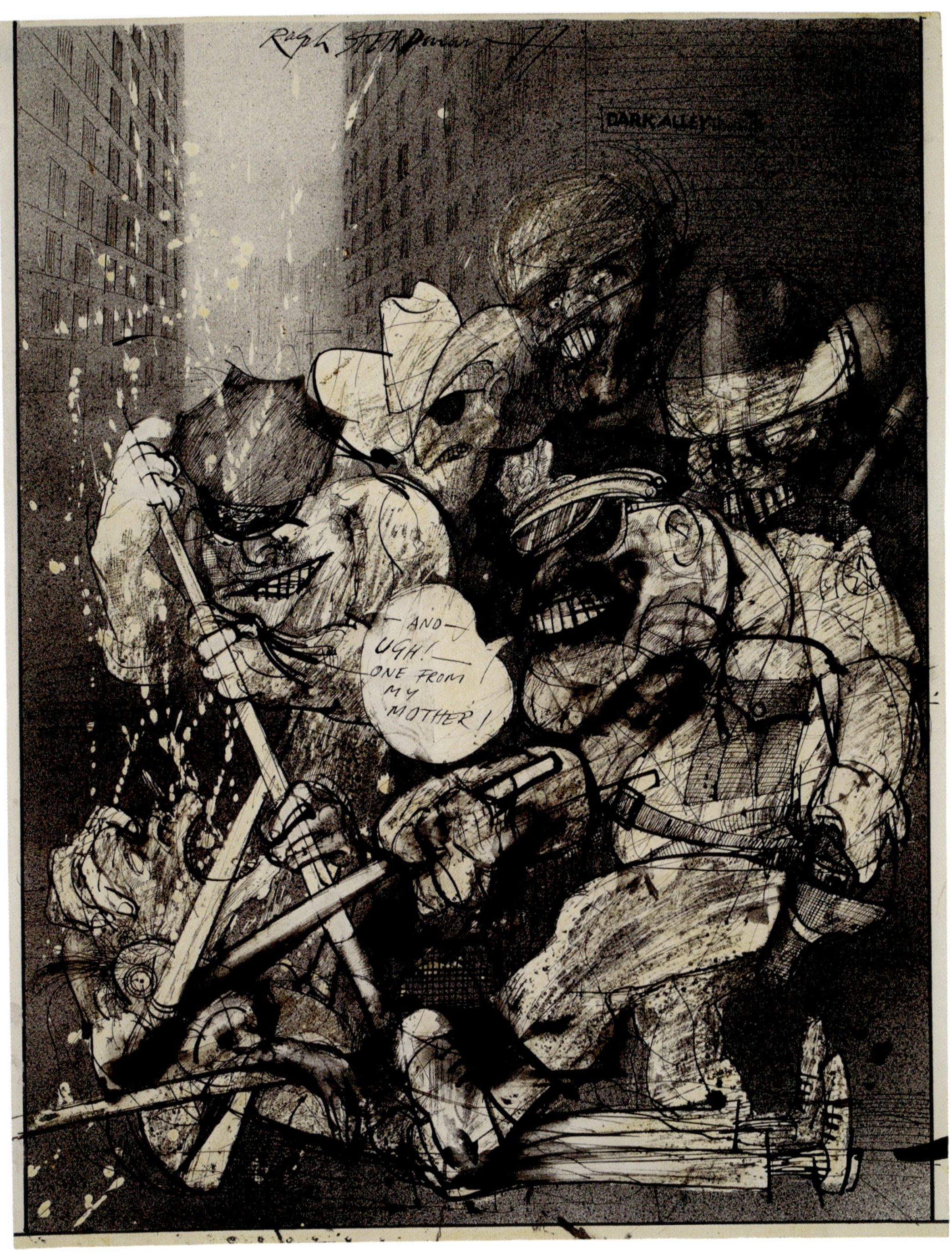

"You see, when you look at these images, you have to wonder if anything has changed. I think I recognised the violence still lurking in America, residue of the Wild West." *Police Authority, ca. 1975*

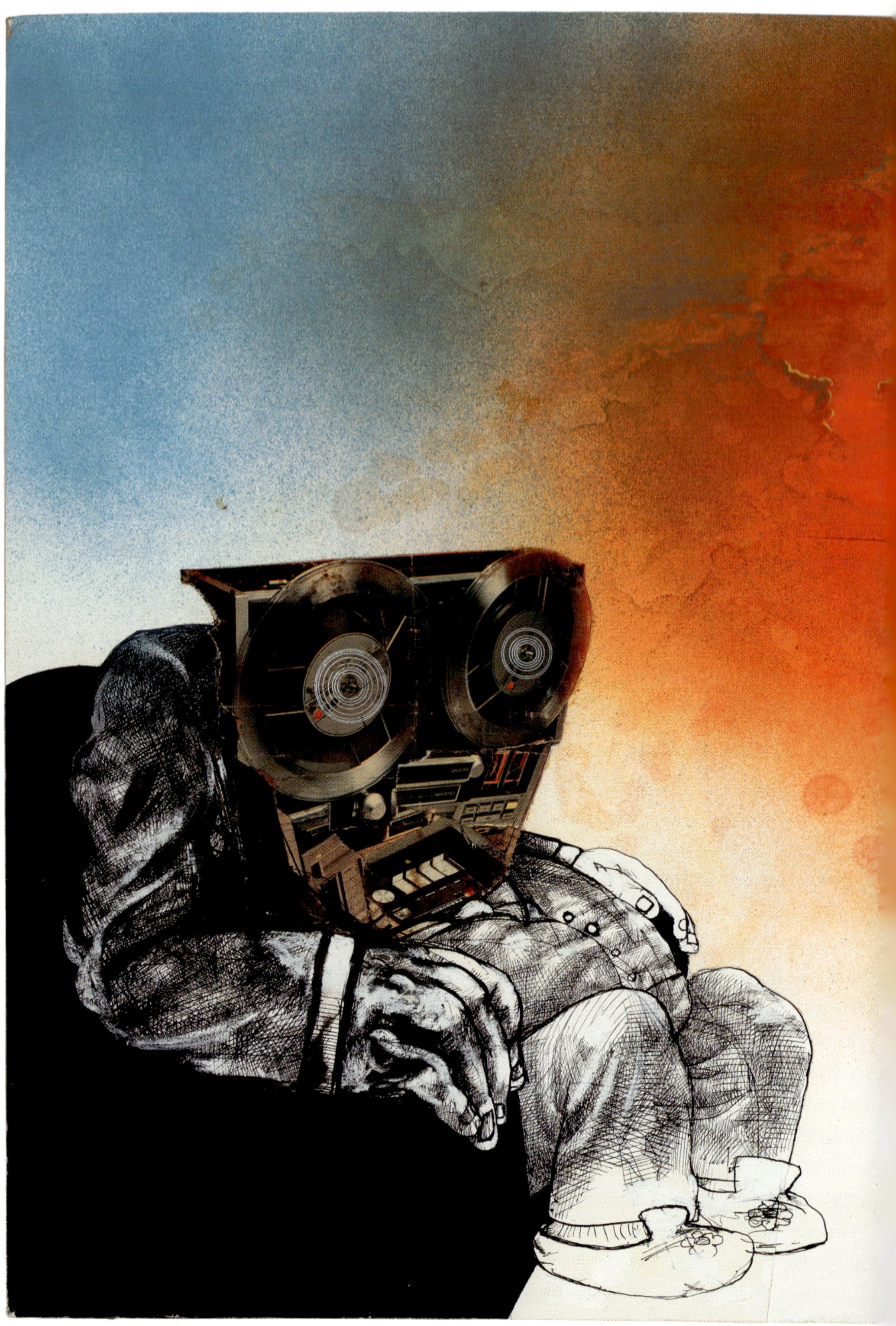

New Technology, ca. 1972

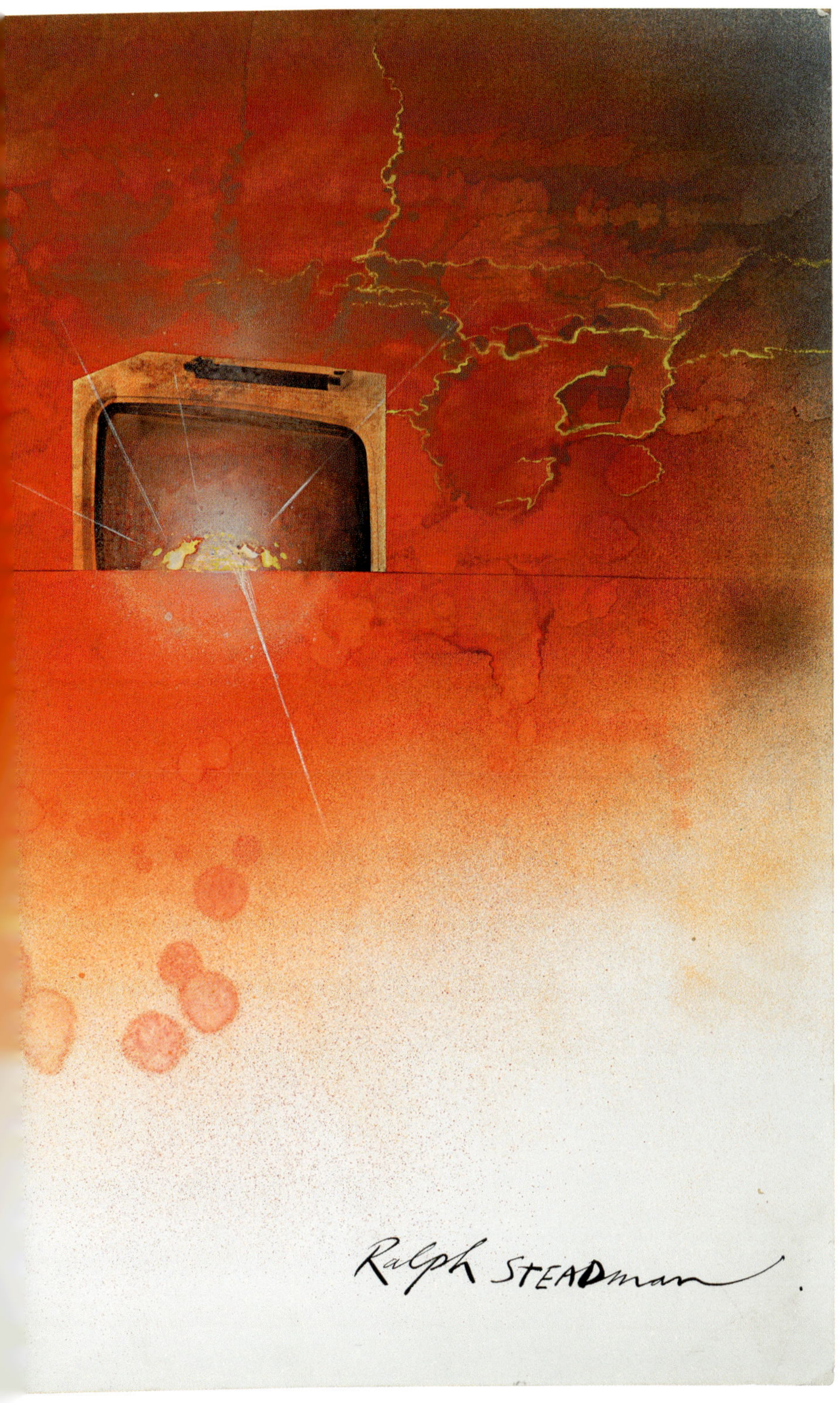

"I have an iPad mini that my wife bought me a few years ago for Xmas. I can just about get the news up on it and read my emails!"

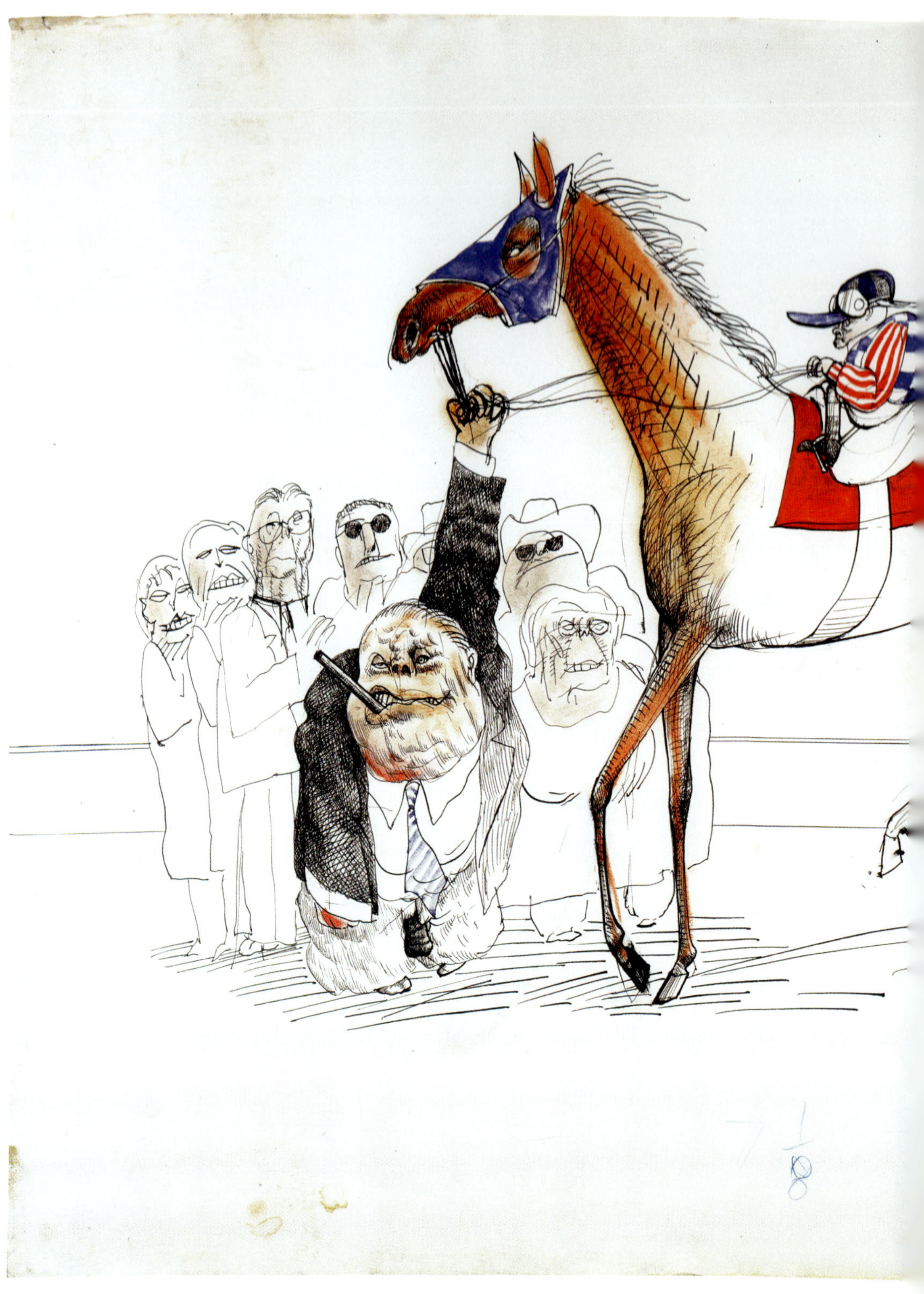

"We had looked for each other for three days. When we finally met, Hunter called me a matted-haired geek with string warts.
 To this day I still do not know what string warts are!"

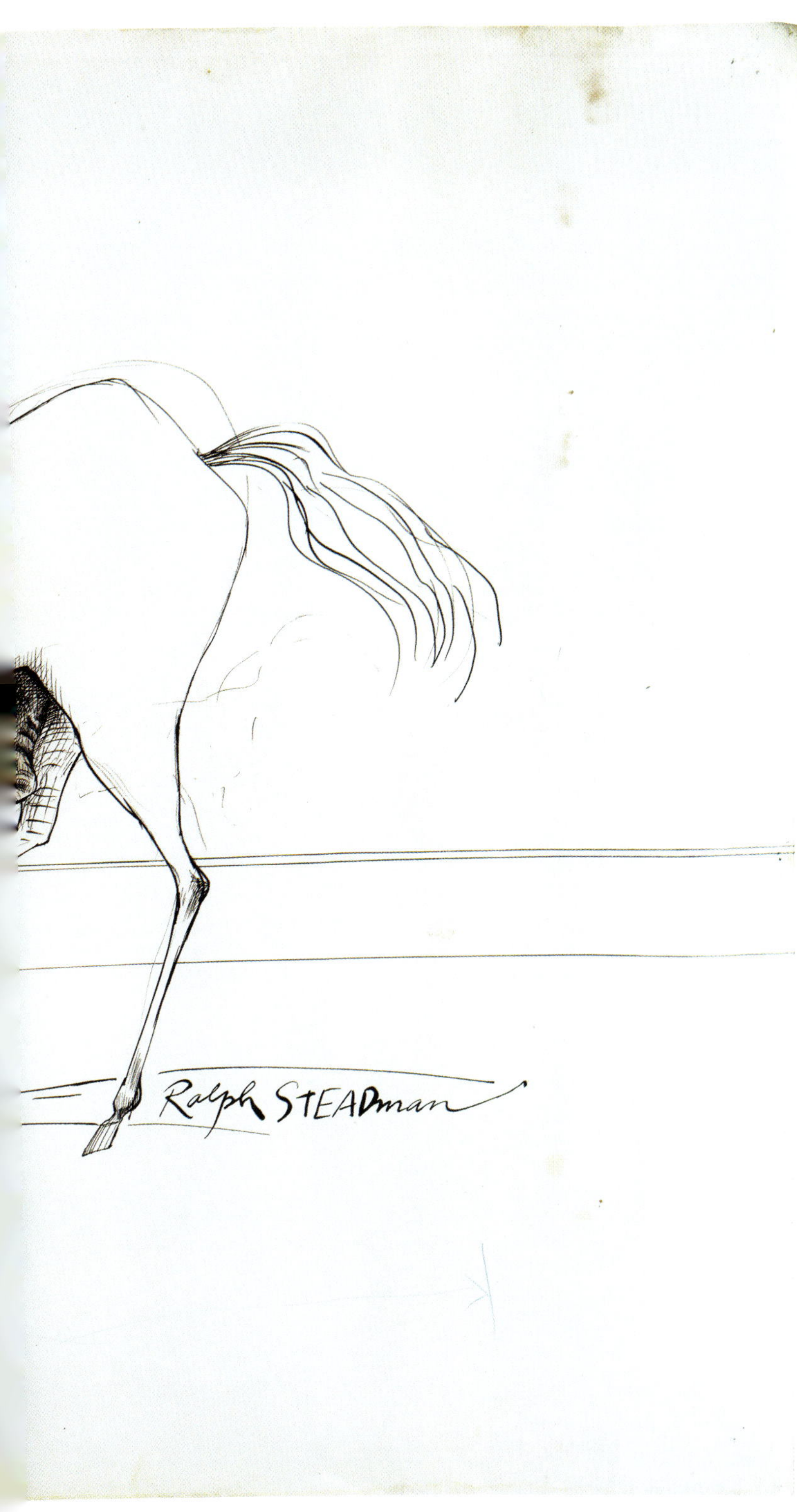

The Kentucky Derby, Winner's Circle, 1970

Admission of Defeat, Trying to Change the World, 1971

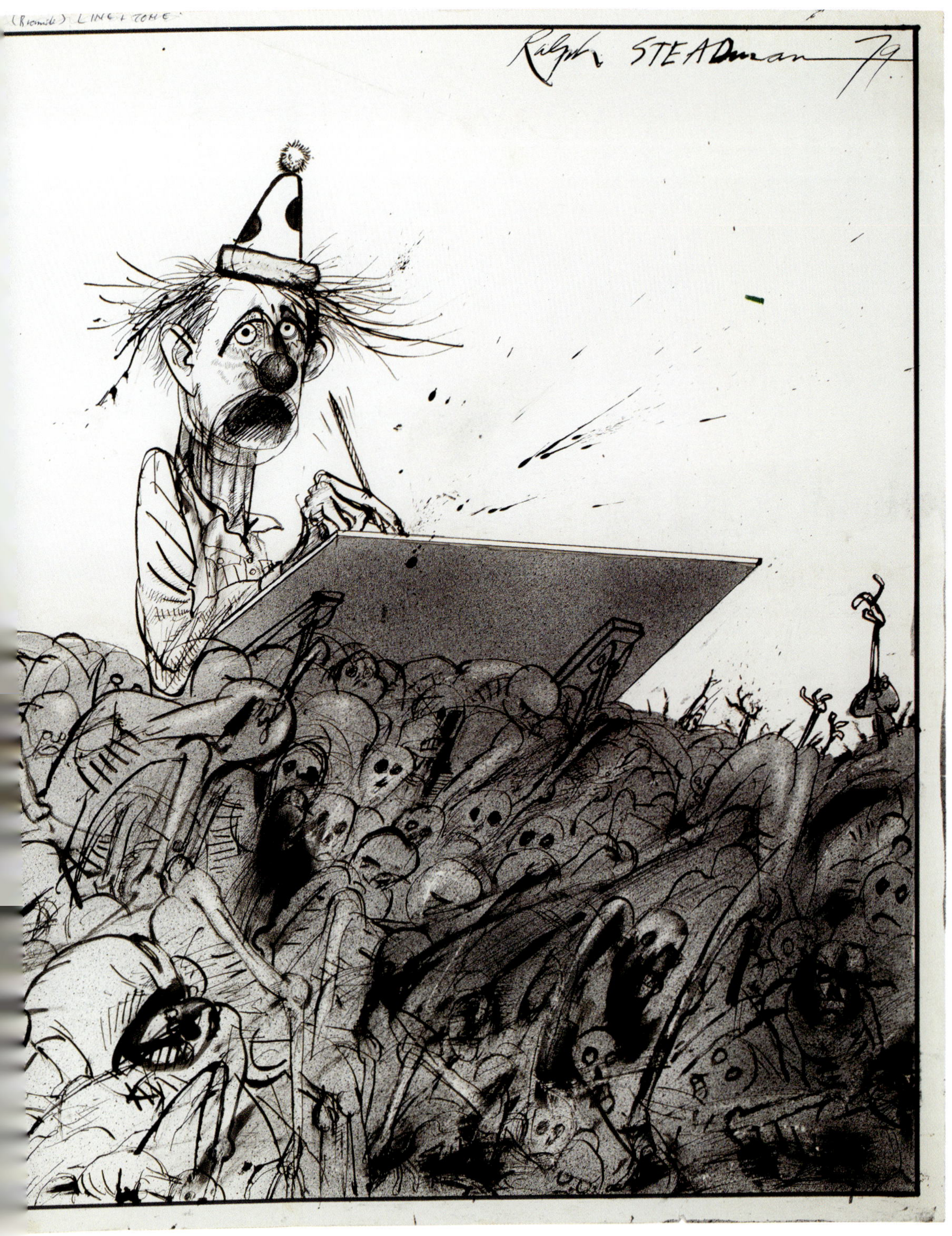

"When I started out, I wanted to change the world. I have succeeded; it's got worse!"

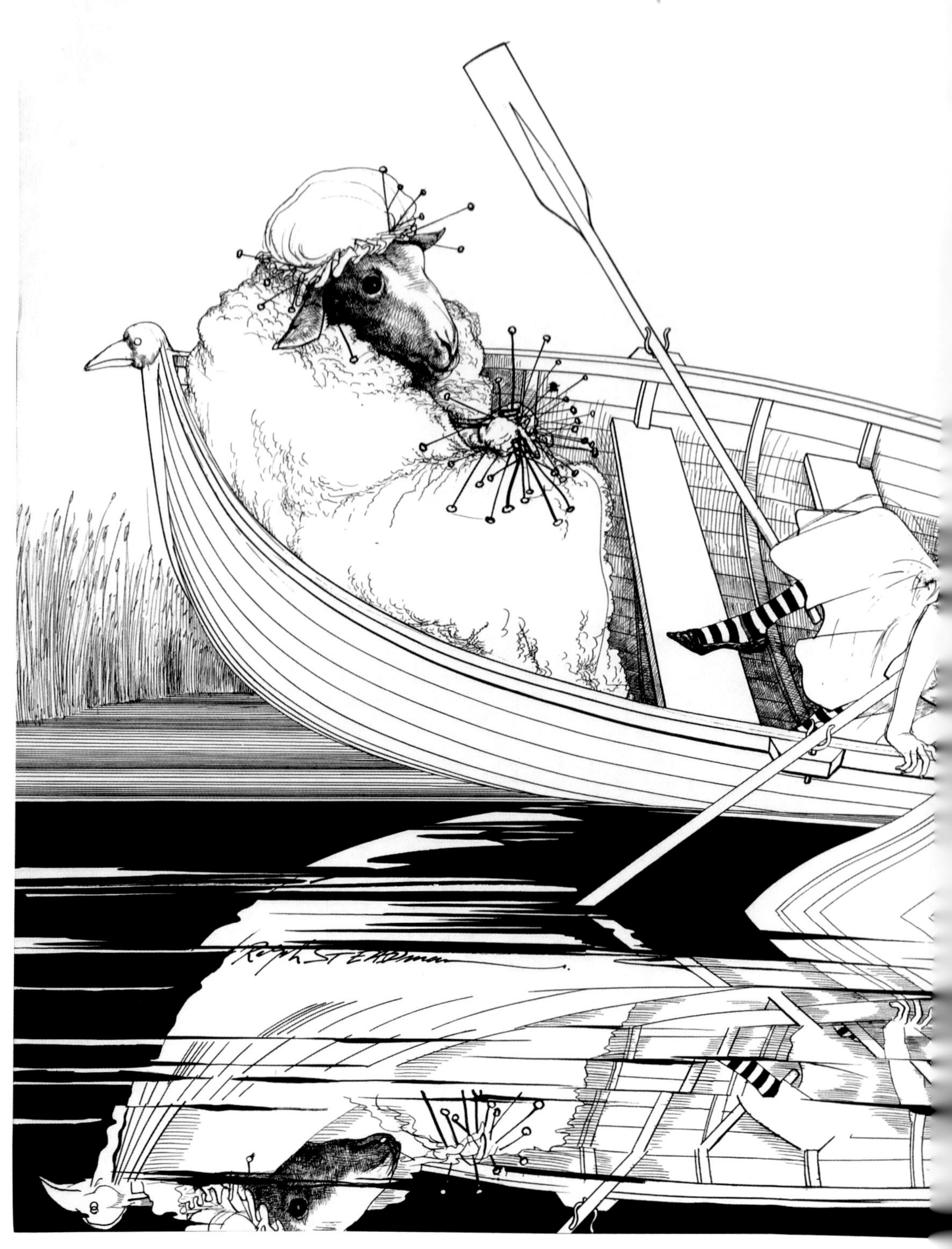

"I got the water effects by tracing the top image and then folding the tracing underneath and upside down and working on that."

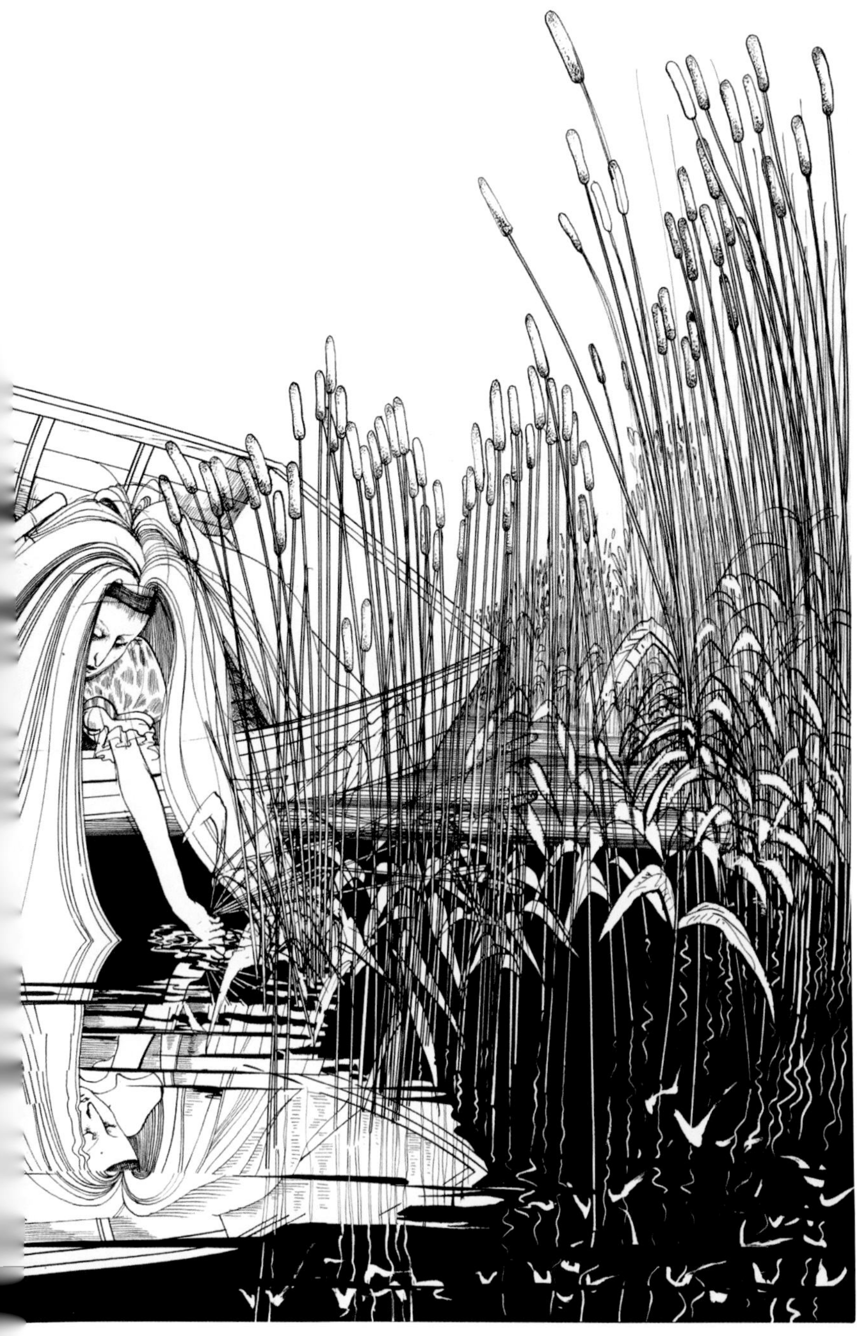

*Wool and Water from **Alice Through the Looking Glass**, 1971*

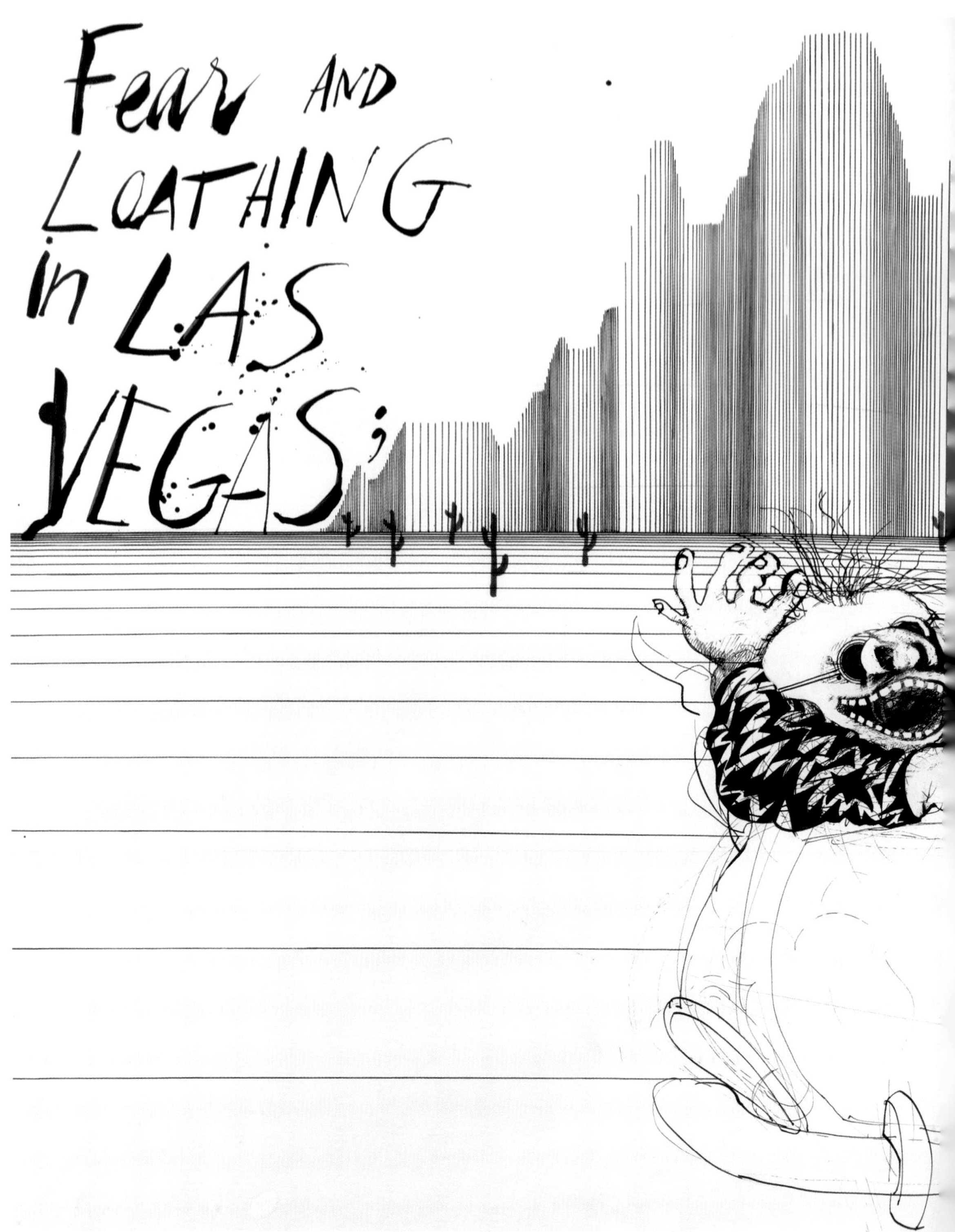

Fear and Loathing in Las Vegas;

"I only realised it recently, but I drew Hunter driving a British car, on the right."

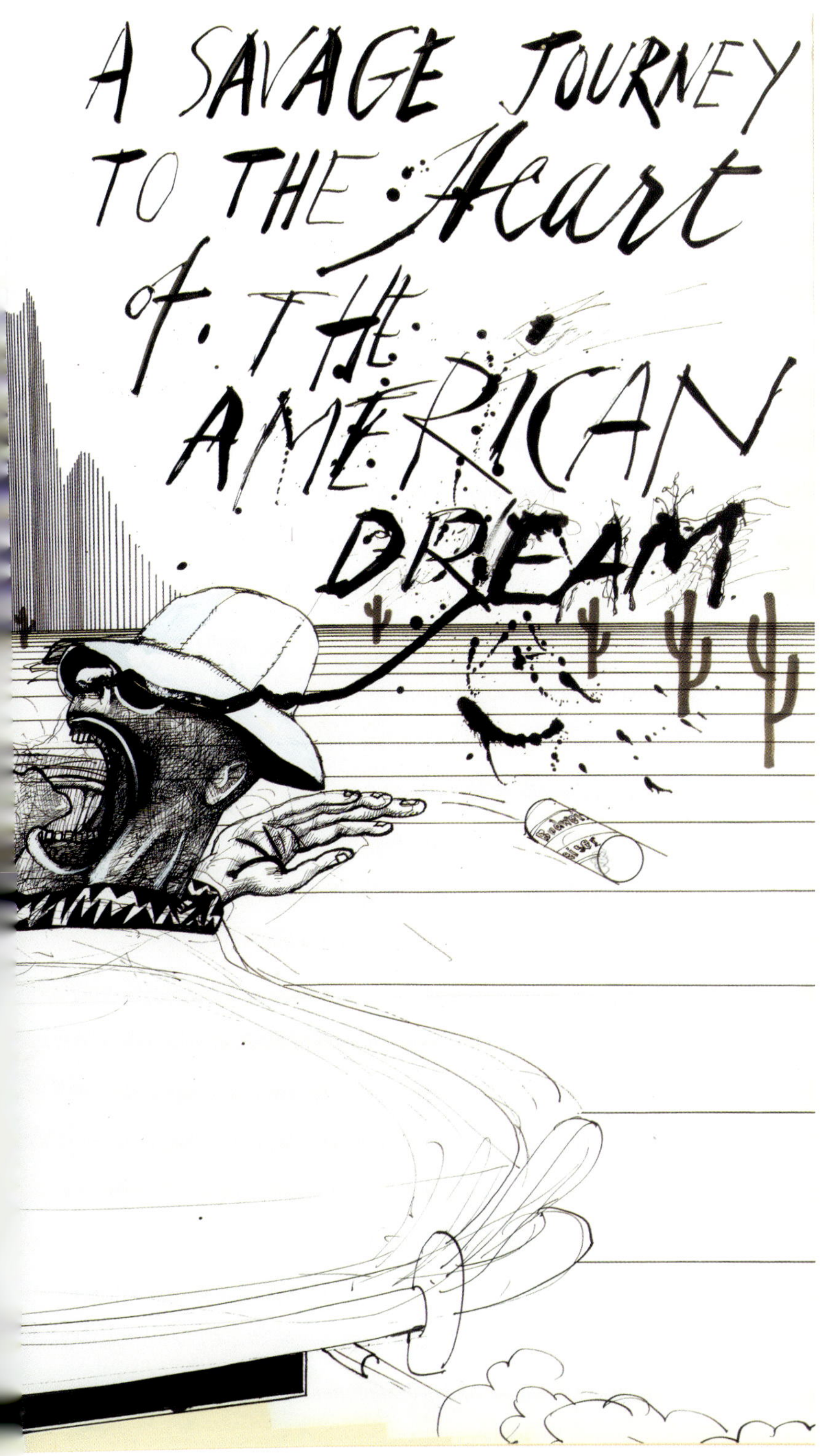

Savage Journey, *Fear and Loathing in Las Vegas*, ca. 1974

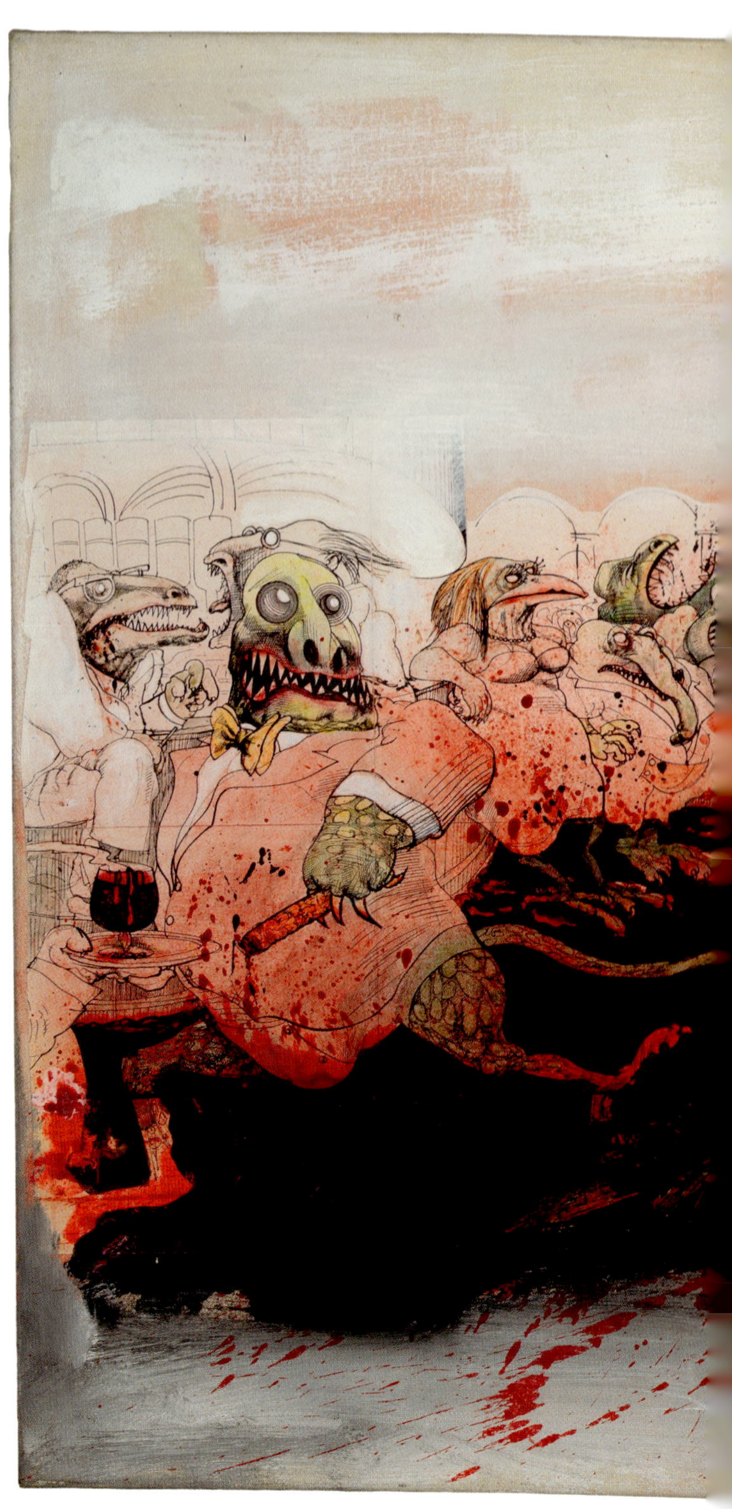

Gonzo the Art, Lizard Lounge Reworked, ca. 1991

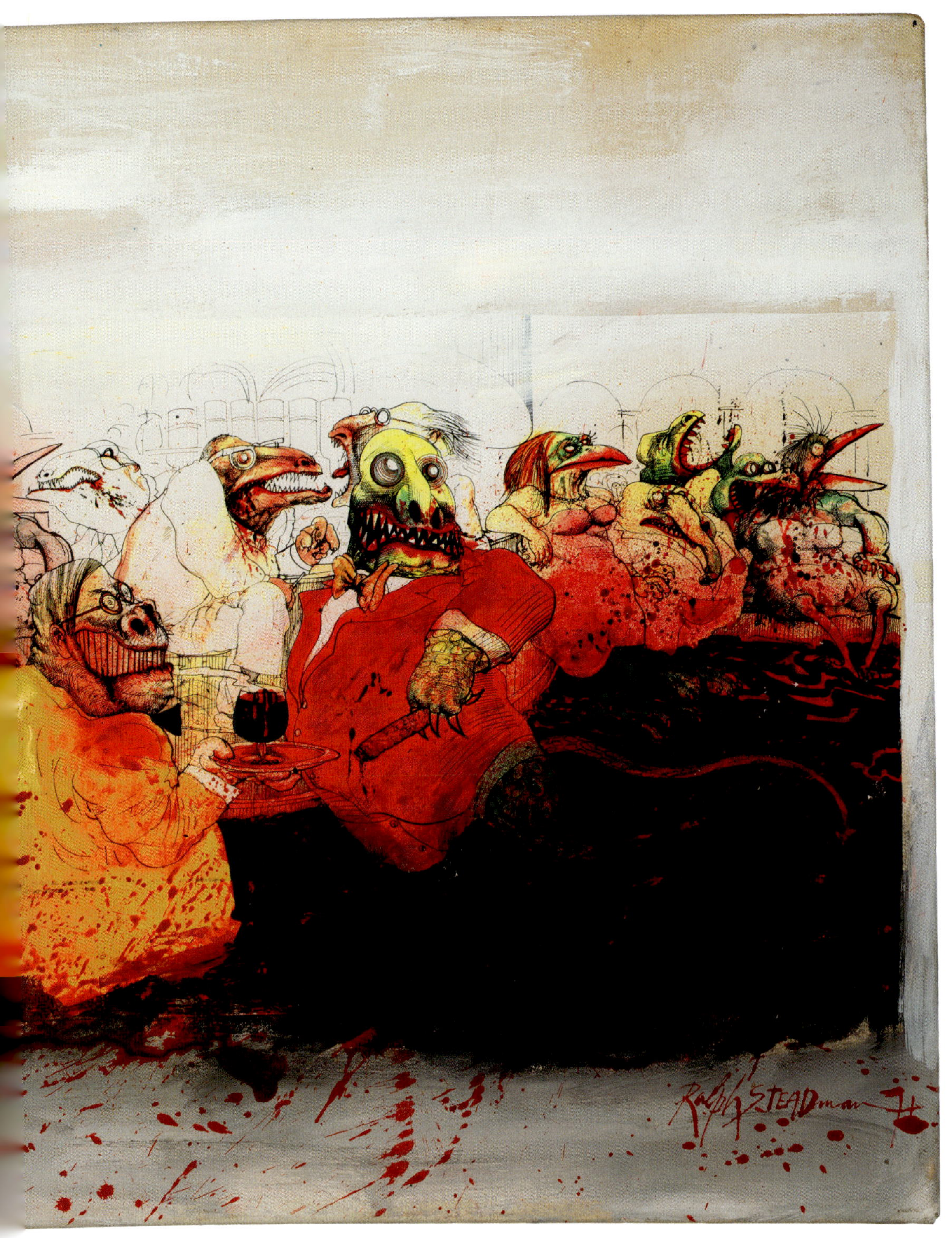

"Jann Wenner bought the original of the Lizard Lounge shortly after it was drawn. This is actually a photocopy, stuck onto canvas and recoloured."

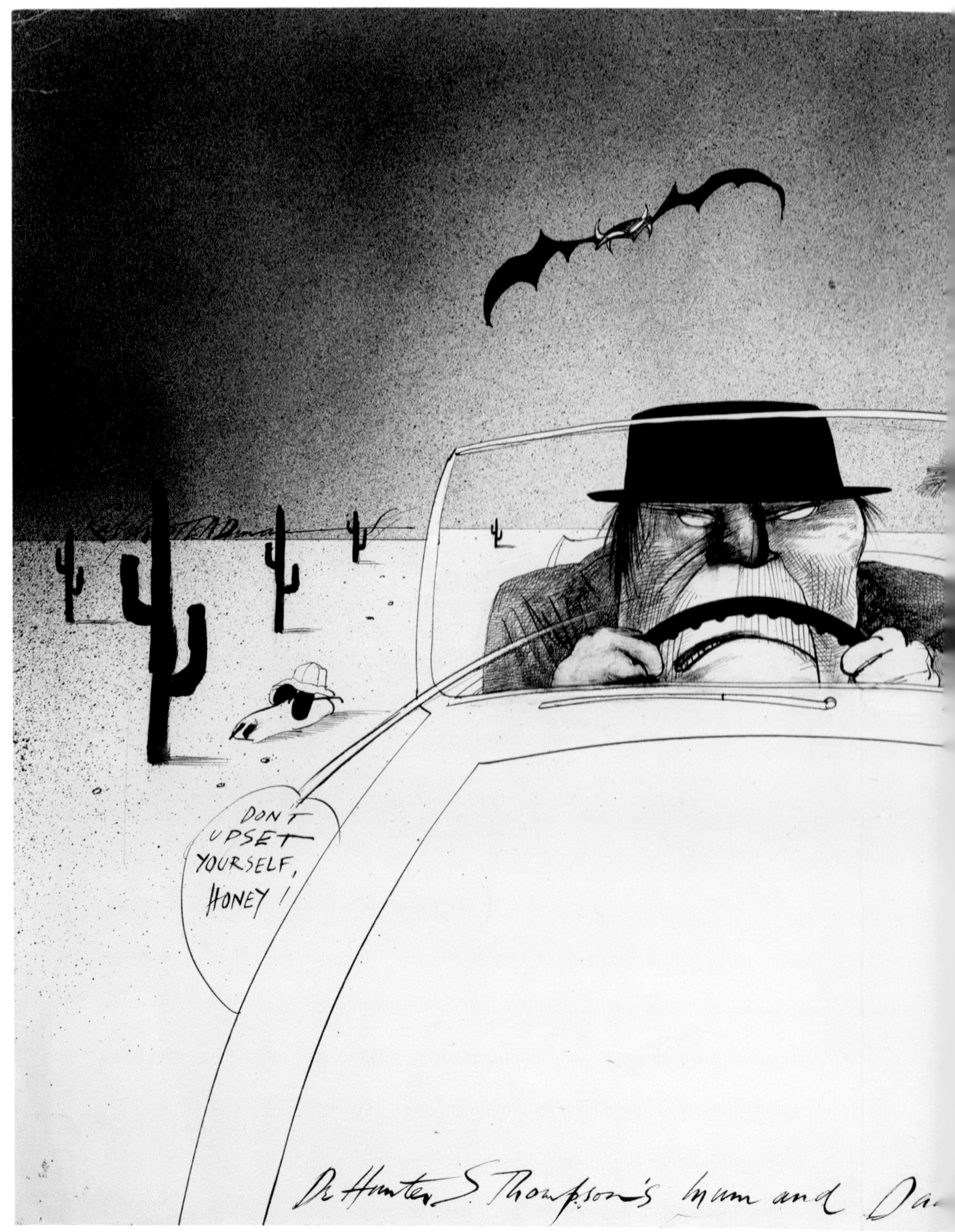

"His mother worked at the Louisville Public Library, so I guess that's where he learned to love reading and language."

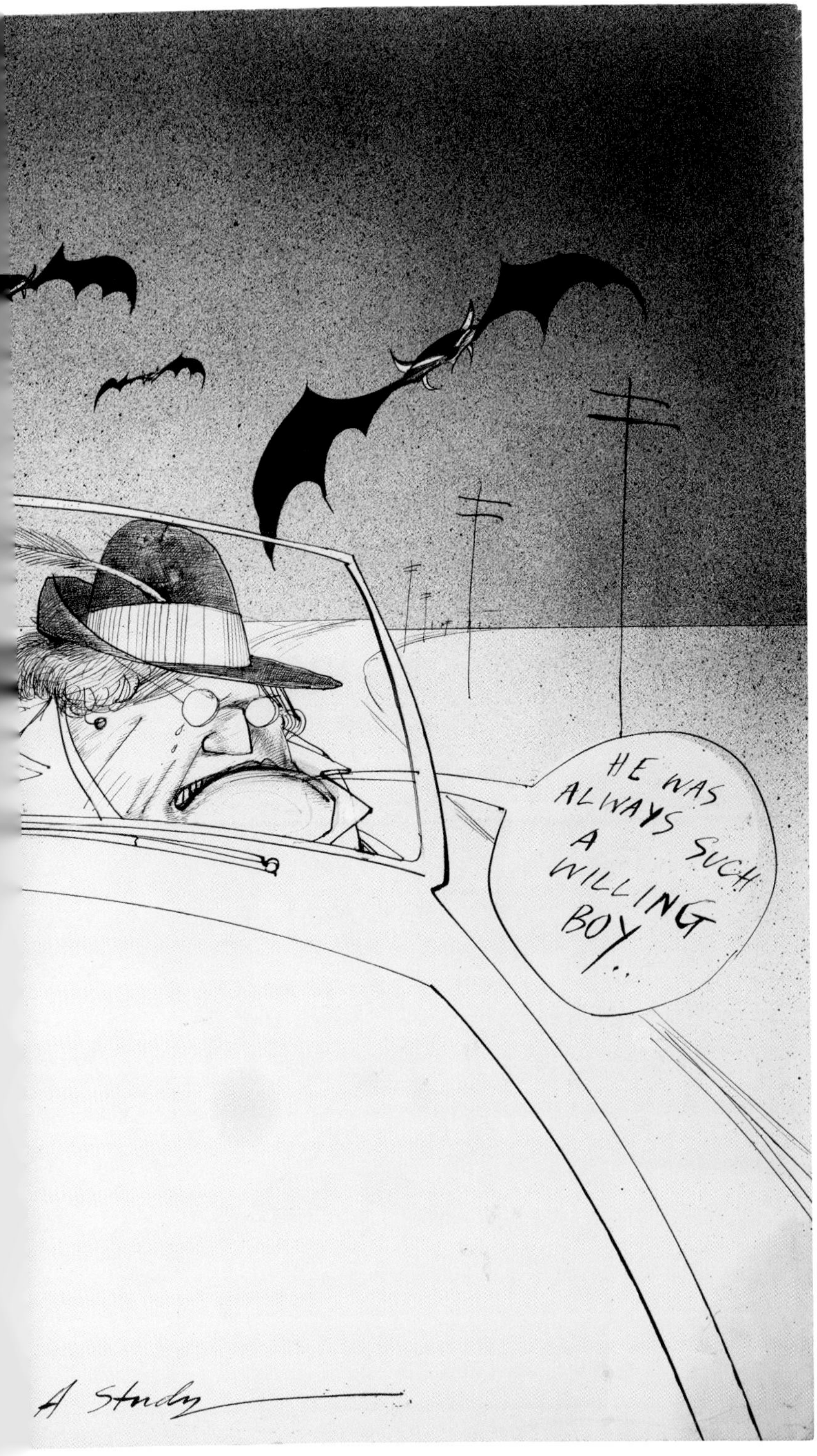

Hunter's "Mum and Dad!" 1981

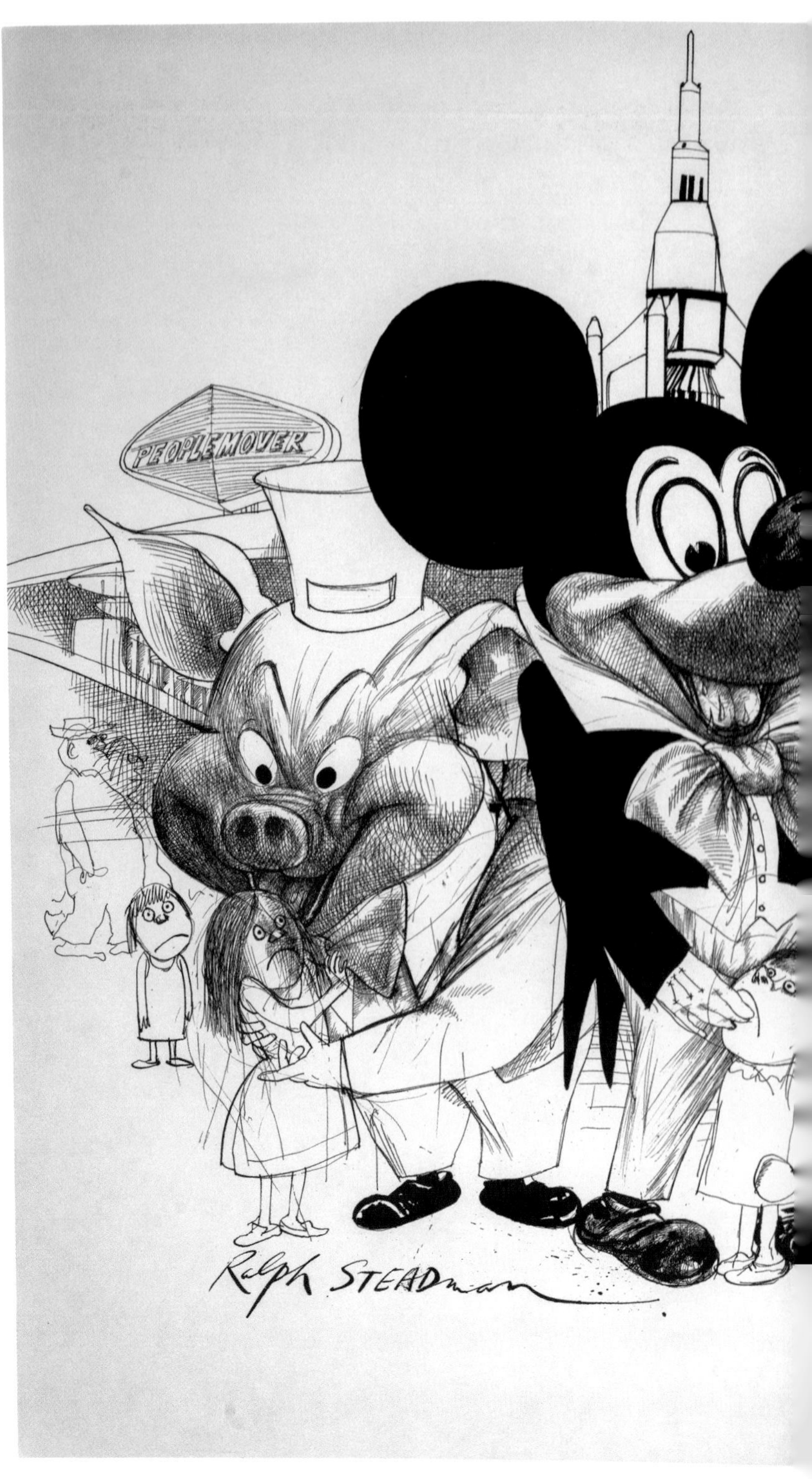

Disneyland! ca. 1982

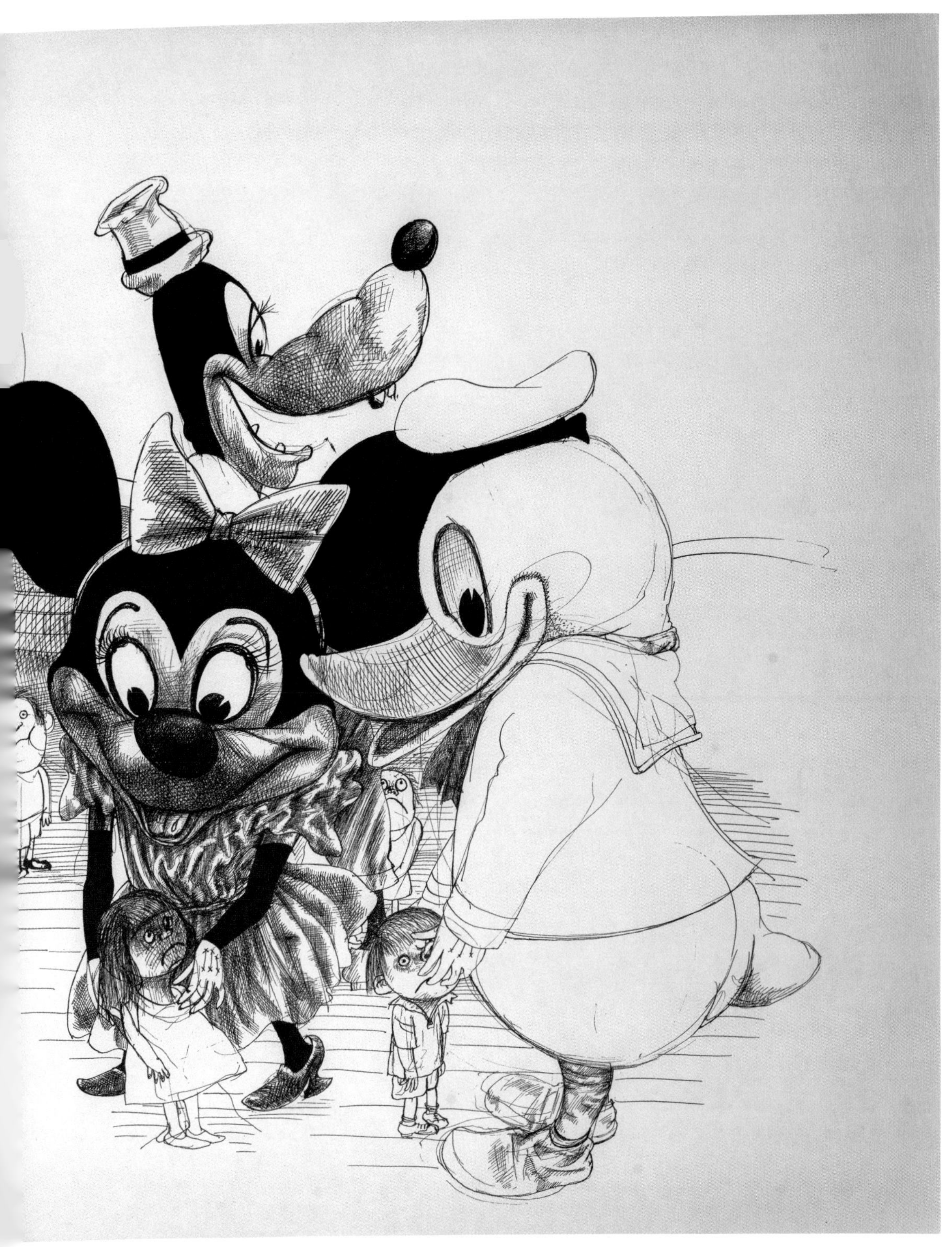

"It was a puzzle, who was actually inside those massive suits. Some of the children looked almost stunned, hypnotised by the exaggerated characters. It was sinister."

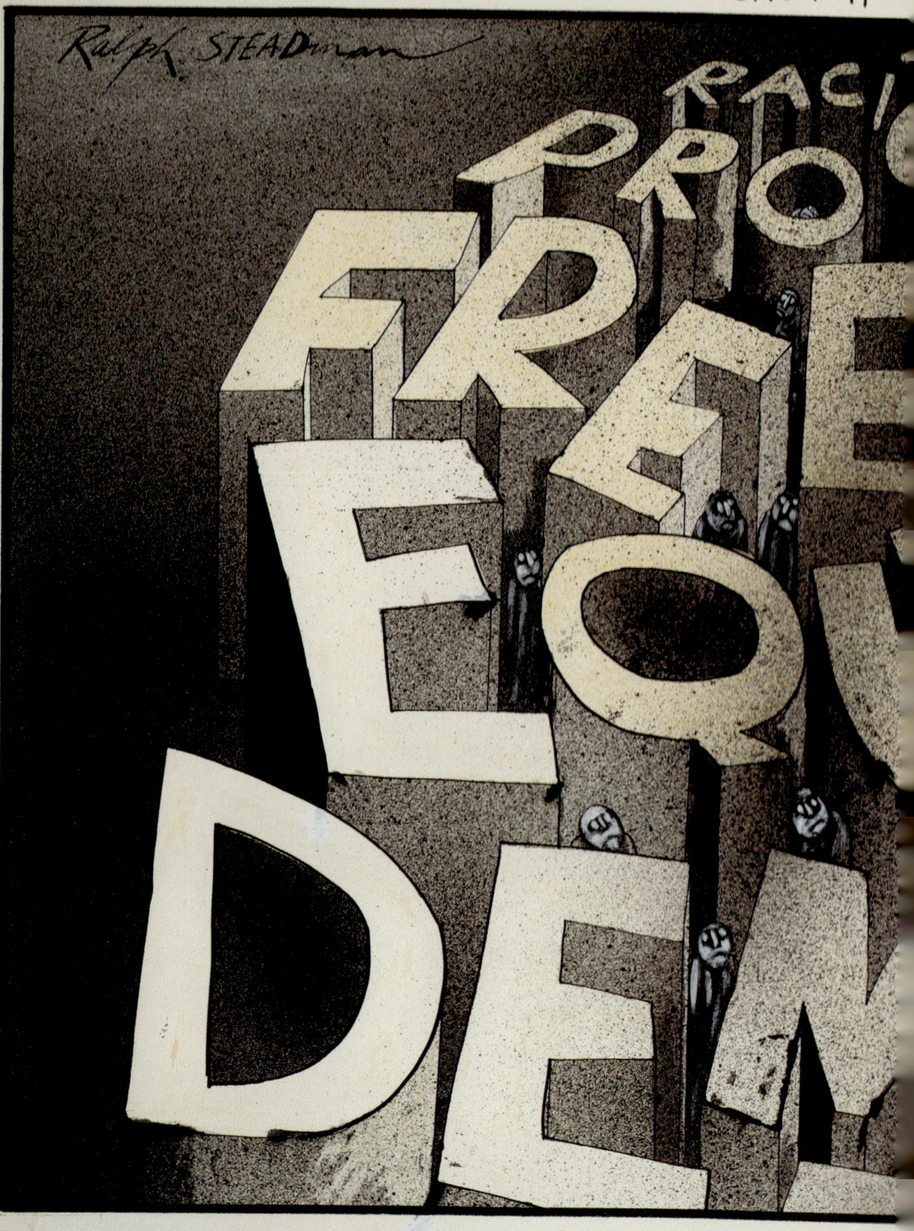
Ralph STEADman
RACI
PRO
FREE
FOU
DE

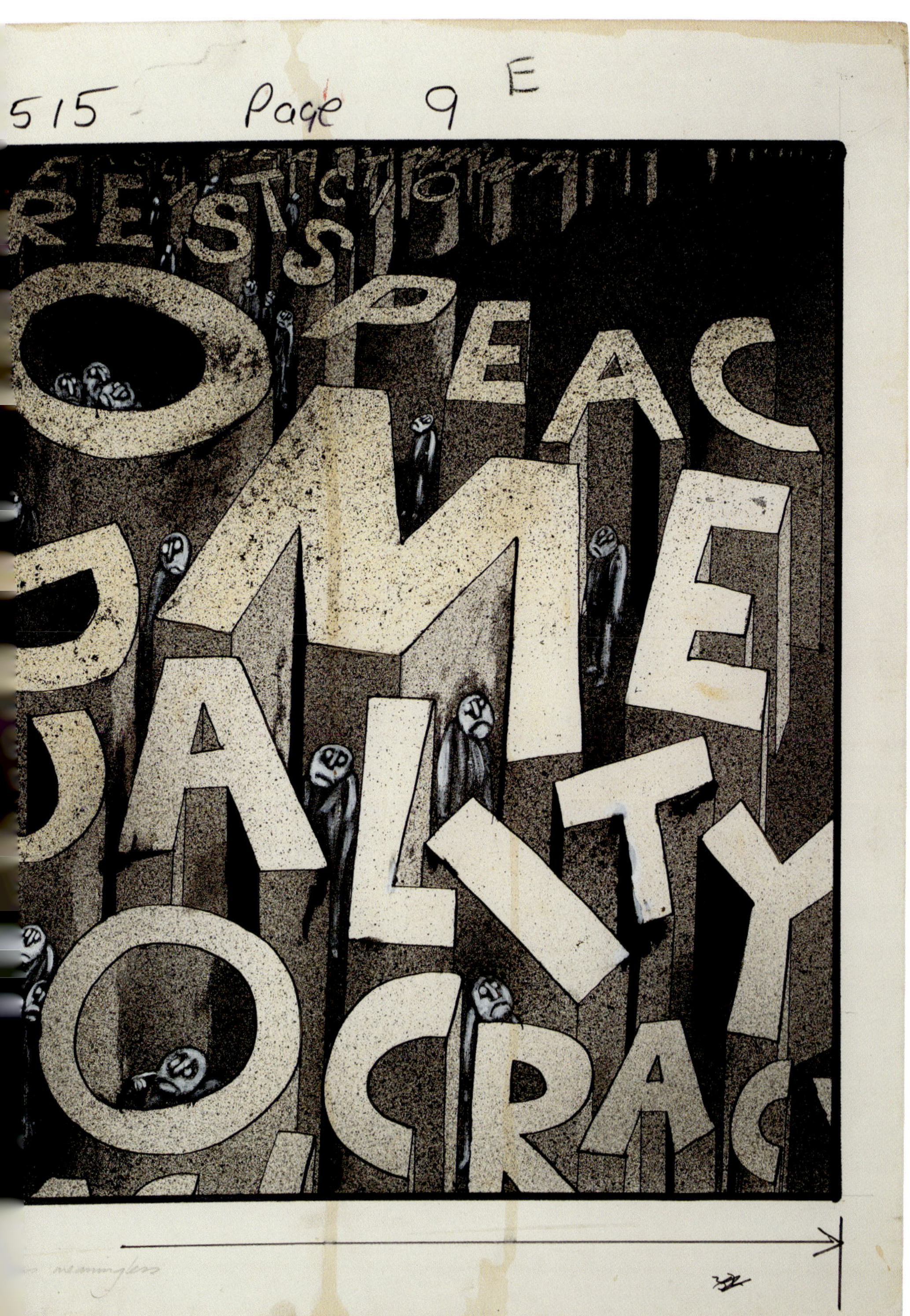

*Moral Maze, for **The Telegraph**, ca. 1972*

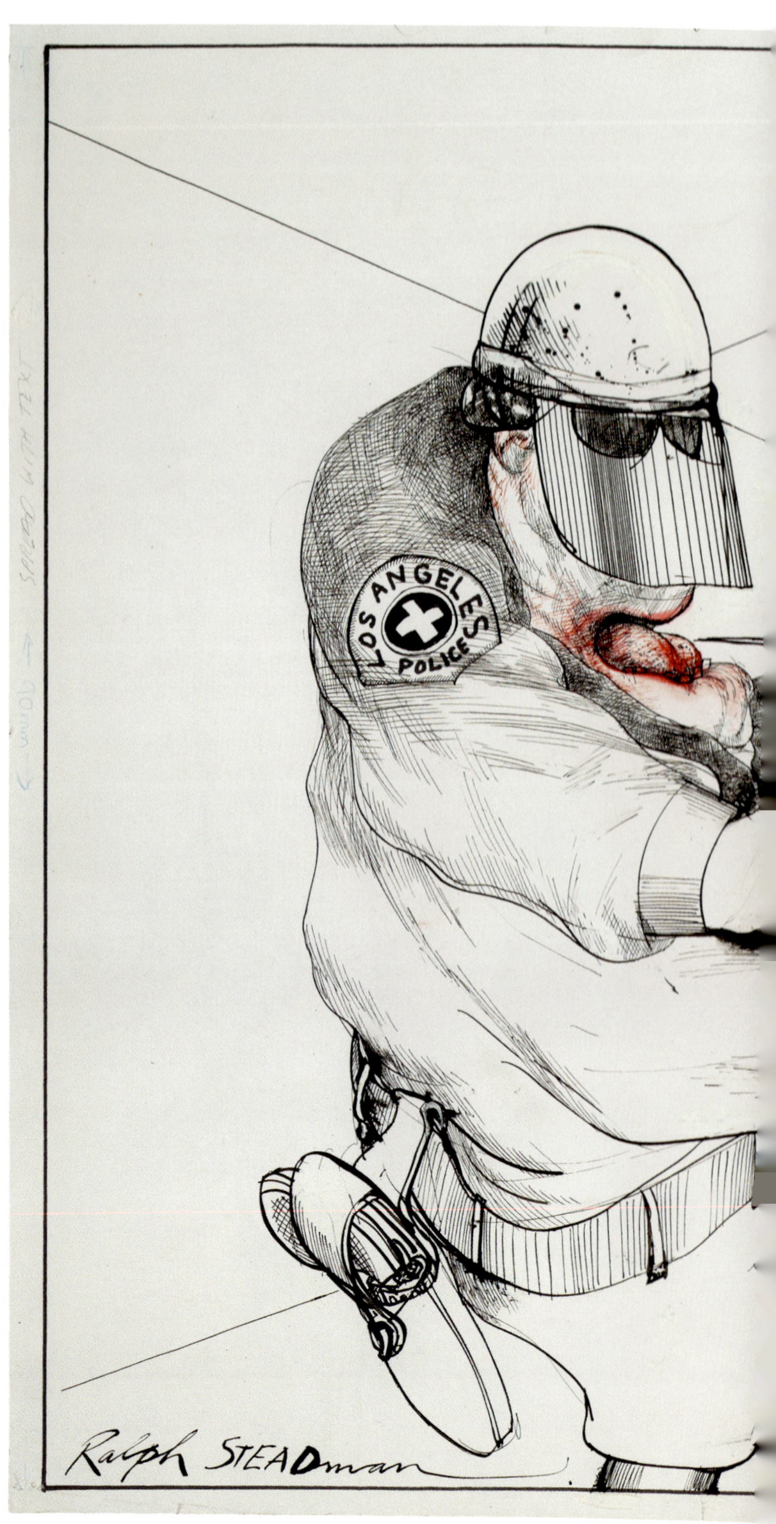

Police Brutality, ca. 1972

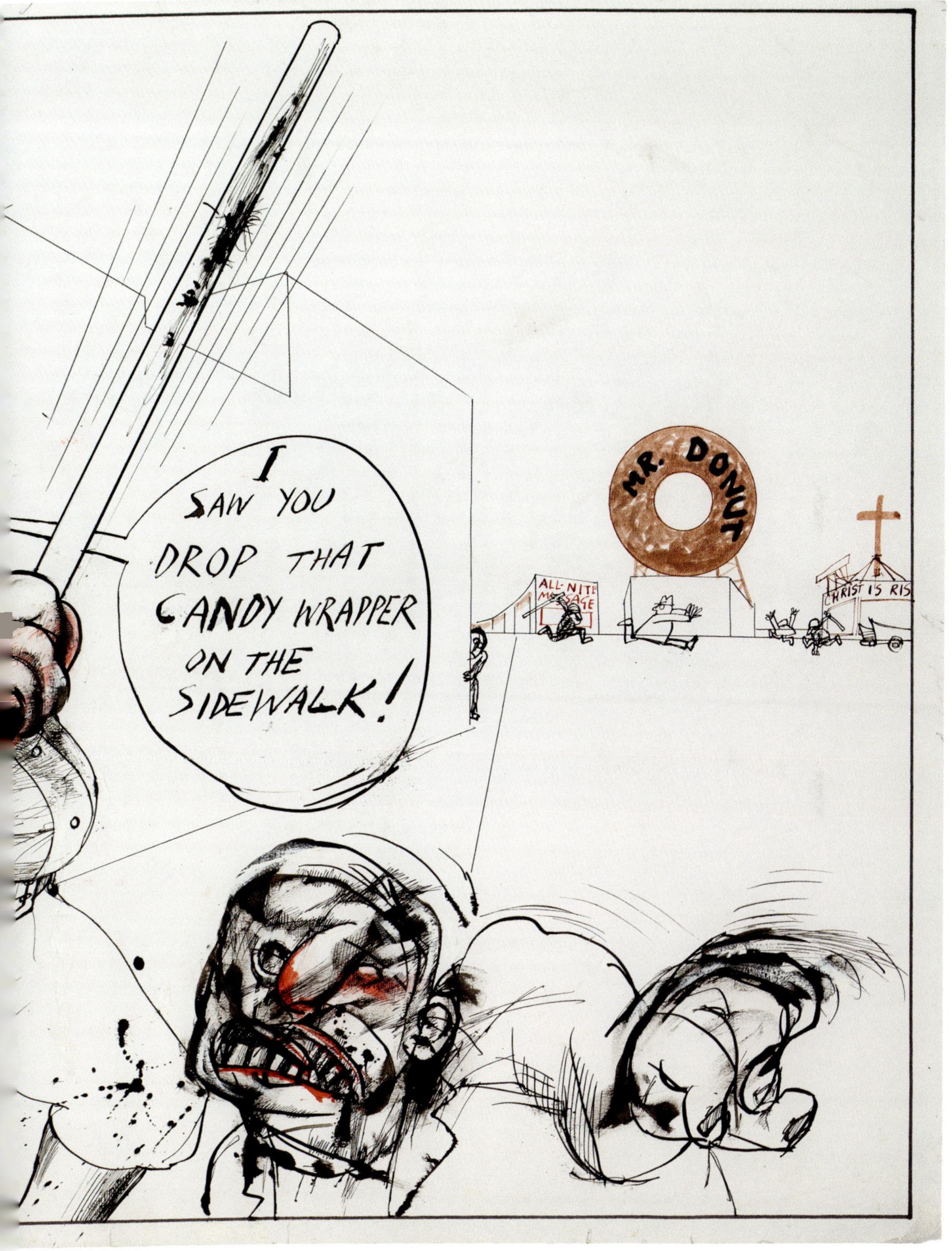

I SAW YOU DROP THAT CANDY WRAPPER ON THE SIDEWALK!
MR. DONUT
ALL-NITE MASSAGE
CHRIST IS RIS

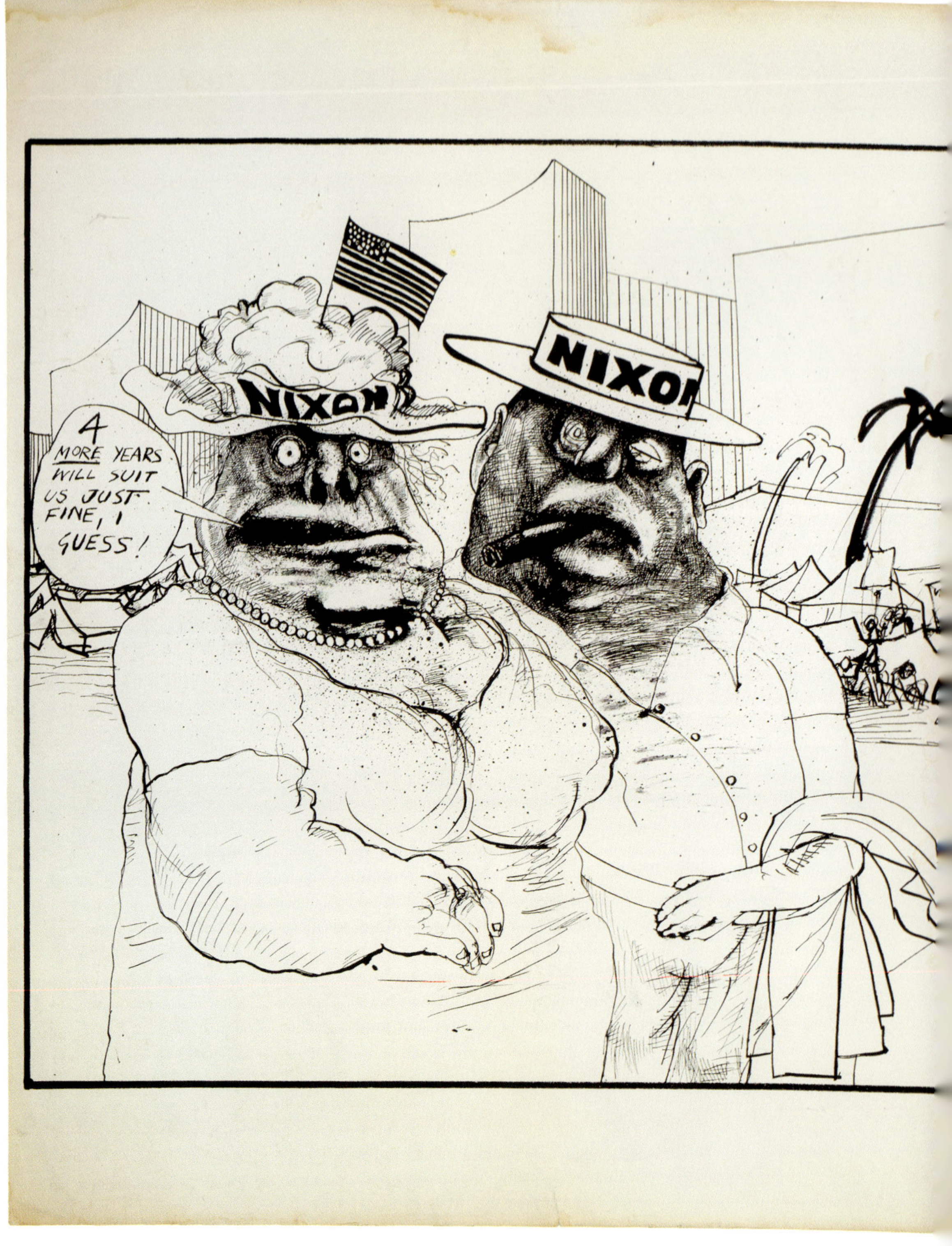

"We were visiting Dallas for the twentieth anniversary of the assassination of JFK. This was a typical couple at the Elks Convention."

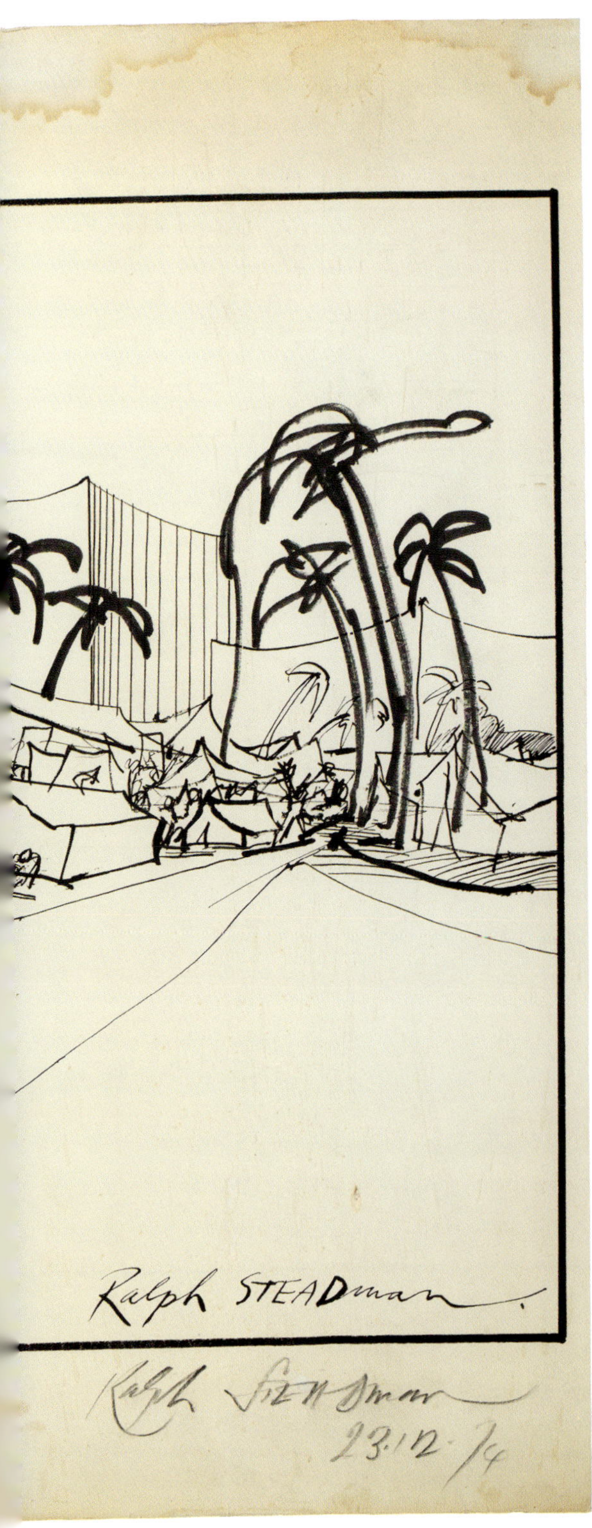

An Elks Convention, ca. 1983

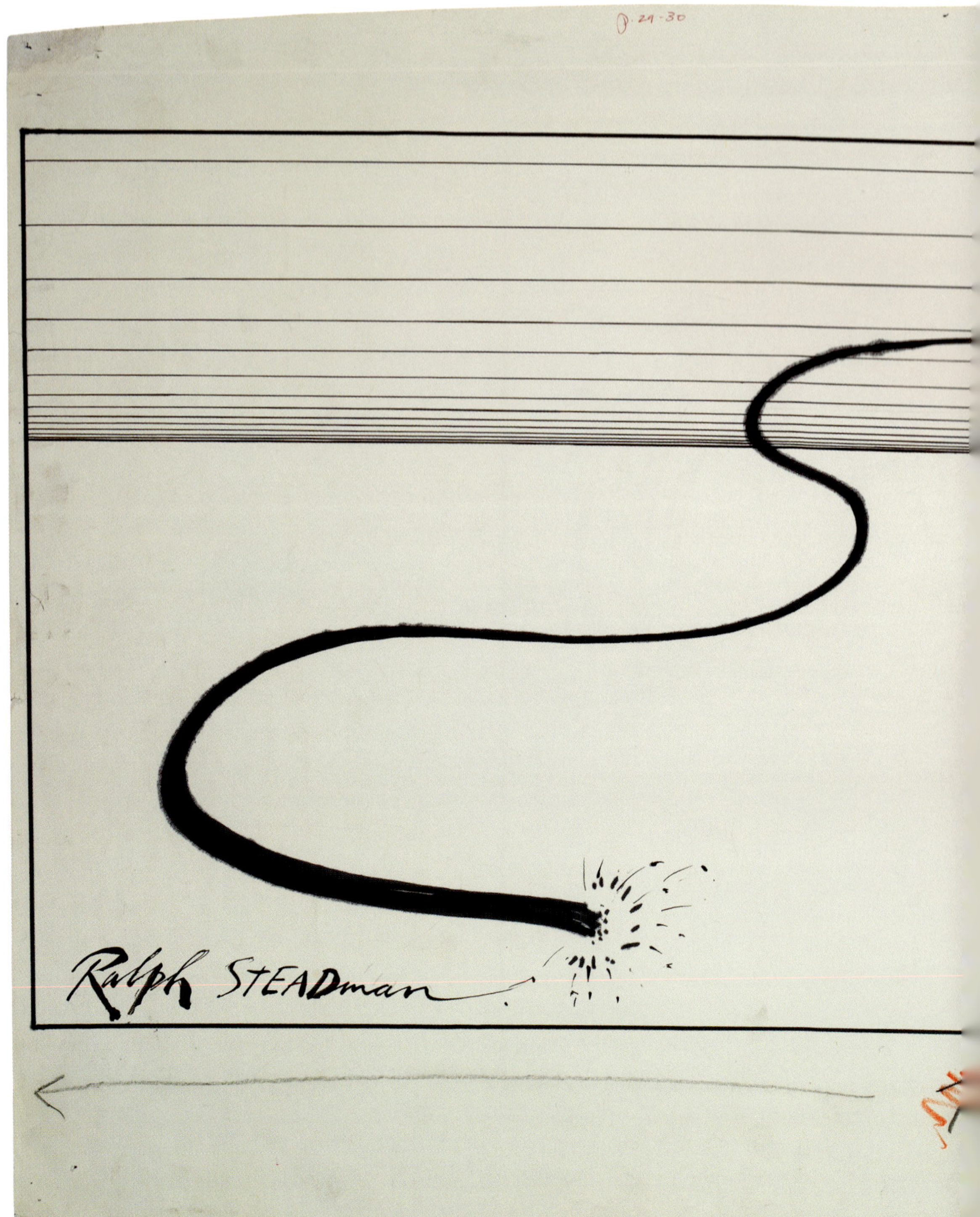

Nixon Trying to Be Funny, ca. 1972

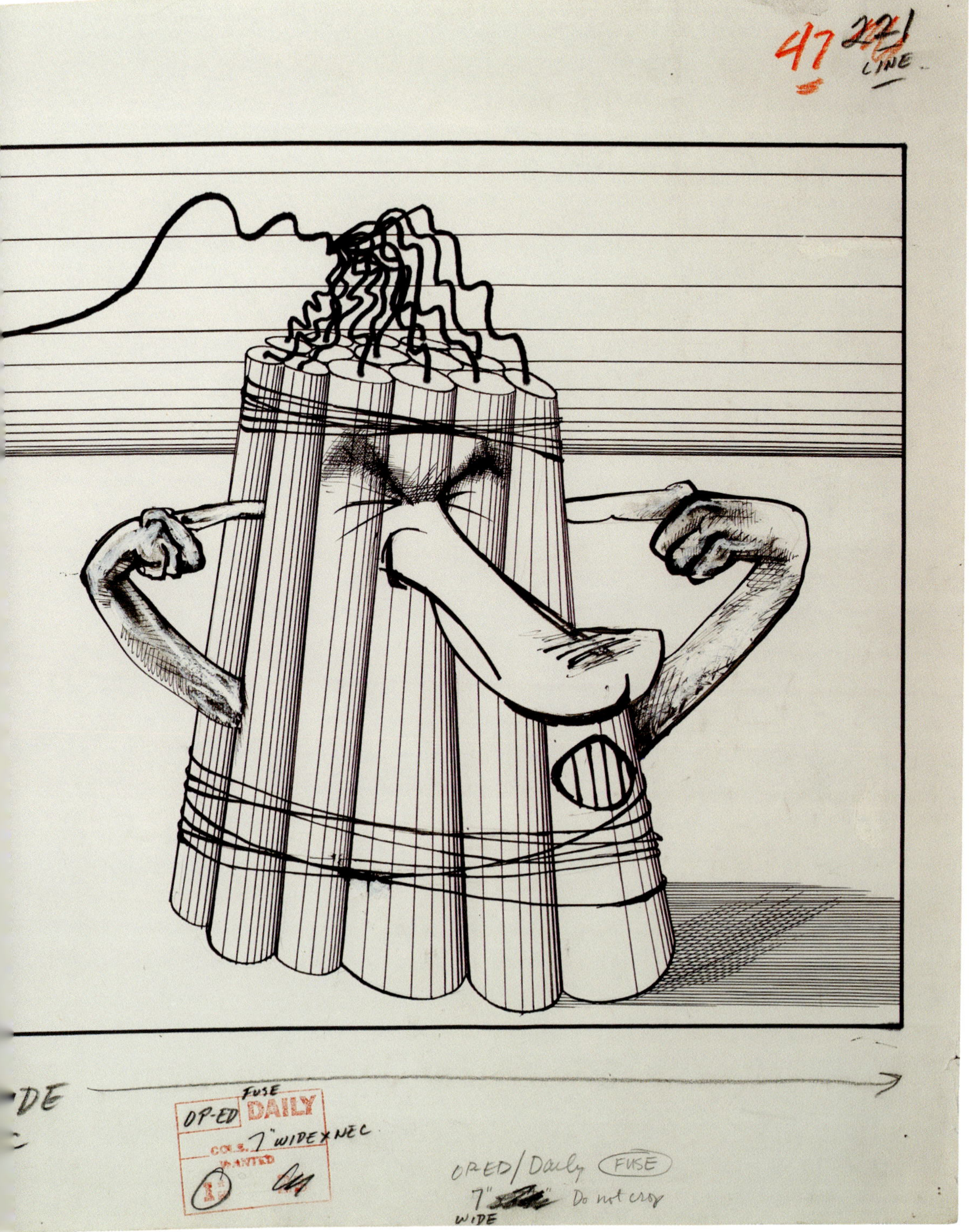

"Would you scribble notes on a Picasso? That's what I want to know—and then they even scribbled it out."

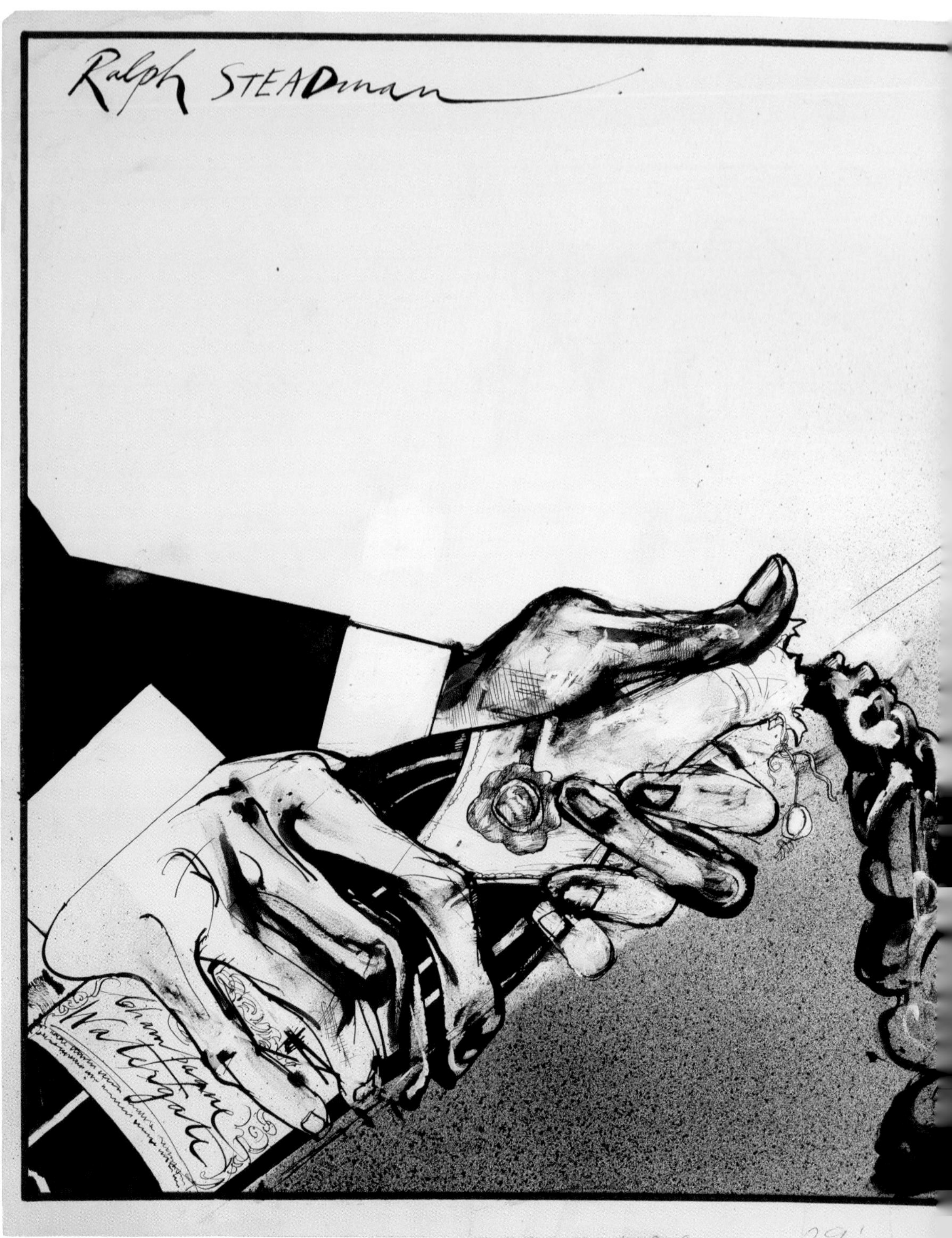

"Nixon might have been a villain, but at least he was an honest-to-goodness politician, tricky or not! Not like these dreadful people we have today."

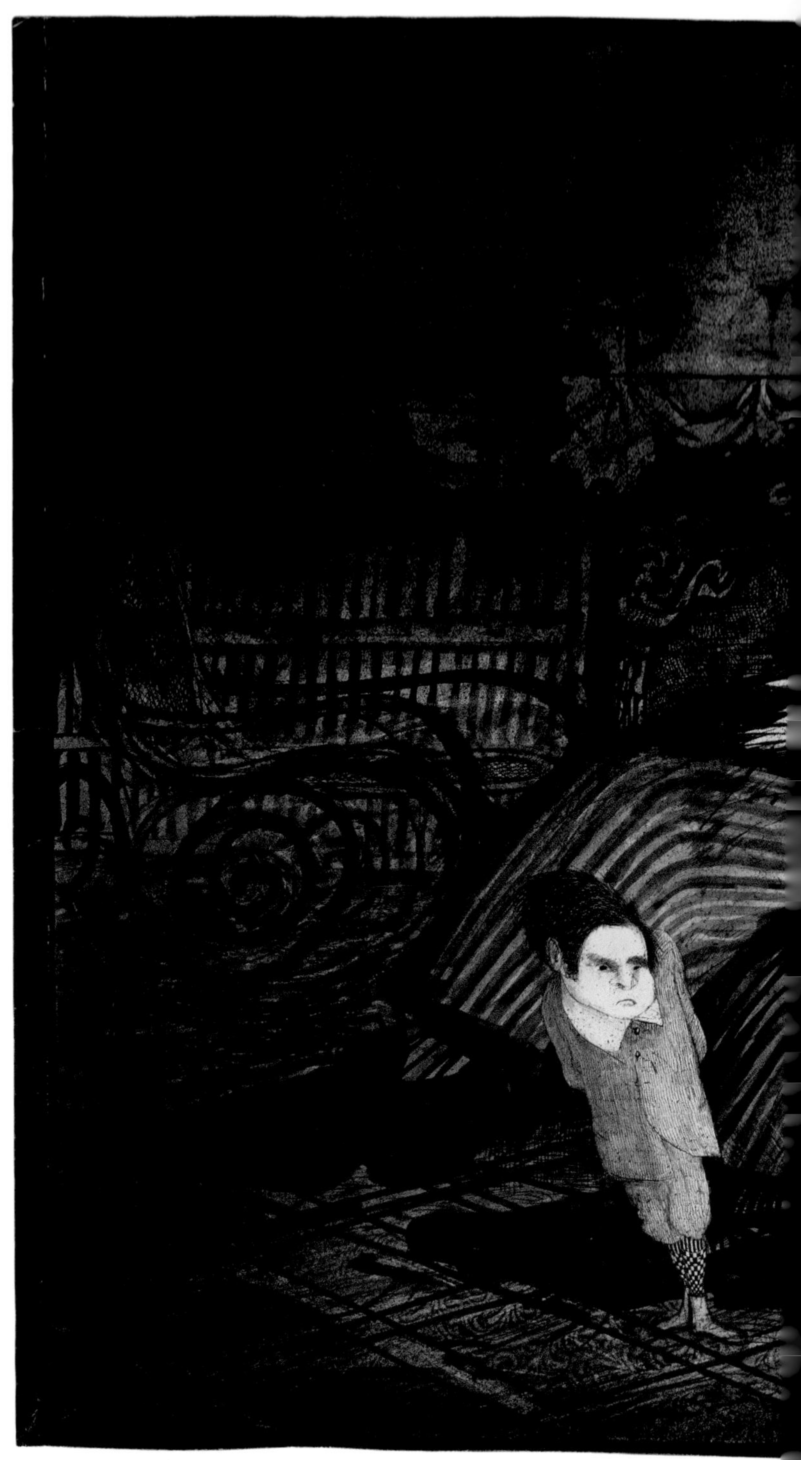

From **Sigmund Freud**, 1979

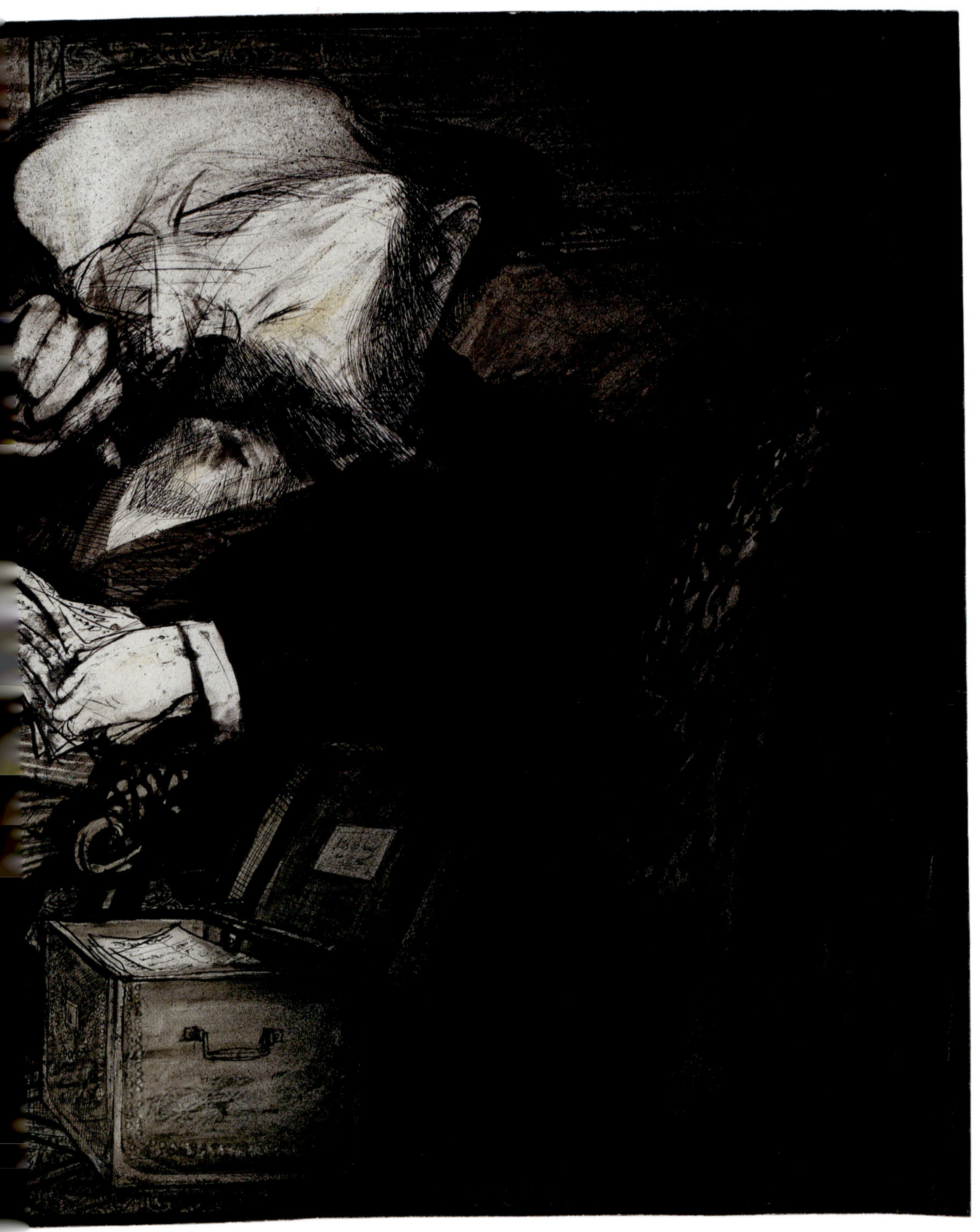

"Herr Freud reproves his son for natural boyhood habits."

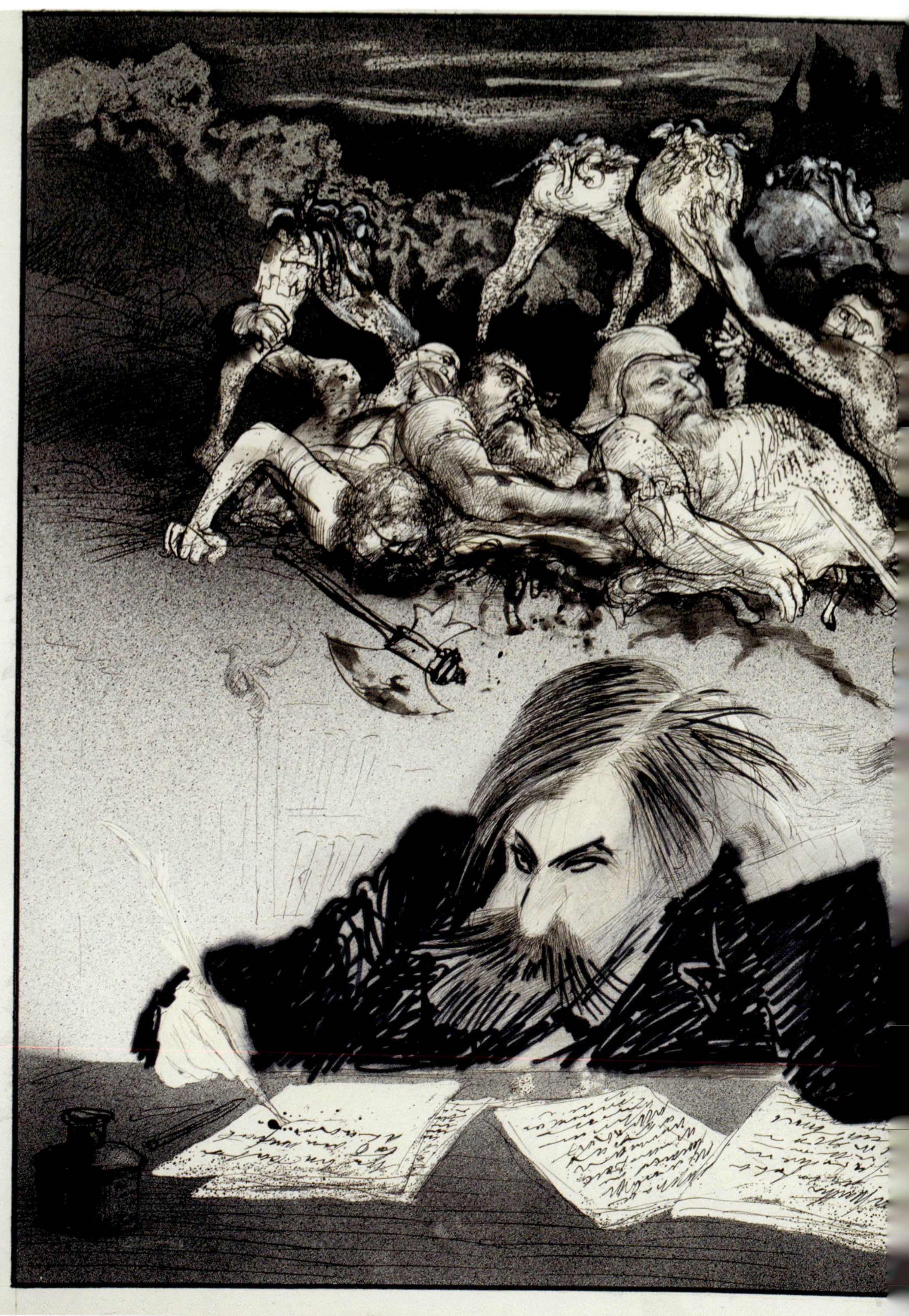

"Ha, sometimes I do use pencil!"

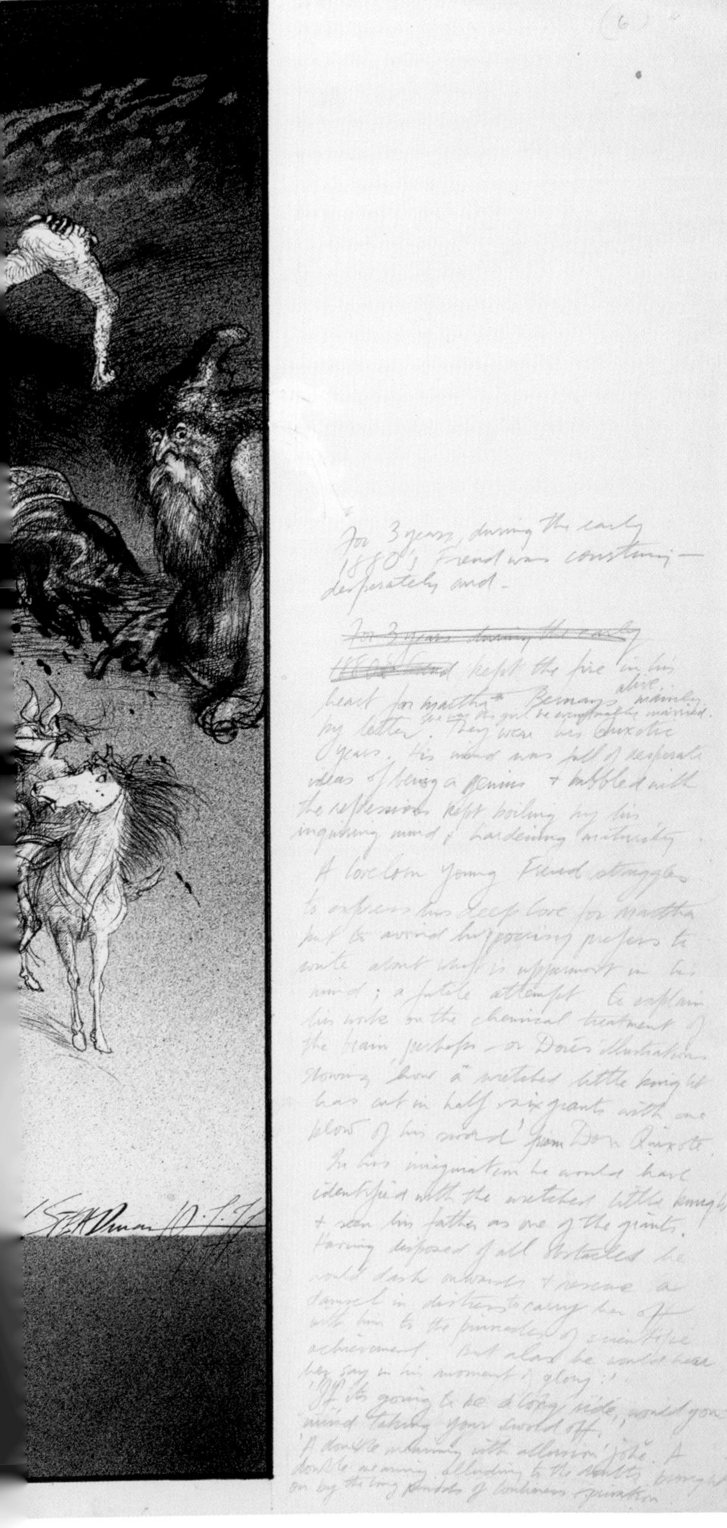

For 3 years, during the early
1880's Freud was courting —
desperately and —

For 3 years during the early
Freud kept the fire in his
heart for Martha Bernays alive.
By letter. They were his quixotic
years. His mind was full of desperate
ideas of being a genius & bubbled with
the reflections kept boiling by his
inquiring mind & hardening intensity.

A lovelorn young Freud struggles
to express his deep love for Martha
but to avoid his pouring prefers to
write about what is uppermost in his
mind; a futile attempt to explain
his work on the chemical treatment of
the brain, perhaps — or Doré's illustration
showing "how a wretched little knight
was cut in half six giants with one
blow of his sword" from Don Quixote.
In his imagination he would have
identified with the wretched little knight
& seen his father as one of the giants.
Having disposed of all obstacles he
would dash onwards & rescue a
damsel in distress to carry her off
with him to the pinnacles of scientific
achievement. But alas he would have
been gay in his moment of glory —
If it's going to be a long ride, would you
mind taking your sword off.'
'A double meaning with allusion' joke. A
double meaning alluding to the
on by the long periods of continuous separation

Sigmund Freud, Natural Aggressive Principles, 1977

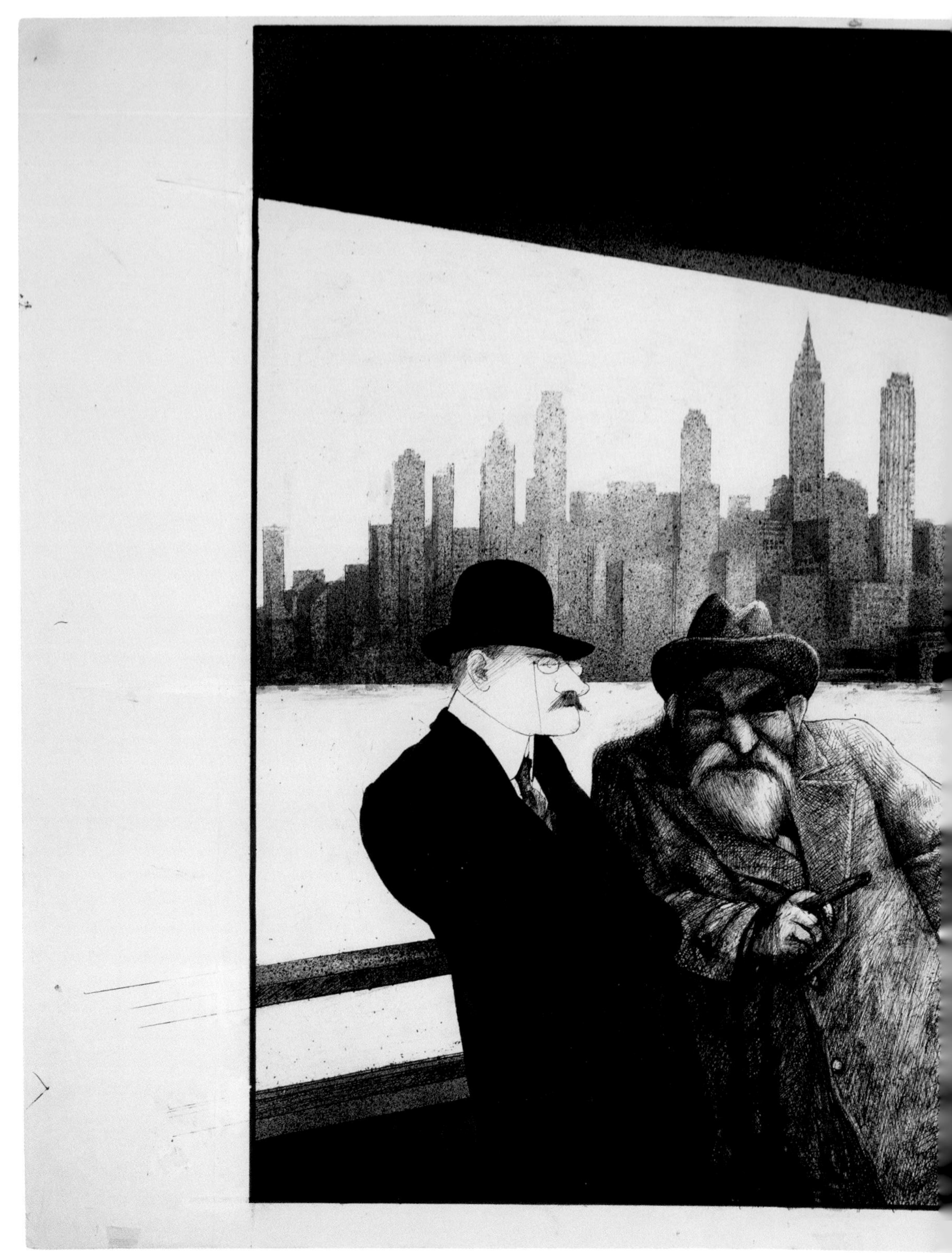

Sigmund Freud, *Carl Jung and Sigmund Freud on the Way to New York City, 1978*

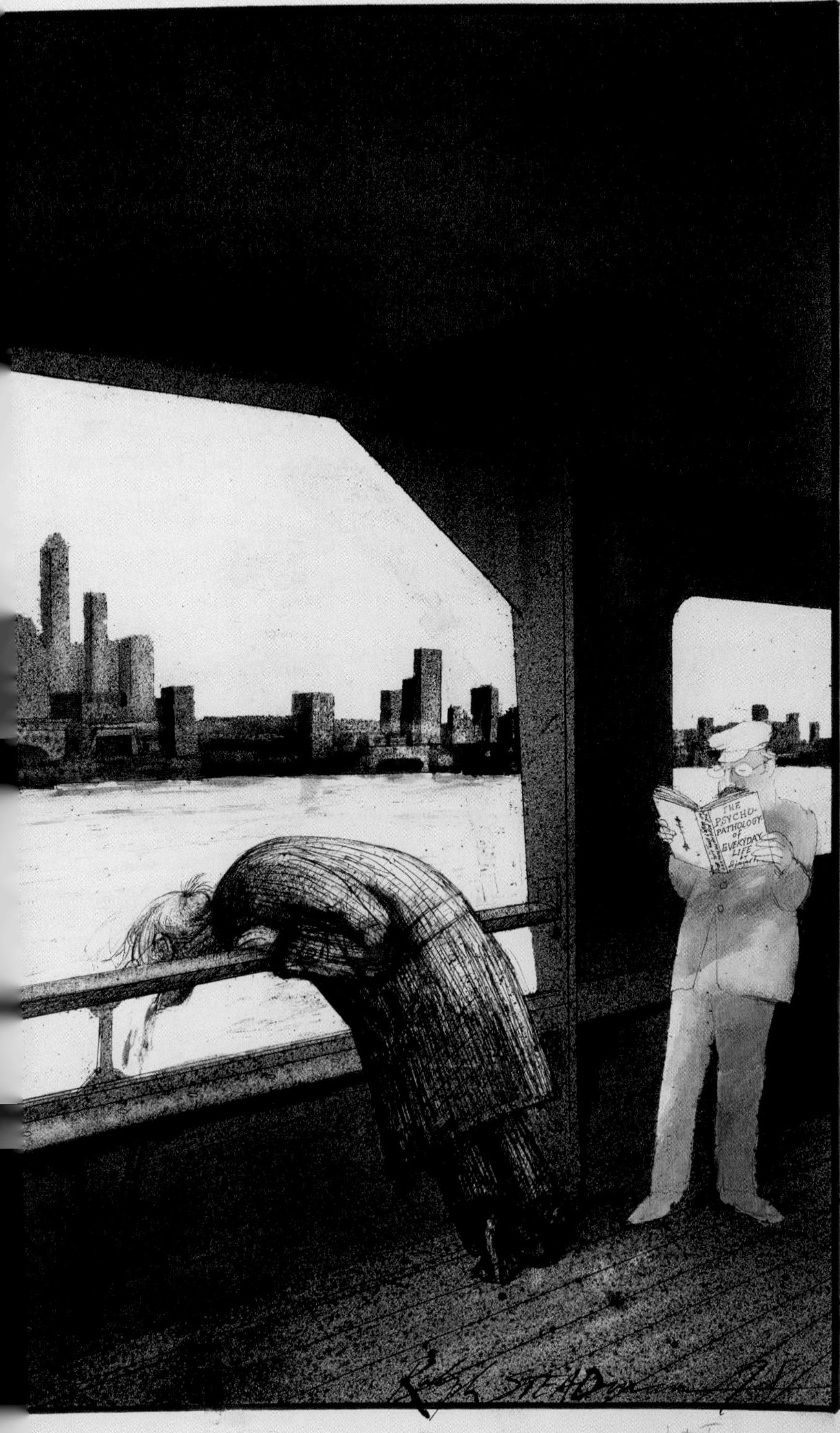

THE
PSYCHO-
PATHOLOGY
of
EVERYDAY
LIFE
Freud

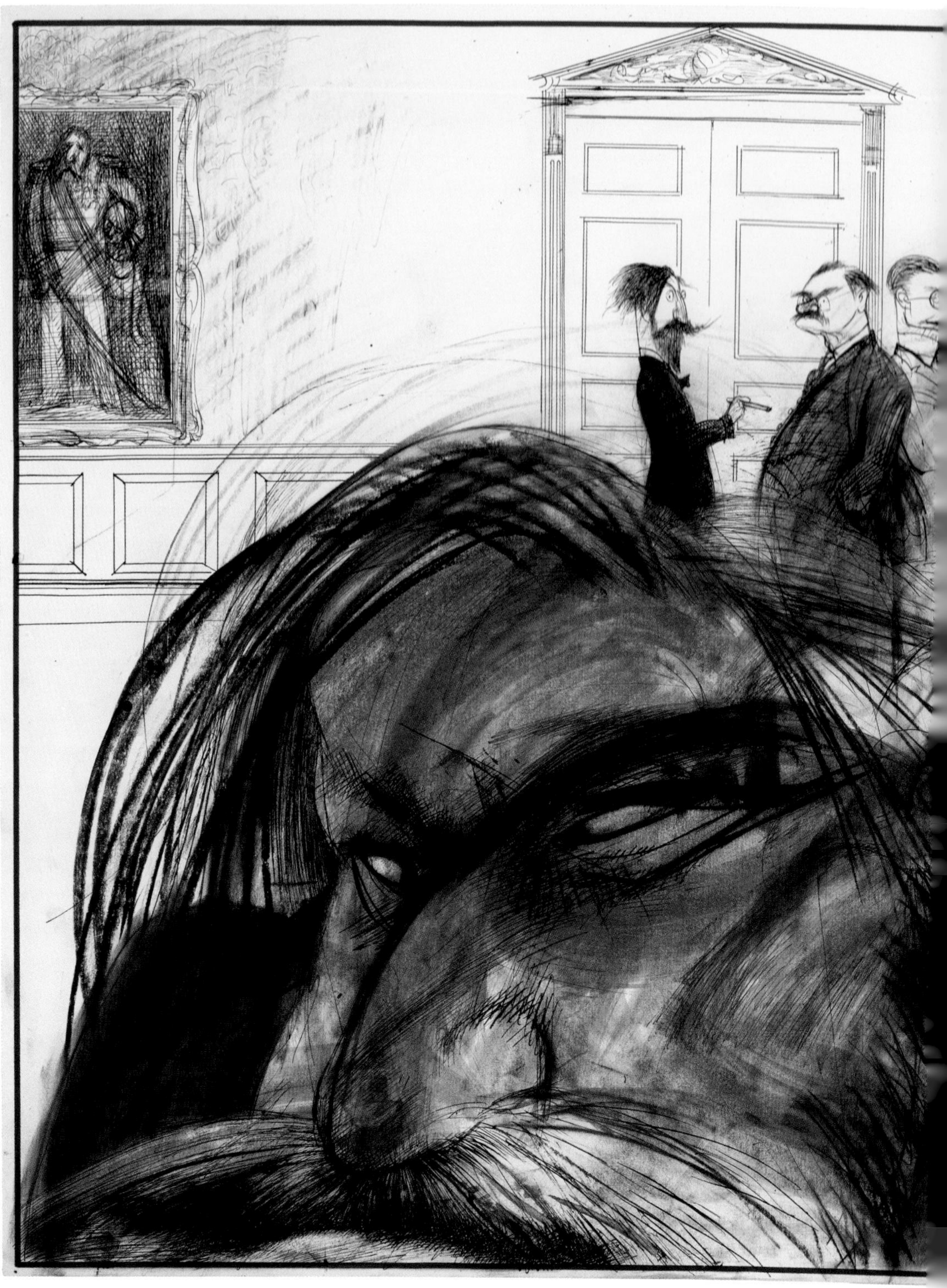

"Wilhem Stekel, one of the 'Big Three Dissenters' within the psychoanalytical movement who was noted for his understanding of dream symbolism, was fond of claiming that he had surpassed Freud's success."

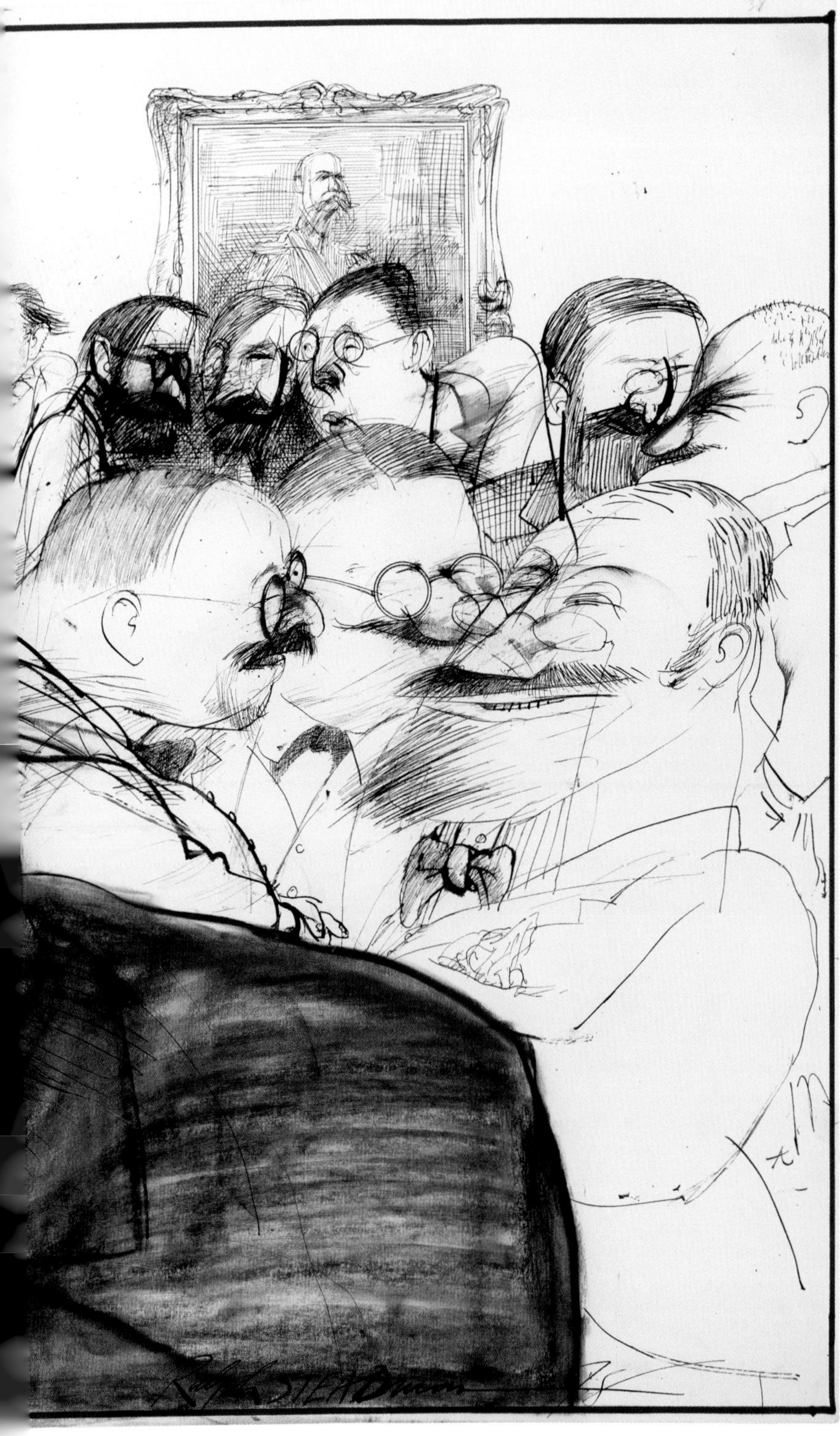

From **Sigmund Freud**, 1978

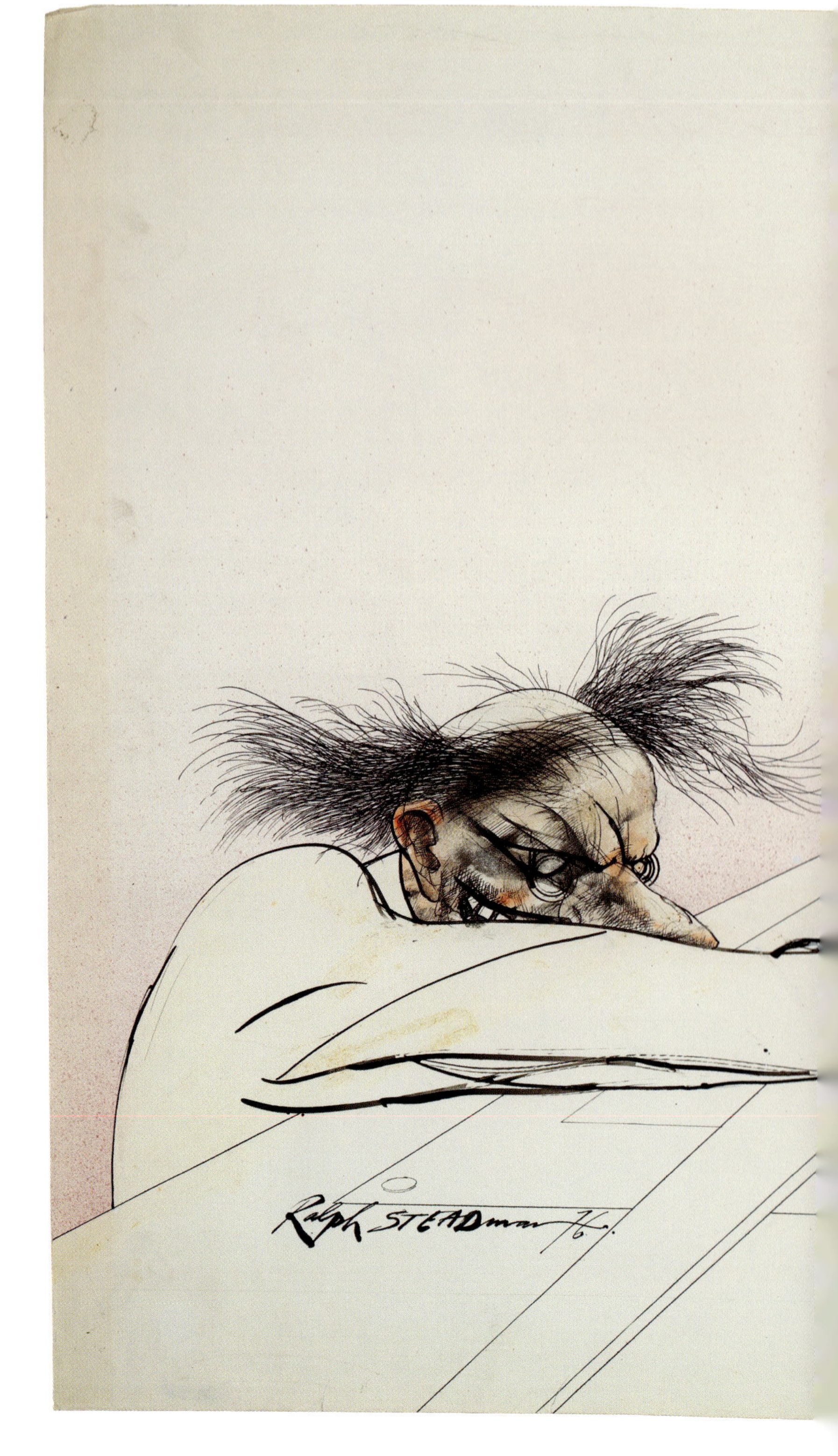

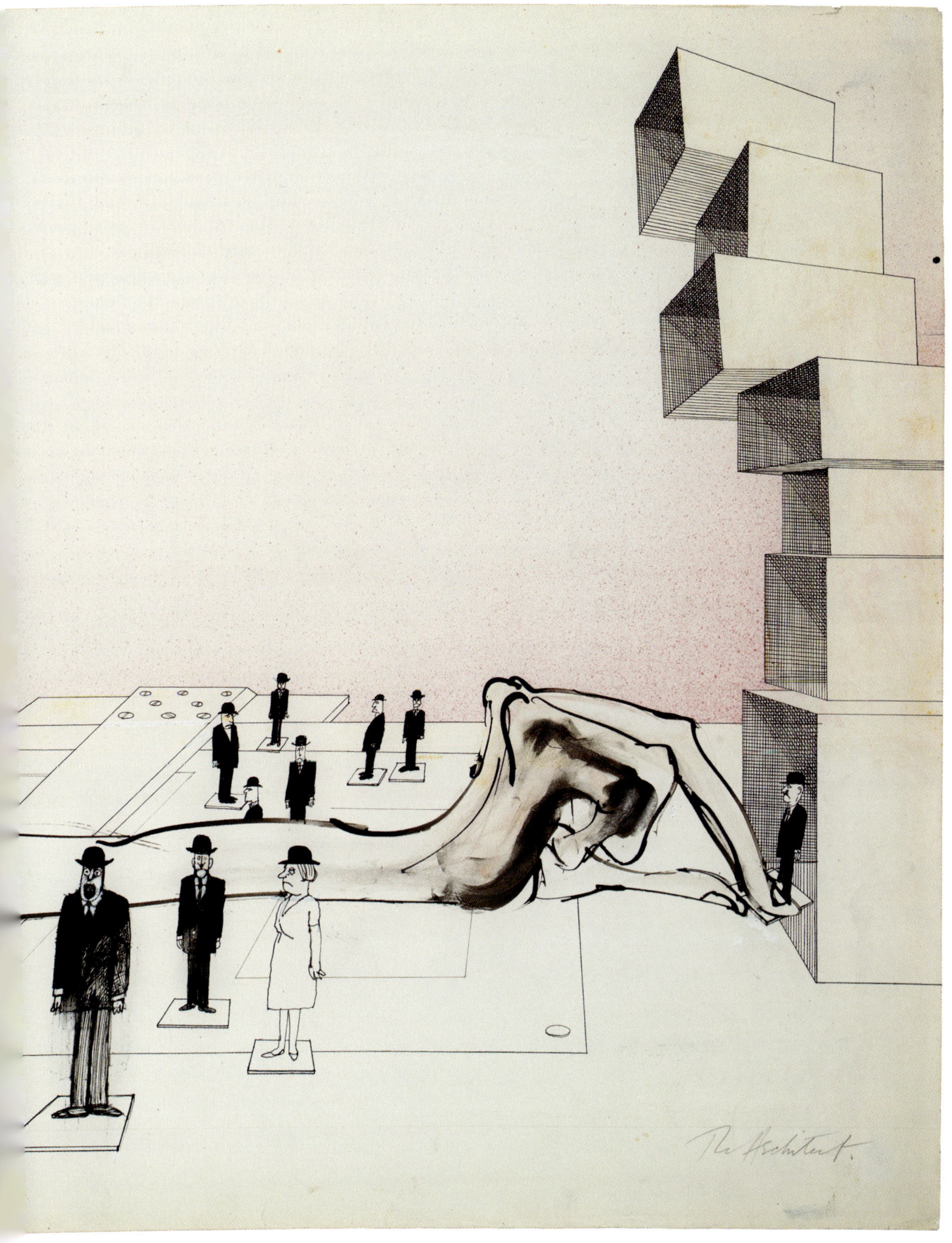

Der Architekt.

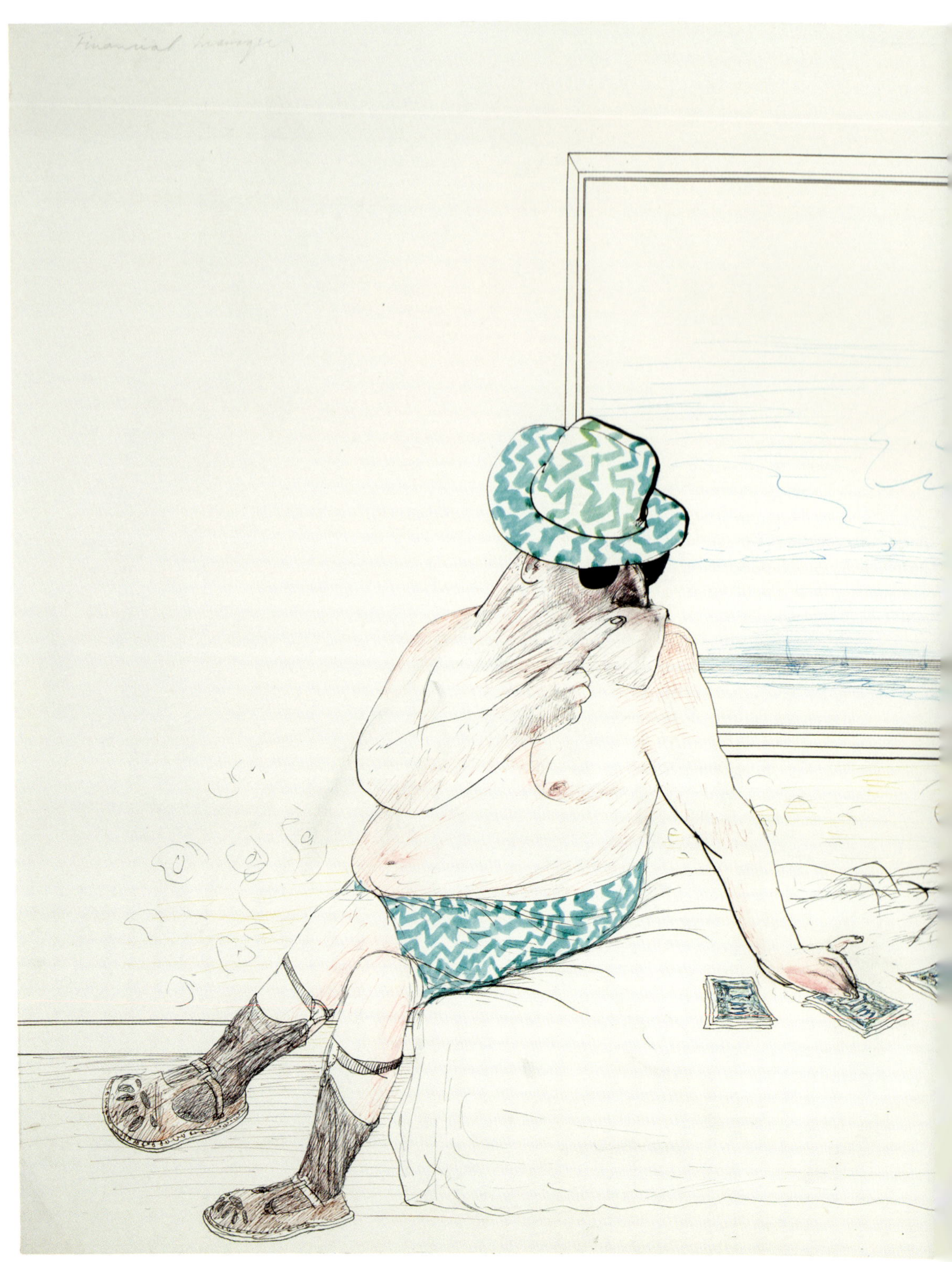

"Those gentleman's sandals were such an iconic piece of 1960s and '70s fashion. They also turned up in *Alice Through the Looking Glass*, on the Lion."

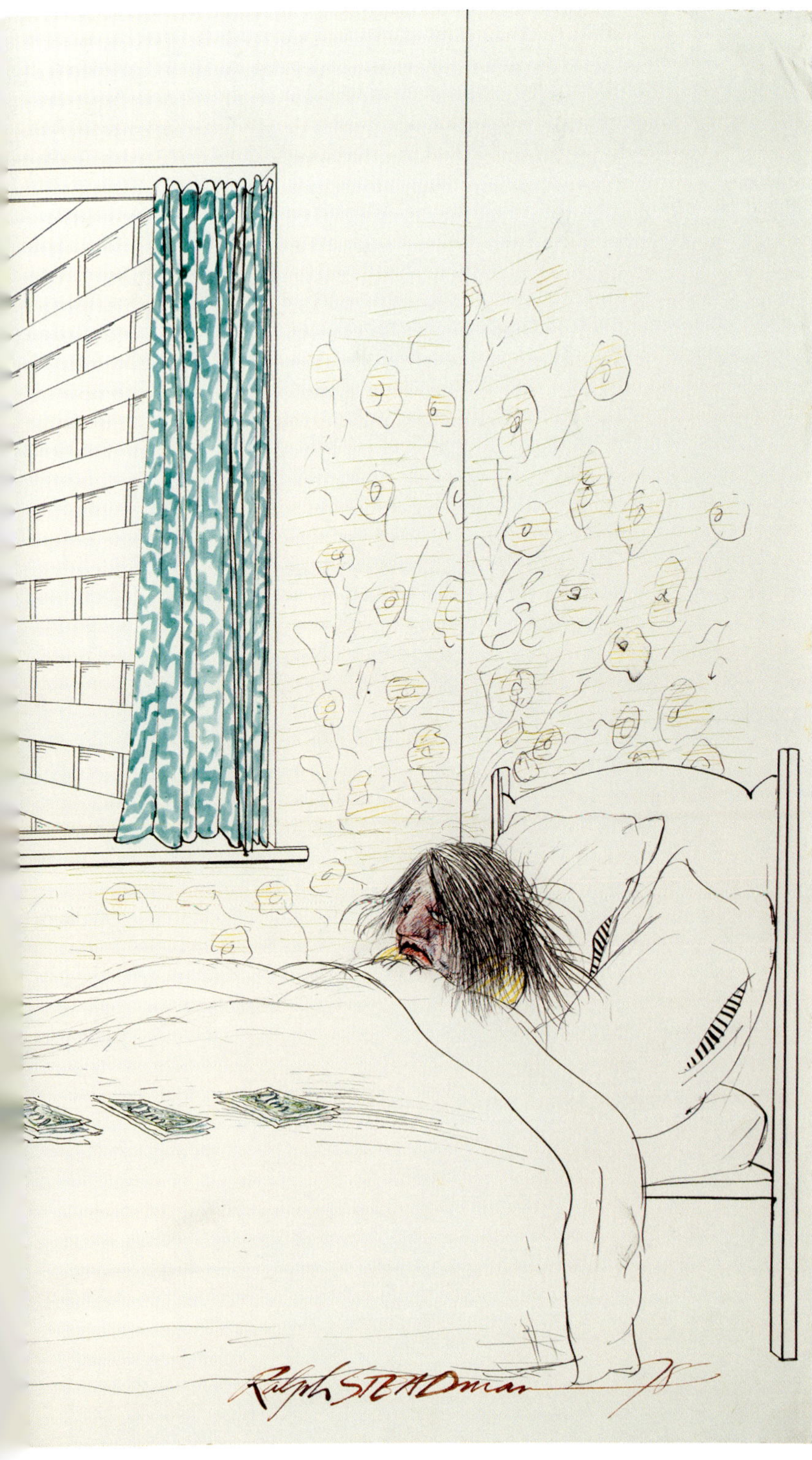

Holiday Picture, 1975

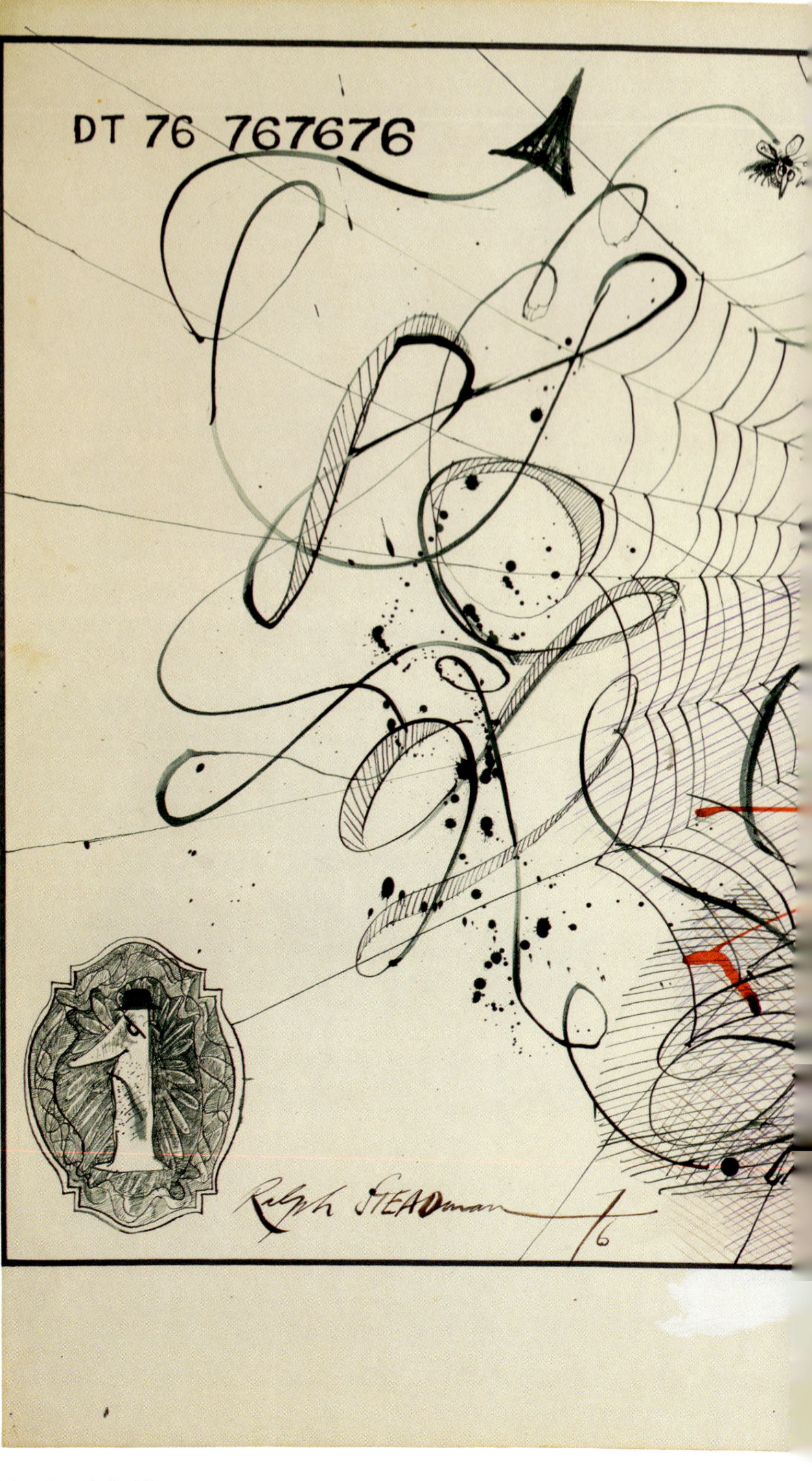

Defamation of the Bank Note, 1976

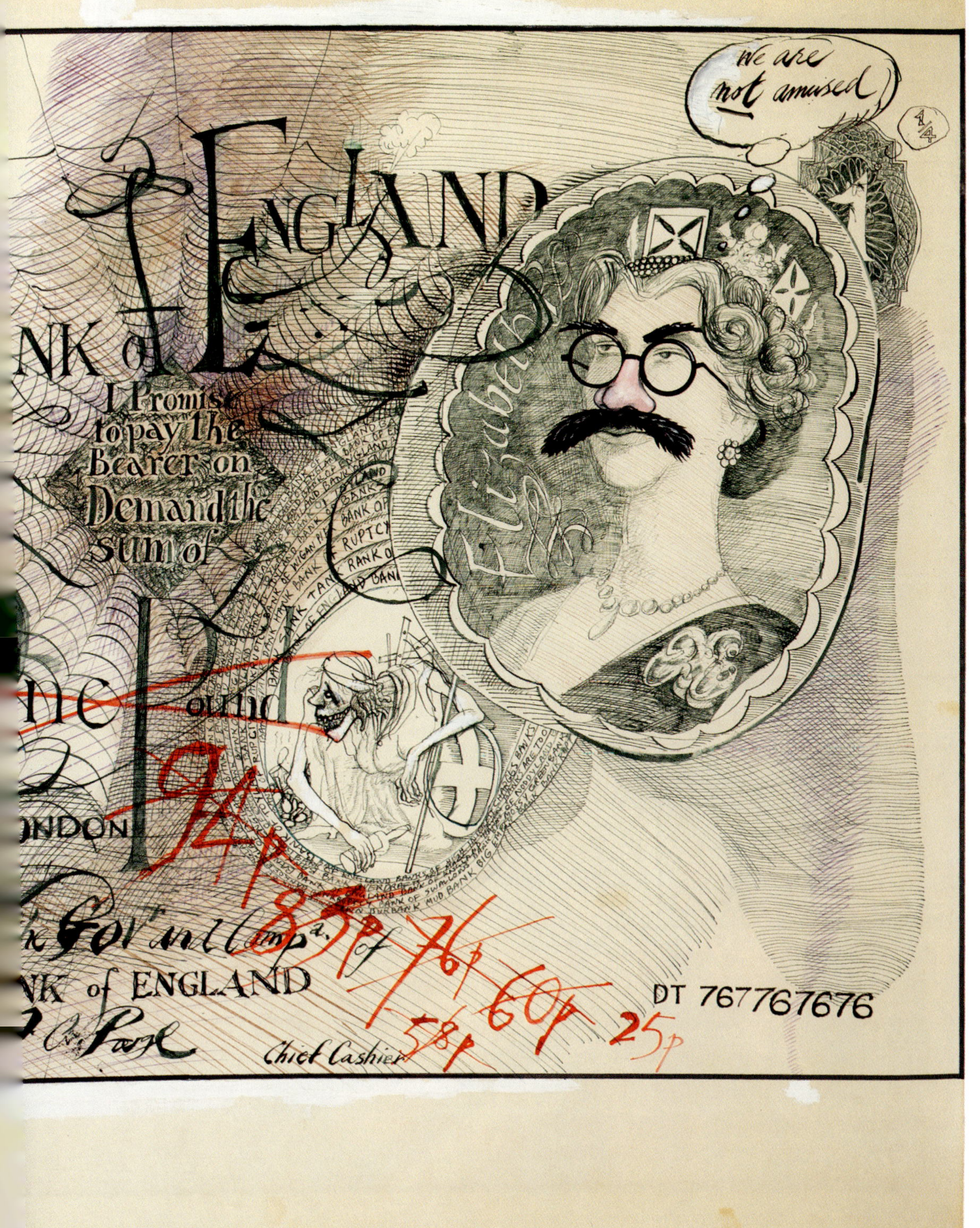

"I don't like the feel of today's bank notes. They feel like they want to slip out of your grasp."

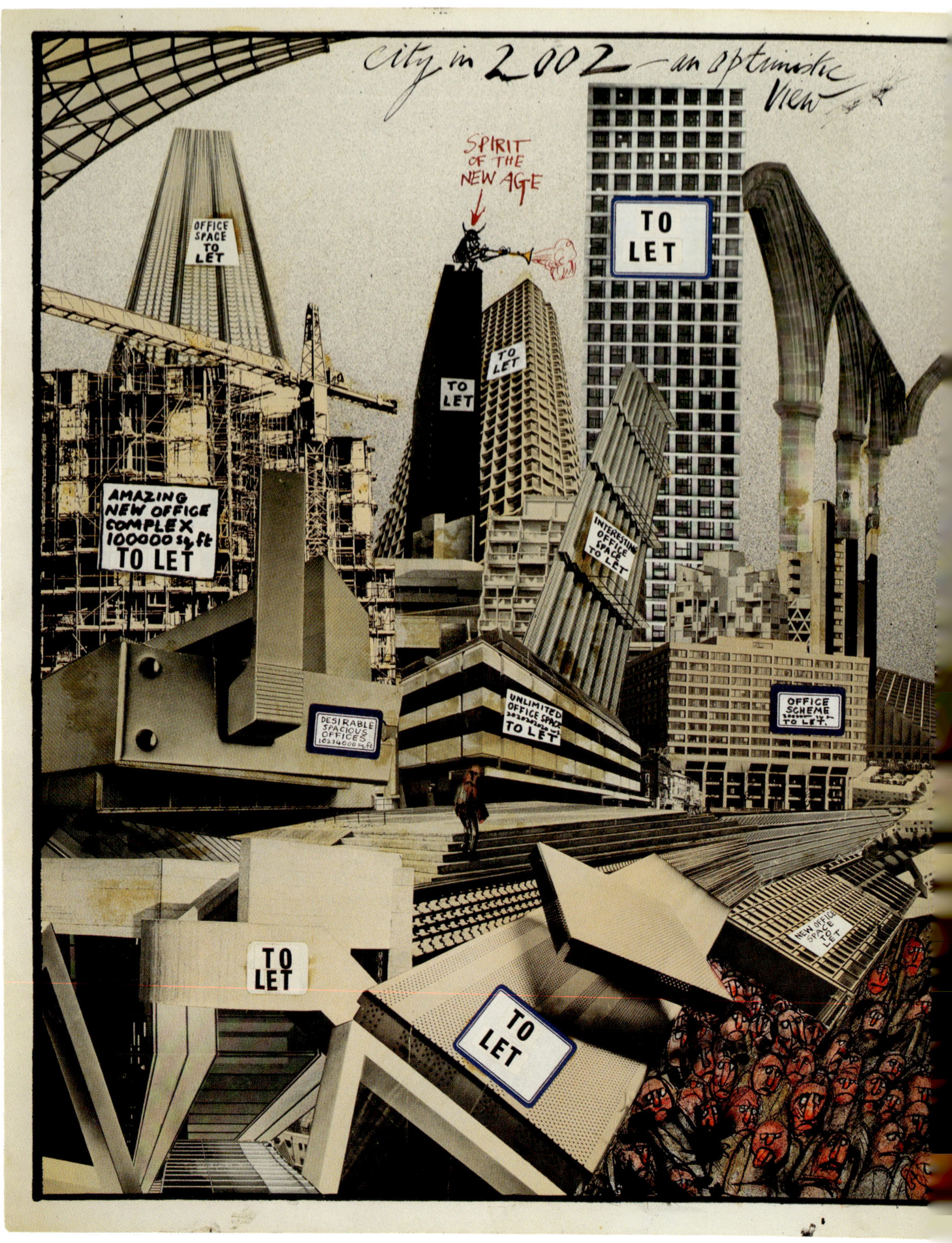

"We went to Toronto in 2015 to launch the film *For No Good Reason*. There were so many cranes and new buildings going up—this reminds me of that."

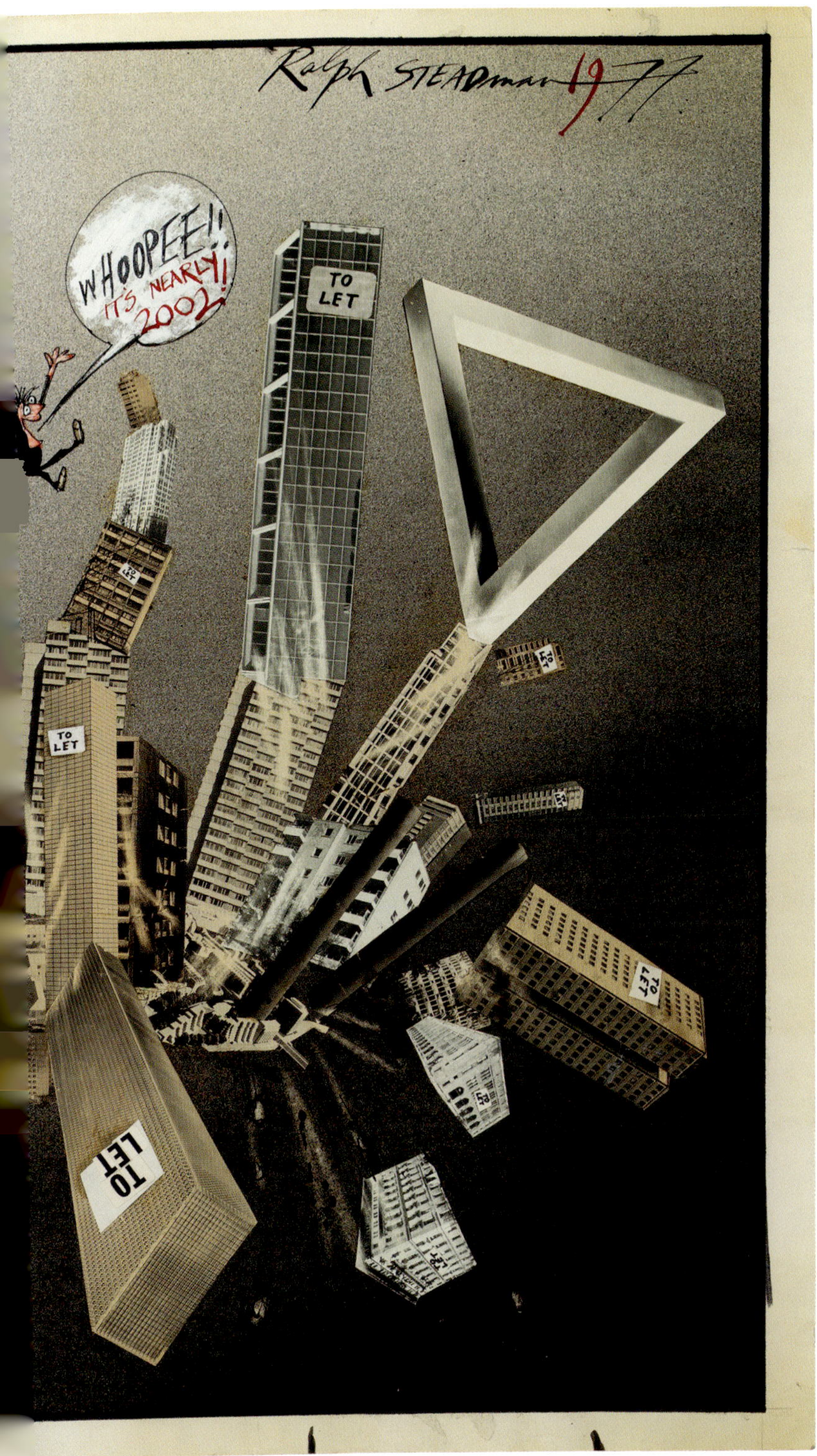

Railing Against Property Developers, 1977

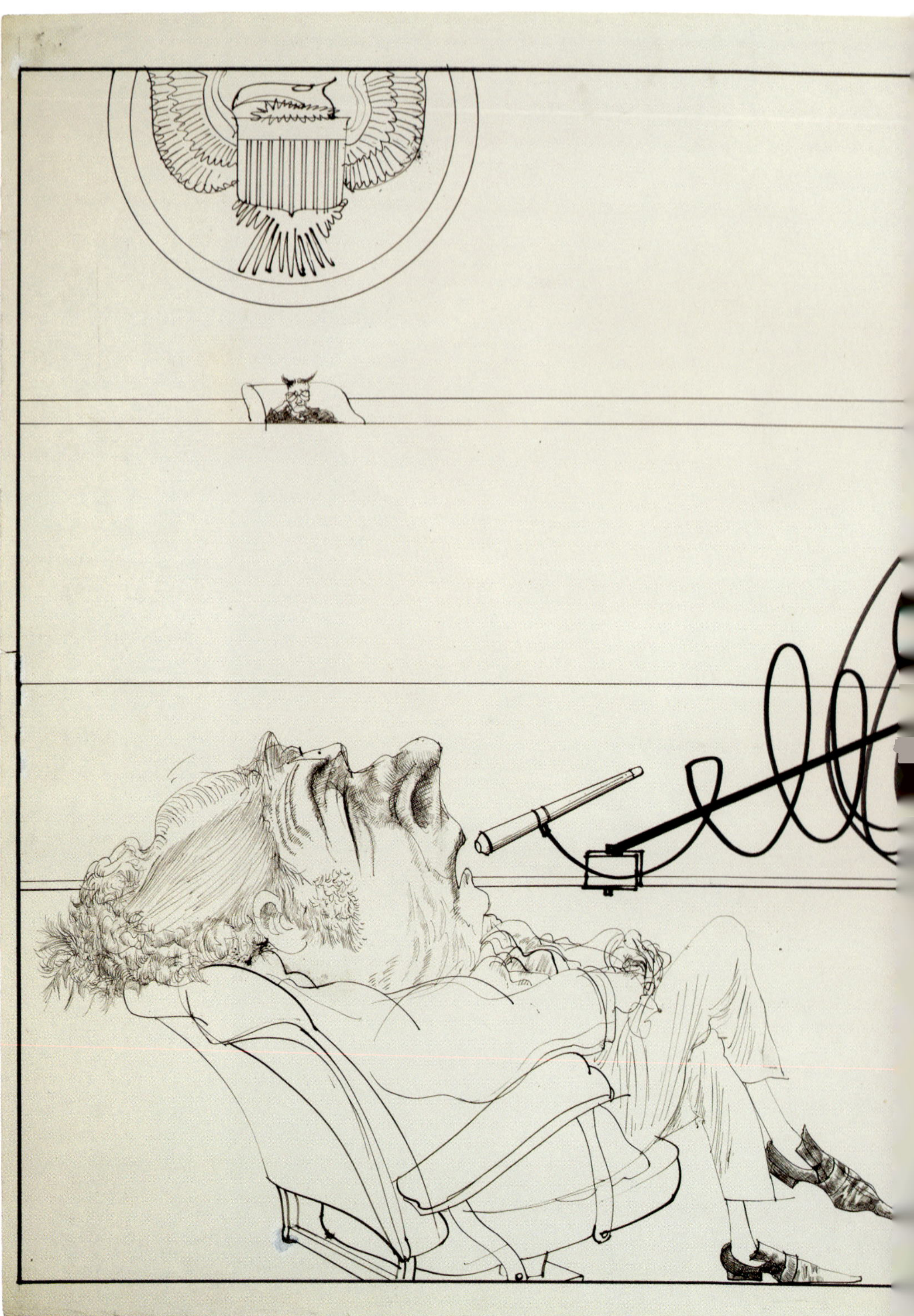

Interviewing Media, 1976

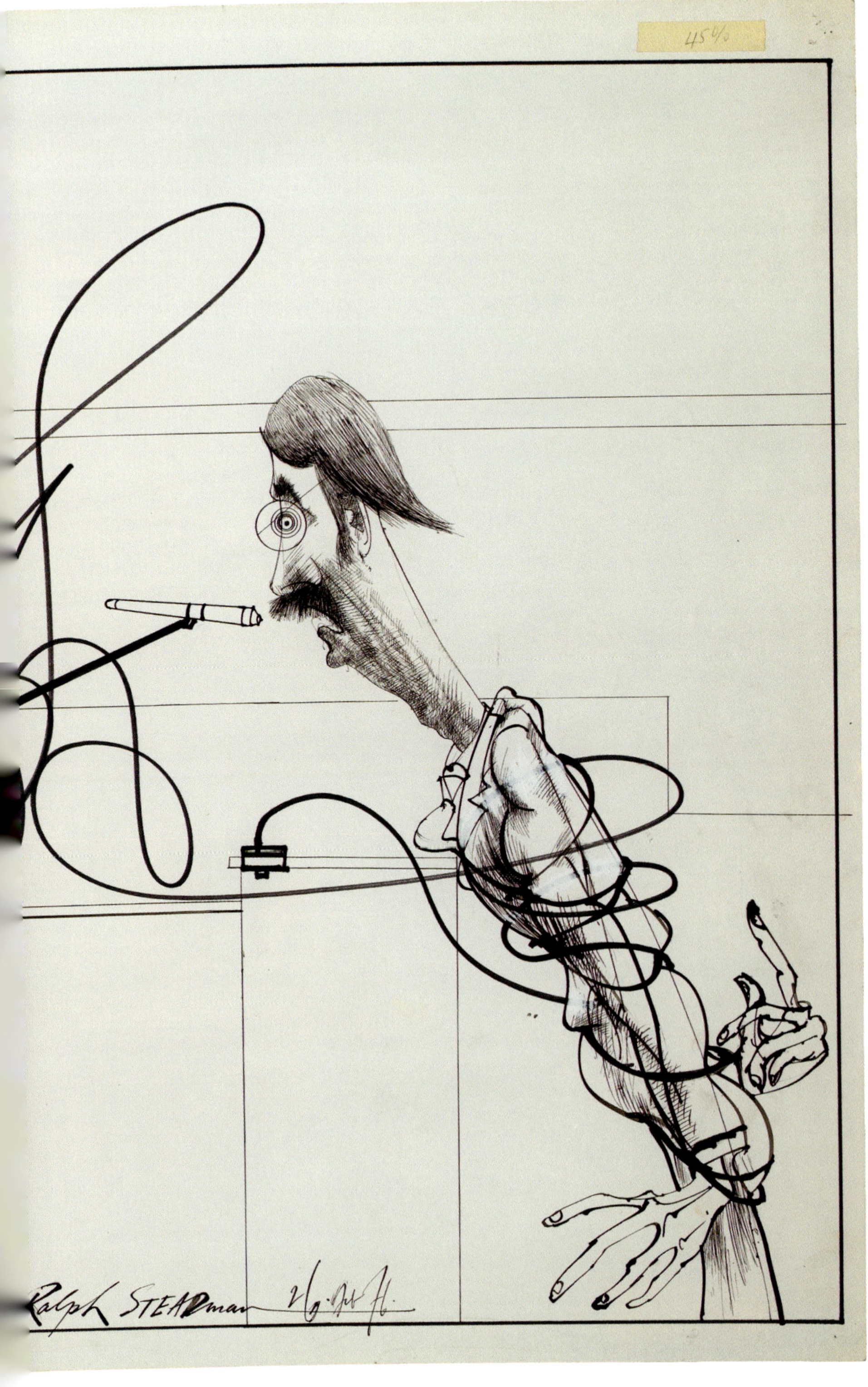

Ralph STEADman

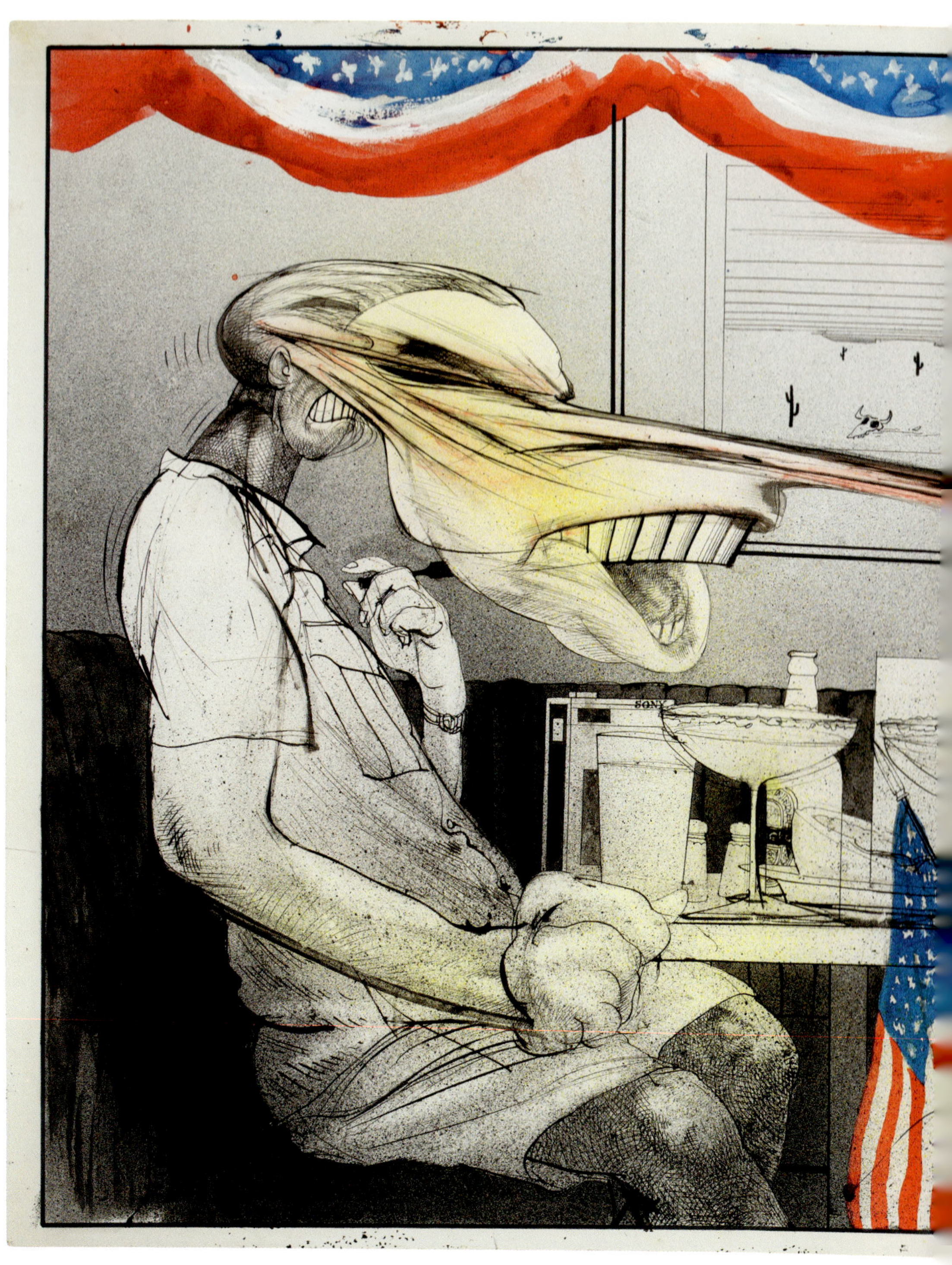

"We went on set of **Where the Buffalo Roam** and were invited into Bill Murray's trailer. My daughter Sadie was with us; she was about five! Bill asked her to sit on his lap. Then he asked if she liked toys. She nodded. He asked if she'd like a trapdoor. She nodded, a bit unsure. Bill opened up his legs, and she fell straight through. It was cruel but funny!"

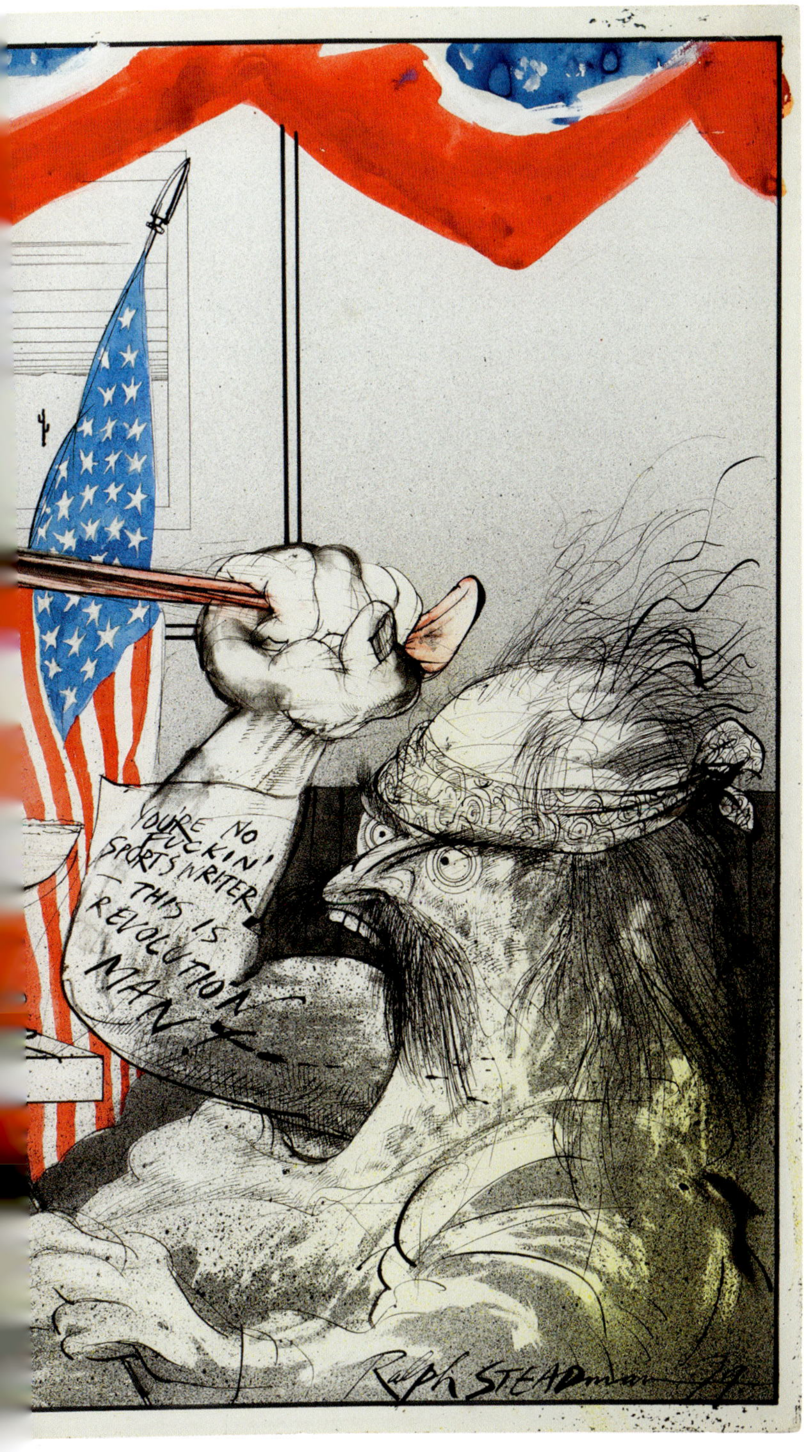

Where the Buffalo Roam, Hunter and Peter Boyle, 1979

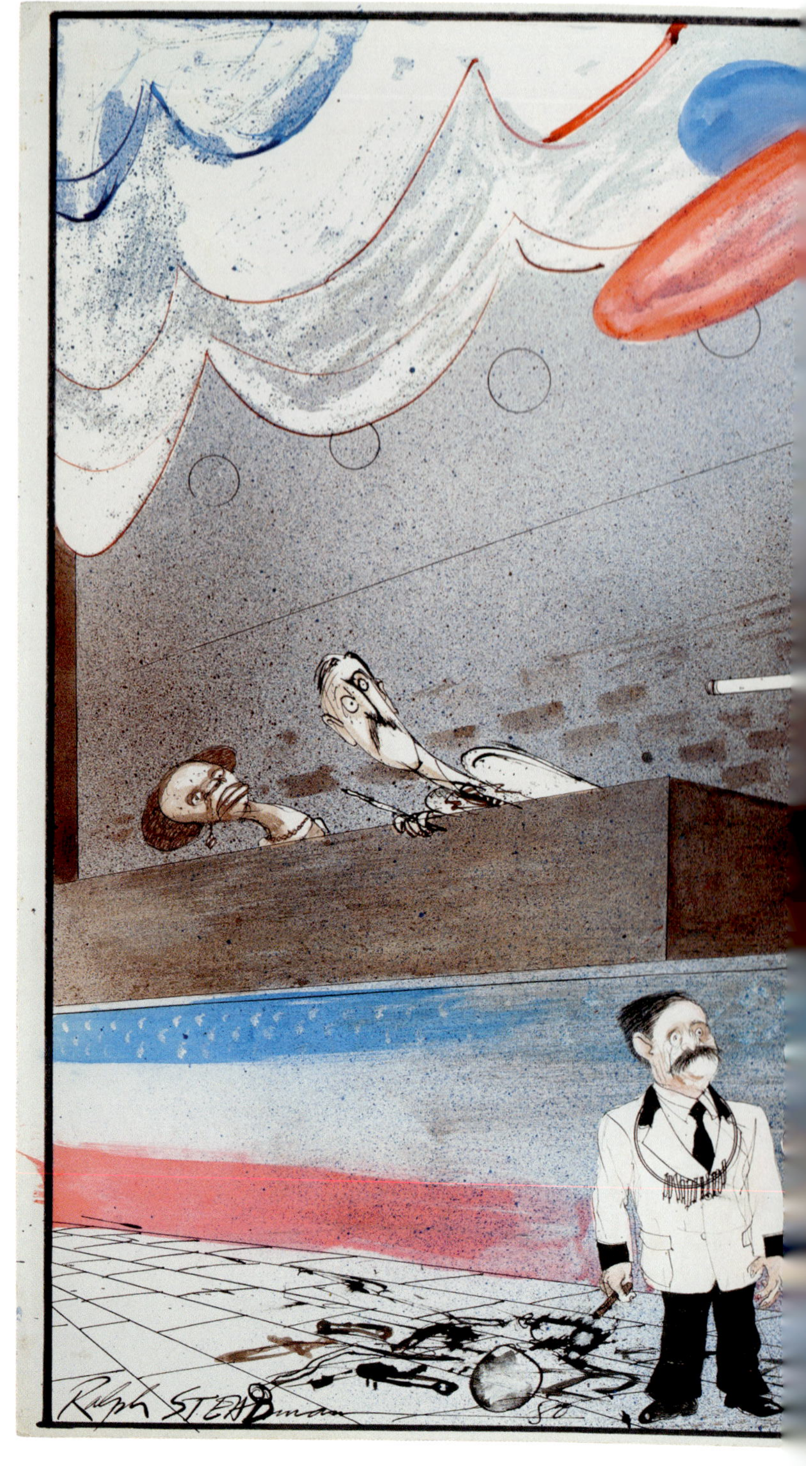

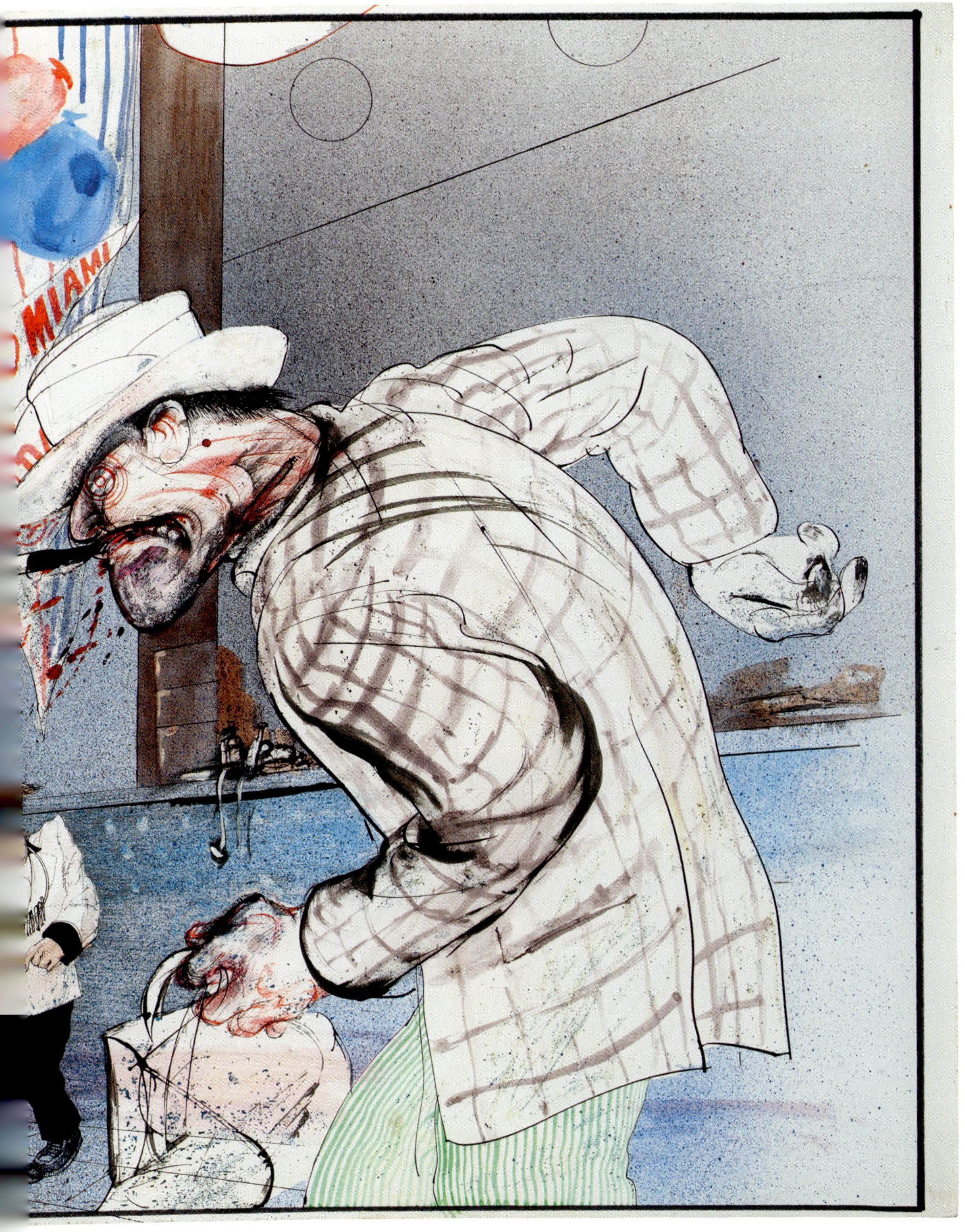

Where the Buffalo Roam, Hunter at the Hotel, 1979

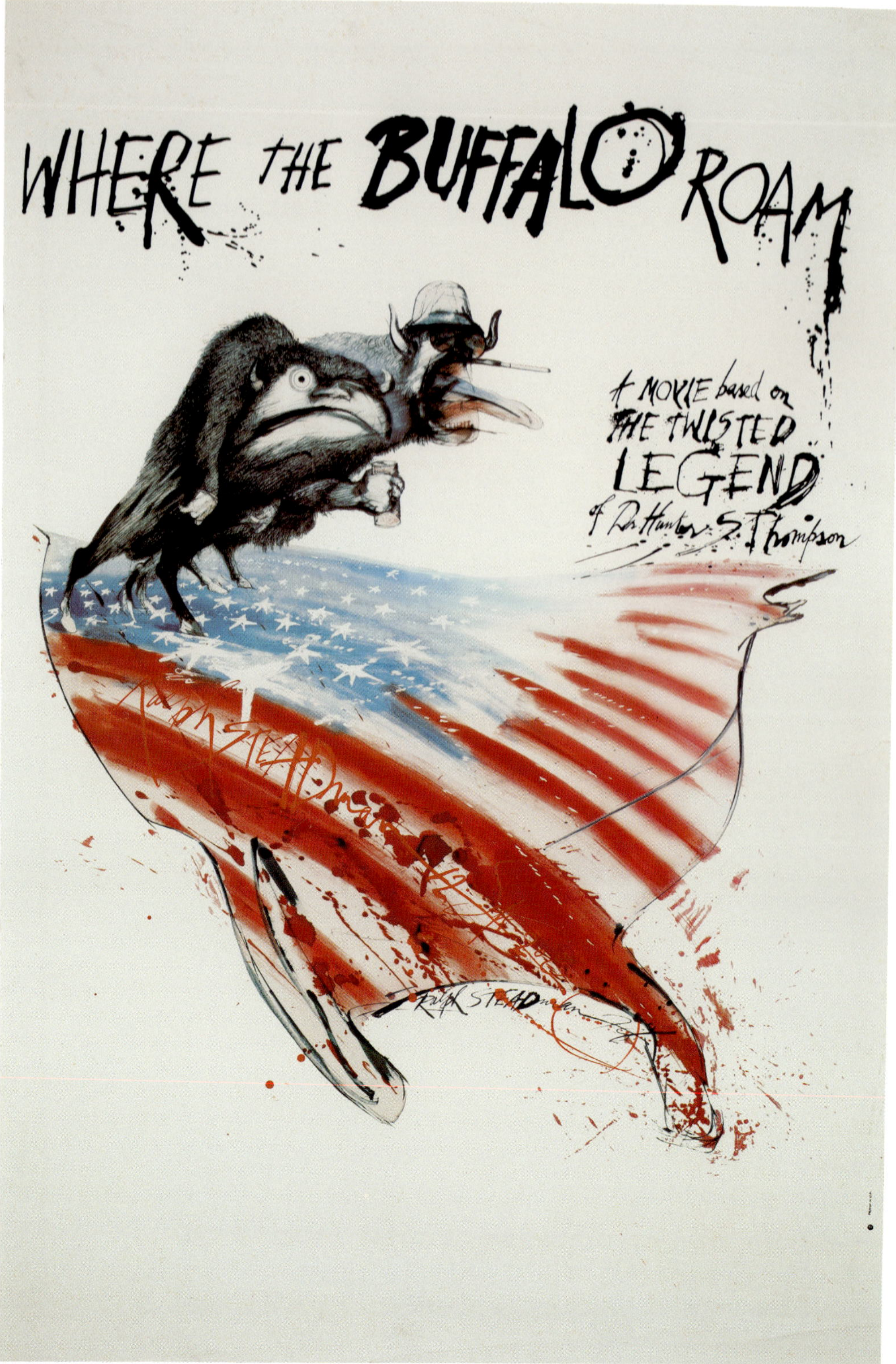

Where the Buffalo Roam *Poster, 1979*

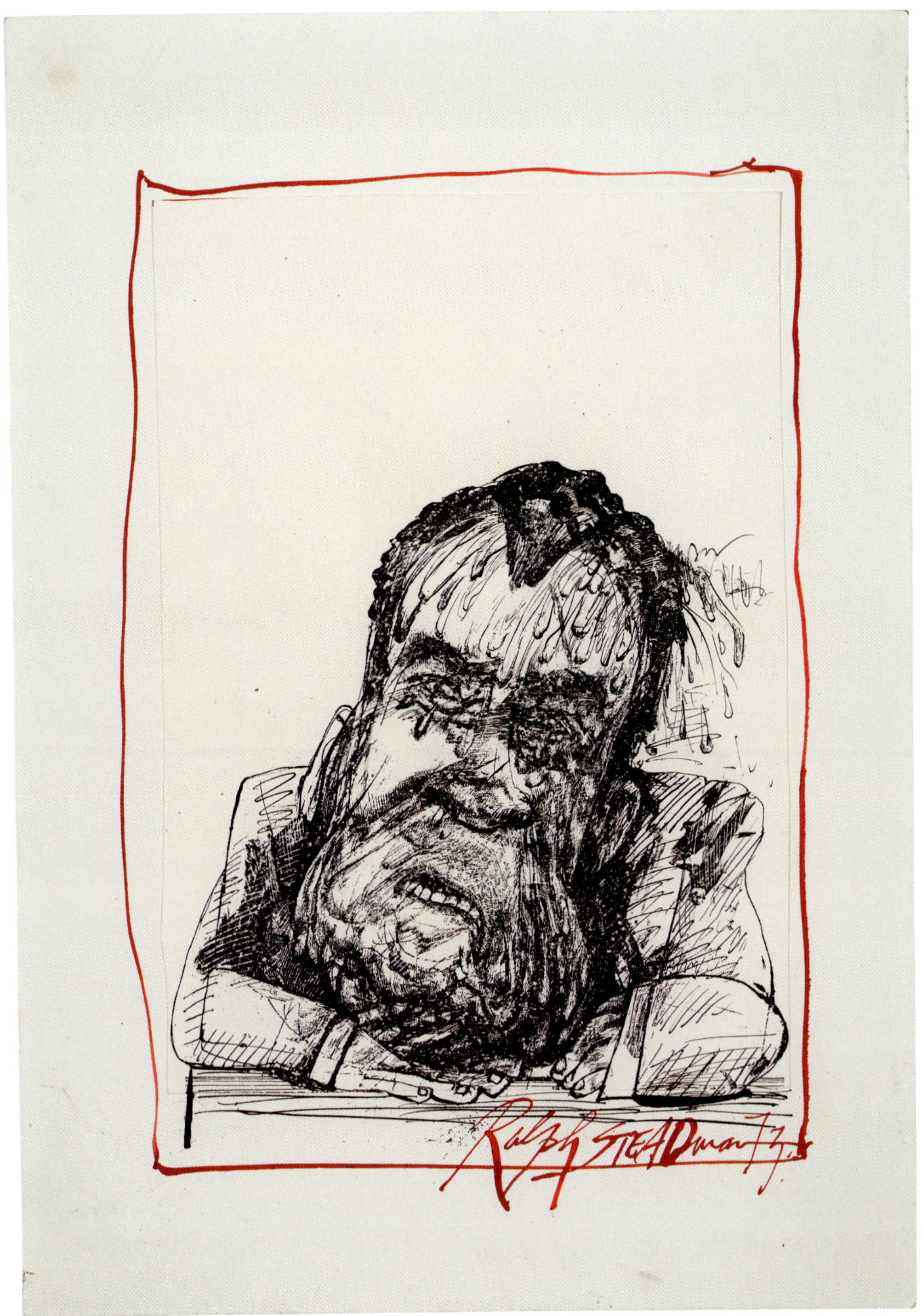

Melting Portrait of Nixon, 1973

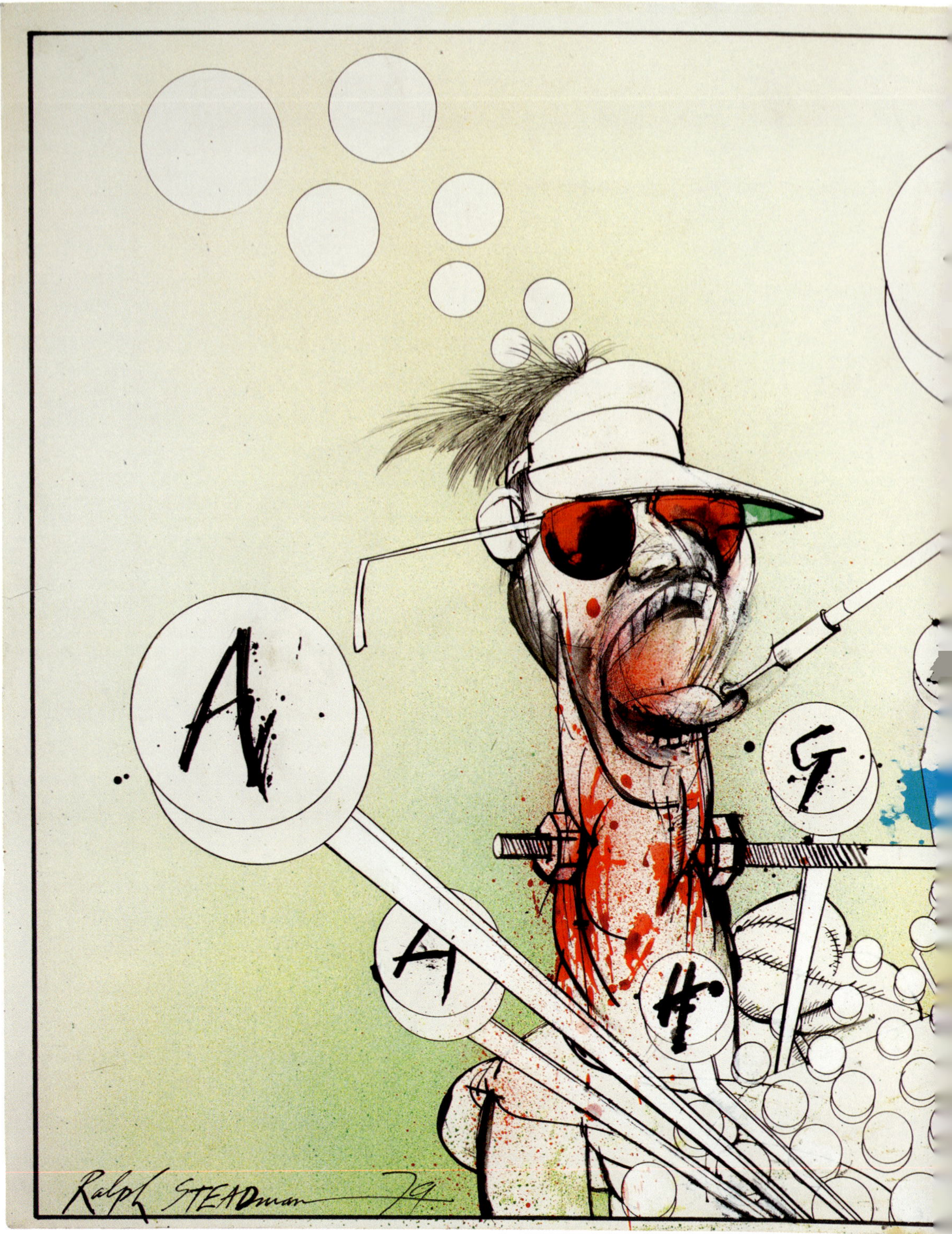

"Hunter always used a typewriter. I wonder if he would ever have swapped to a computer."

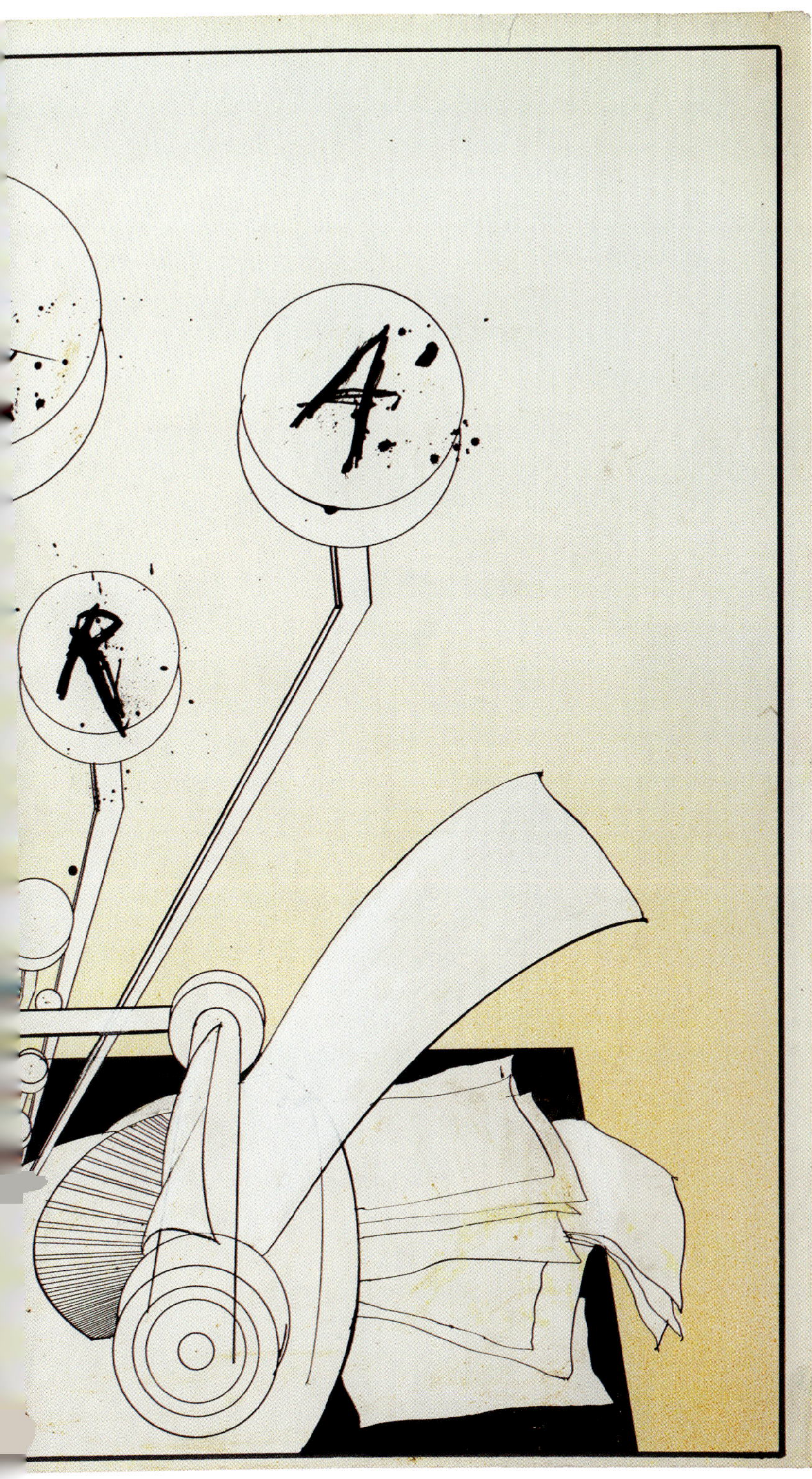

Aaarrgh! Hunter at Work! 1979

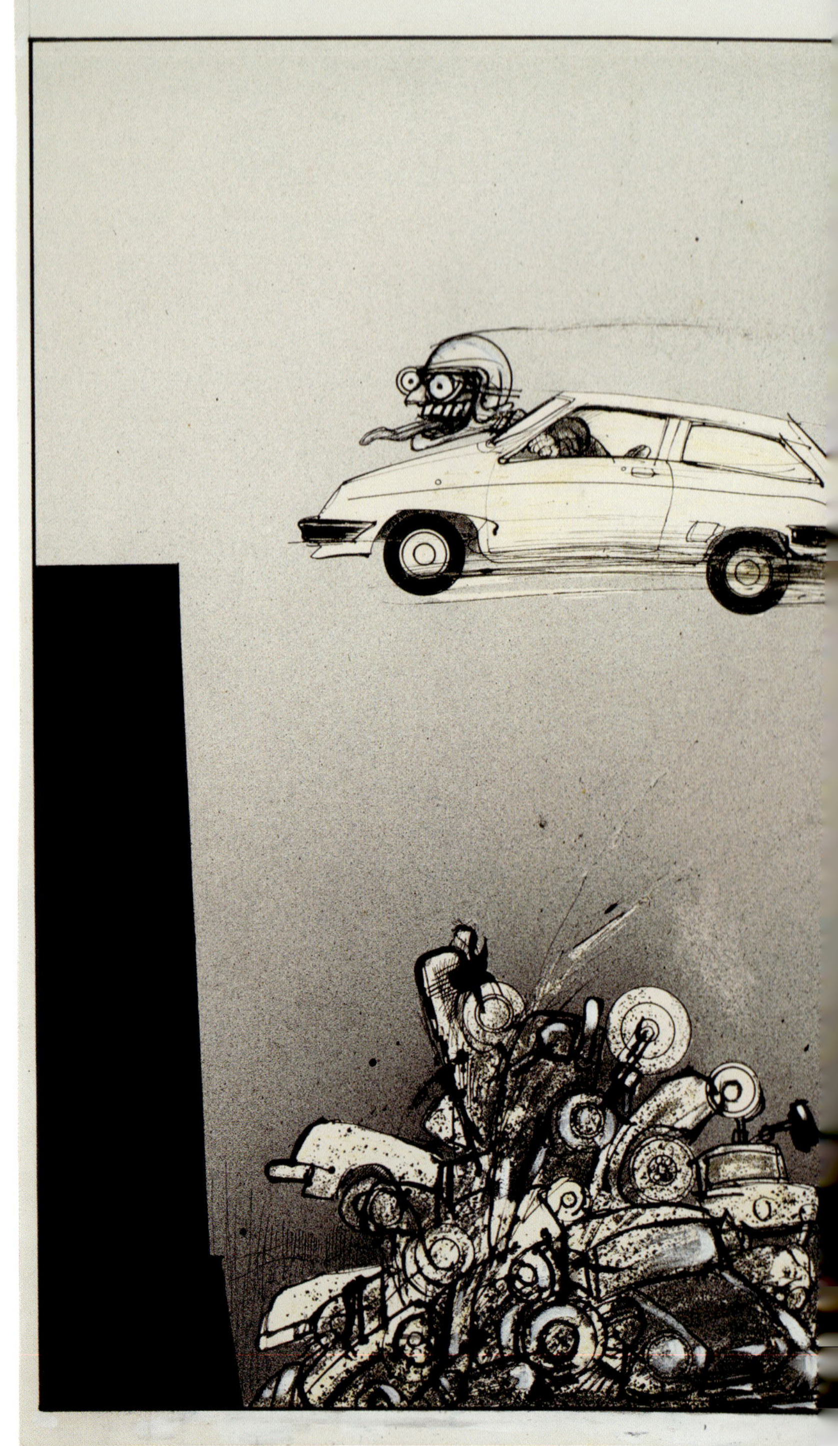

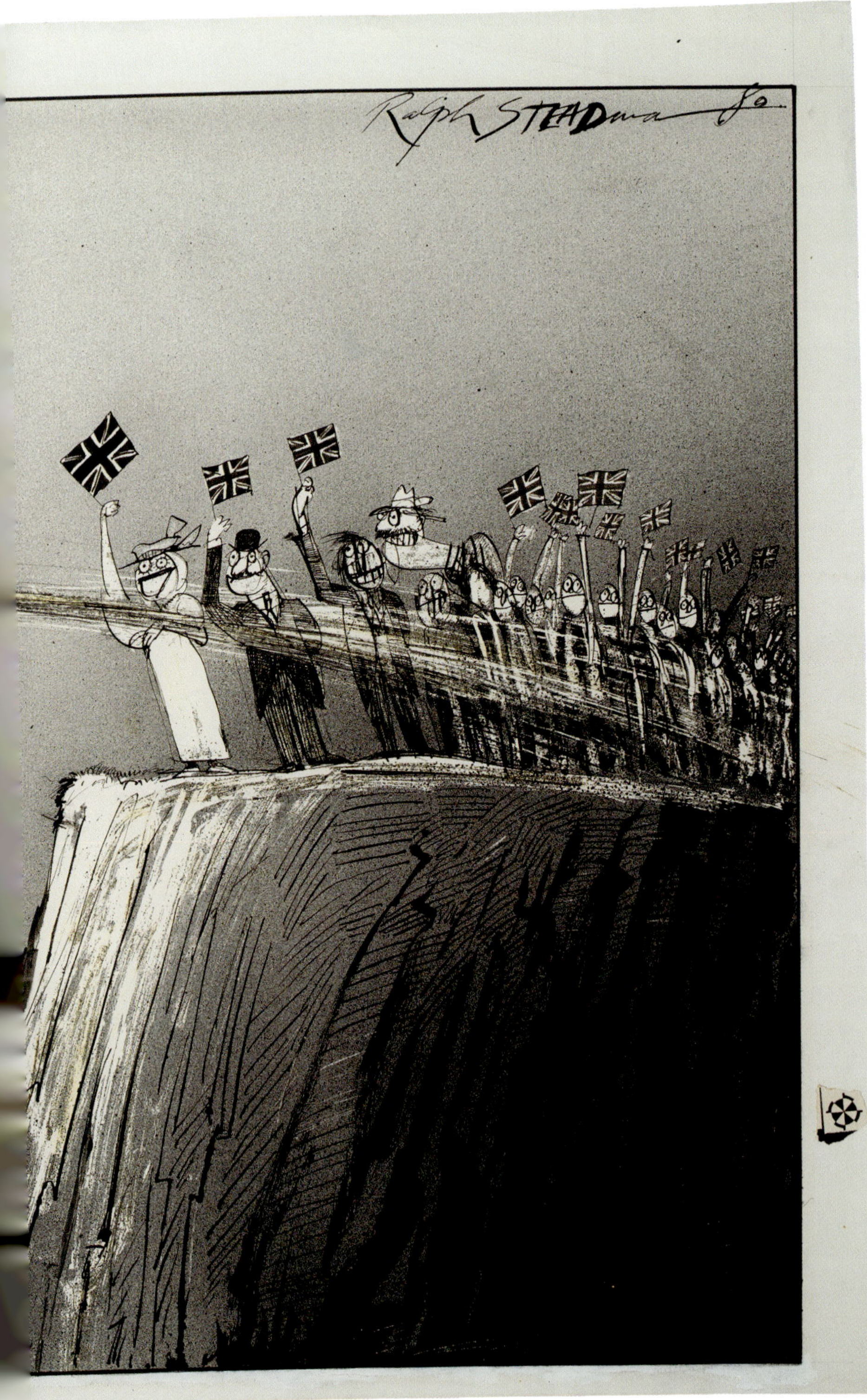

Britain's Relationship with Europe, 1980

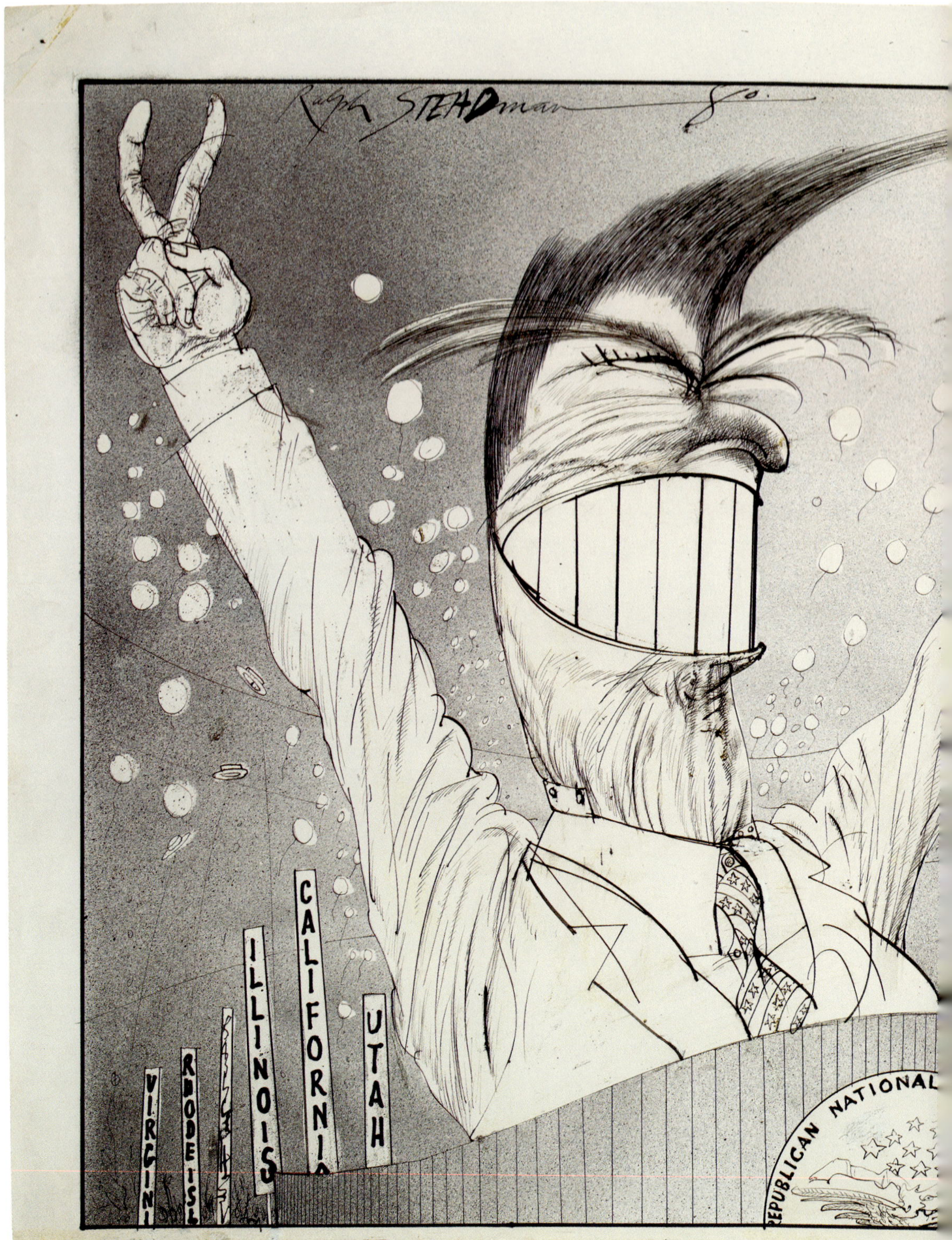

Ronald Reagan and "Running Mate," 1980

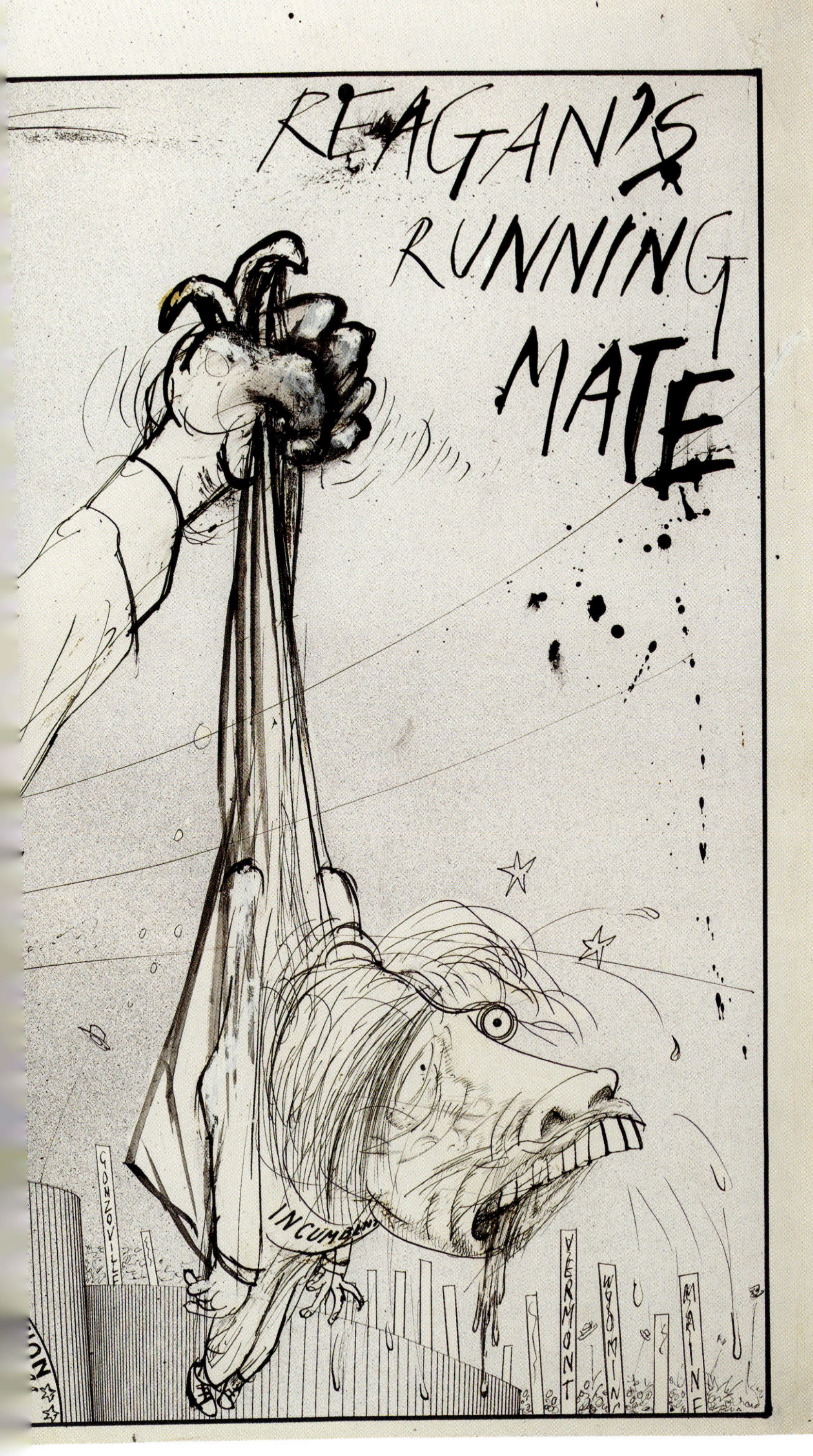

REAGAN'S
RUNNING
MATE
GONZOVILLE
IN CUMBENT
VERMONT
WYOMING
MAINE

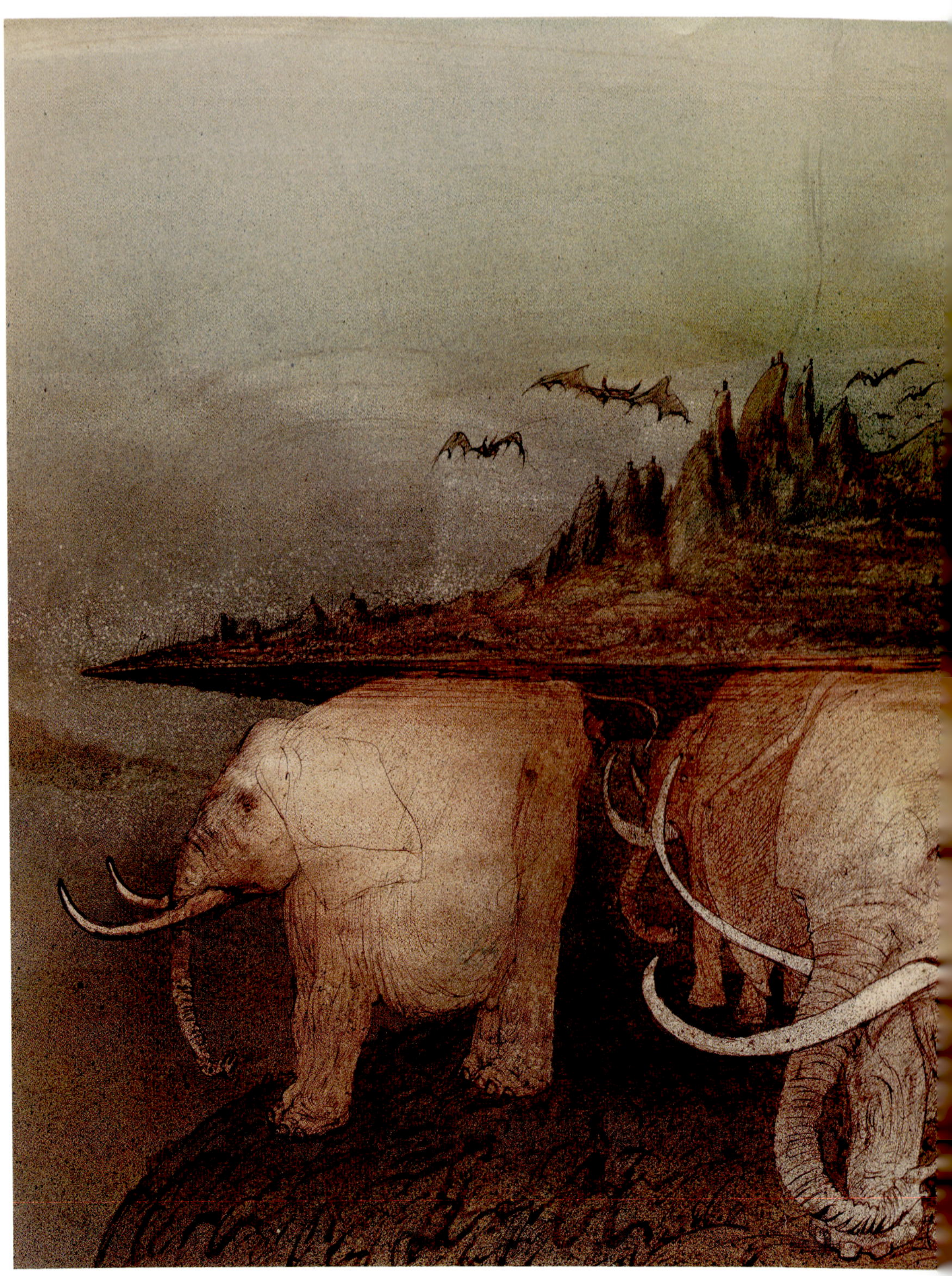

*Opening Picture from **I Leonardo**, 1981*

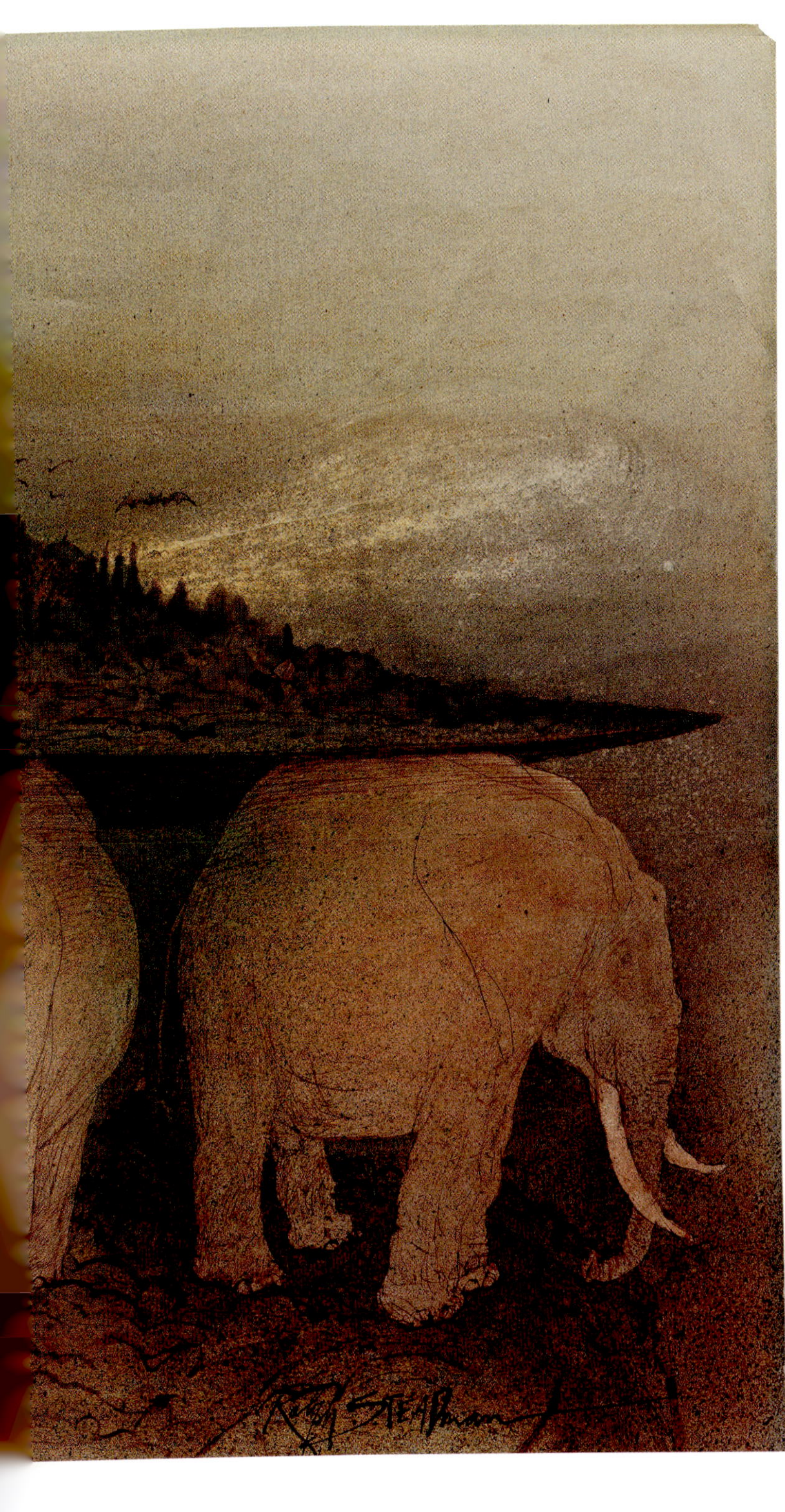

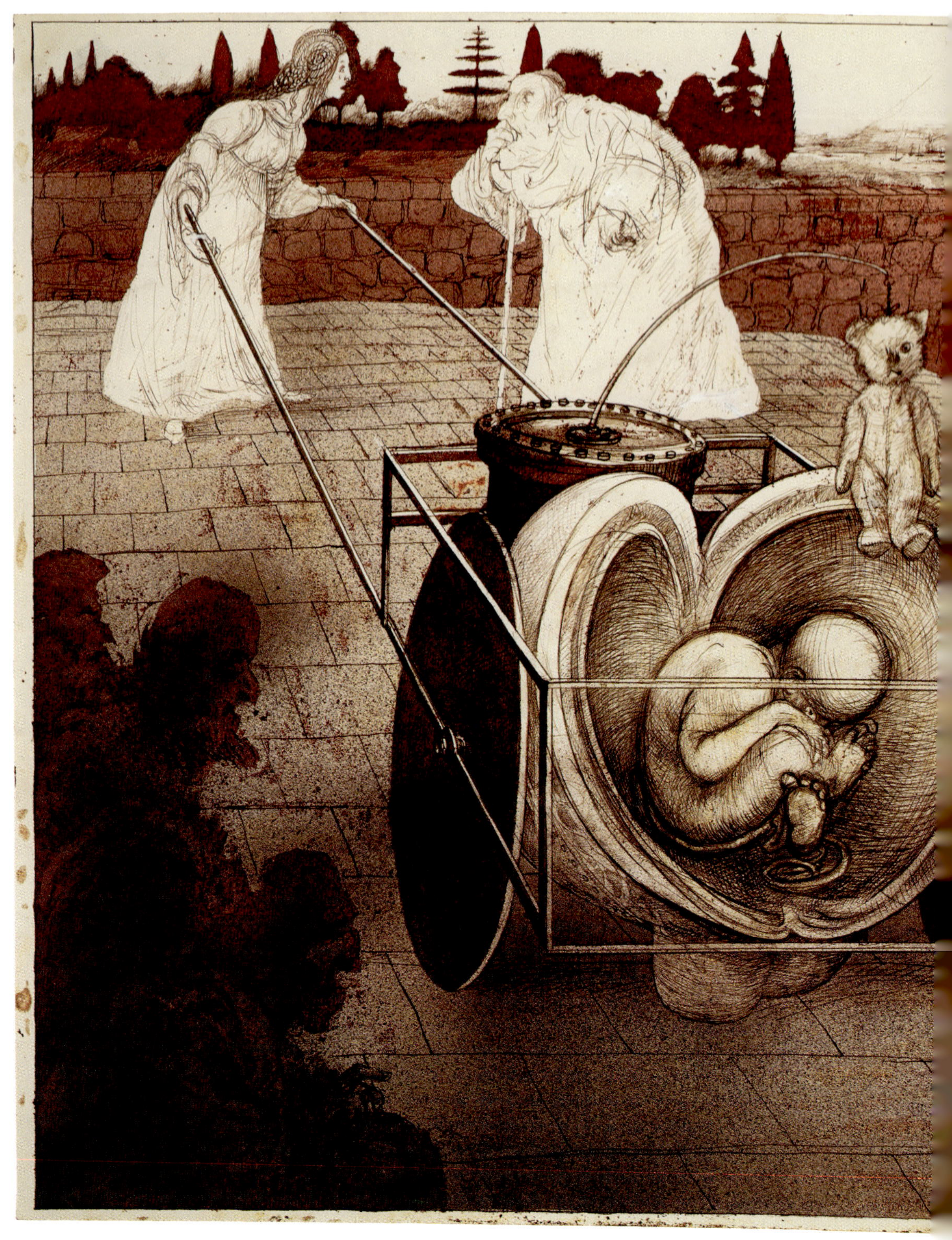

Leonardo, a personal hero, in his mother's womb. The teddy bear is actually a portrait of Ralph's wife, Anna's, childhood teddy bear, Christopher, who would also eventually appear as the main character in Ralph's children's book **Teddy Where Are You?**

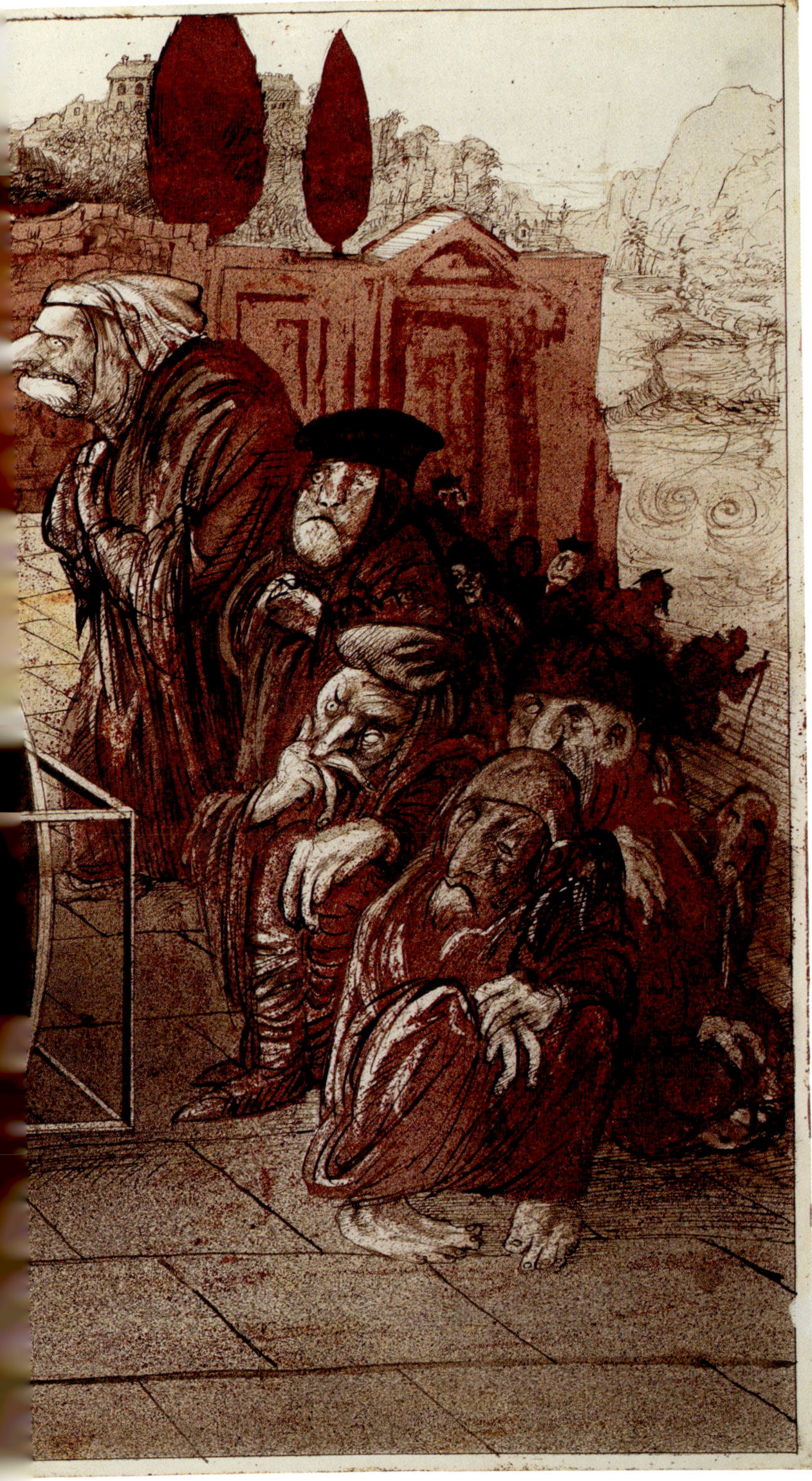

*From **I Leonardo**, 1981*

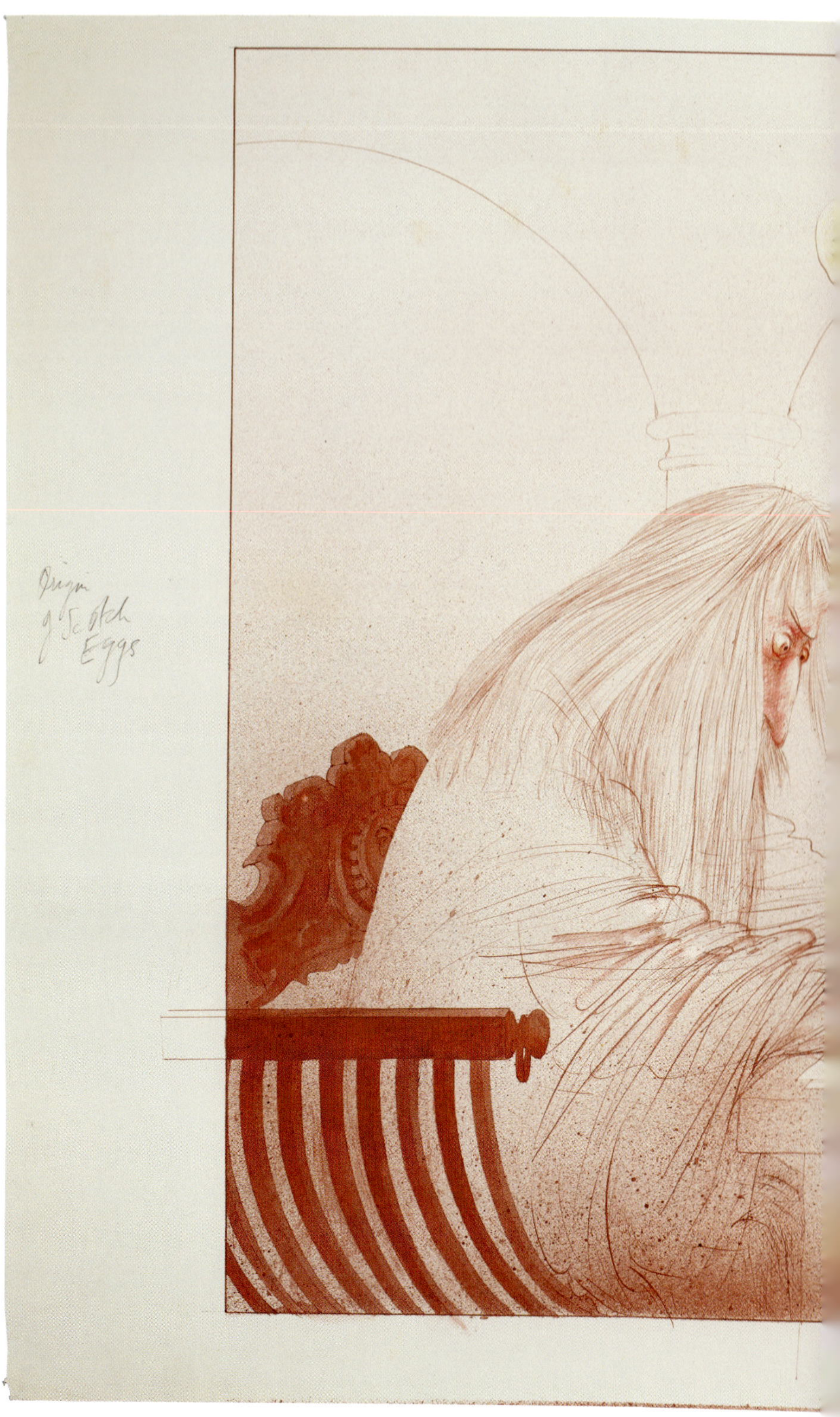

I Leonardo, *Leonardo Cutting and Examining the Anatomy of the Eye, 1981*

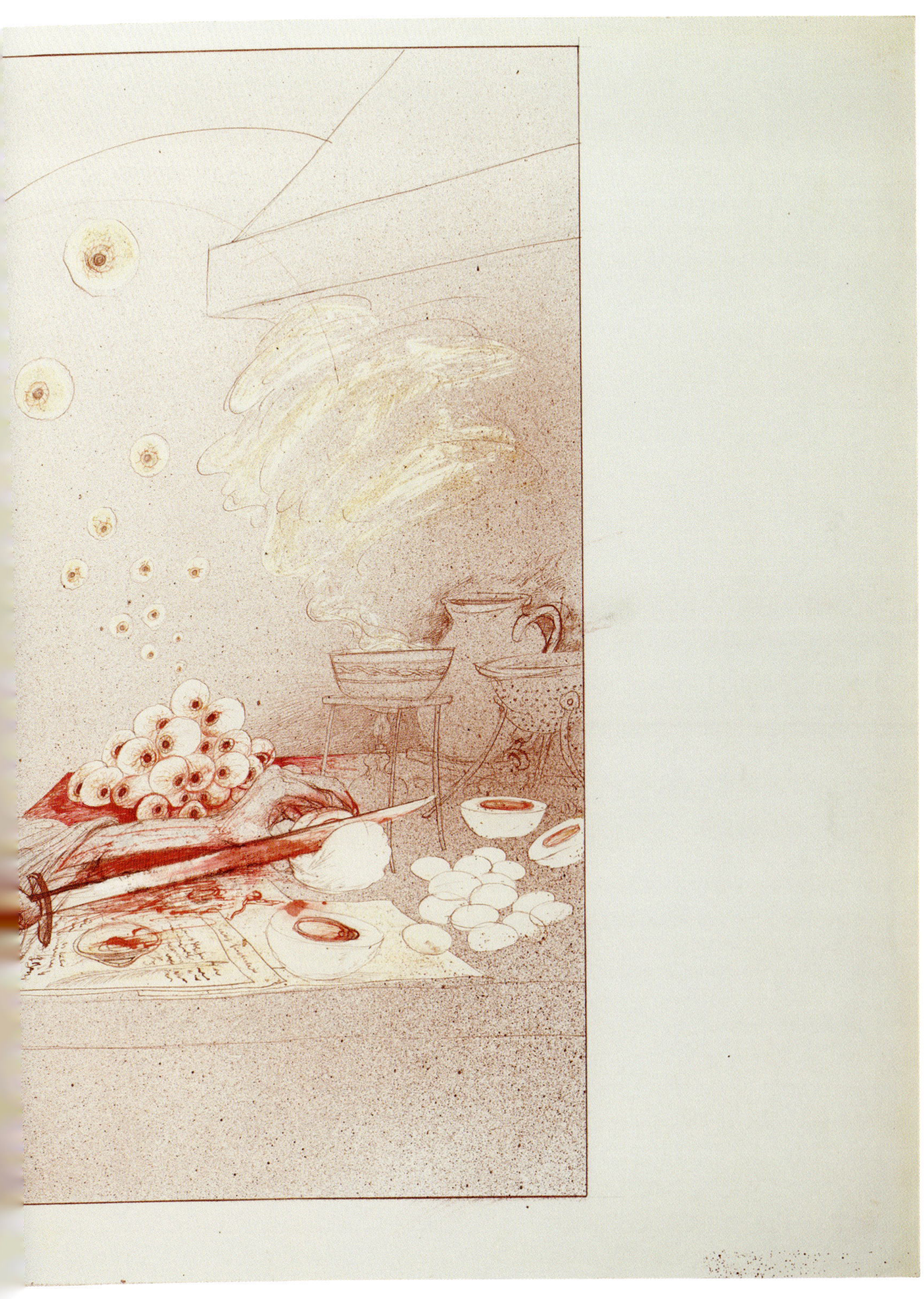

"He was the consummate observer of the natural world. He wanted to understand it. Freud called Leonardo da Vinci 'the man who woke up in the dark'."

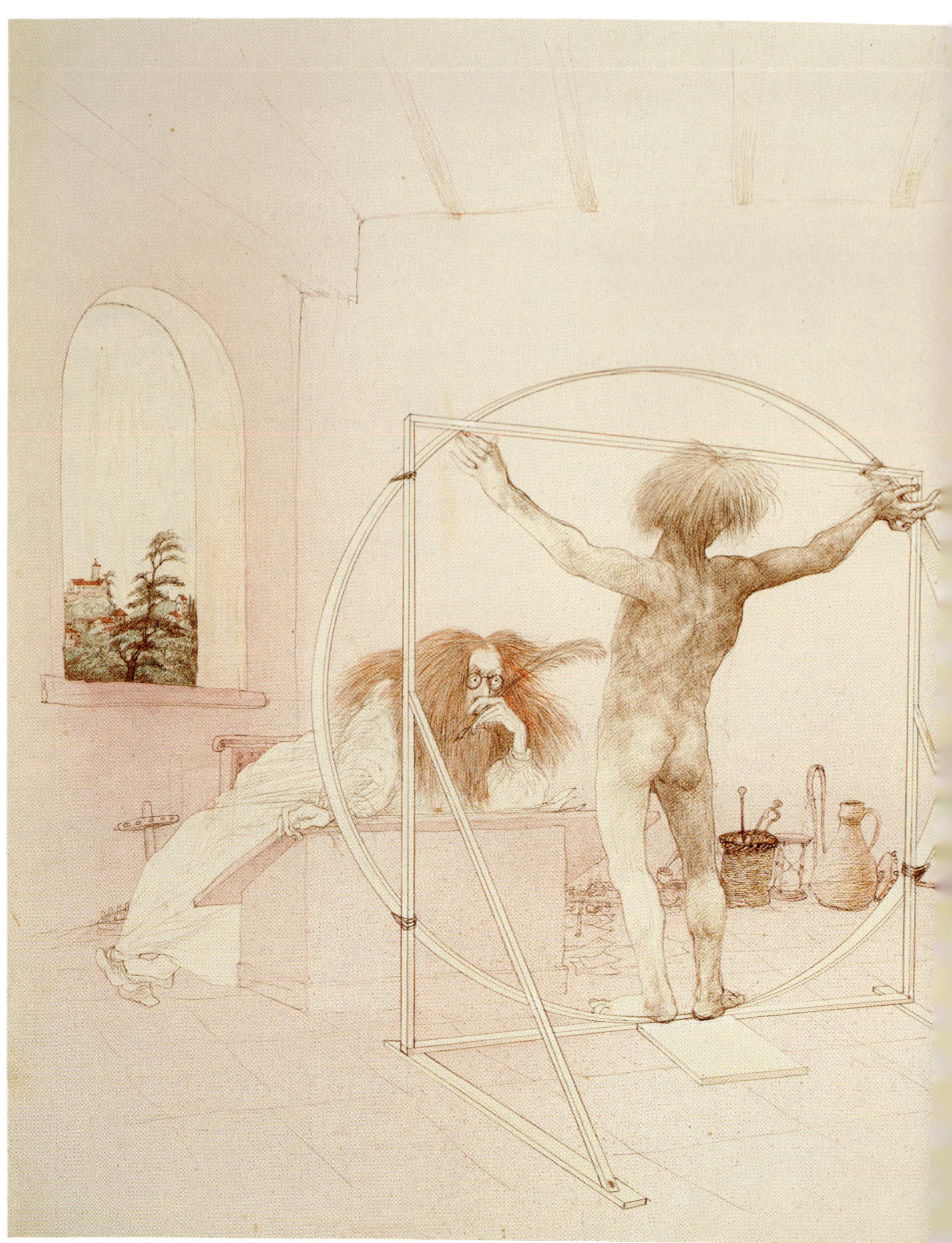

"The Kate Moss of his day!"

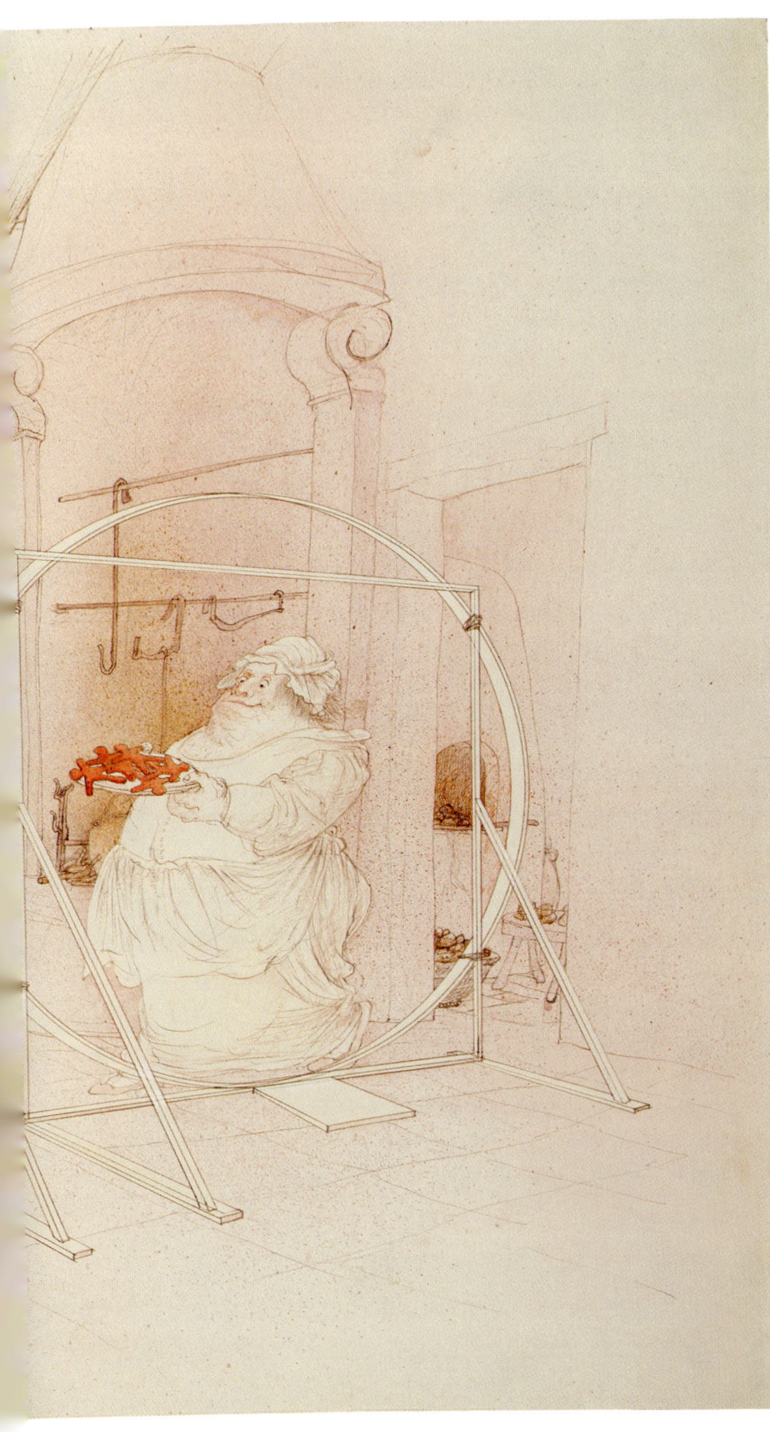

I Leonardo, *Leonardo and Vitruvian Man Model, 1981*

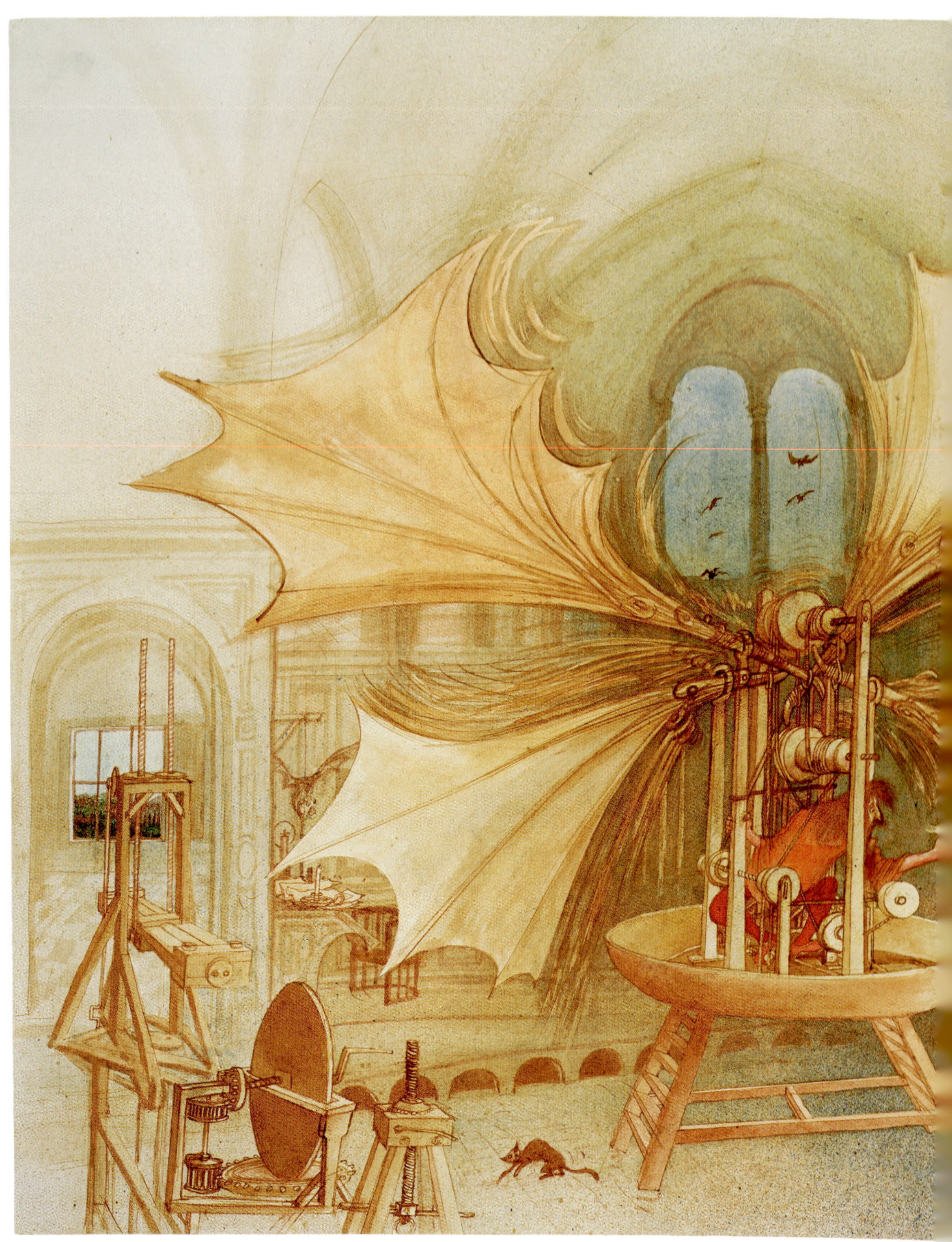

I Leonardo, Leonardo Building a Helicopter, 1981

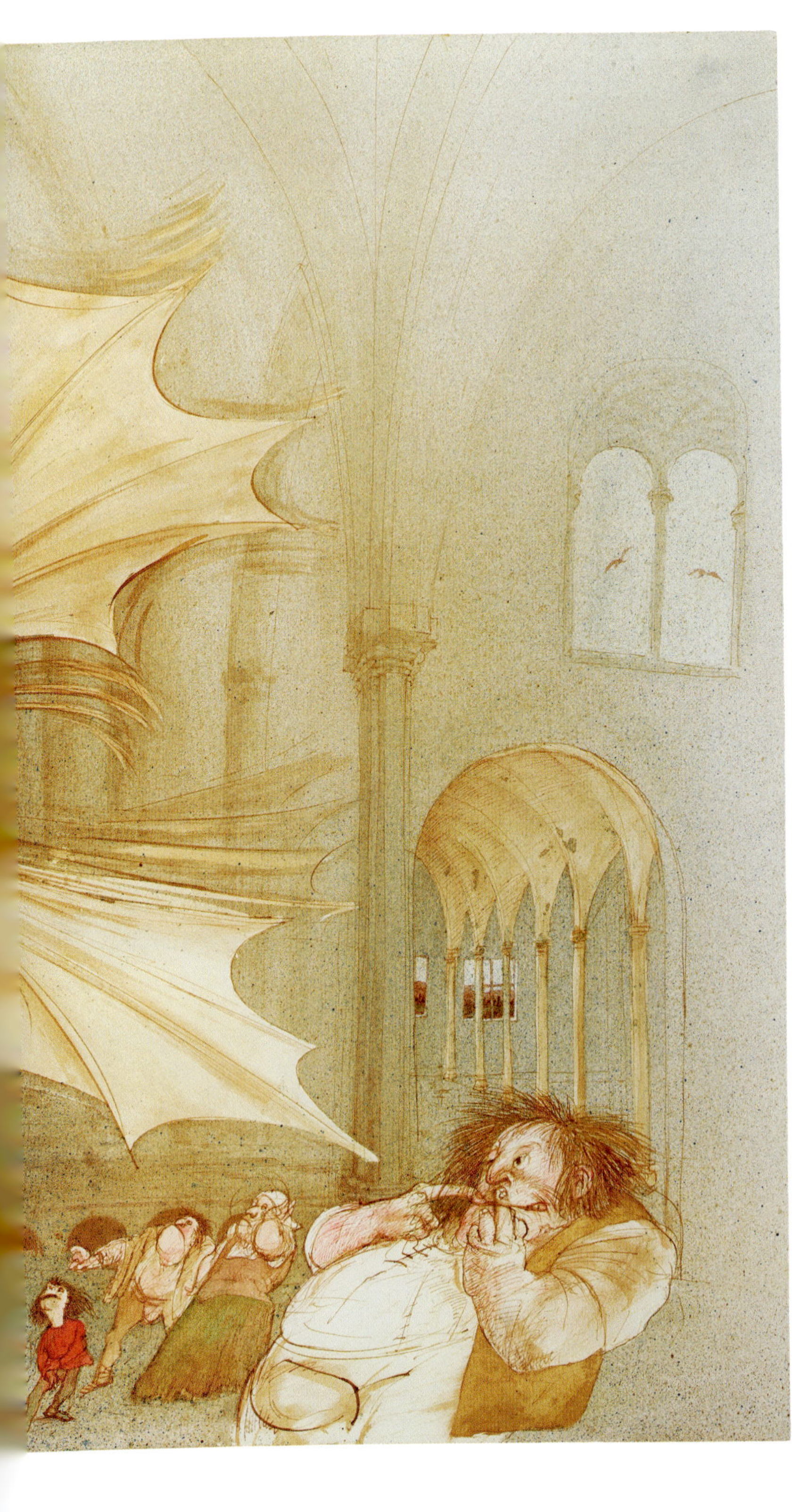

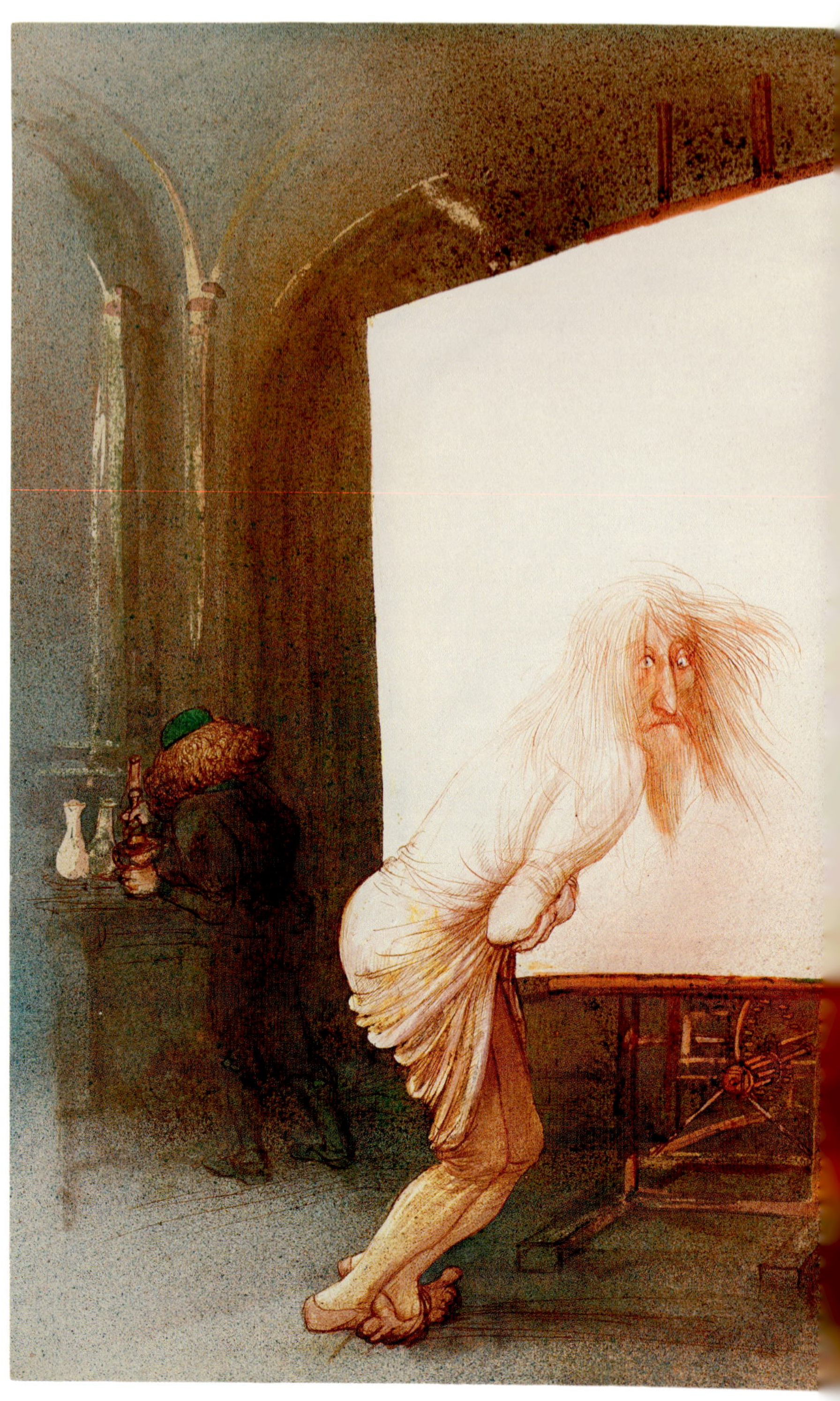

I Leonardo, *Leonardo's Fear of the Blank Canvas, 1981*

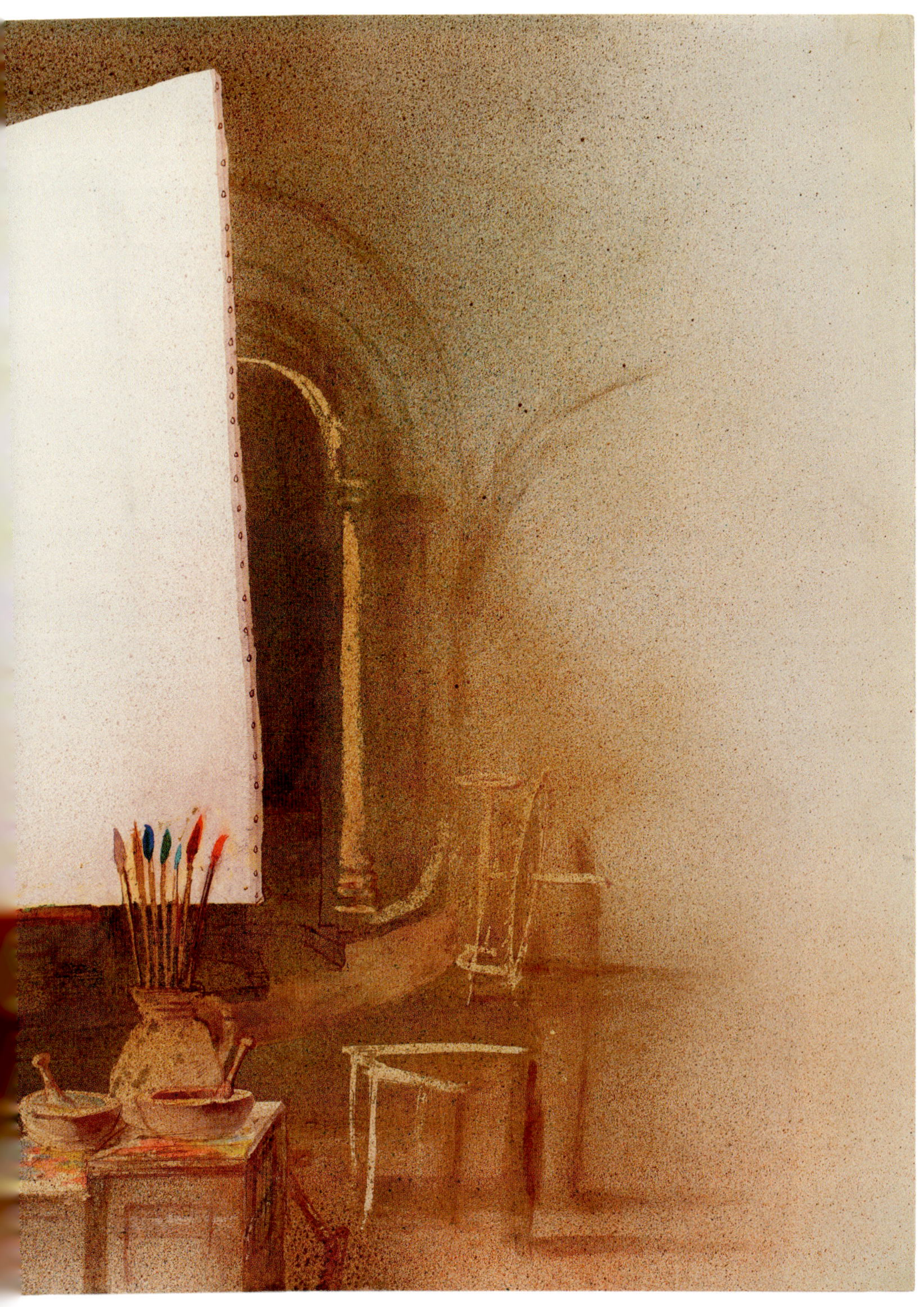

"The white page is the most intimidating thing—that's why you must always make a positive, definitive mark."

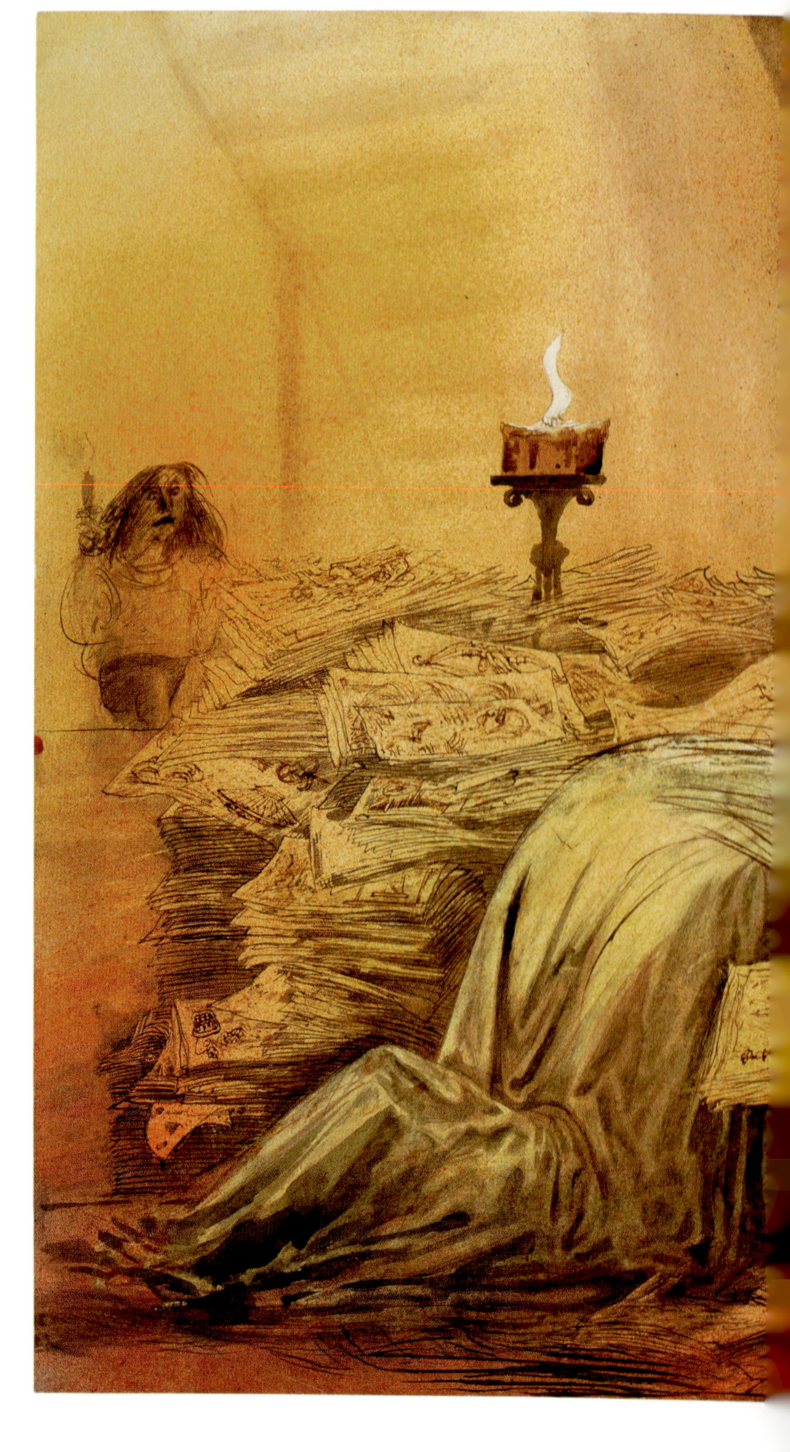

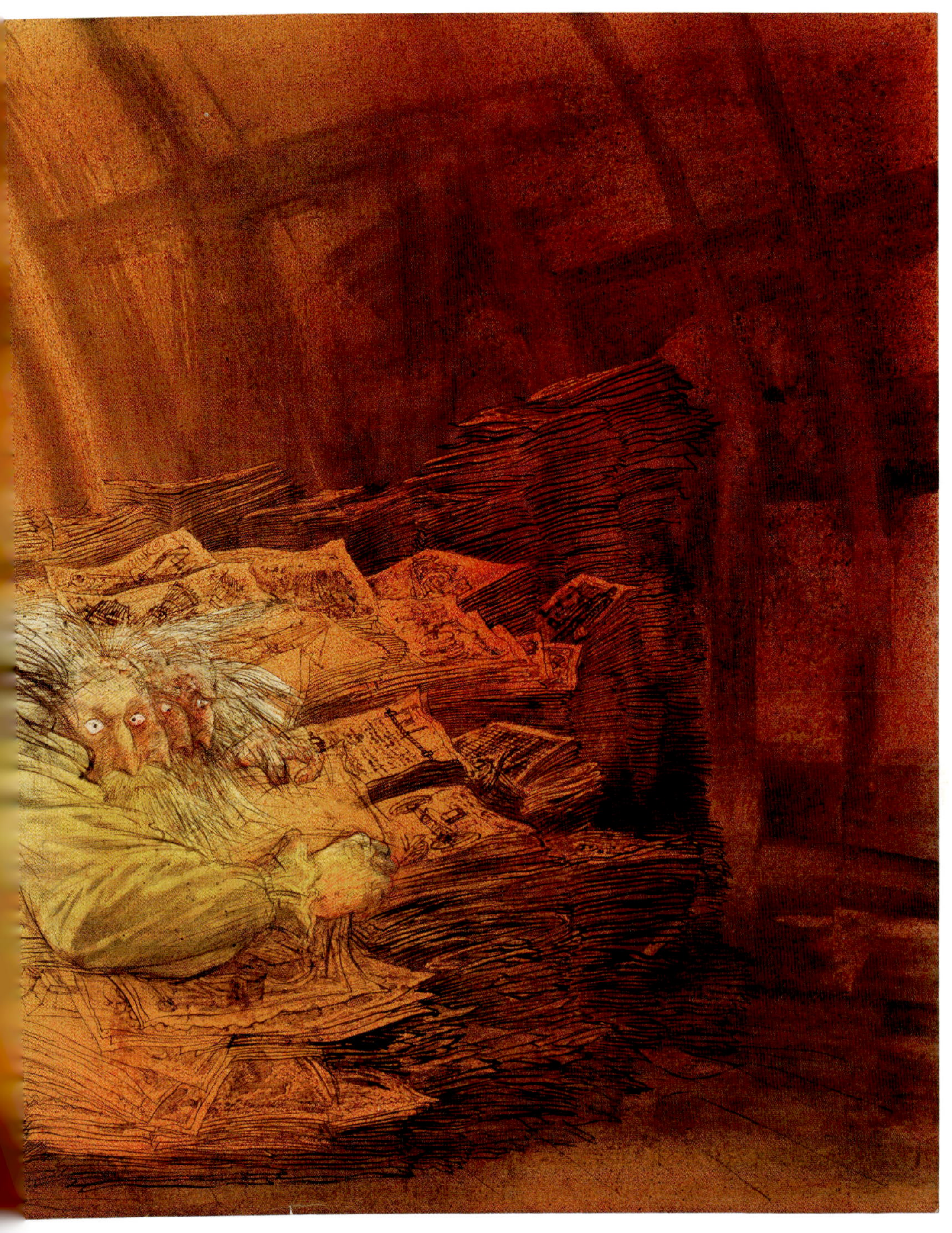

I Leonardo, *Leonardo With All His Papers, 1981*

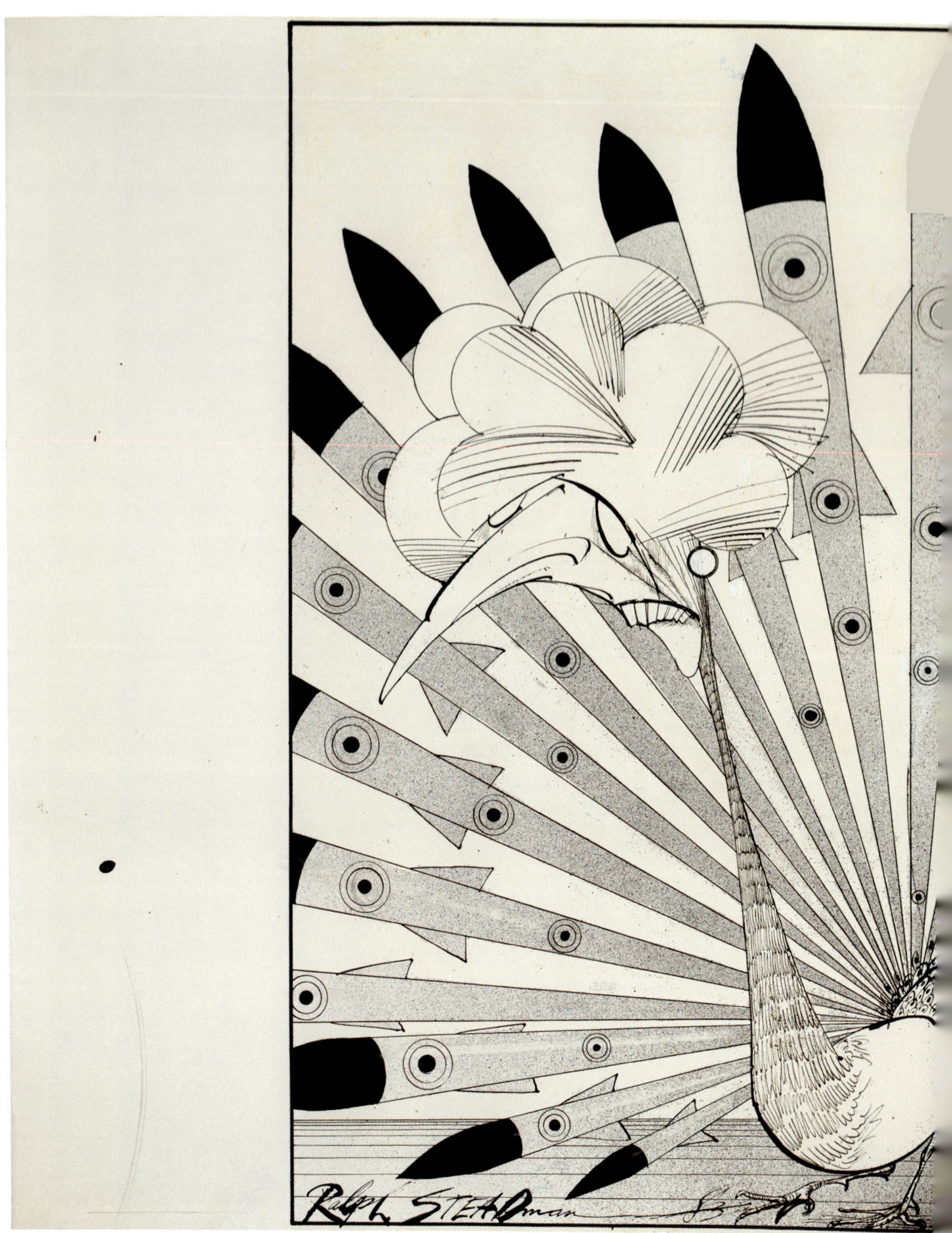

Tor-Peacock! 1983

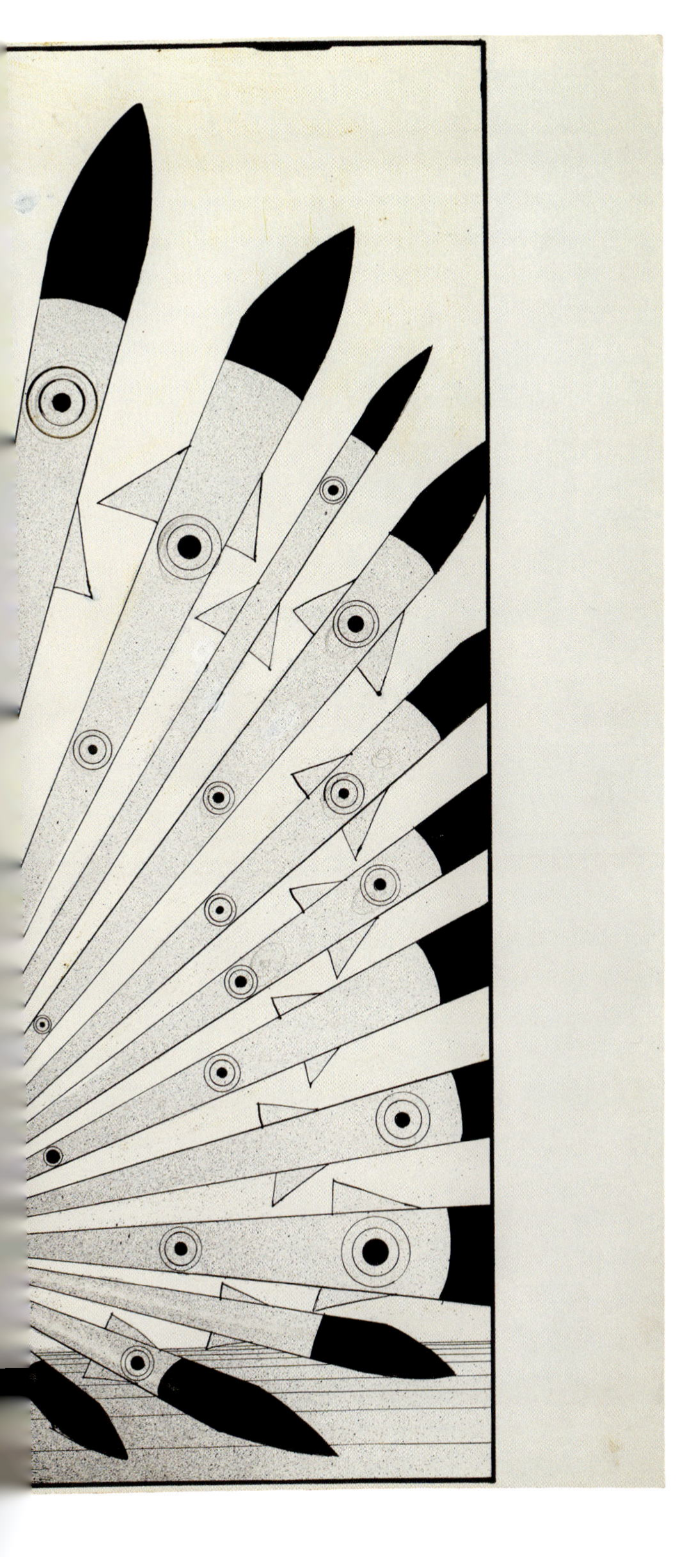

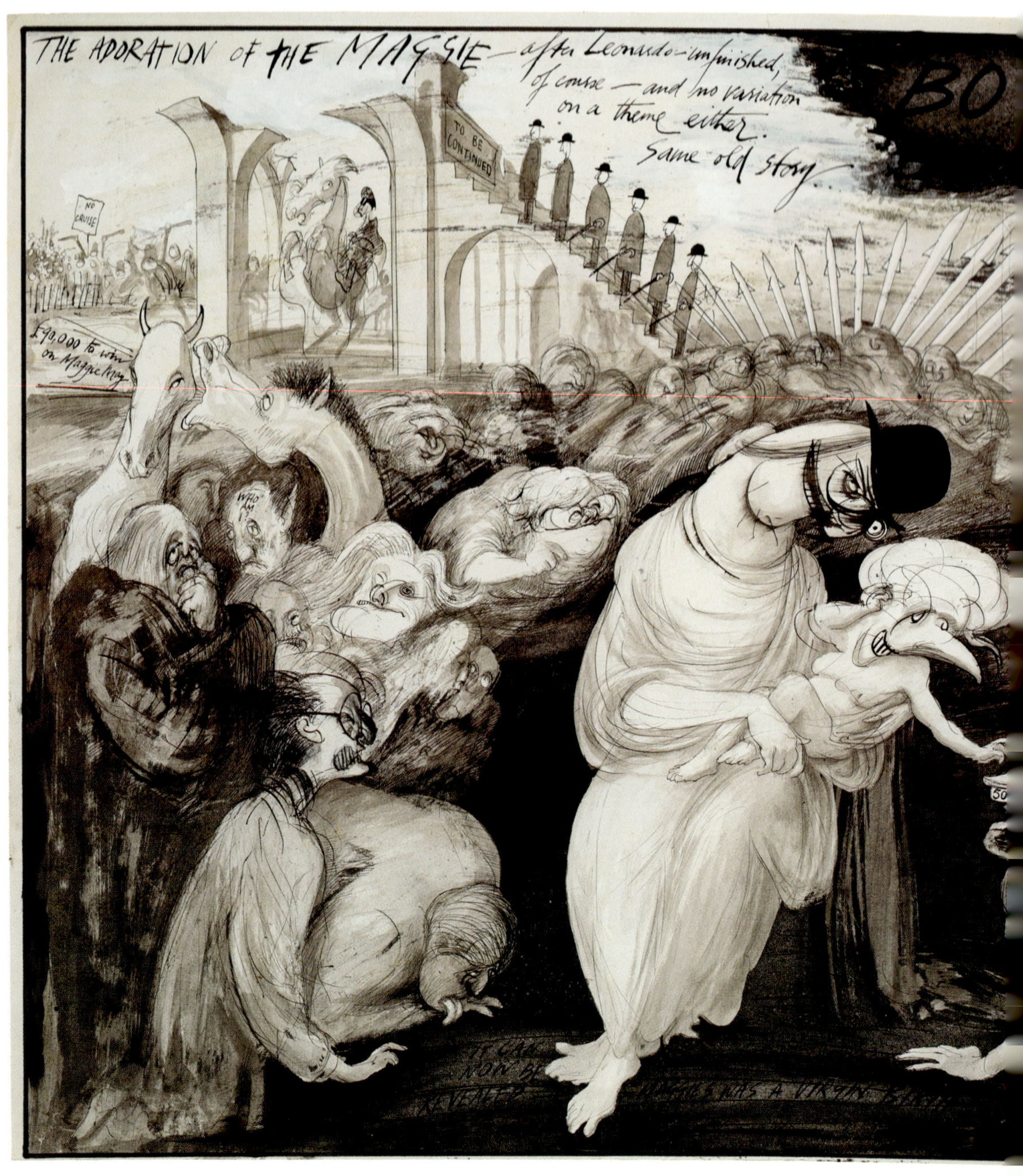

"In comparison to today's politicians, Maggie was a Saint."

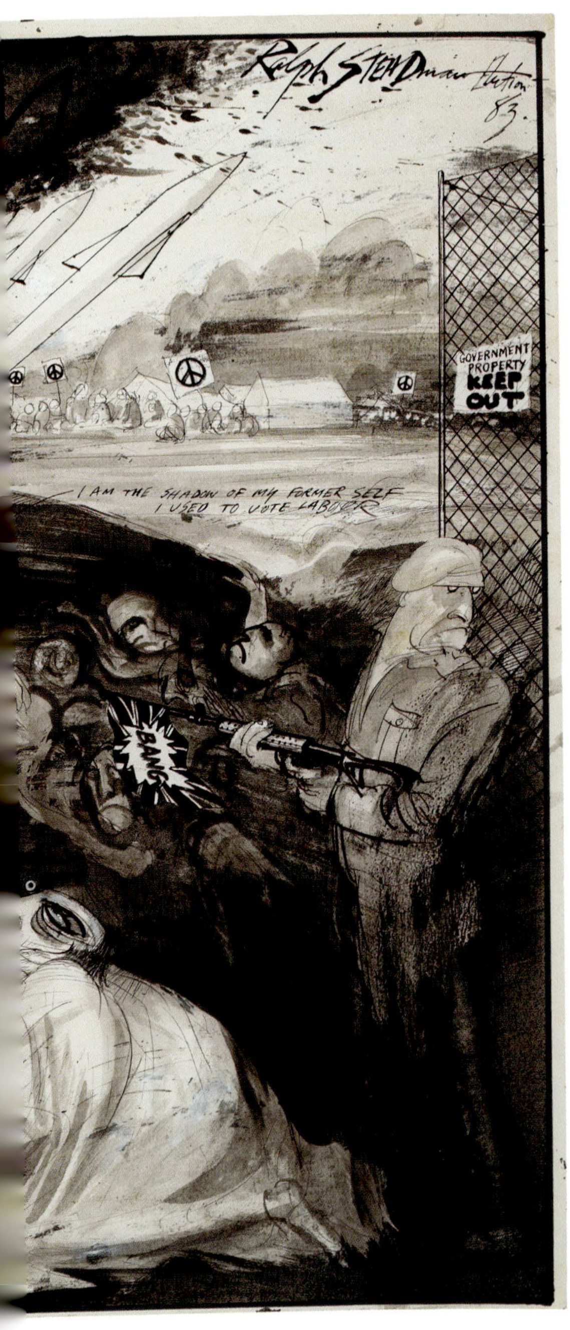

The Adoration of the Maggie, 1983

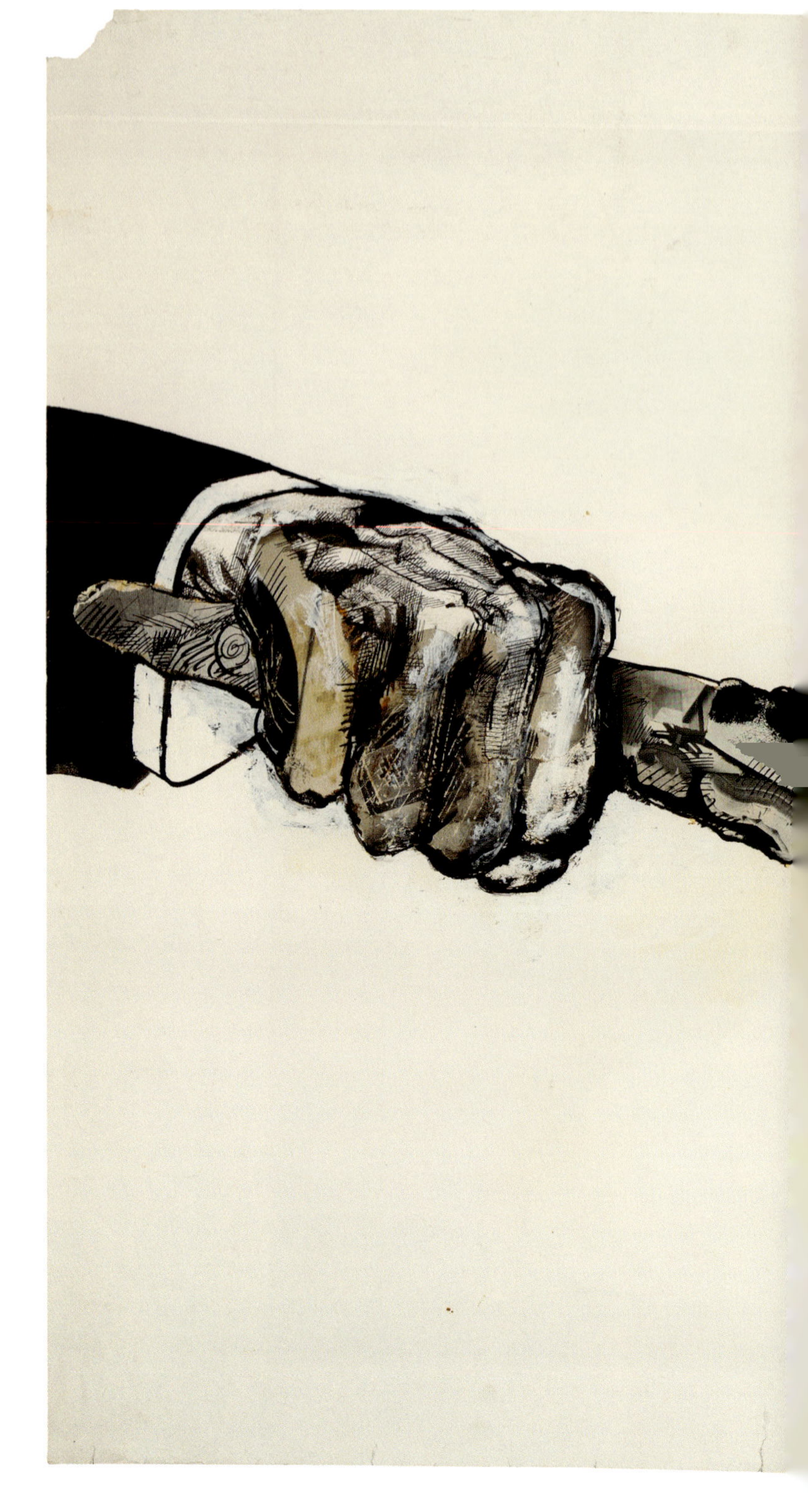

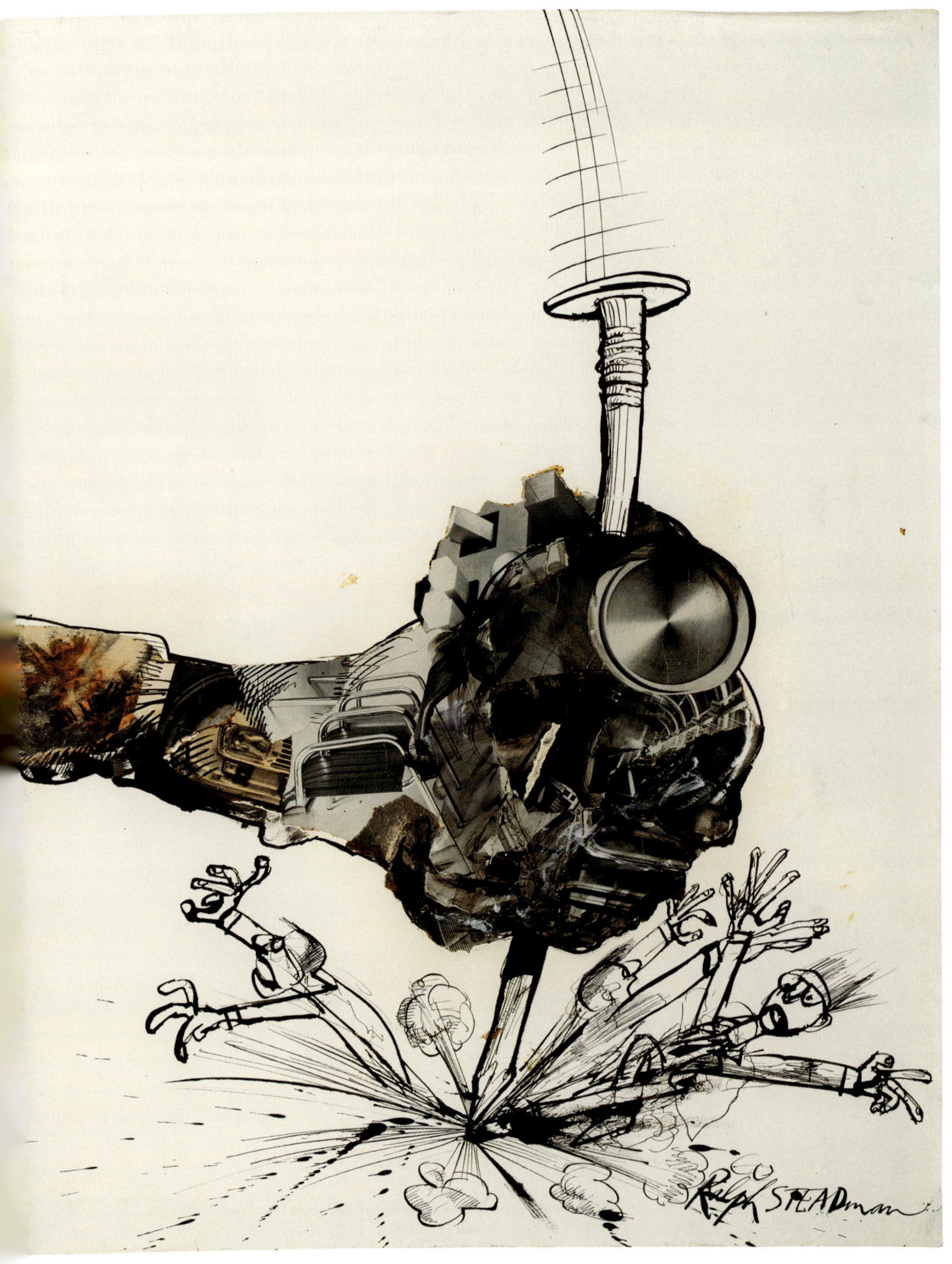

Authority Against Protest, ca. 1970

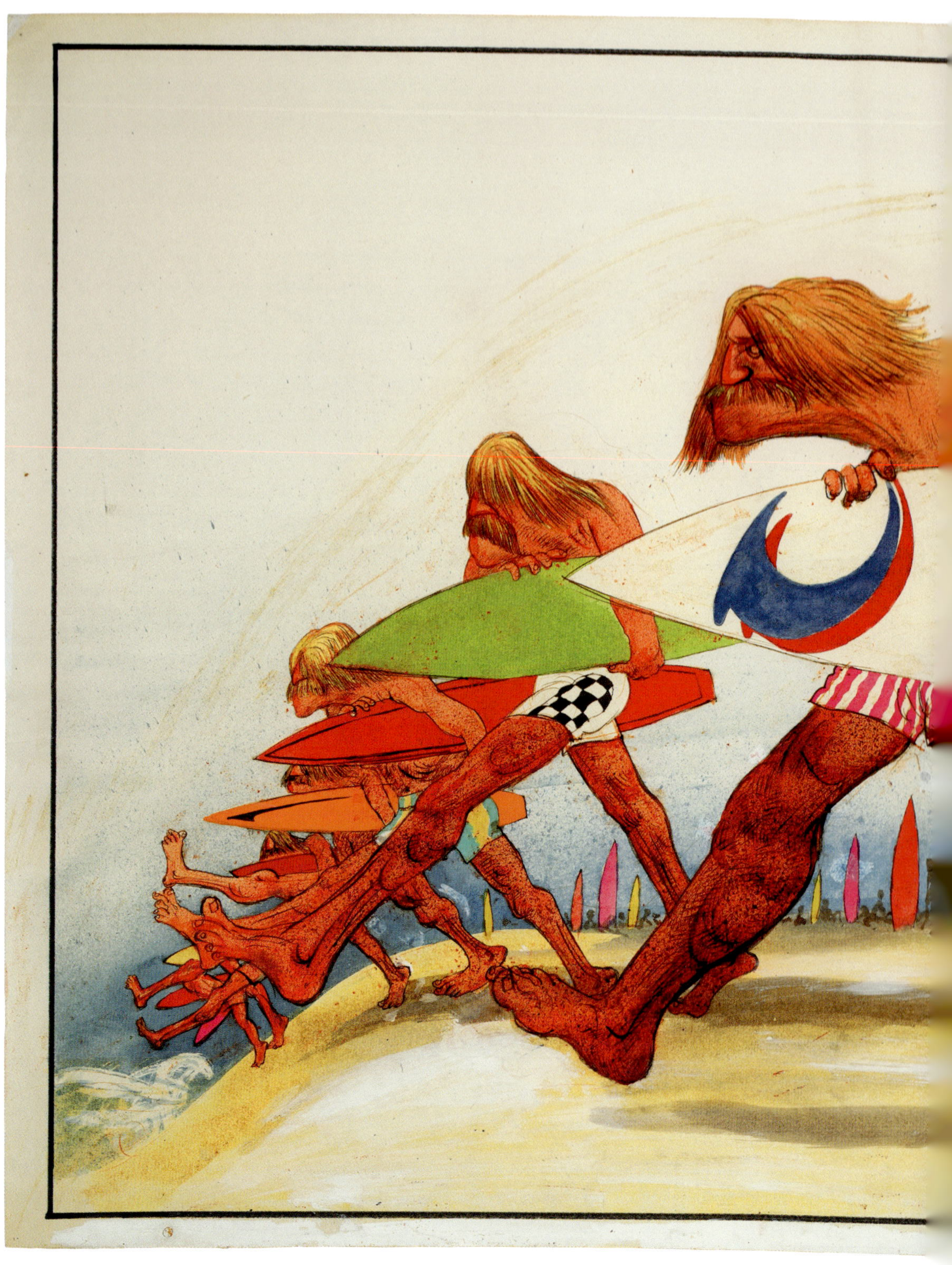

Surfers in Hawaii, **The Curse of Lono**, *ca. 1980*

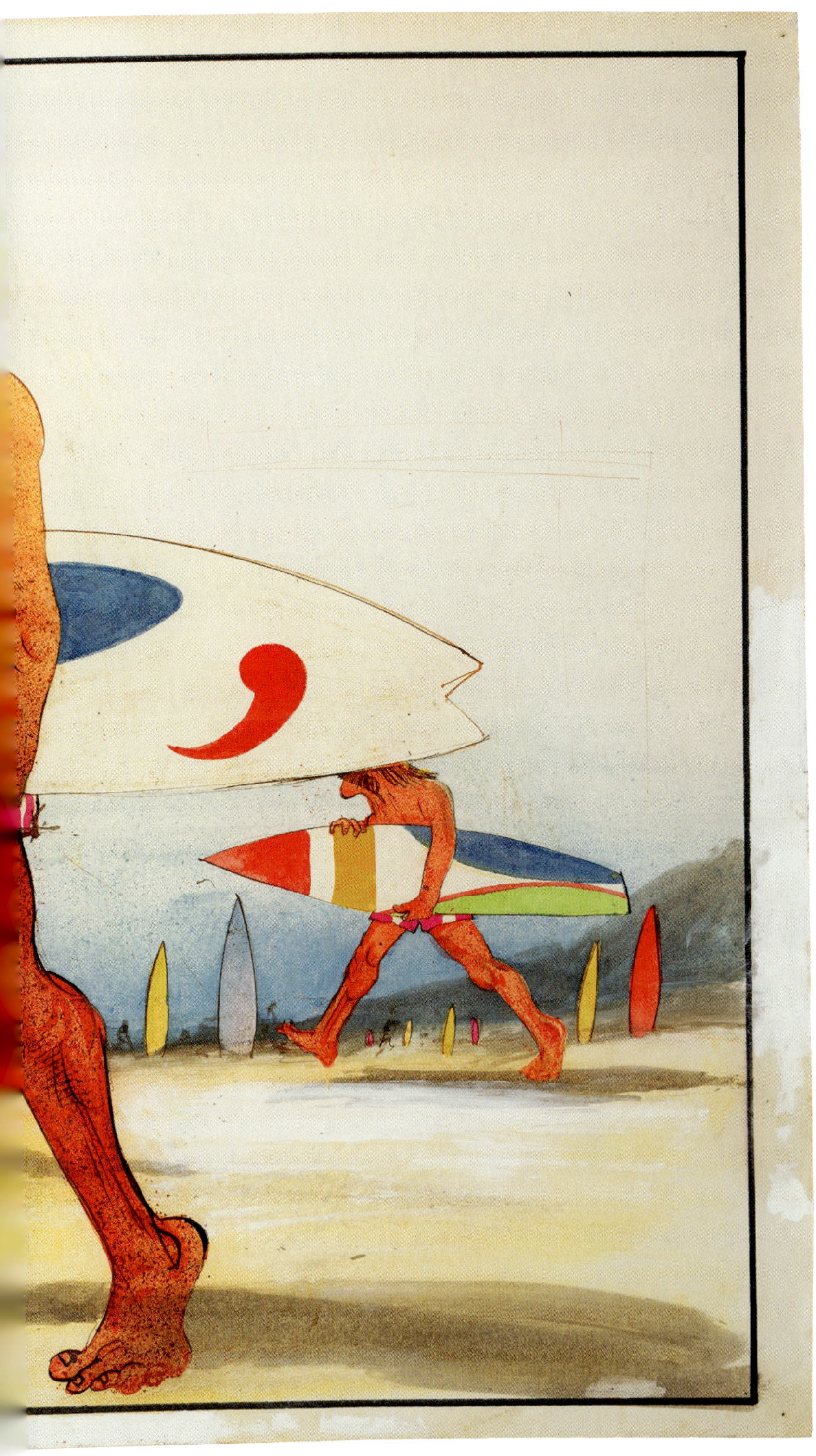

"They seem to be social distancing!"

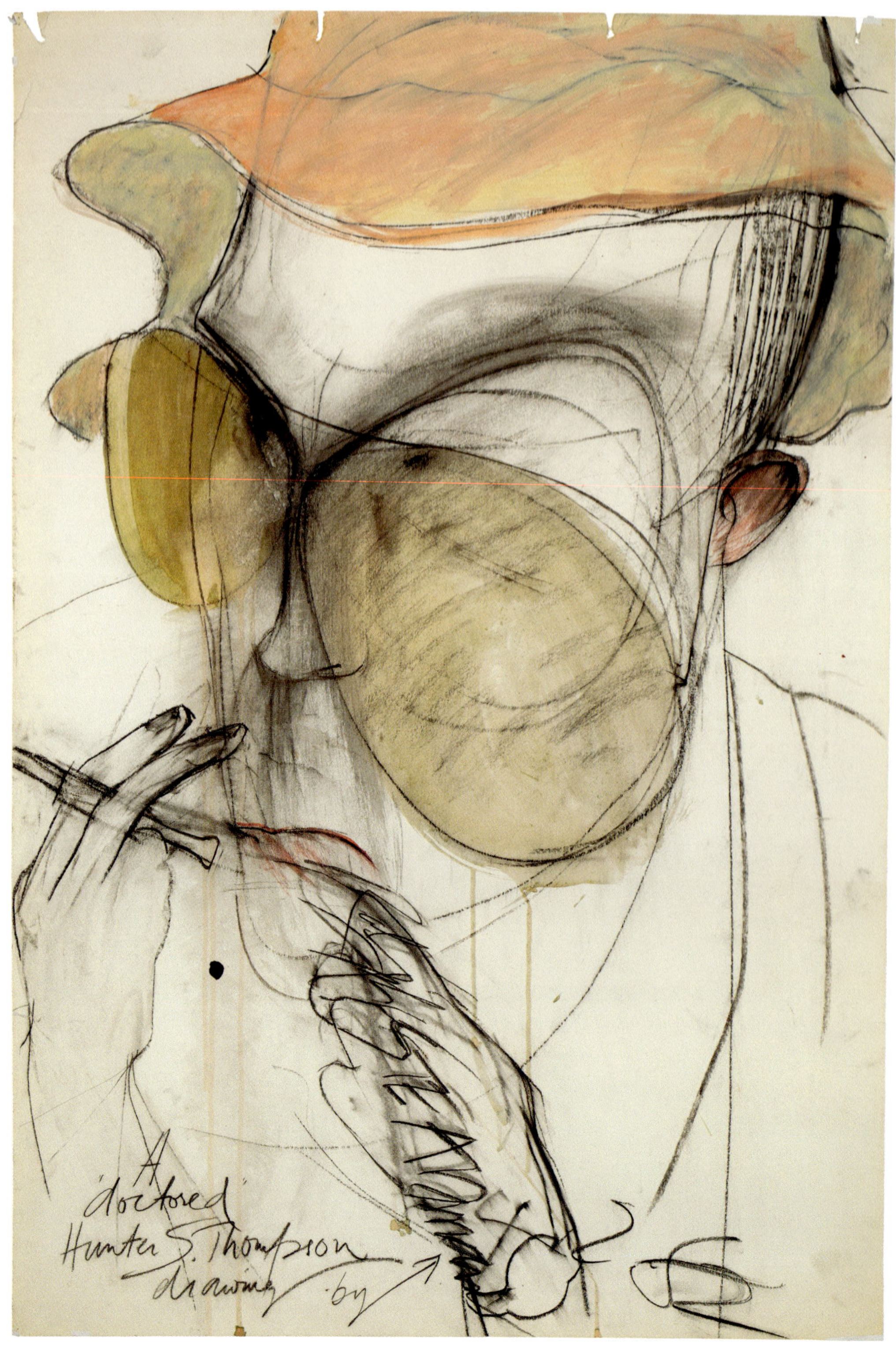

A Doctored Hunter S. Thompson, 1982

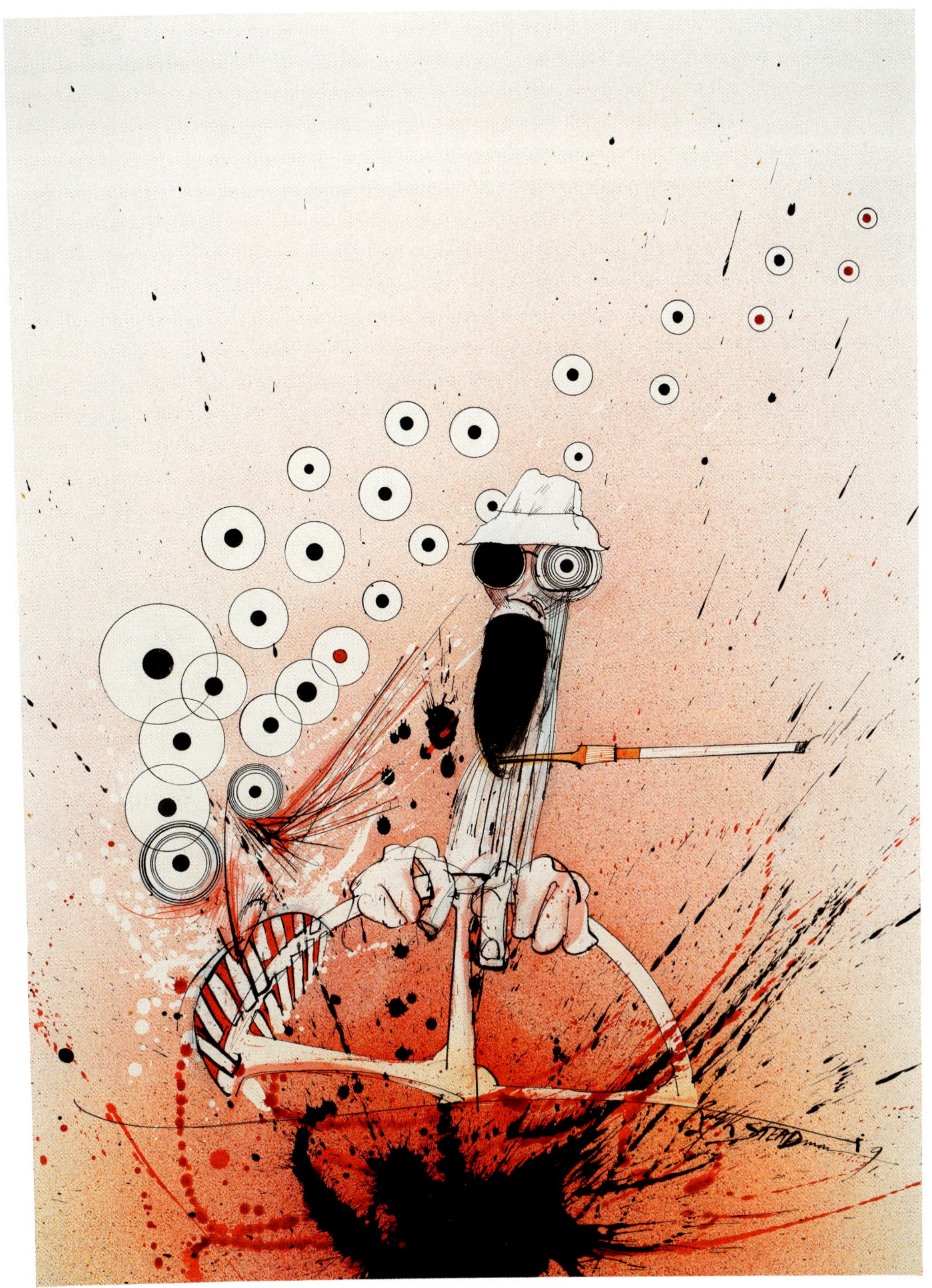

"Hunter would drive his Red Shark, steering with one hand, gripping a bottle of Chivas Regal with the other." *Hunter at the Wheel, 1991*

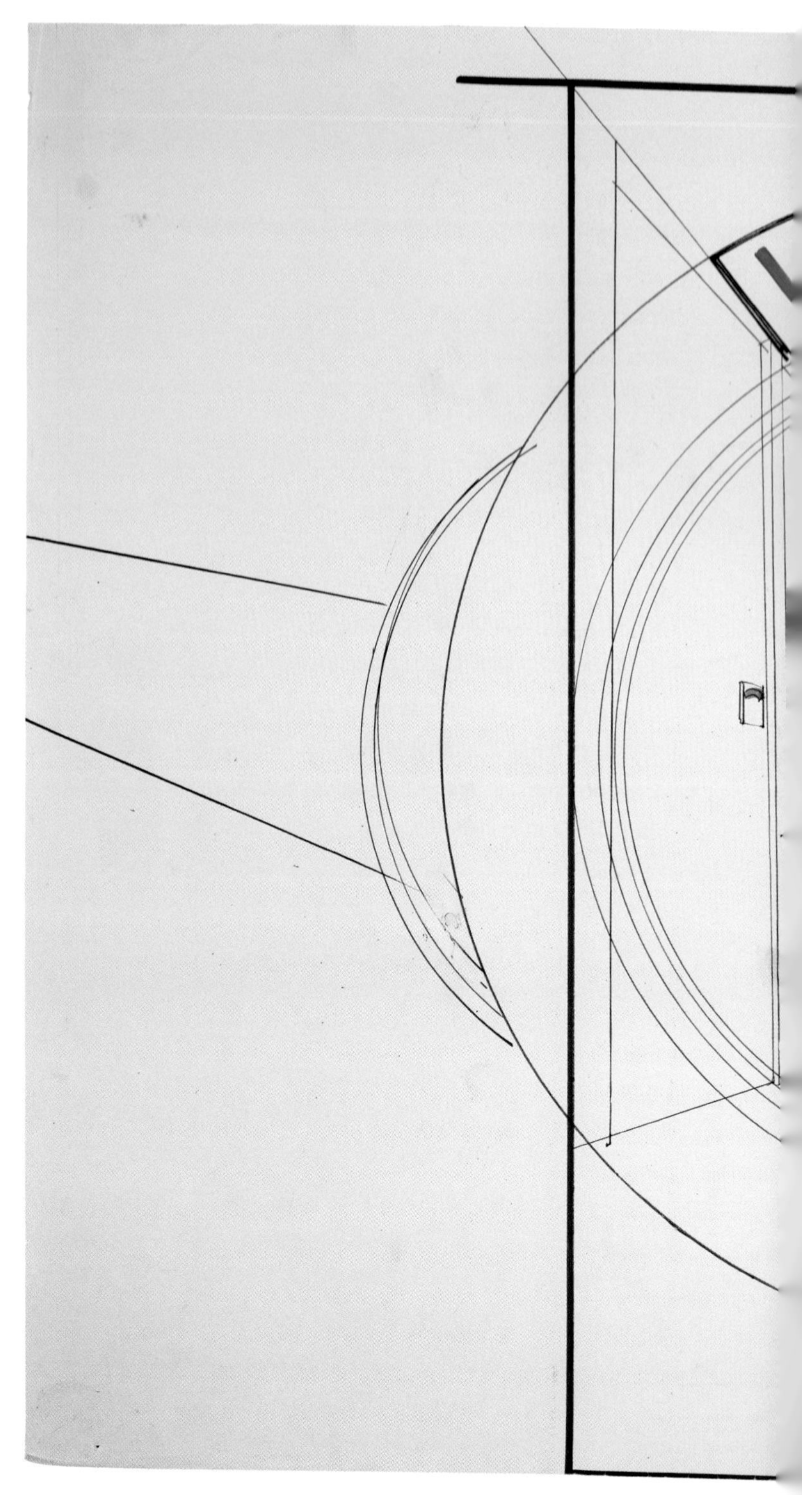

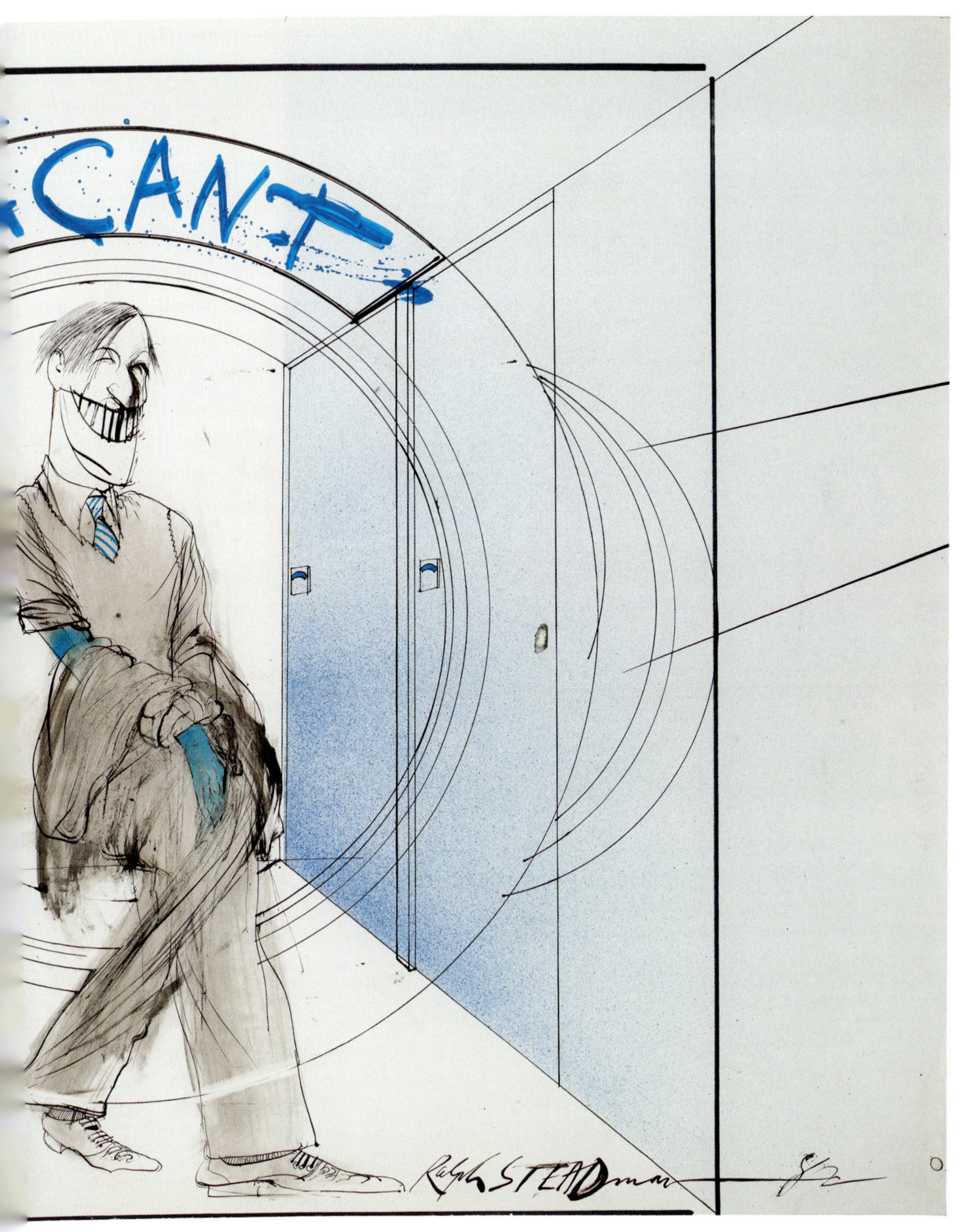

The Curse of Lono, Man with Blue-Stained Hand Toilet Accident, 1980

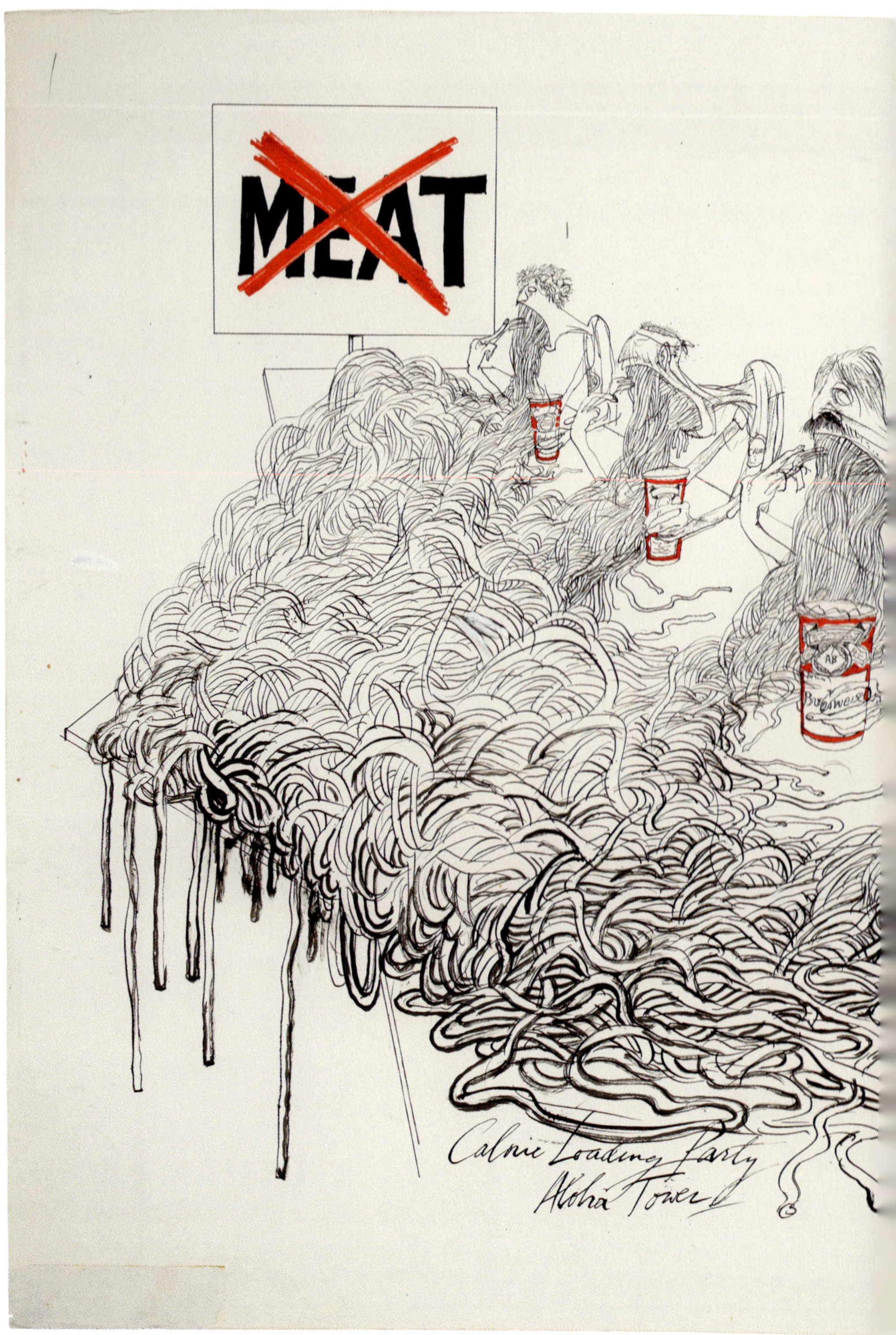

The Curse of Lono, *Pre-Race Carb Binge at the Honolulu Marathon, 1980*

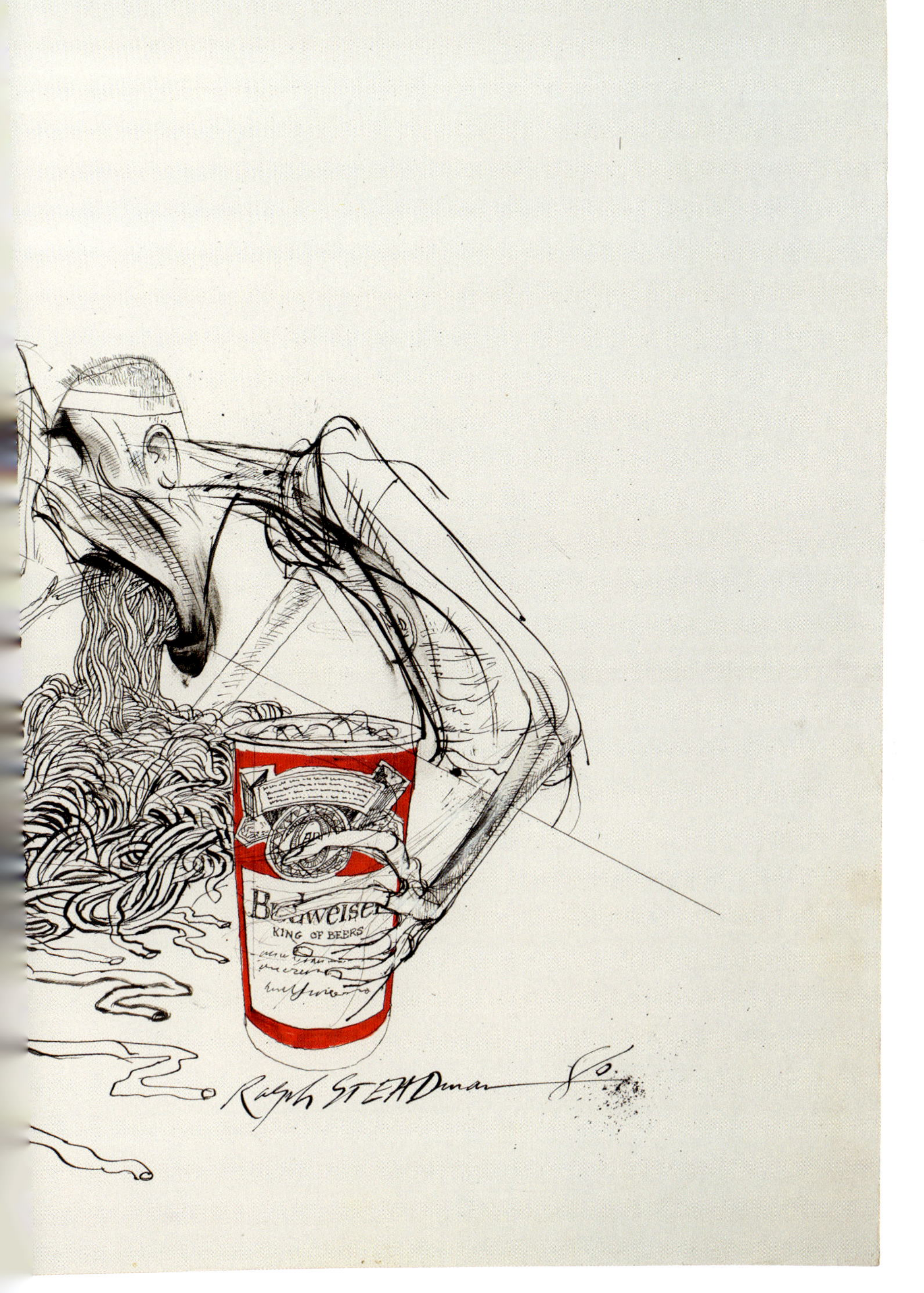
Budweiser
KING OF BEERS

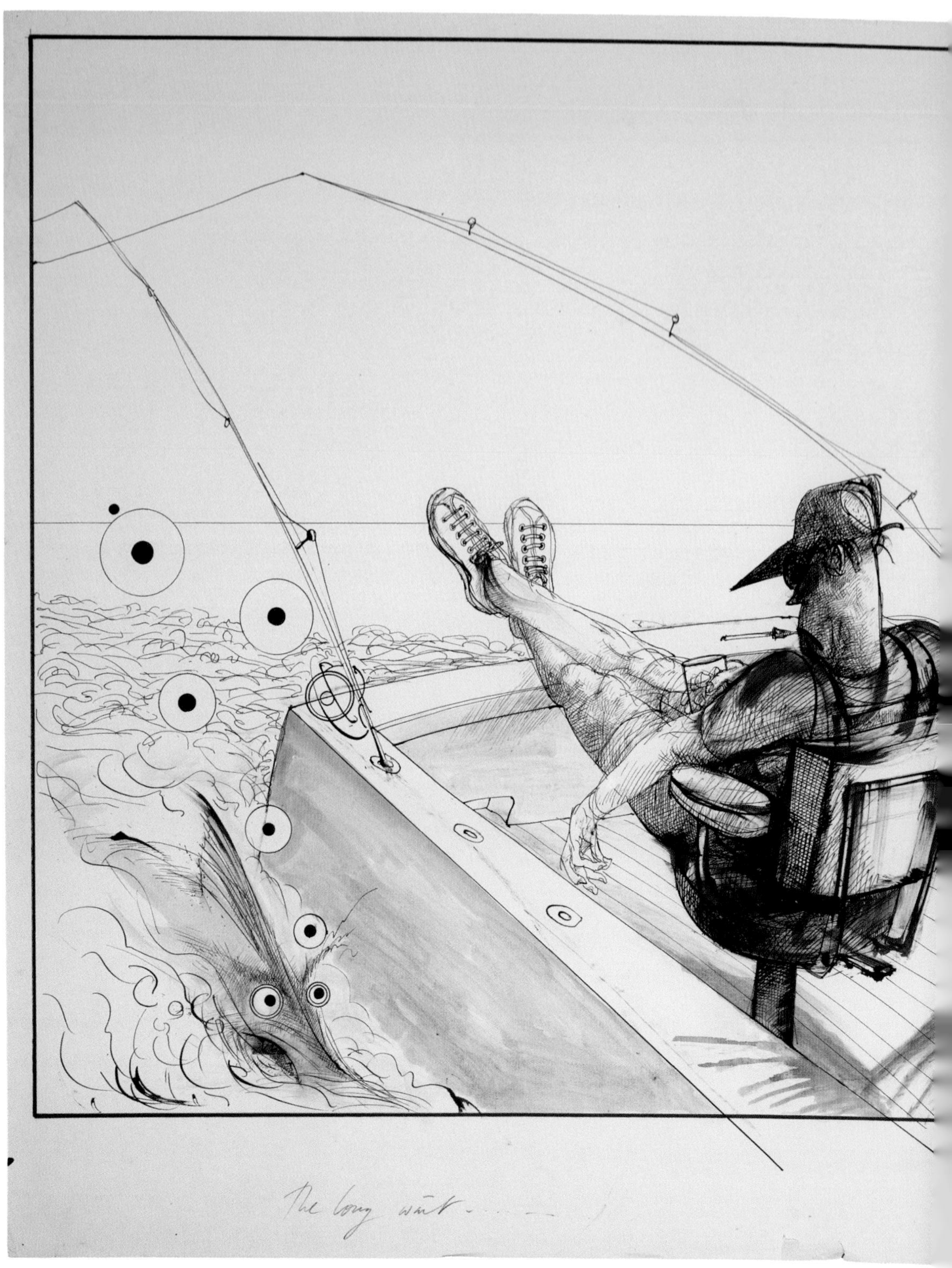

"He looked so much more relaxed in that moment than I had ever seen him. Calm before the tsunami."

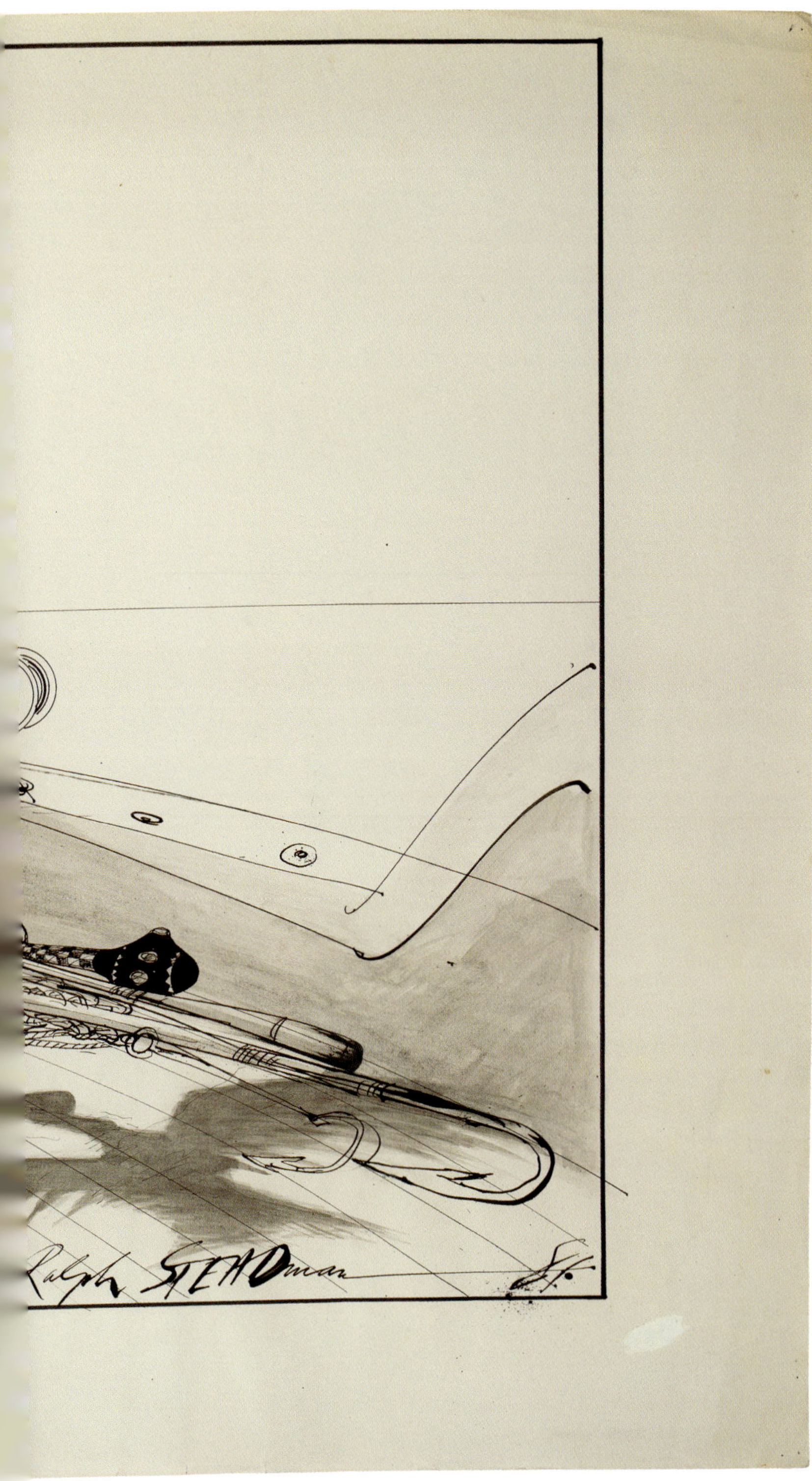

The Curse of Lono, Hunter Fishing, 1980

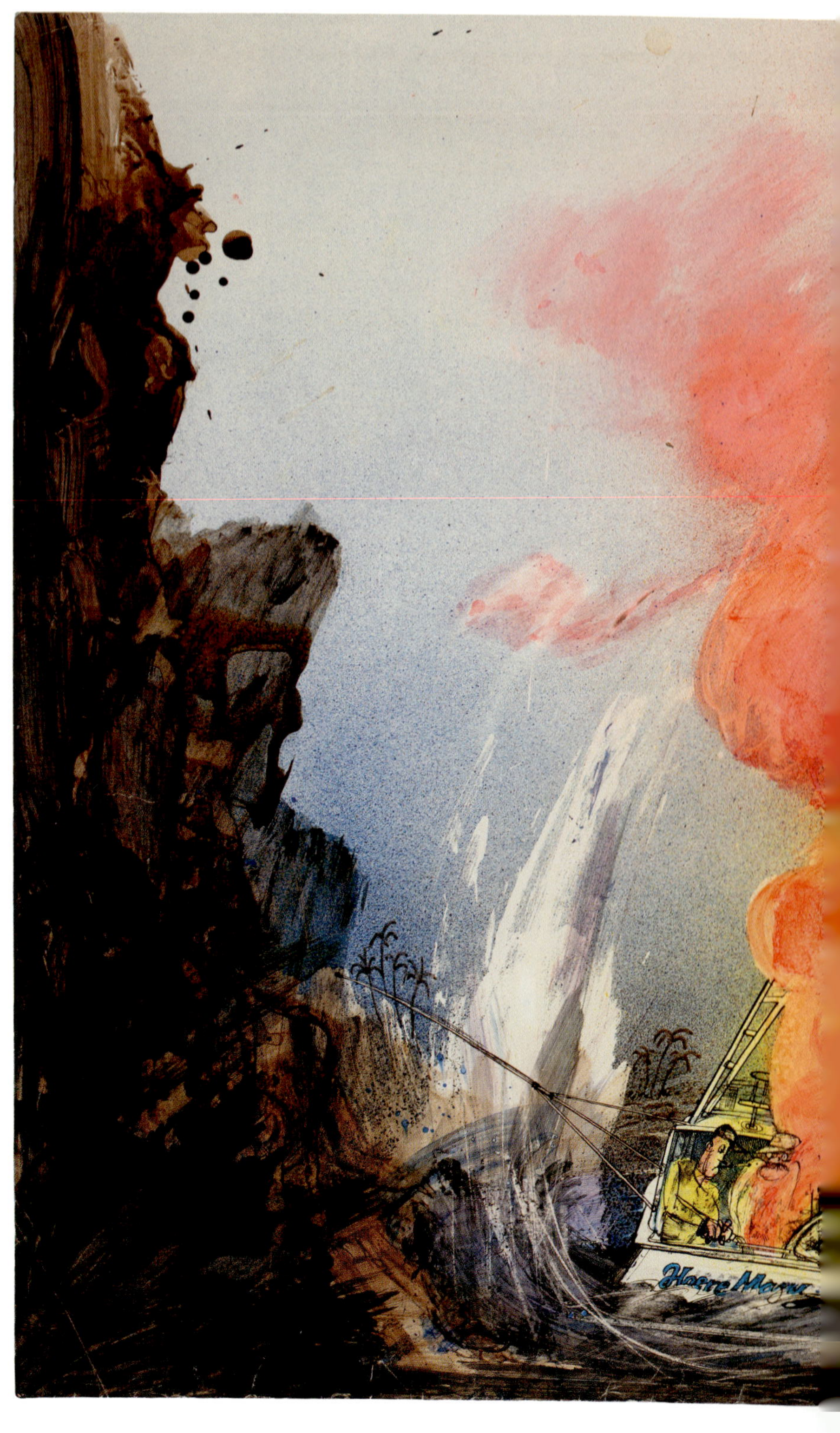

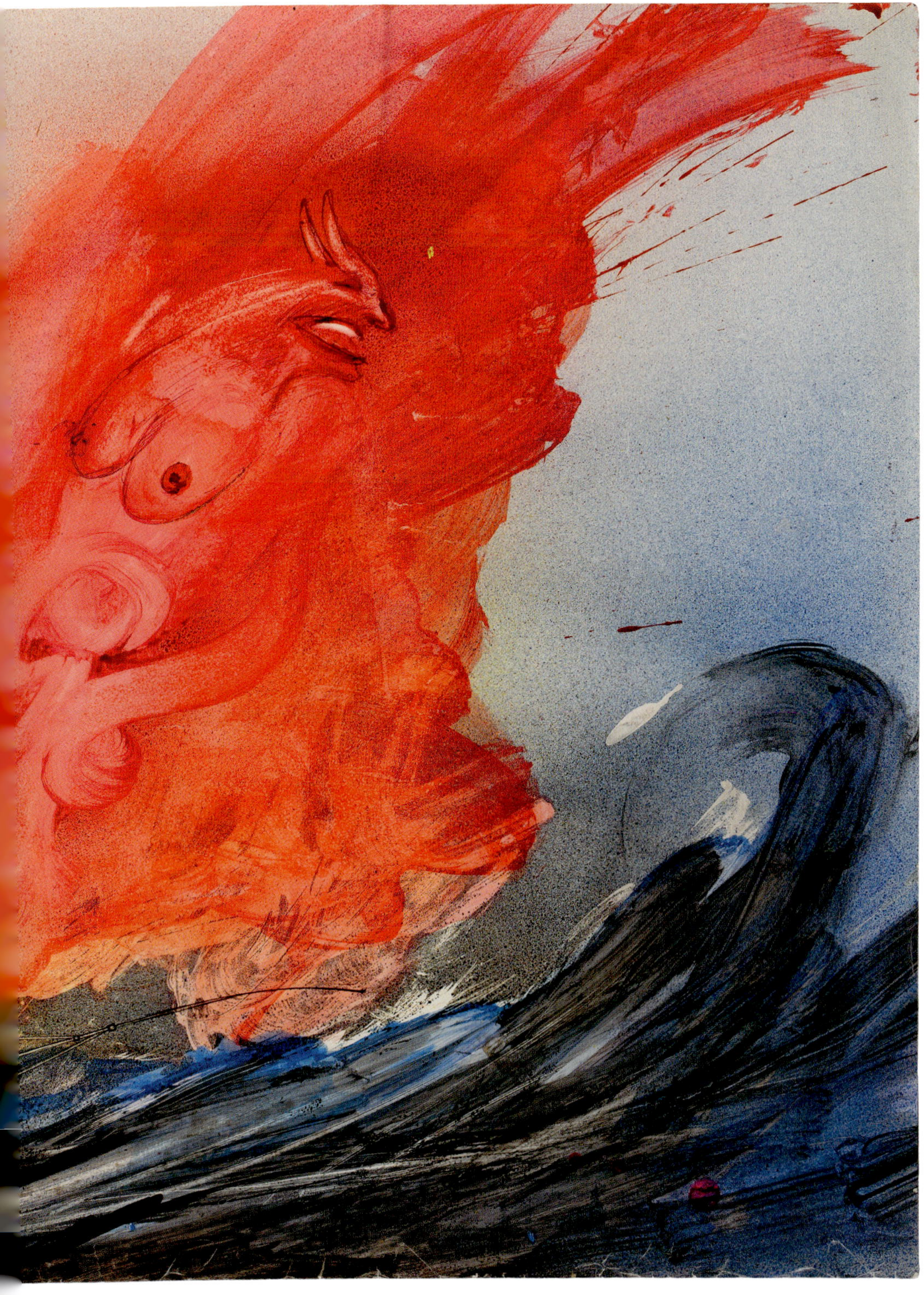

The Curse of Lono, Goddess Pele in Hawaii, 1980

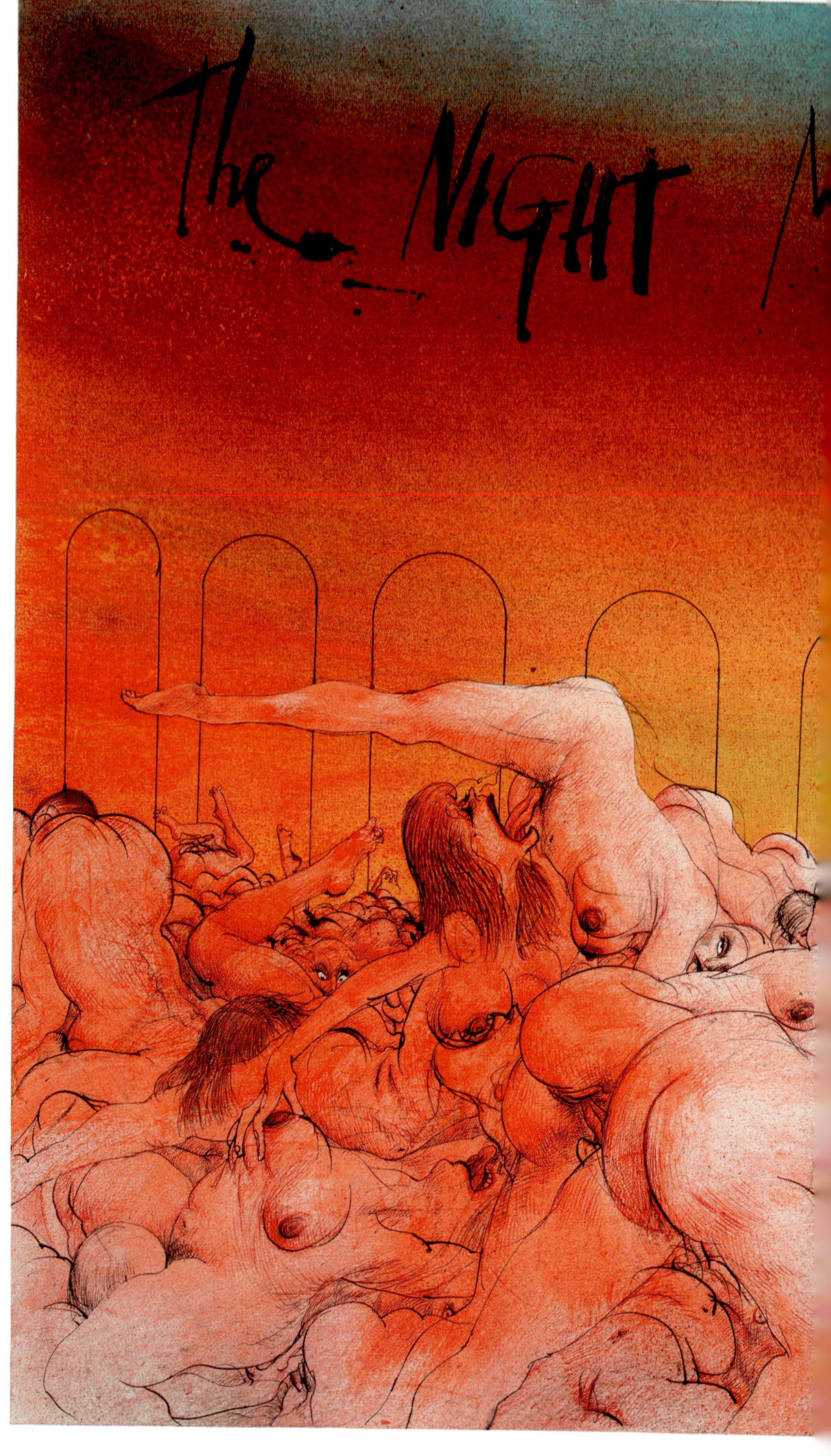
The NIGHT

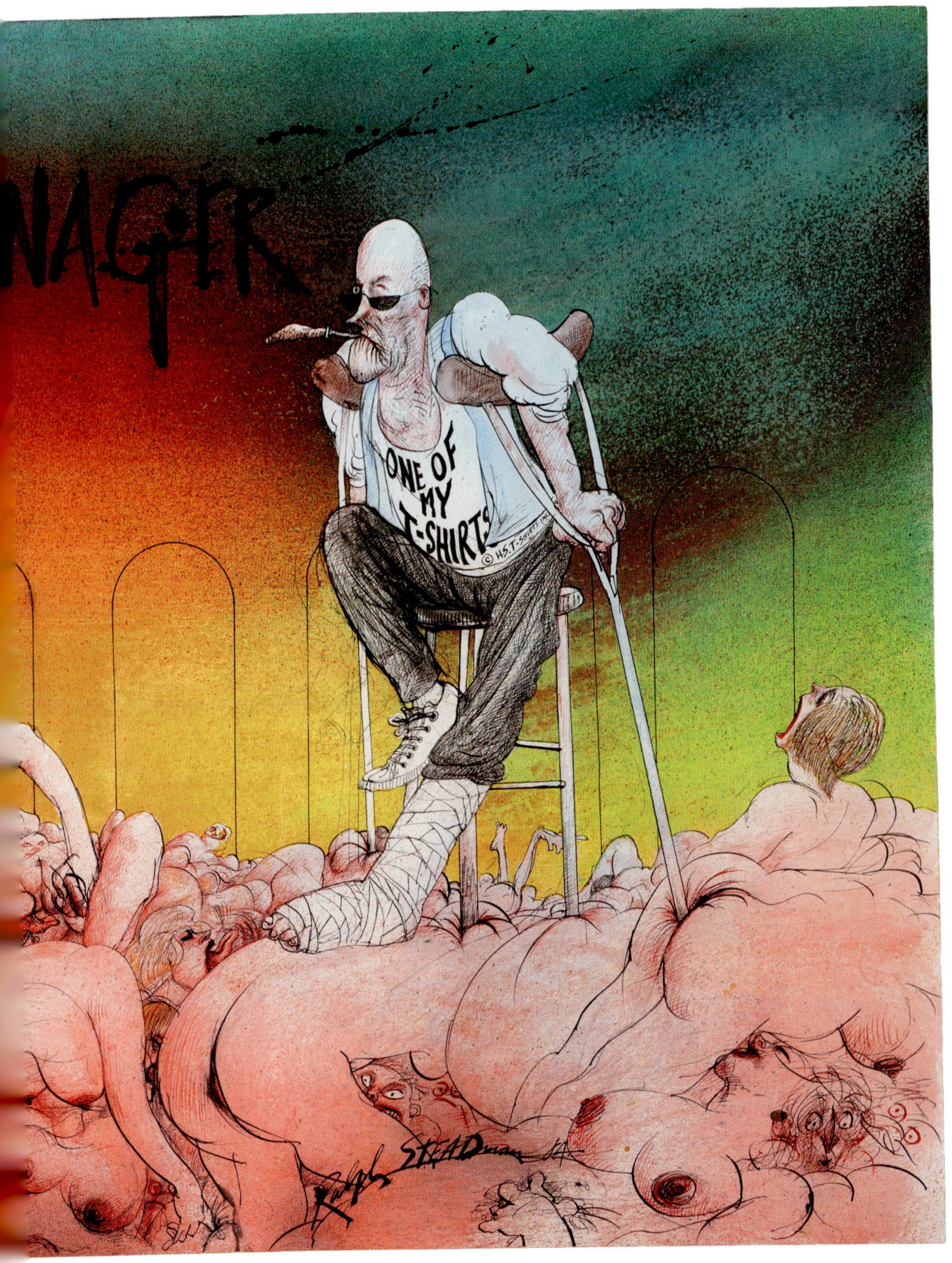

Hunter as "Night Manager" in San Francisco with Broken Leg, 1984

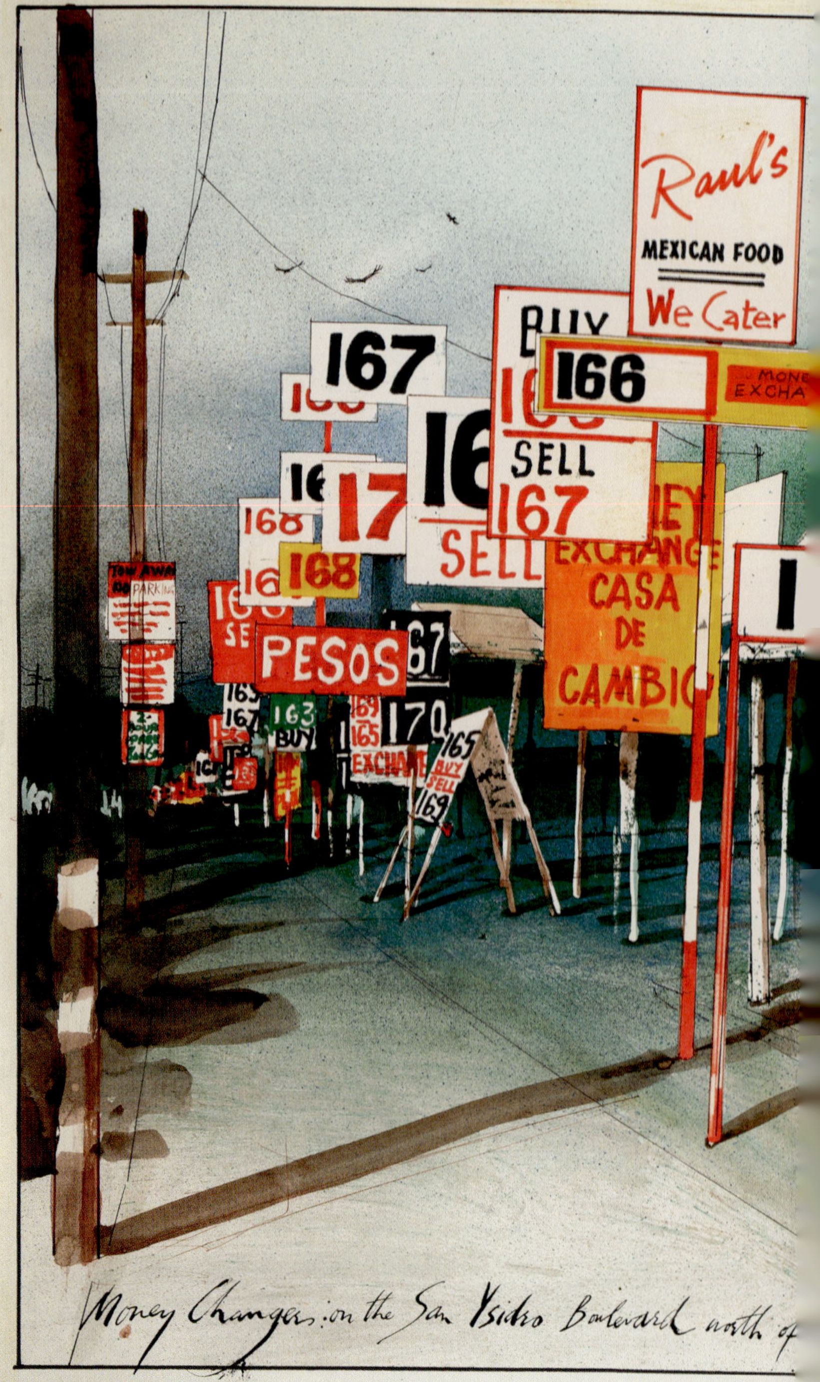

Money Changers on the San Ysidro Boulevard north of

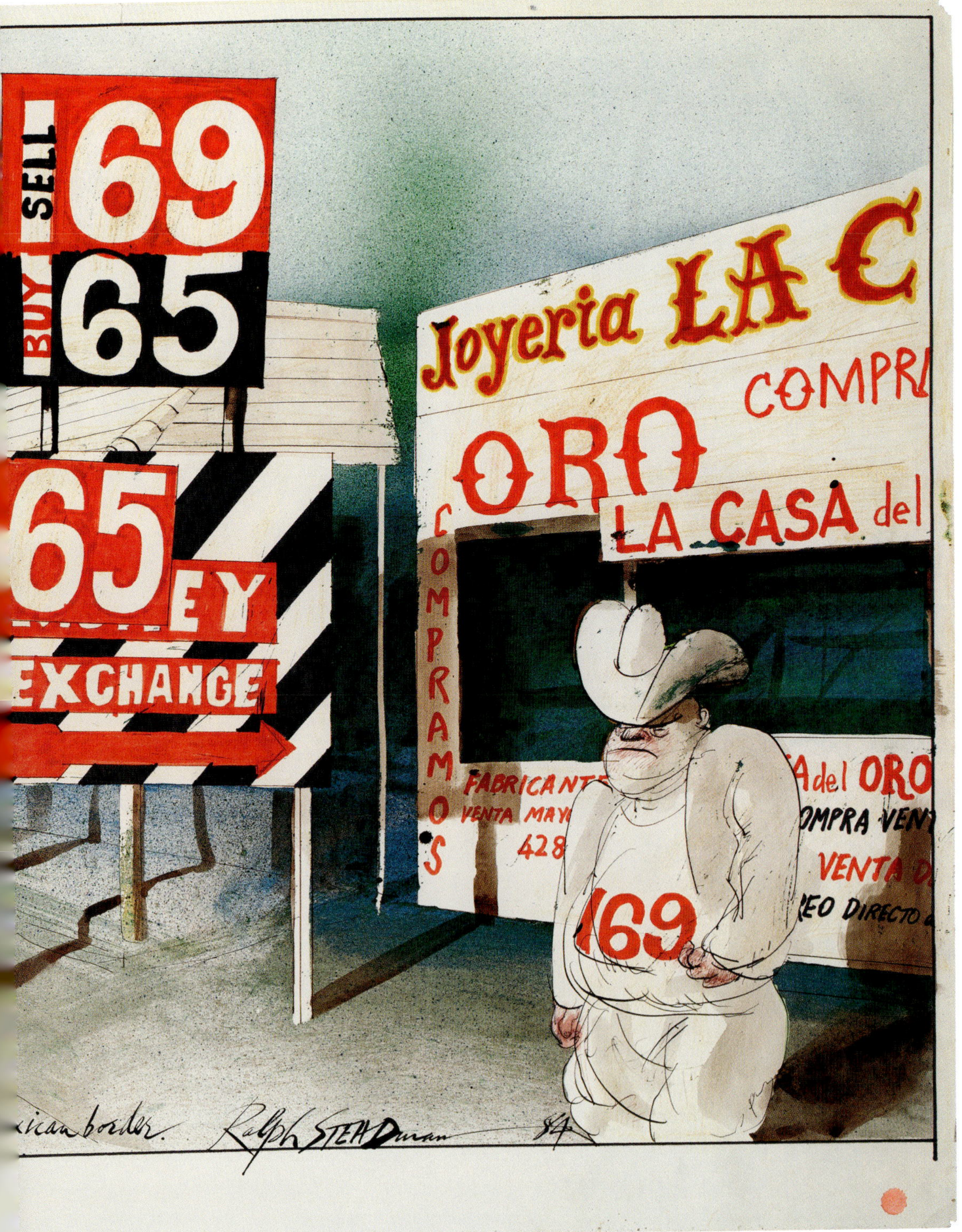

Money Changers at the Mexican Border, 1984

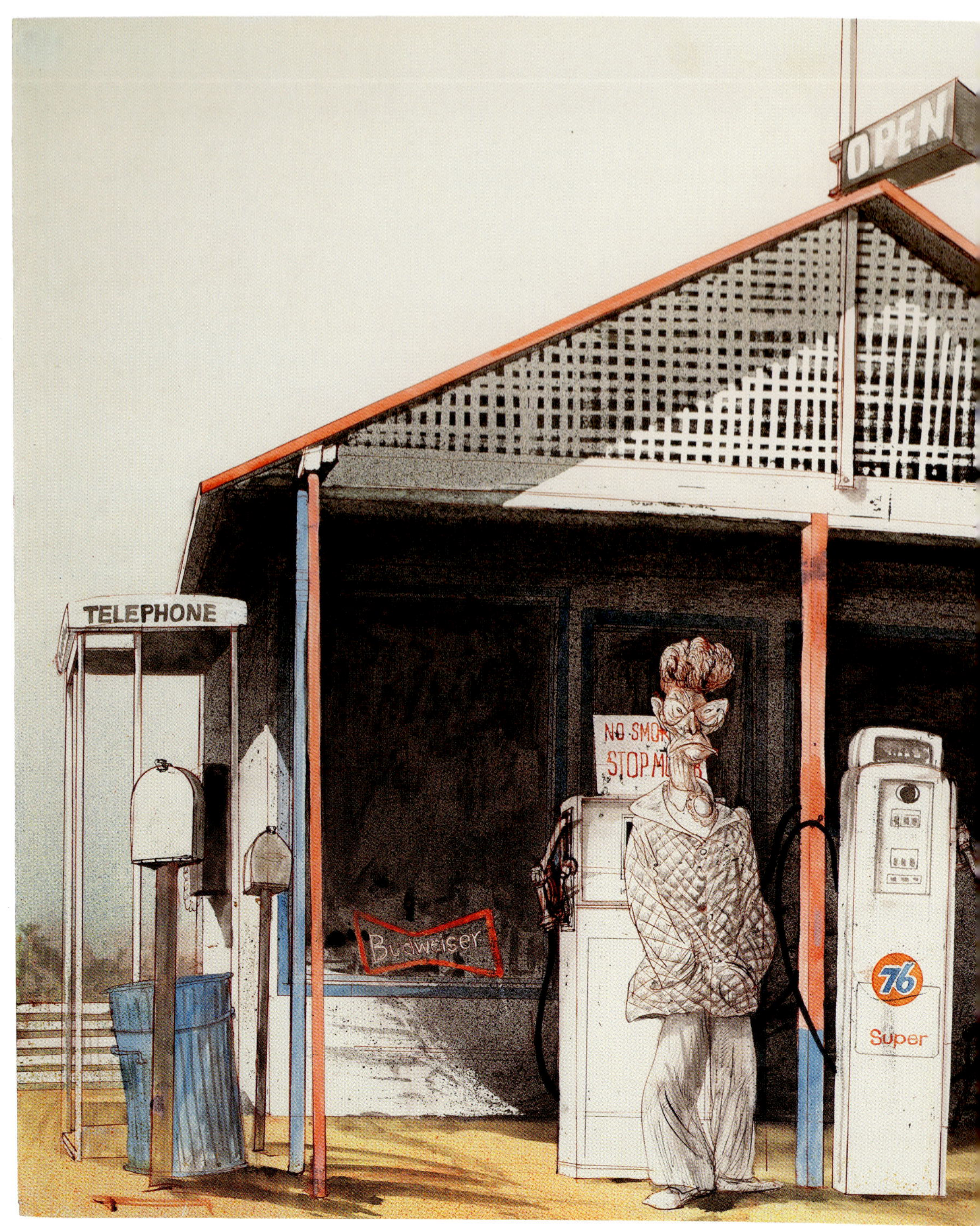

"When you really get out into 'Merica, some of the characters are almost unbelievable. Sometimes the ordinary is the most extraordinary thing."

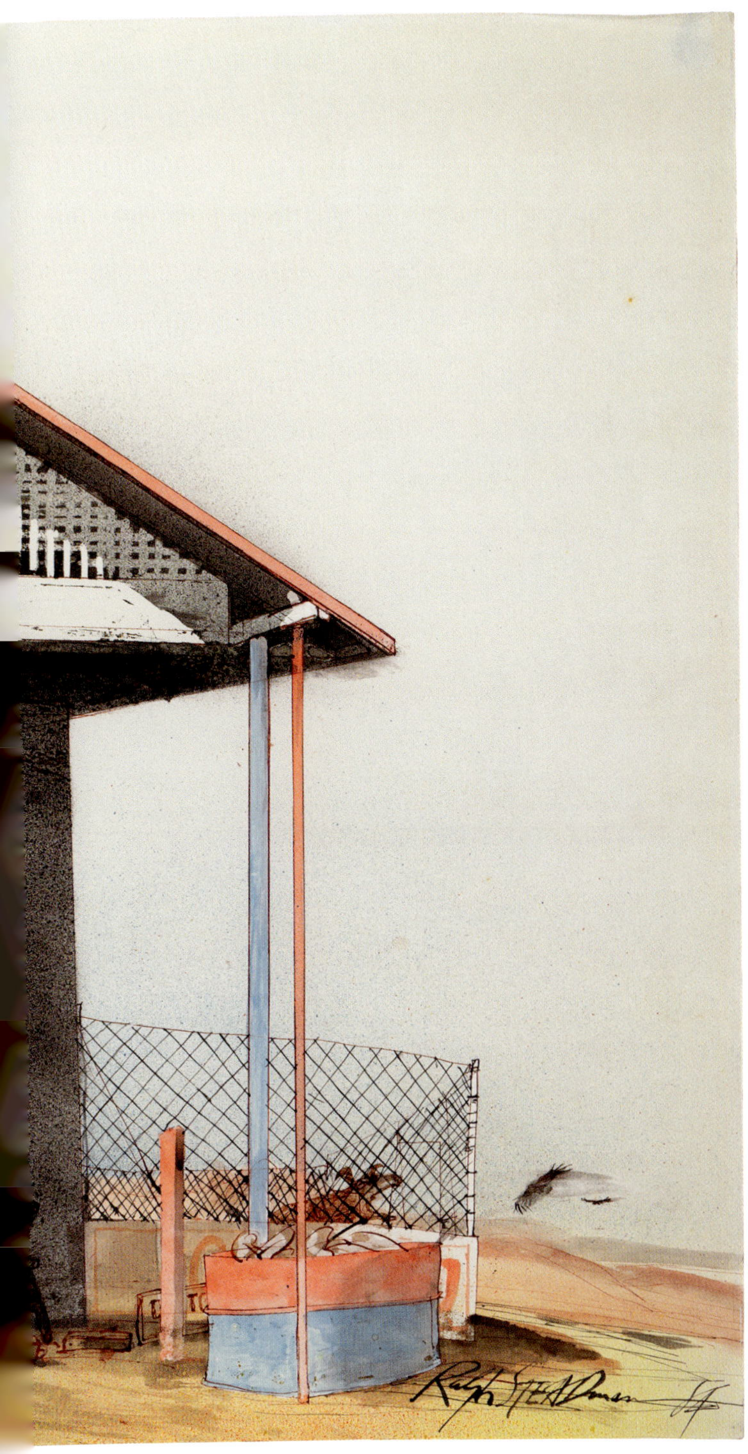

Gas Station in Dallas, 1984

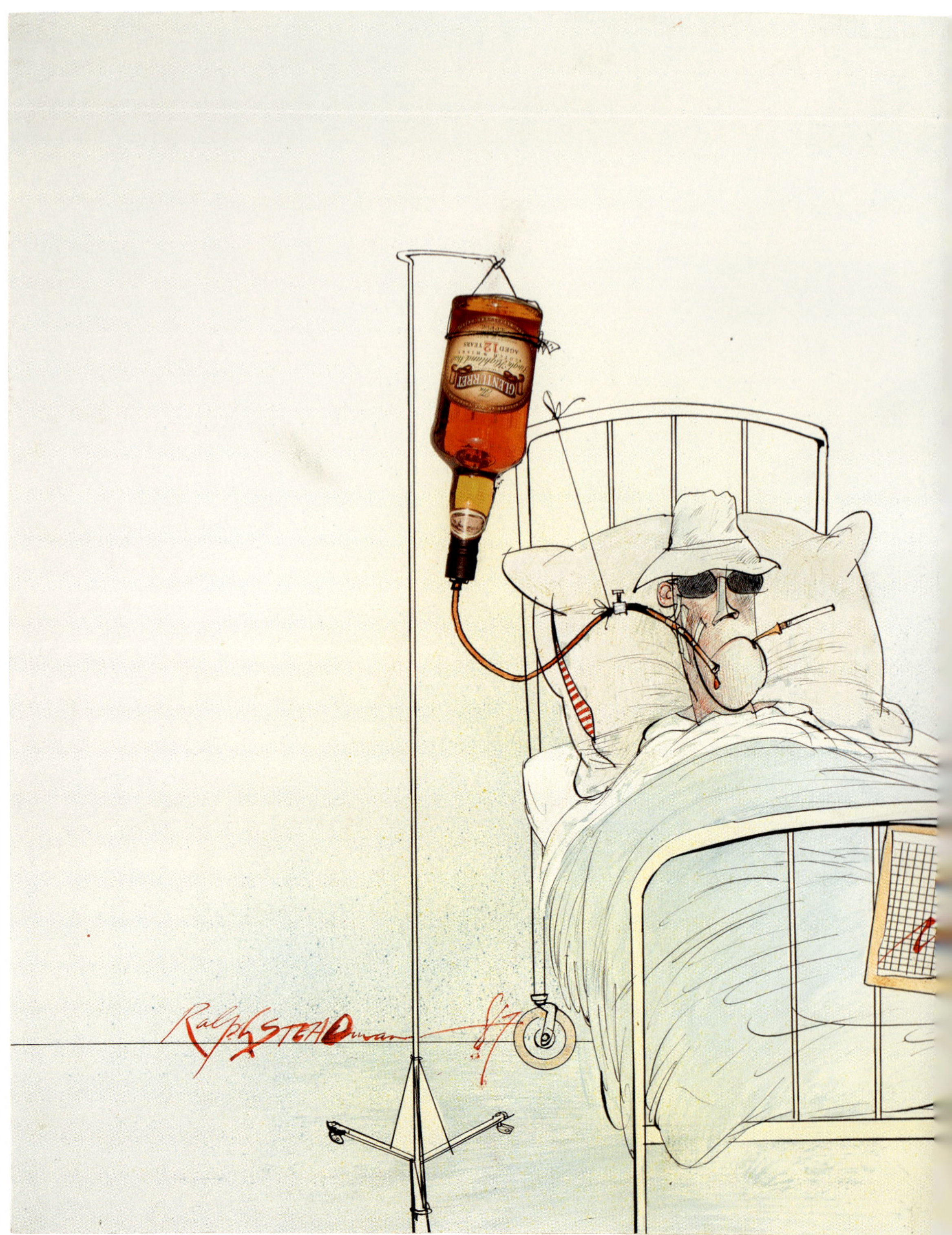

Hunter on a "Whiskey Drip," 1987

"Hunter used to order six Bloody Marys for breakfast."

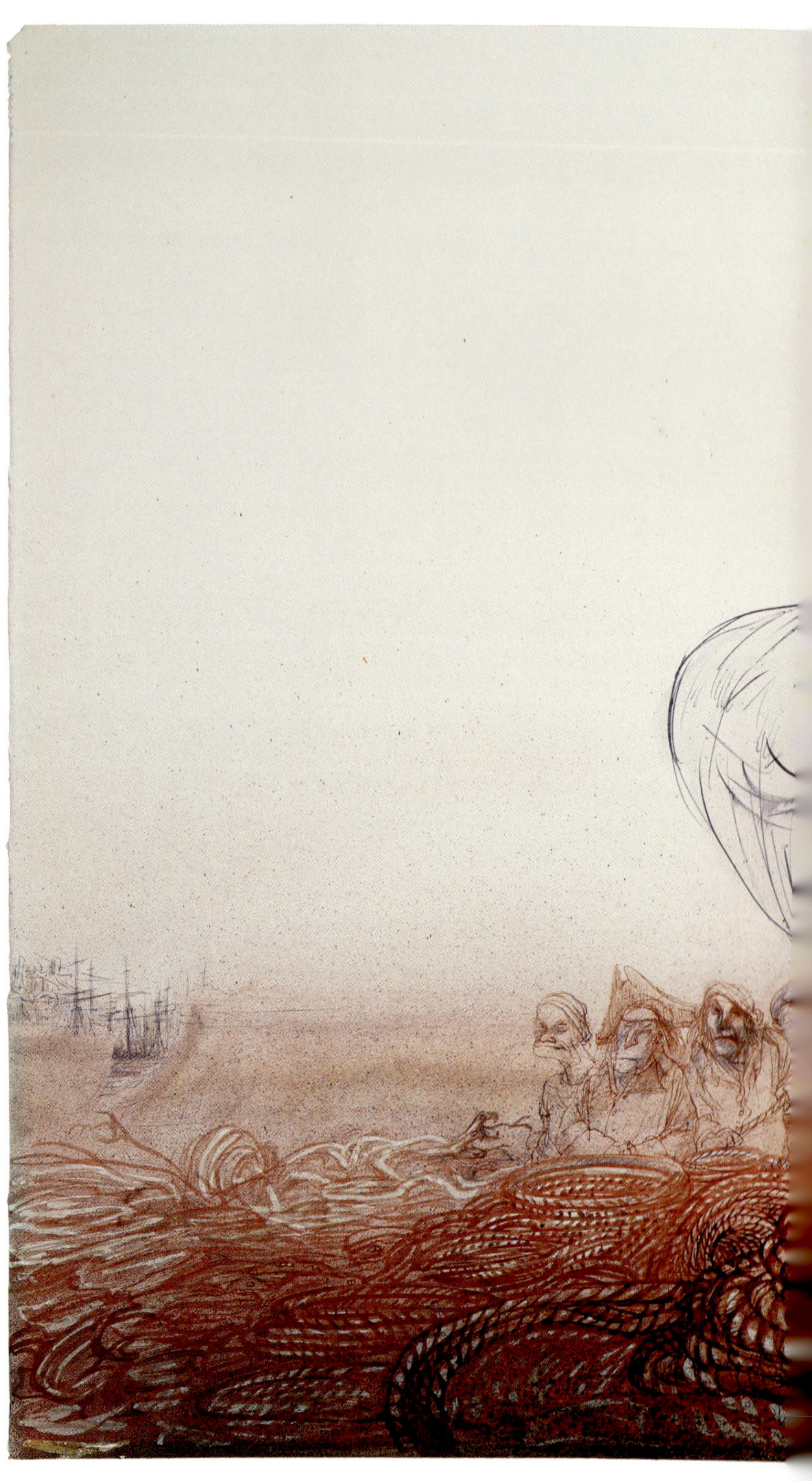

Crew Member from **Treasure Island**, 1985

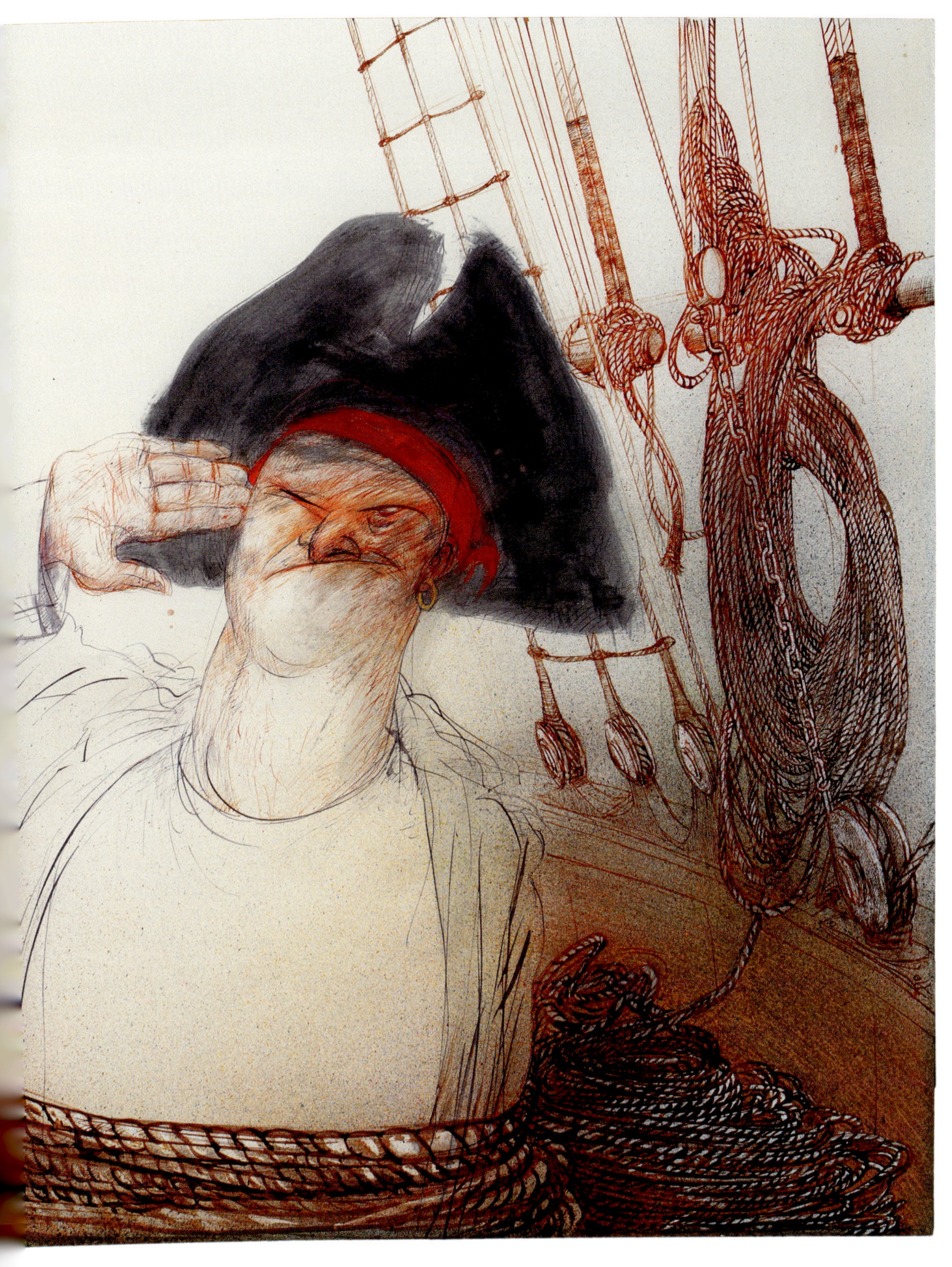

"We held the launch party for *Treasure Island* at our local pub, The Chequers in Loose, that I had used as the Admiral Benbow Inn in the book."

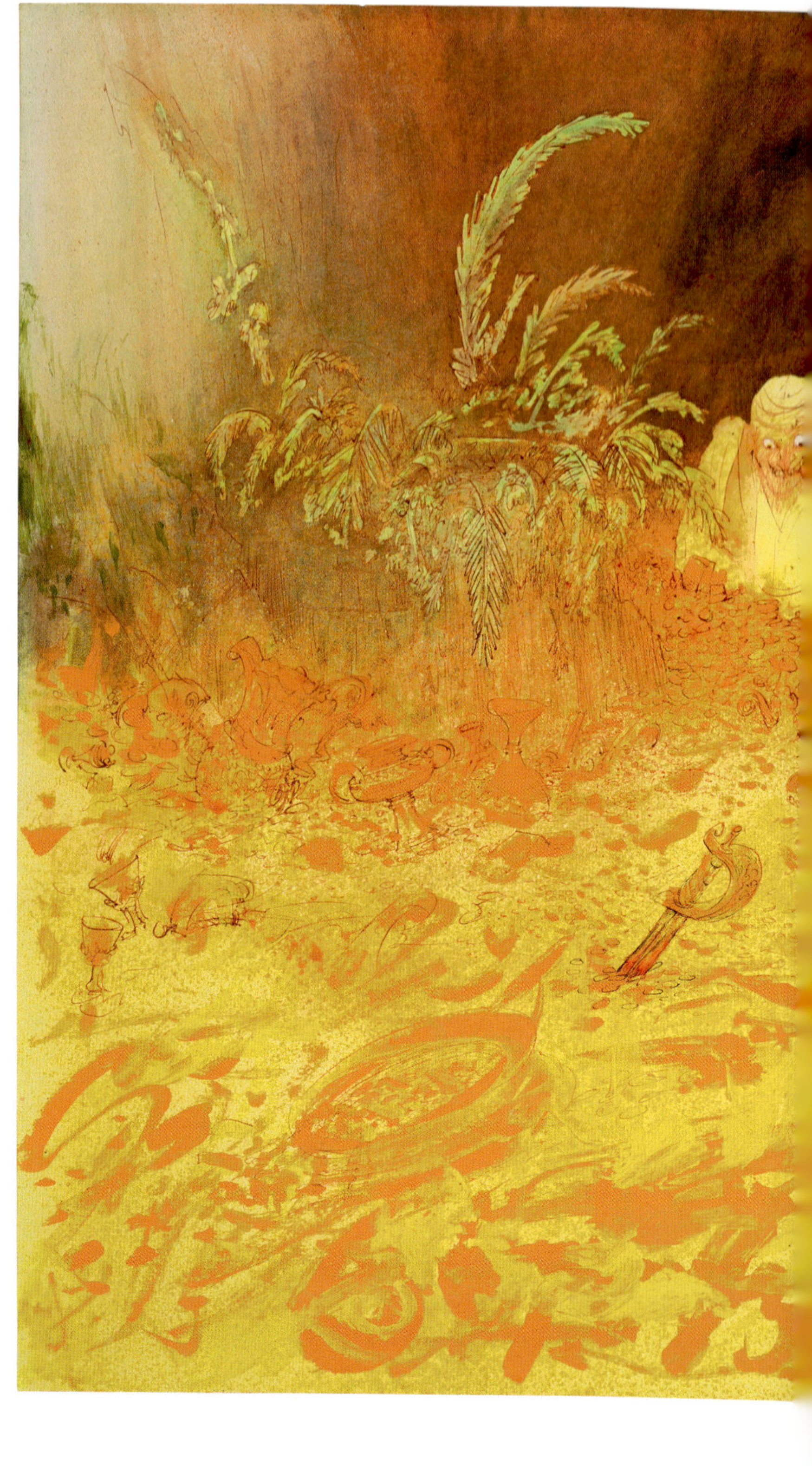

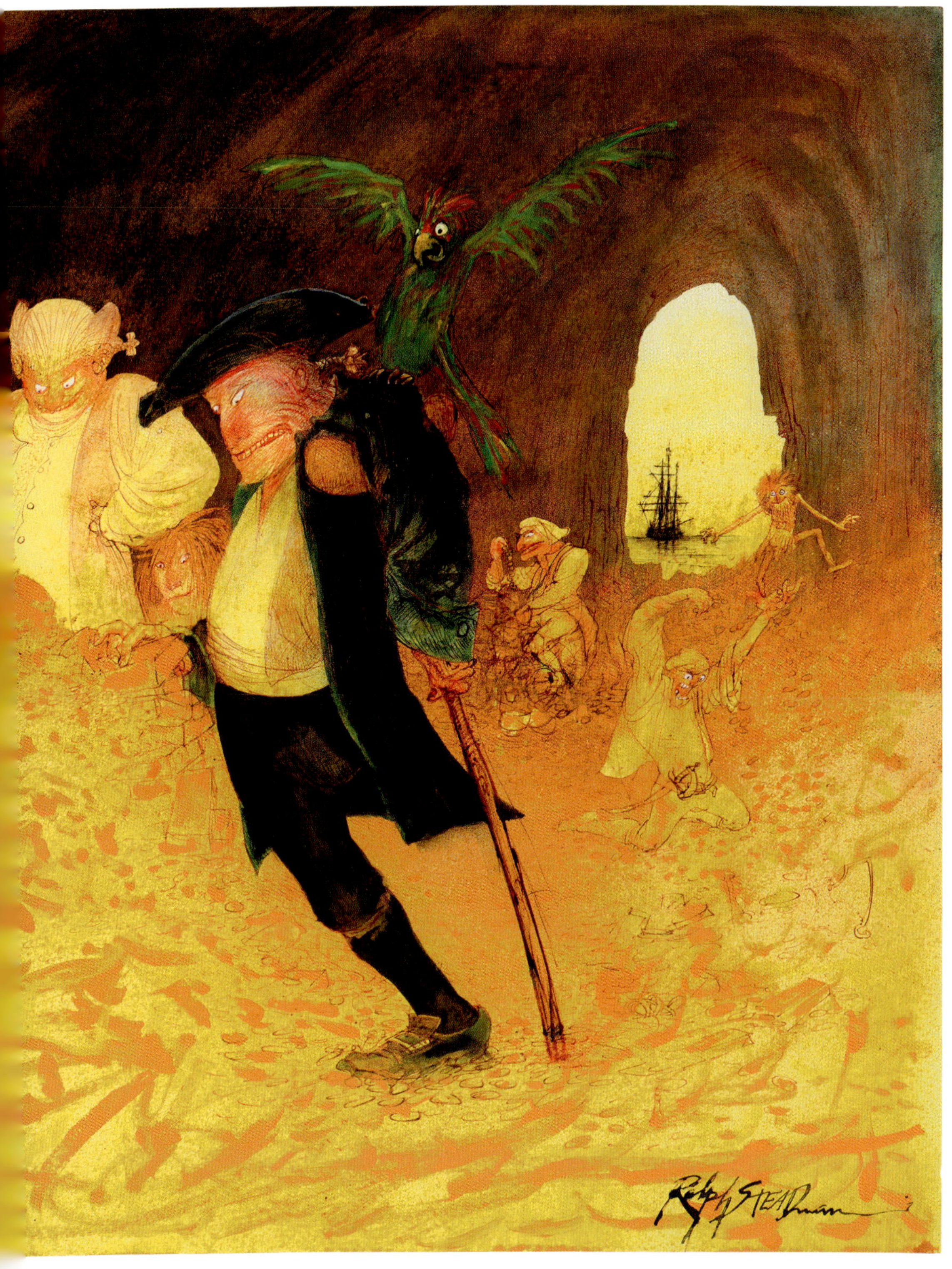

Cap'n Silver Looks at the Gold, 1985

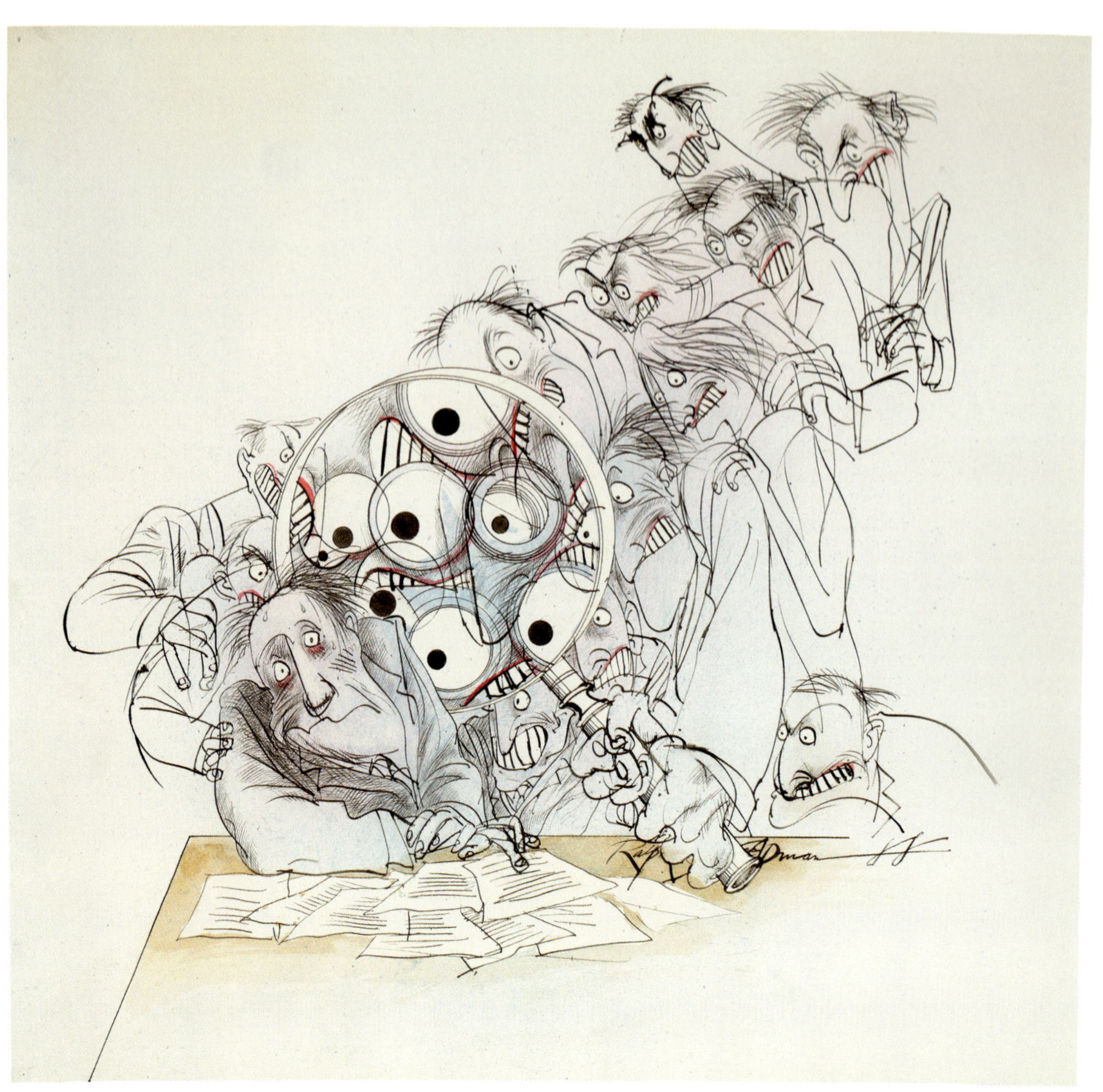

Being Watched, 1988 "I now think that some of this social media pressure feels a bit like this."

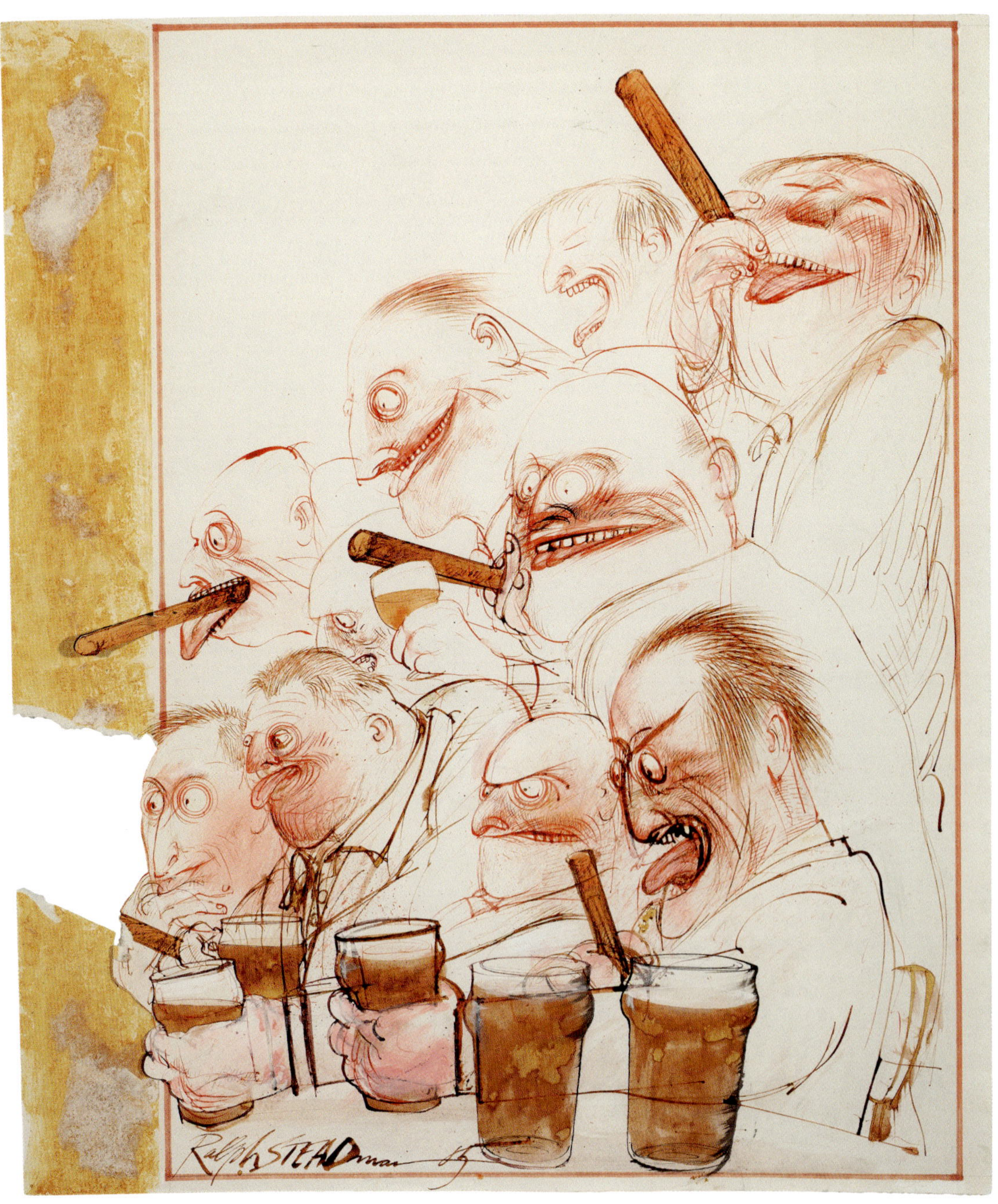

Men in a Pub, 1985

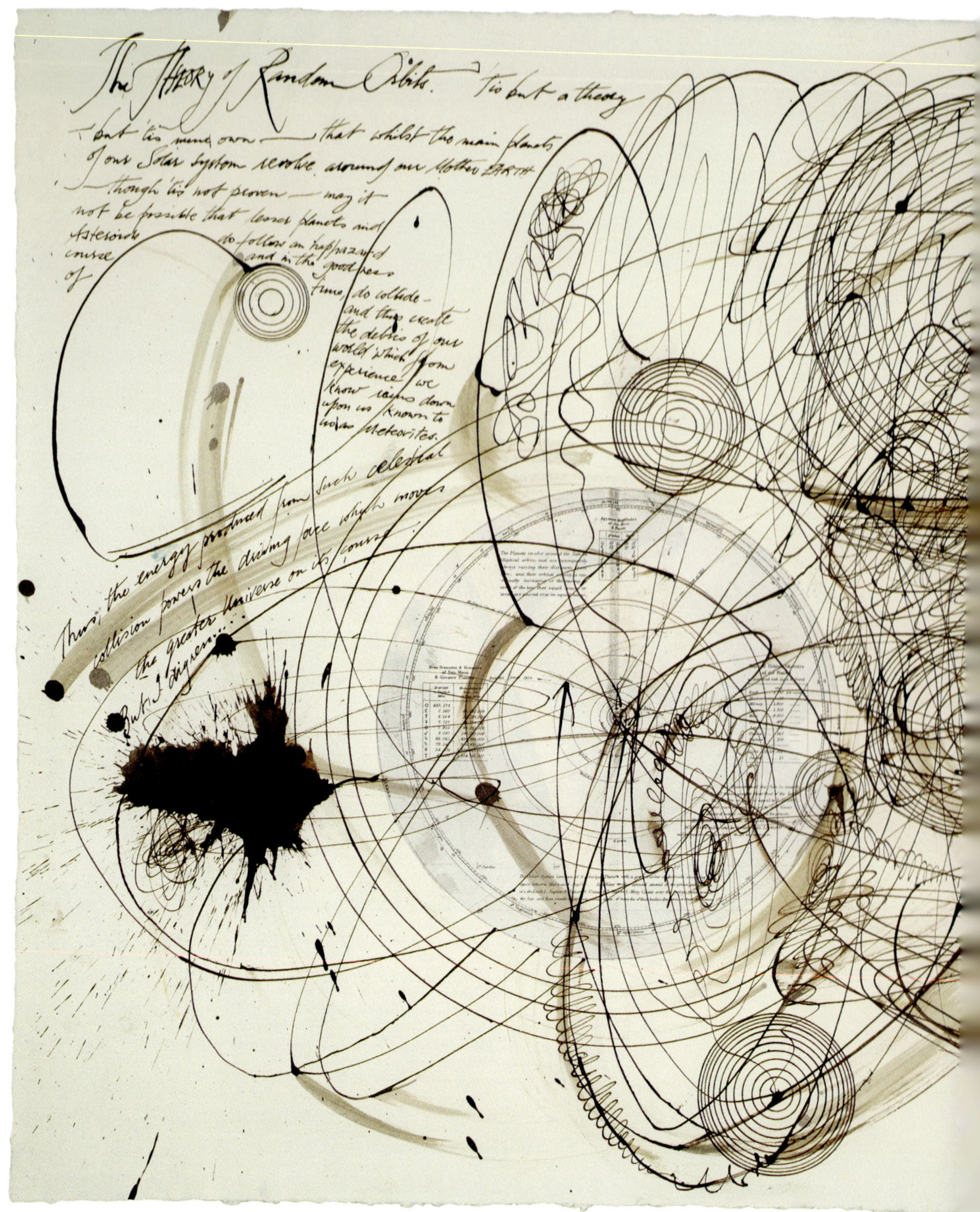

"I have continued to use elements of technical drawing, concentric circles, etc., in my work since I trained in Radar at de Havilland Airplane Company, but back then I would get told off for doodling in the margins!"

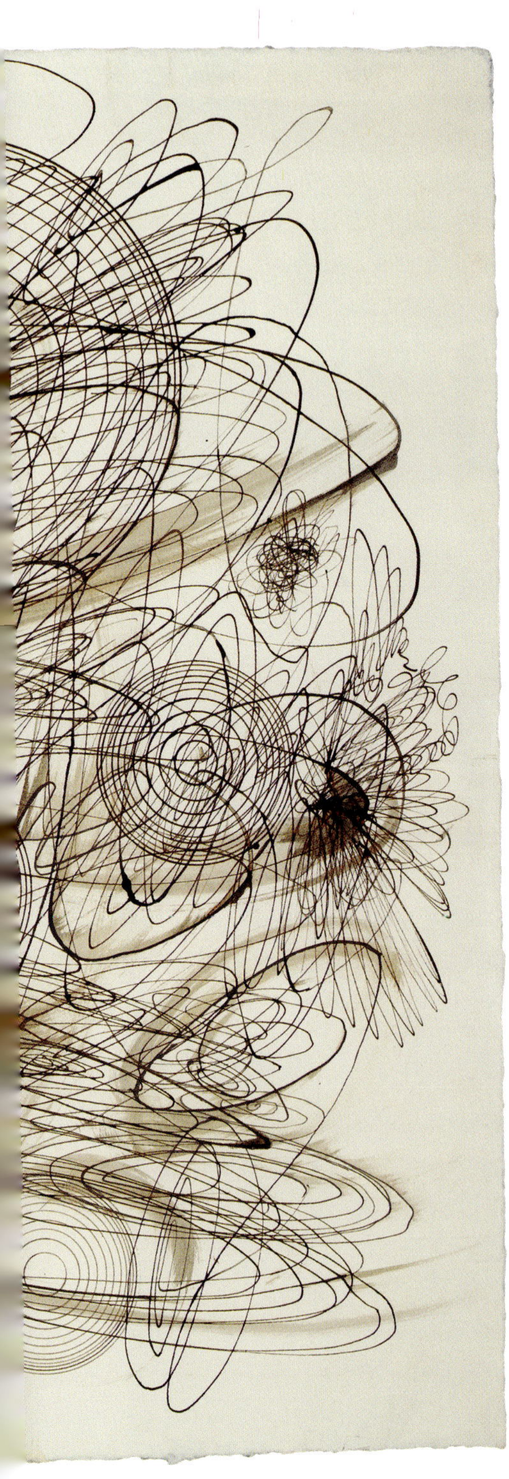

The Theory of Random Orbits, ca. 1985

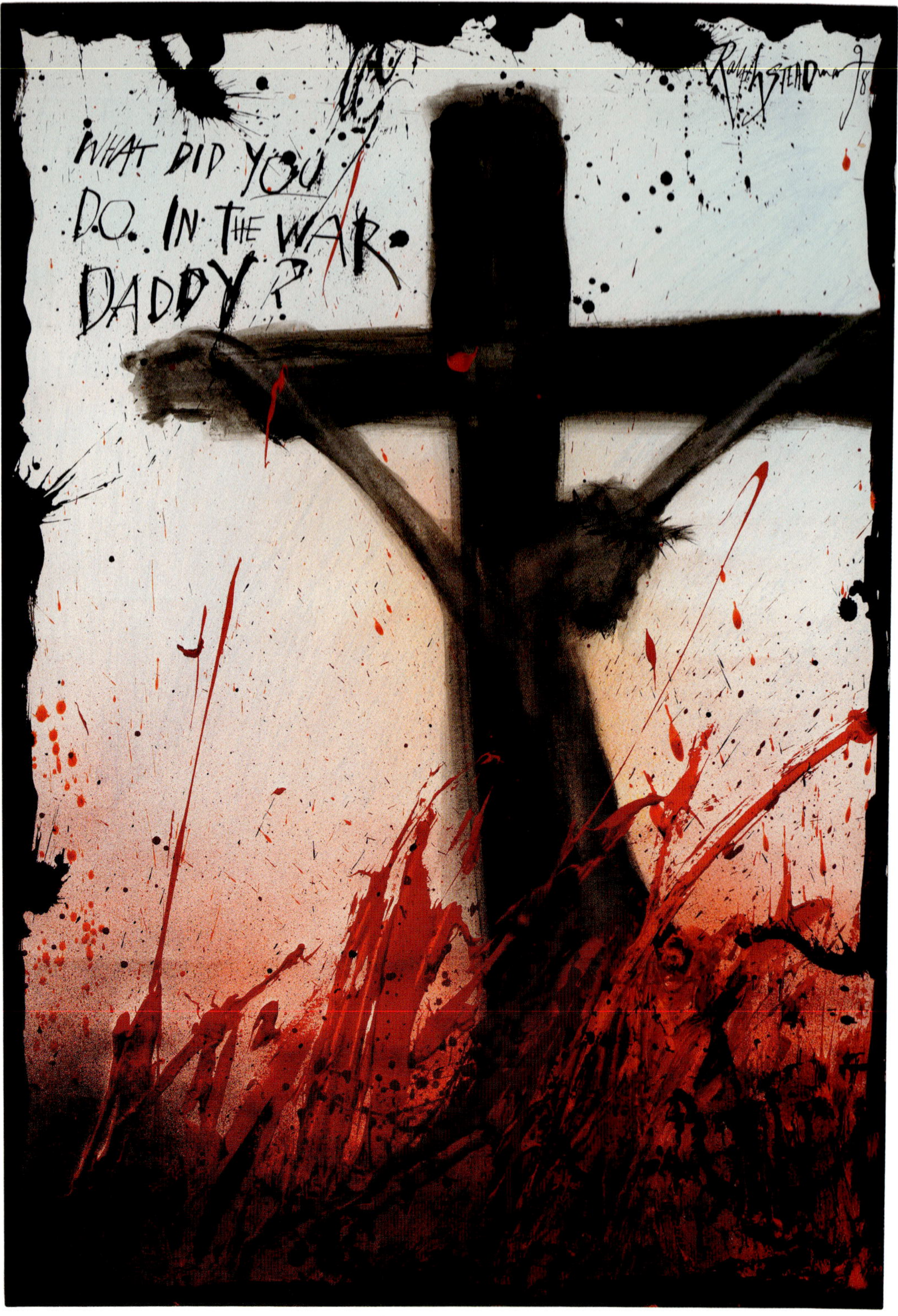

What Did You Do in the War, Daddy? 1998

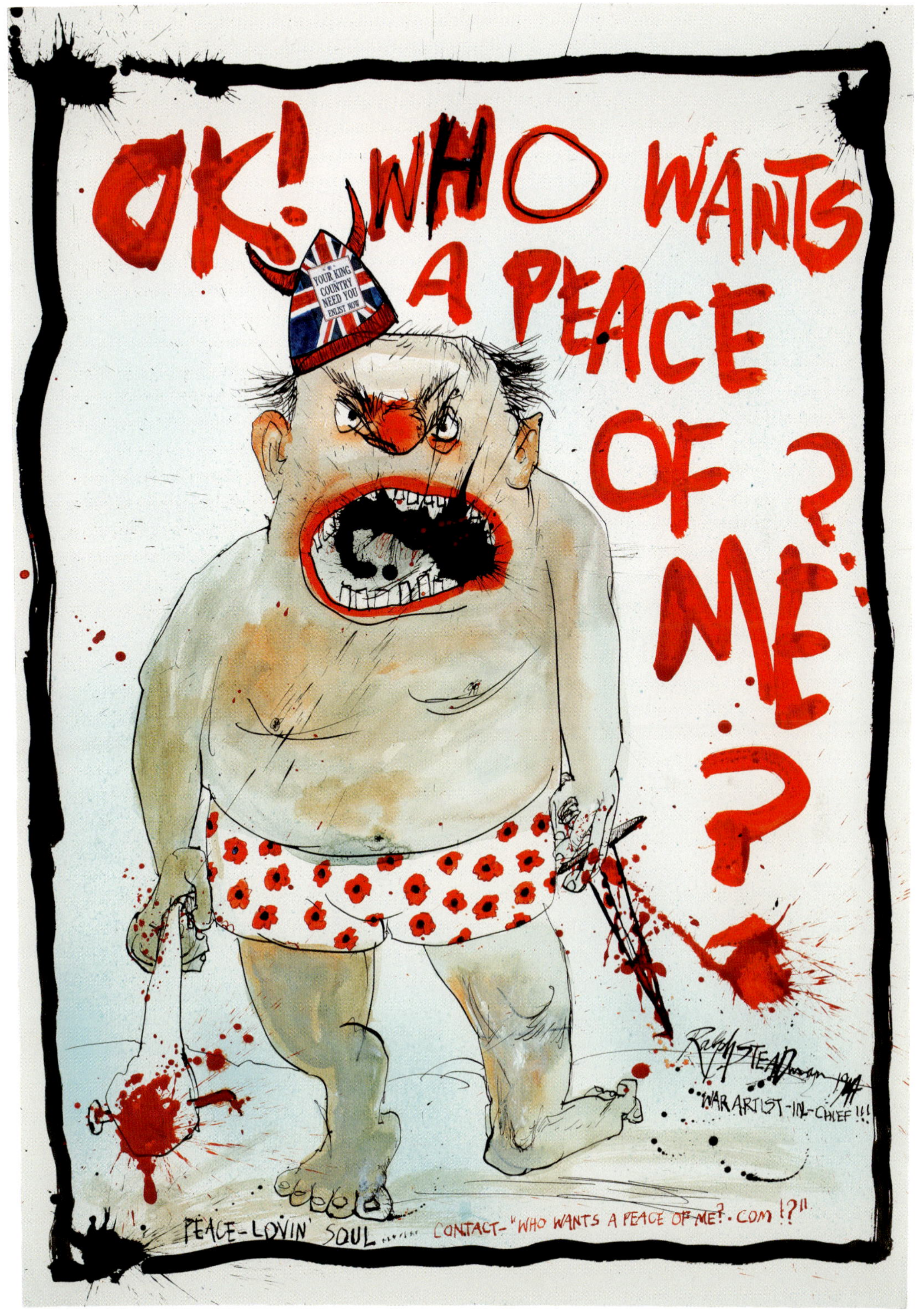

"I don't pencil in first, I go straight in with the ink!" *OK, Who Wants a Piece of Me?* 1994

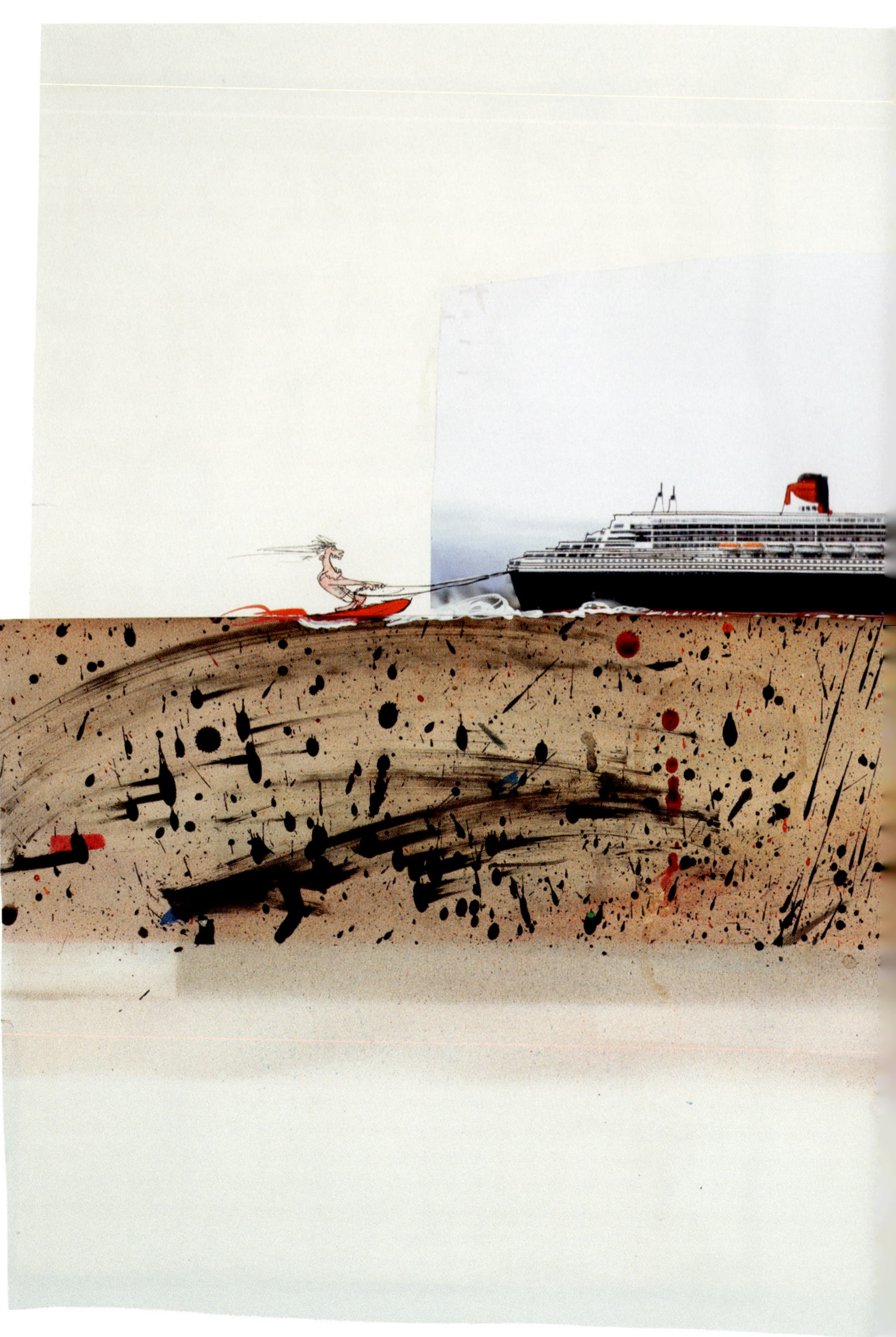

"The sea is a piece of backing paper that would have been on my drawing board to protect it from extra splats and blots."

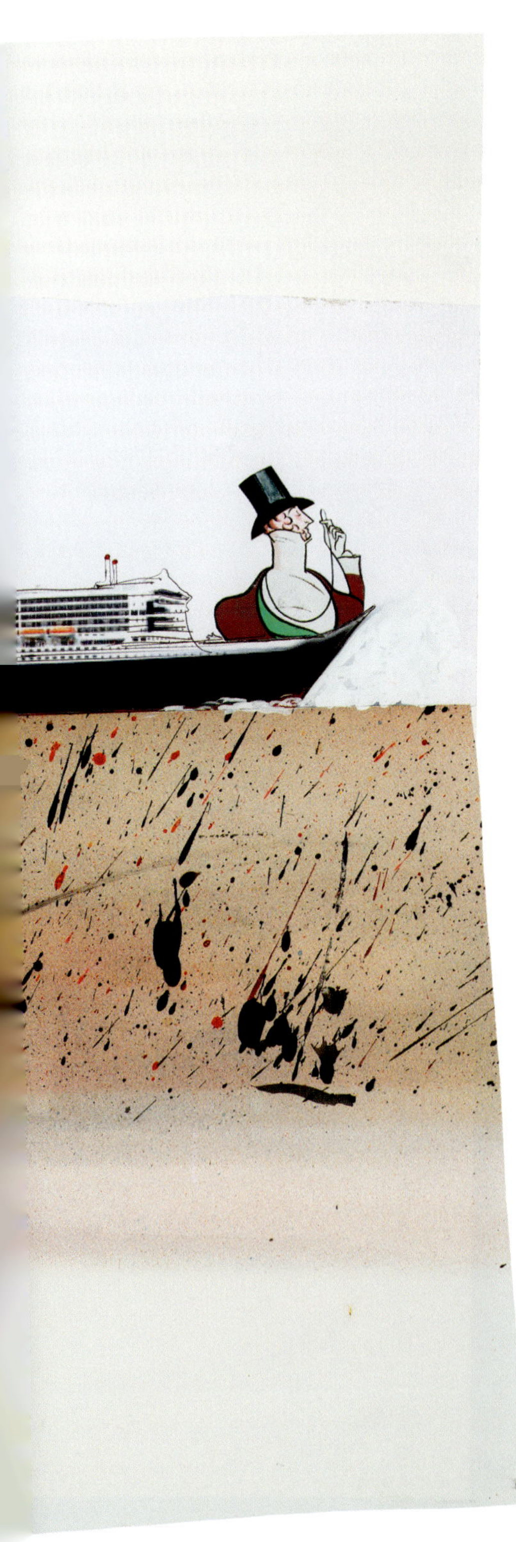

Ocean Going Liner for **The New Yorker**, *ca. 1994*

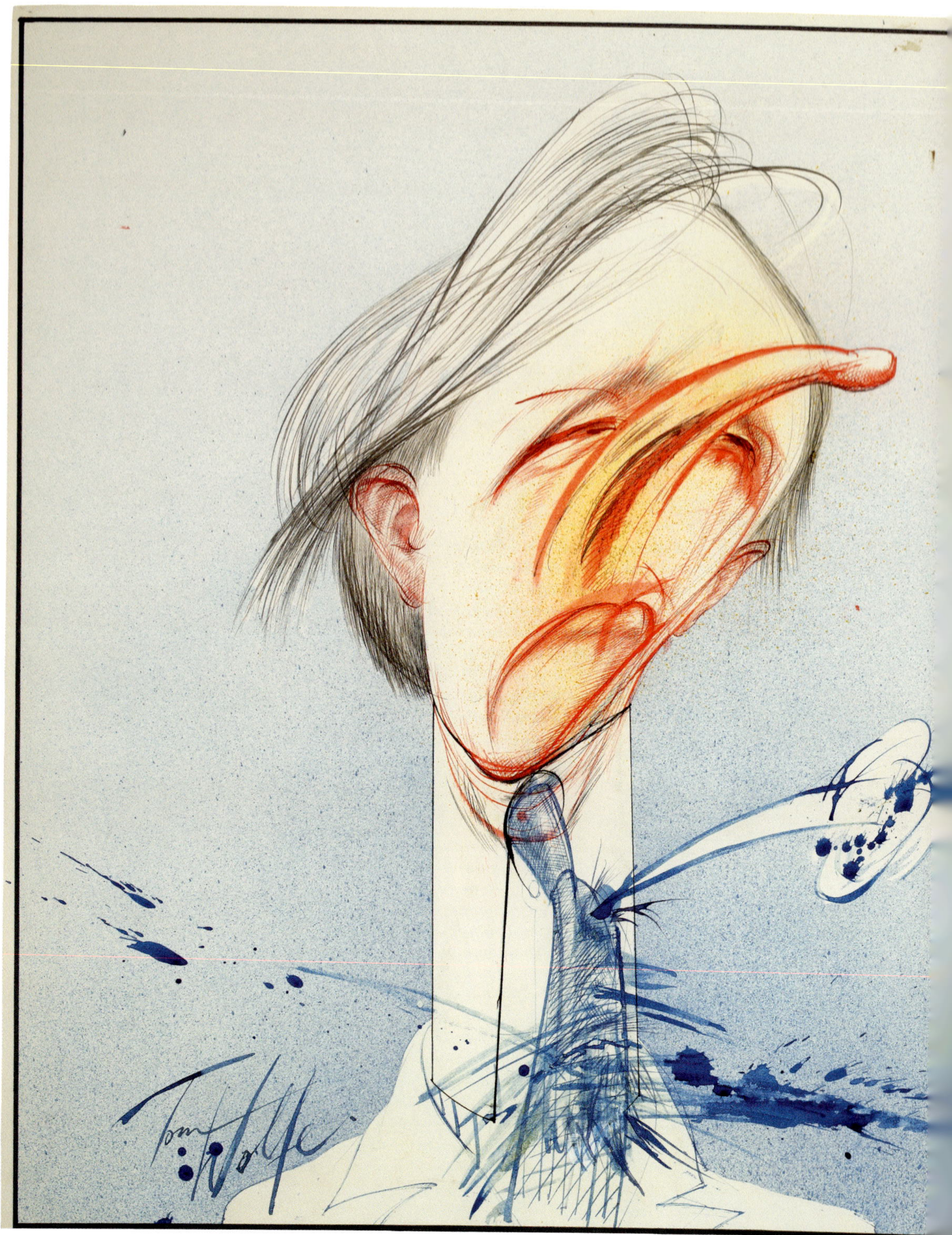

Tom Wolfe Portrait, 1980

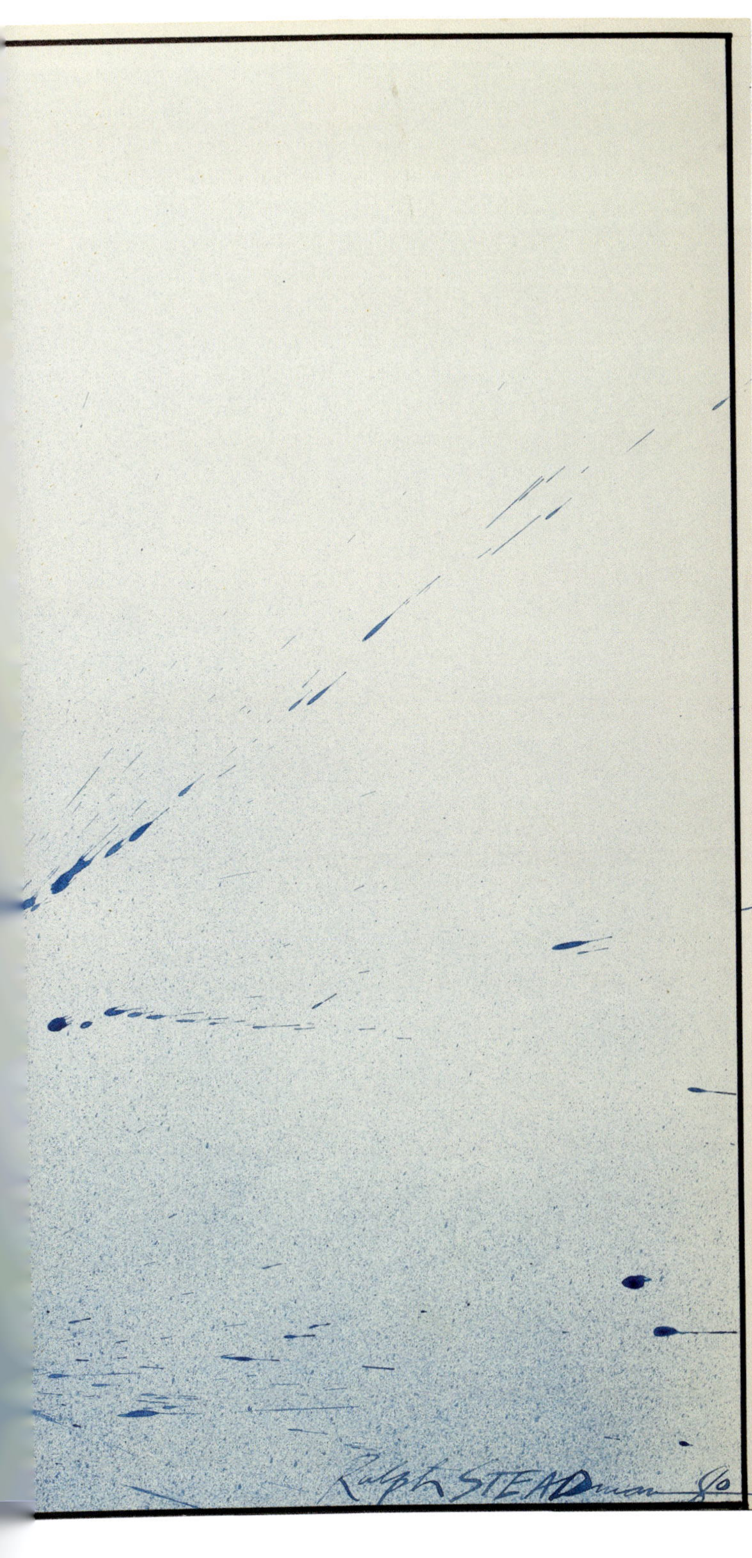

Ralph STEADman 80

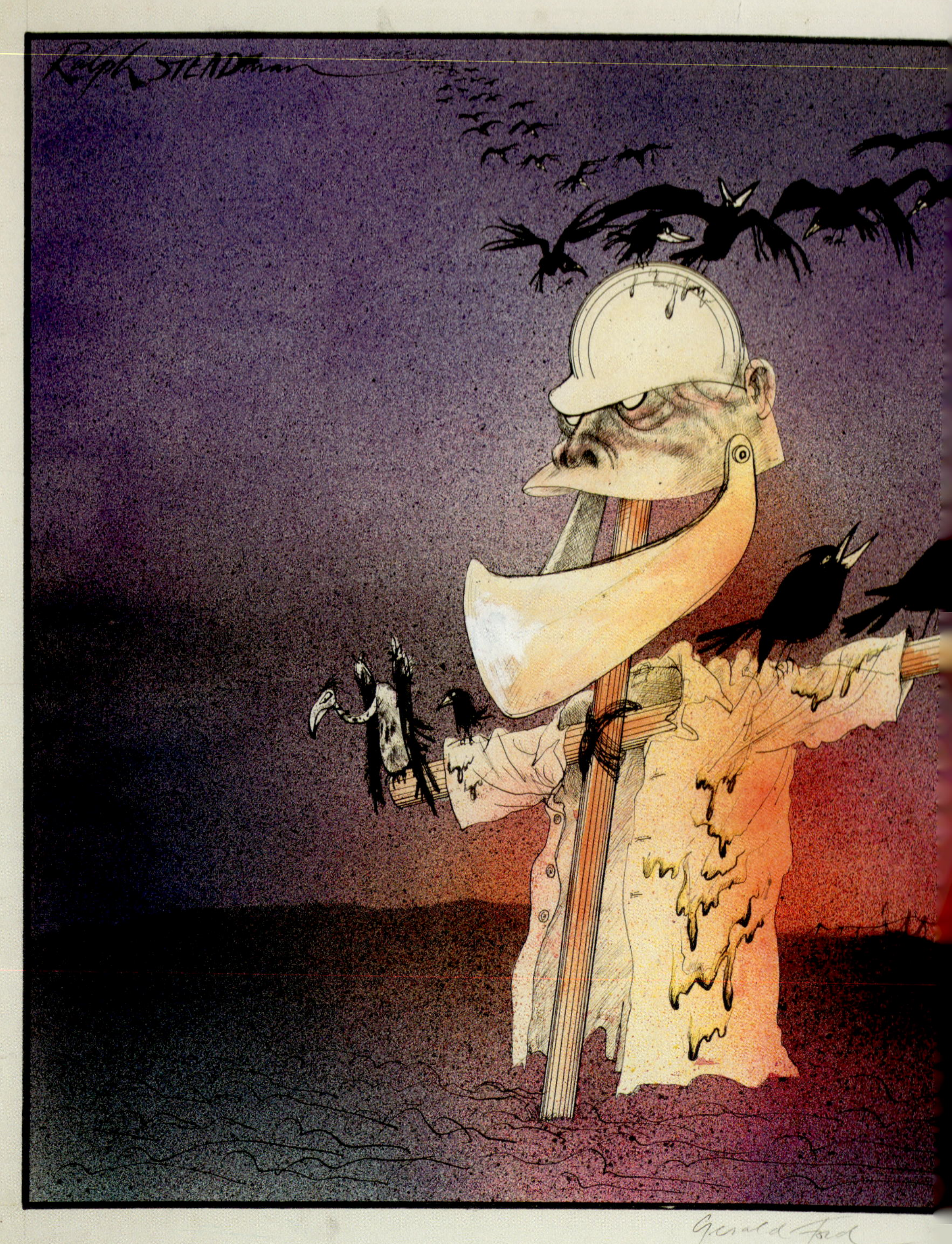

Political Scarecrow, Hague, ca. 1976

"I use an atomiser to get that fine splatter effect. There is still some randomness to it."

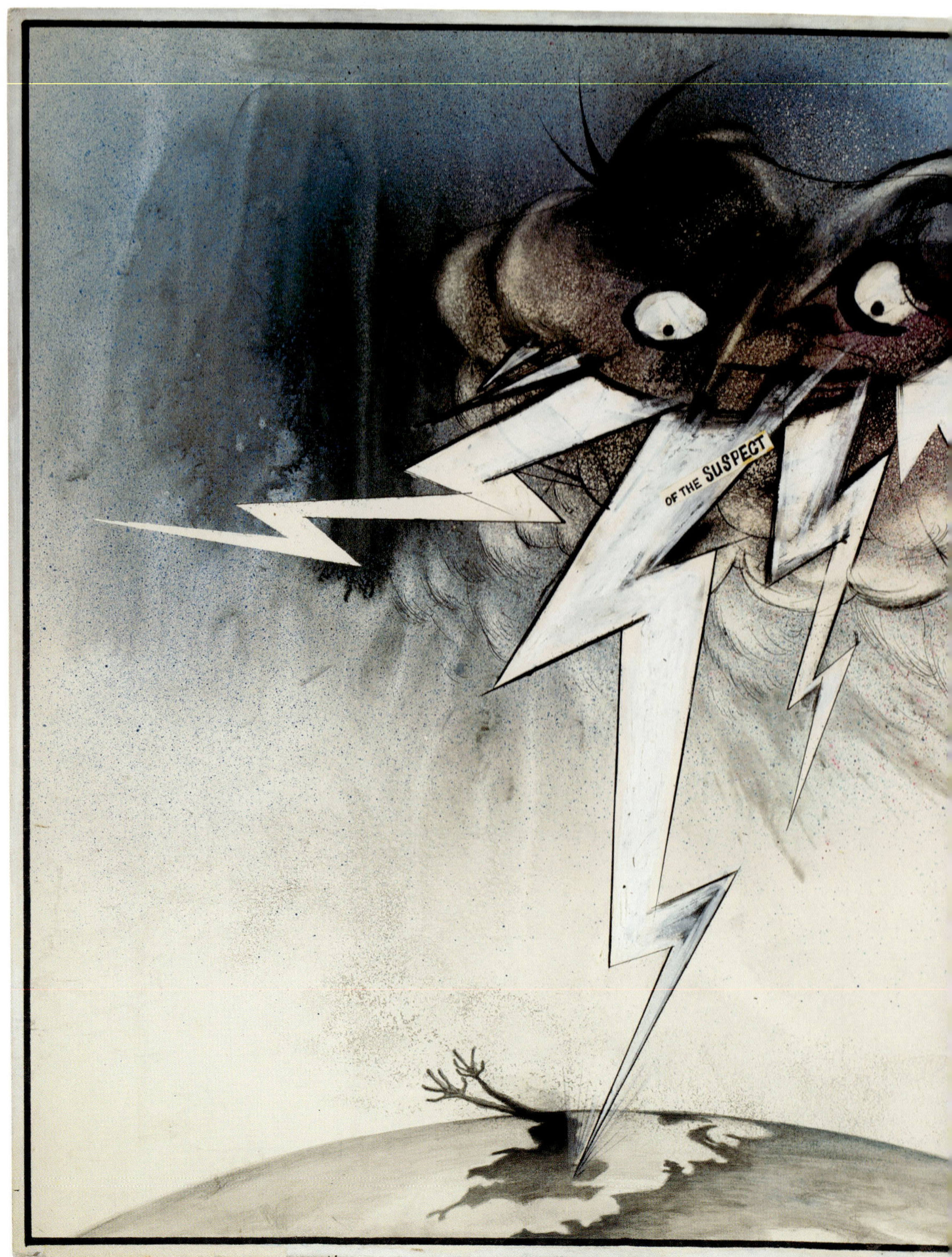

"I think the UK has always felt itself apart from the EU, which it is geographically, but I am not sure we ever fully committed."

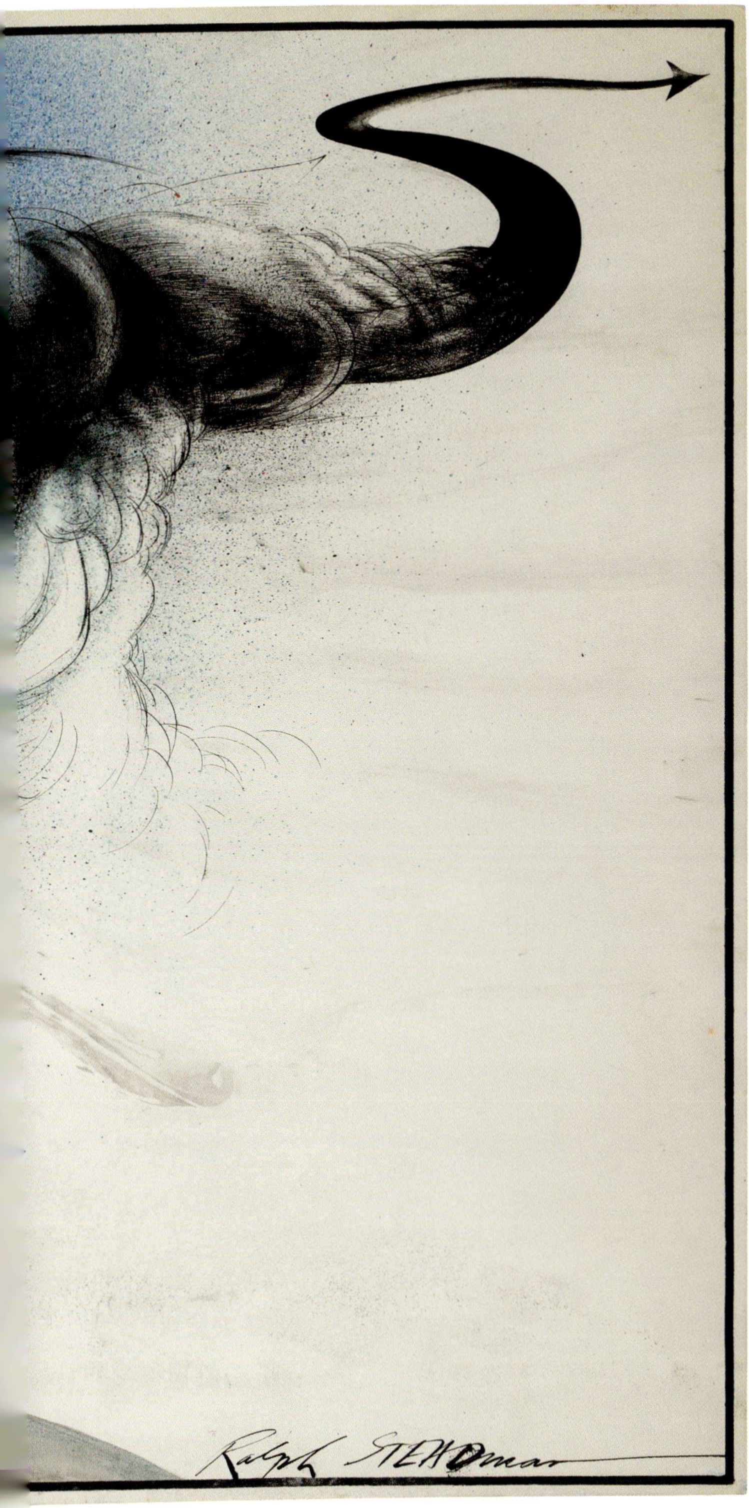

The United Kingdom, Un-Uniting, ca. 1980

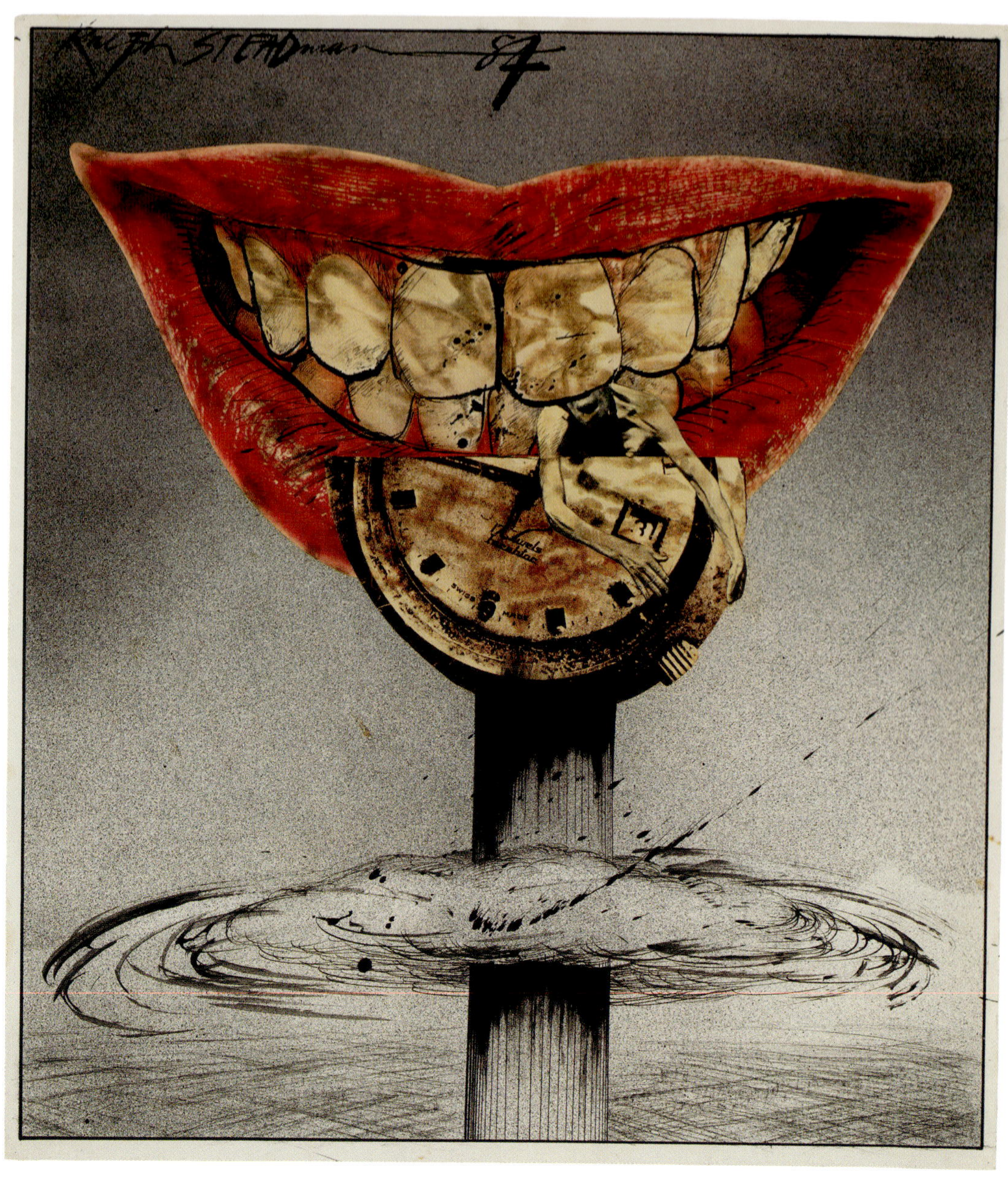

Nuclear Smile, 1984 "I often use collage in my work: sometimes from old magazines, sometimes from old anatomical and medical books, and sometimes from old drawings of machinery."

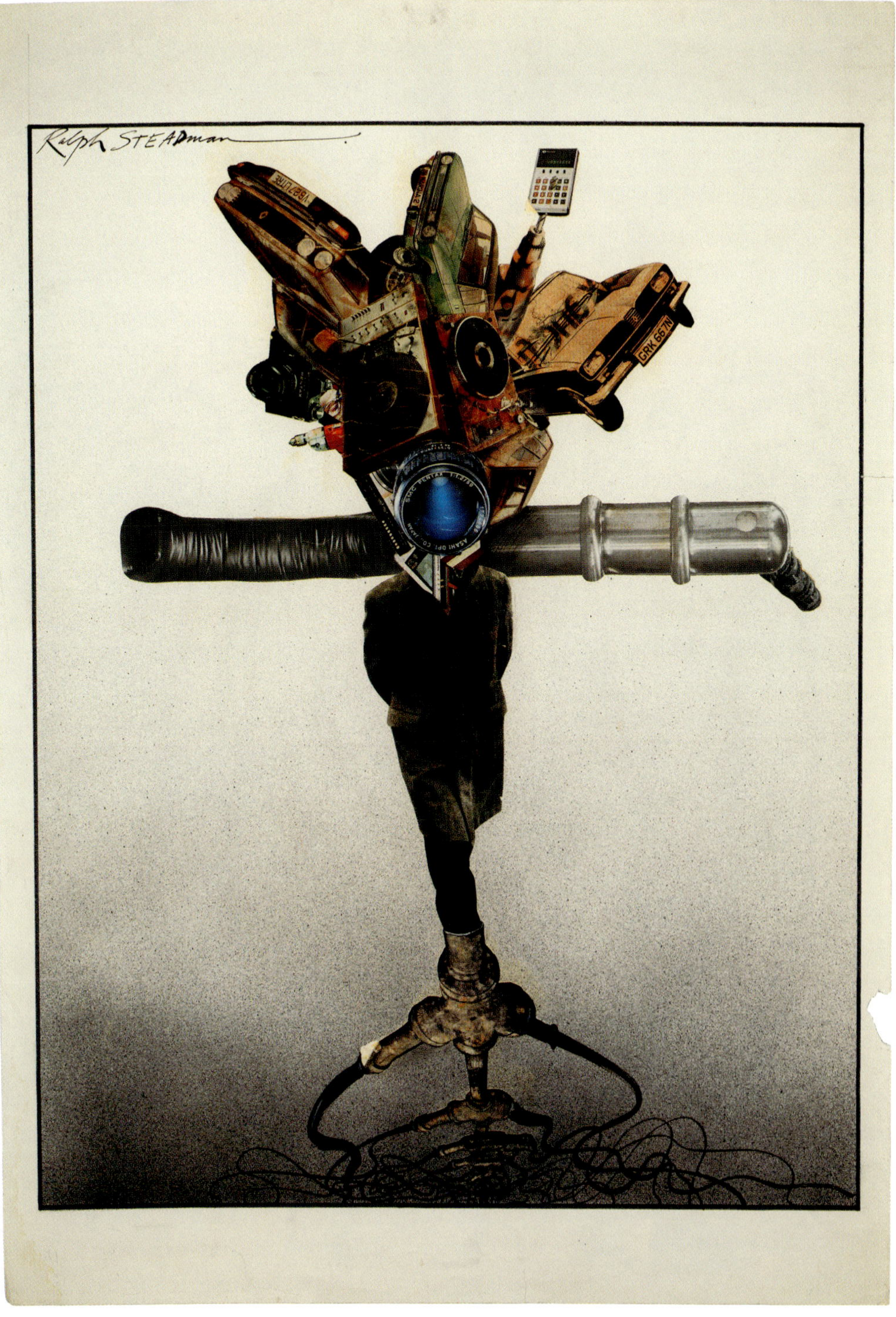

Ralph STEADman

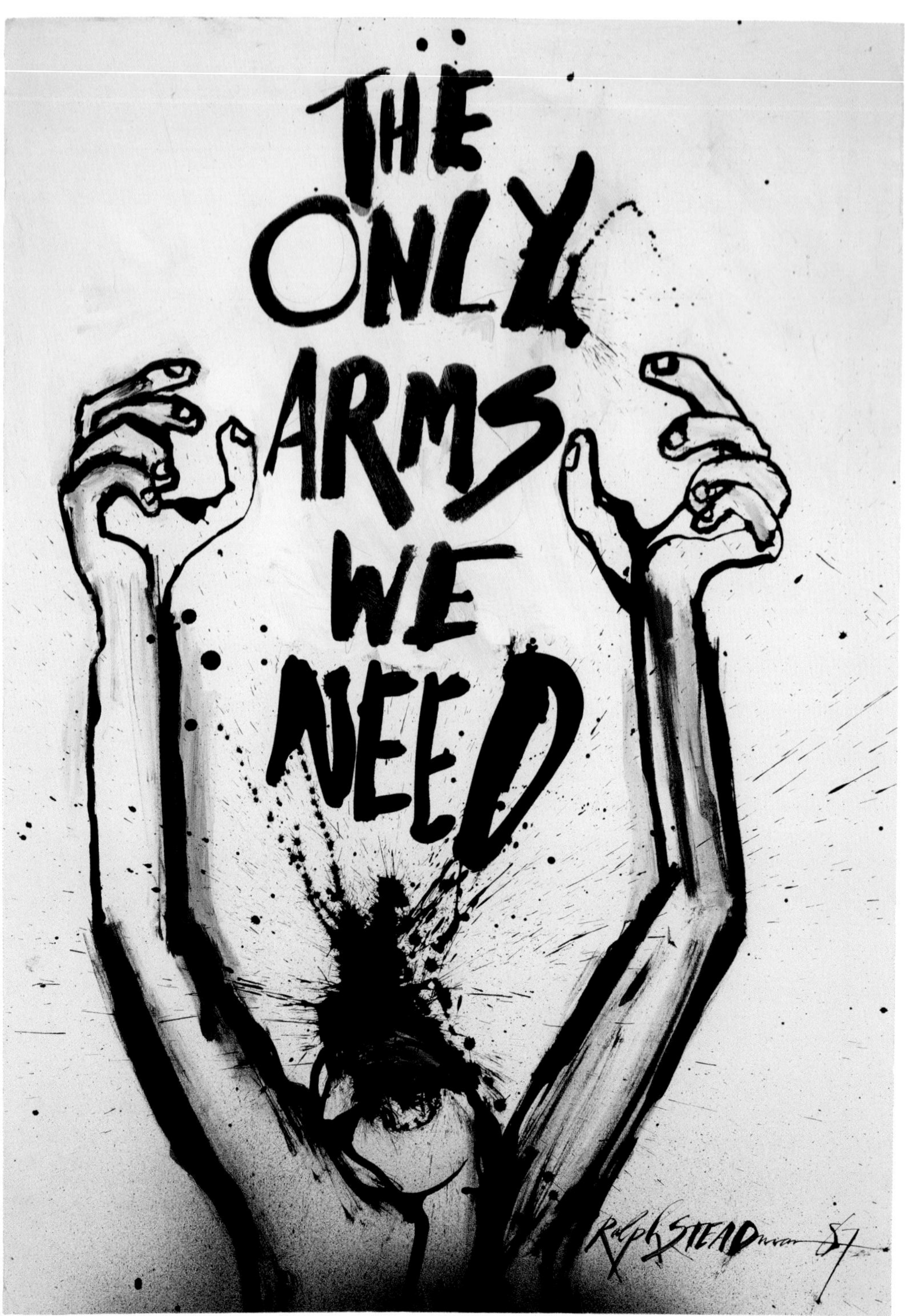

Anti-War Poster, *The Only Arms We Need*, 1987

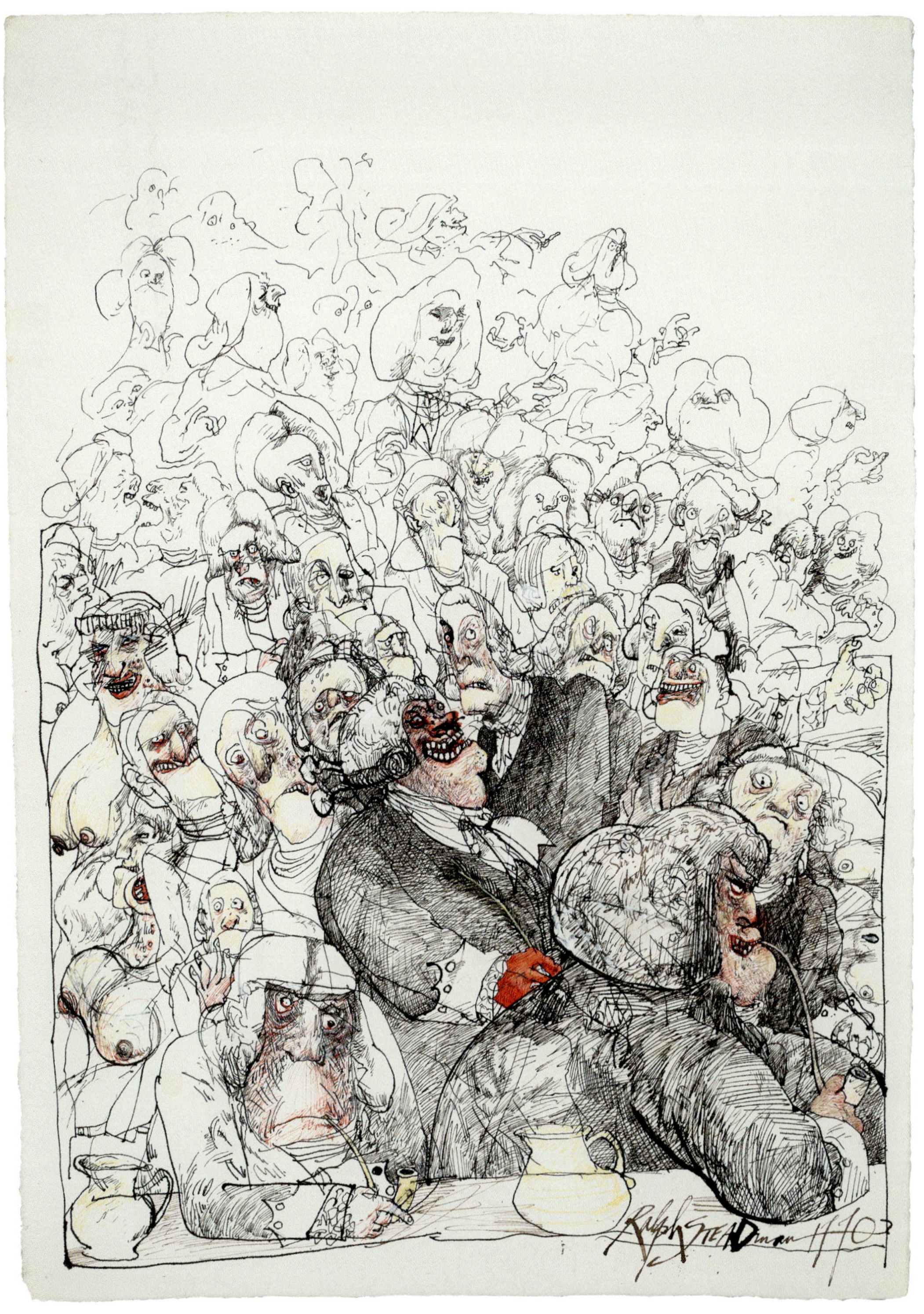

18th Century Legal, Samuel Pepys, ca. 1990

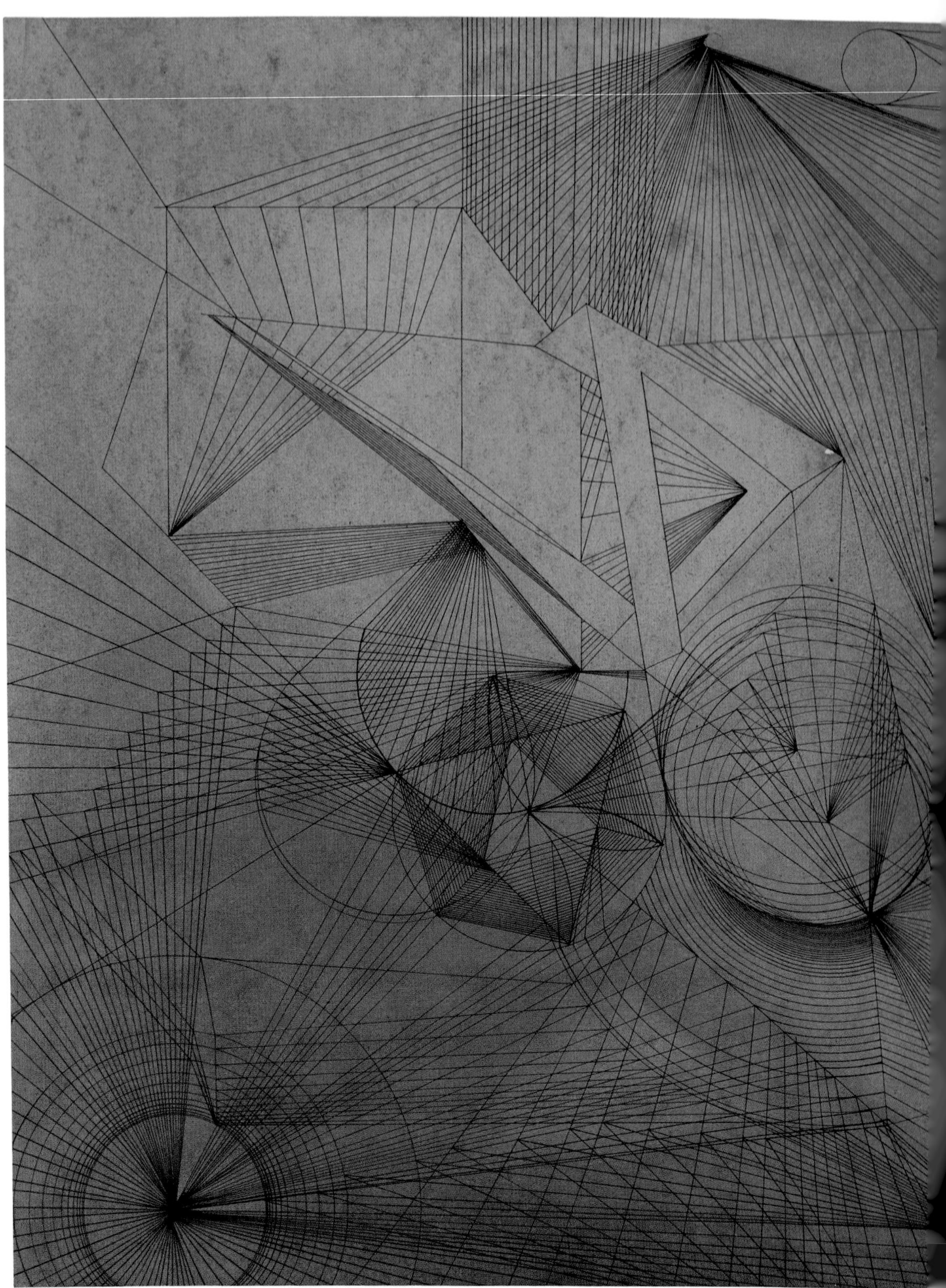

"I always carried what I learnt draughting with me. The pure straight lines and precision still fascinate, but I like to contrast them with chaos."

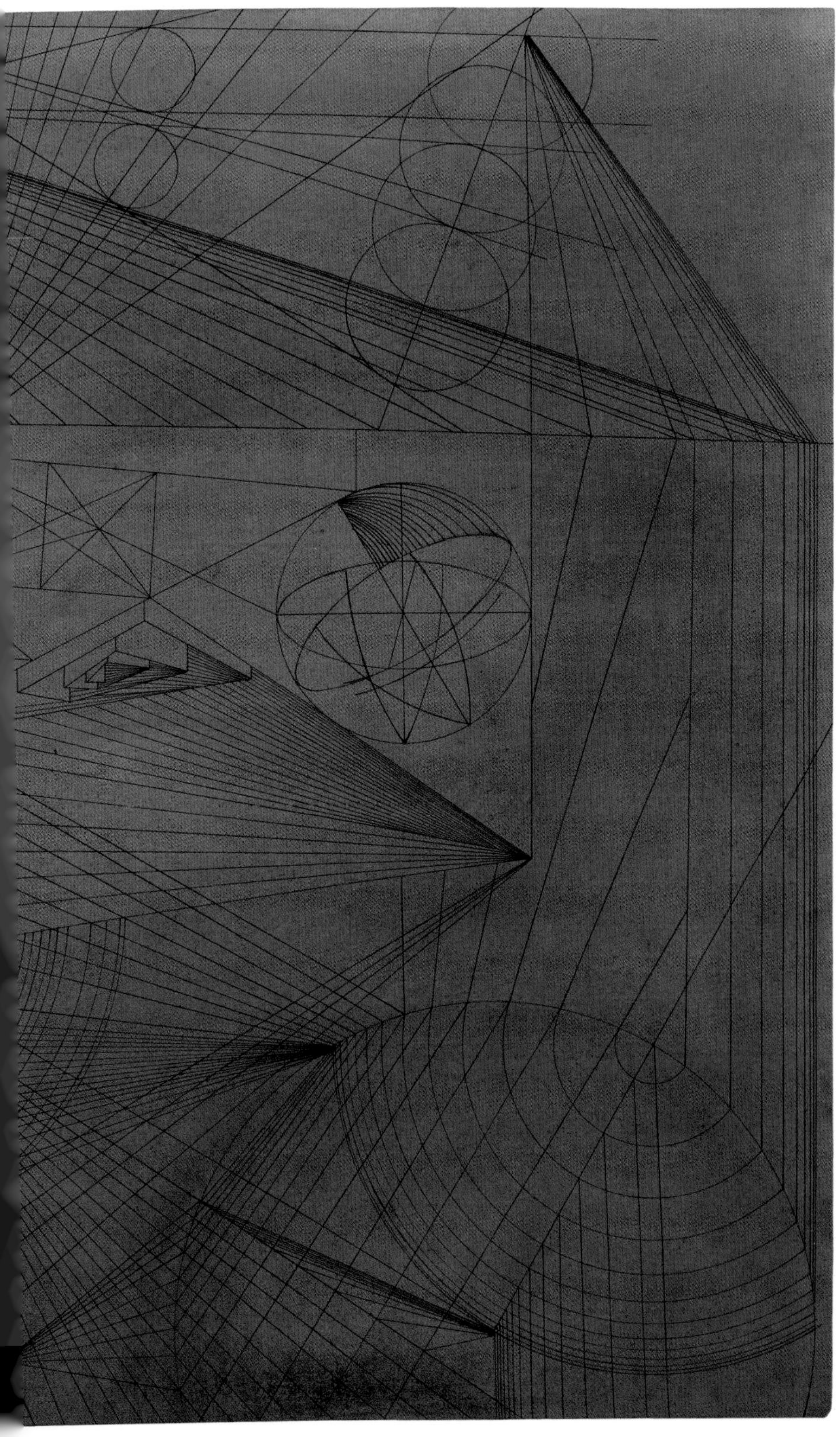

*End Papers from **The Big I Am**, 1995*

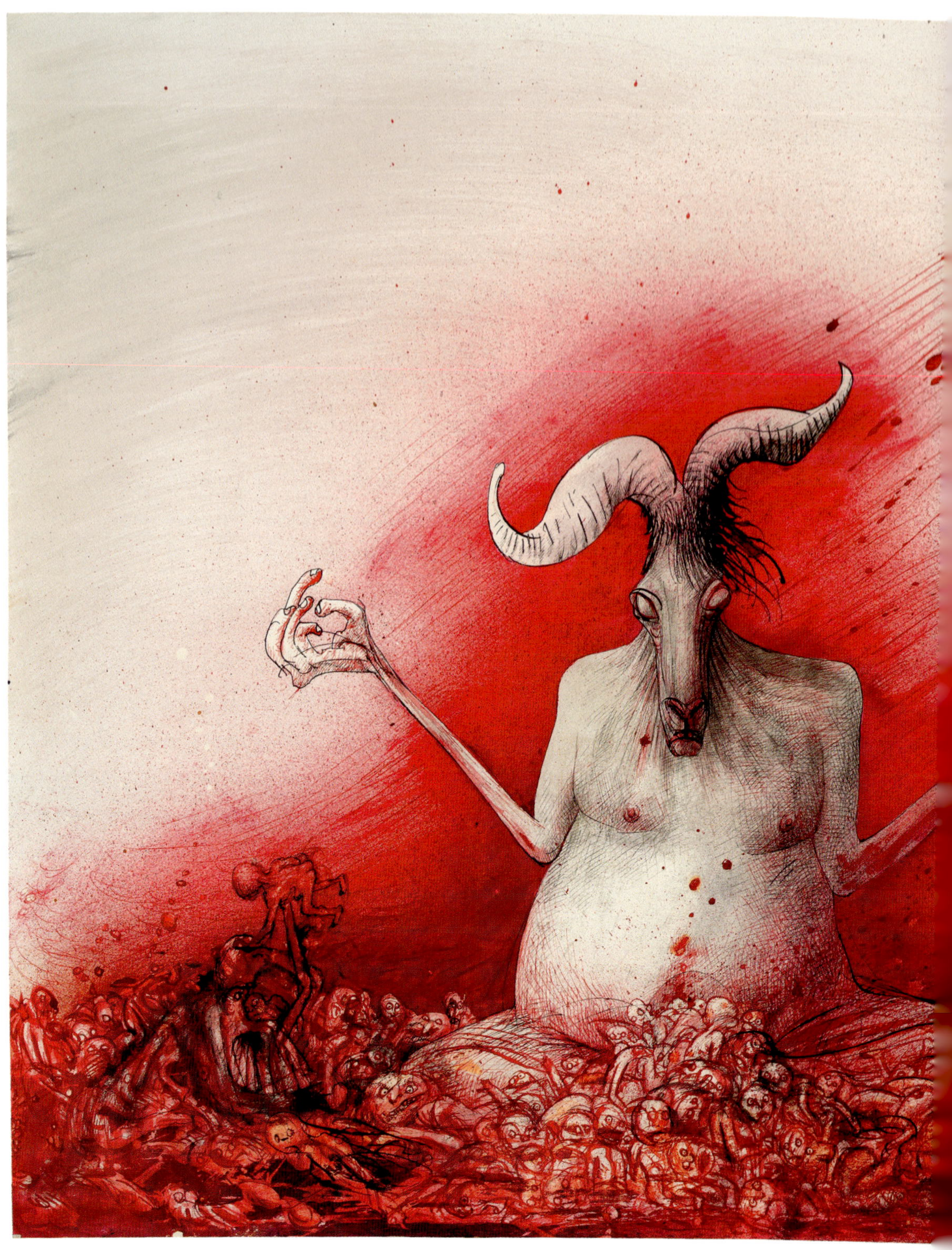

*The Devil from **The Big I Am**, 1995*

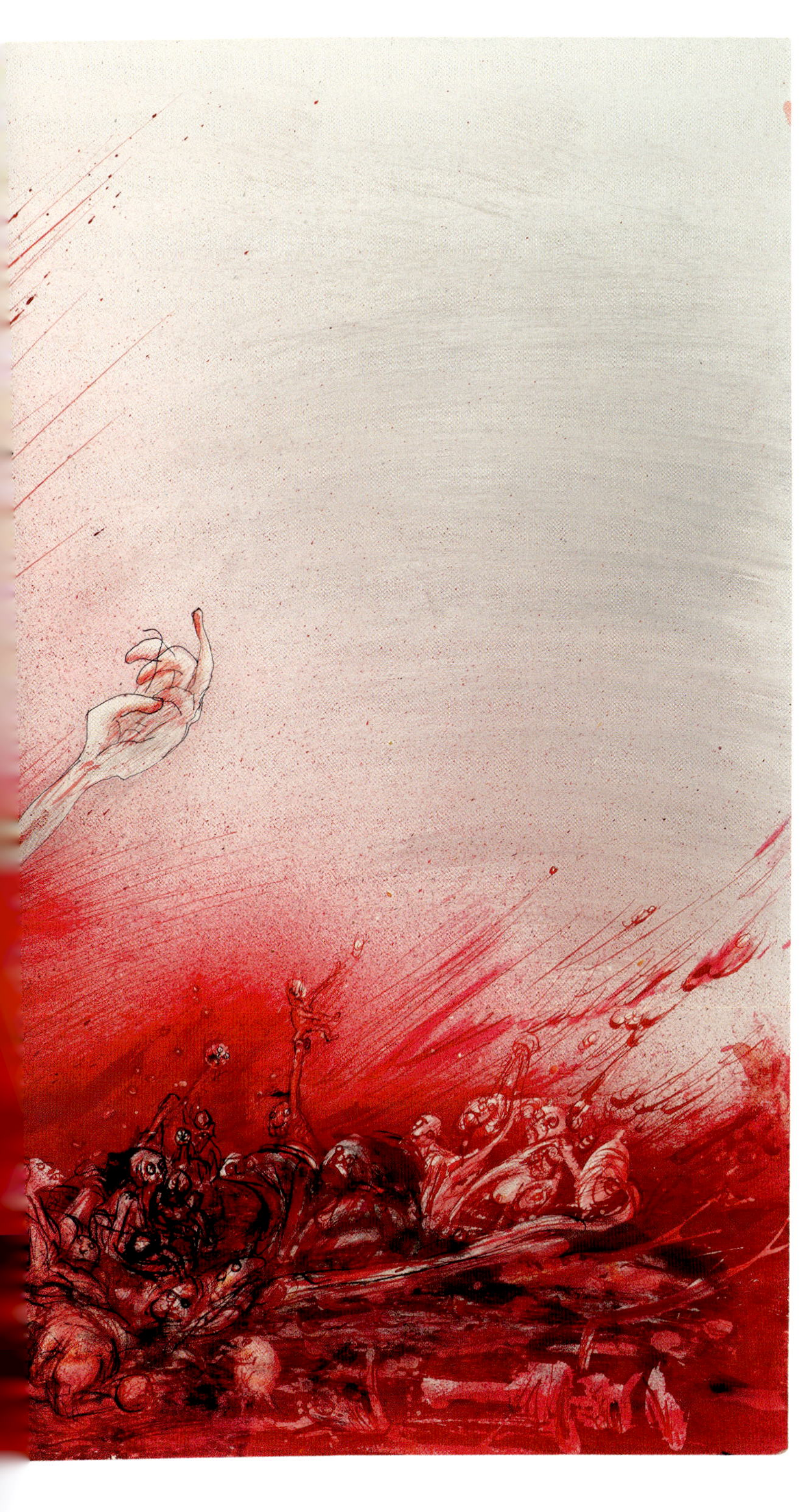

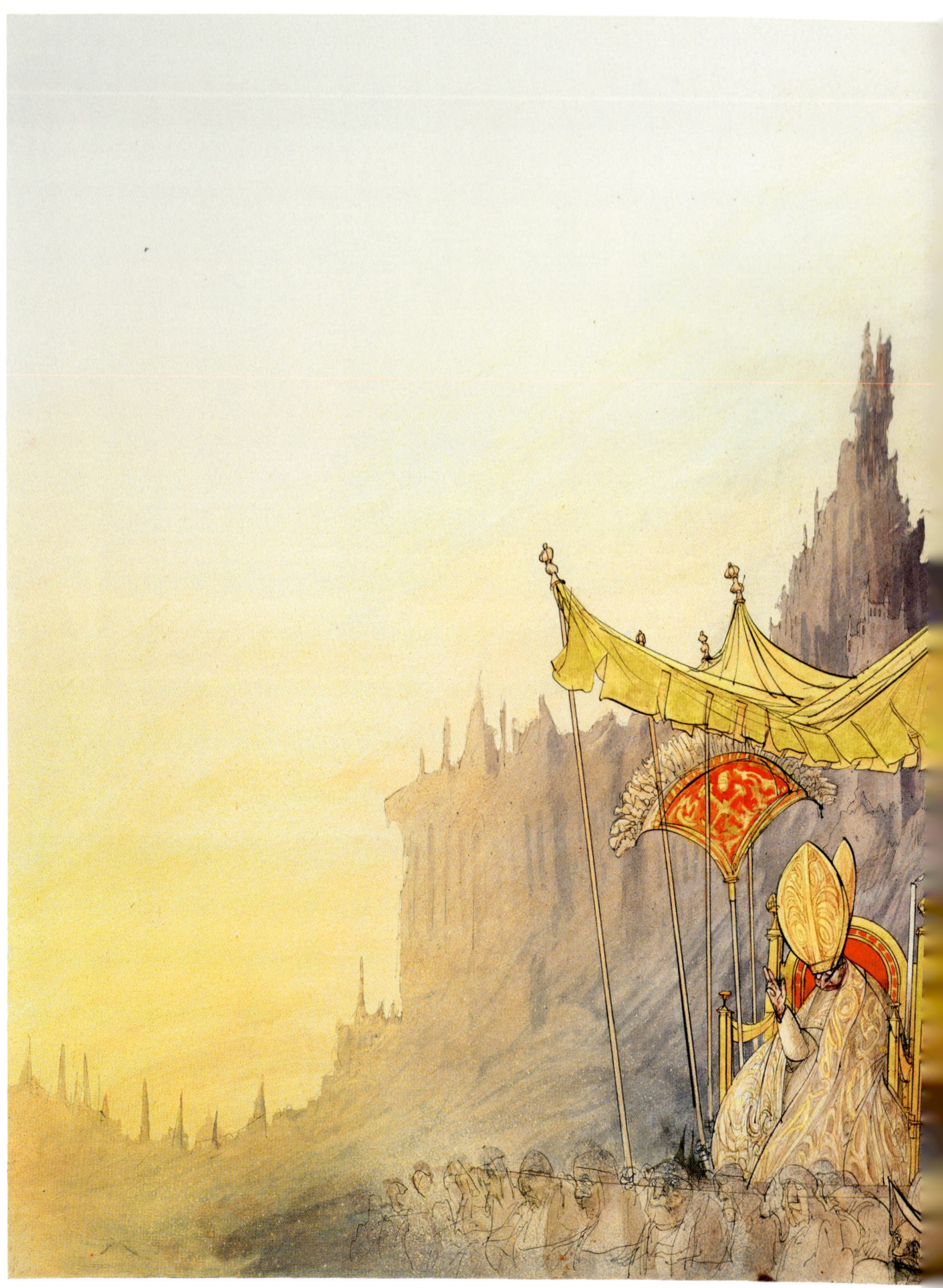

Religious Authority from **The Big I Am**, *1995*

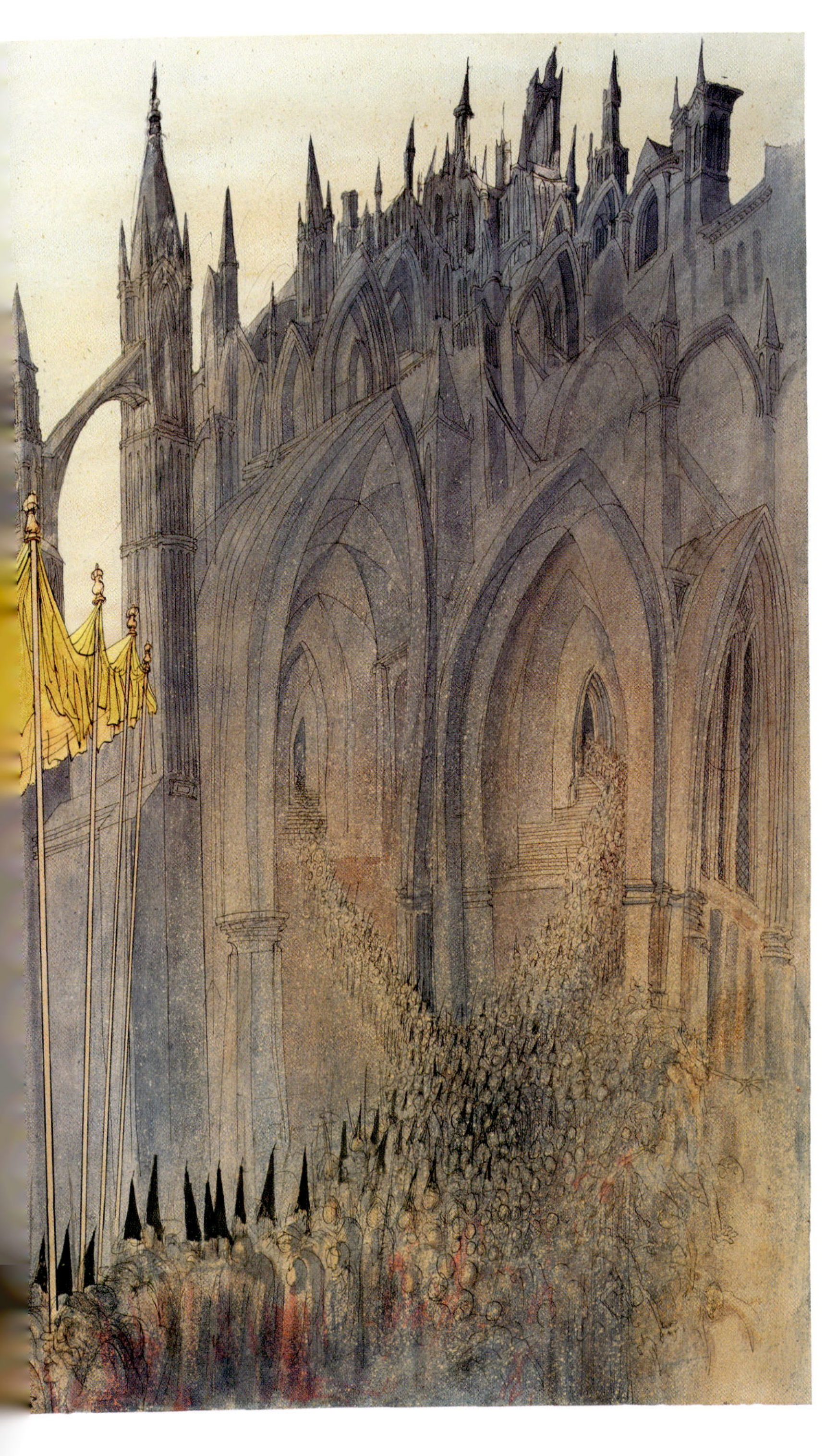

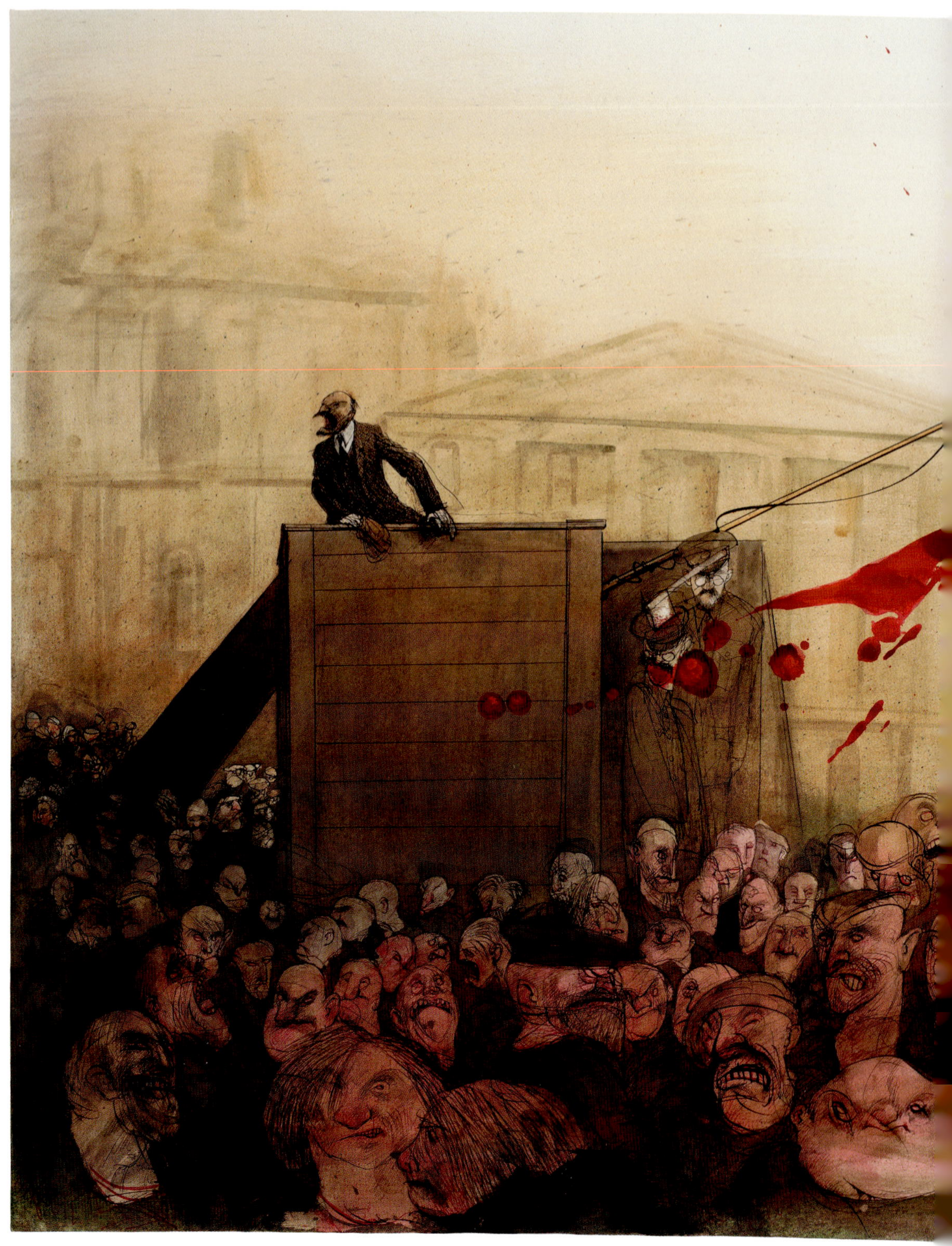

The Birth of Communism from **The Big I Am**, 1995

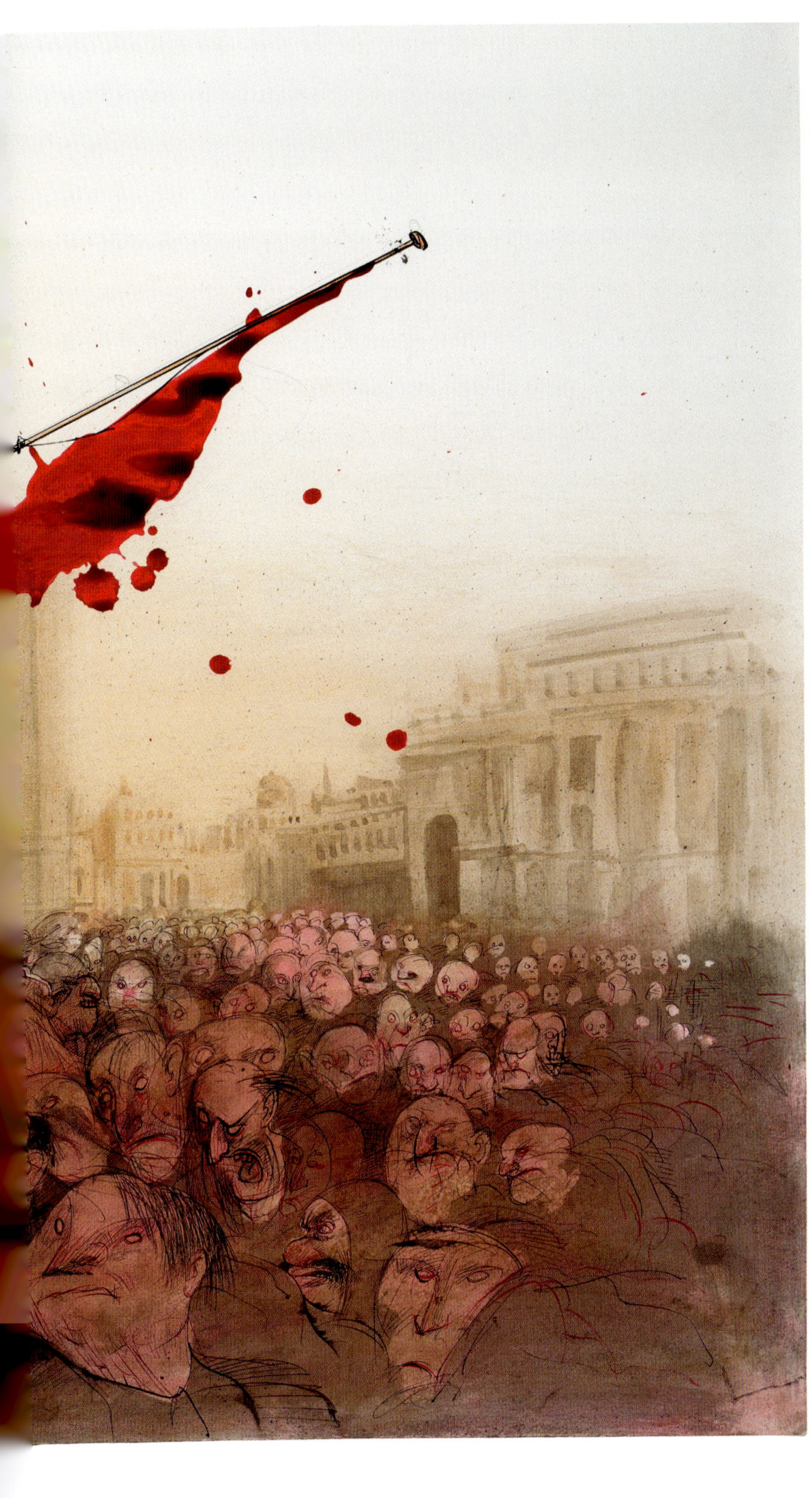

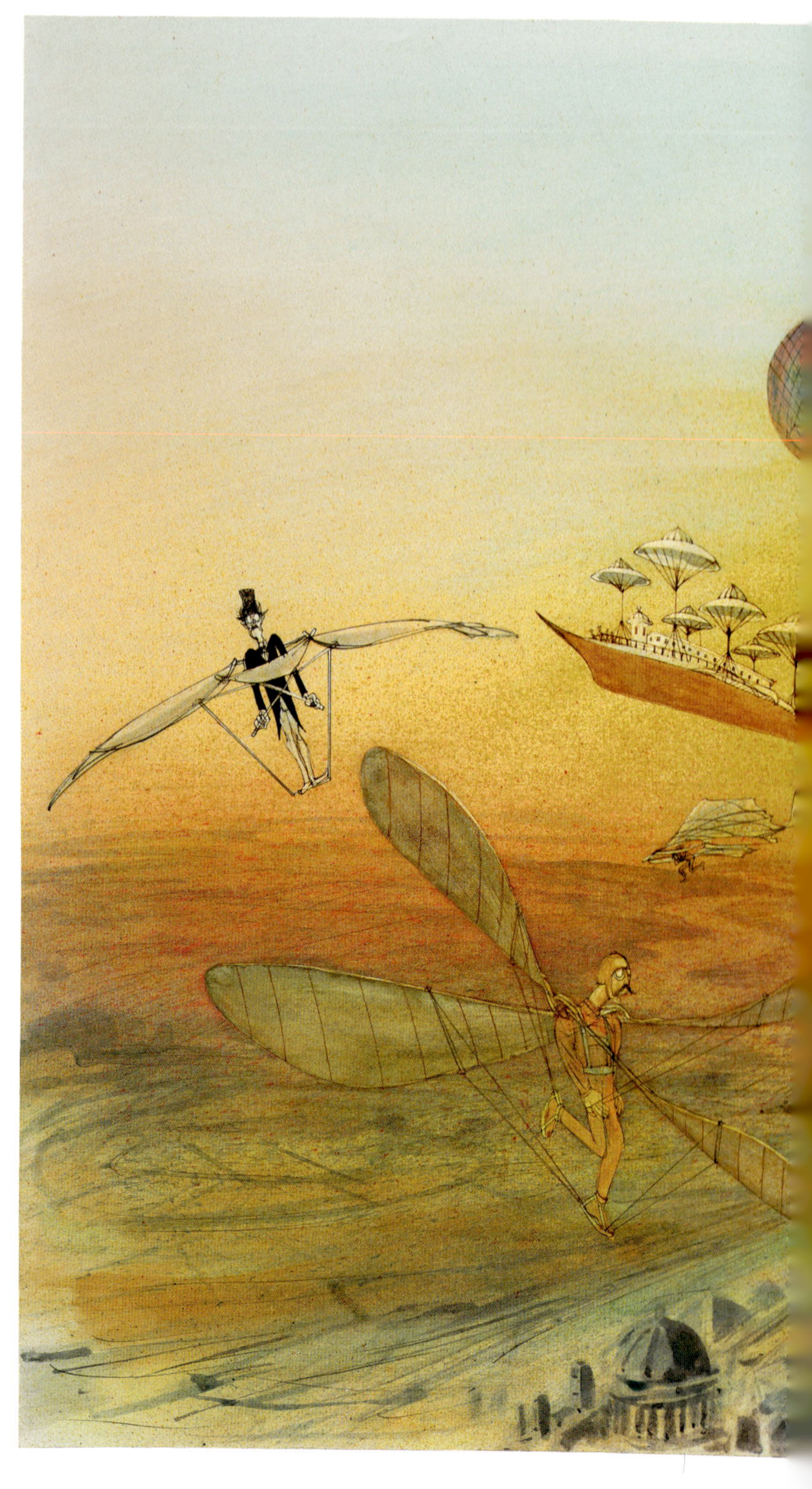

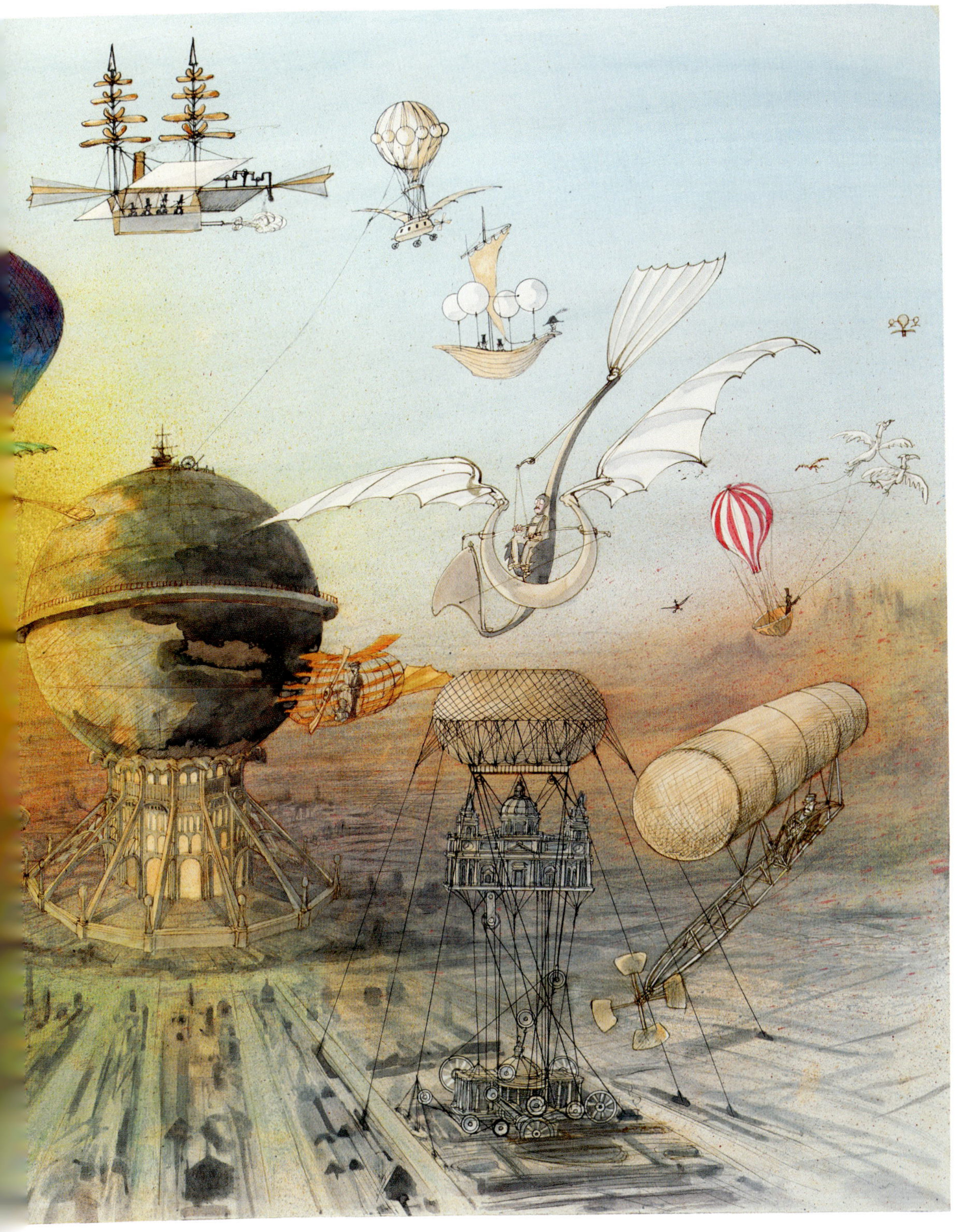

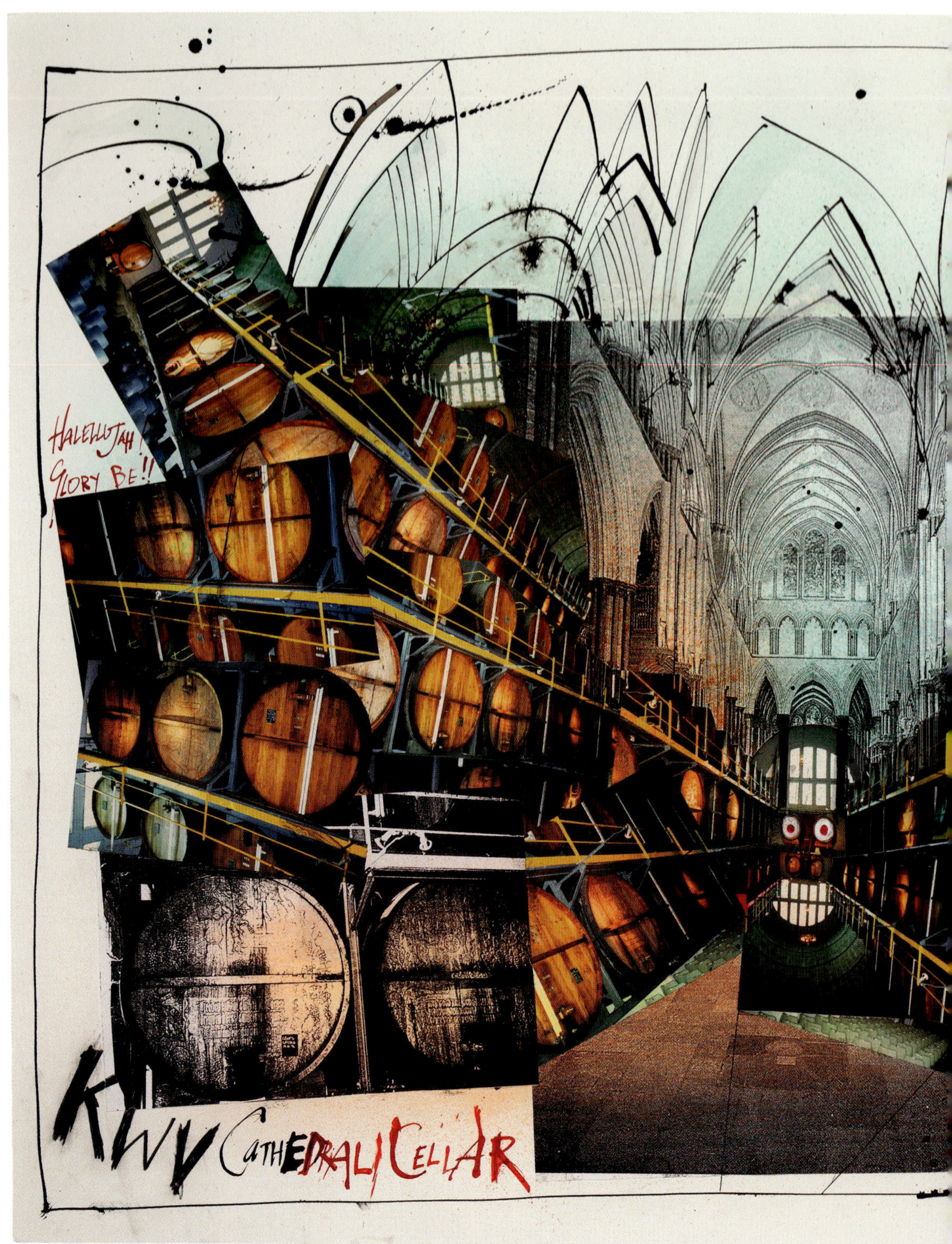

"That was an unsettling trip for Oddbins, the way the wealth was so divided between the races."

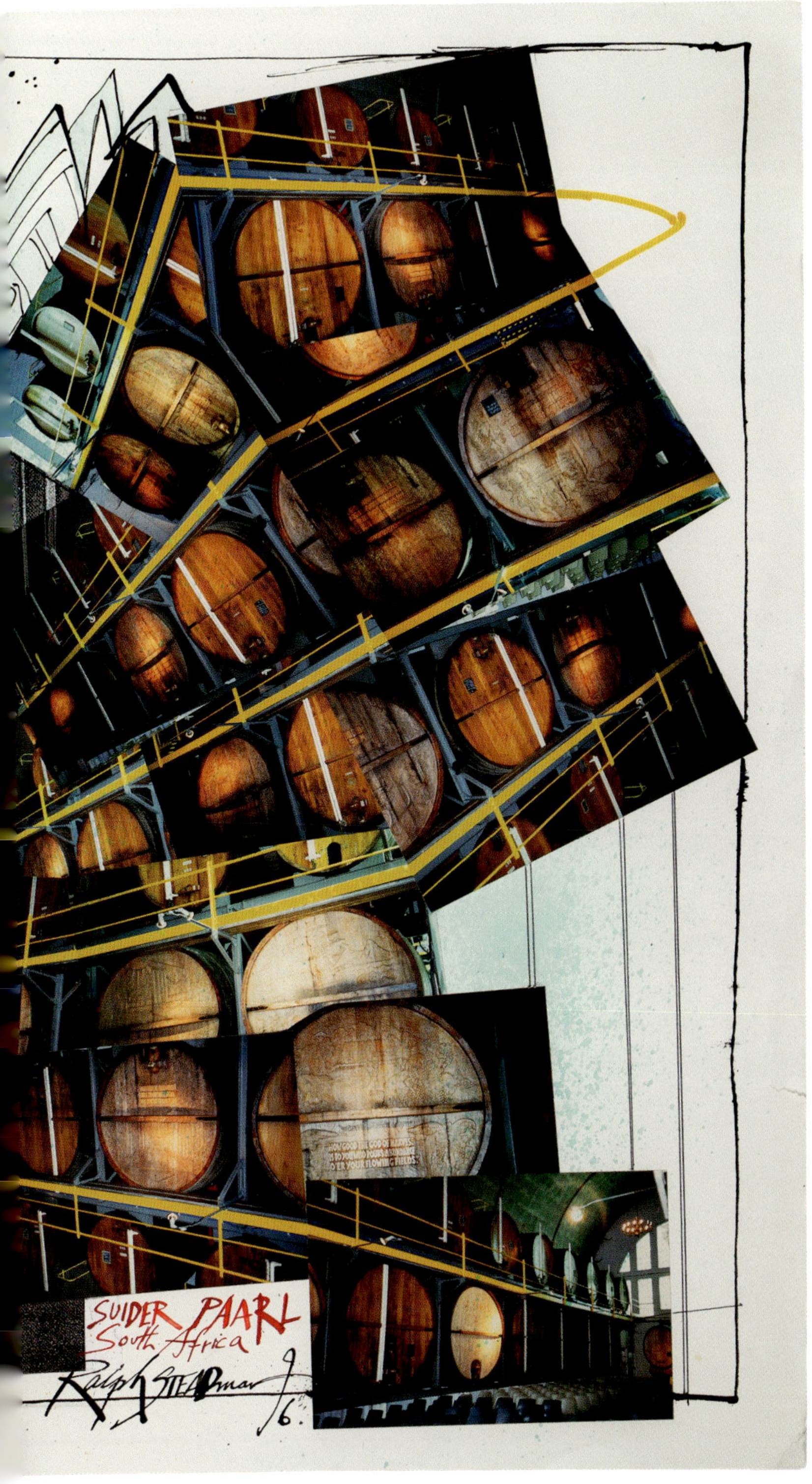

South African Wine Cellar, 1996

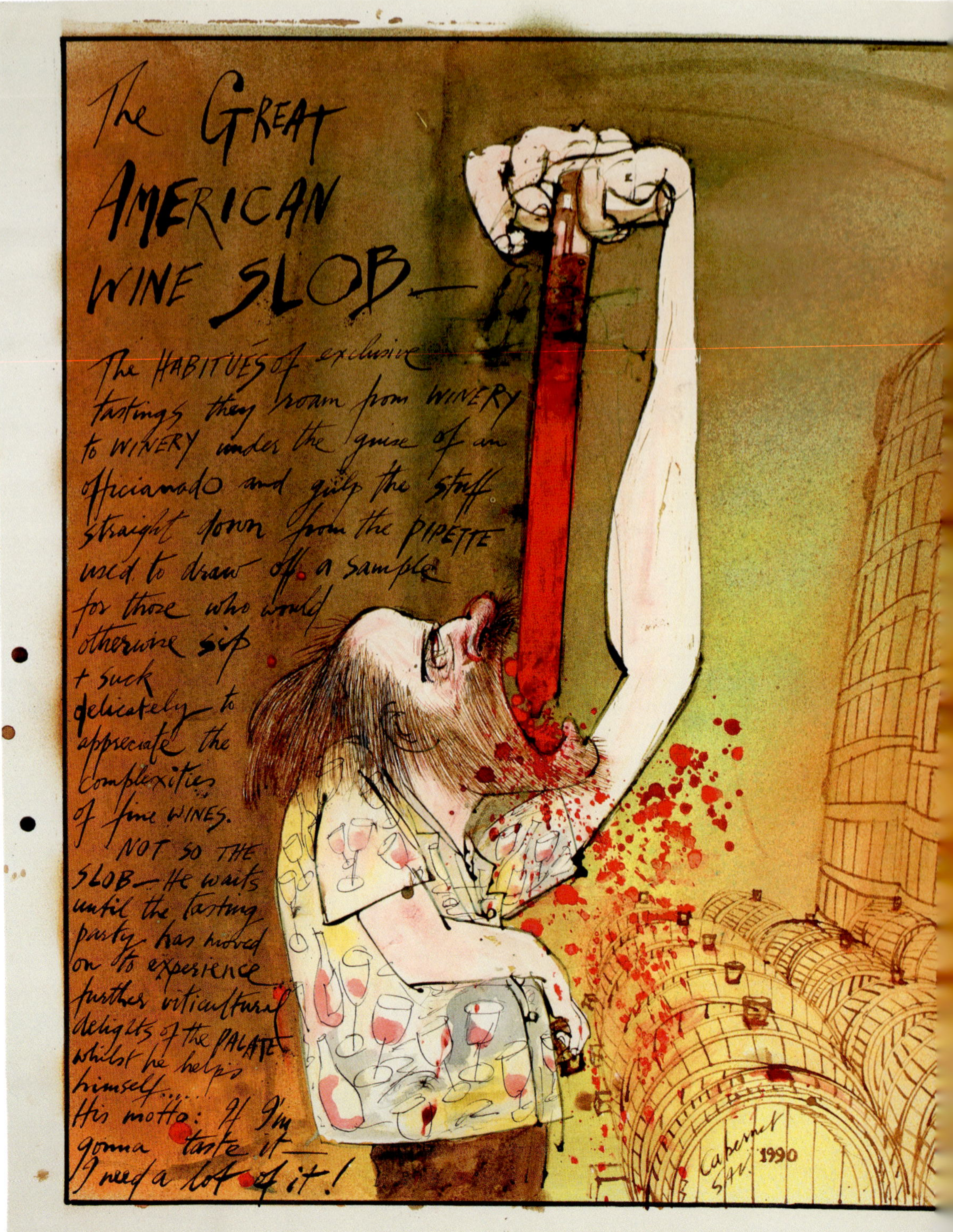

The Great American Wine Slob, 1990

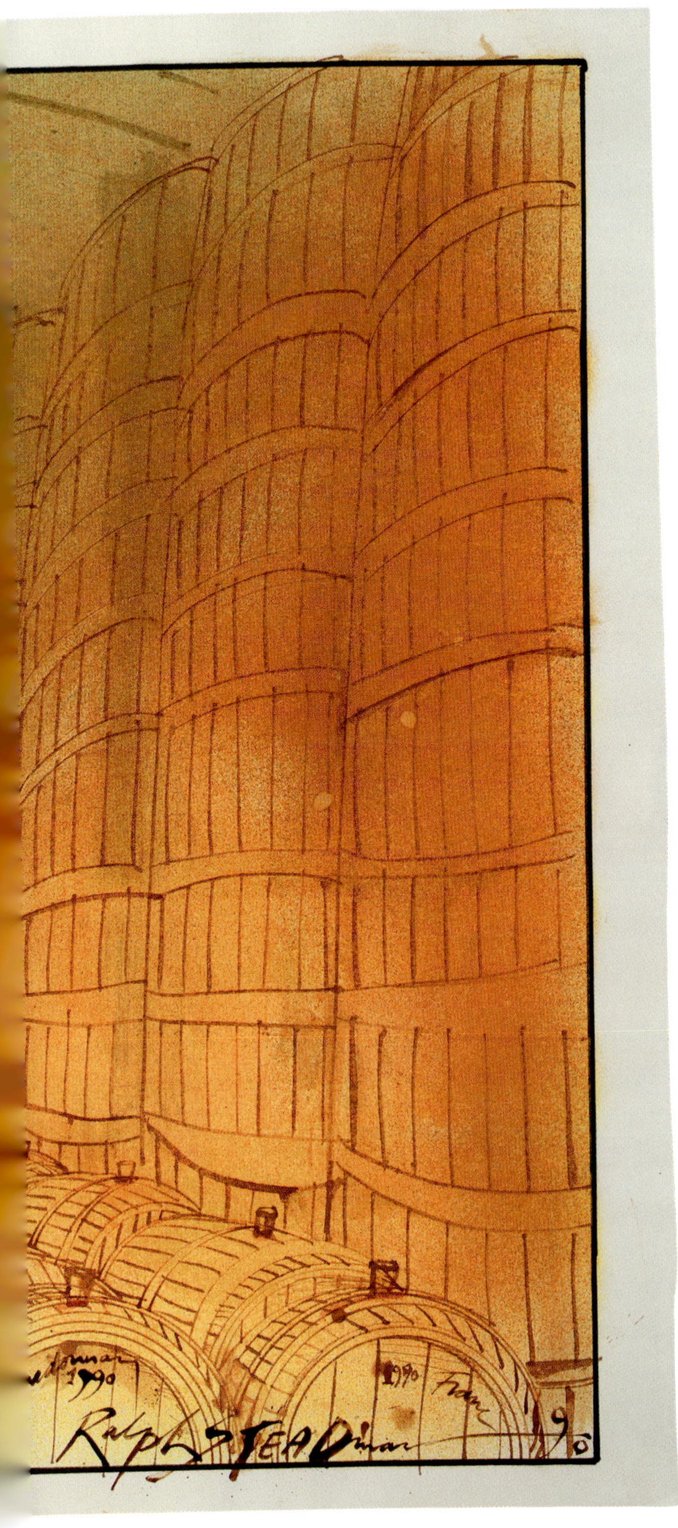

"In memory of Hal Willner, lost to Covid 19."

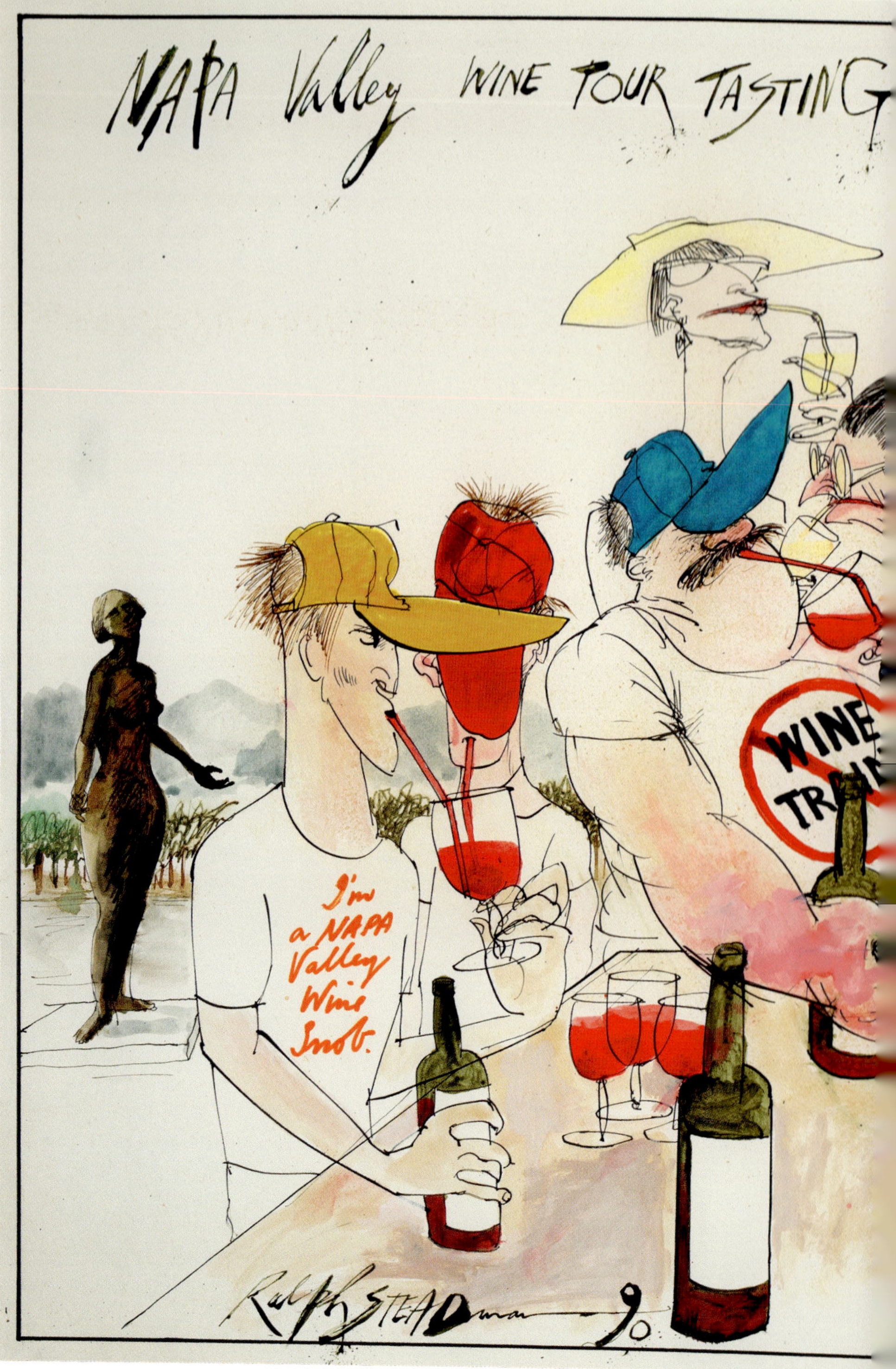

NAPA Valley WINE TOUR TASTING
I'm a NAPA Valley Wine Snob.
WINE TRAIN
Ralph STEADman 90

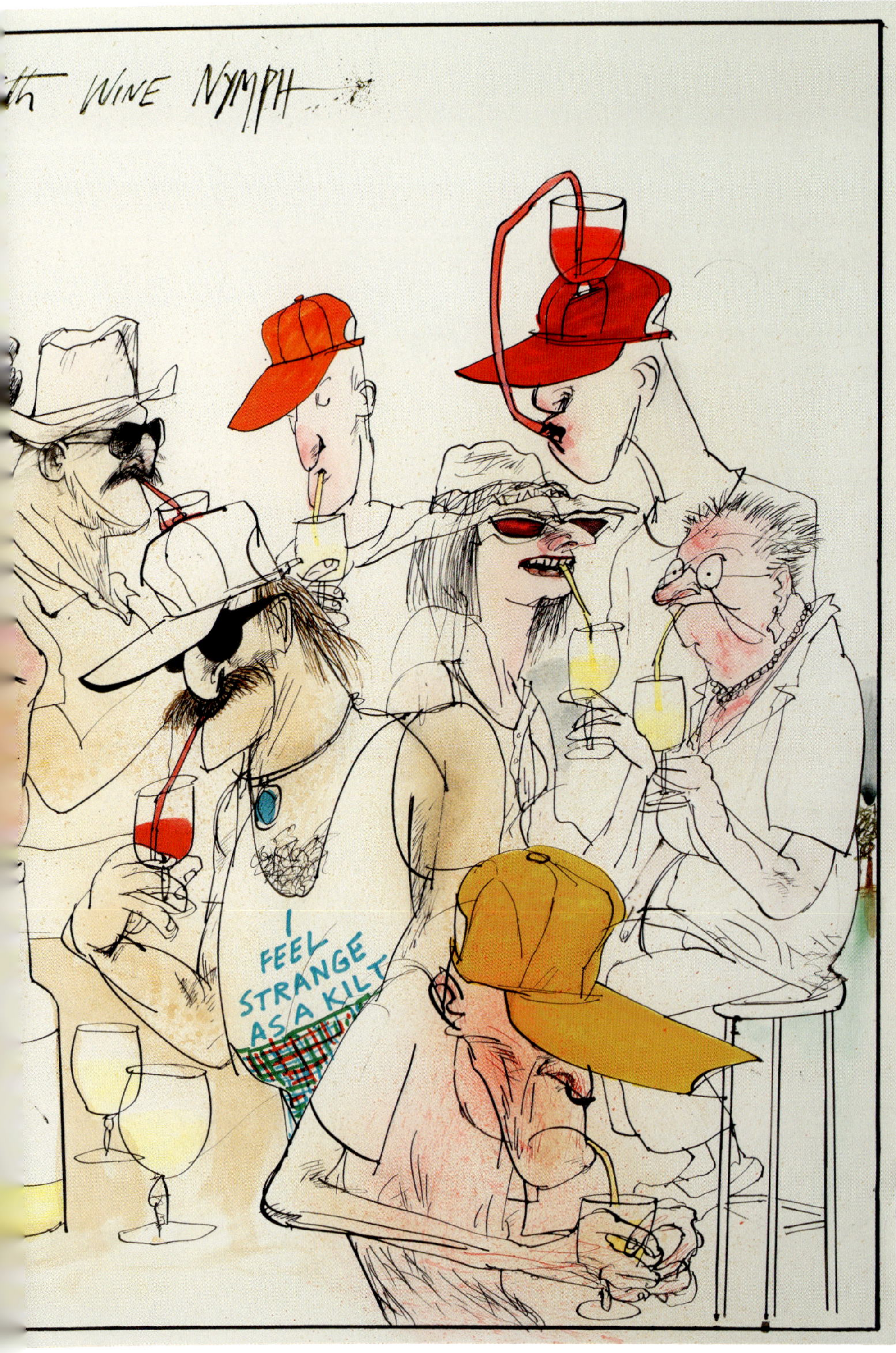

Napa Valley Wine Tasting—the Ultimate Tourist Experience, 1990

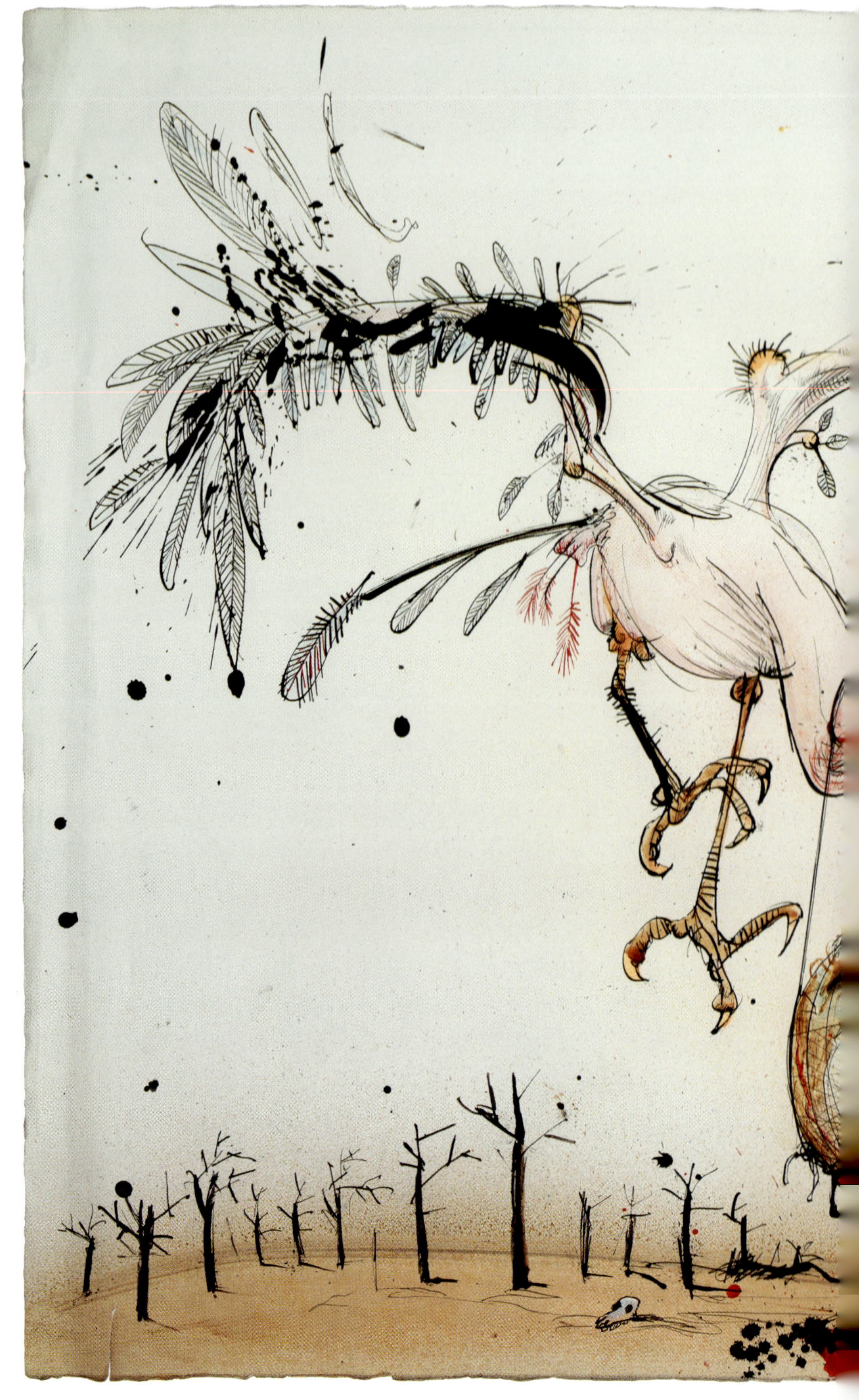

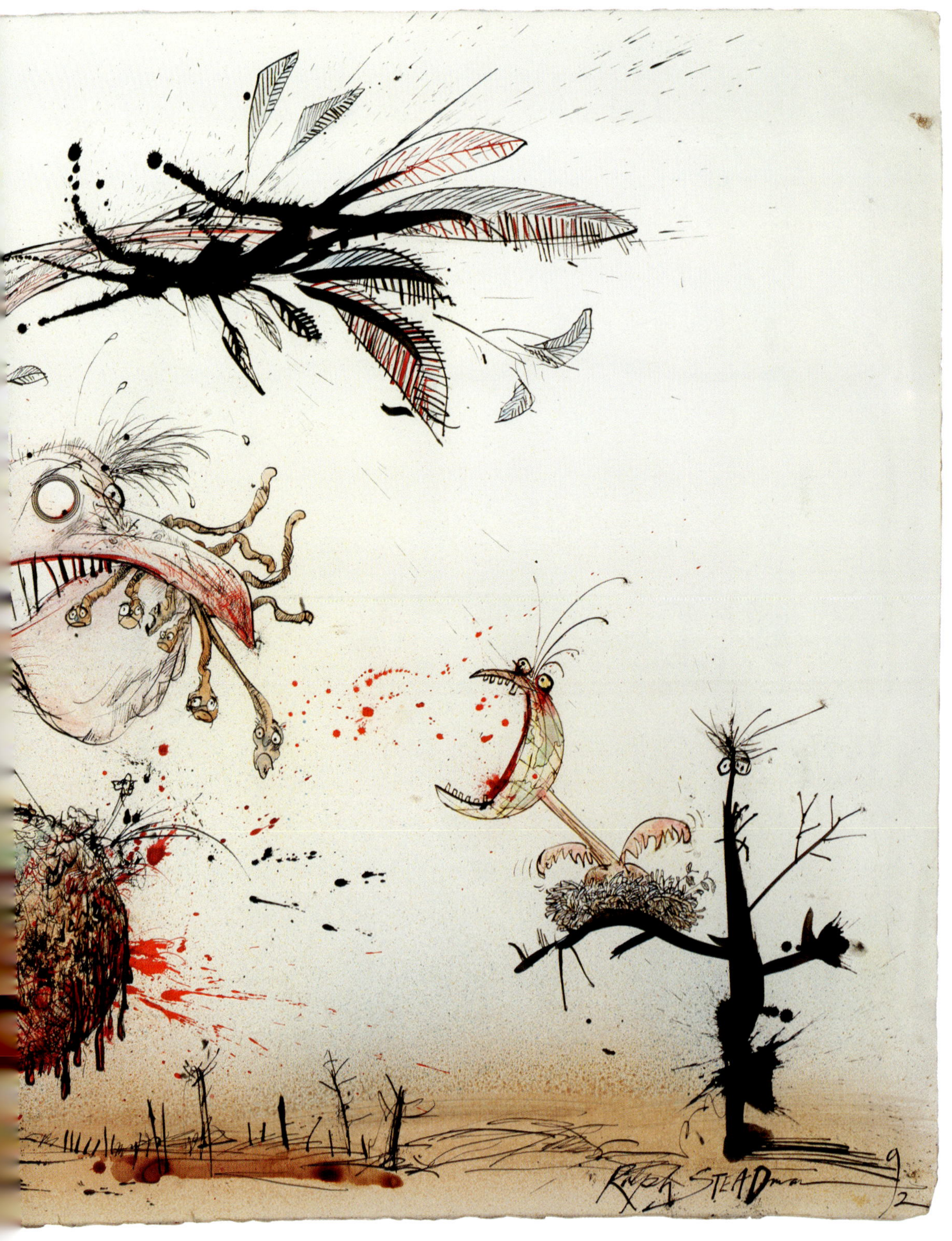

World Pollution, 1992

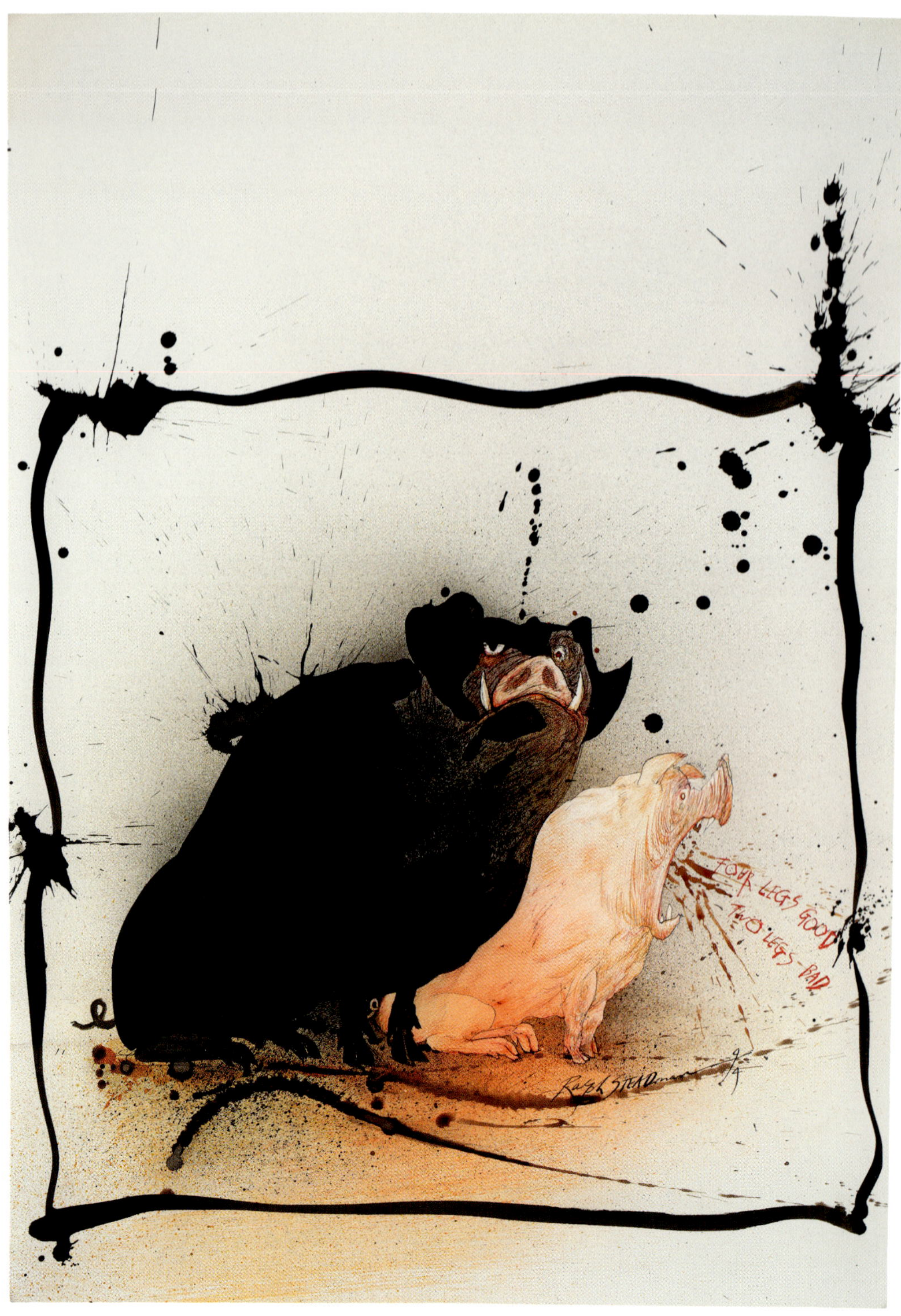

Cover of **Animal Farm** *with Napoleon and Snowball, 1995*

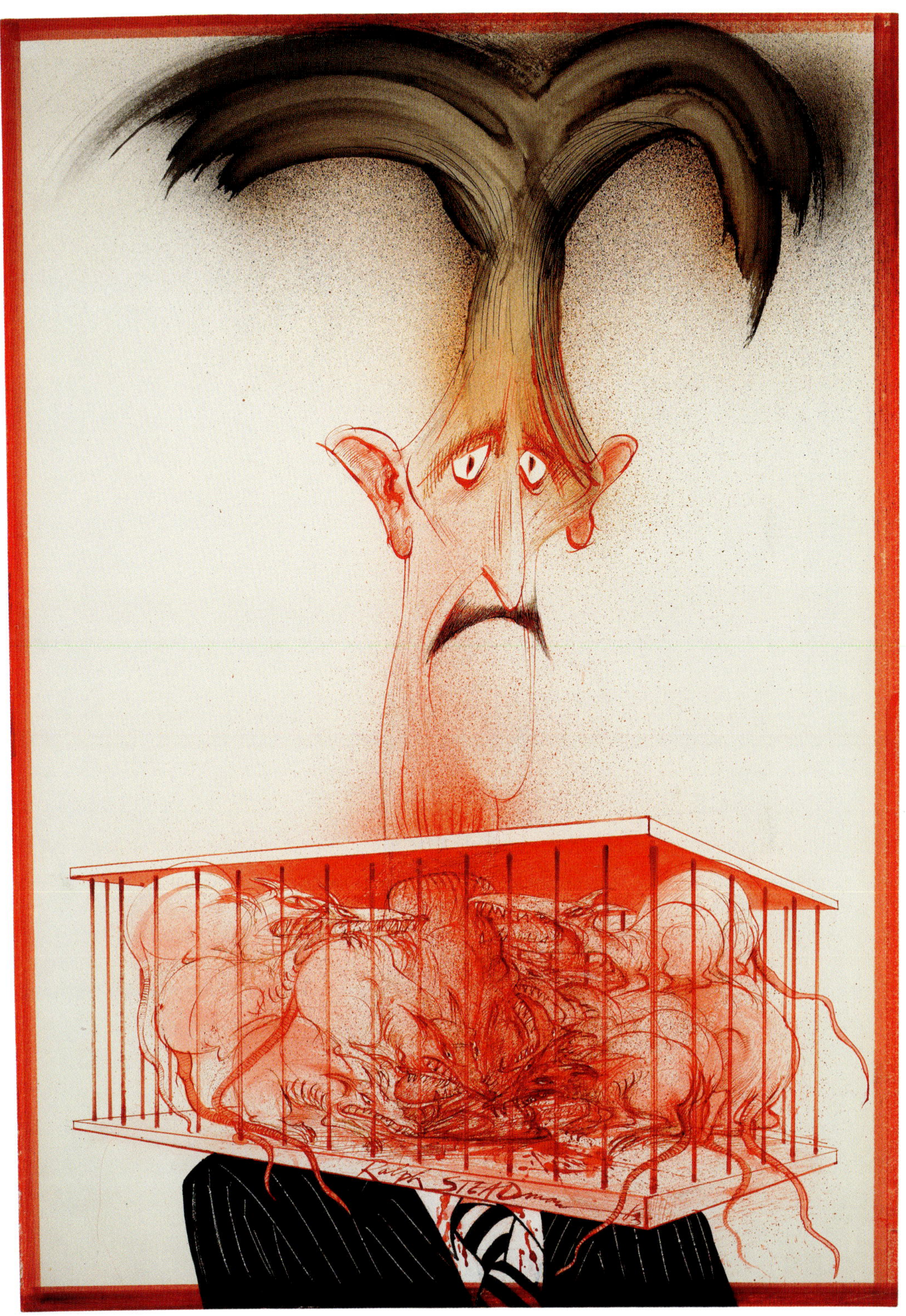

Portrait of George Orwell, 1995

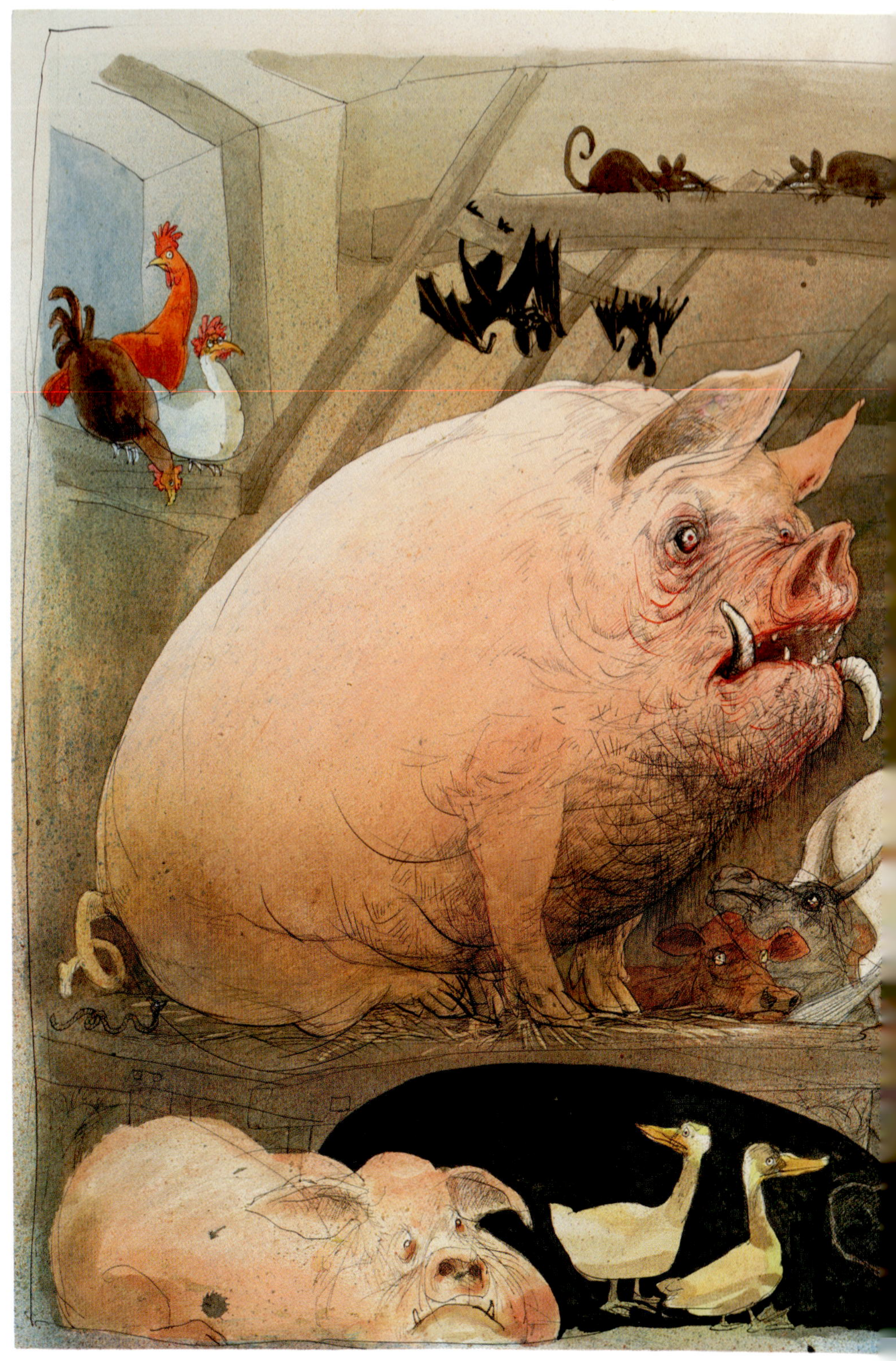

Animal Farm, War Council, 1995

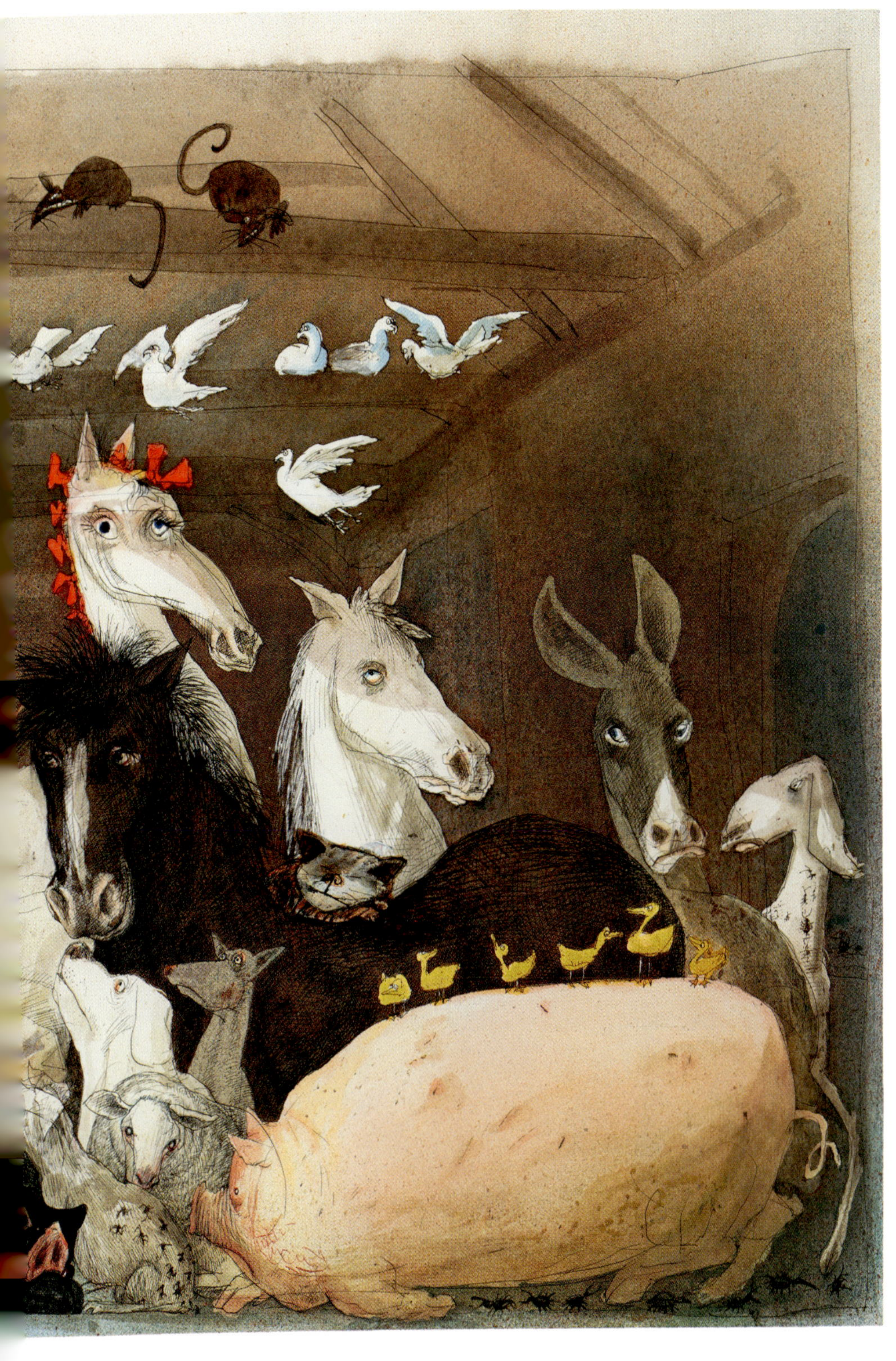

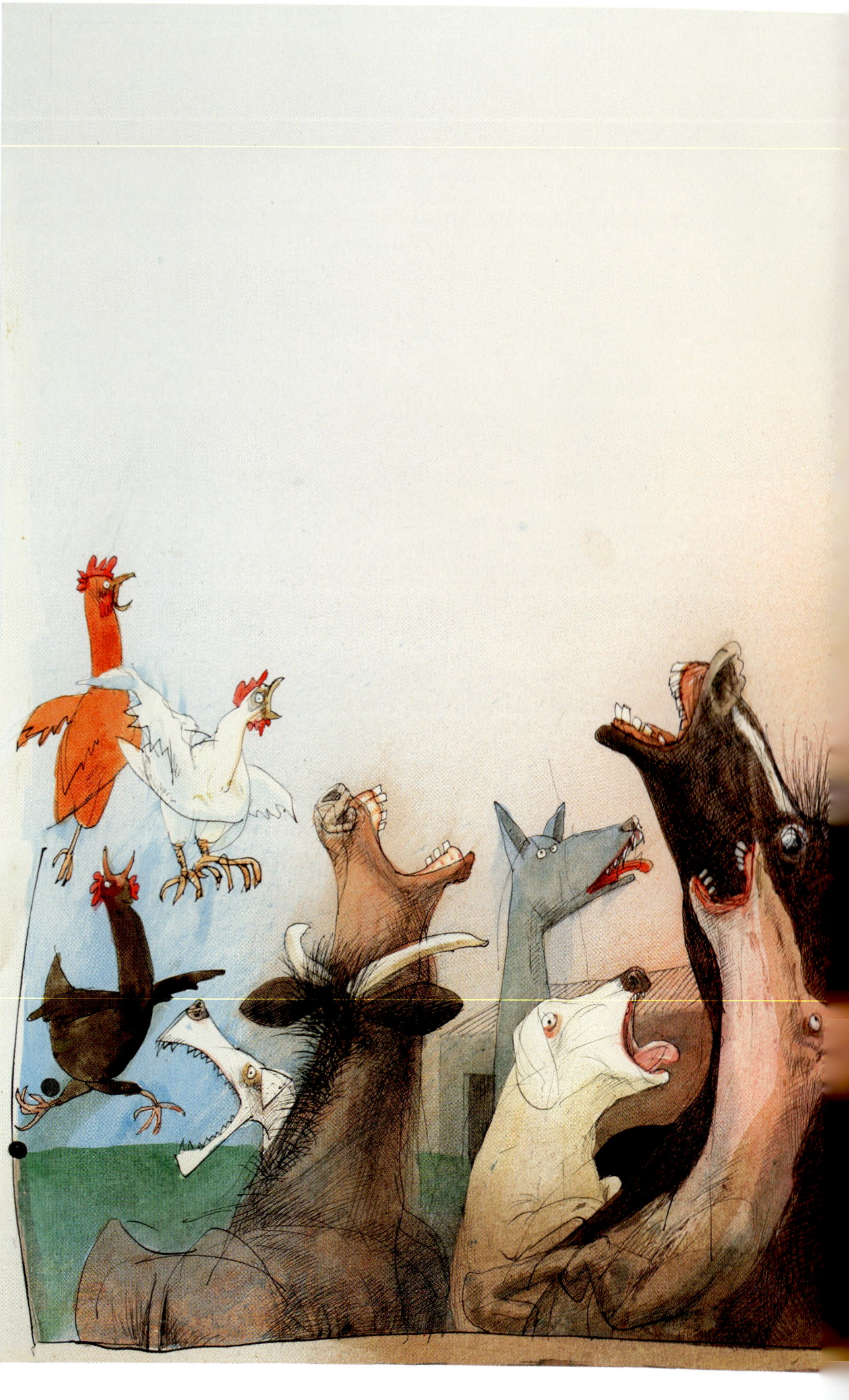

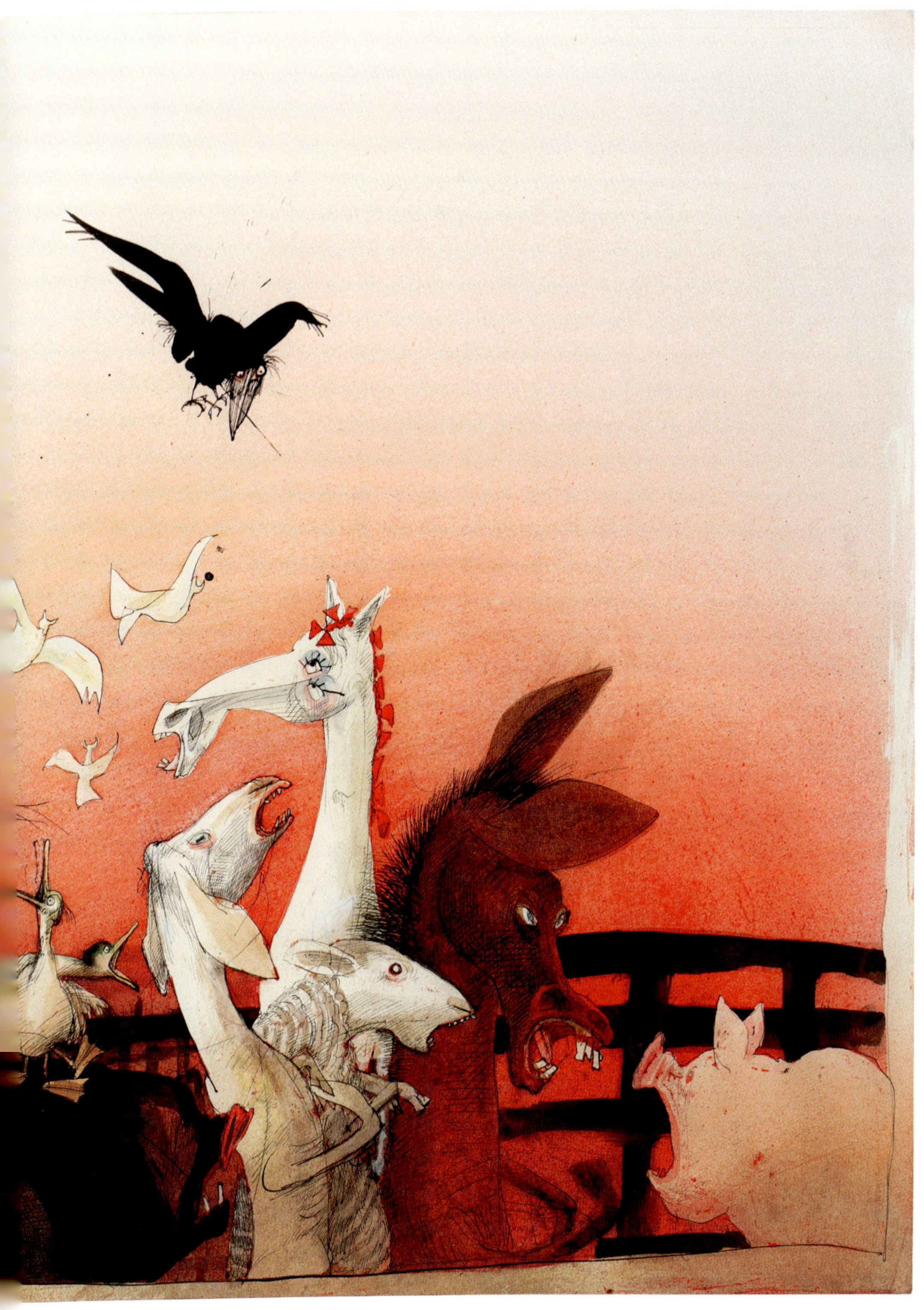

***Animal Farm**, The Animals Aspiring to Sing Their Anthem, 1995*

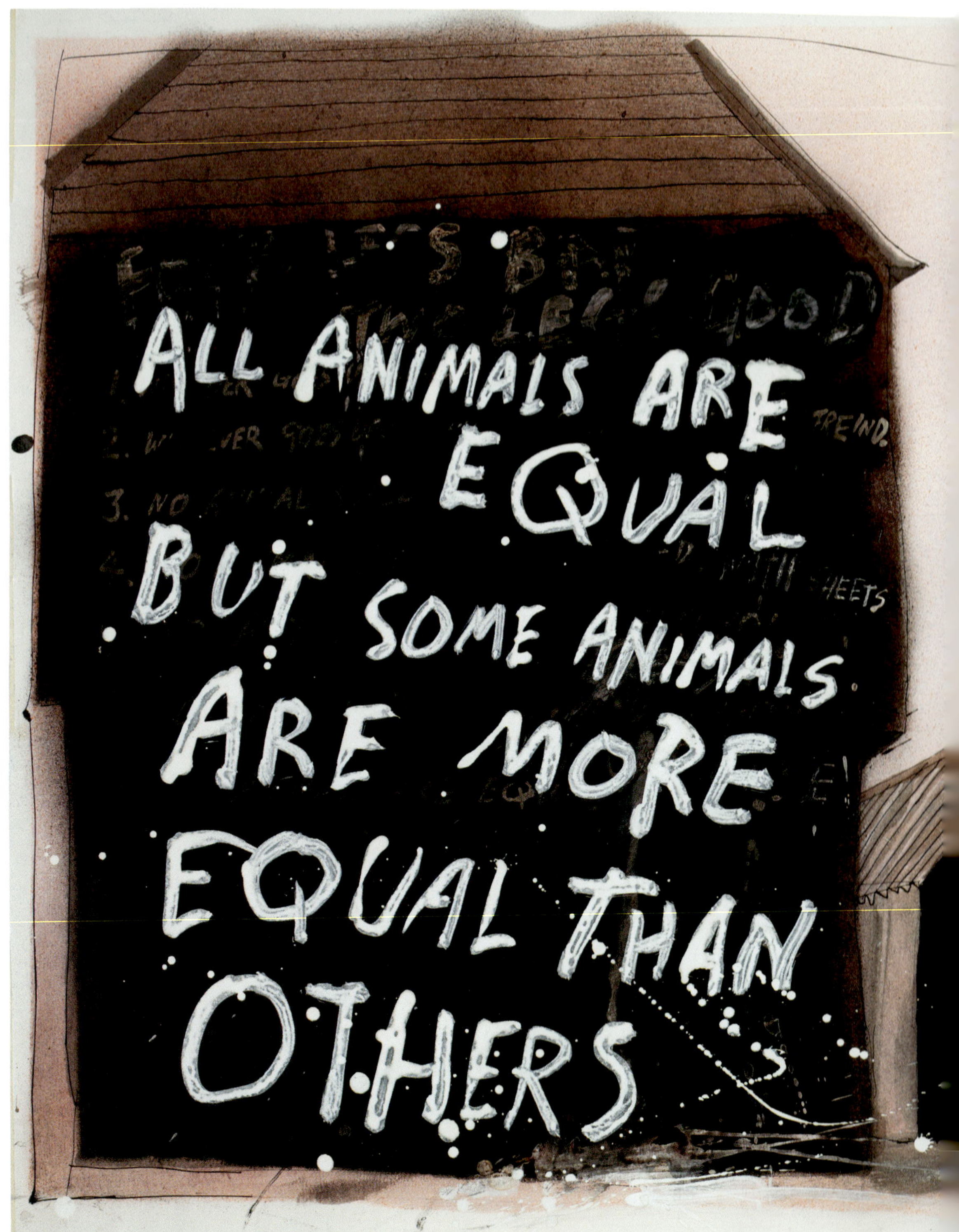

Animal Farm, Some Animals Are More Equal than Others, 1995

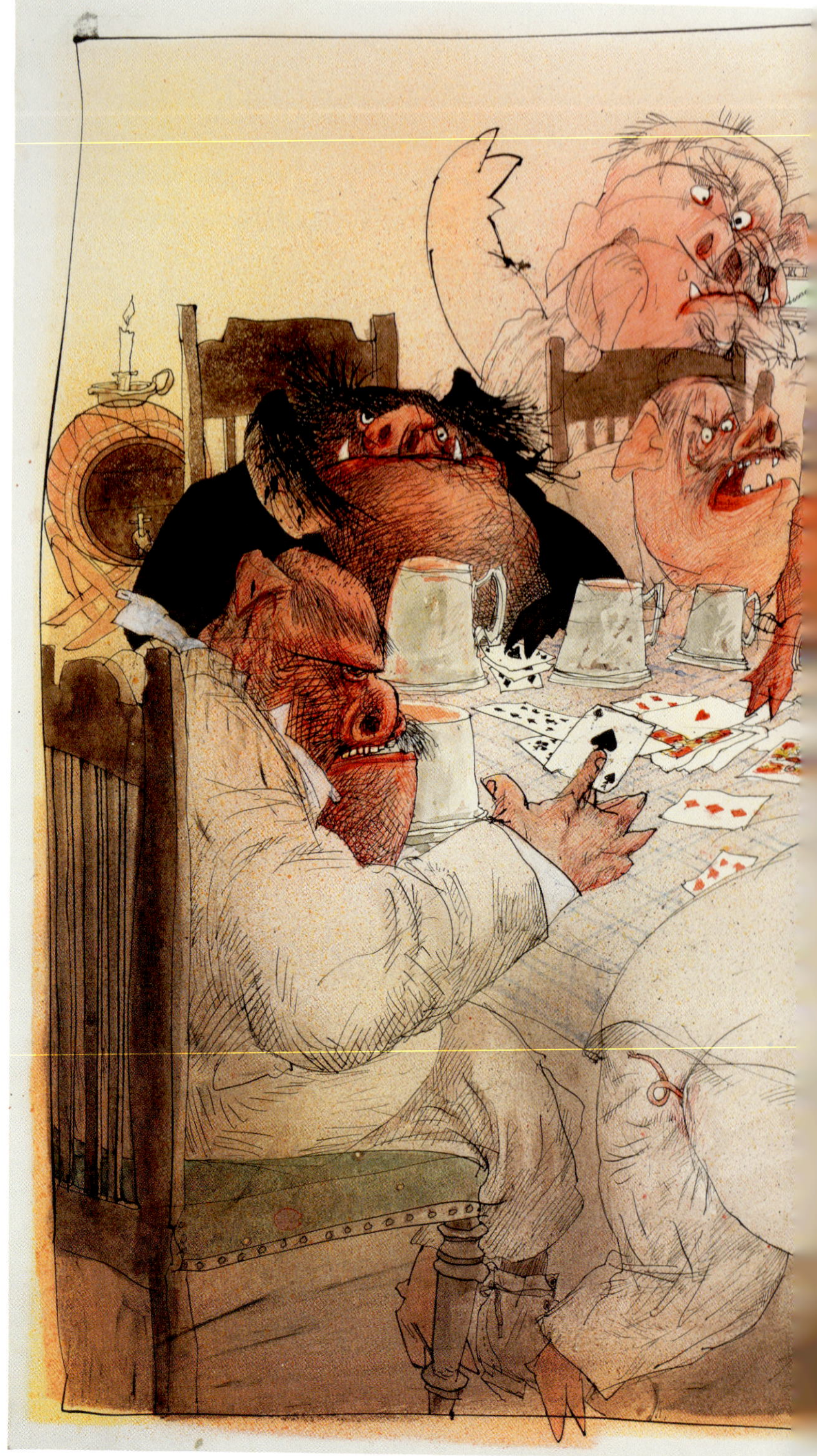

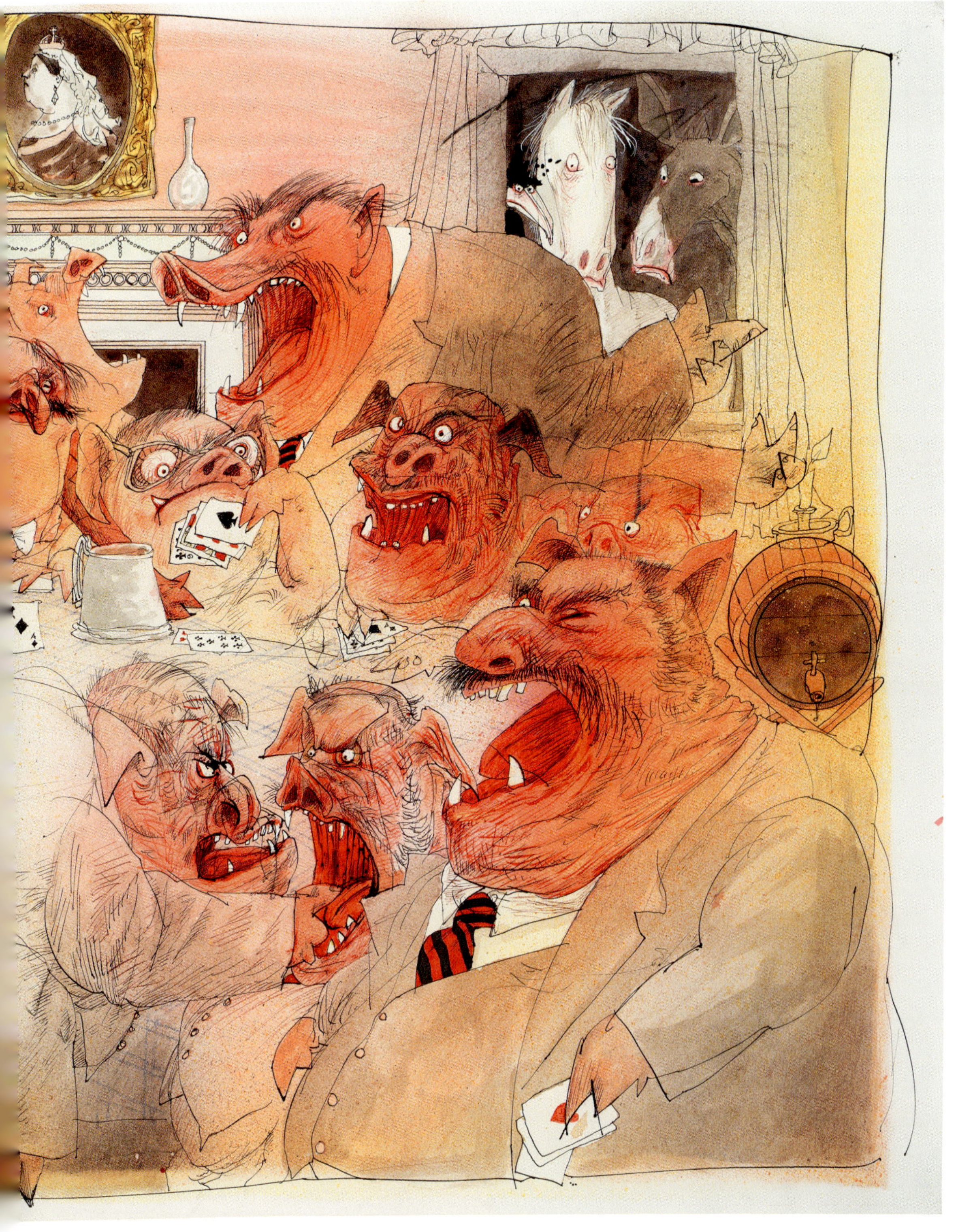

The Pigs Become Men, The Enemy Within, 1995

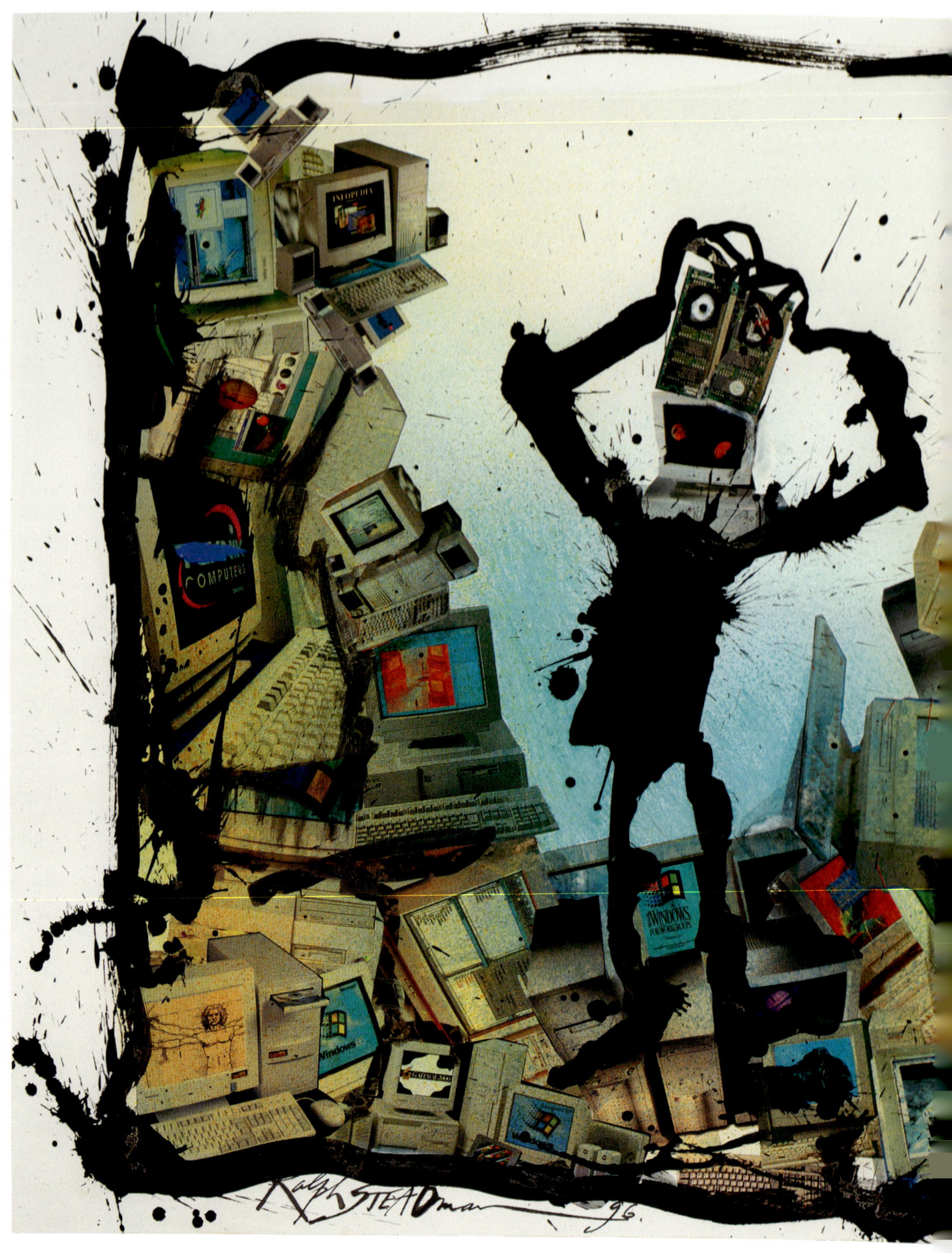

The Trough of Disillusionment as Electronics Take Over the World, 1996

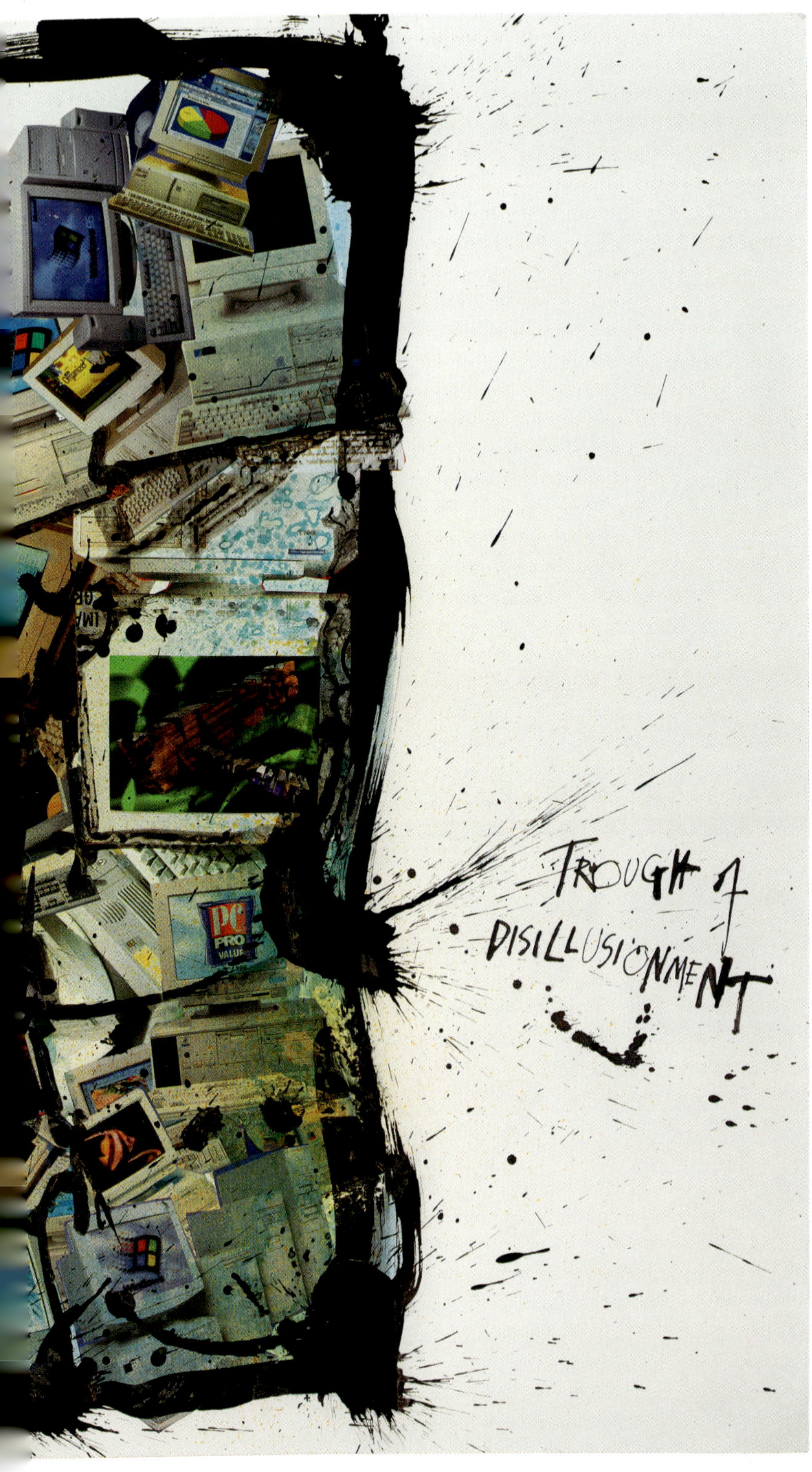

"I have tried to embrace the digital age—with varying degrees of success. But it has made sending artwork simpler."

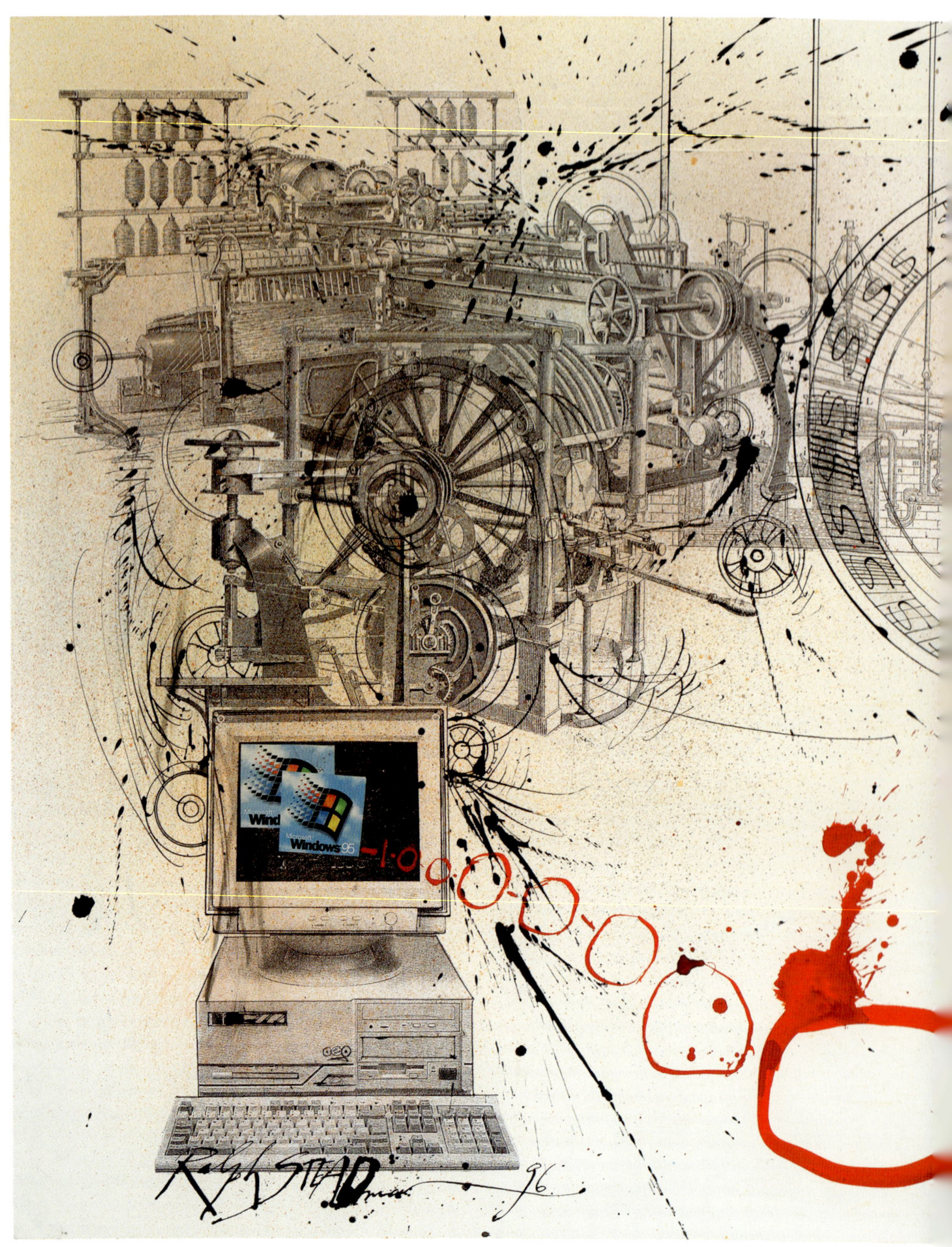

The Treadmill of Computerisation, 1996

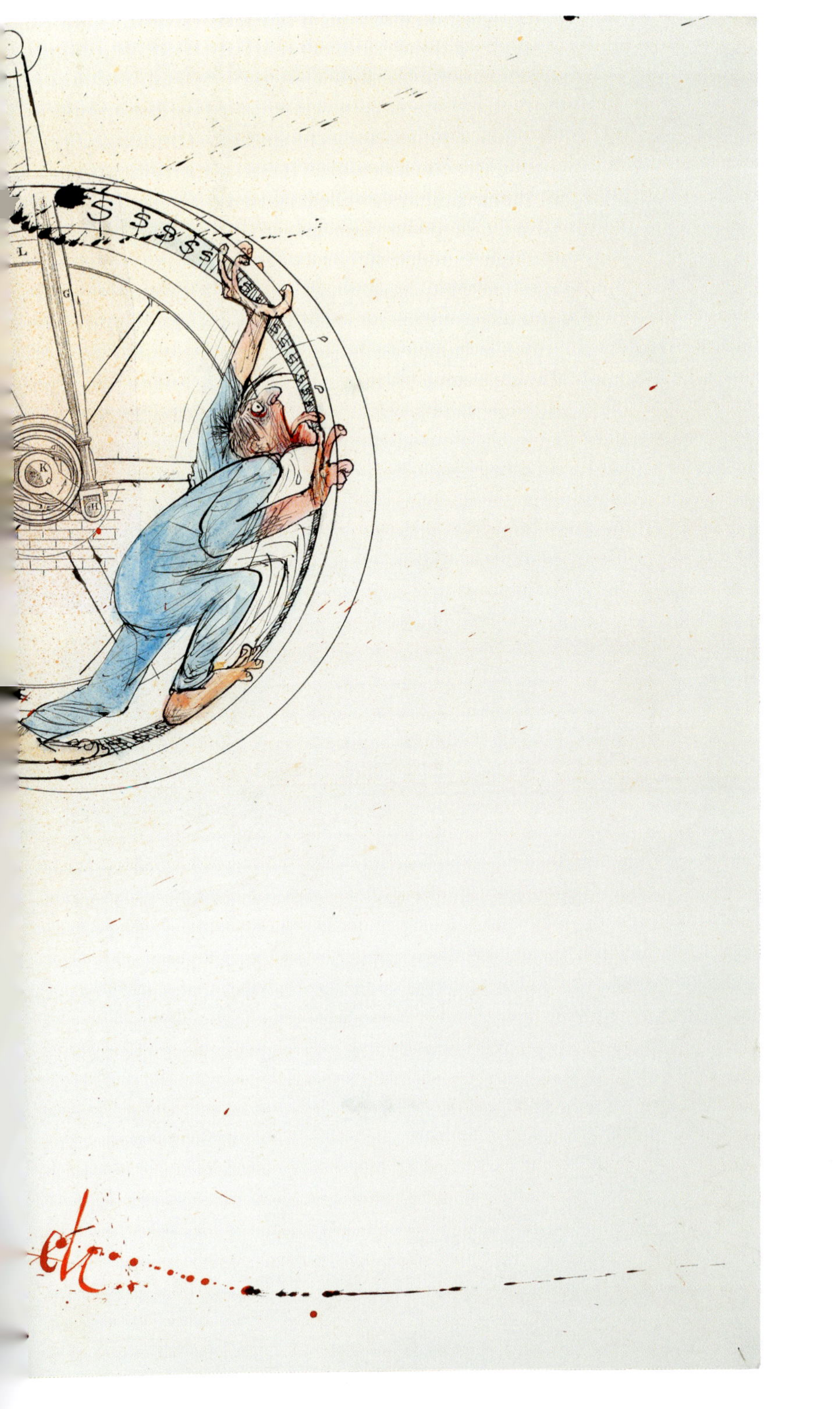

etc.........

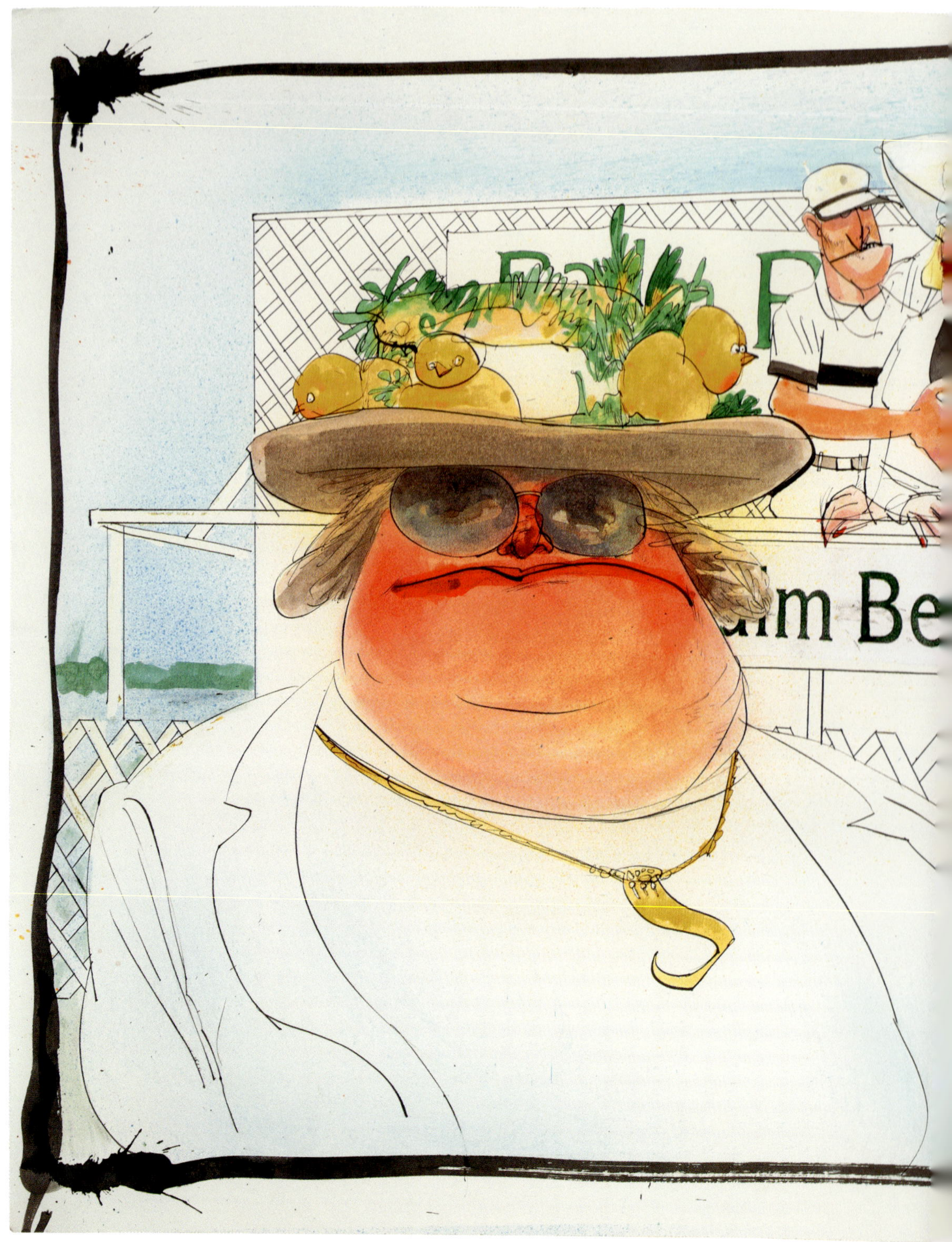

Polo is My Life, 1995, which Hunter never finished

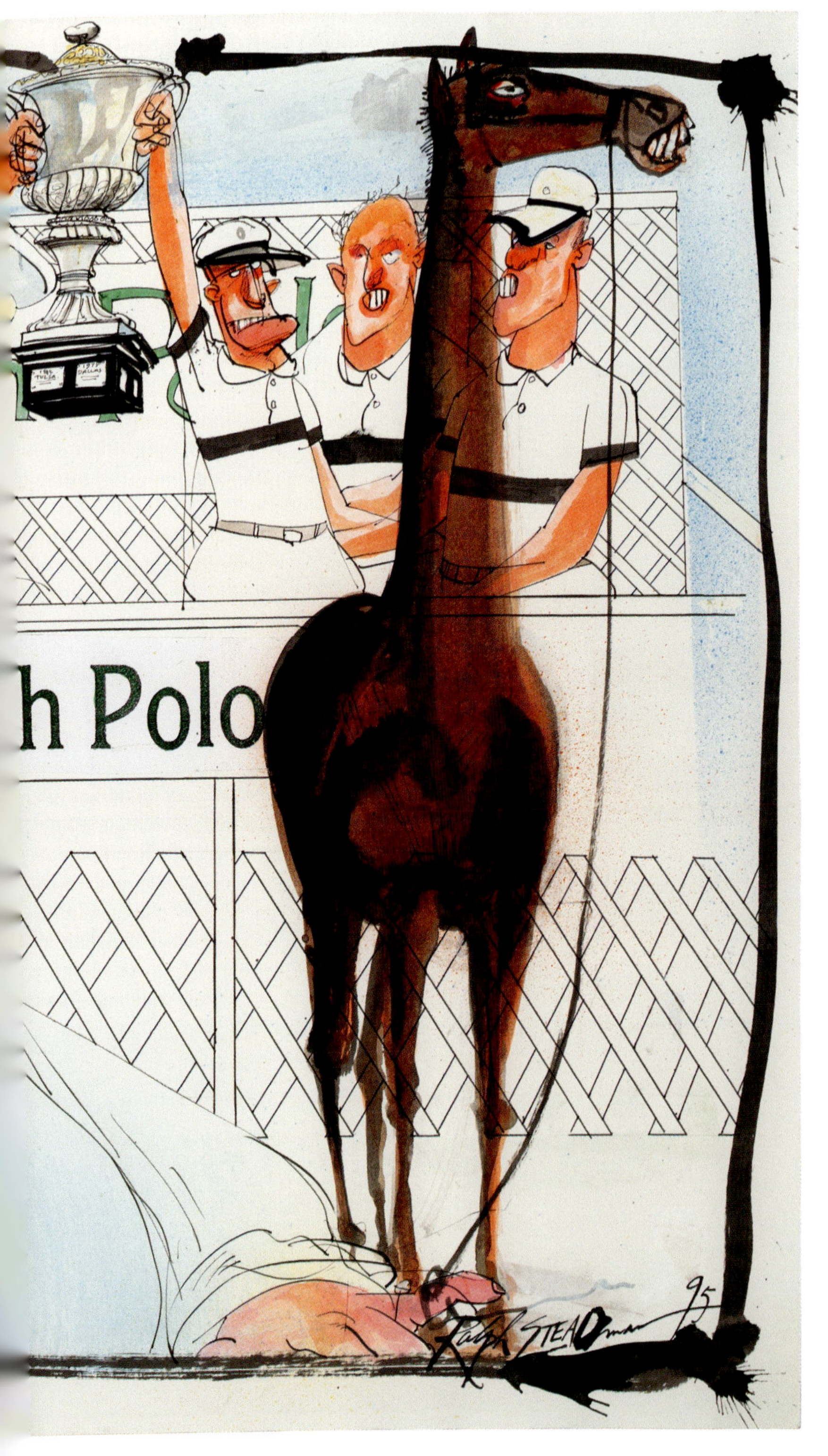

h Polo

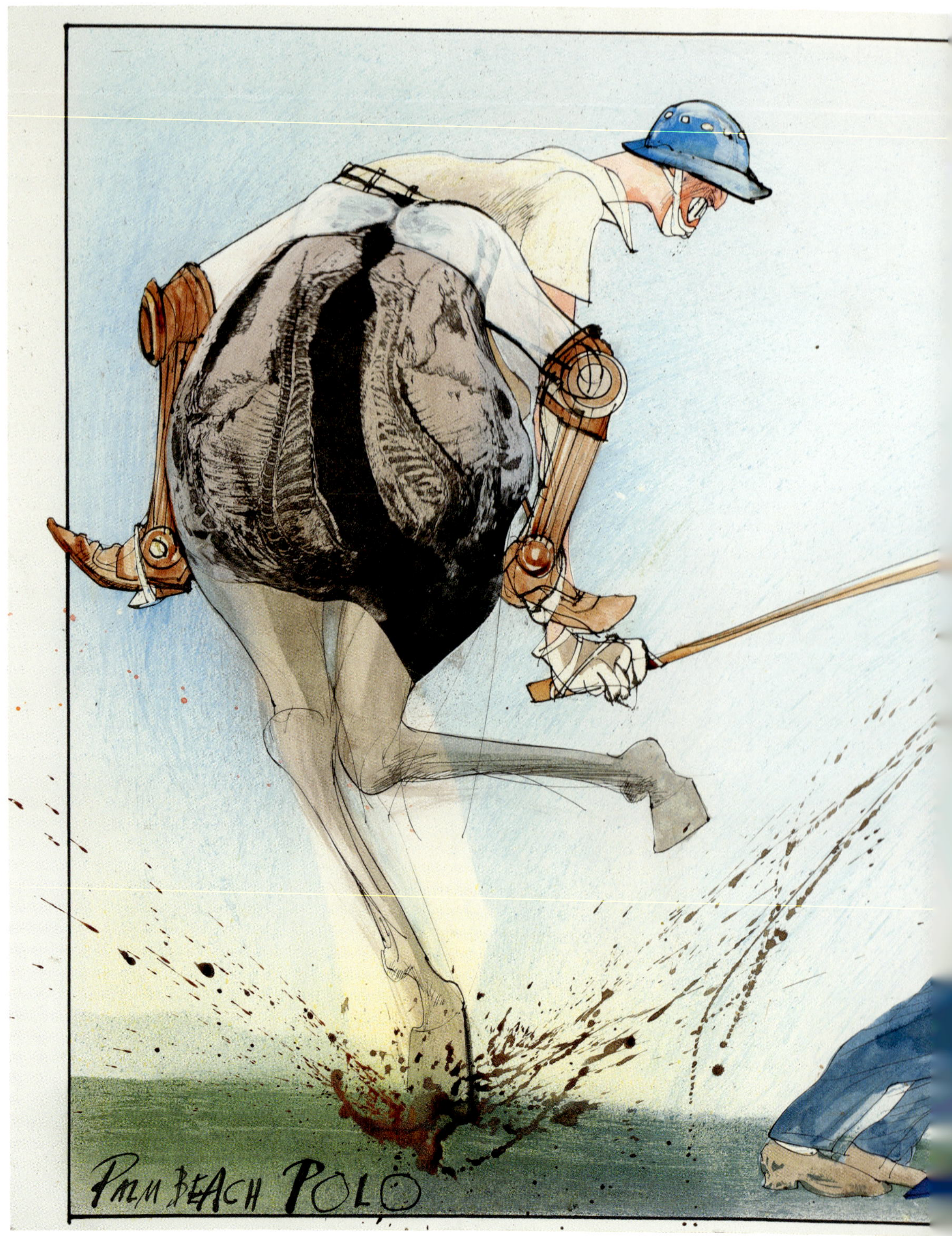

Polo is My Life, 1995

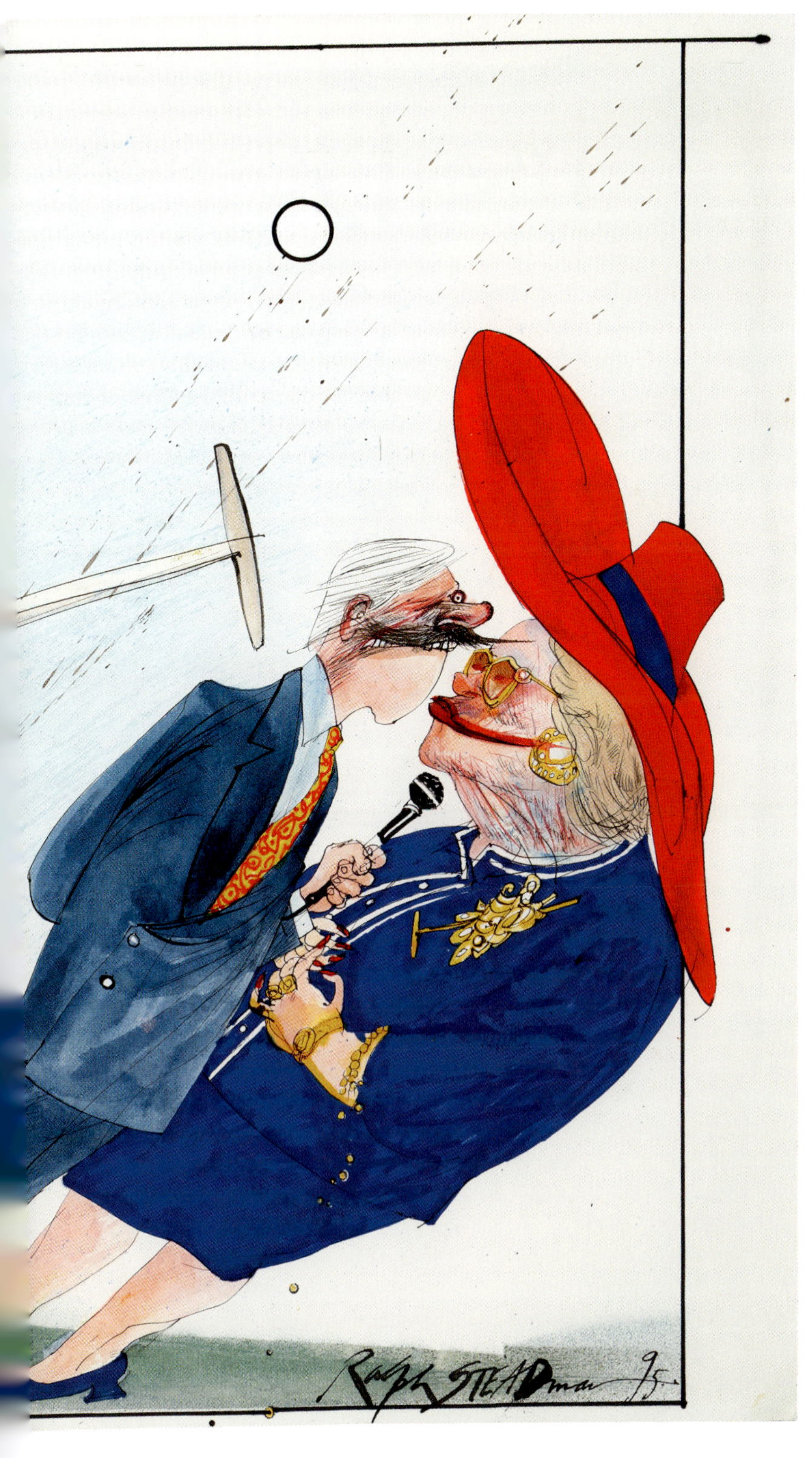

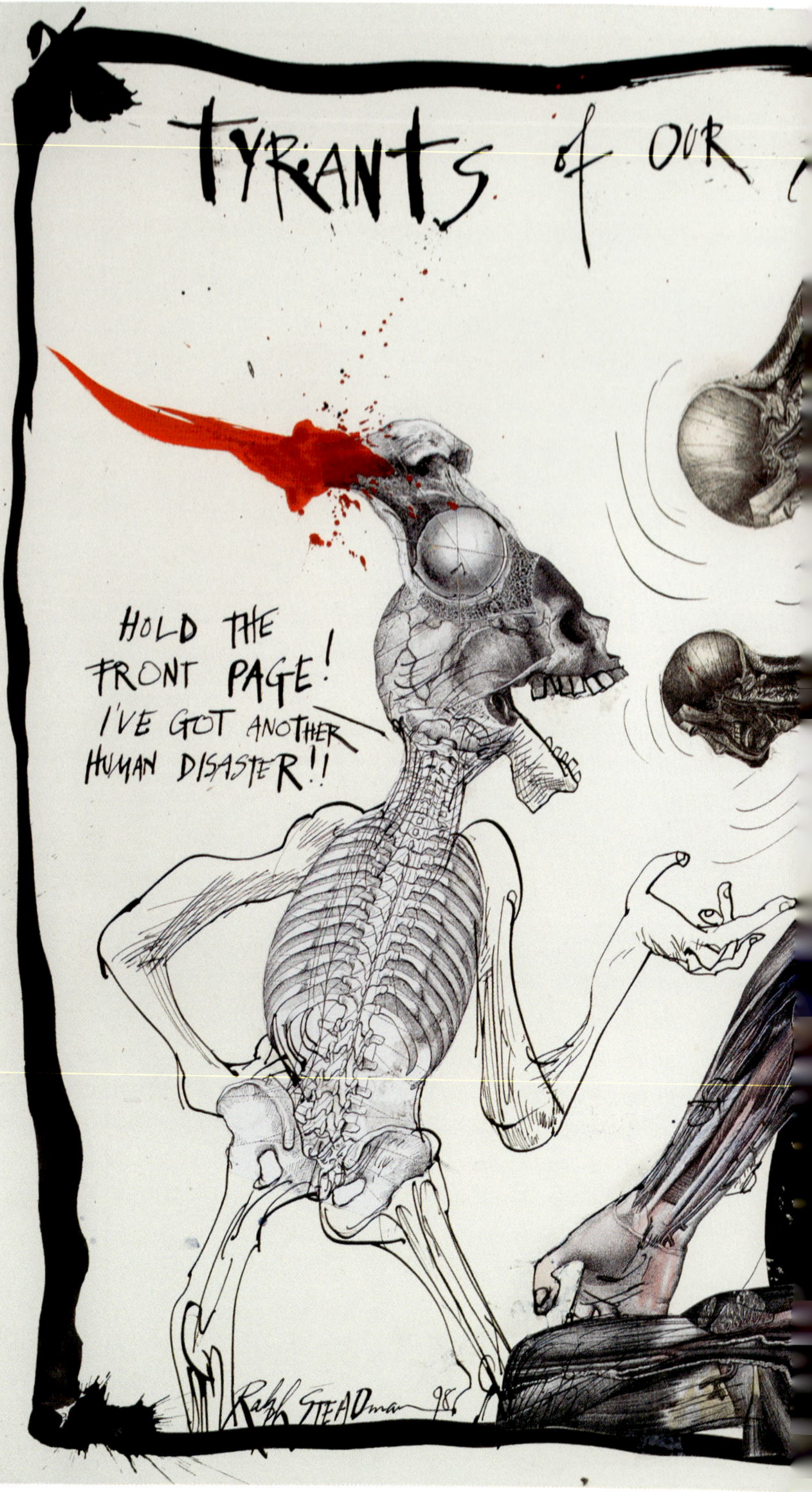

TYRANTS of OUR
HOLD THE FRONT PAGE!
I'VE GOT ANOTHER HUMAN DISASTER!!
Ralph STEADman 98

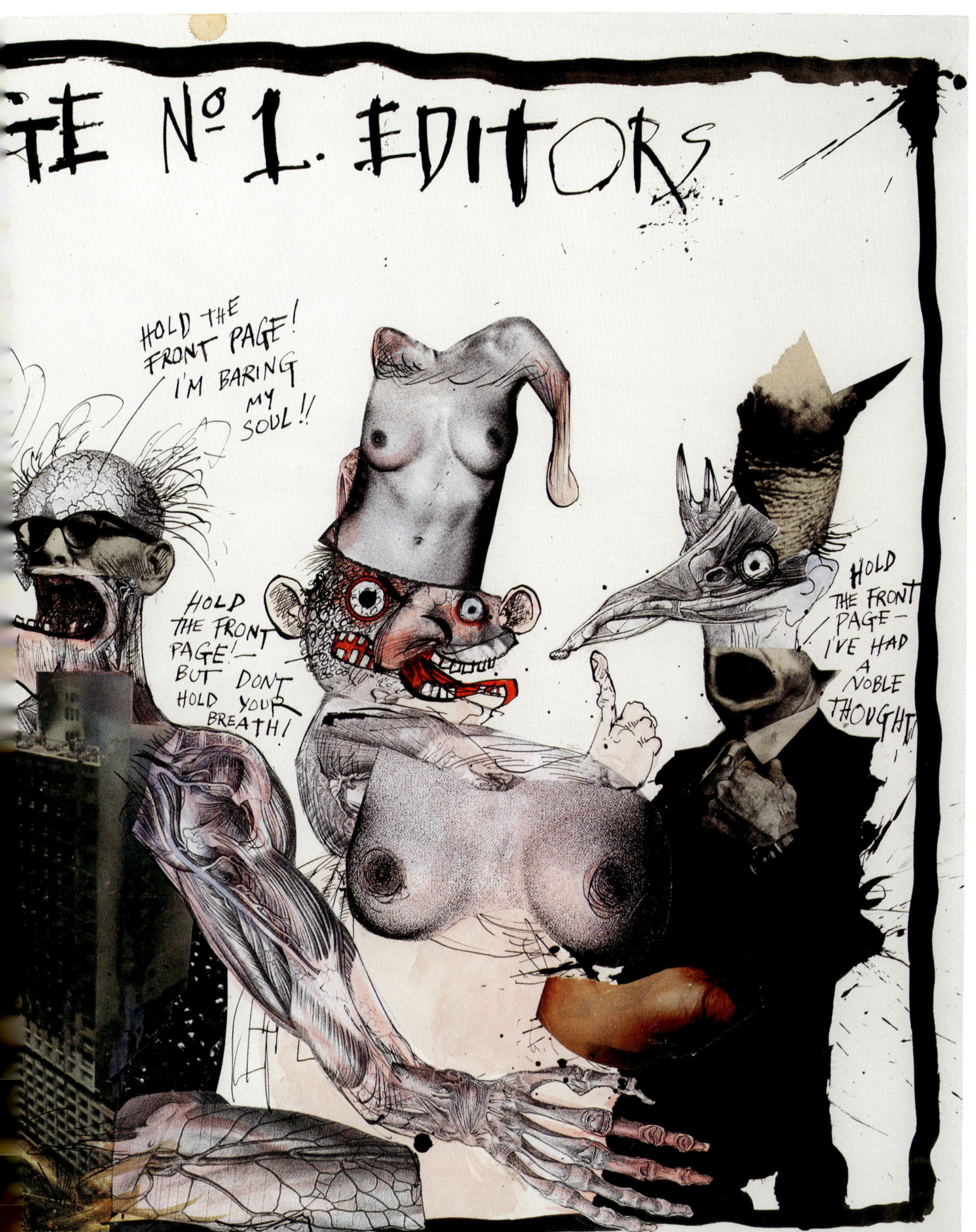

Tyrants of Our Age No. 1: Editors, 1998

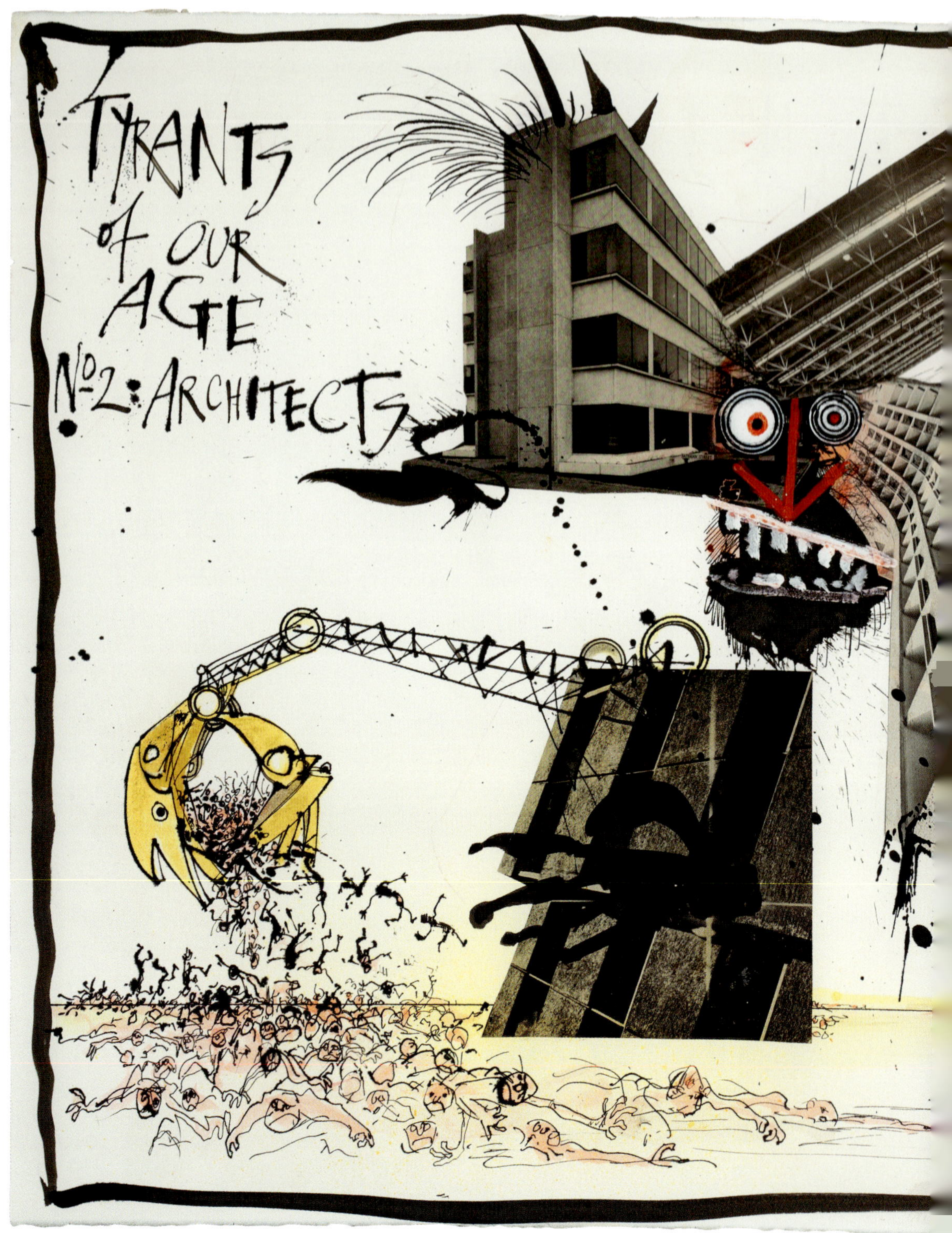

"There is a building in Maidstone that looks like a stack of toilet rolls. The architect must have been in a really bad mood to inflict that on us."

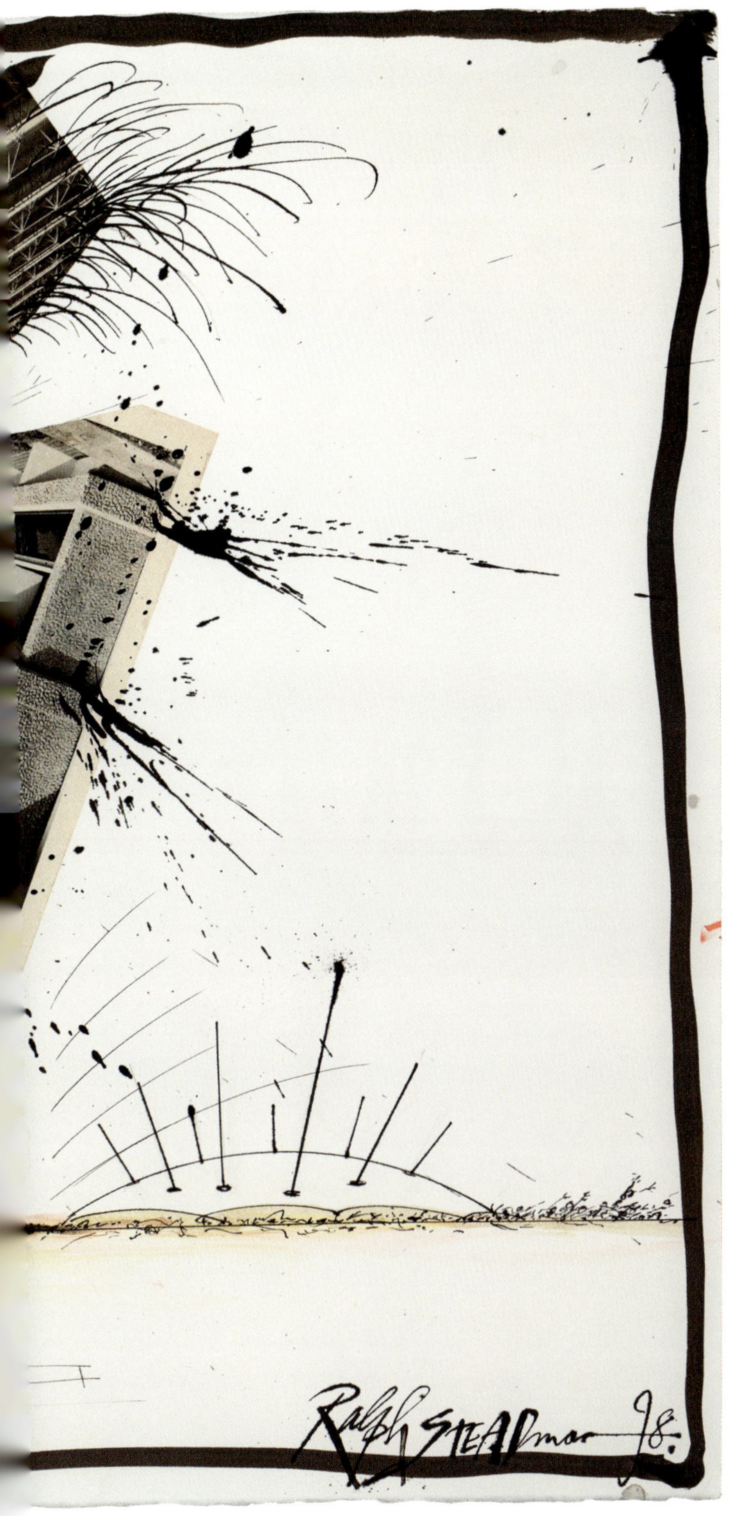

Tyrants of Our Age No. 2: Architects, 1998

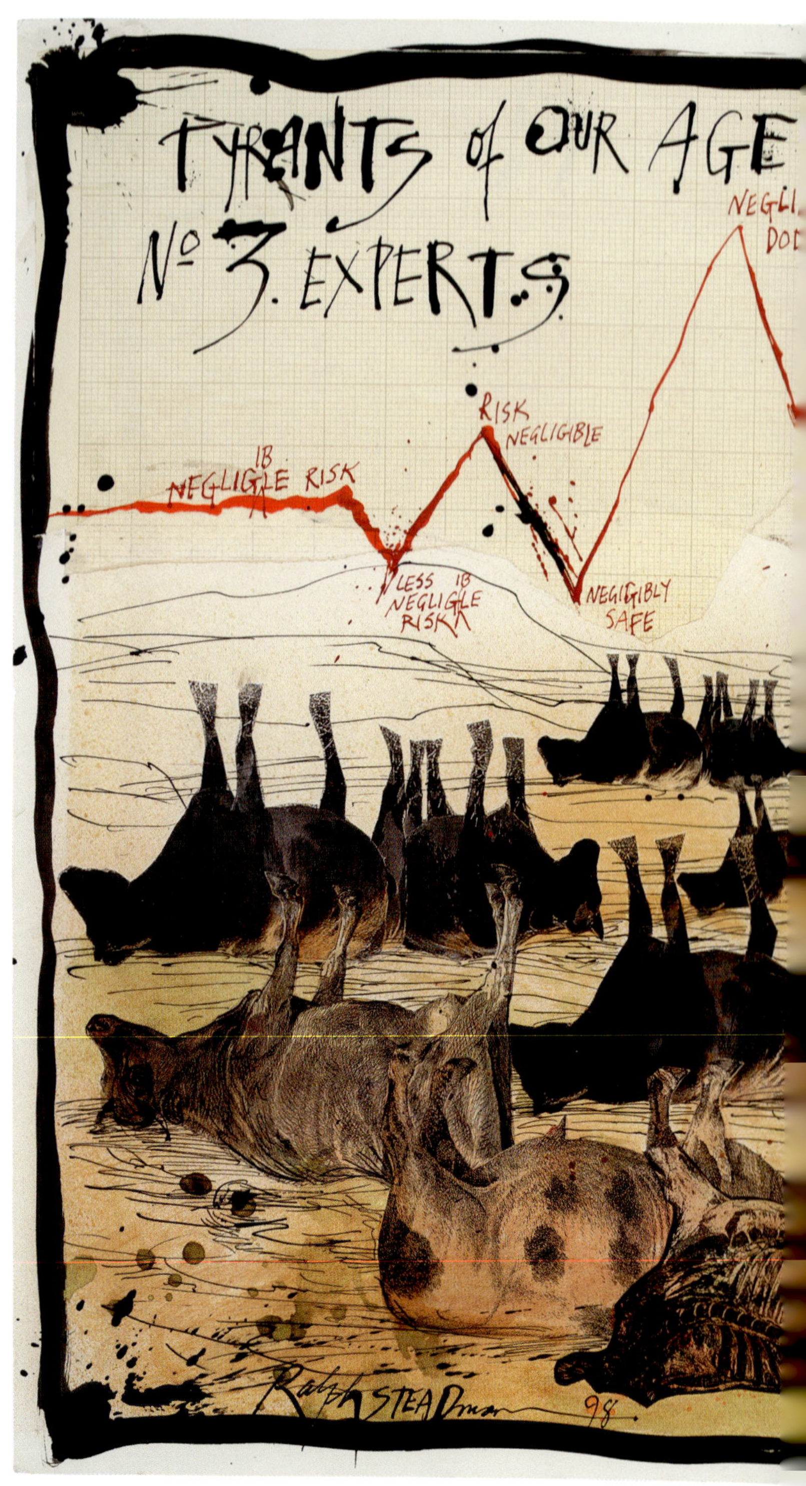

Tyrants of Our Age No. 3: Experts, 1998

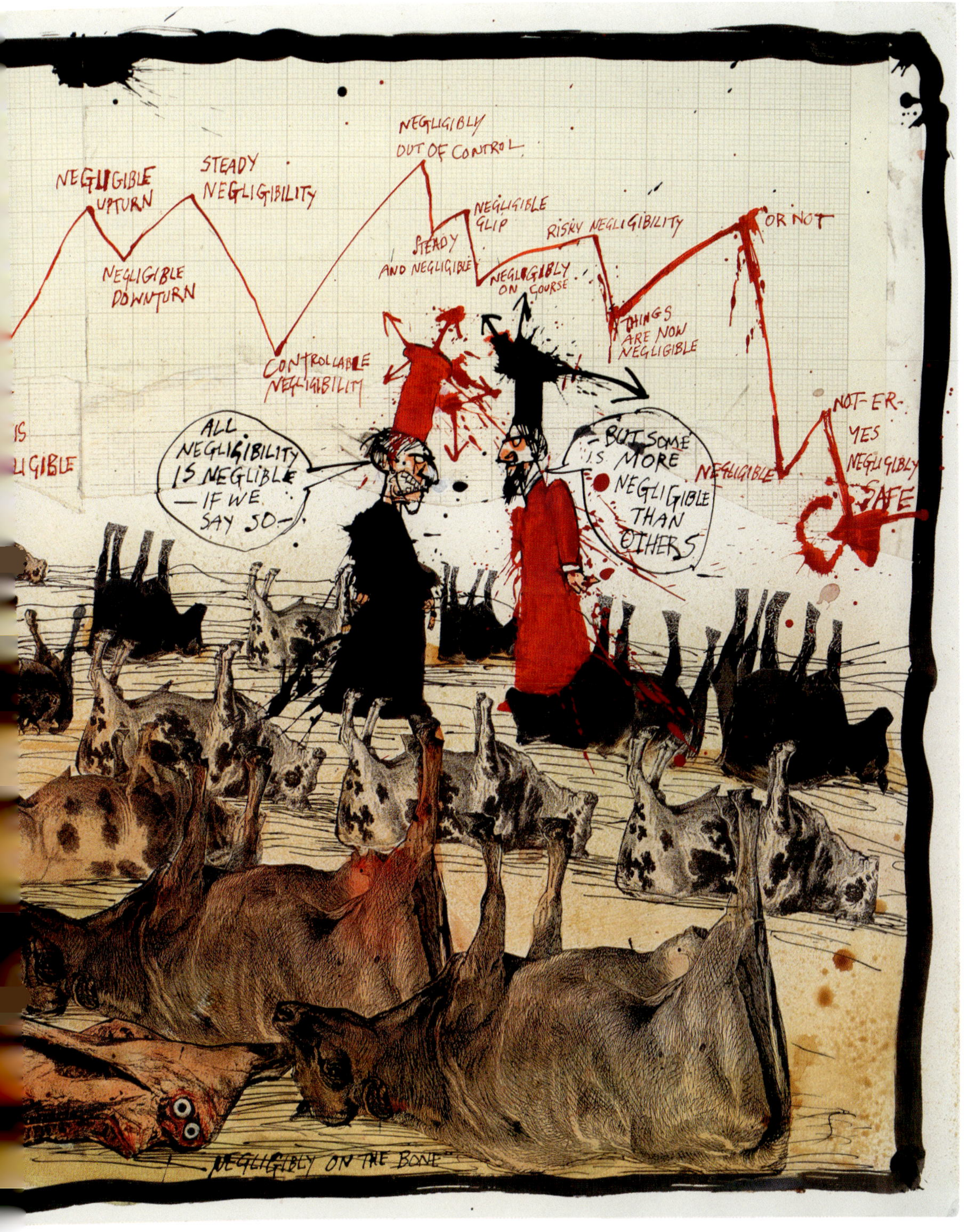

"I wish our government would listen to a few of these."

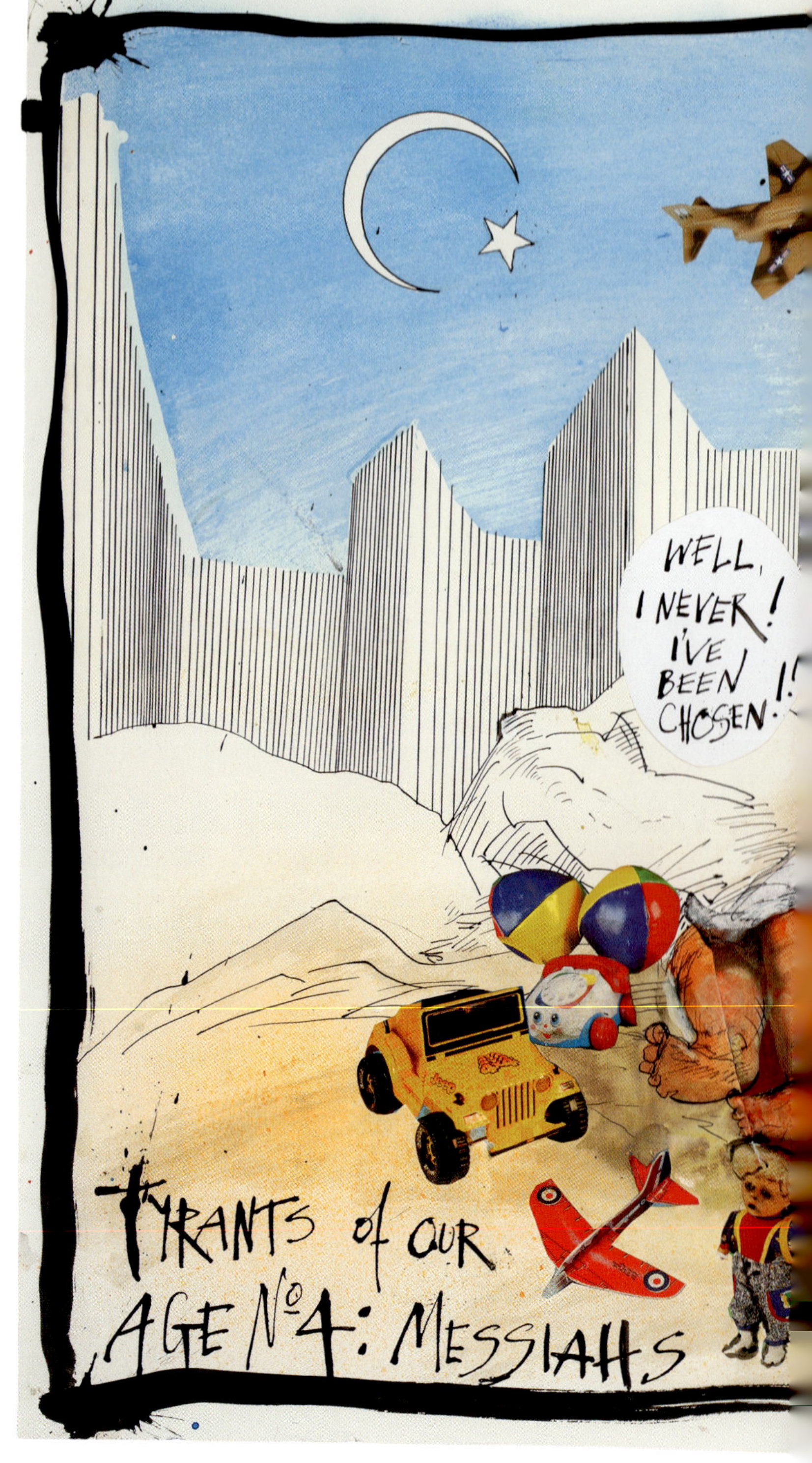

WELL, I NEVER! I'VE BEEN CHOSEN!!
TYRANTS of OUR AGE Nº 4: MESSIAHS

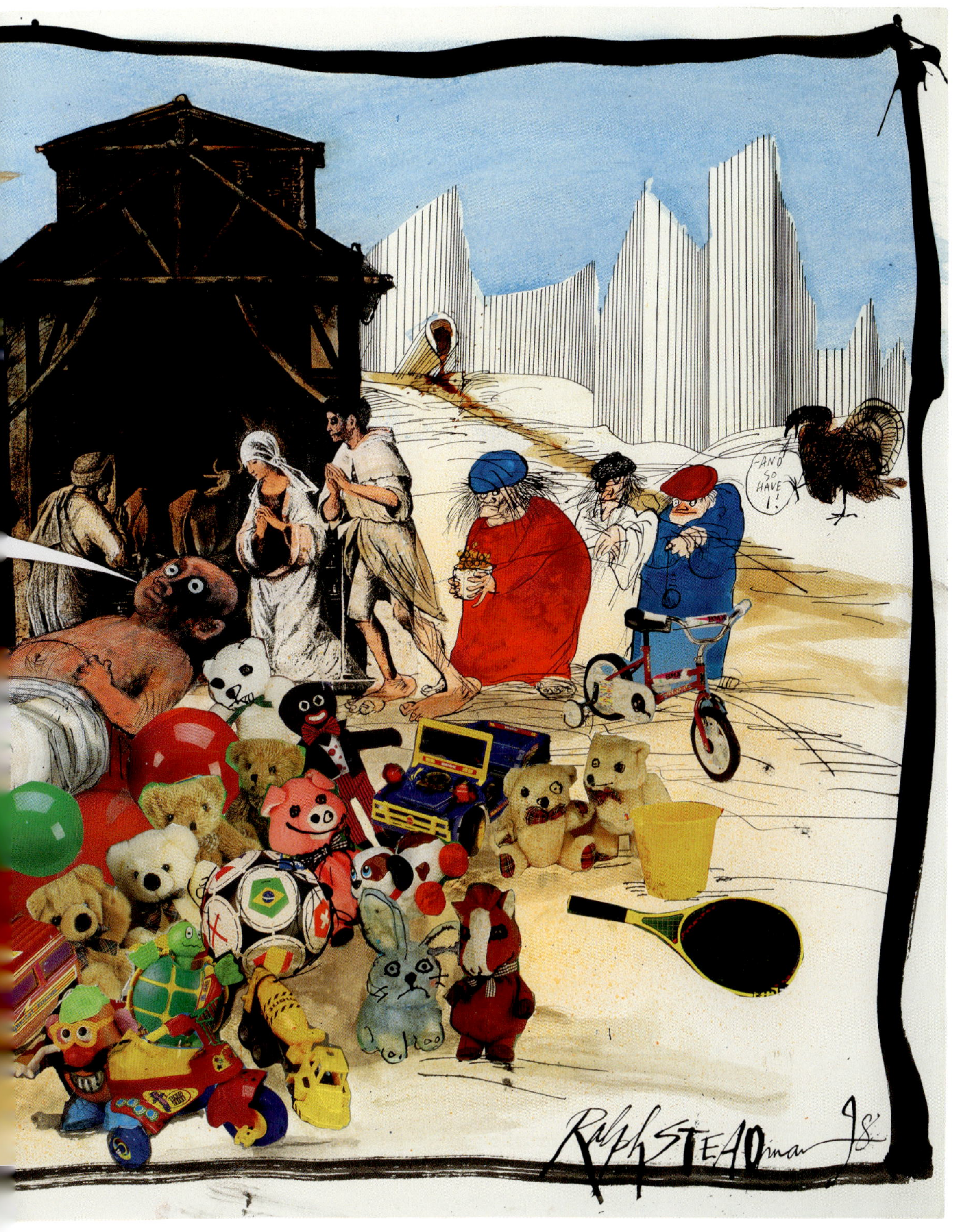

Tyrants of Our Age No. 4: Messiahs, 1998

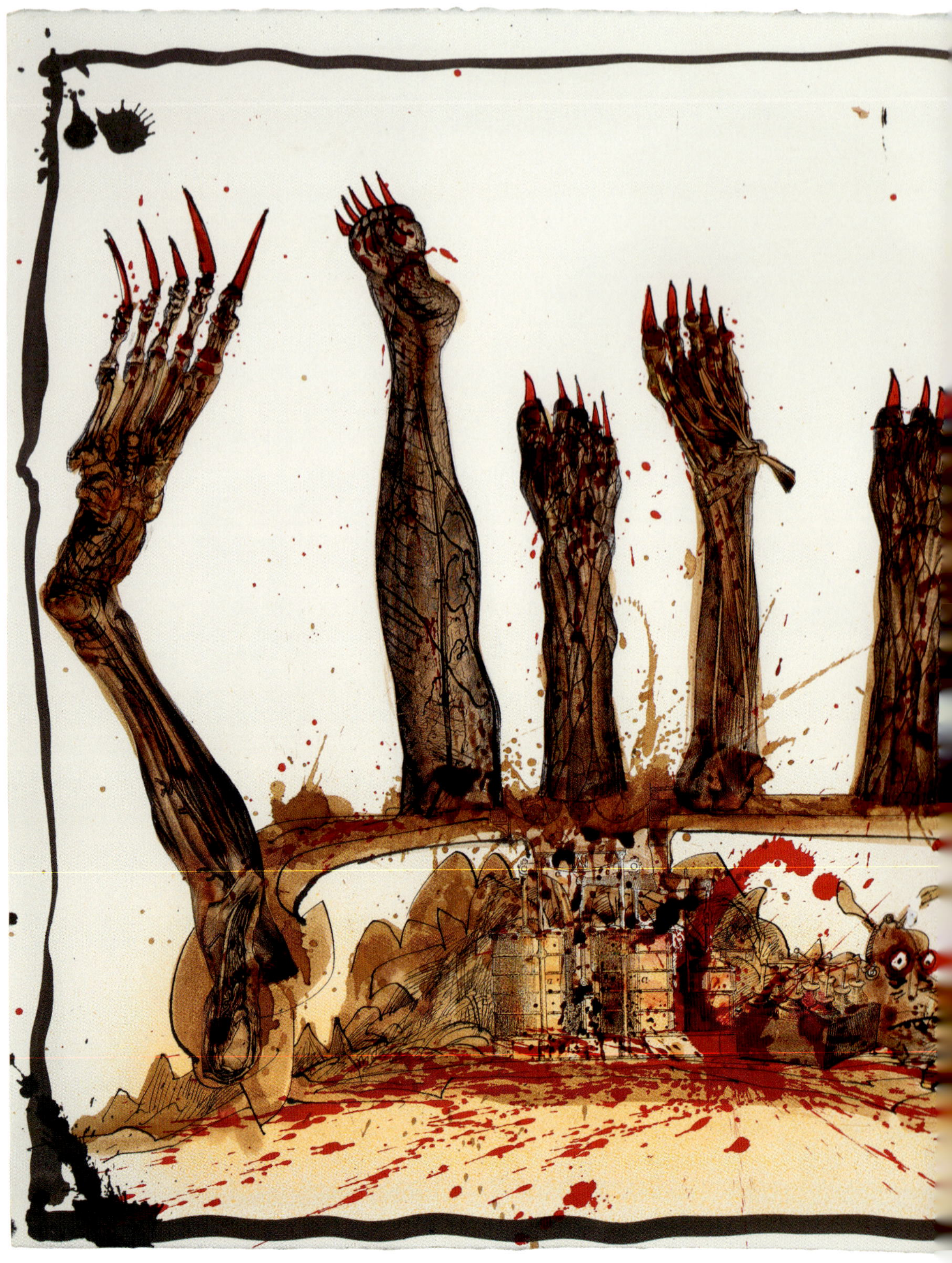

Tyrants of Our Age No. 5: Us, 1998

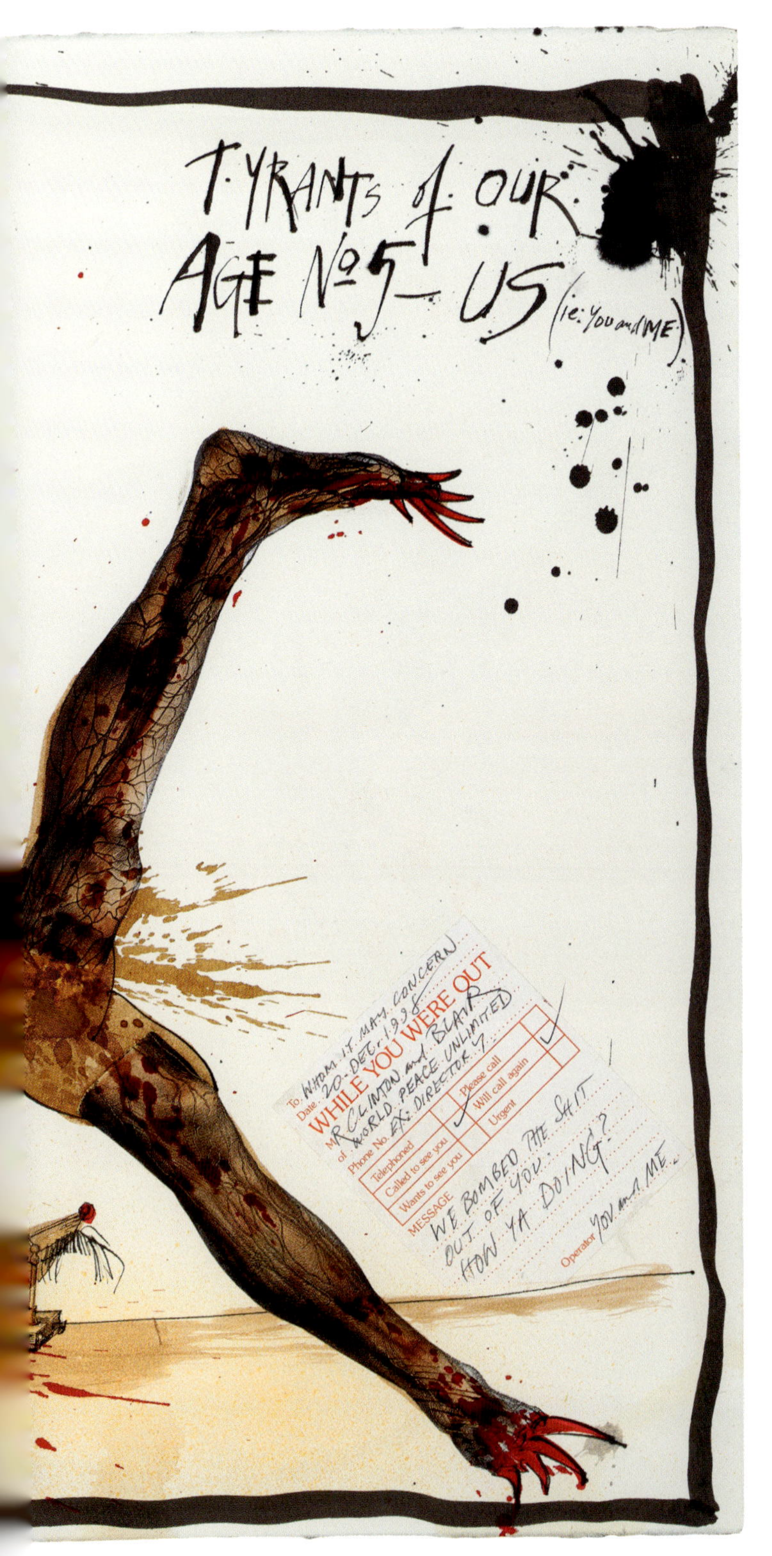
TYRANTS of OUR
AGE No 5 — US (ie. YOU and ME)
To, WHOM IT MAY CONCERN
Date 20-DEC-1998
WHILE YOU WERE OUT
MR CLINTON and BLAIR
of WORLD PEACE UNLIMITED
Phone No. EX: DIRECTOR 7
Telephoned
Called to see you
Wants to see you
Please call
Will call again
Urgent
MESSAGE
WE BOMBED THE SHIT
OUT OF YOU.
HOW YA DOING?
Operator YOU and ME.

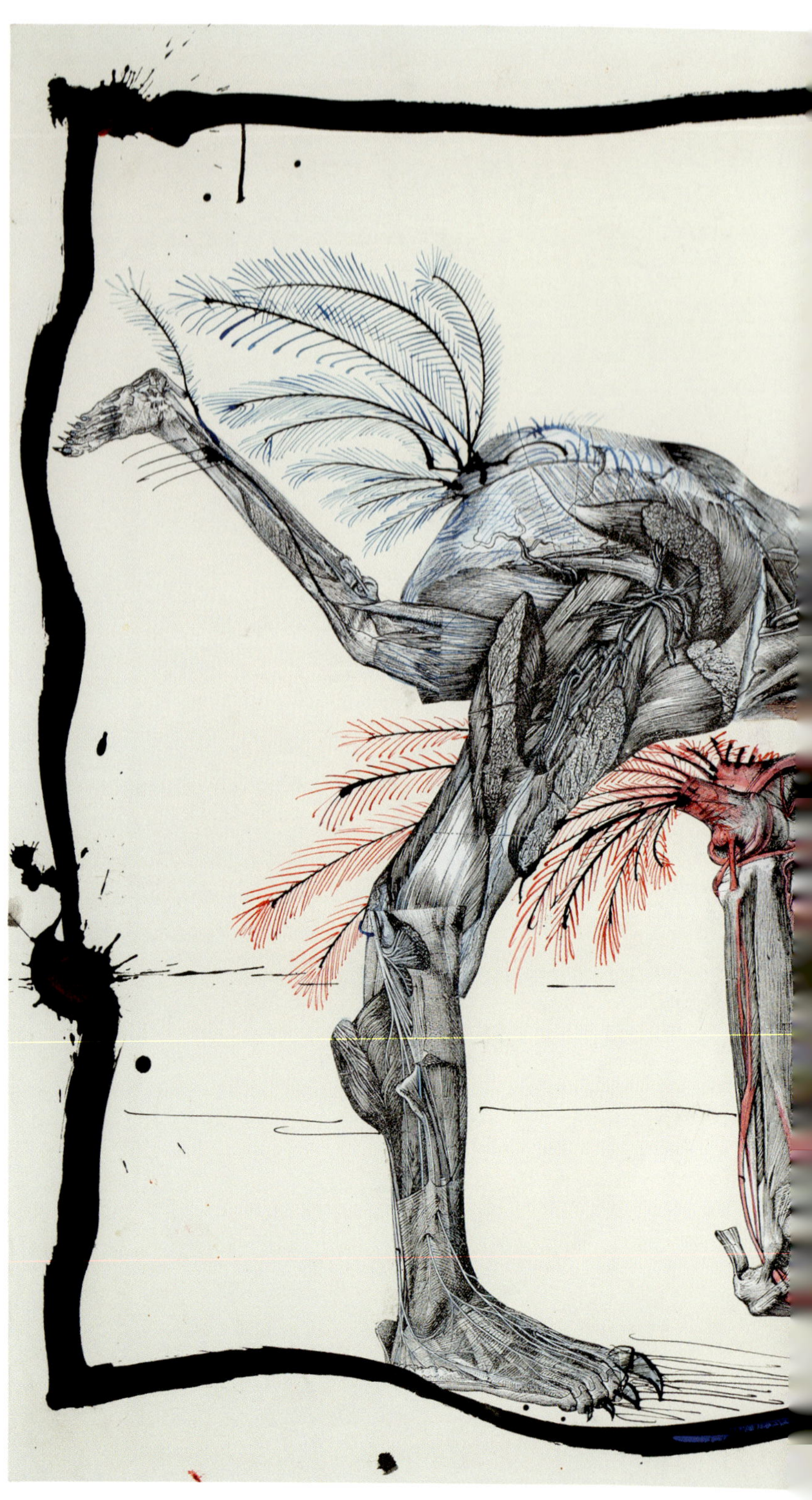

Elections, Kiss My Ass Lip Service, 1997

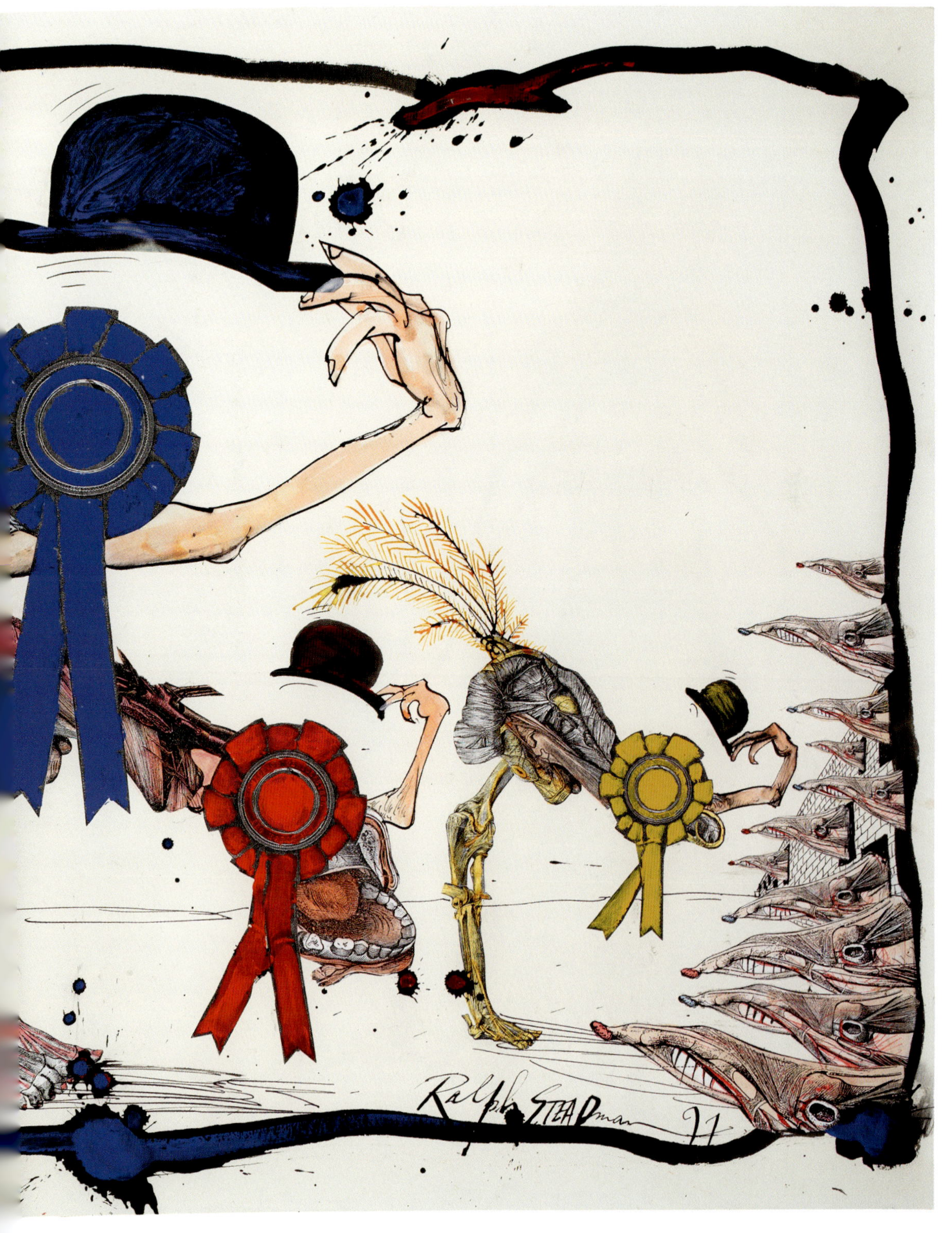

"During the 1997 election I just wanted to get the Tories out of government. That year Labour won, so I hope I helped!"

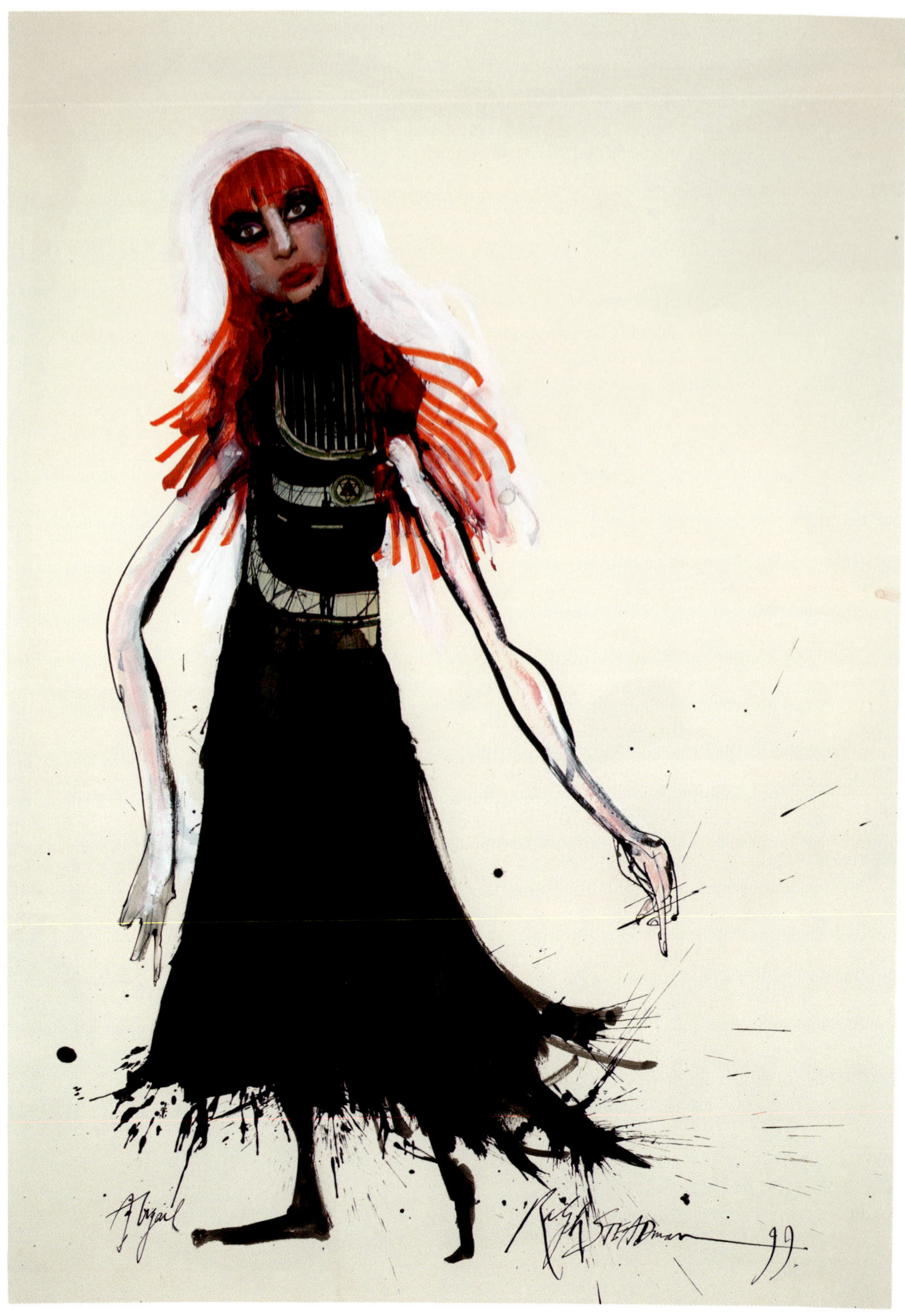

Abigail, **The Crucible** *ballet, The Royal Opera House, 1999*

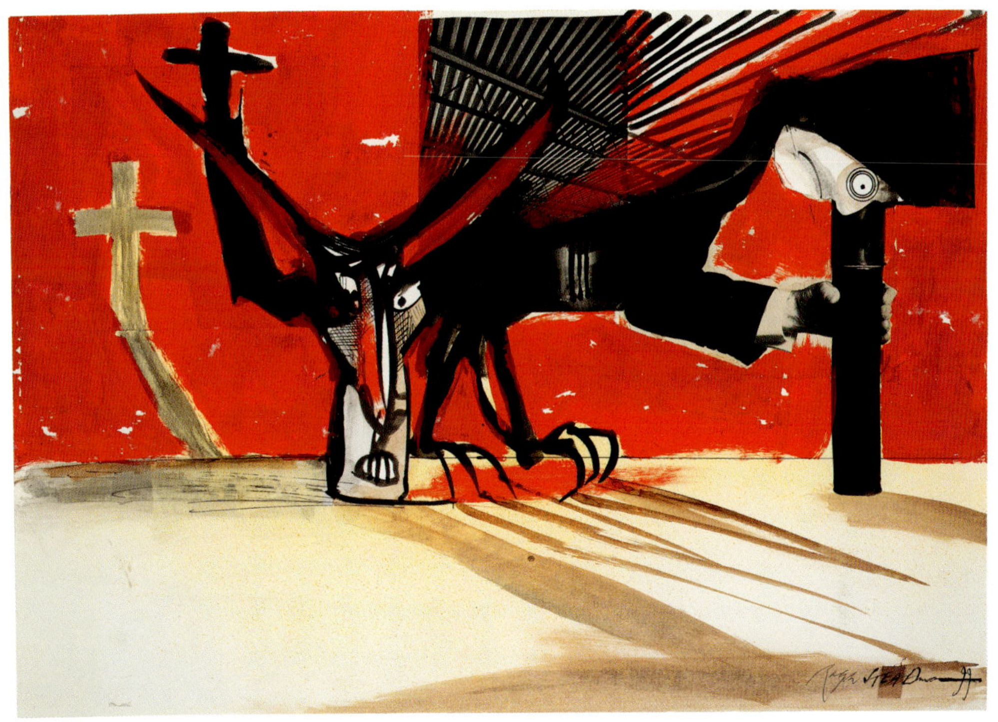

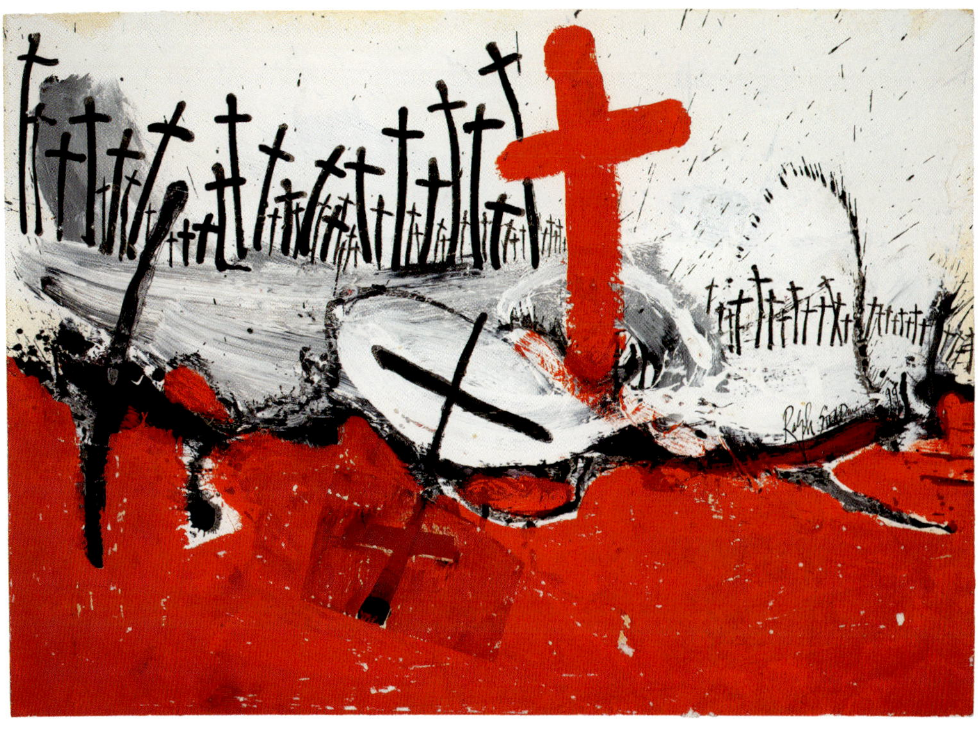

*Scenes from **The Crucible** ballet, The Royal Opera House, 1999*

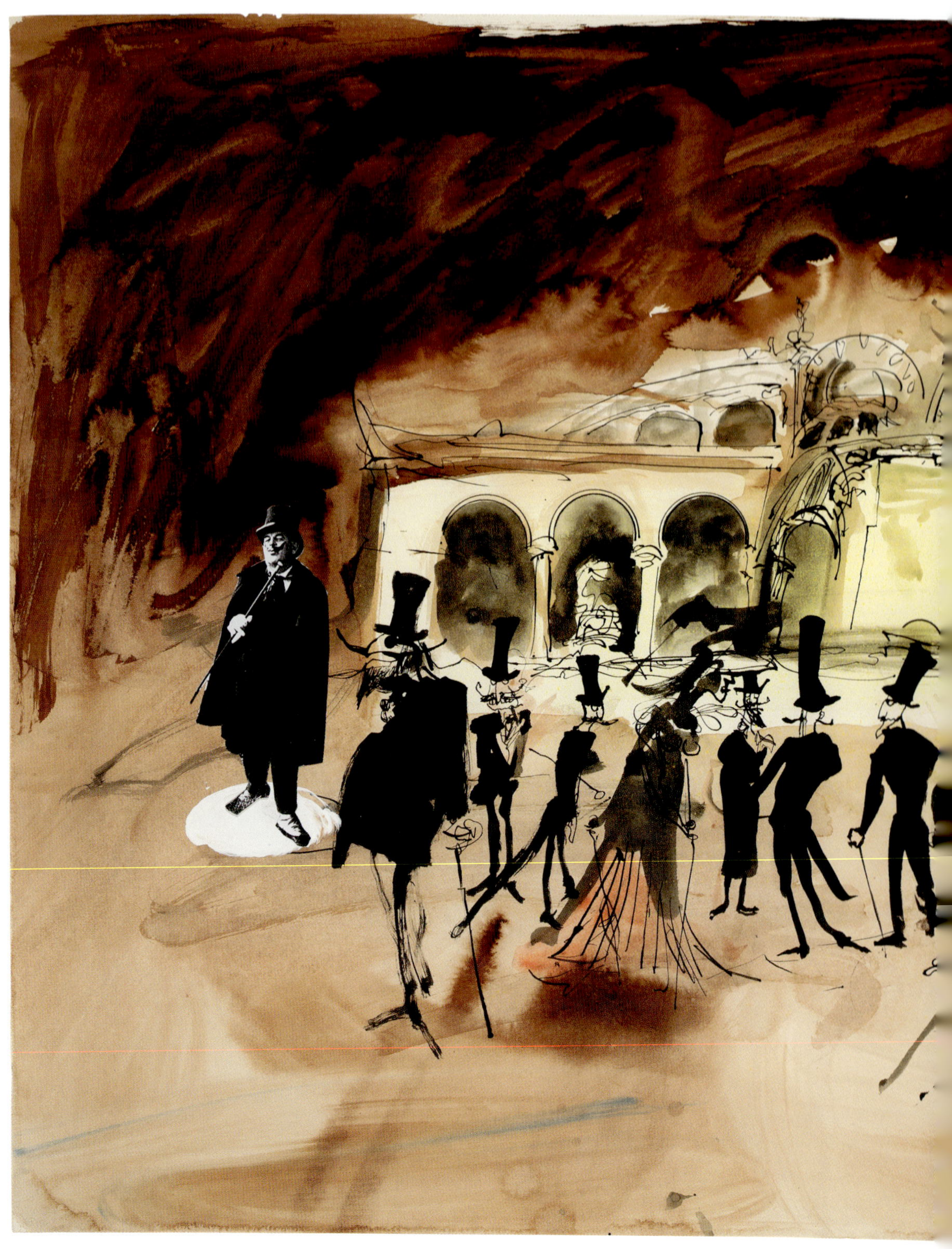

"For the TV show *Leviathan*, late 1990s. They made me dress up a lot. I got my Equity Card through it. Not sure I ever needed to use it again though."

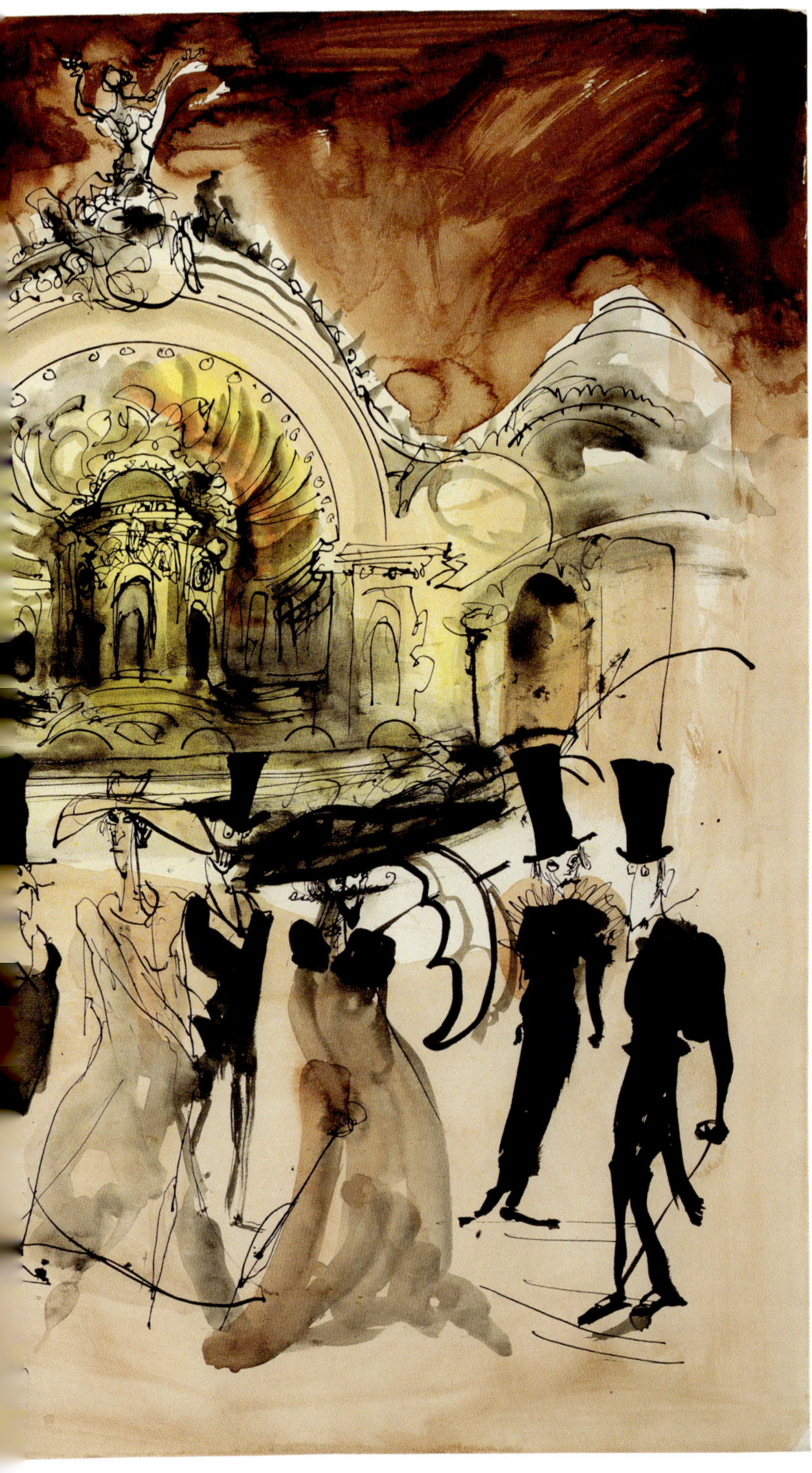

The Hoi-Polloi! ca. 1995

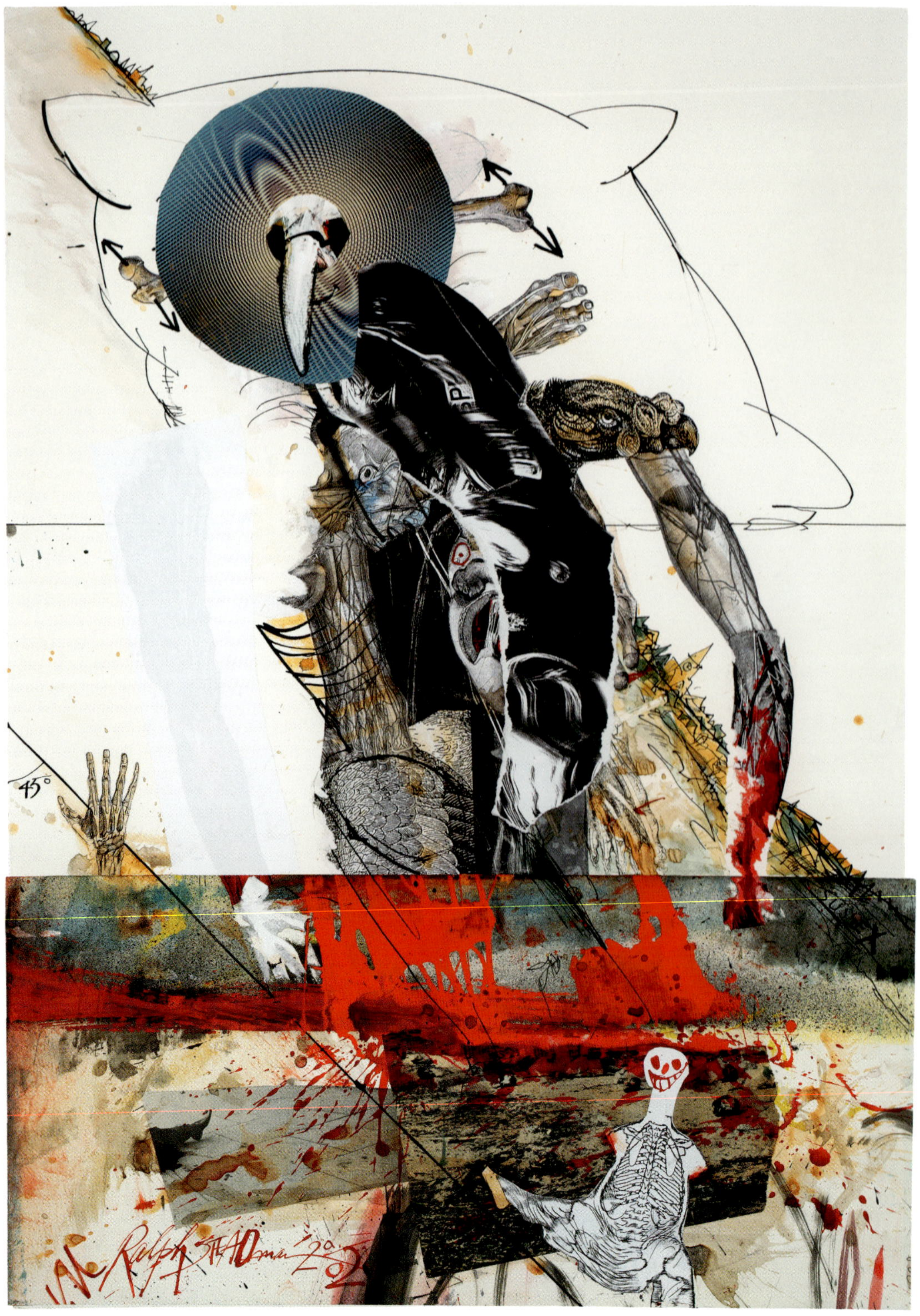

Spiritual Symbol Right, 2002

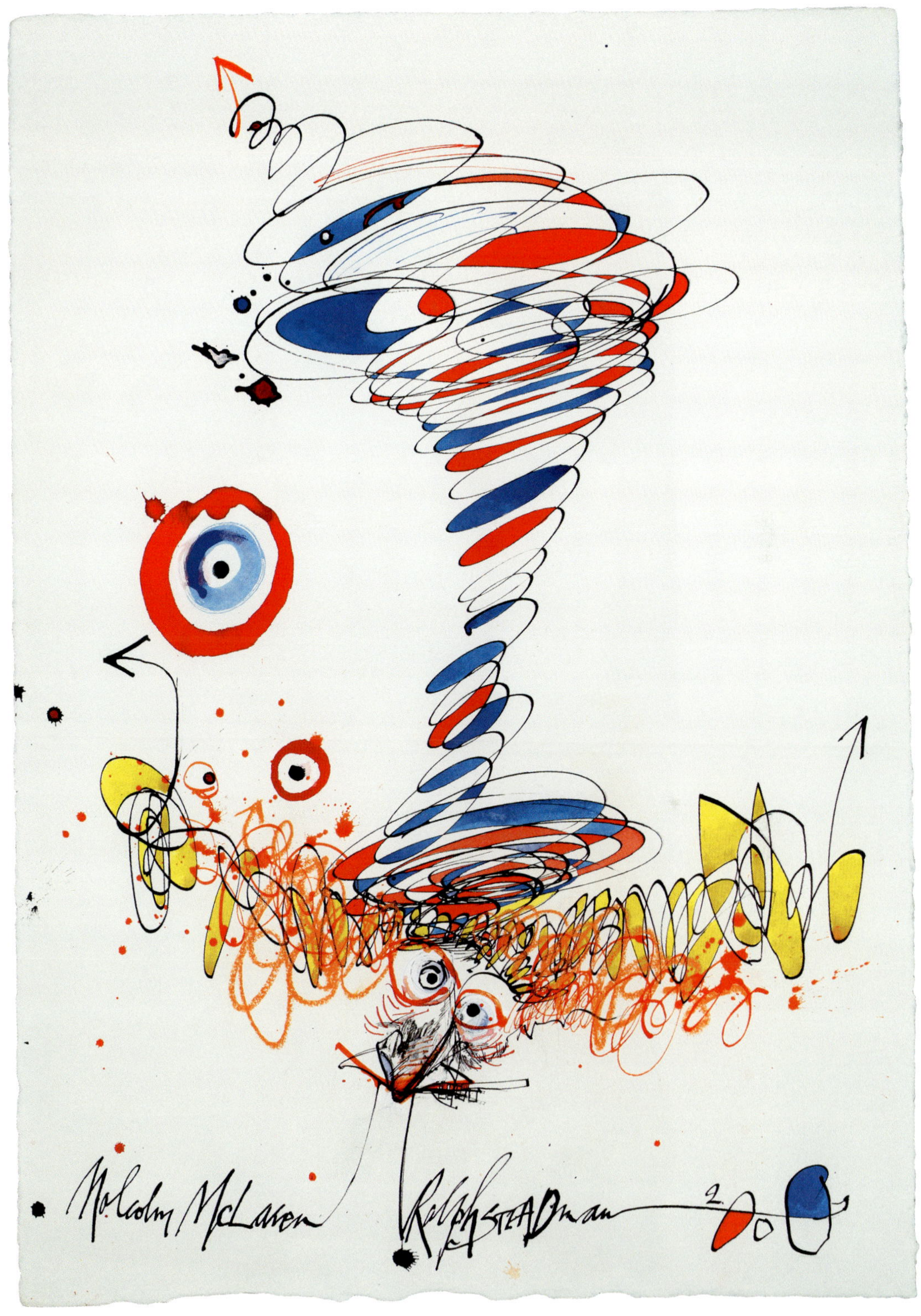

Malcolm McLaren
Ralph STEADman
2000

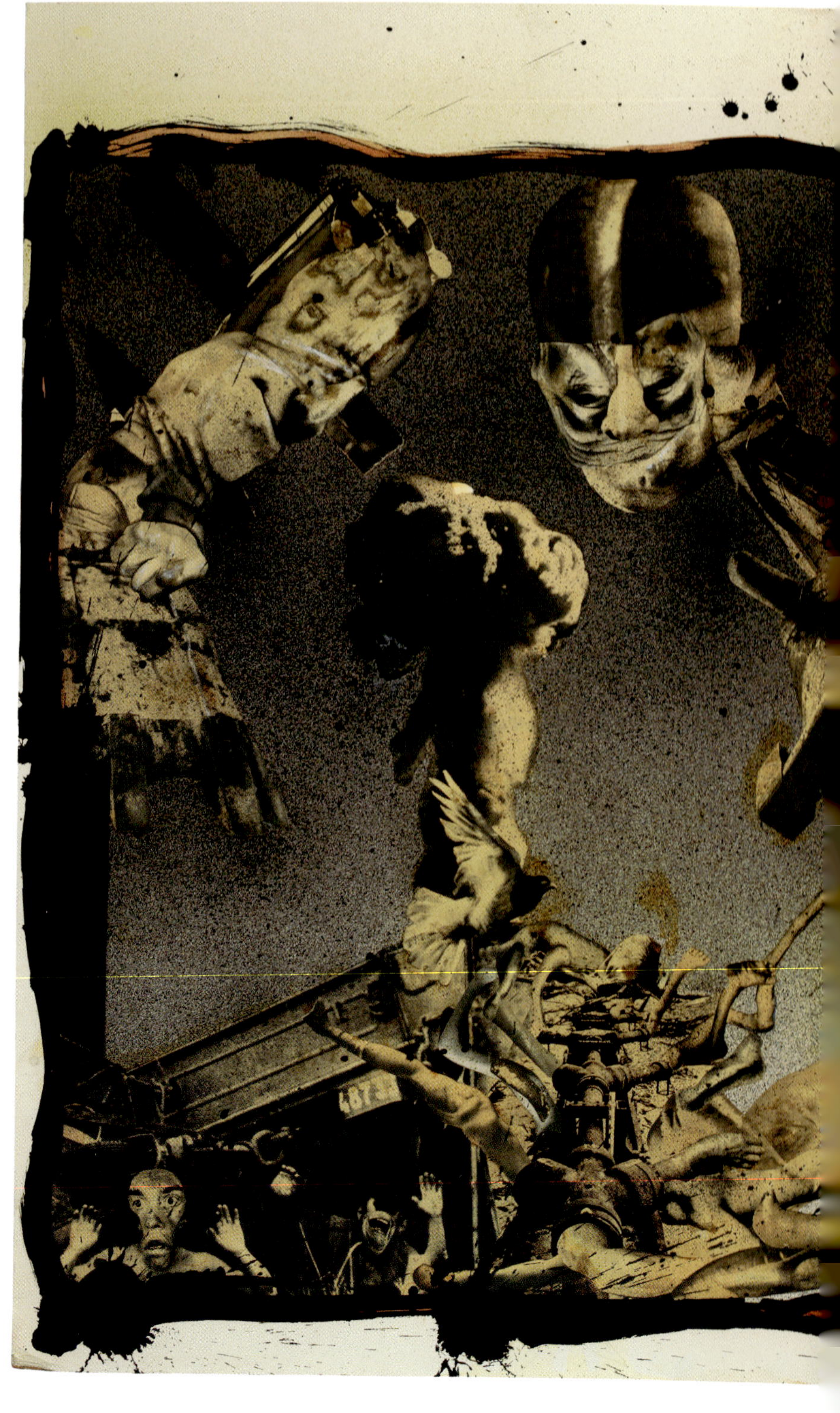

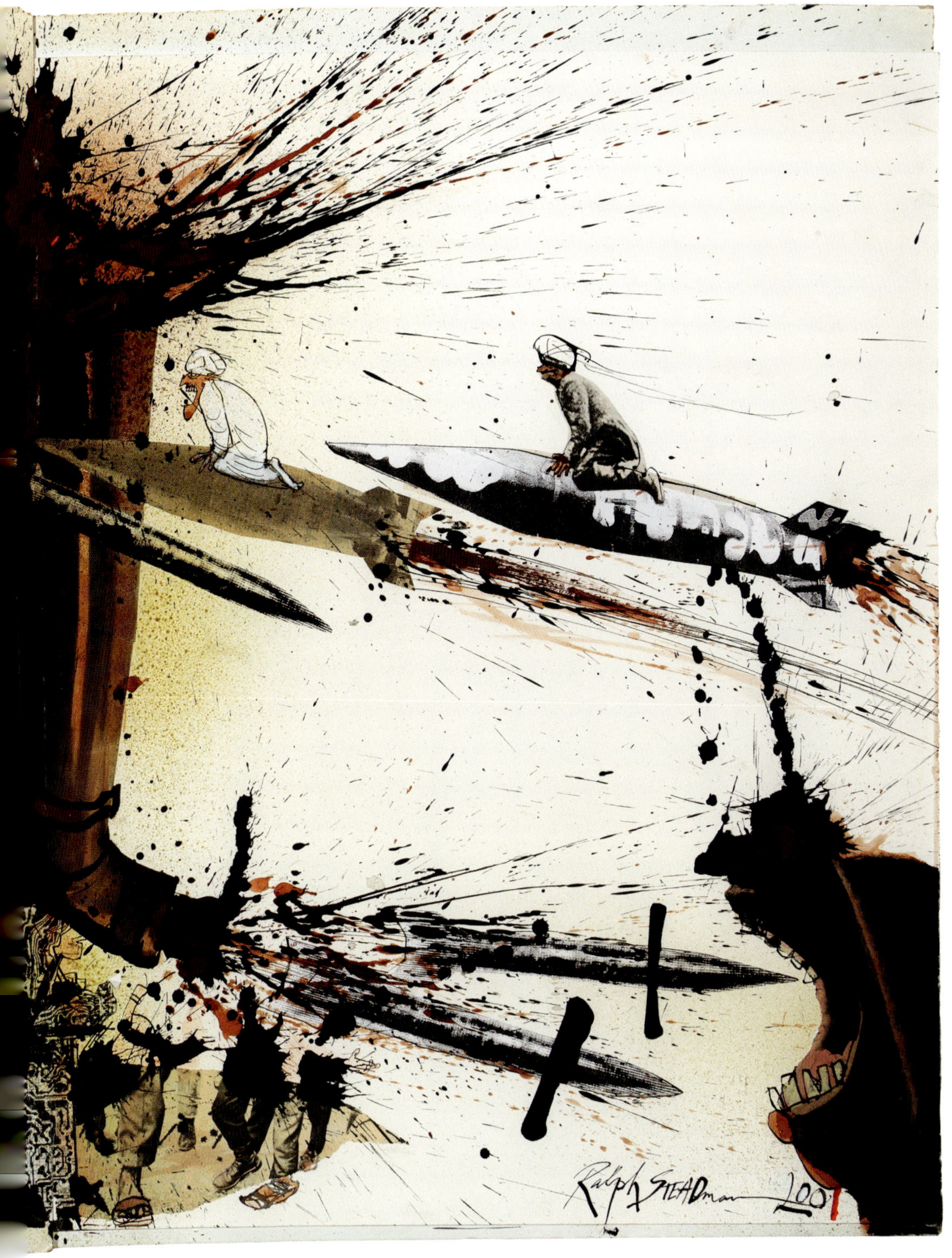

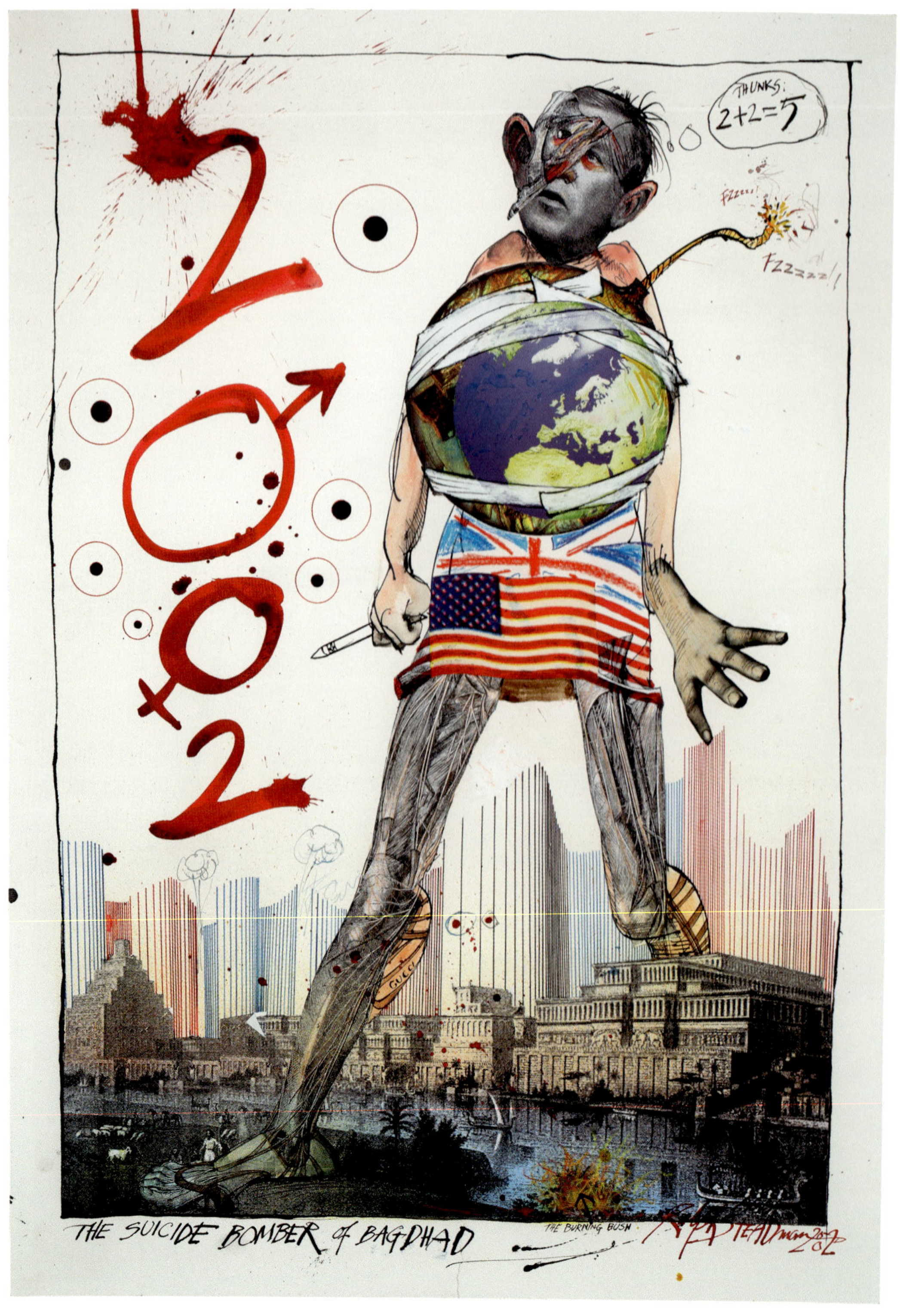

George Bush Jr., The Bomber of Baghdad, 2002 "Really I thought that George Bush Junior was as low as the presidency could sink. How wrong I was!"

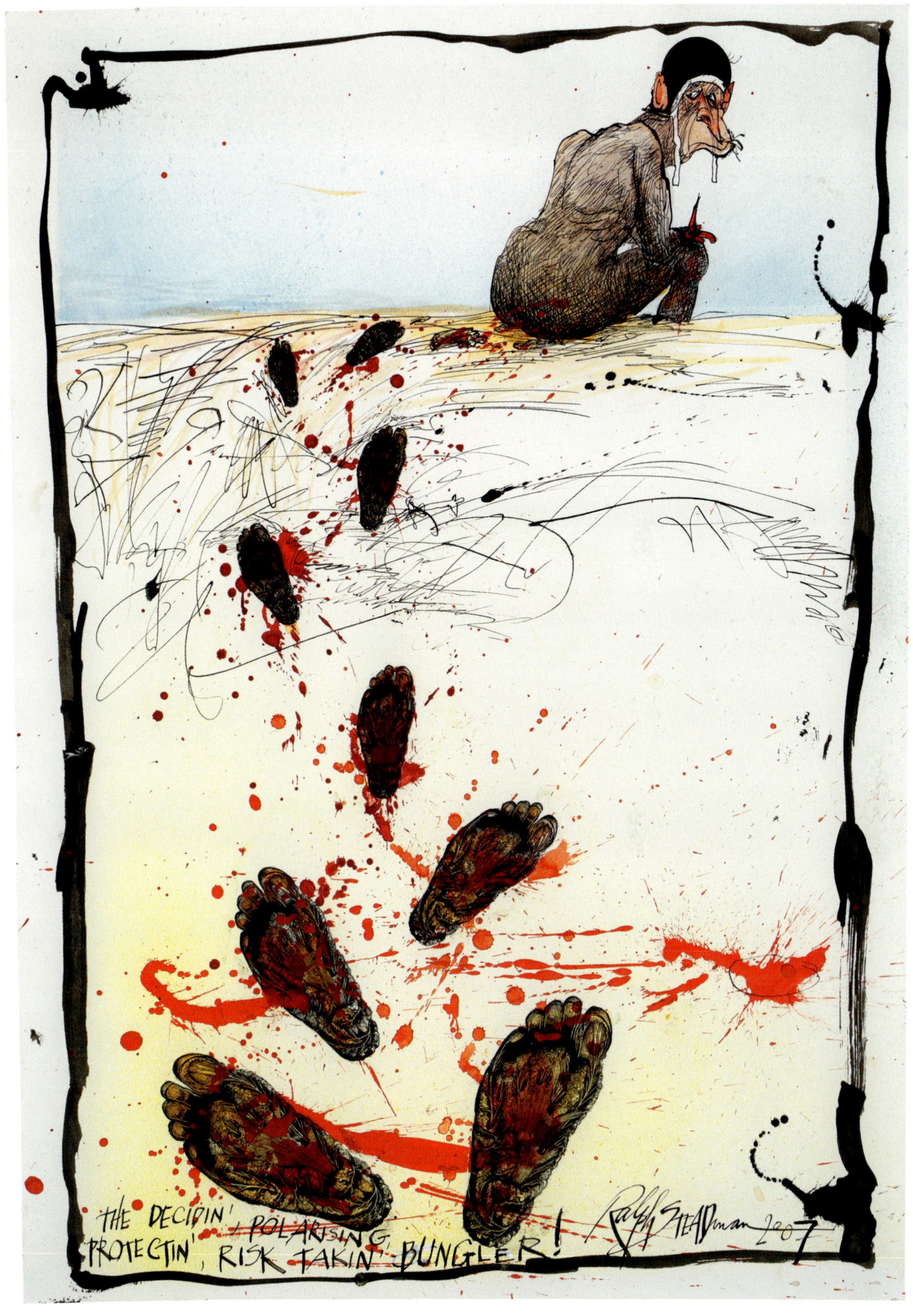

THE DECIDIN'
PROTECTIN', POLARISING
RISK TAKIN' BUNGLER!

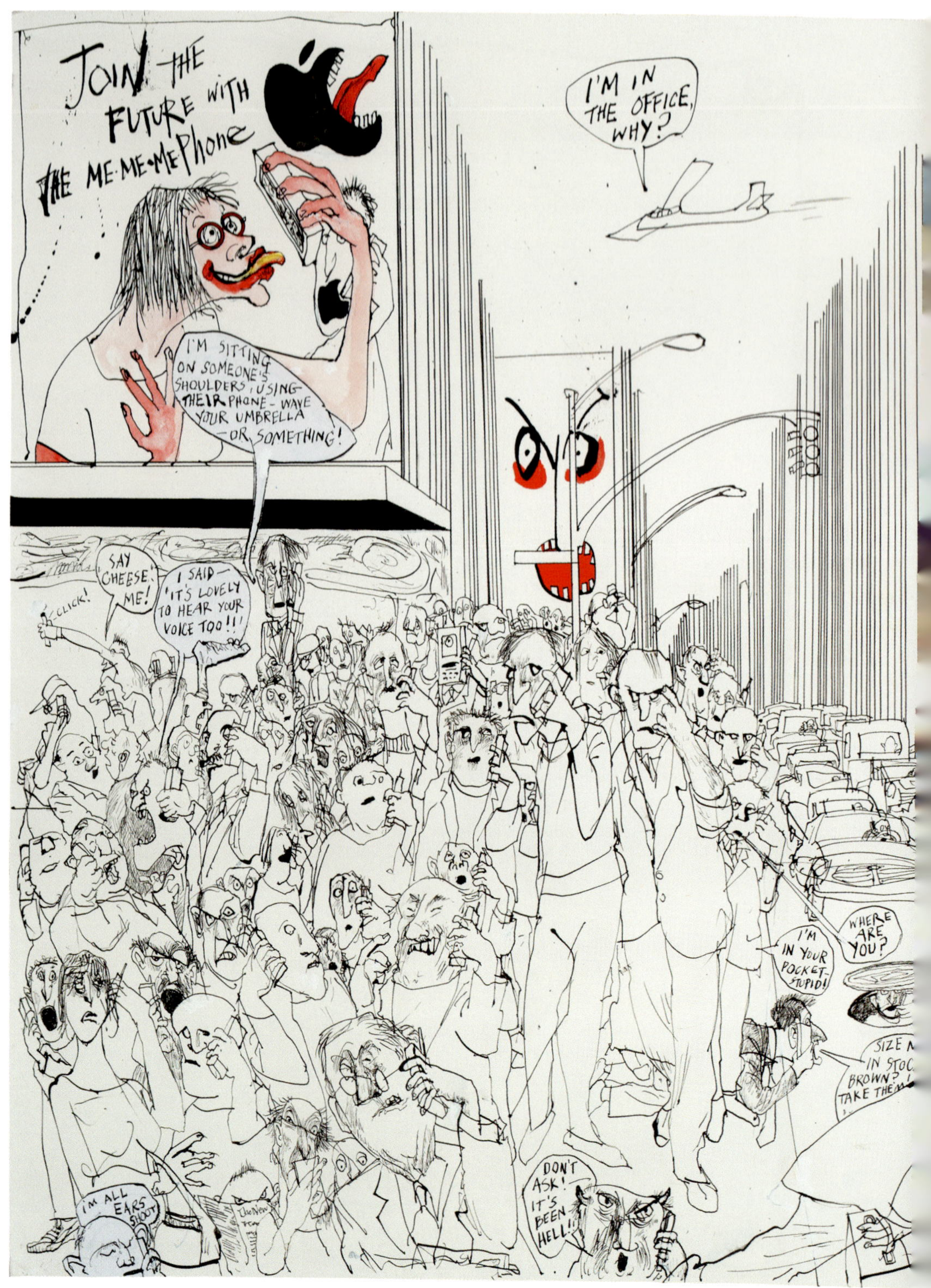

Pedestrian Landscape—Birth of the Mobile Phone, **The New Yorker**, *2008*

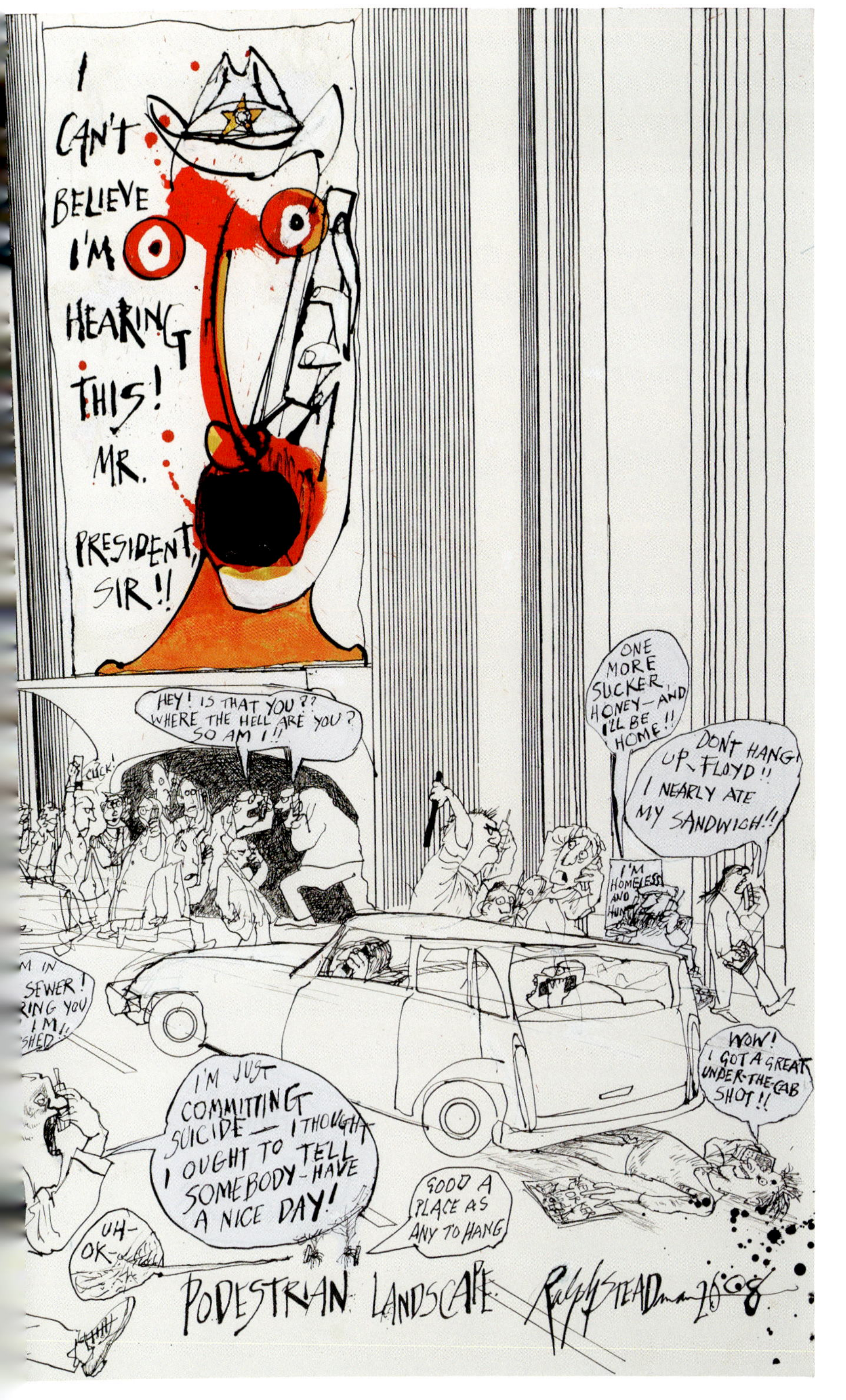

I CAN'T BELIEVE I'M HEARING THIS! MR. PRESIDENT, SIR!!
ONE MORE SUCKER HONEY—AND I'LL BE HOME!!
DON'T HANG UP, FLOYD!! I NEARLY ATE MY SANDWICH!!
HEY! IS THAT YOU?? WHERE THE HELL ARE YOU? SO AM I!!
CLICK
I'M HOMELESS AND HUNGRY
I'M IN SEWER! RING YOU I'M SHED
WOW! I GOT A GREAT UNDER-THE-CAB SHOT!!
I'M JUST COMMITTING SUICIDE — I THOUGHT I OUGHT TO TELL SOMEBODY — HAVE A NICE DAY!
GOOD A PLACE AS ANY TO HANG
UH-OK-
PODESTRIAN LANDSCAPE.   Ralph STEADman 2008

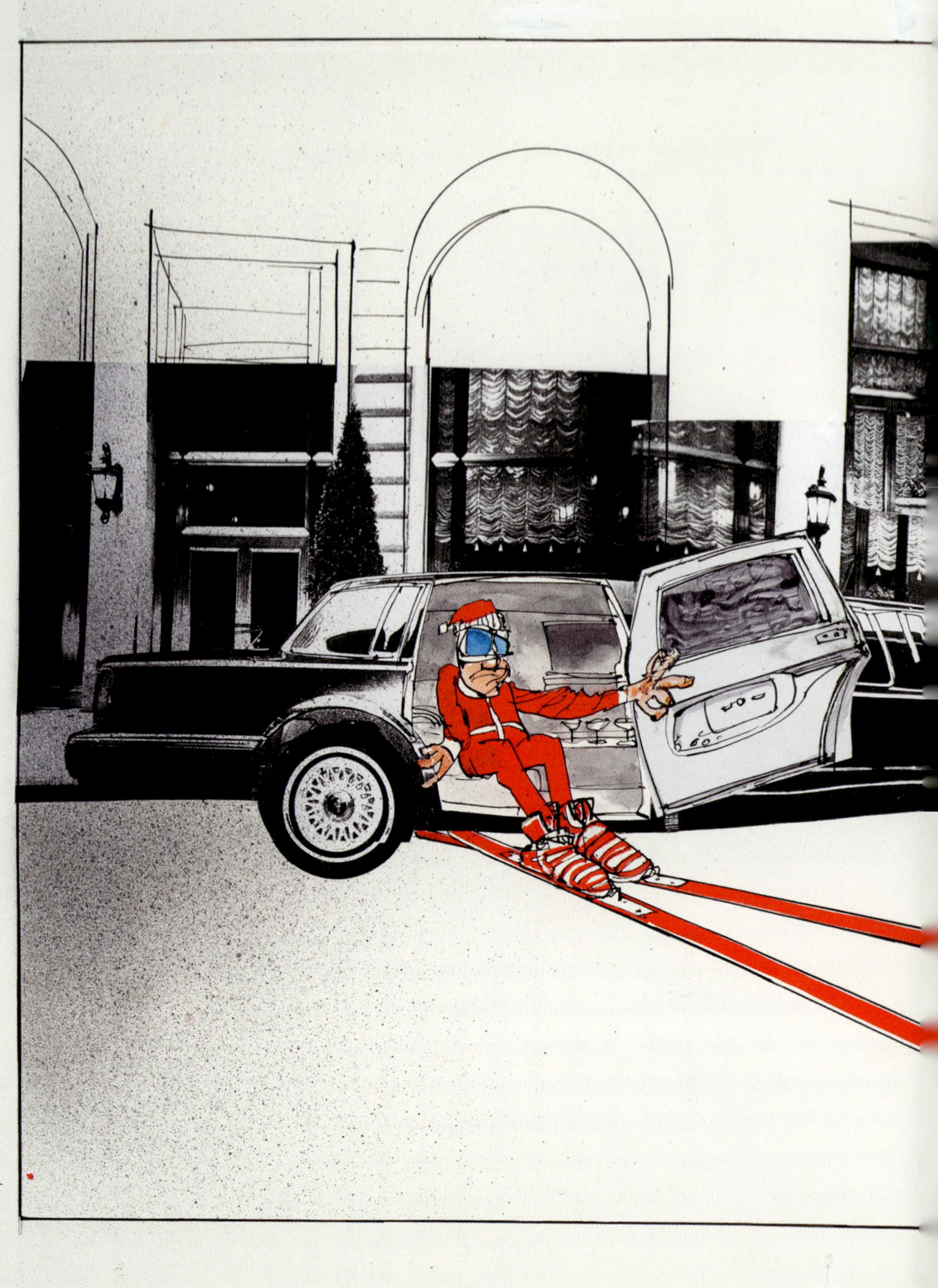

Guest Disembarking at the St. Regis, 2003

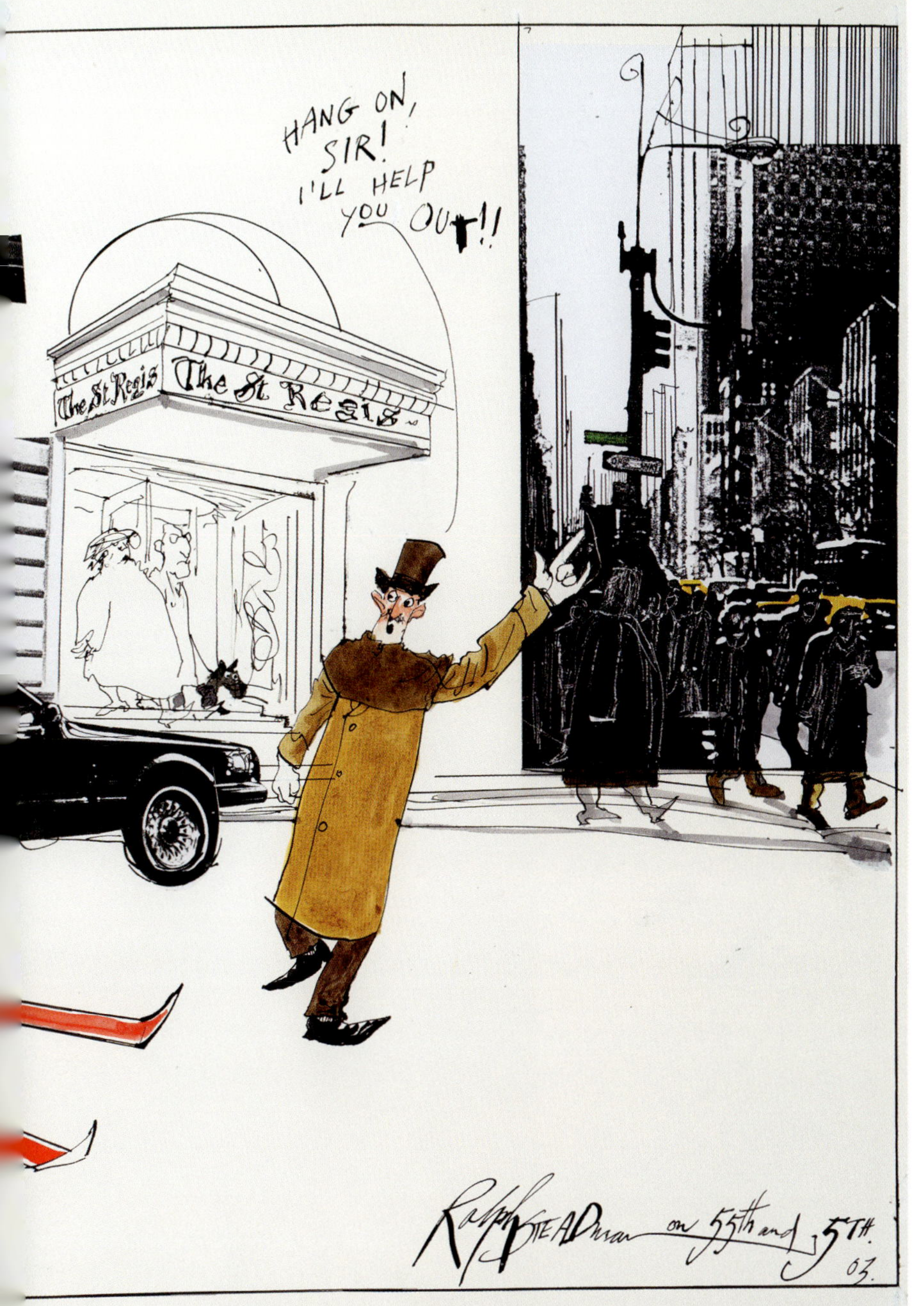

HANG ON, SIR! I'LL HELP YOU OUT!!
The St Regis   The St Regis
Ralph STEADman on 55th and 5TH.
03.

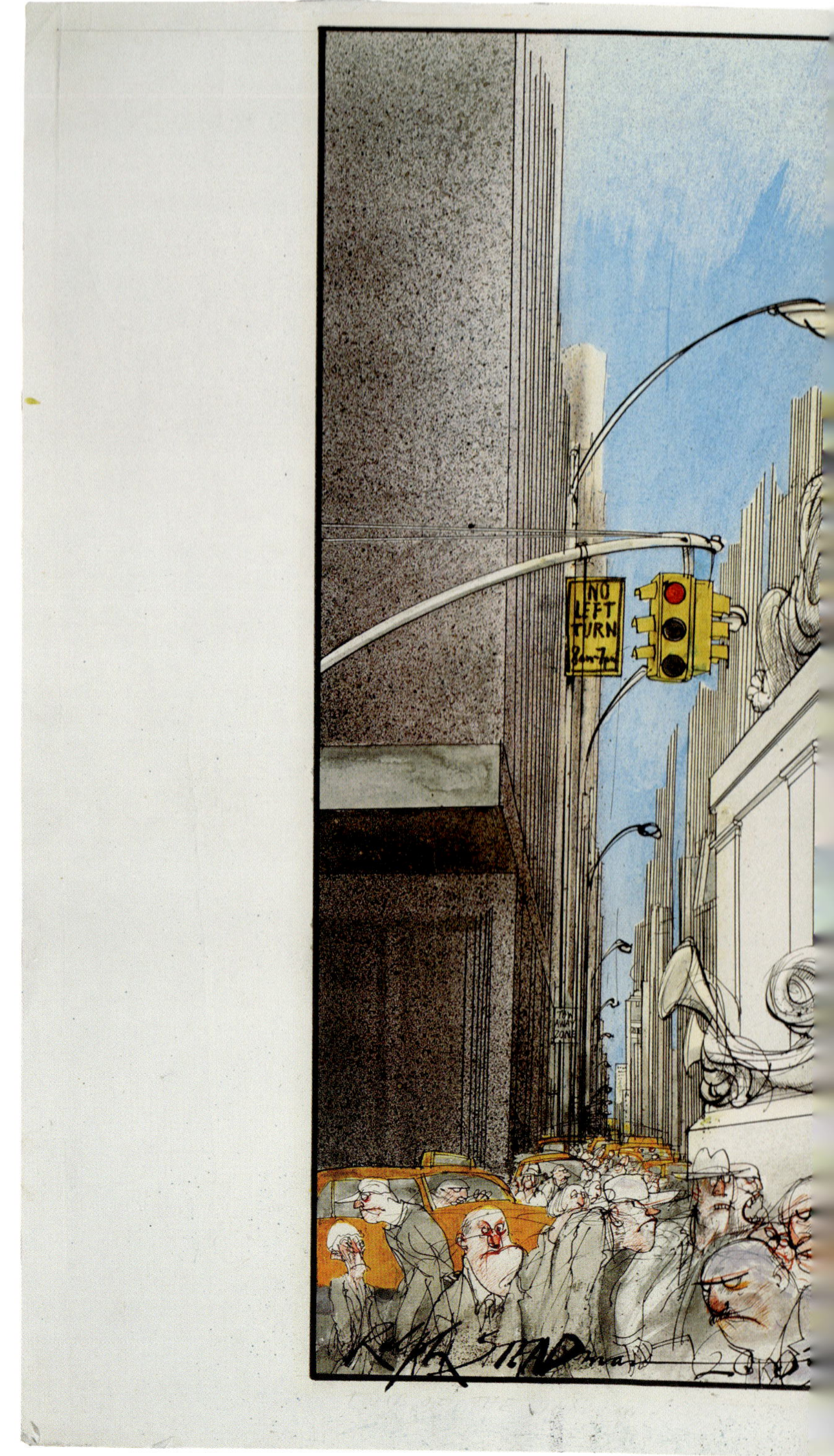

NO
LEFT
TURN
8am-7pm

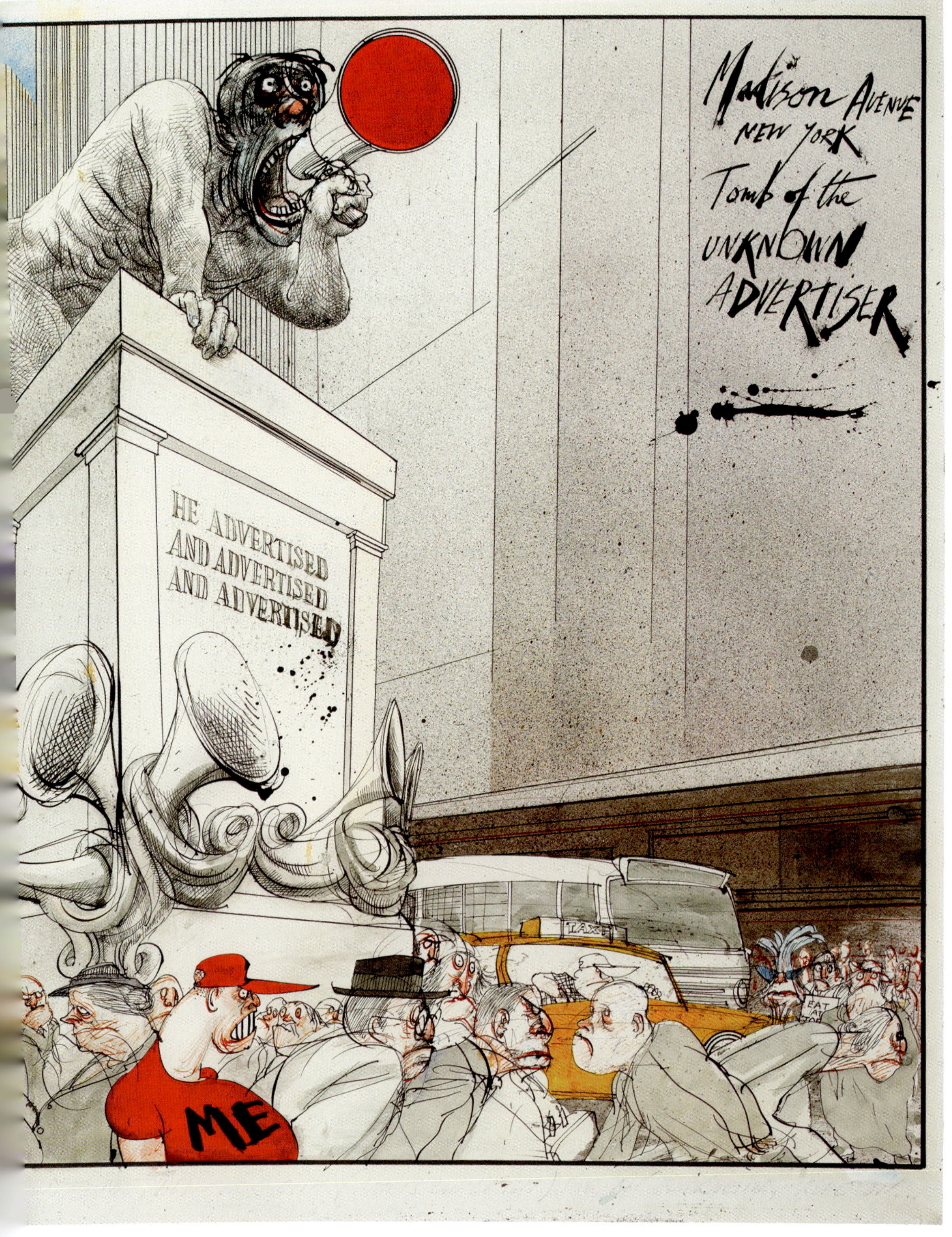

Madison Avenue—The Tomb of the Unknown Advertiser, 2003

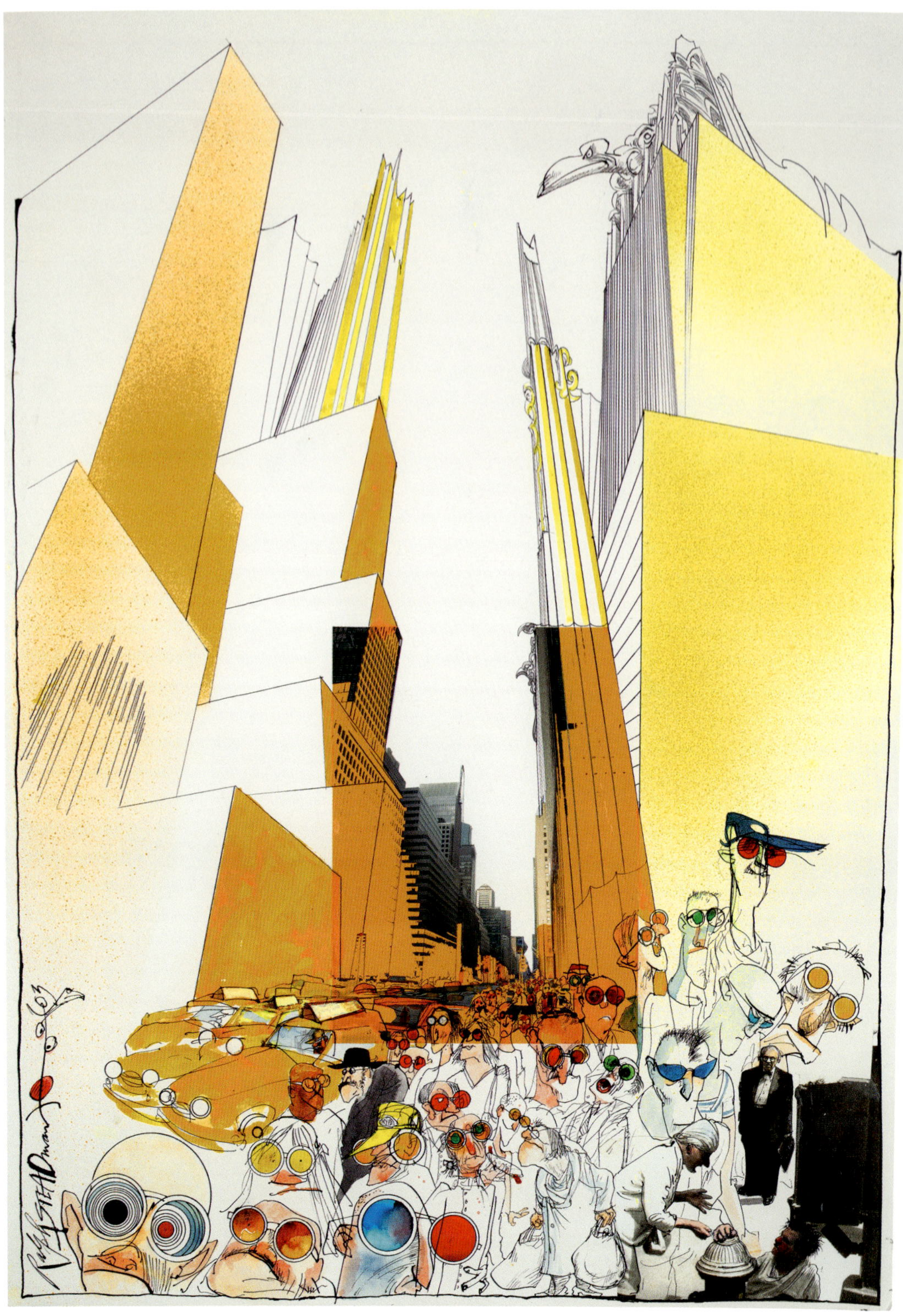

Street Scene, New York, 2000

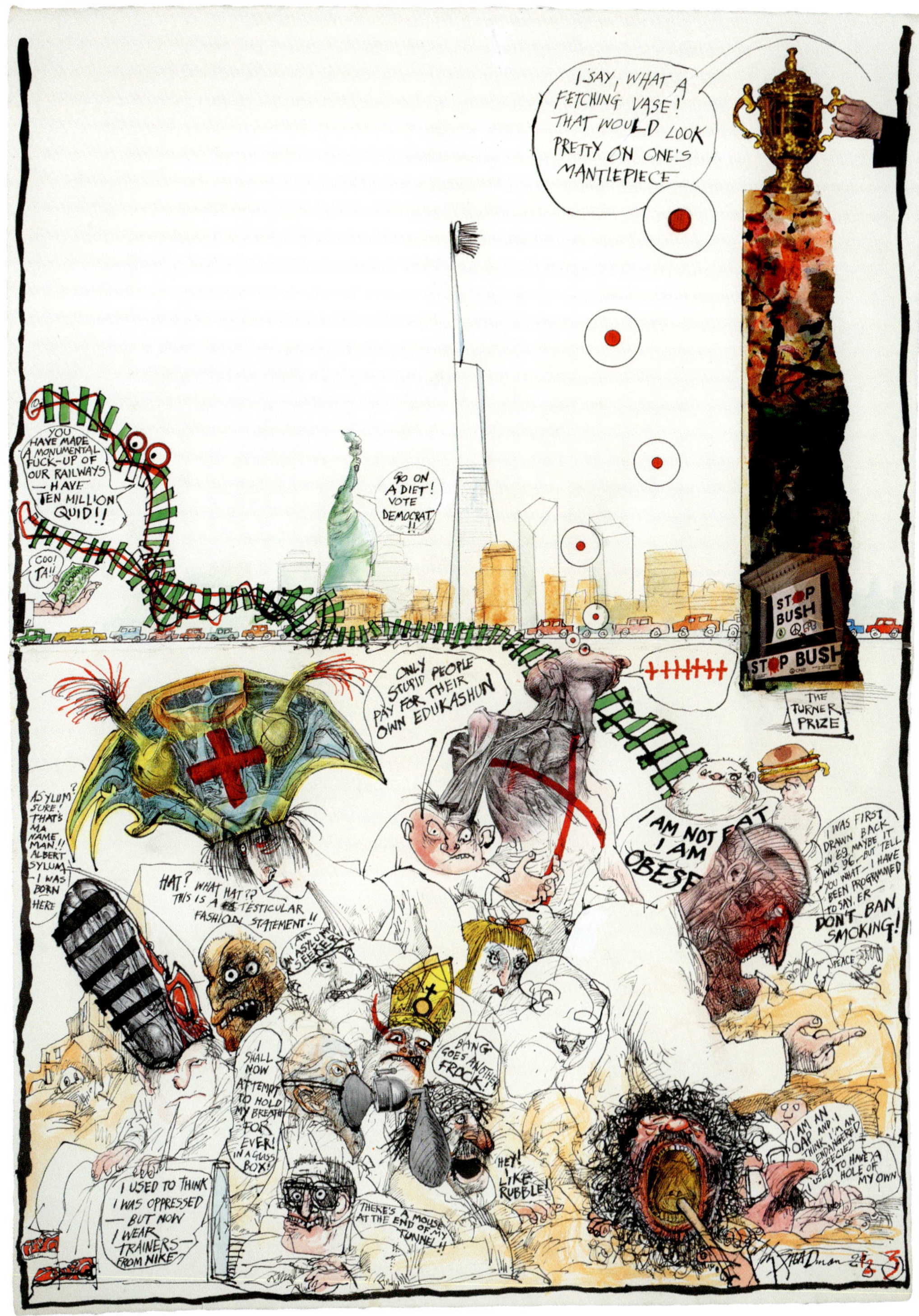

World Cup, 2003

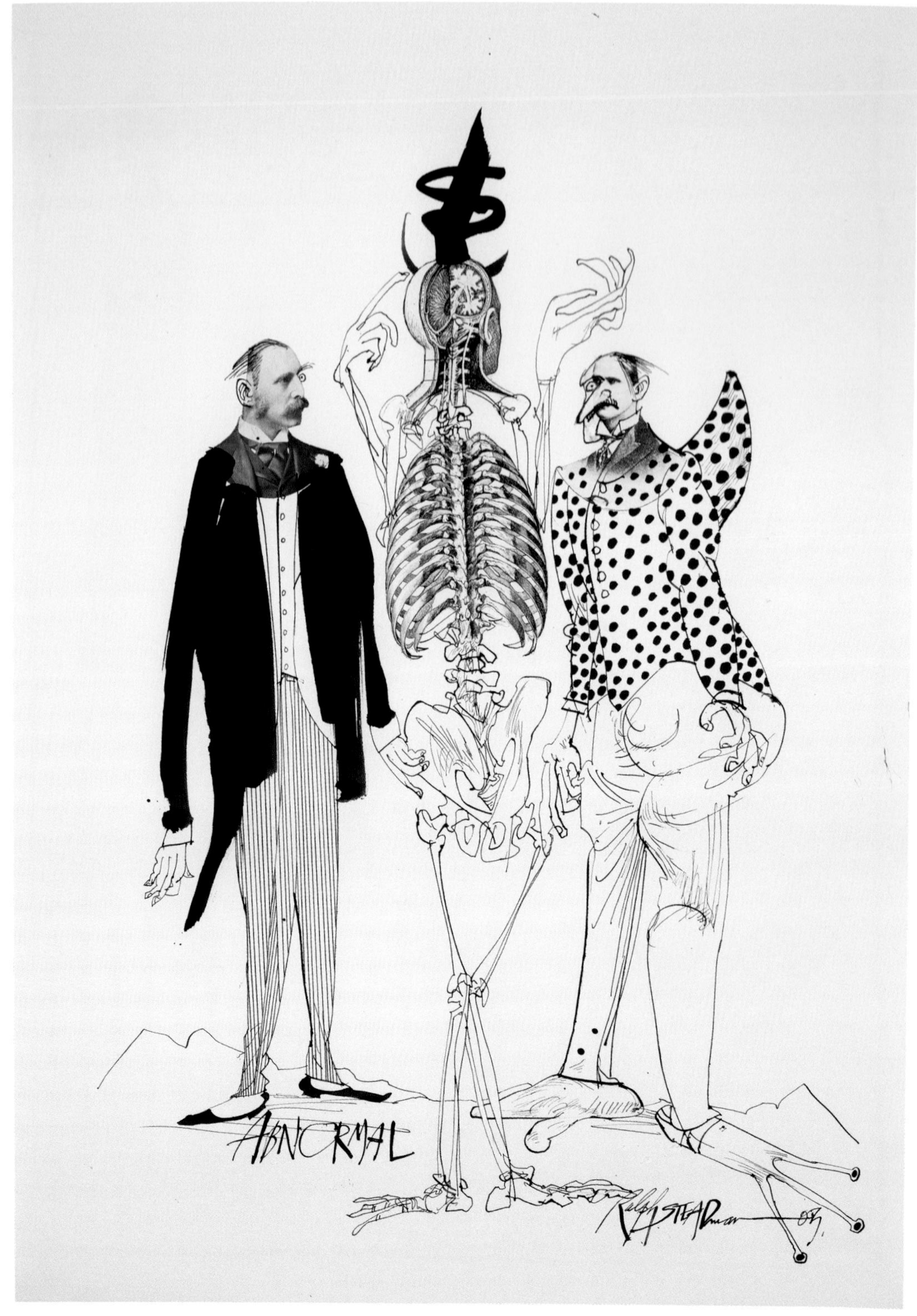

A is for Abnormal, **The Devil's Dictionary** by Ambrose Bierce, 2003

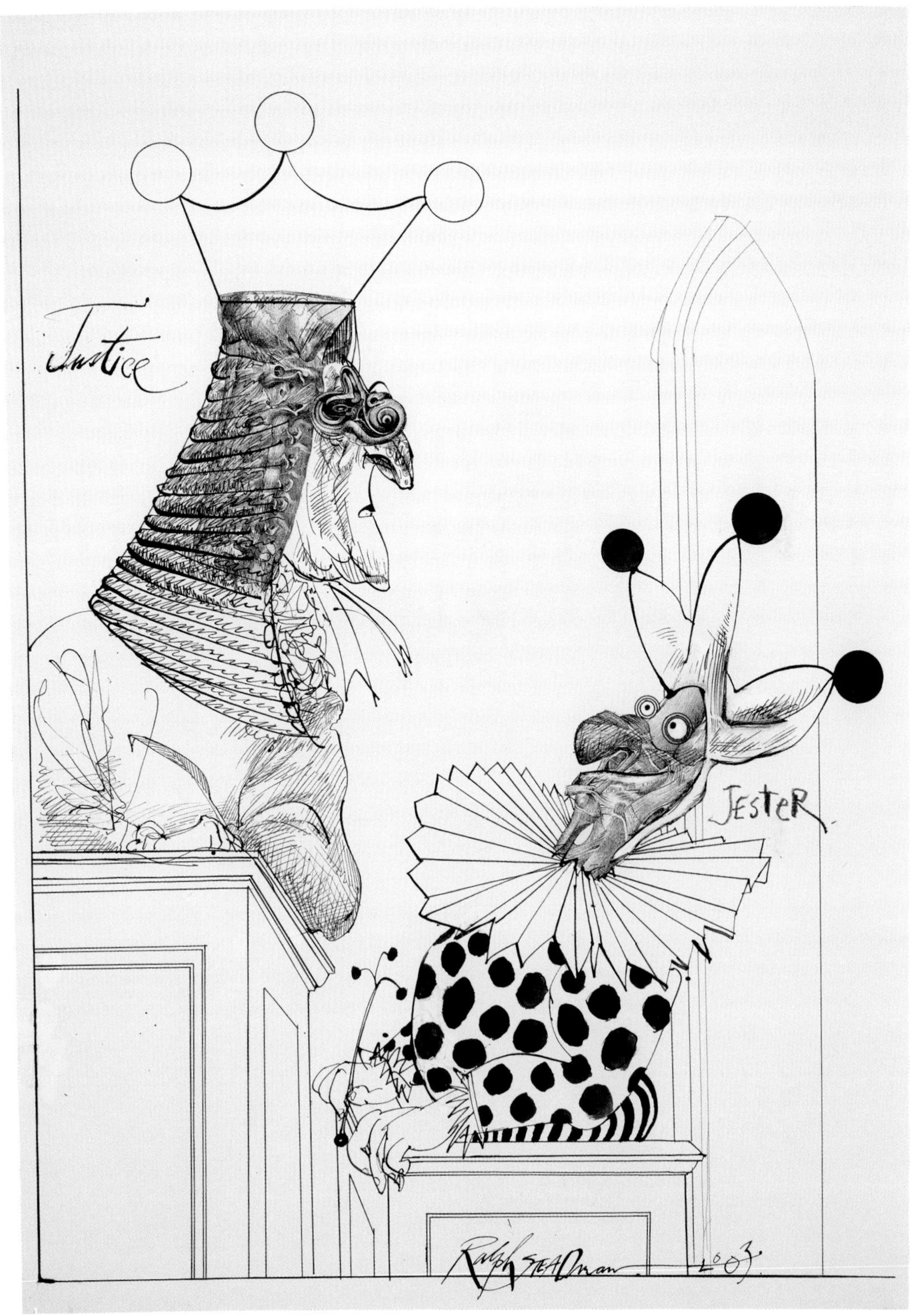

J is for Justice, *The Devil's Dictionary* by Ambrose Bierce, 2003

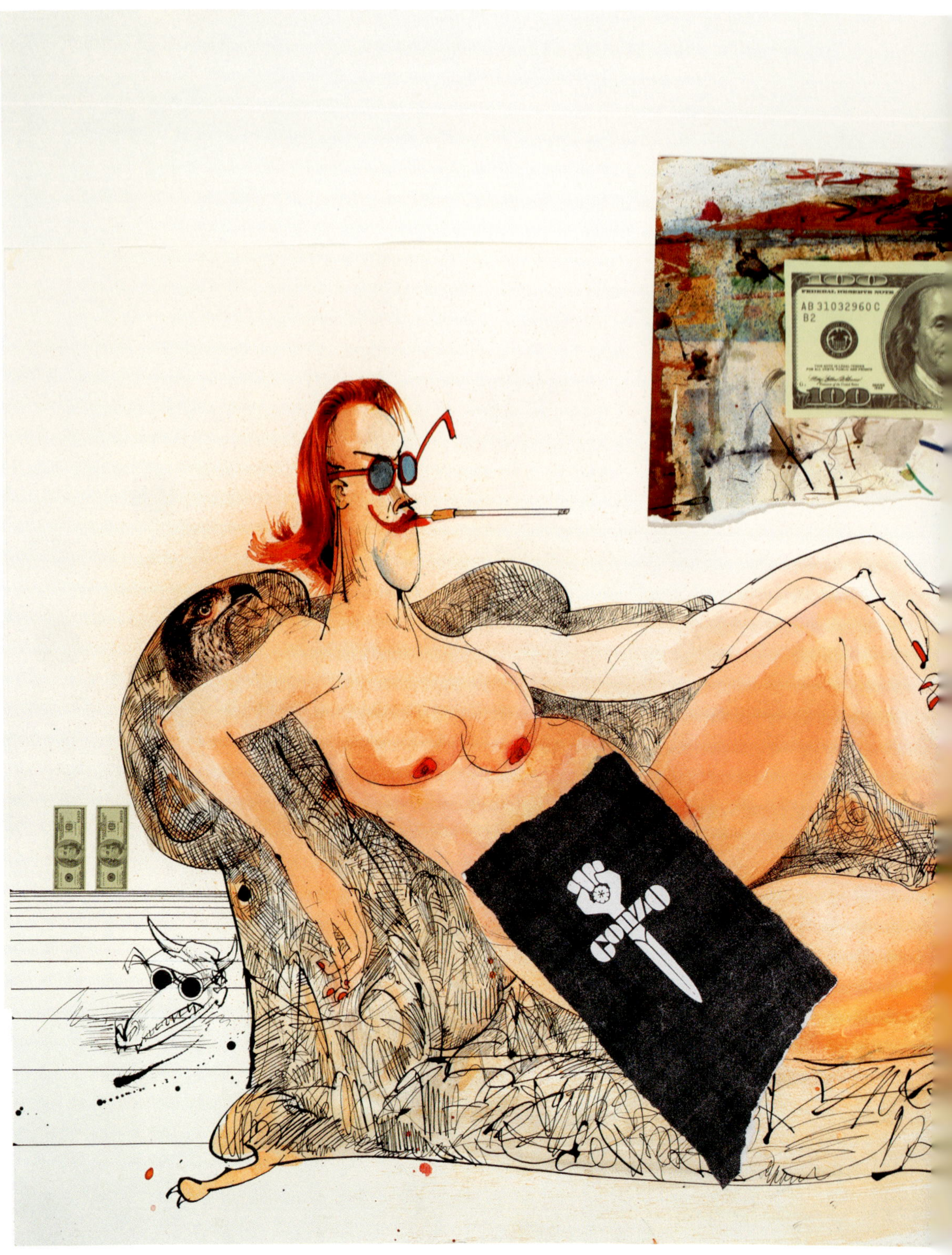

If Hunter Were a Woman... 2003

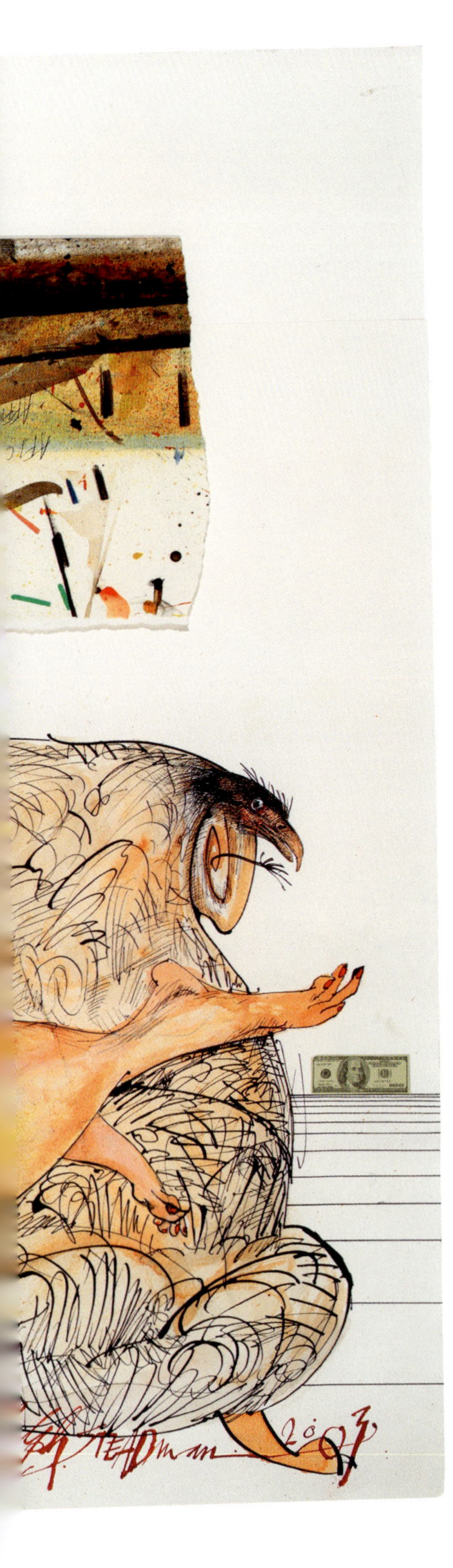

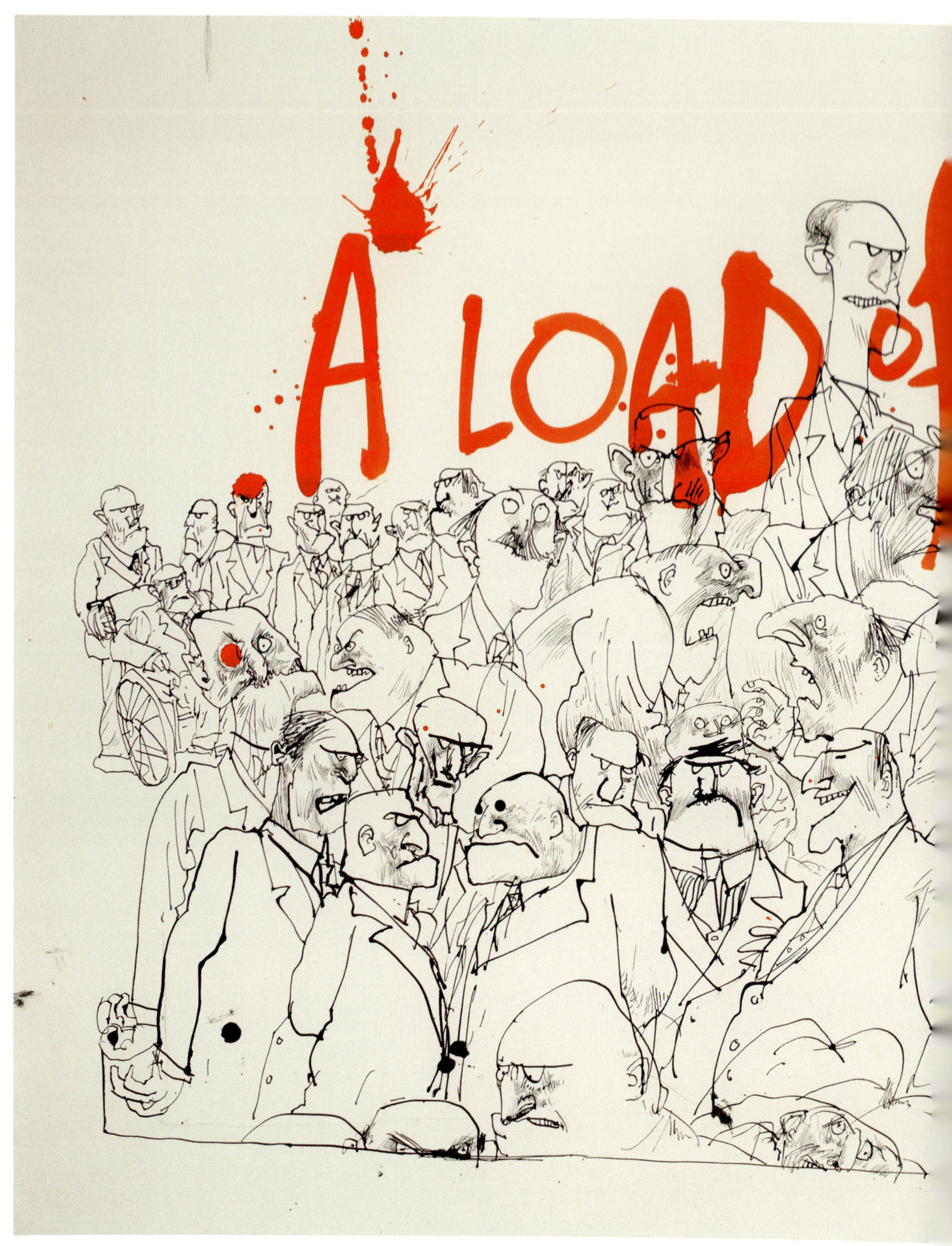

A Load of Bankers, 2002 "I wrote a song called '*We Are Scum*' for my Leonardo musical. It's about bankers!"

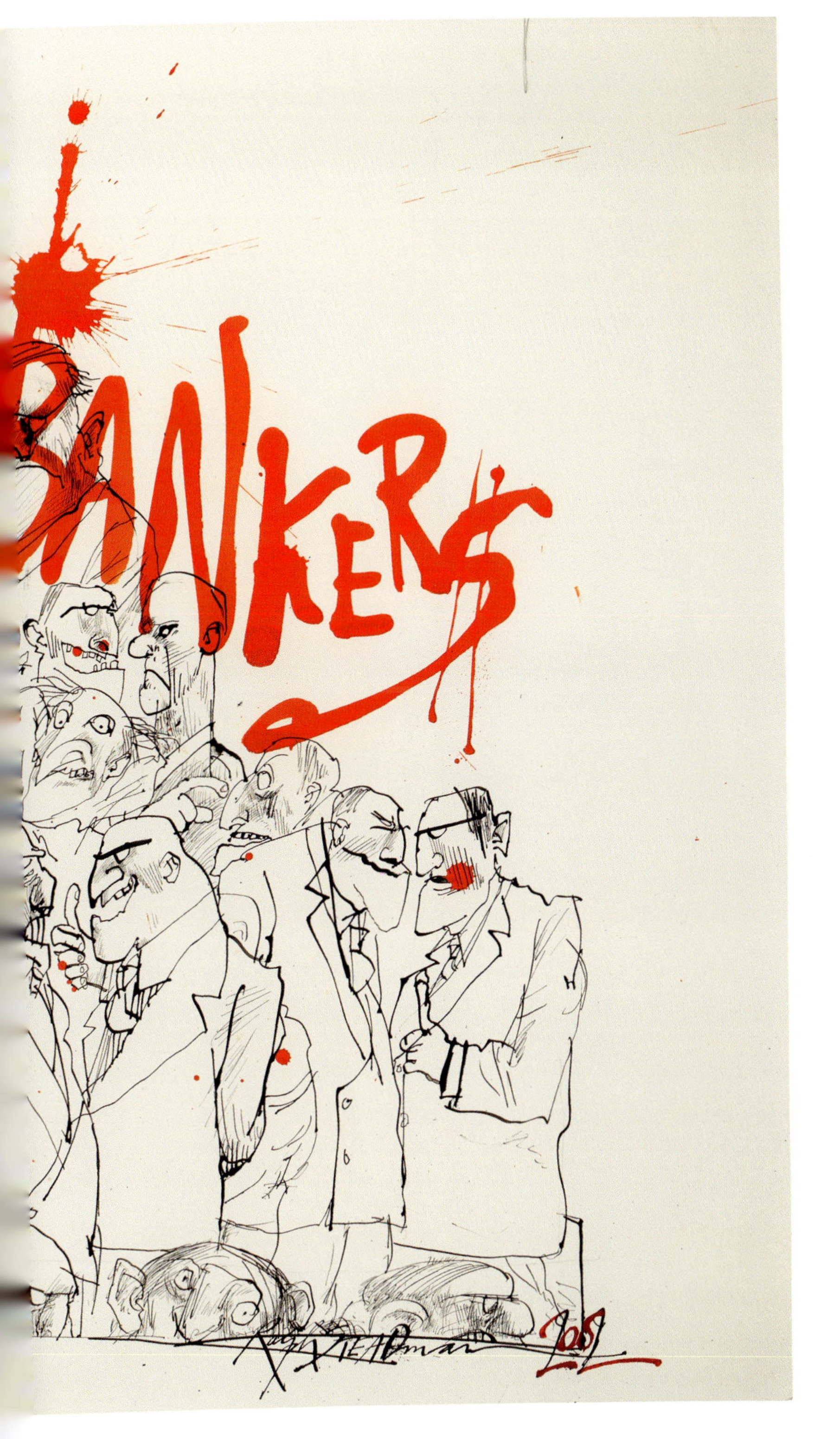

WANKERS

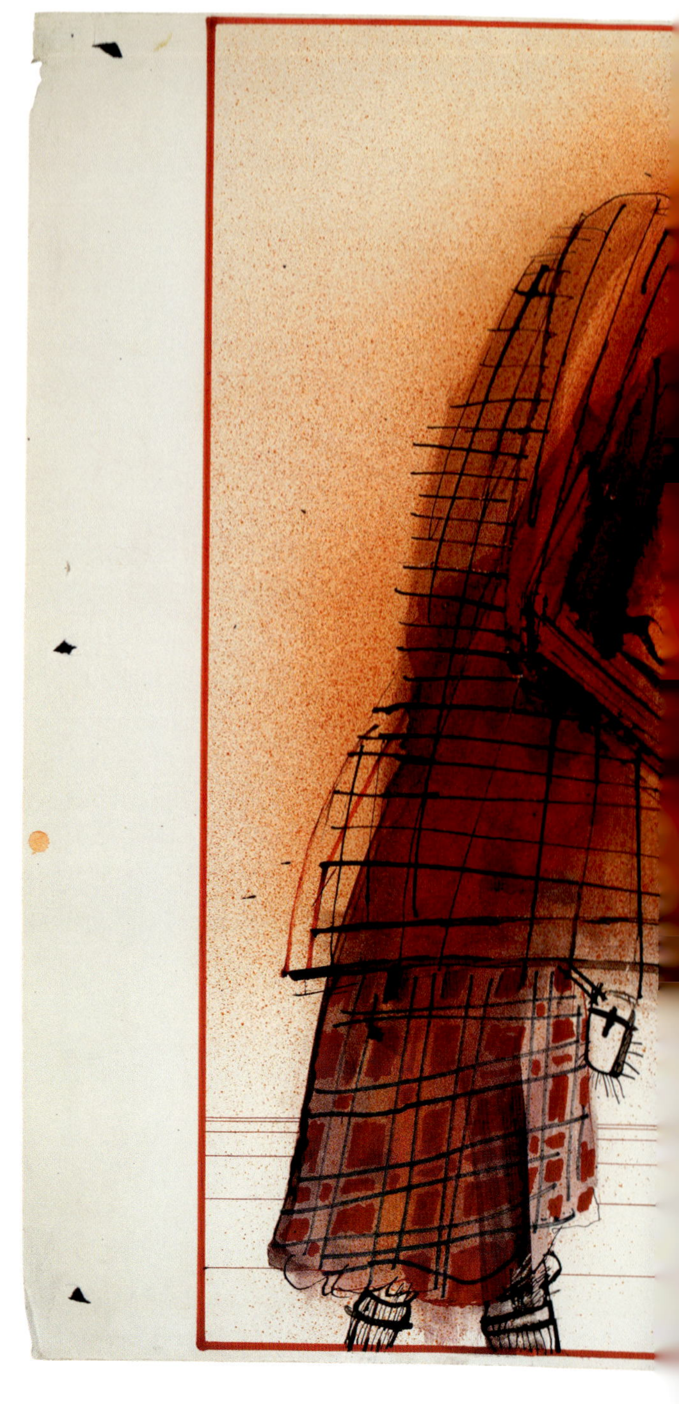

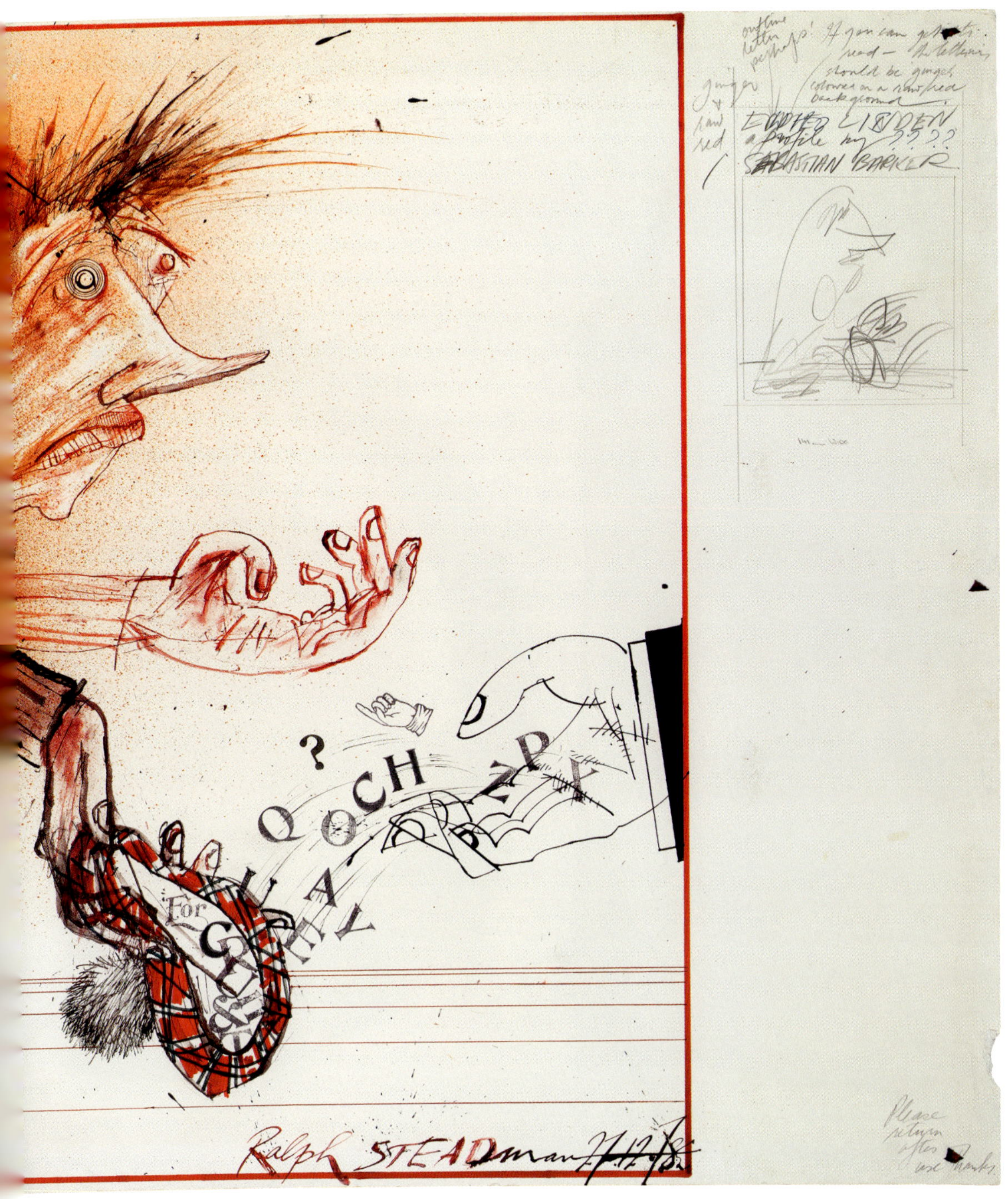

Eddie Linden, Scottish Poet, 1998

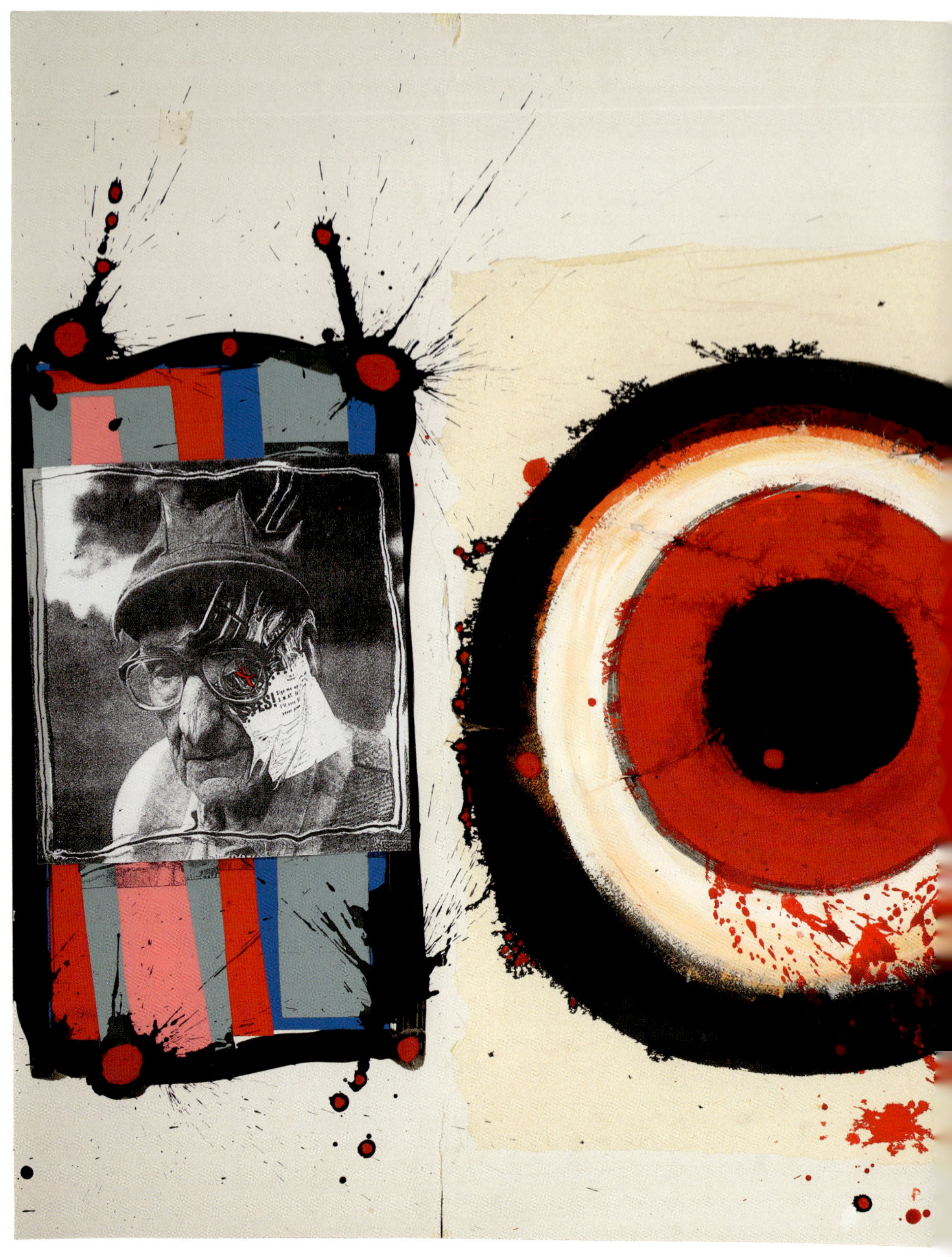

Something New Has Been Added, ca. 1995, William Burroughs at Home in Lawrence, Kansas, shooting target prints.

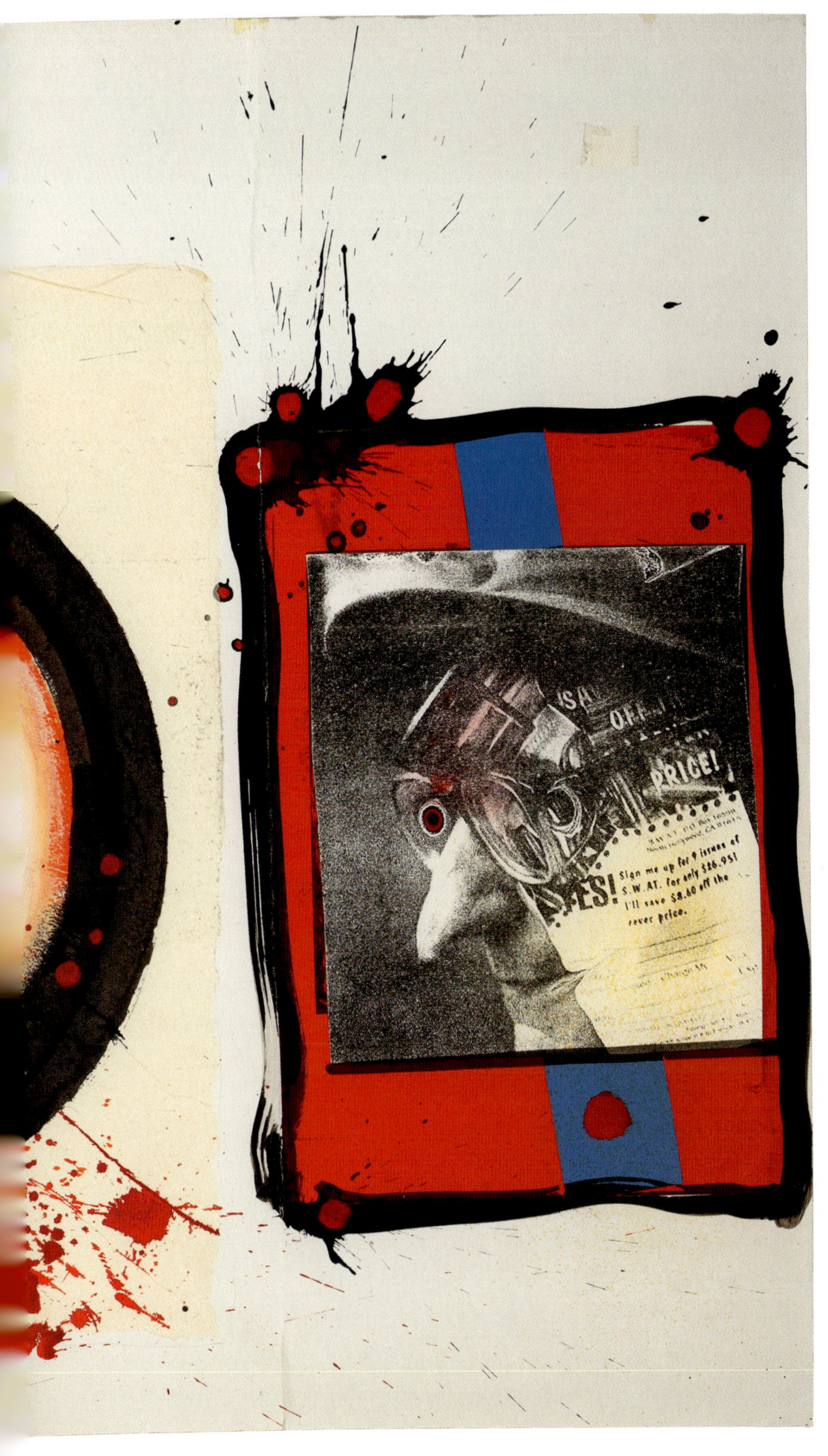

SALE OFF
PRICE!
S.W.A.T. P.O. Box 16000
North Hollywood, CA 91615
YES! Sign me up for 9 issues of
S.W.A.T. for only $26.95!
I'll save $8.60 off the
cover price.

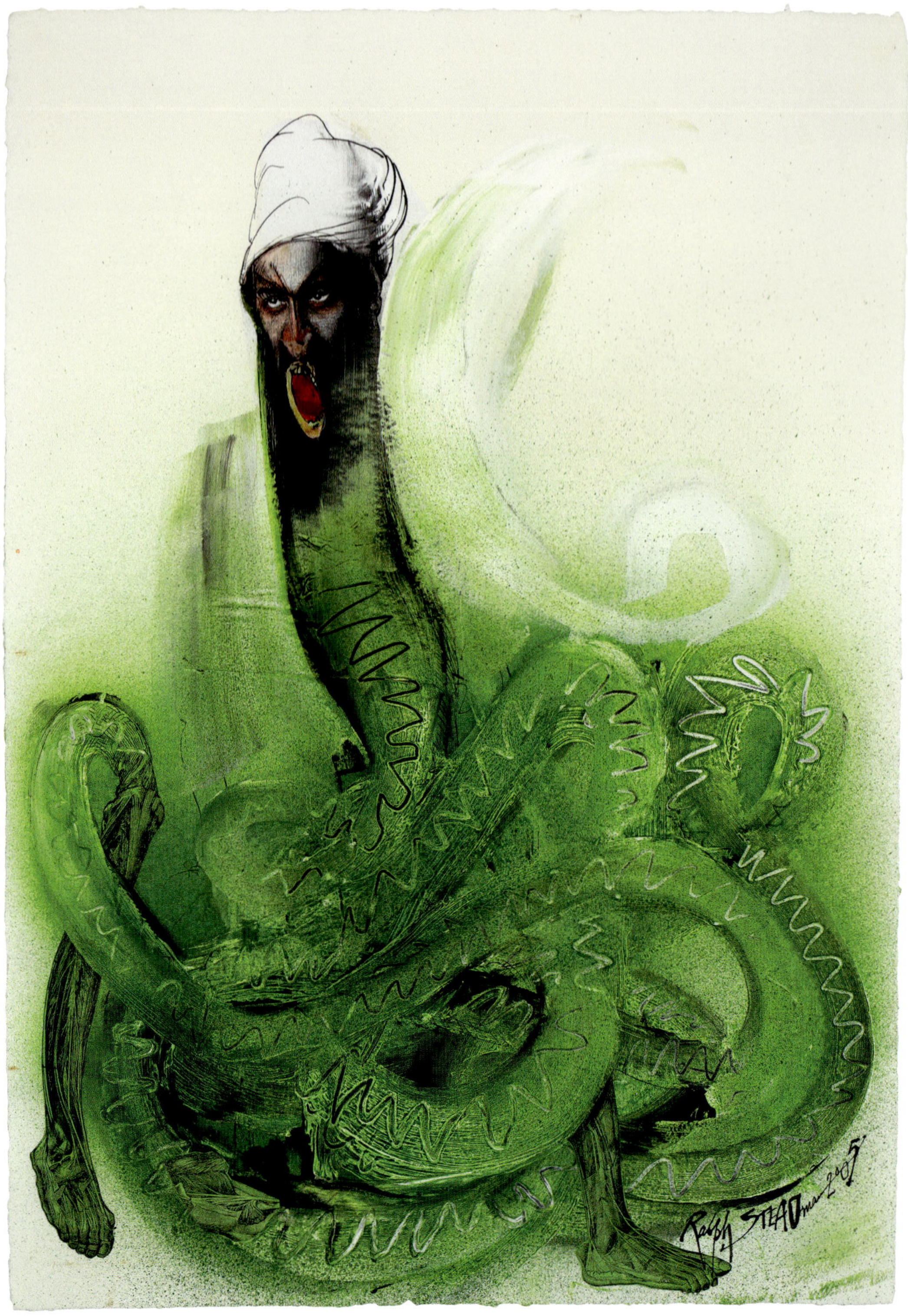

Bin Laden, 2005

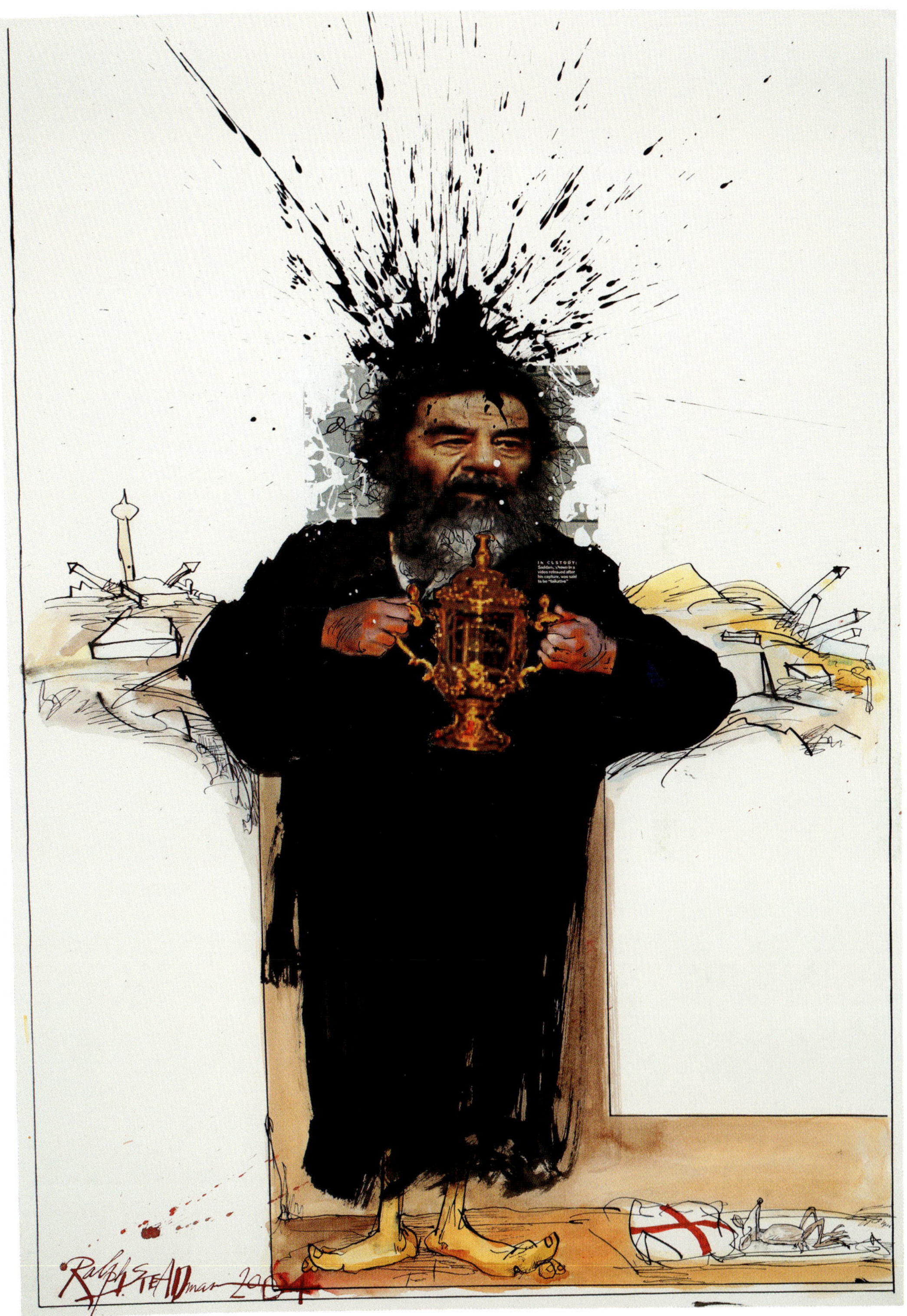

Saddam Hussein, 2004

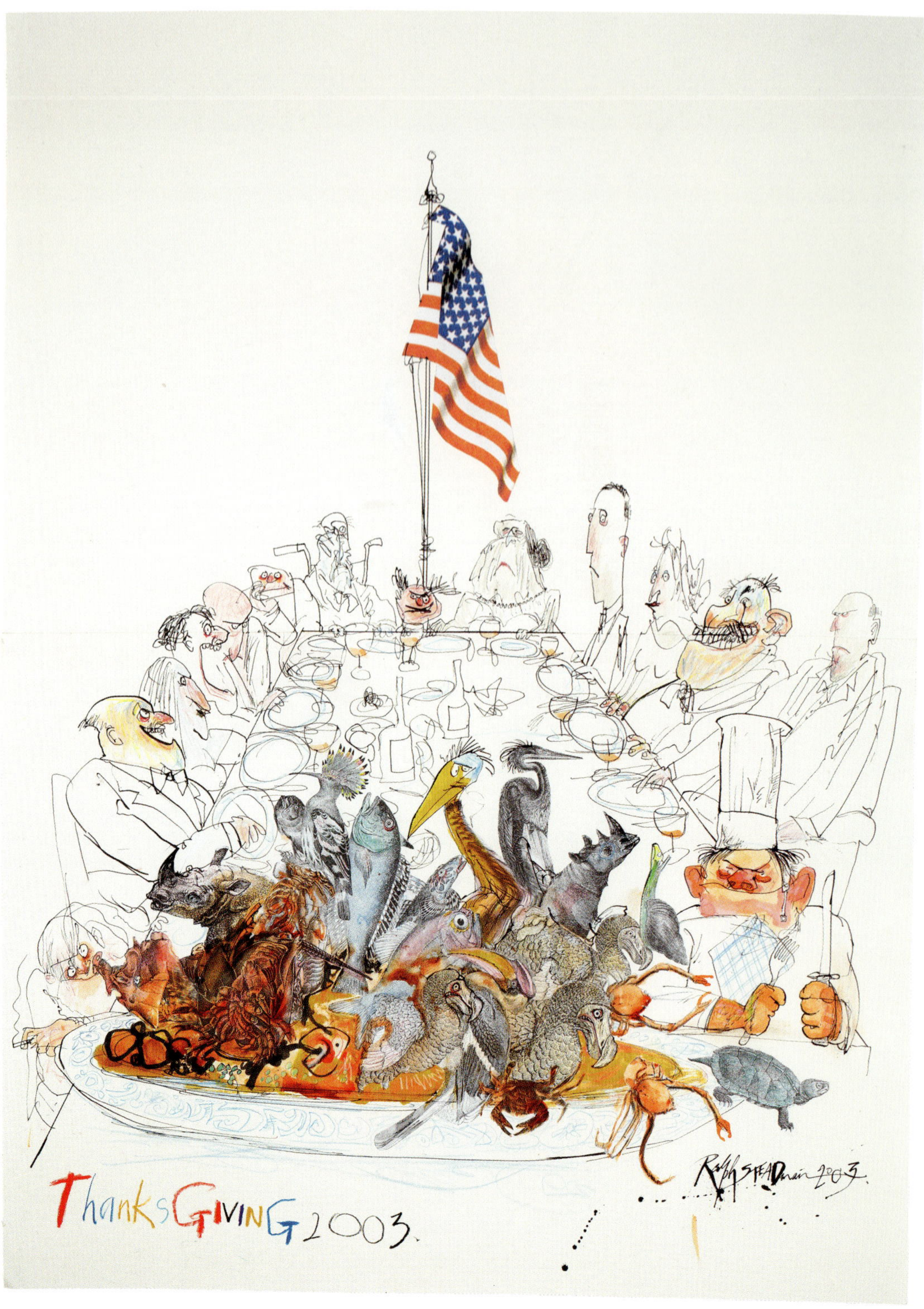

Thanksgiving Dinner, 2003

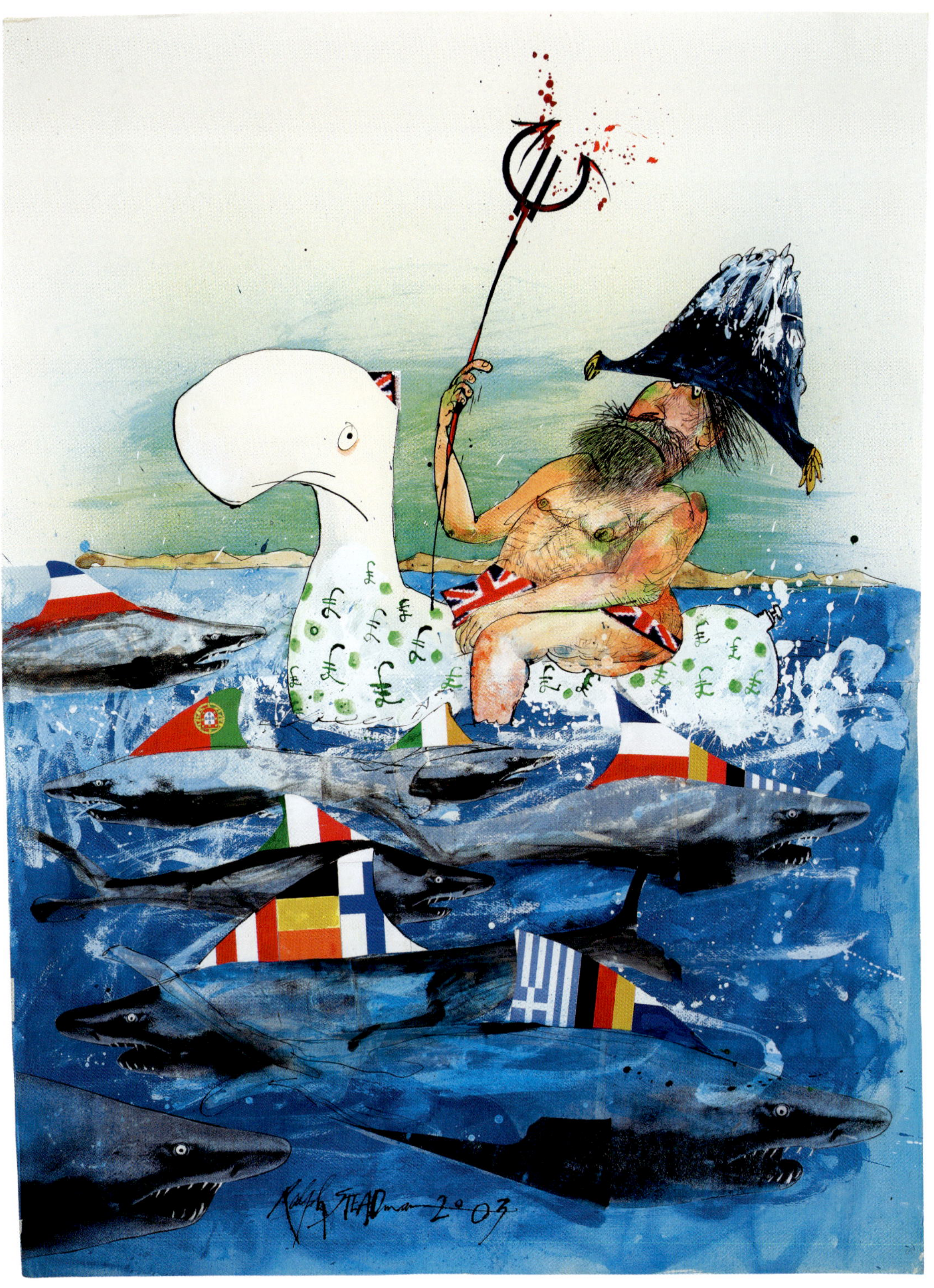

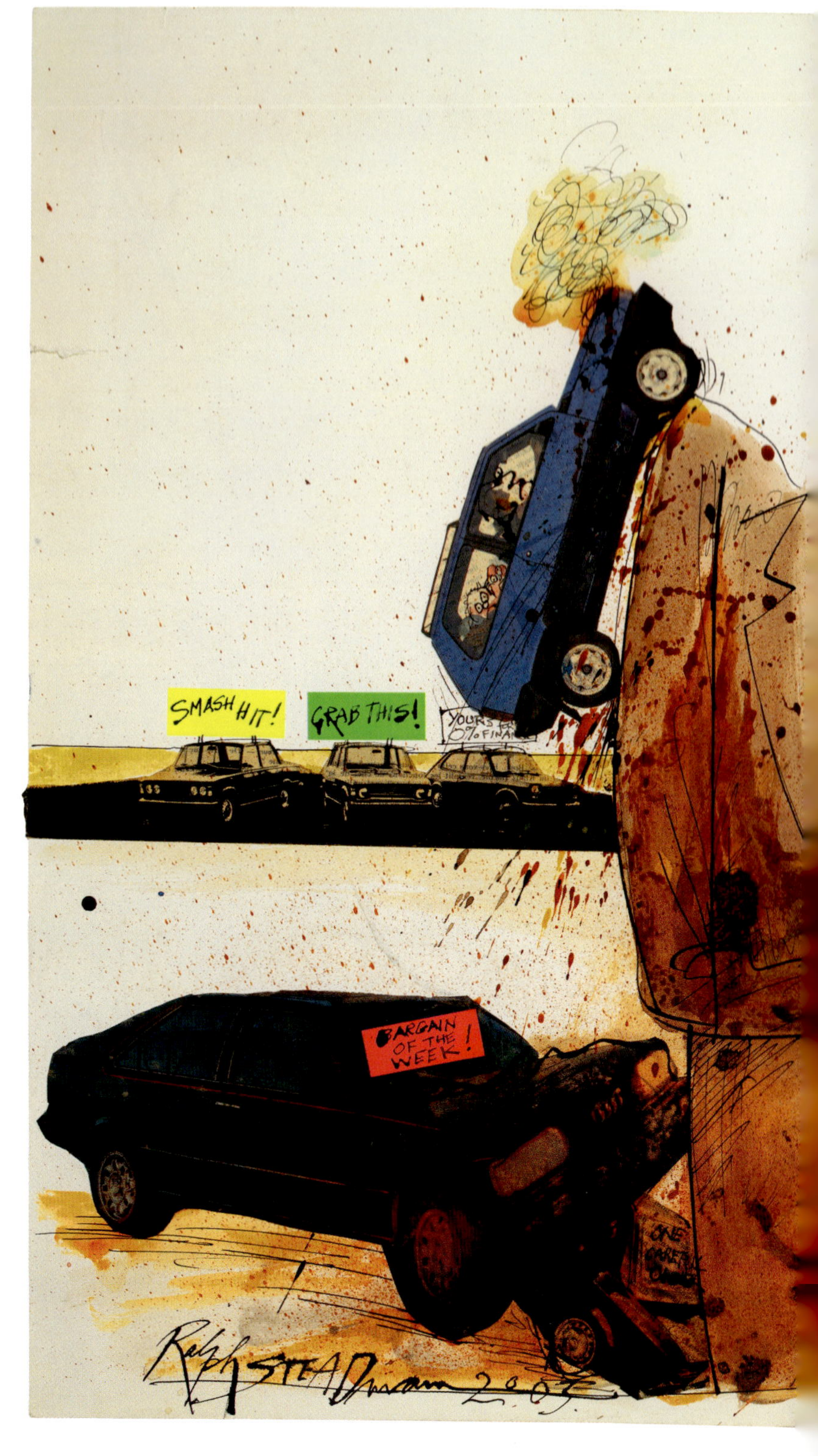

SMASH HIT!
GRAB THIS!
YOURS FOR 0% FINANCE
BARGAIN OF THE WEEK!

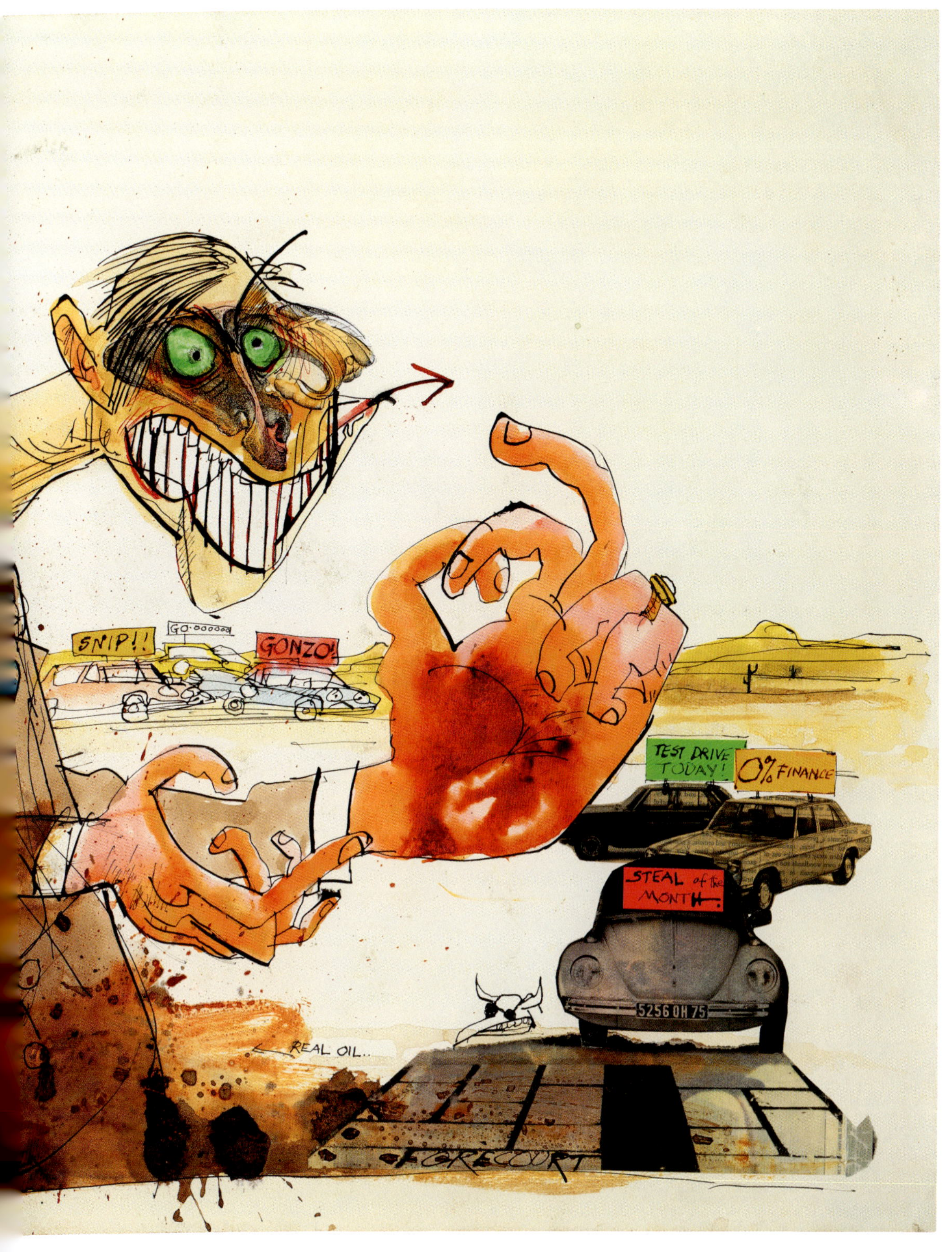

Used Car Salesman, 2003

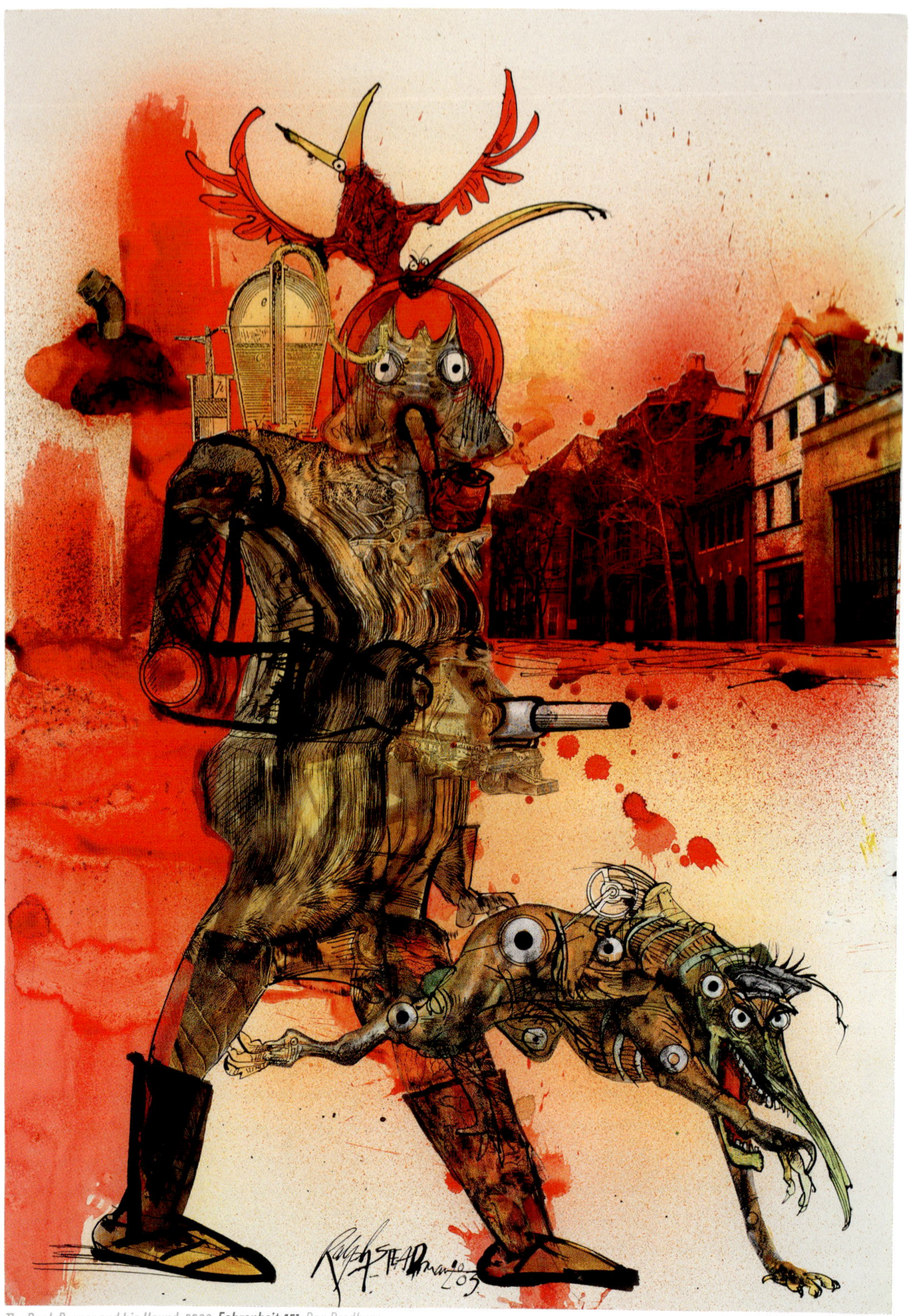

*The Book Burner and his Hound, 2003, **Fahrenheit 451**, Ray Bradbury*

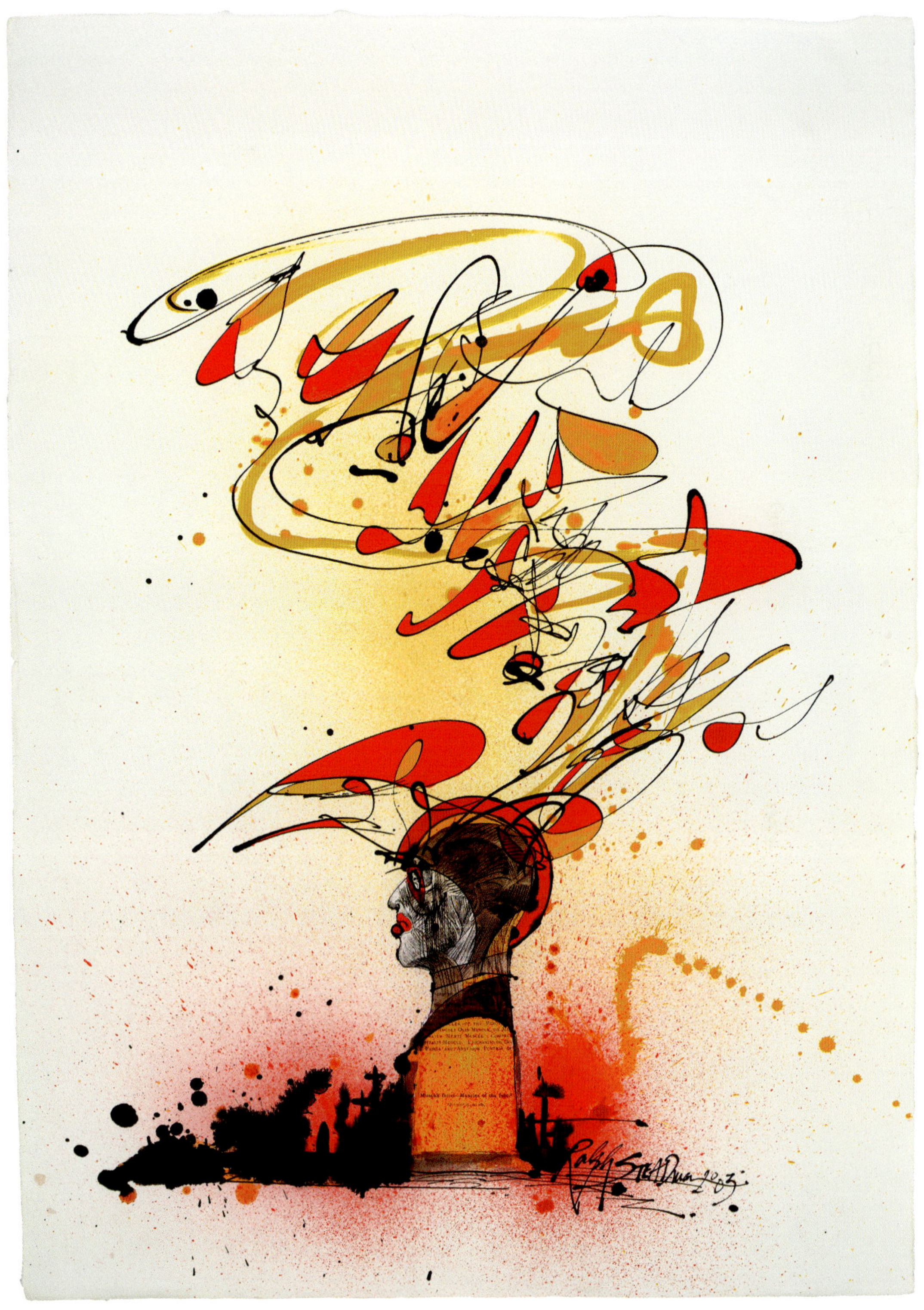

The Mind Machine, 2003, Fahrenheit 451, Ray Bradbury

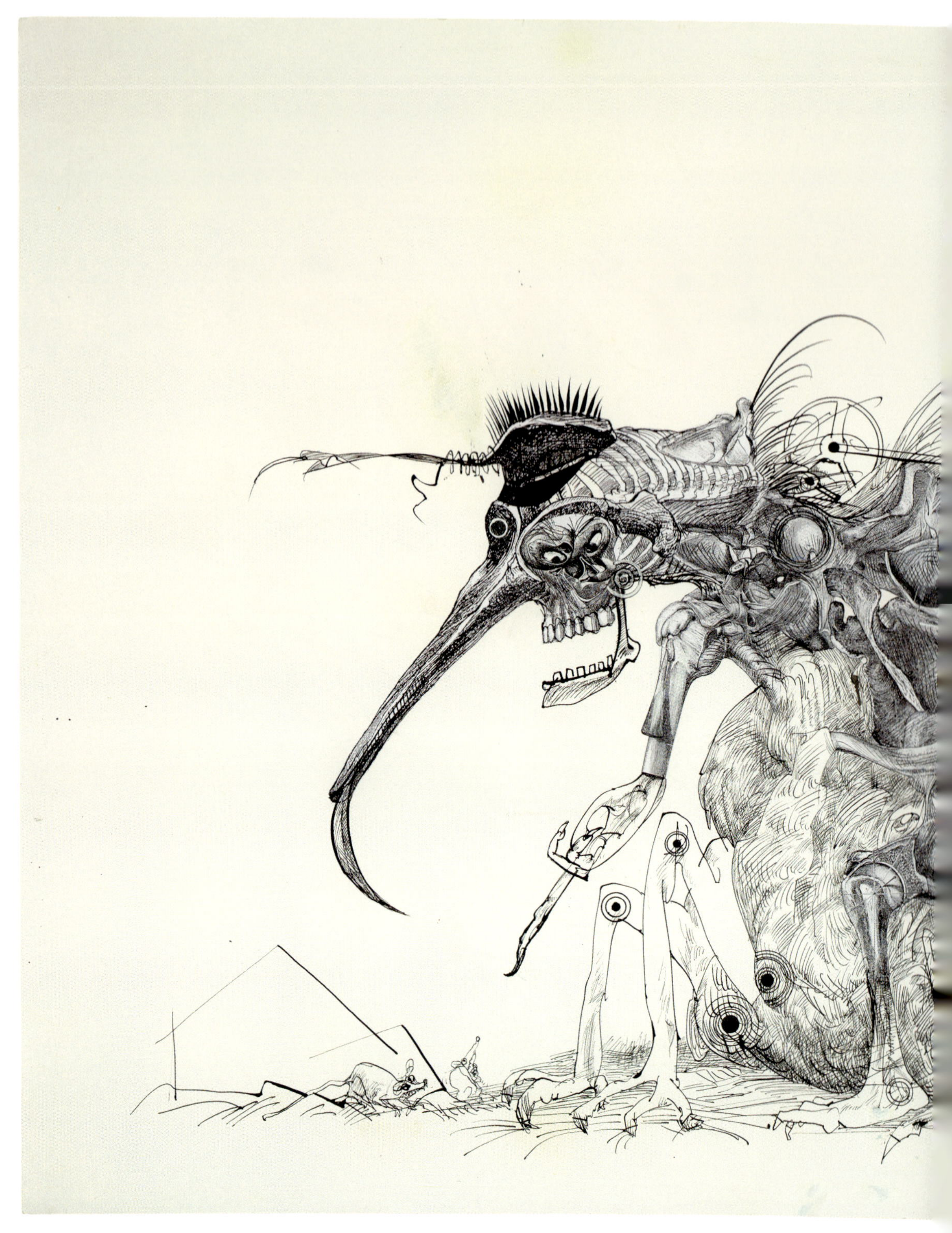

"I have always found anatomical drawing fascinating. It doesn't really matter to me where they actually belong;
I like to see what the different shapes of bone, muscle, and sinew do."

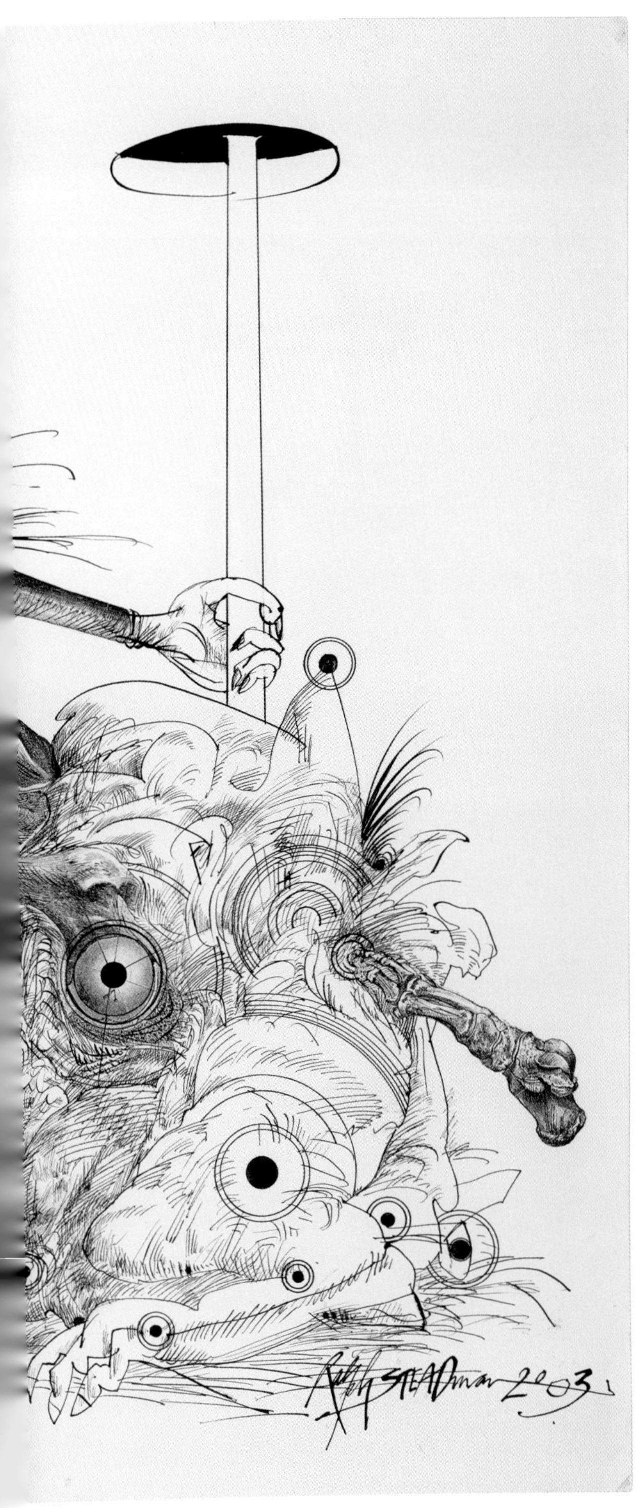

The Hell Hound, 2003, **Fahrenheit 451**, Ray Bradbury

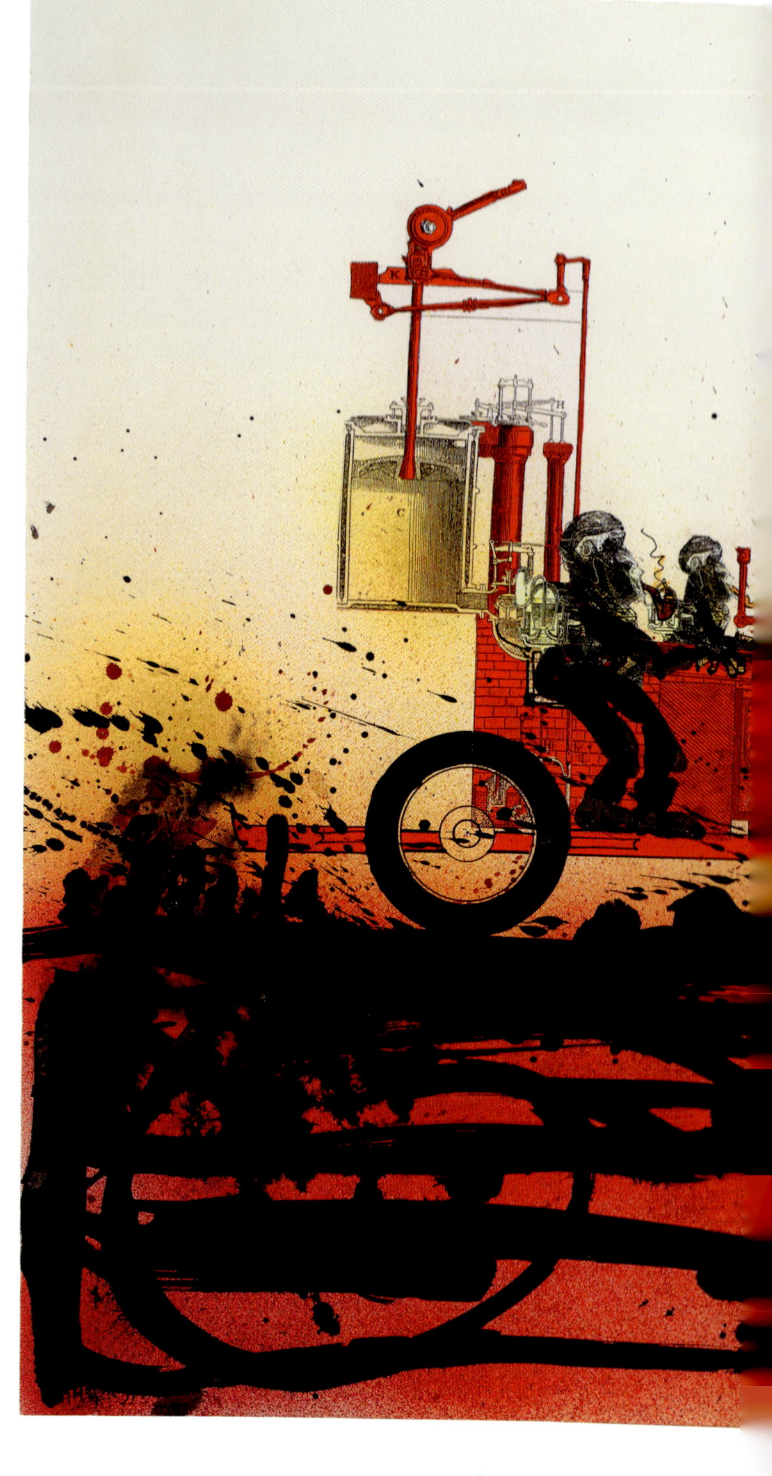

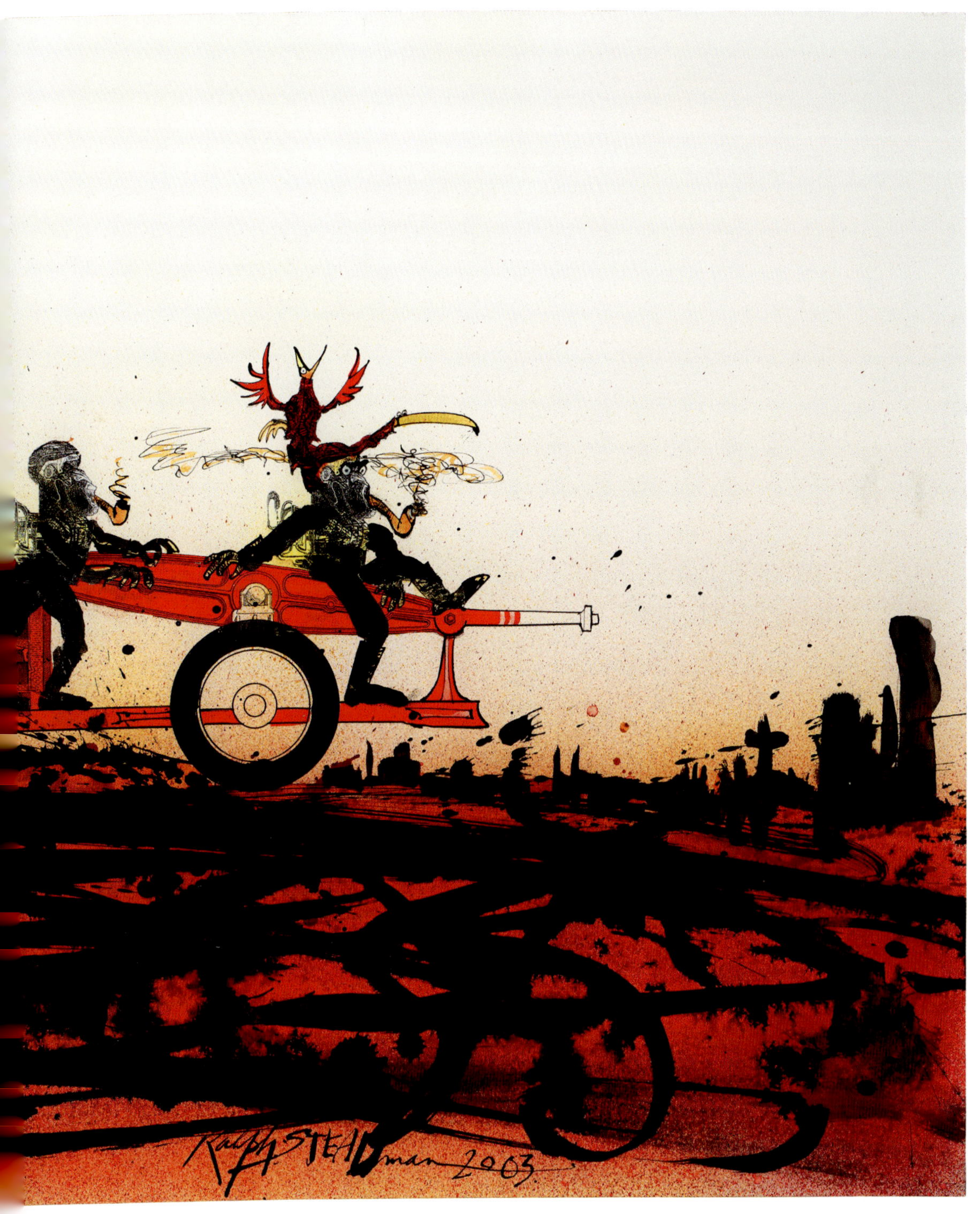

The Fire Engine, 2003, **Fahrenheit 451**, *Ray Bradbury*

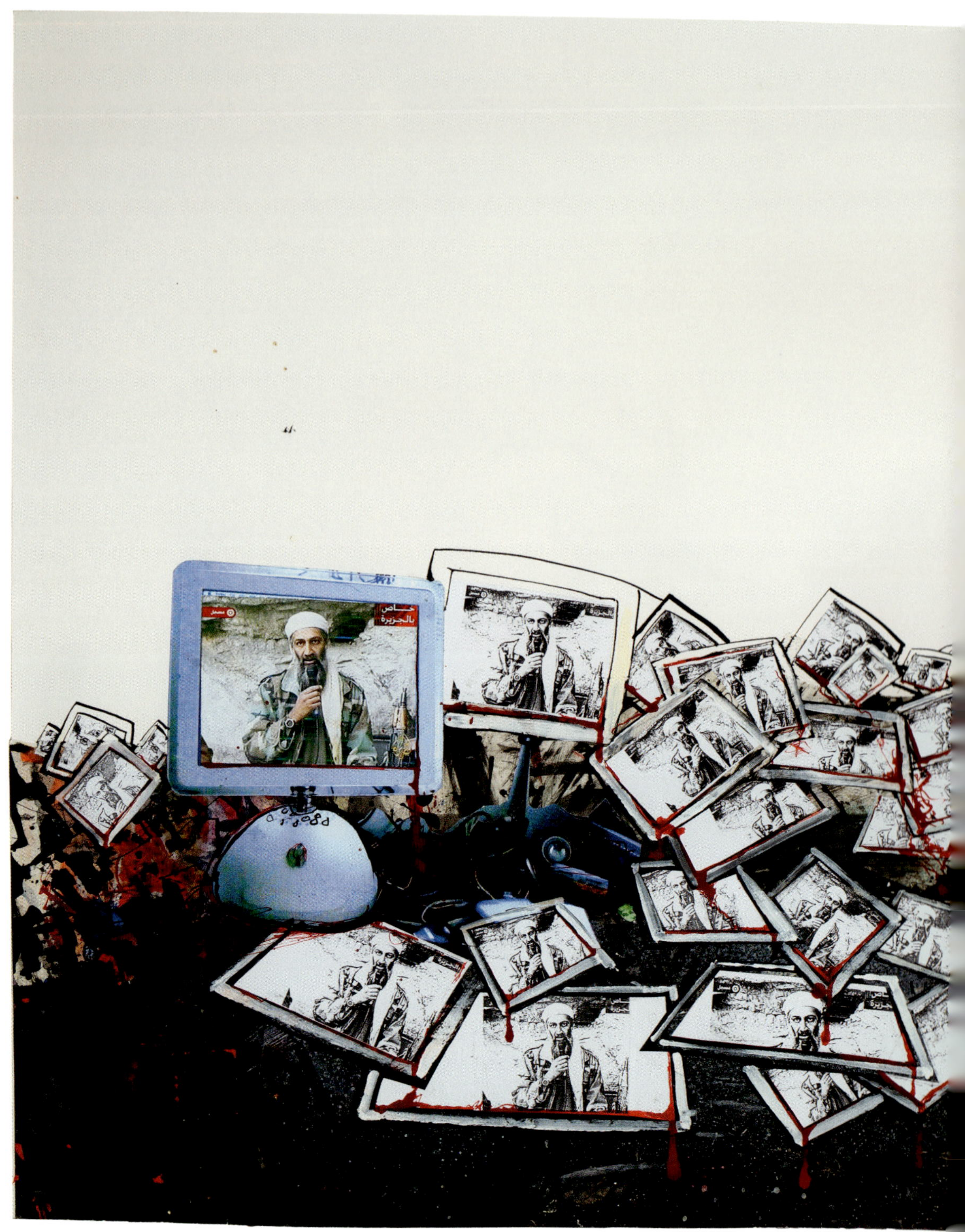

Bin Laden, 2004

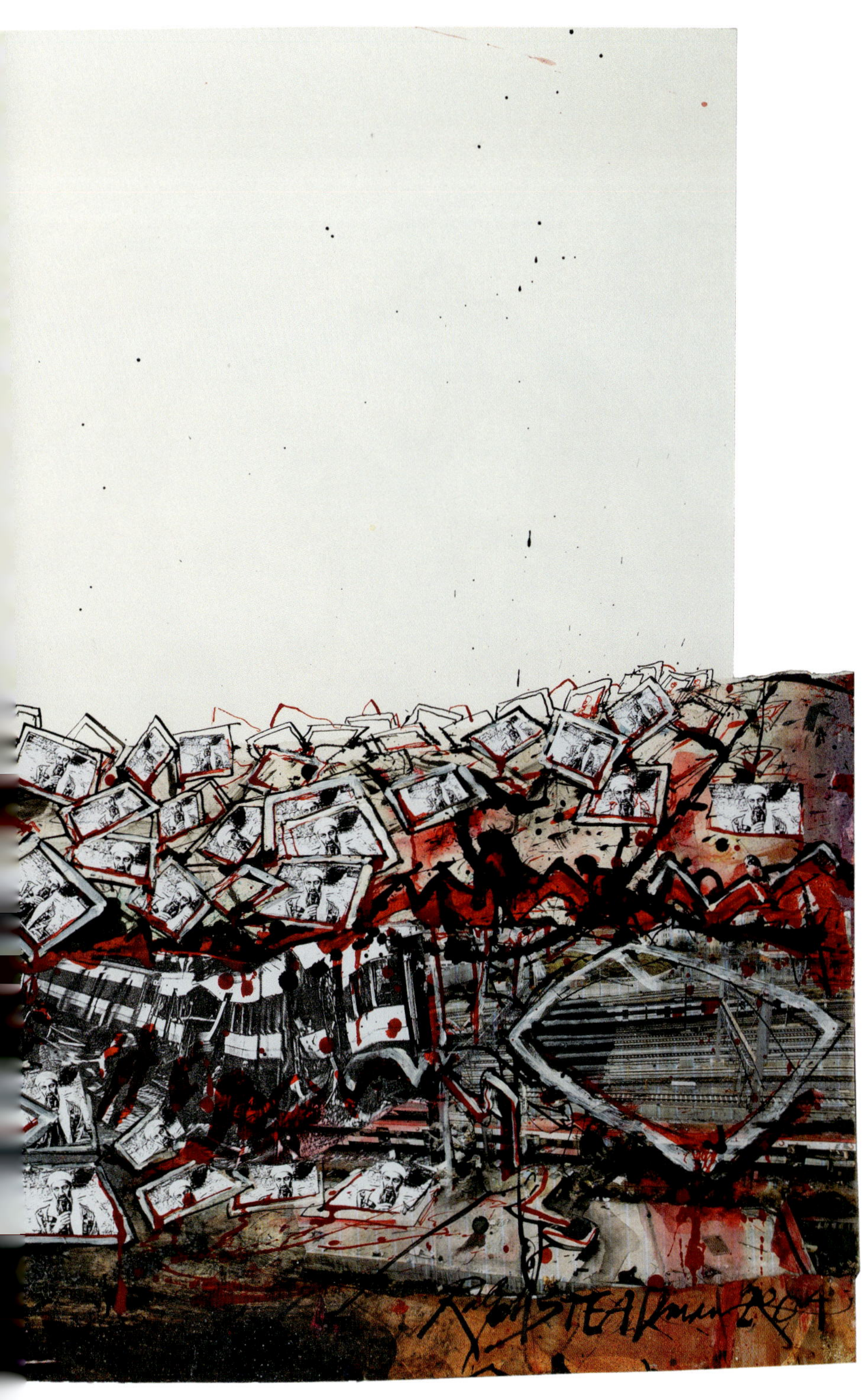

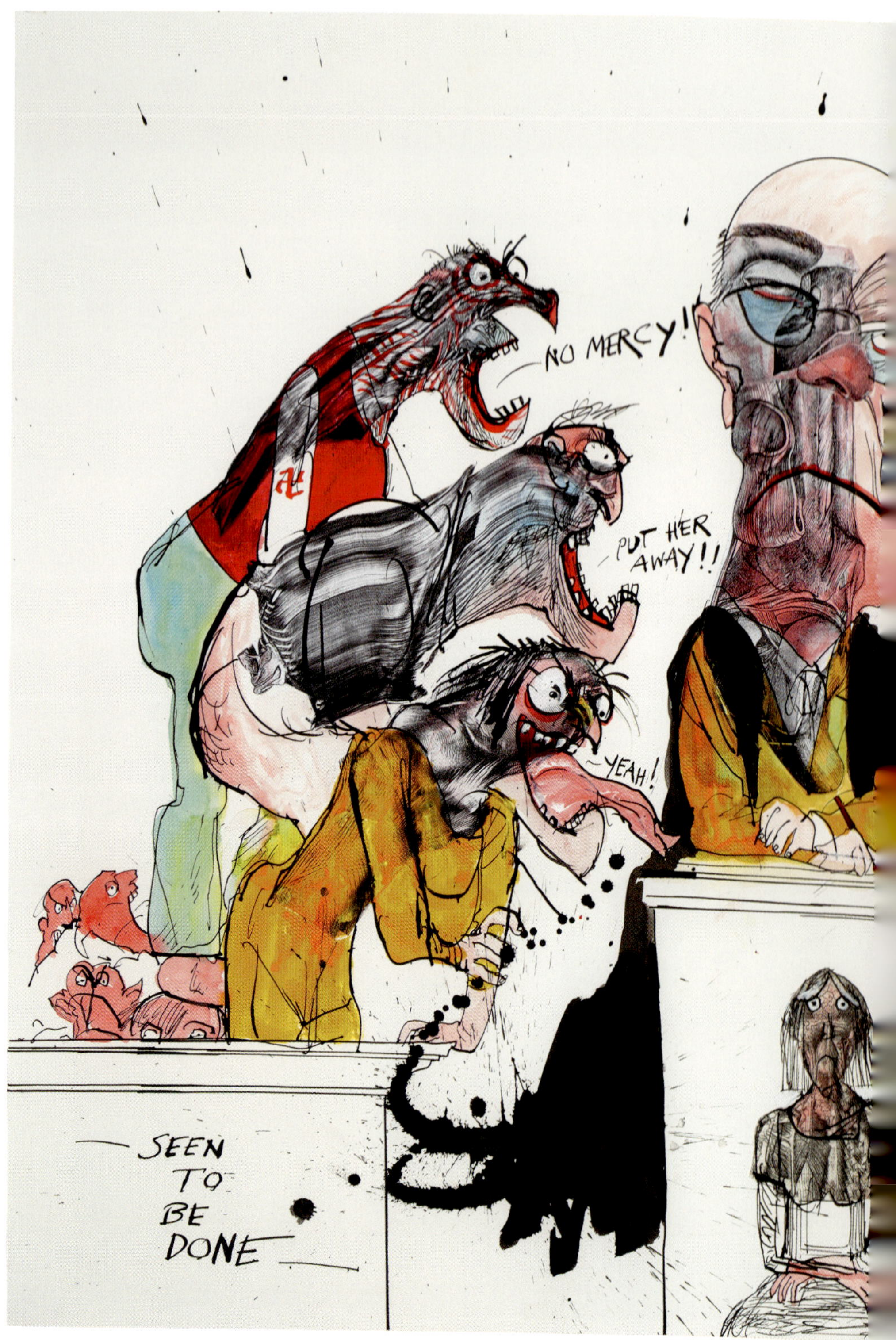

The Trial of Lisl Auman, 2004

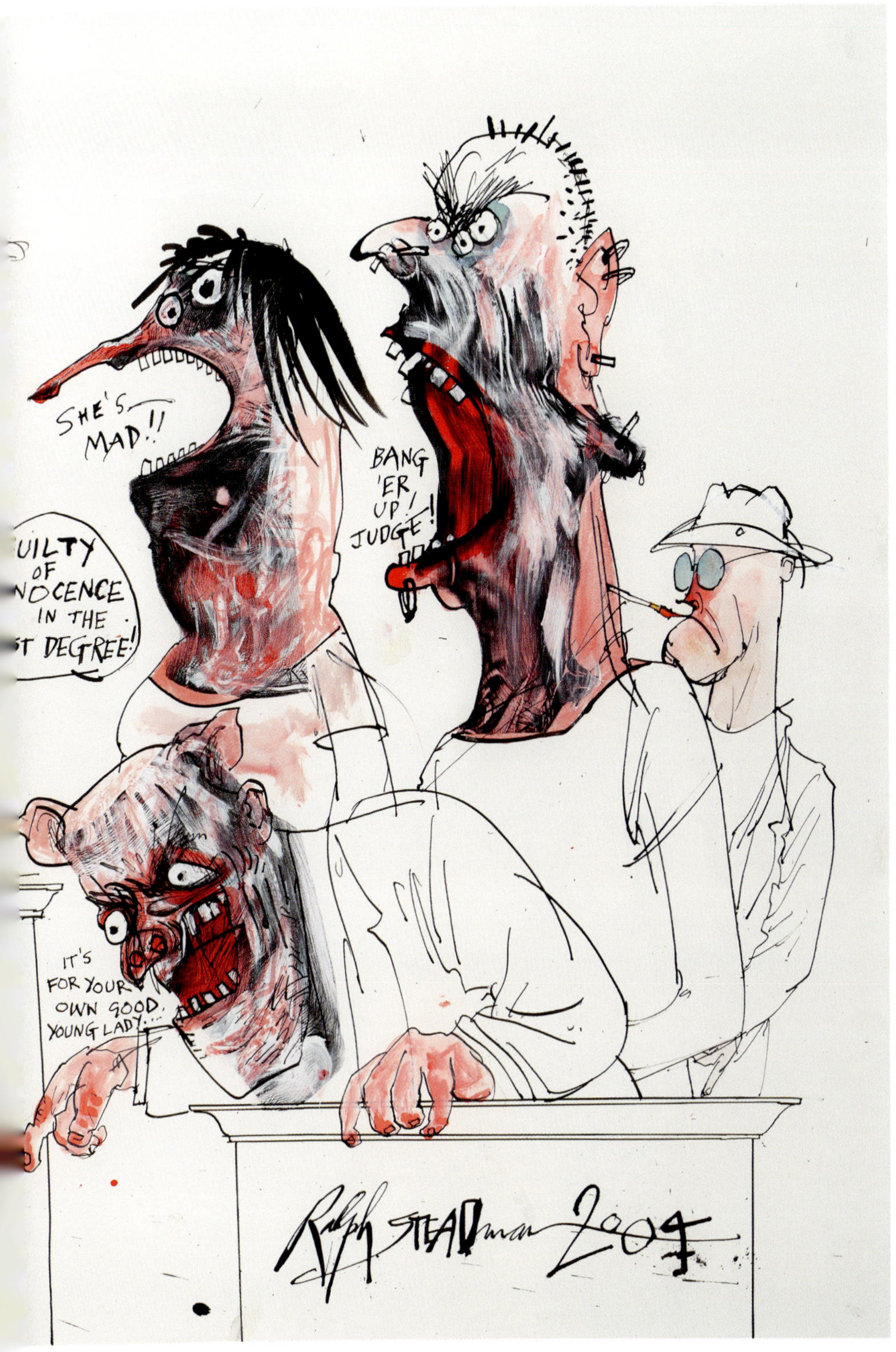

"Hunter thought it was a travesty of justice."

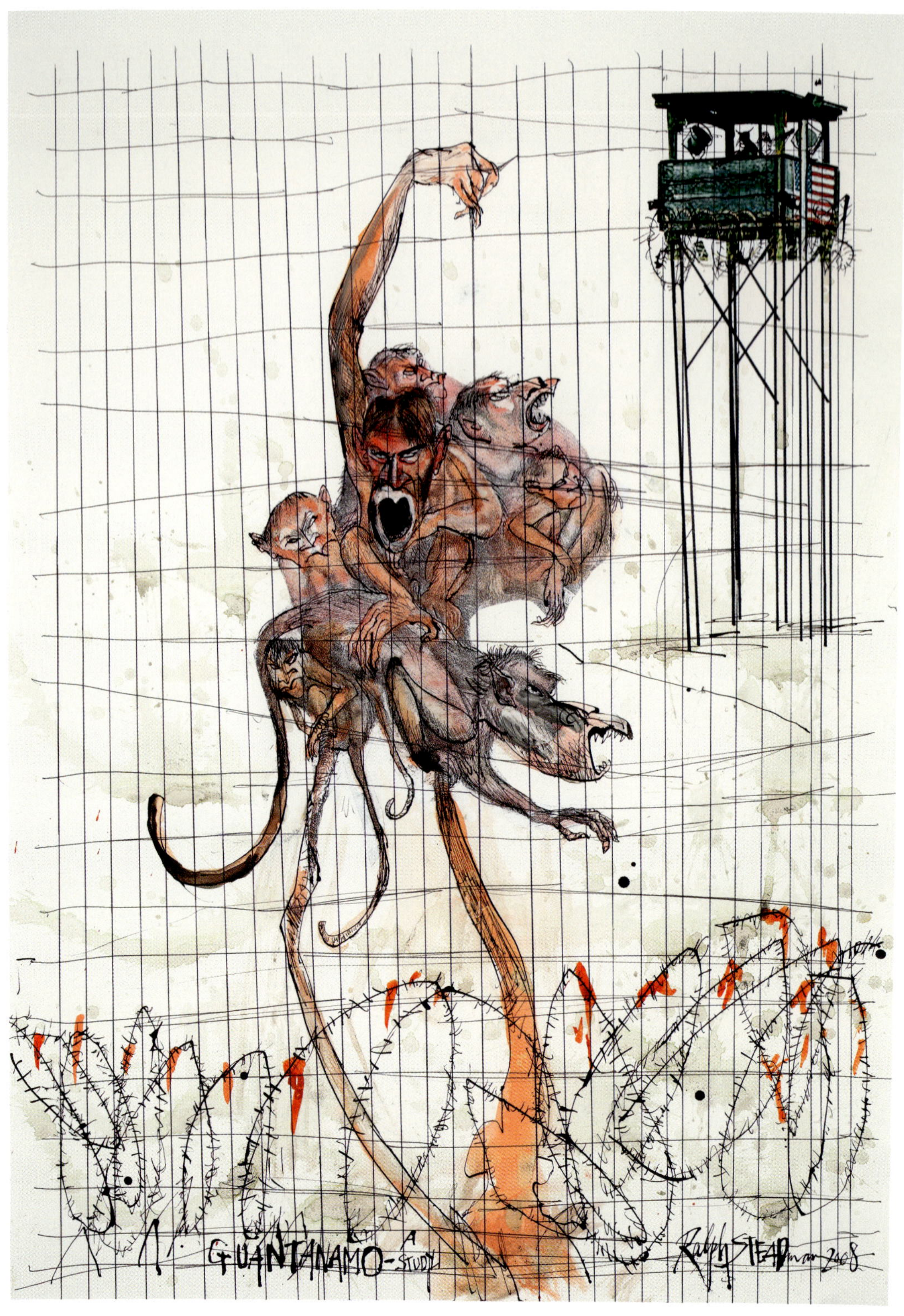

Guantanamo Bay Jail, 2008

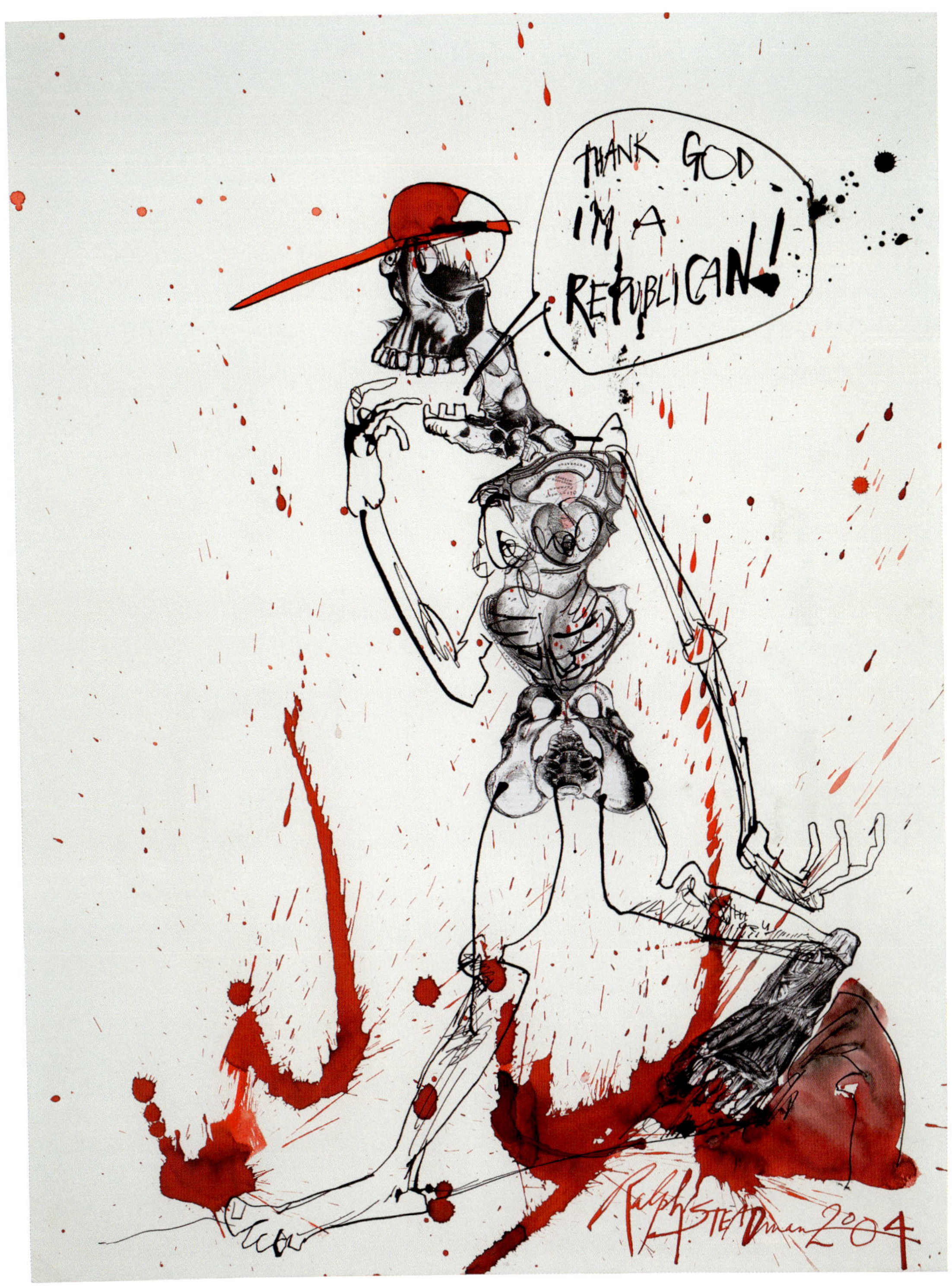

Innocent Republican, 2004

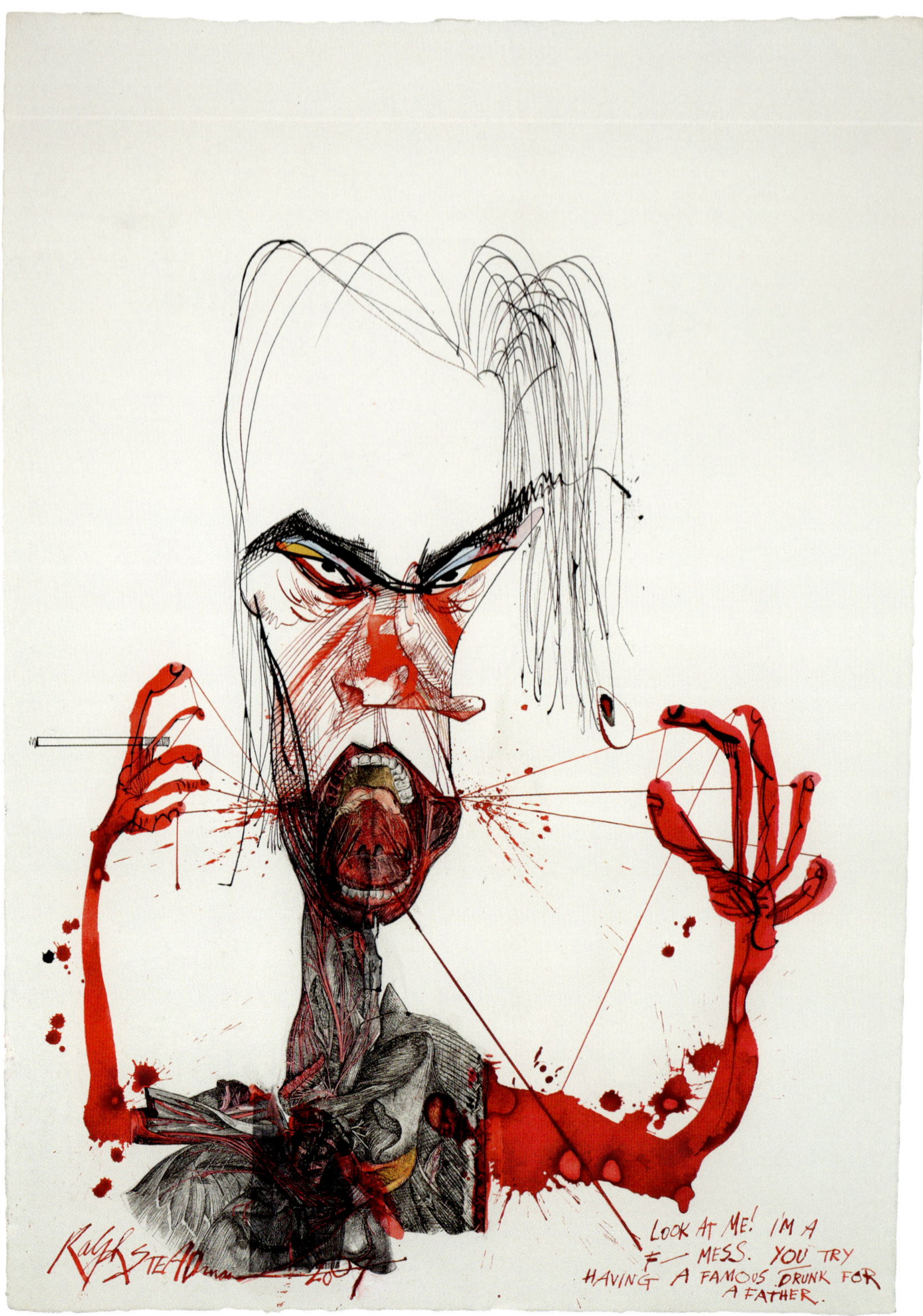

Portrait of Martin Amis, 2007

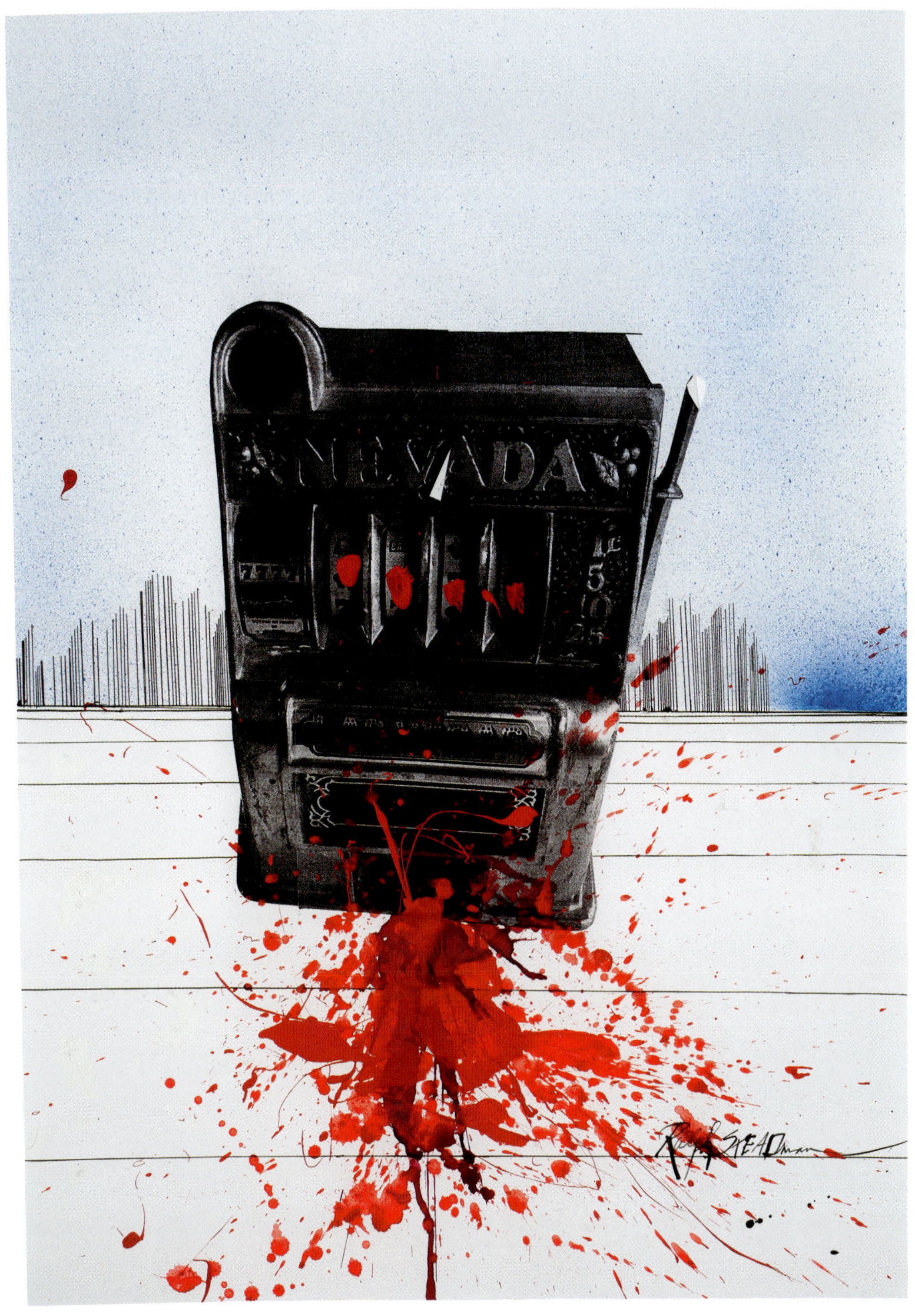

Bleeding One Armed Bandit, 2017, reaction to the shooting in Las Vegas

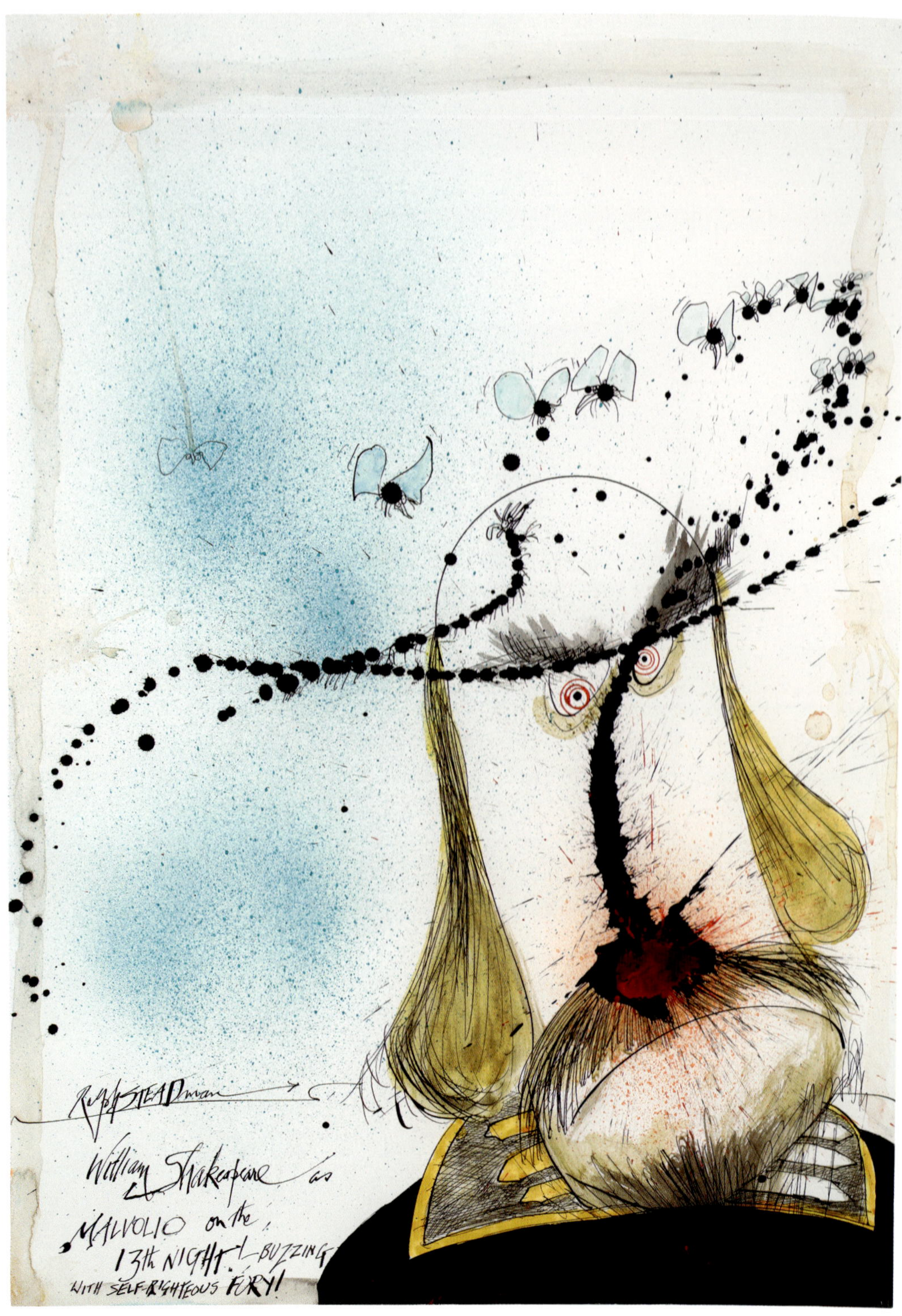

William Shakespeare, ca. 1998

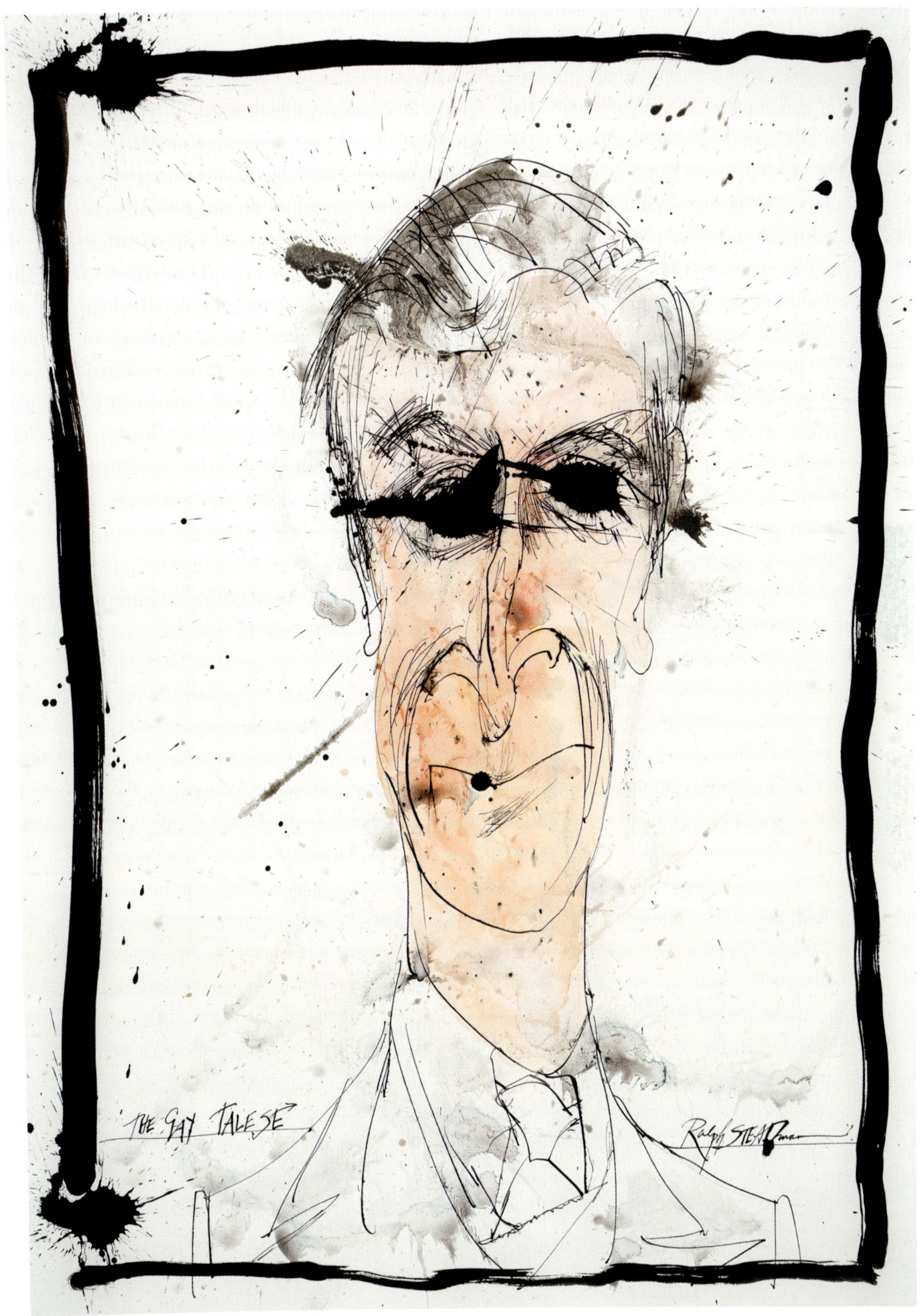

The Gay Talese, ca. 2017

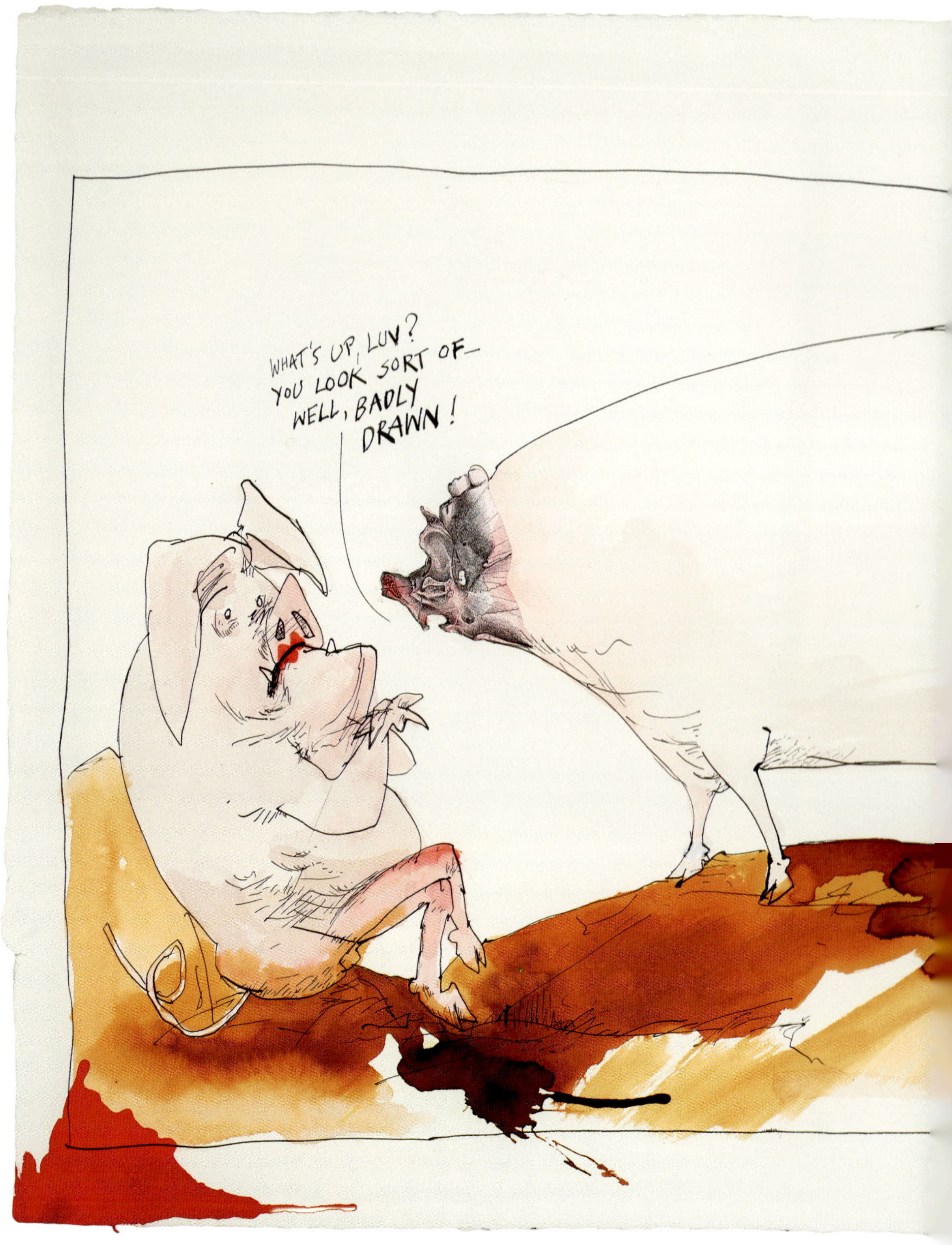

Badly Drawn Pigs, **Animal Behaviourist,** *2002*

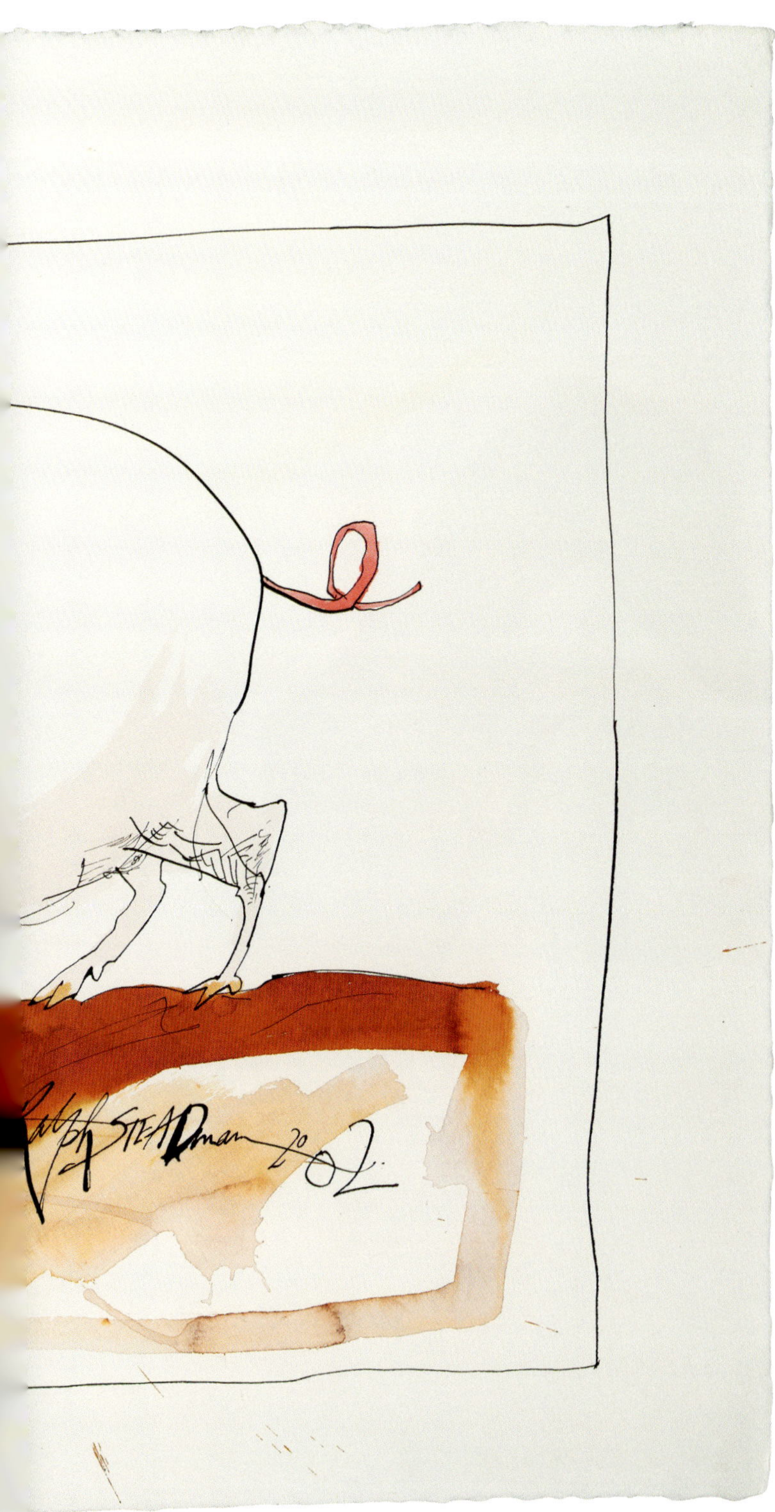

"Never take yourself too seriously."

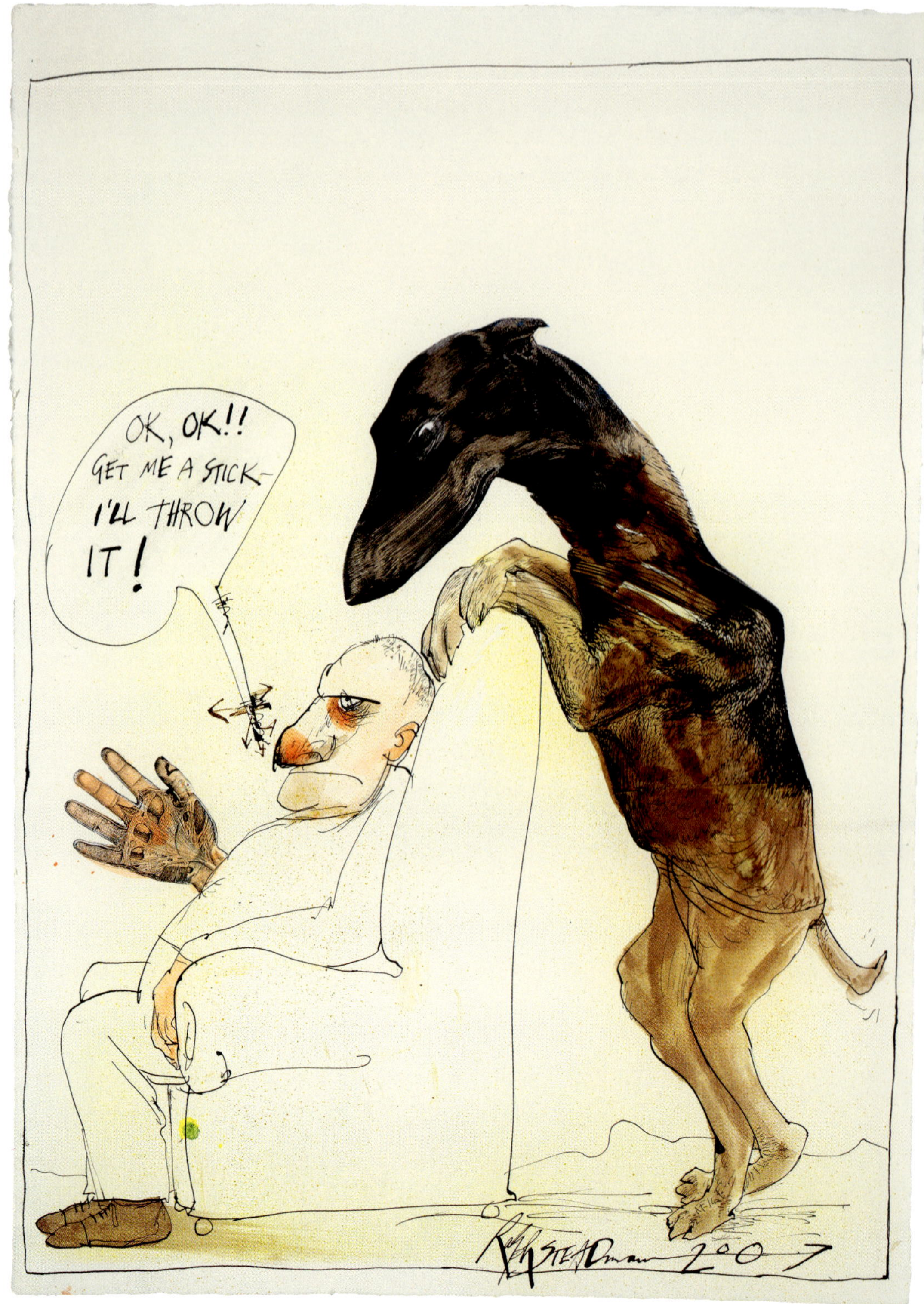

Animal Behaviourist, 2007

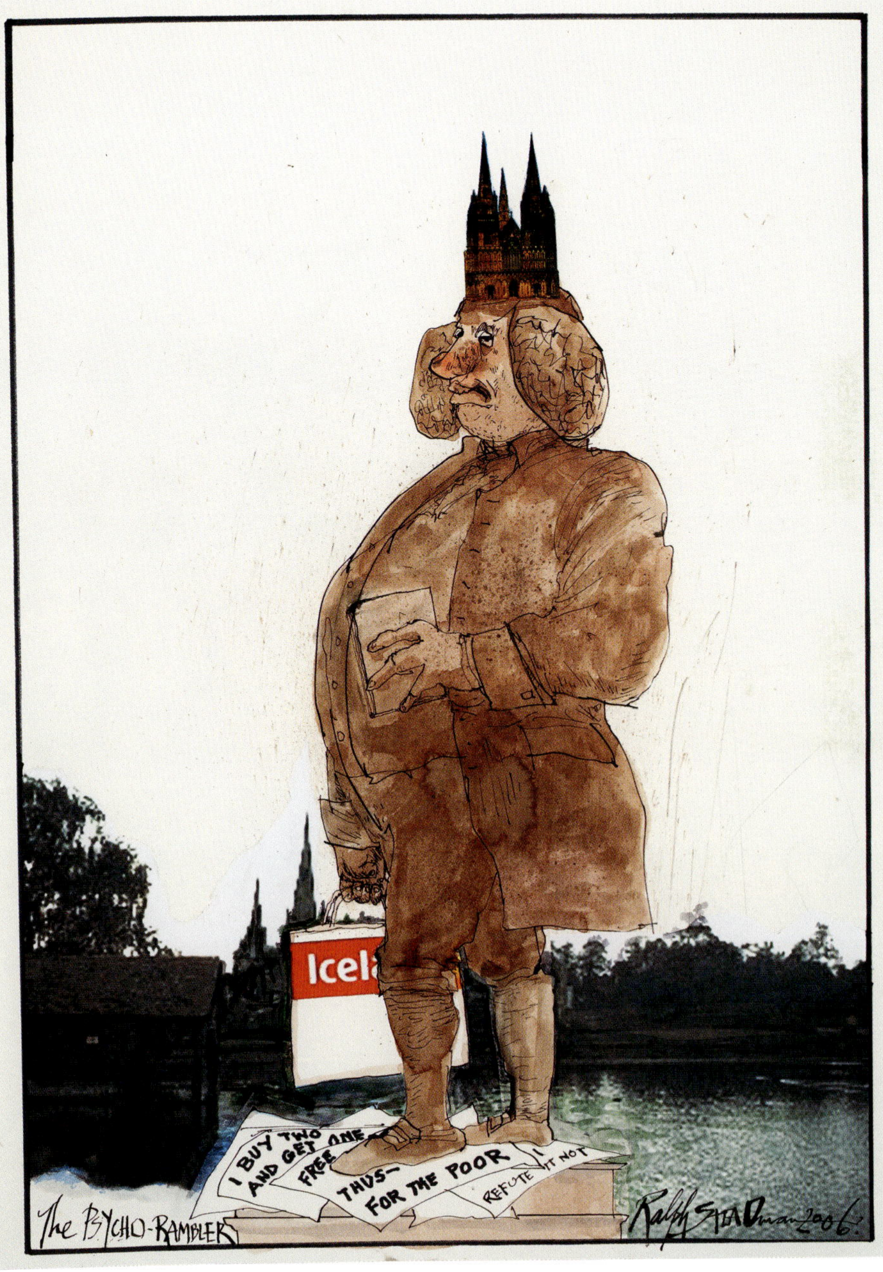
Icela
I BUY TWO AND GET ONE FREE
THUS— FOR THE POOR
REFUTE IT NOT
The PSYCHO-RAMBLER
Ralph STEADman 2006

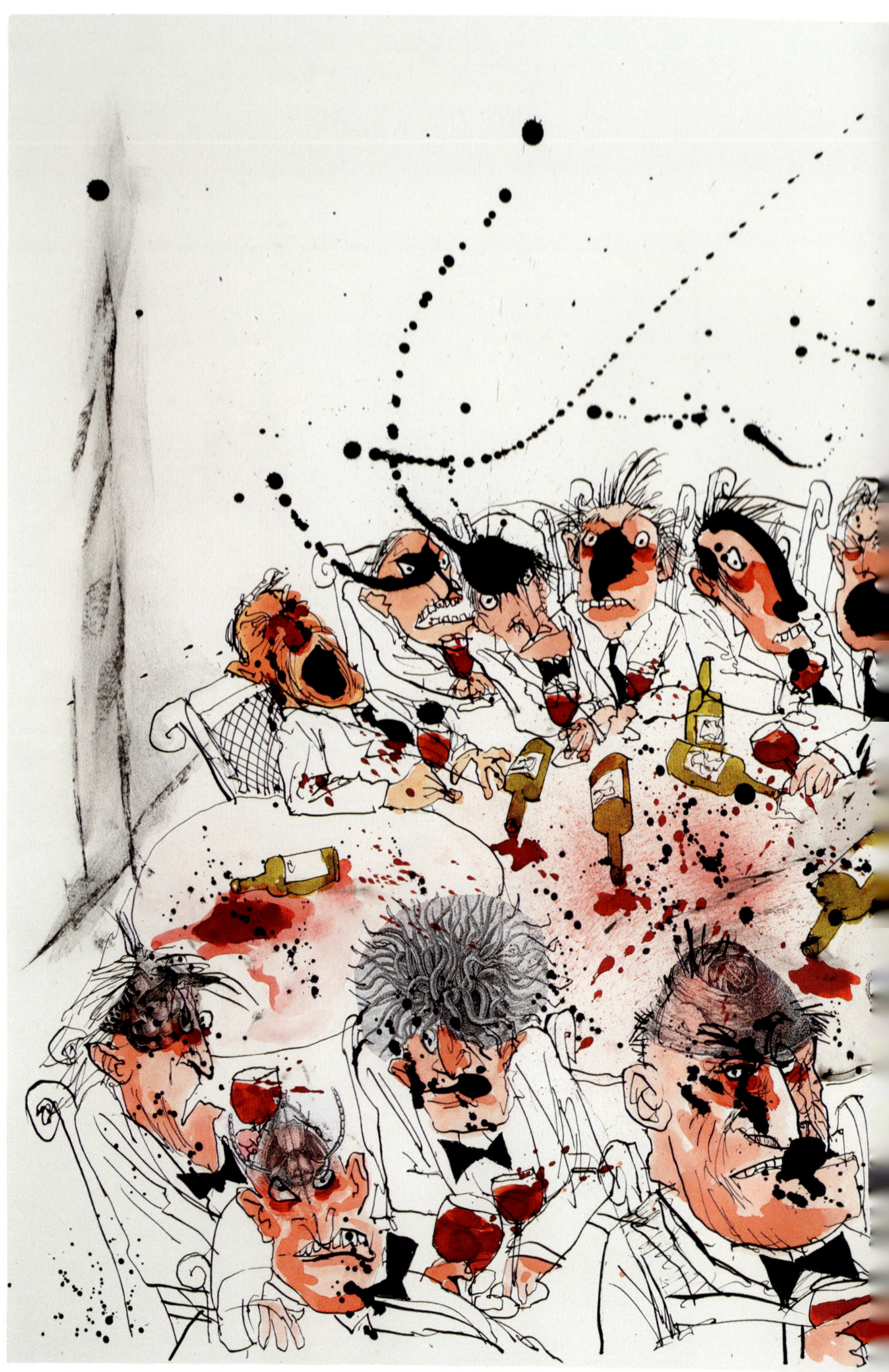

"I always was a messy bugger, so I just turned a vice into a virtue."

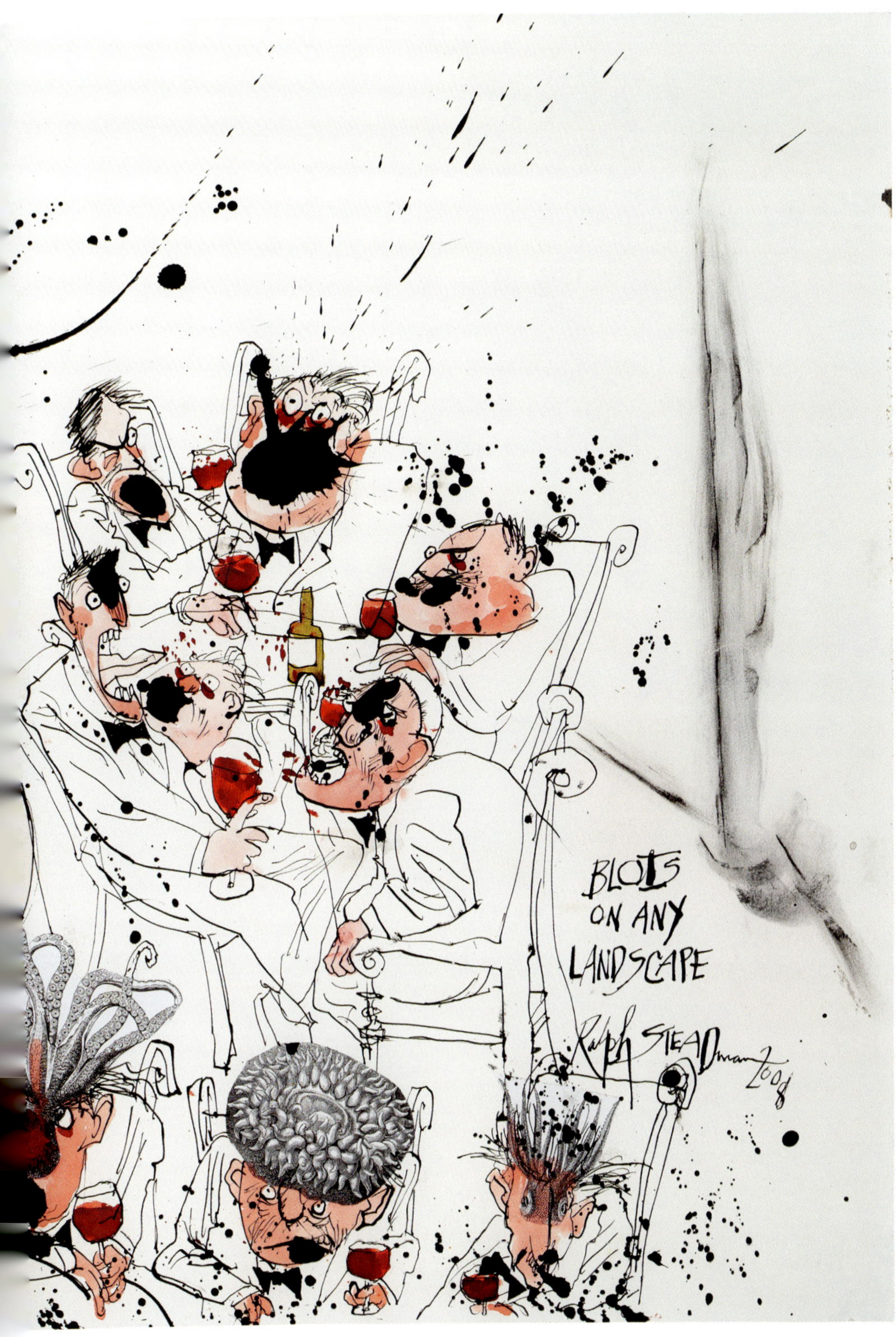

Blots on Any Landscape, 2008

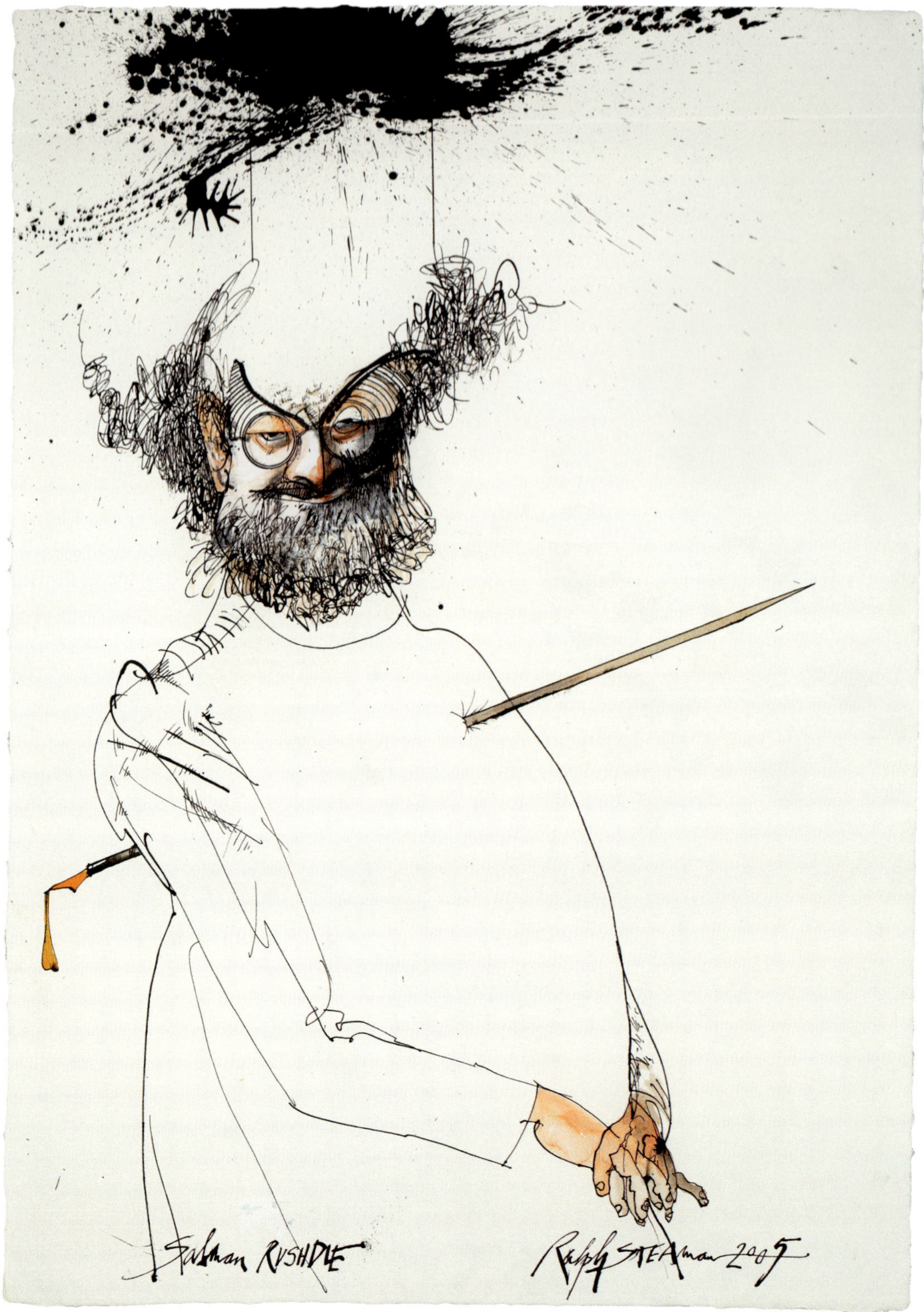

Salman Rushdie, 2005

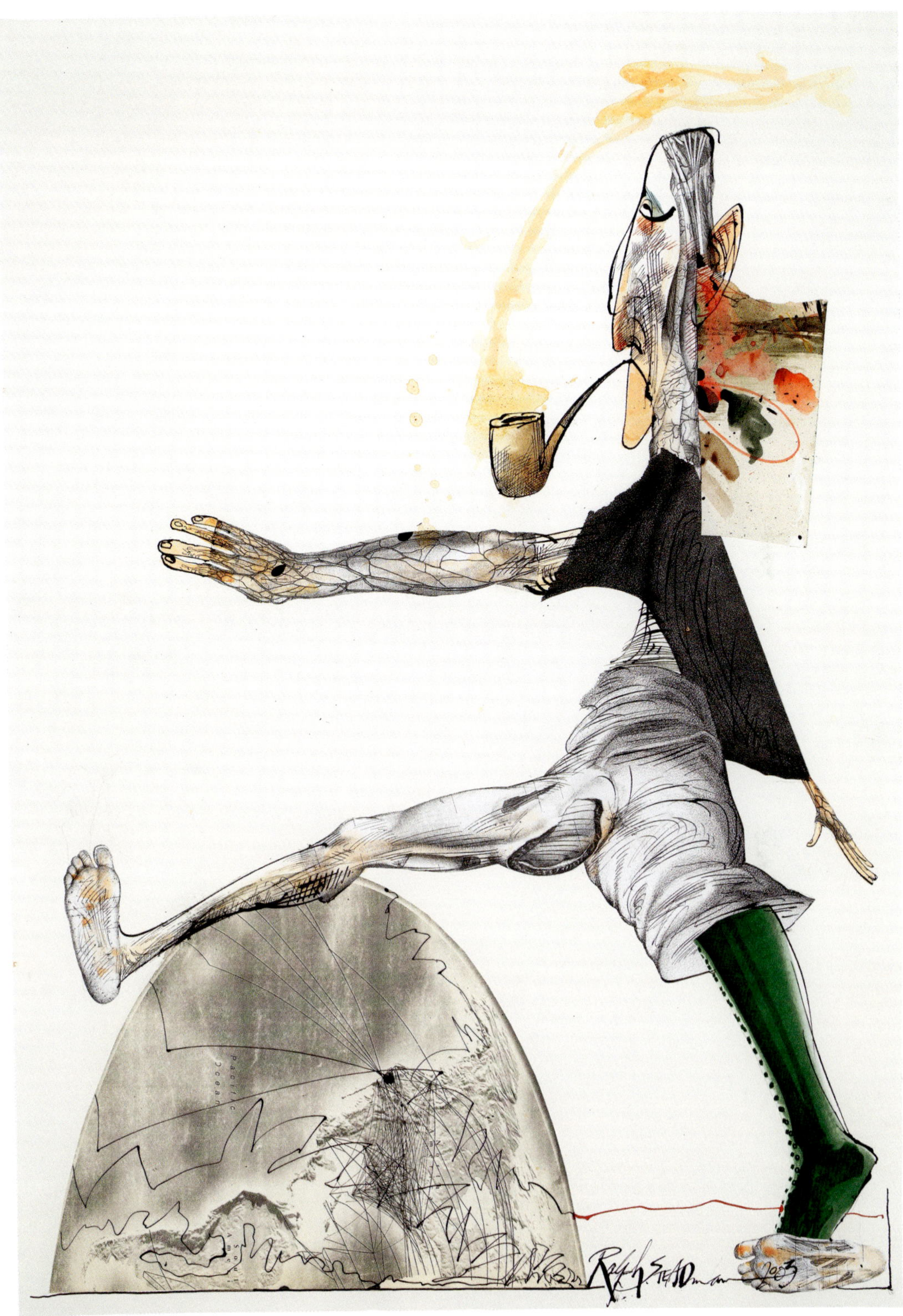

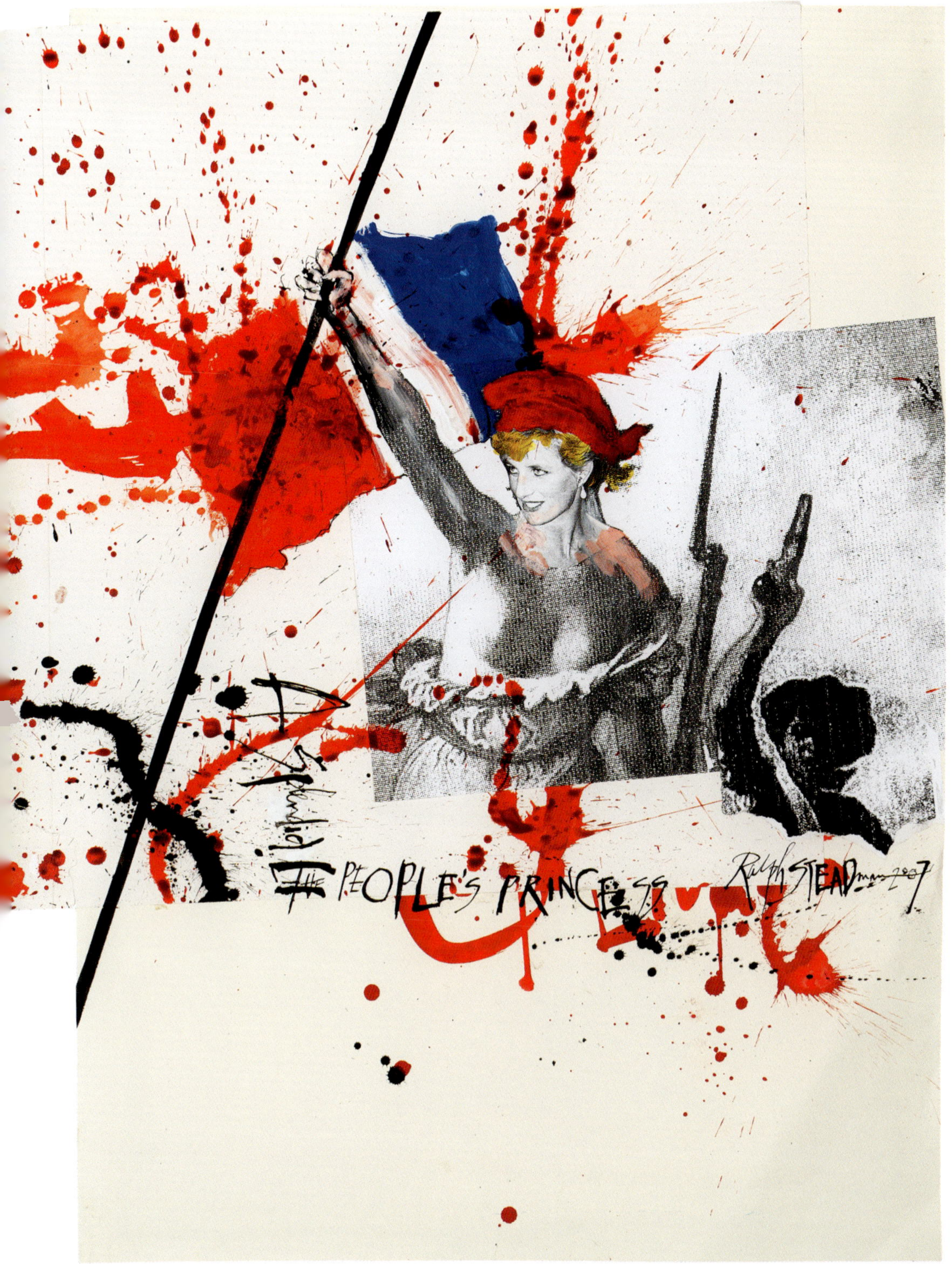

Princess Diana, 2007

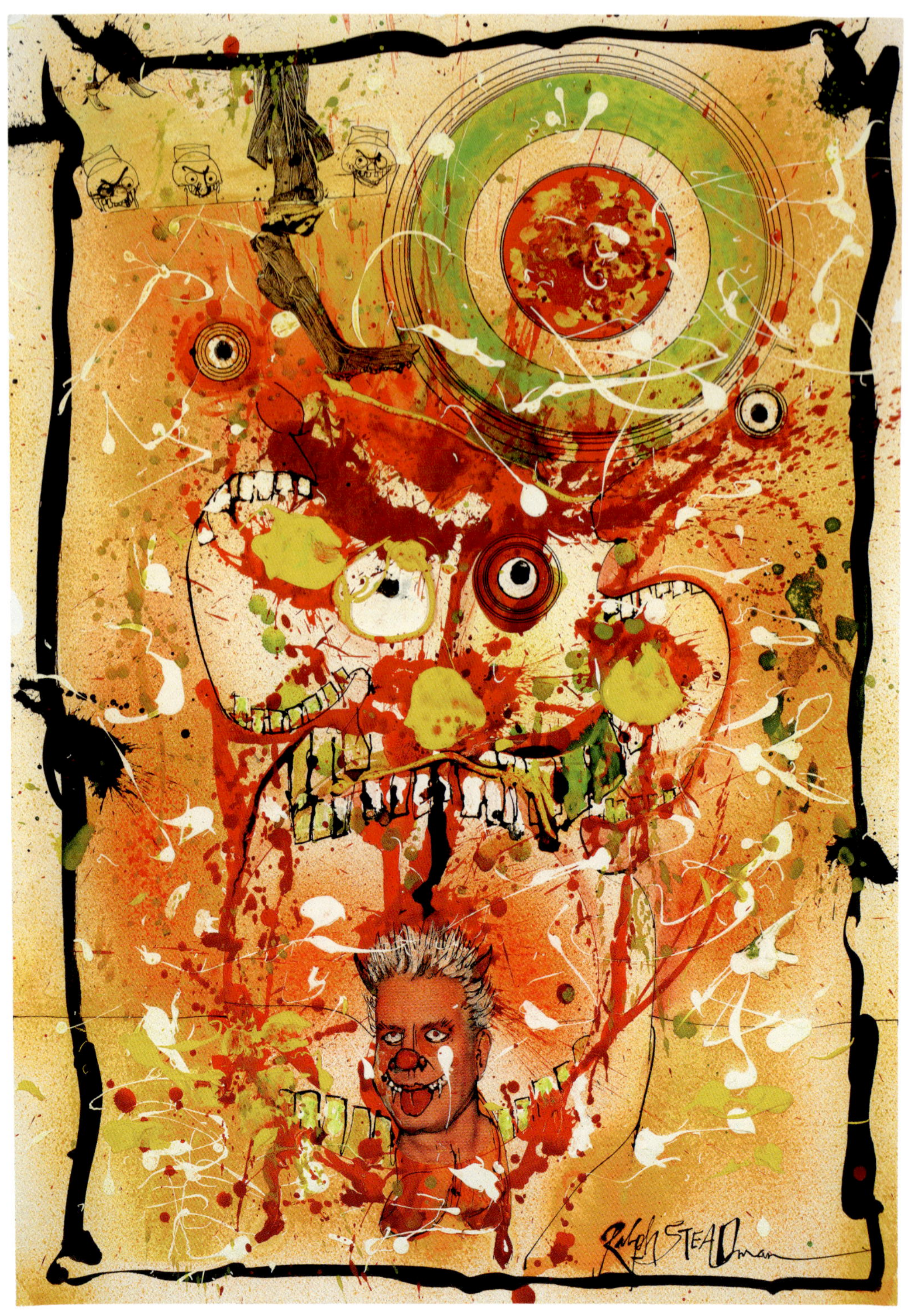

Appetites by Anthony Bourdain, *Book Cover, 2016* "He interviewed me for his series *Parts Unknown*. We went to the Chequers pub in Loose for lunch, and he ordered the Steak and Kidney pie—but he did not eat the base. A year later he was dead. I am not sure if there was a clue there to his sadness at the time."

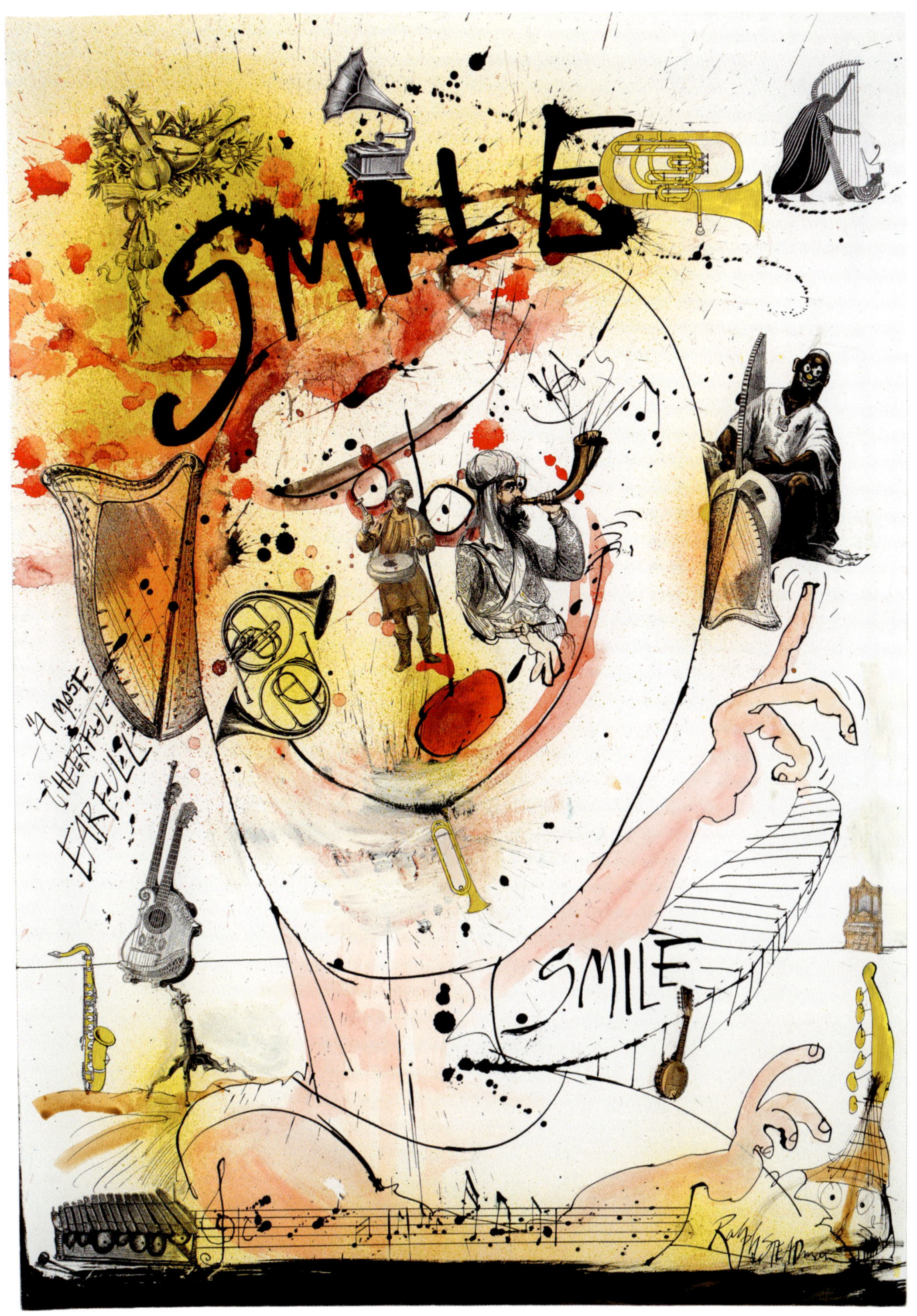

Record Sleeve for Richard Harvey, ca. 2005

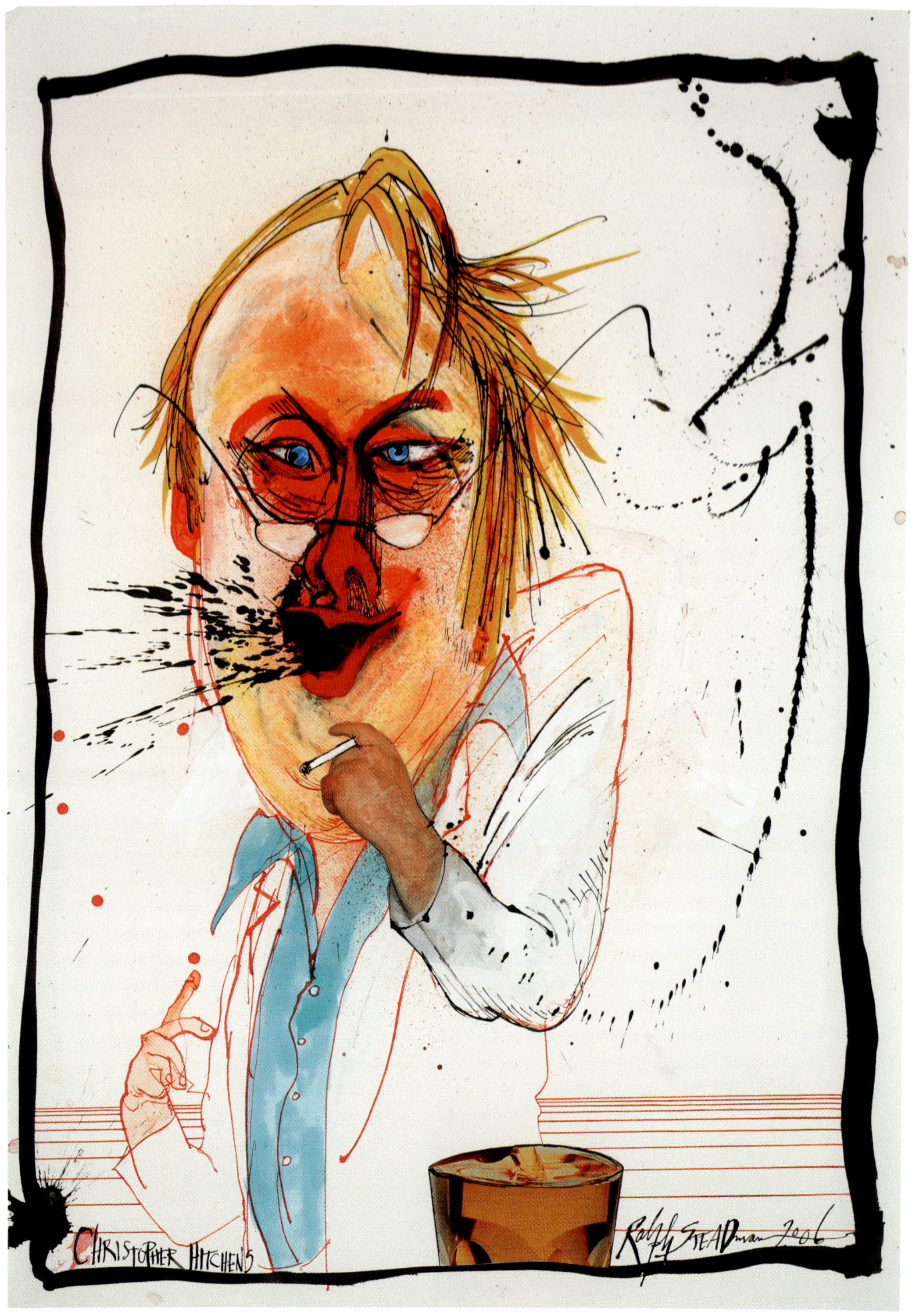

Christopher Hitchens, 2006

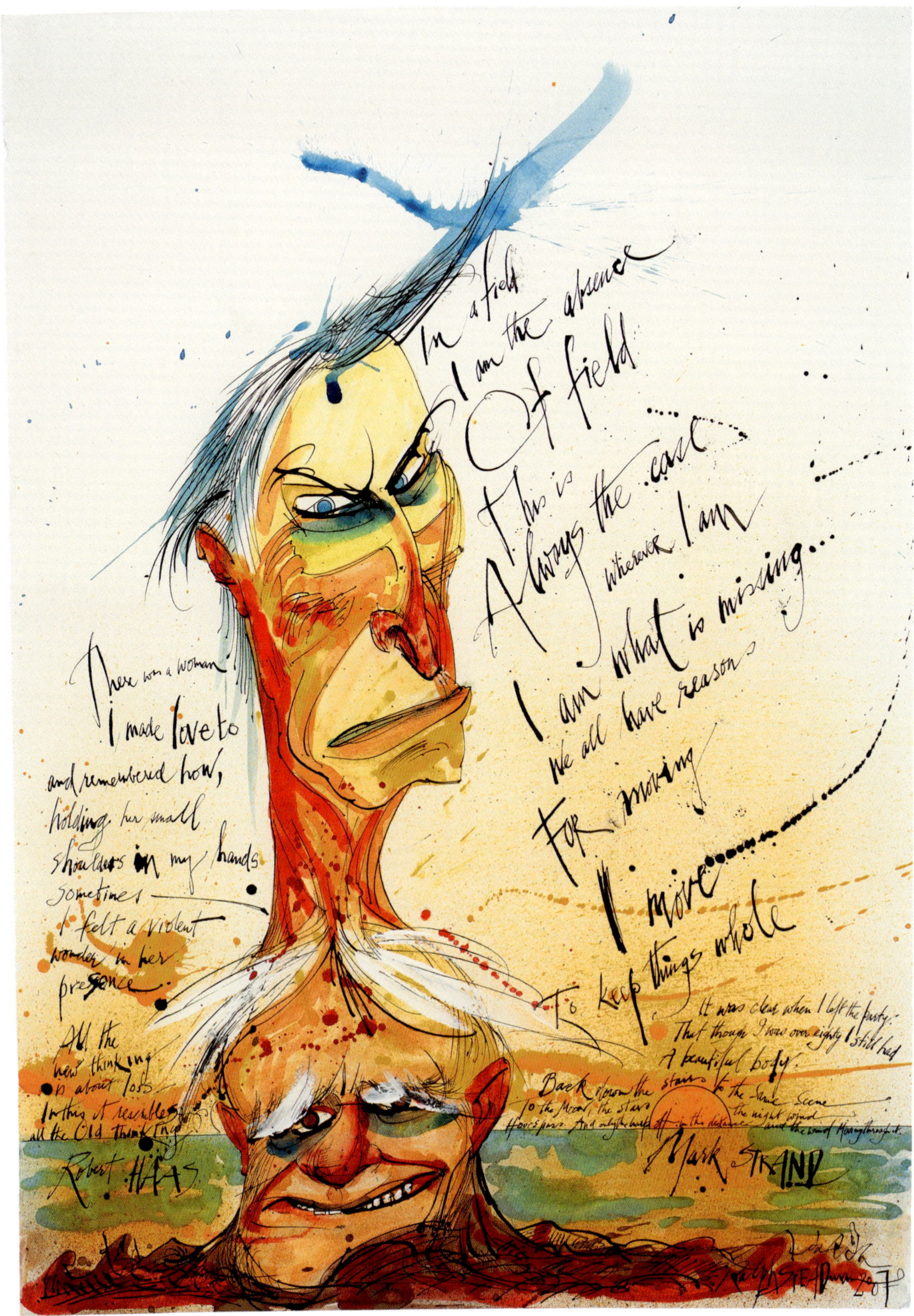

In a field
I am the absence
of field.
This is
always the case.
Wherever I am
I am what is missing.

We all have reasons
for moving.
I move
to keep things whole.

There was a woman
I made love to
and remembered how,
holding her small
shoulders in my hands
sometimes
I felt a violent
wonder in her
presence.

All the
new thinking
is about loss.
In this it resembles
all the old thinking.
Robert HASS

It was clear when I left the party
That though I was over eighty I still had
A beautiful body.

Back down the stars to the same scene
To the Moon, the stars
Hours pass. And night moves off in the distance
MARK STRAND

OK Boys, One Day All This Will Be Yours, 2008

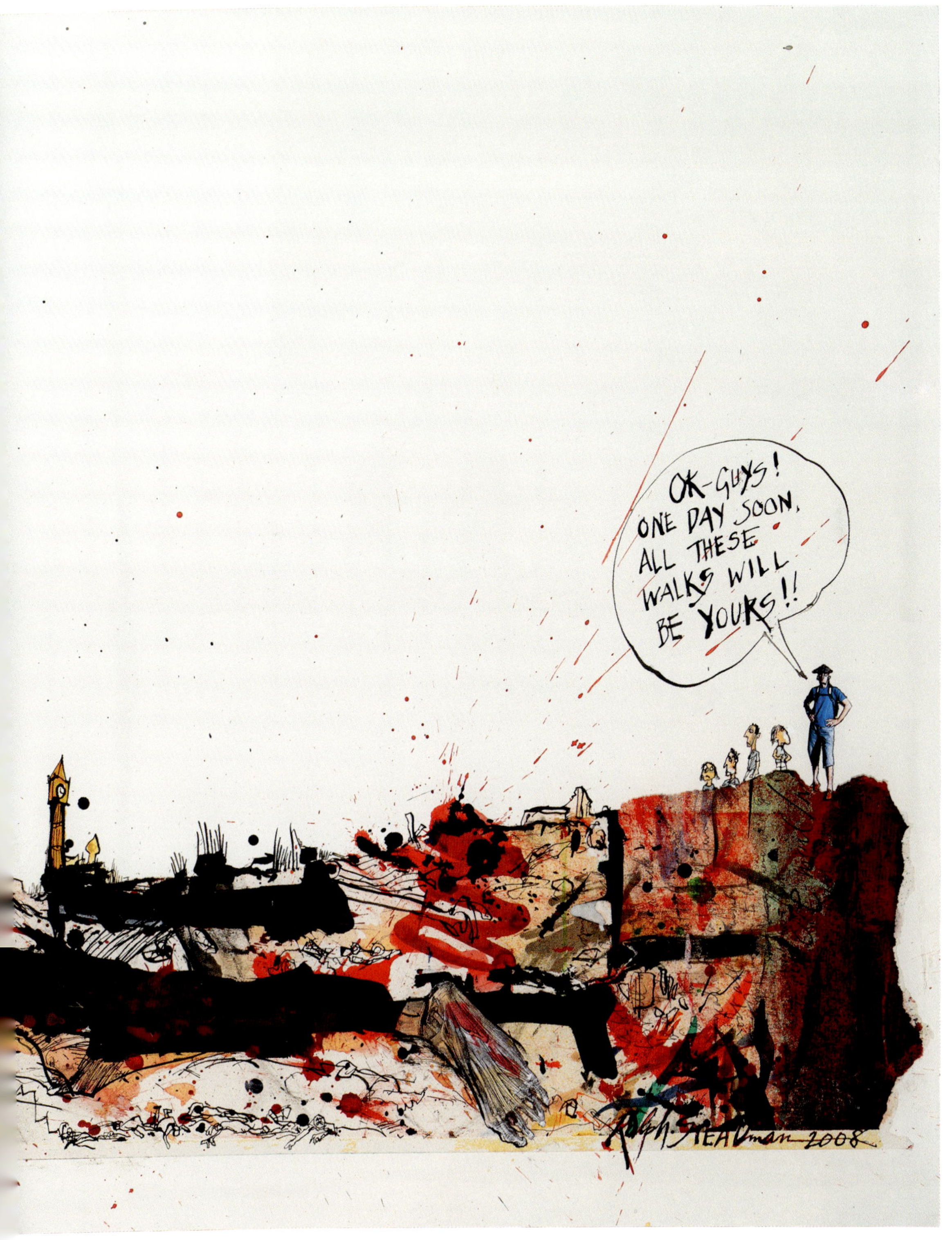

"The landscape is made from a backing paper from my drawing desk. So it's completely random."

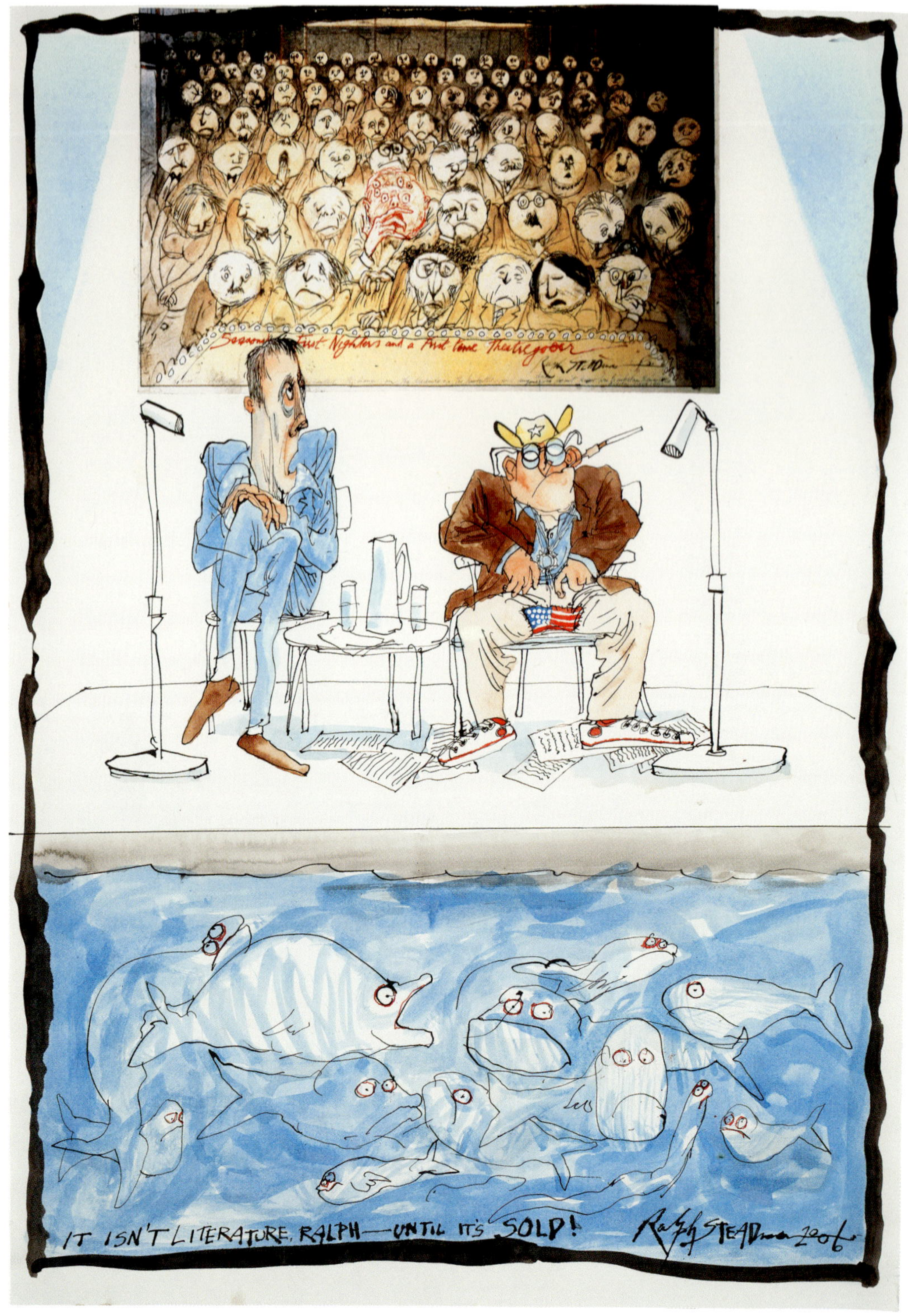

Seasoned first Nighters and a First time Theatregoer
IT ISN'T LITERATURE, RALPH — UNTIL IT'S SOLD!
Ralph STEADman 2006

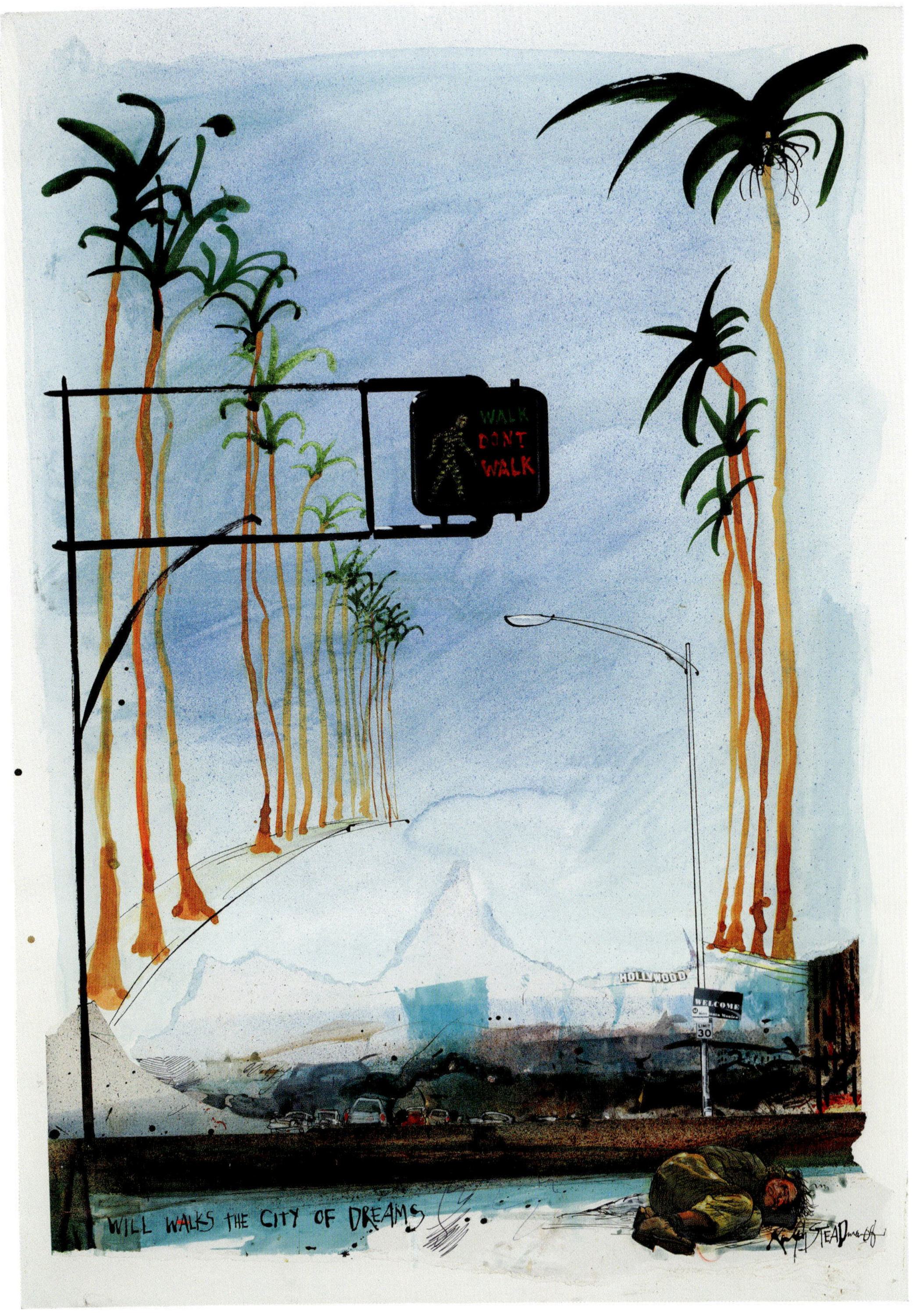

WALK
DON'T
WALK
HOLLYWOOD
WELCOME
LIMIT
30
WILL WALKS THE CITY OF DREAMS

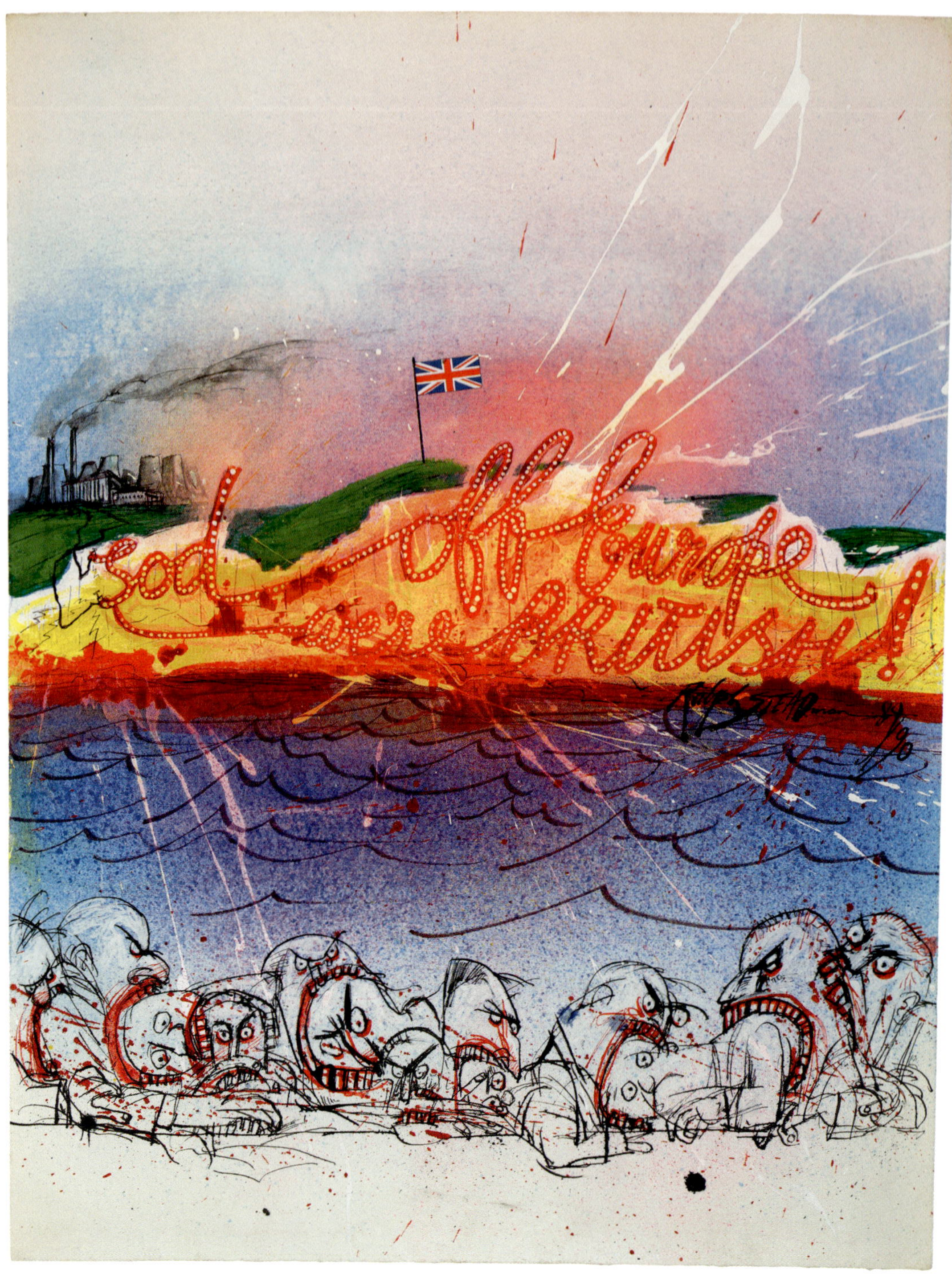

sod off Europe we're british!

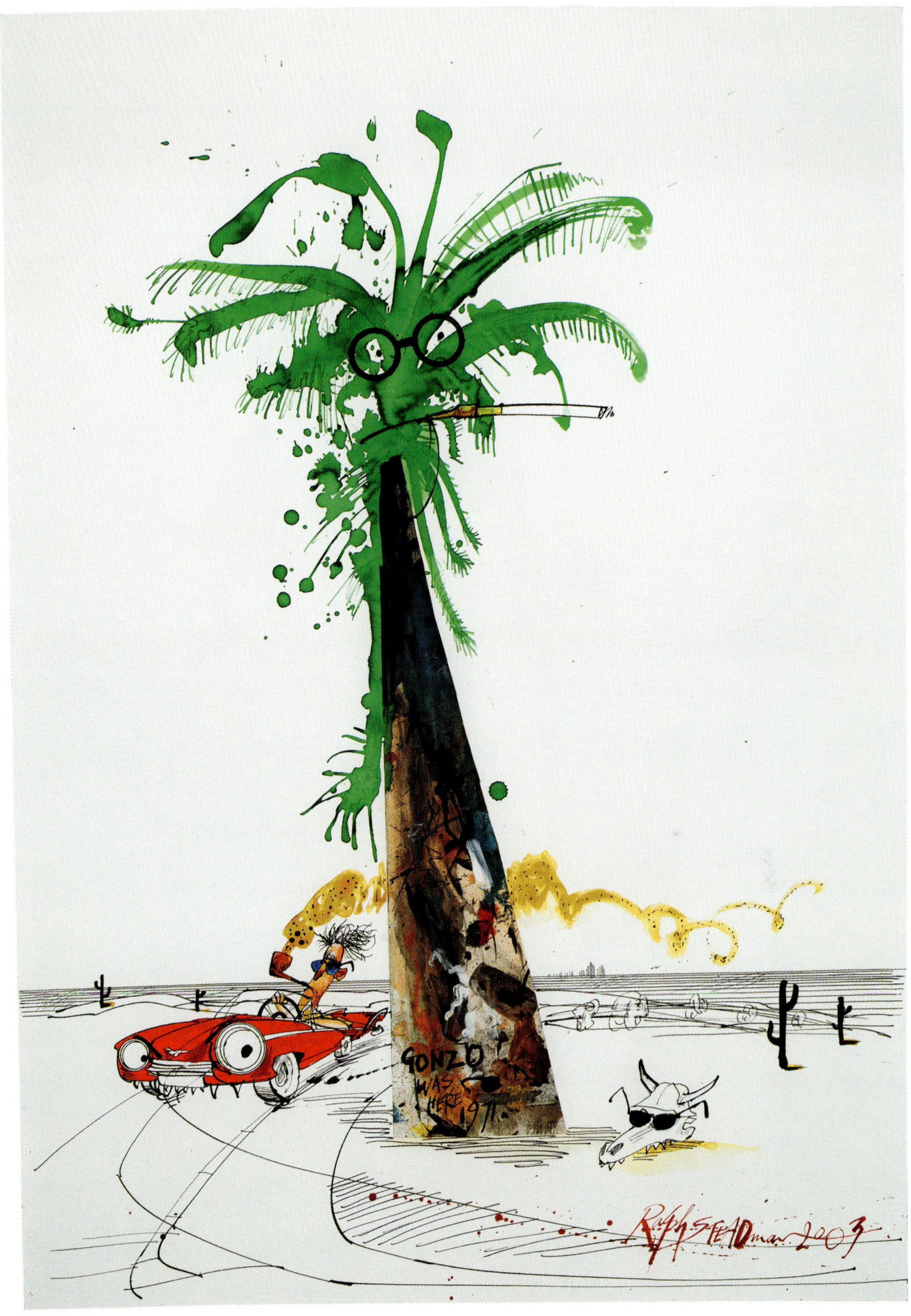

*Fear and Loathing Pastiche from **Psychogeography**, 2003*

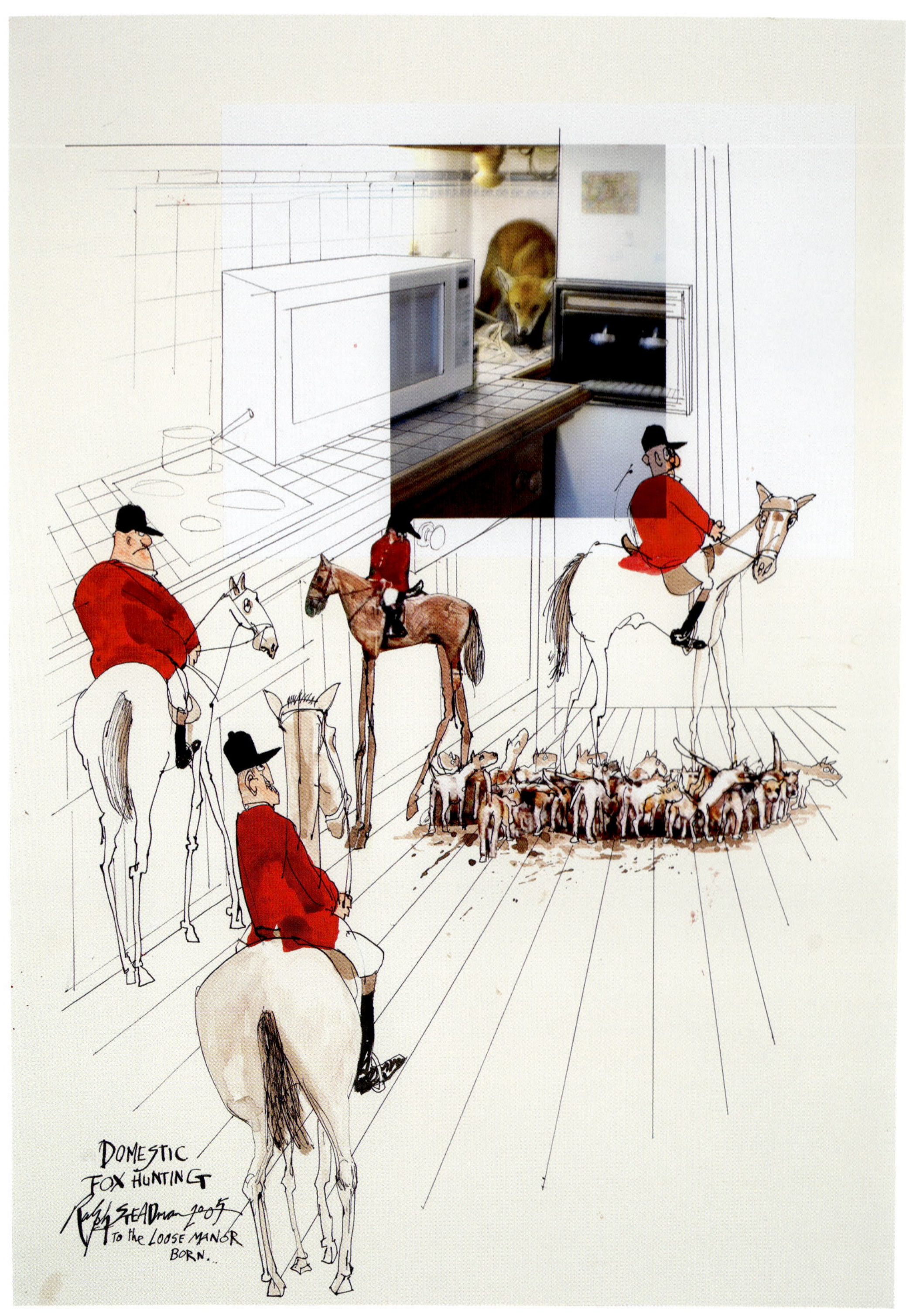

From *Psychogeography*, 2003 "A fox got trapped in our kitchen behind the microwave. I managed to take a photo, and then Will Self wrote a piece about it."

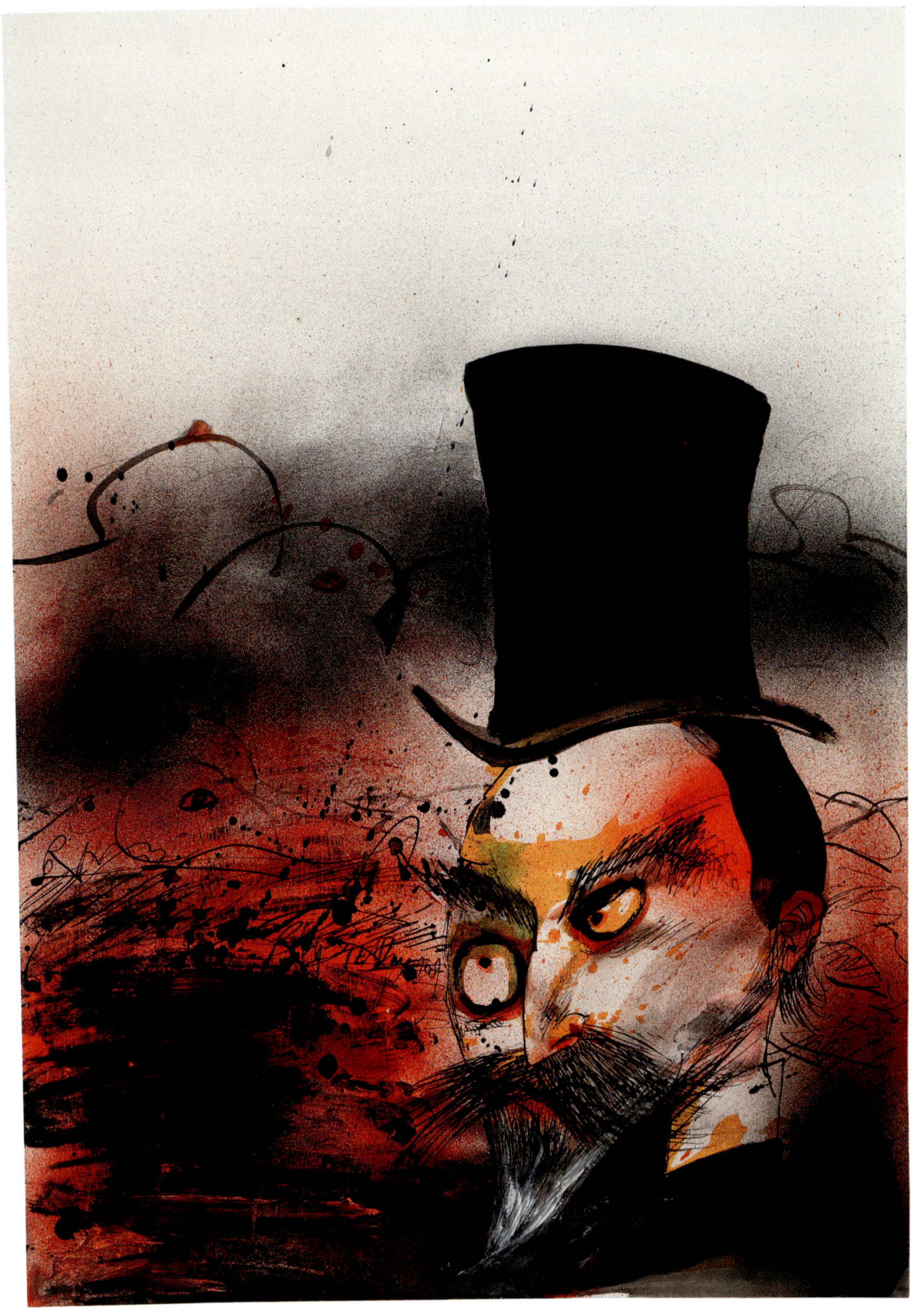

Top Hatted Gentleman, ca. 2002

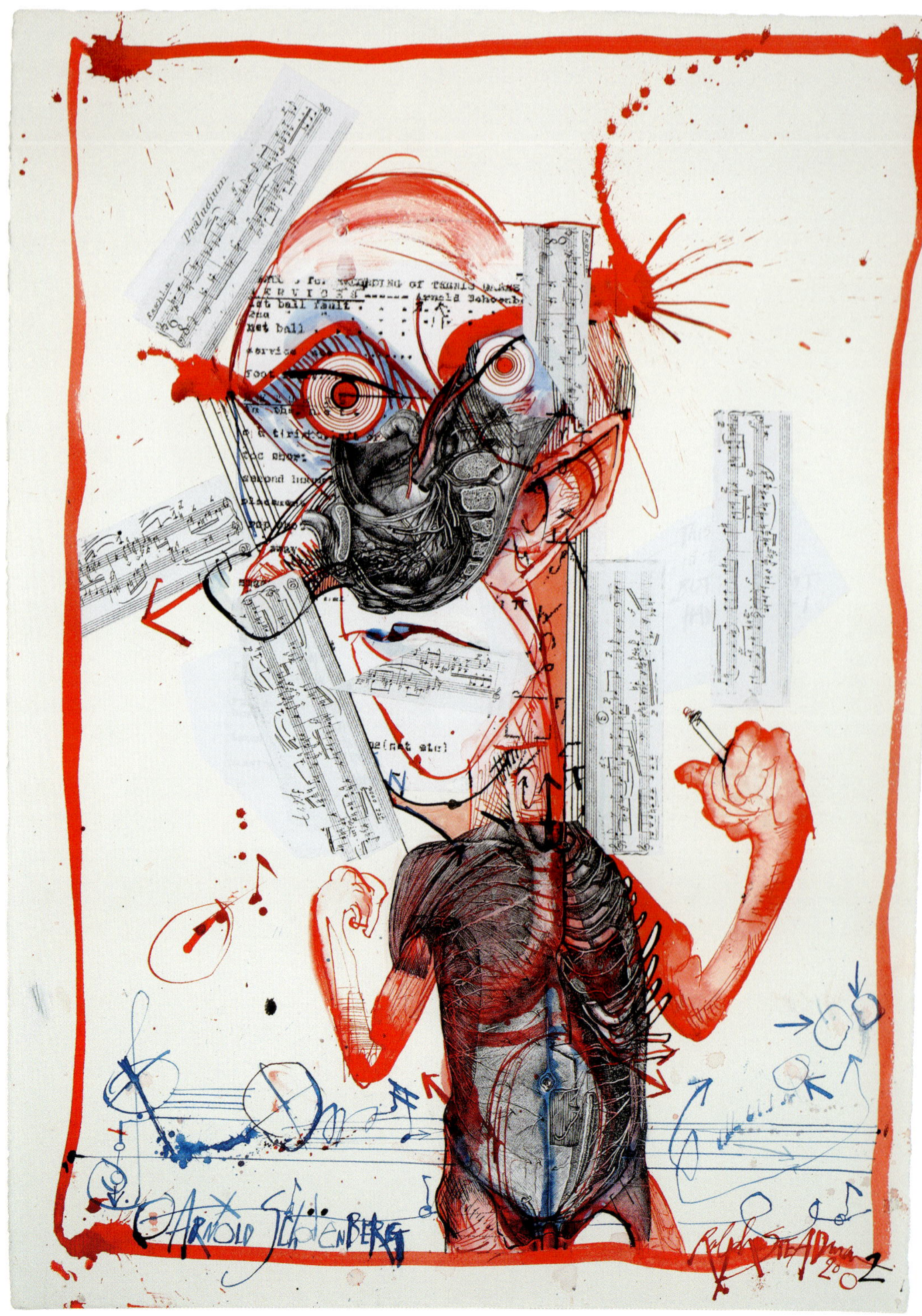

Arnold Schoenberg, 2002

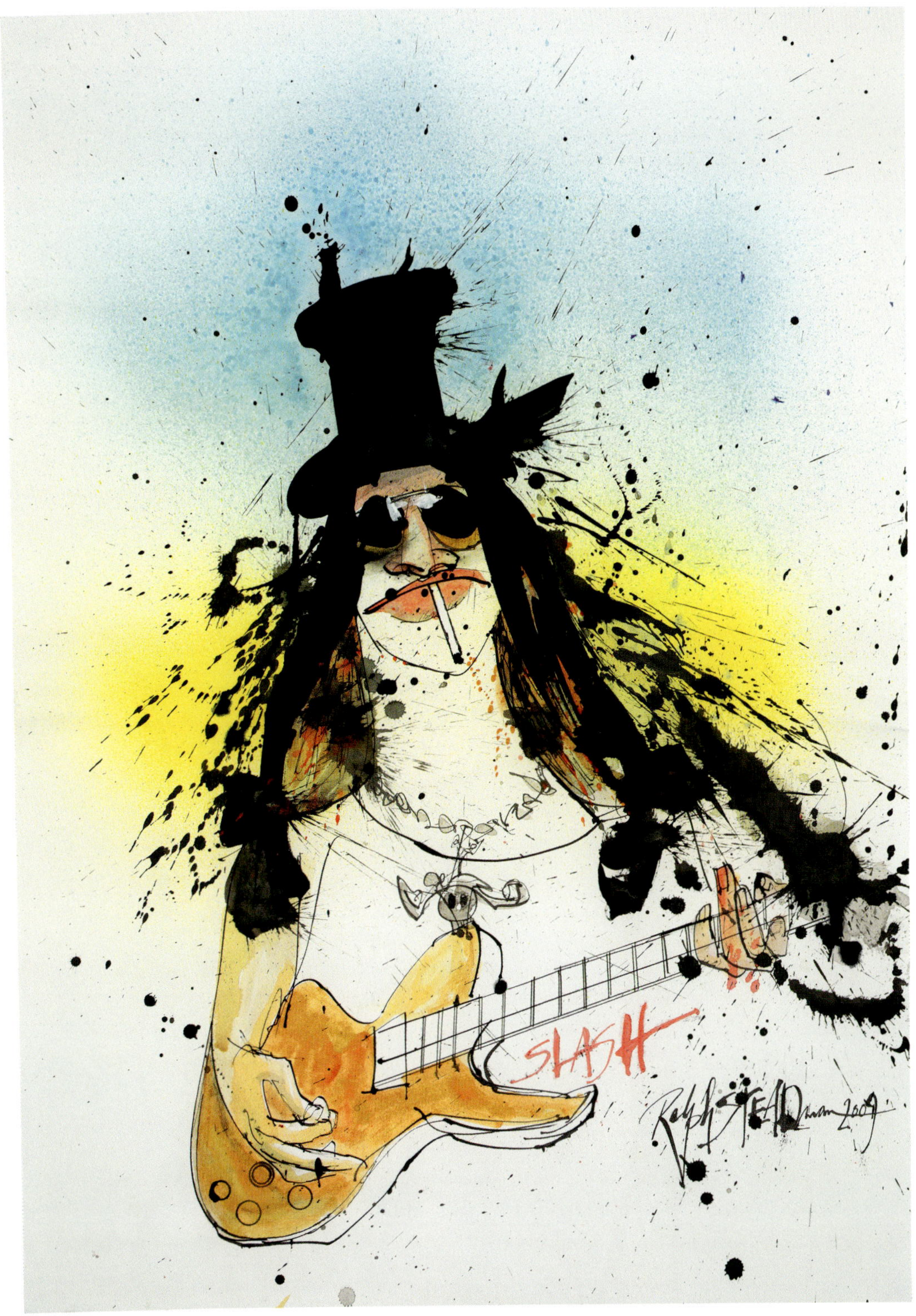
SLASH

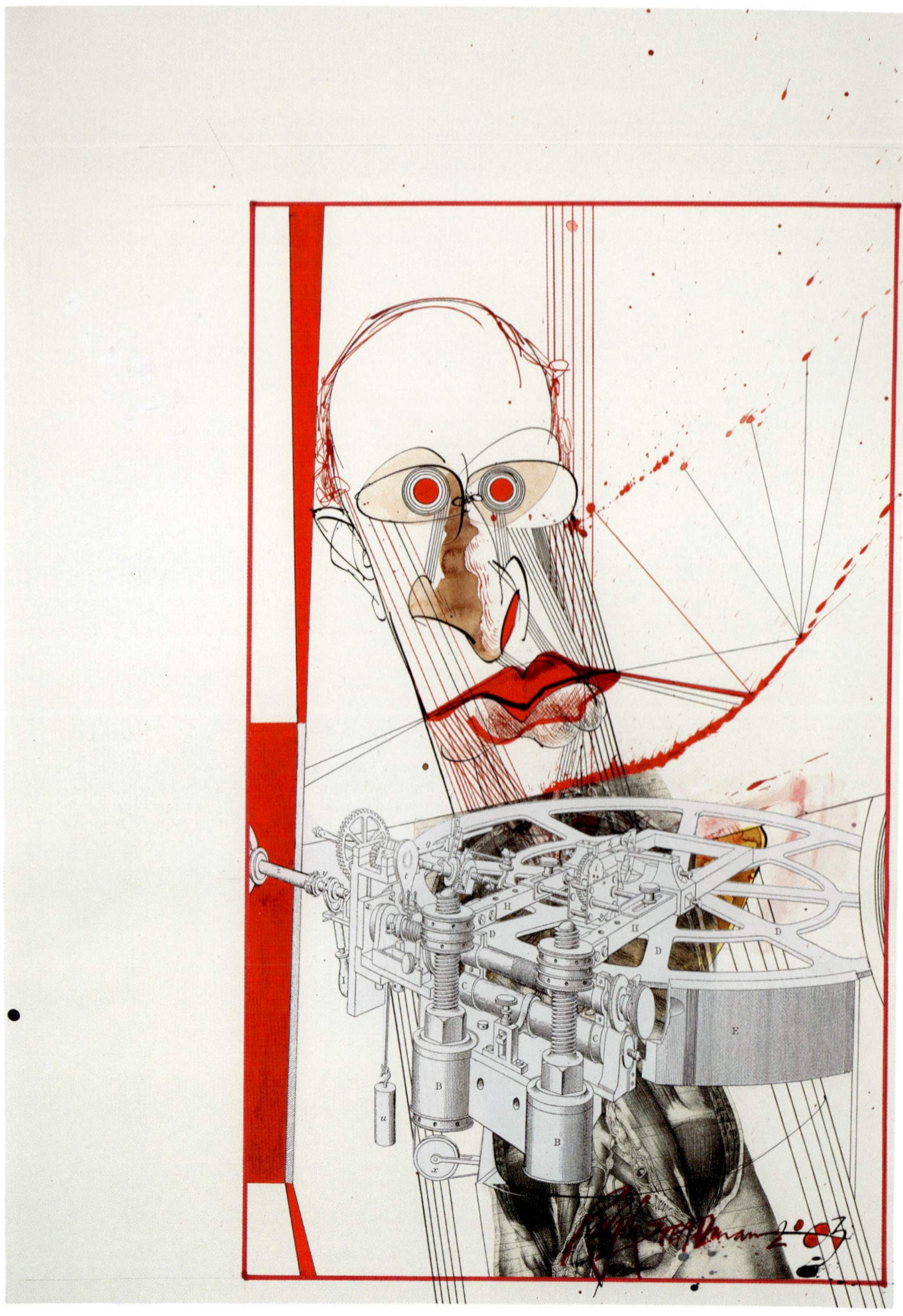

Unknown Portrait, 2003

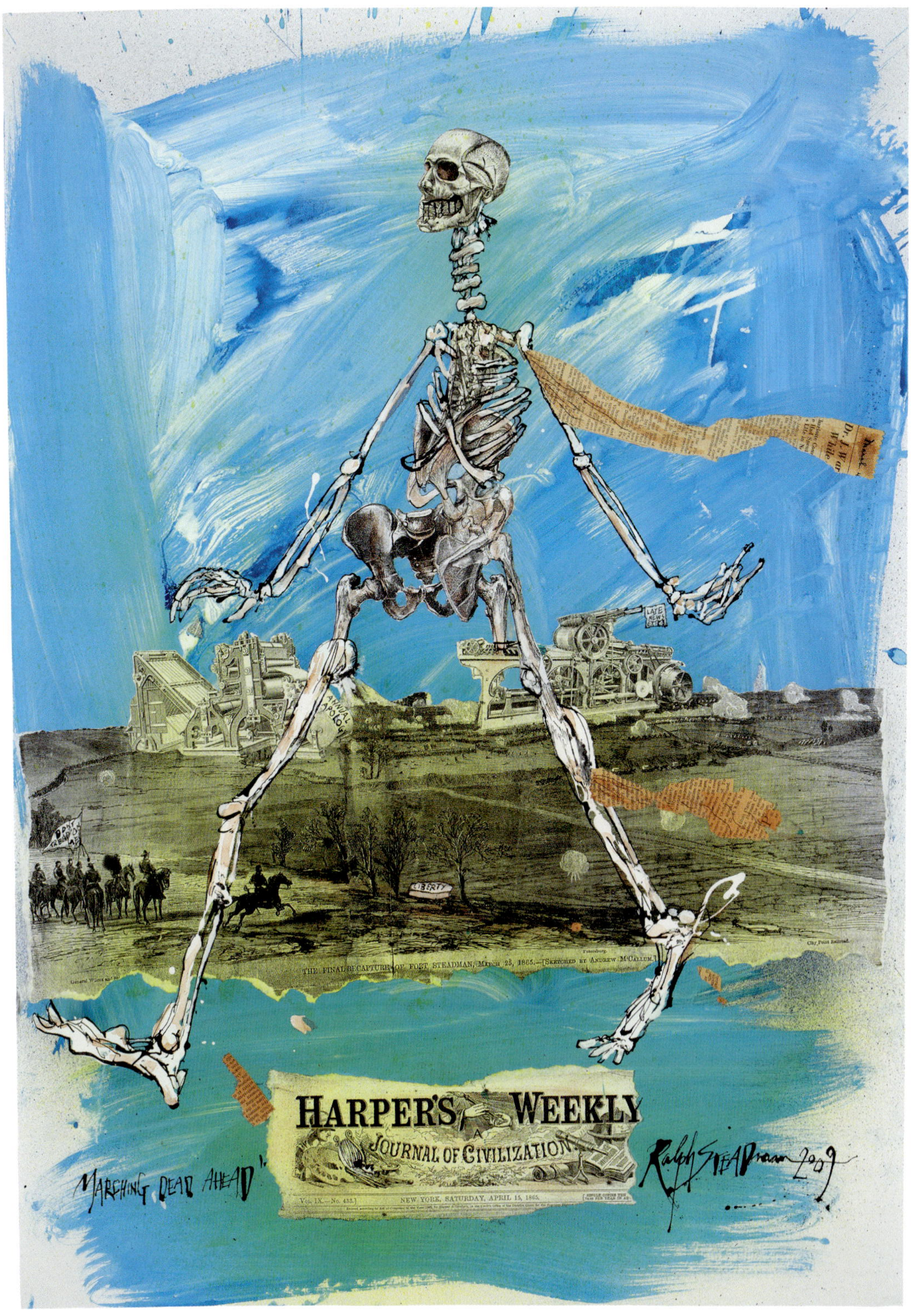

Harper's Weekly, 2009

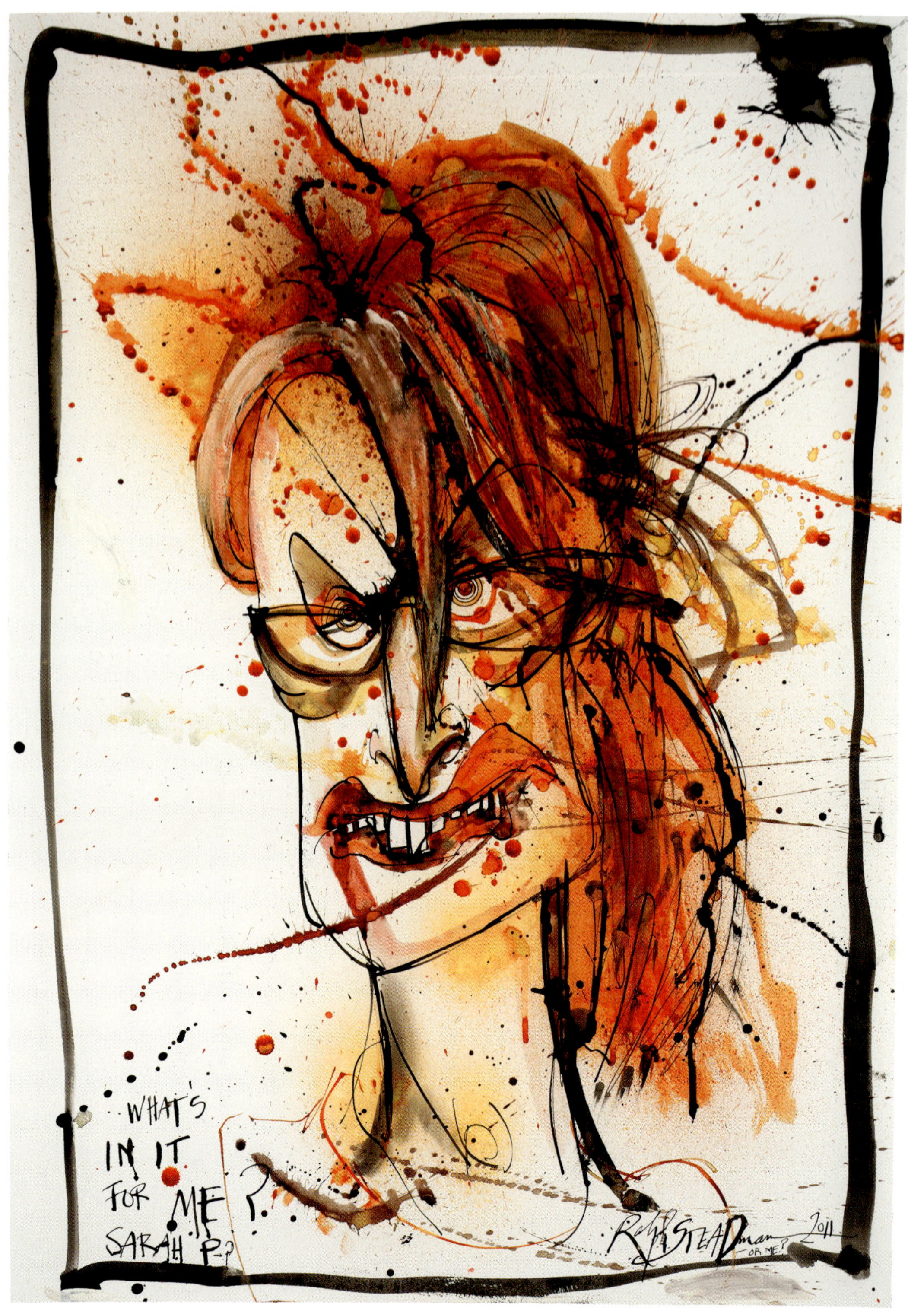

Sarah Palin, 2011

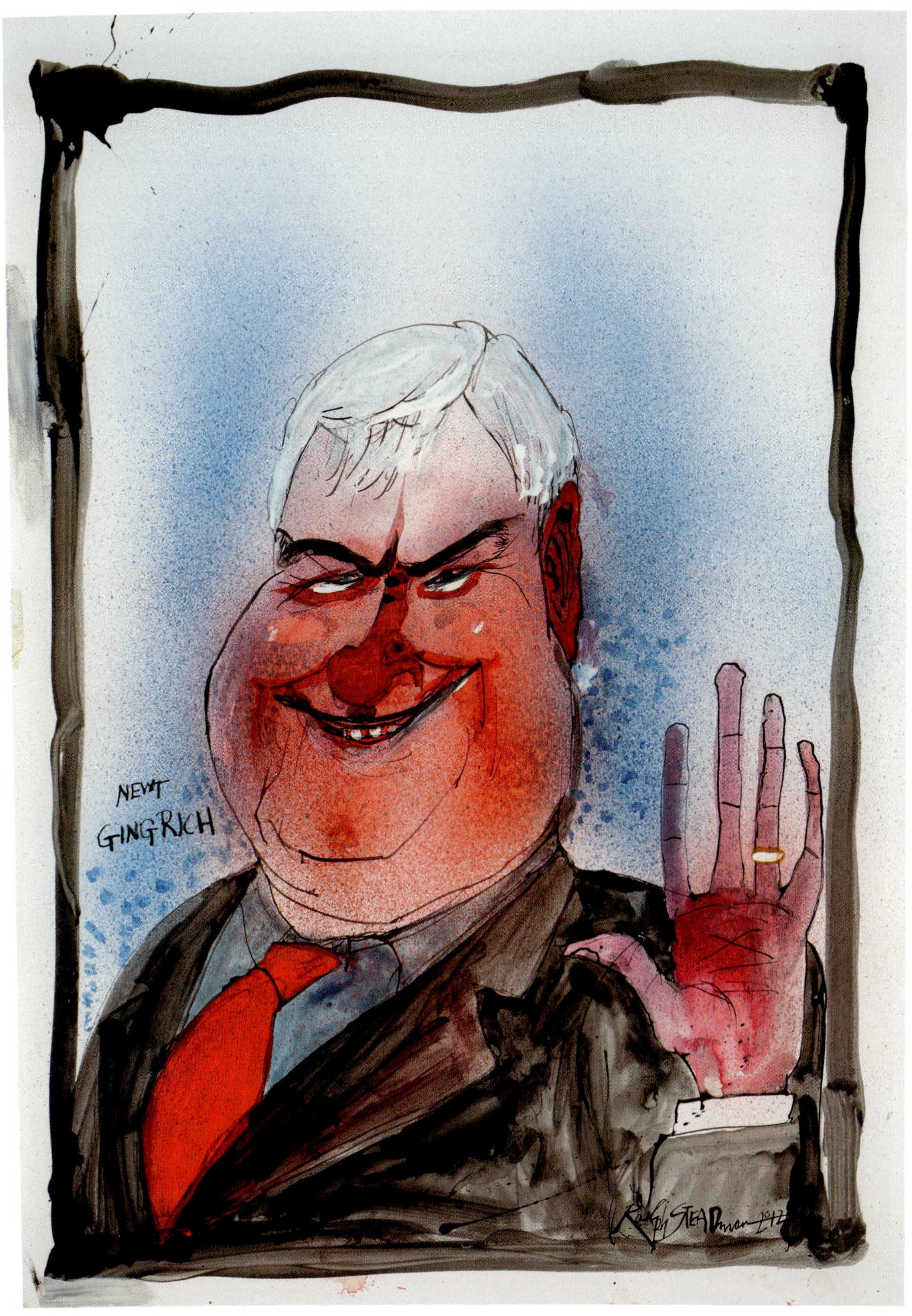

NEWT
GINGRICH

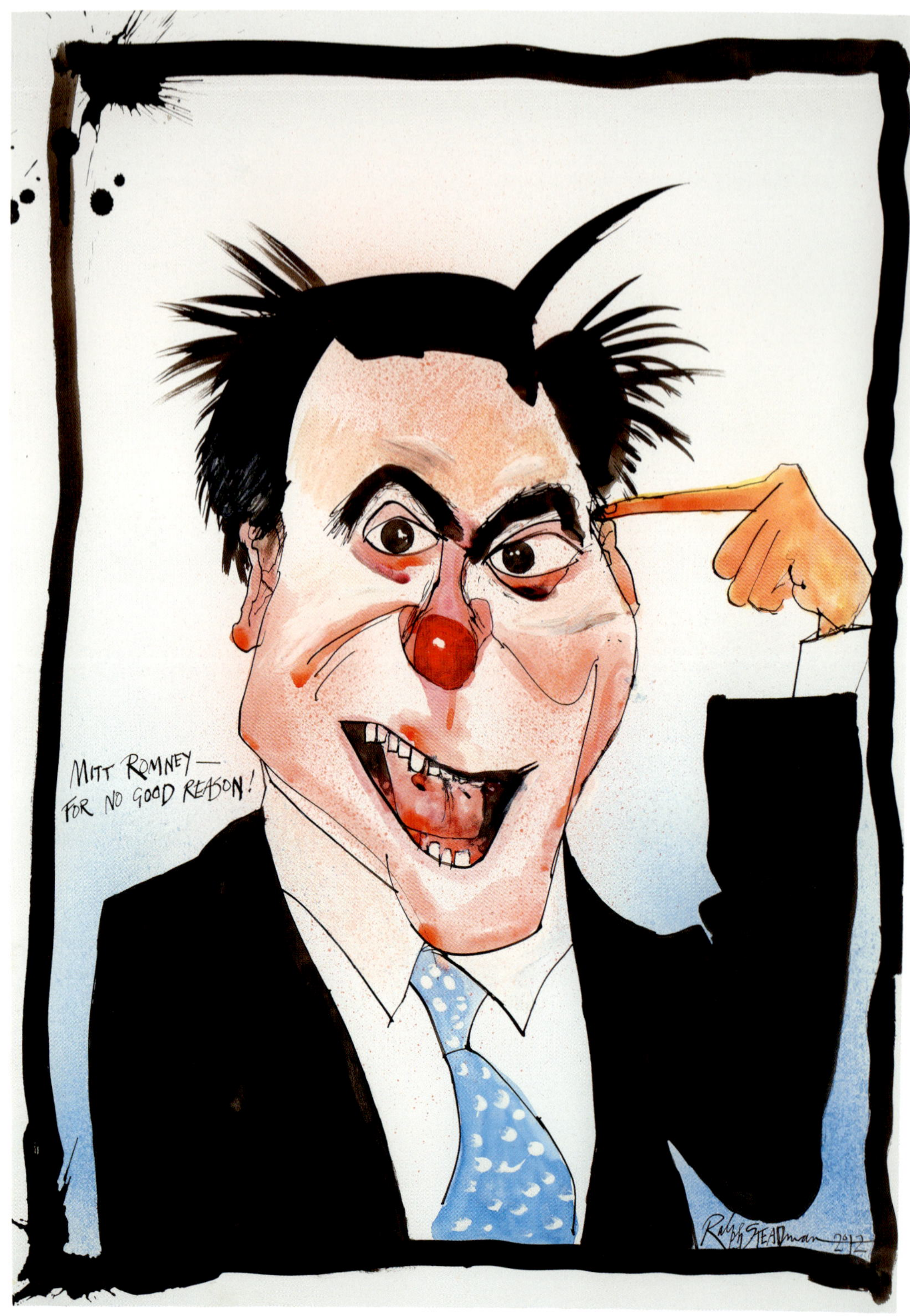

Mitt Romney, 2012

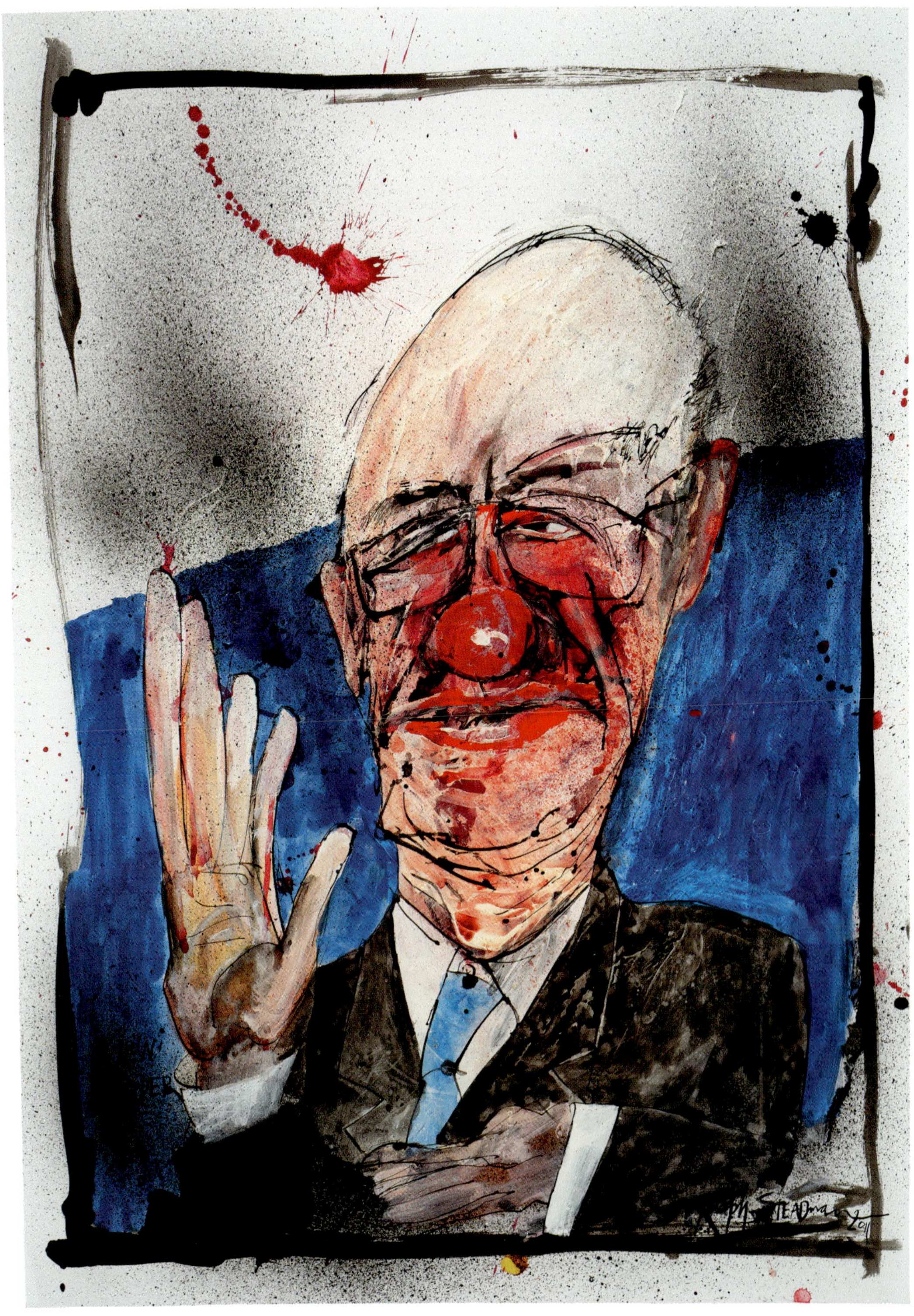

Rupert Murdoch, 2011

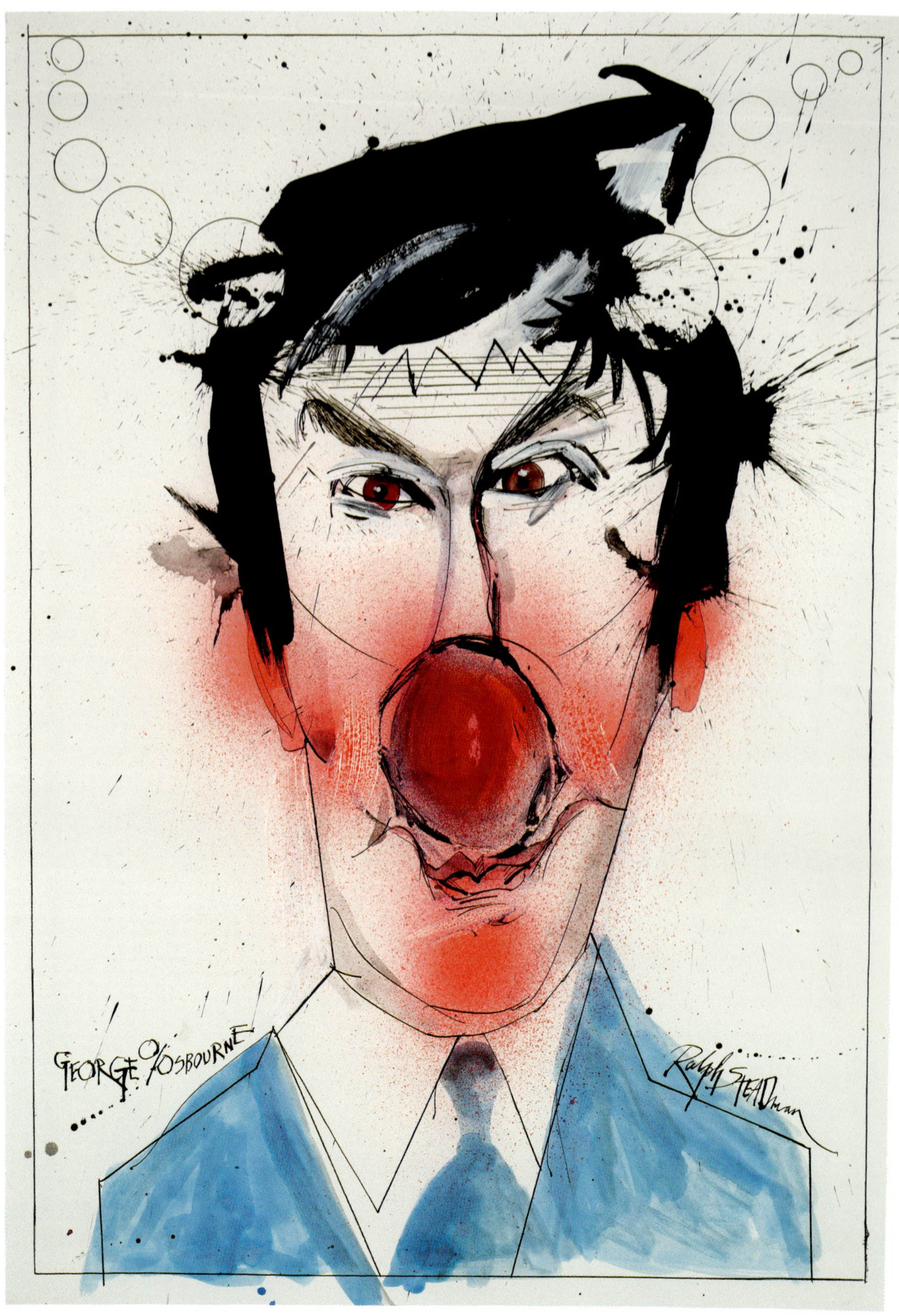

George Osborne, 2015

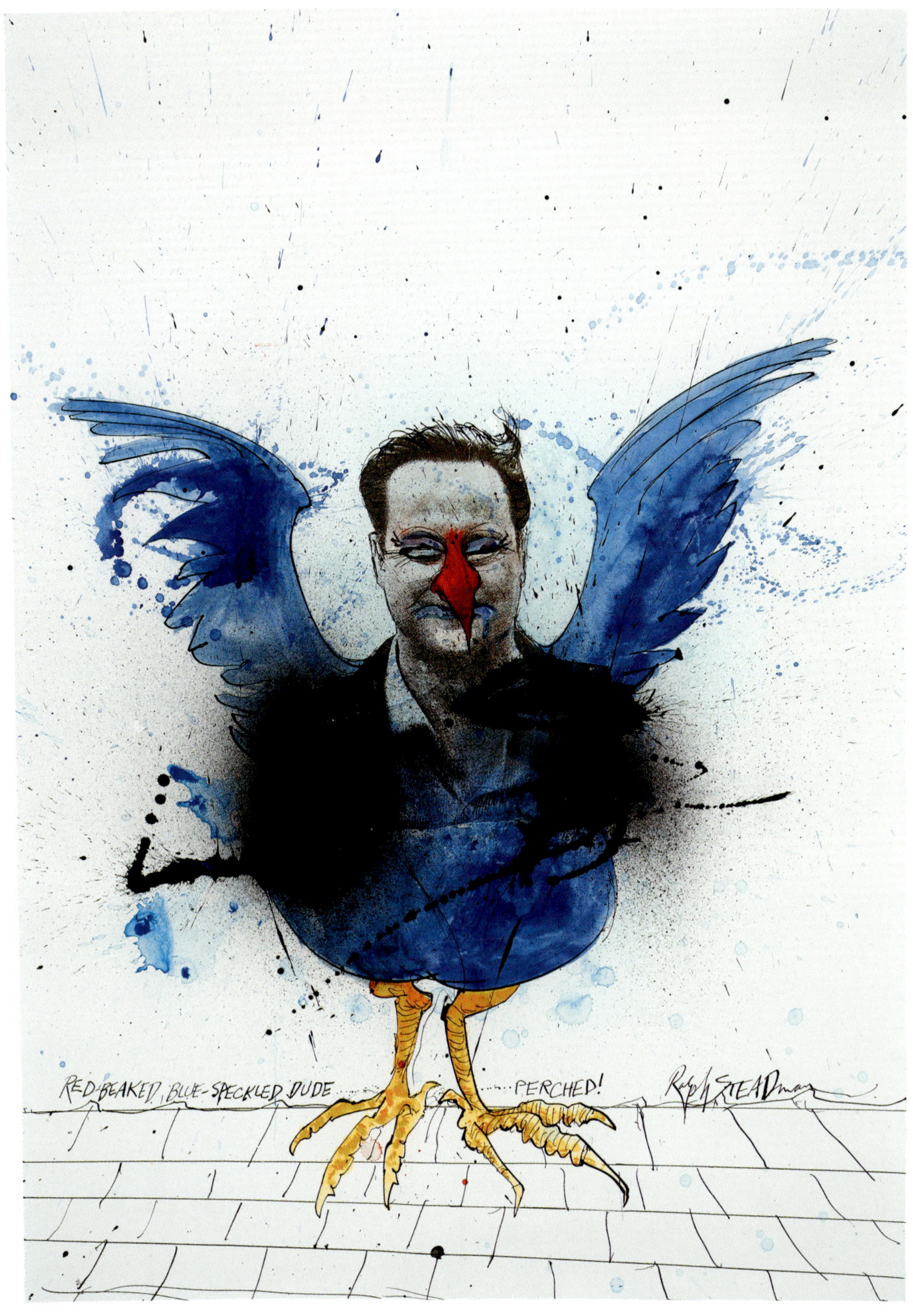

David Cameron, 2015 "He left one helluva mess behind him."

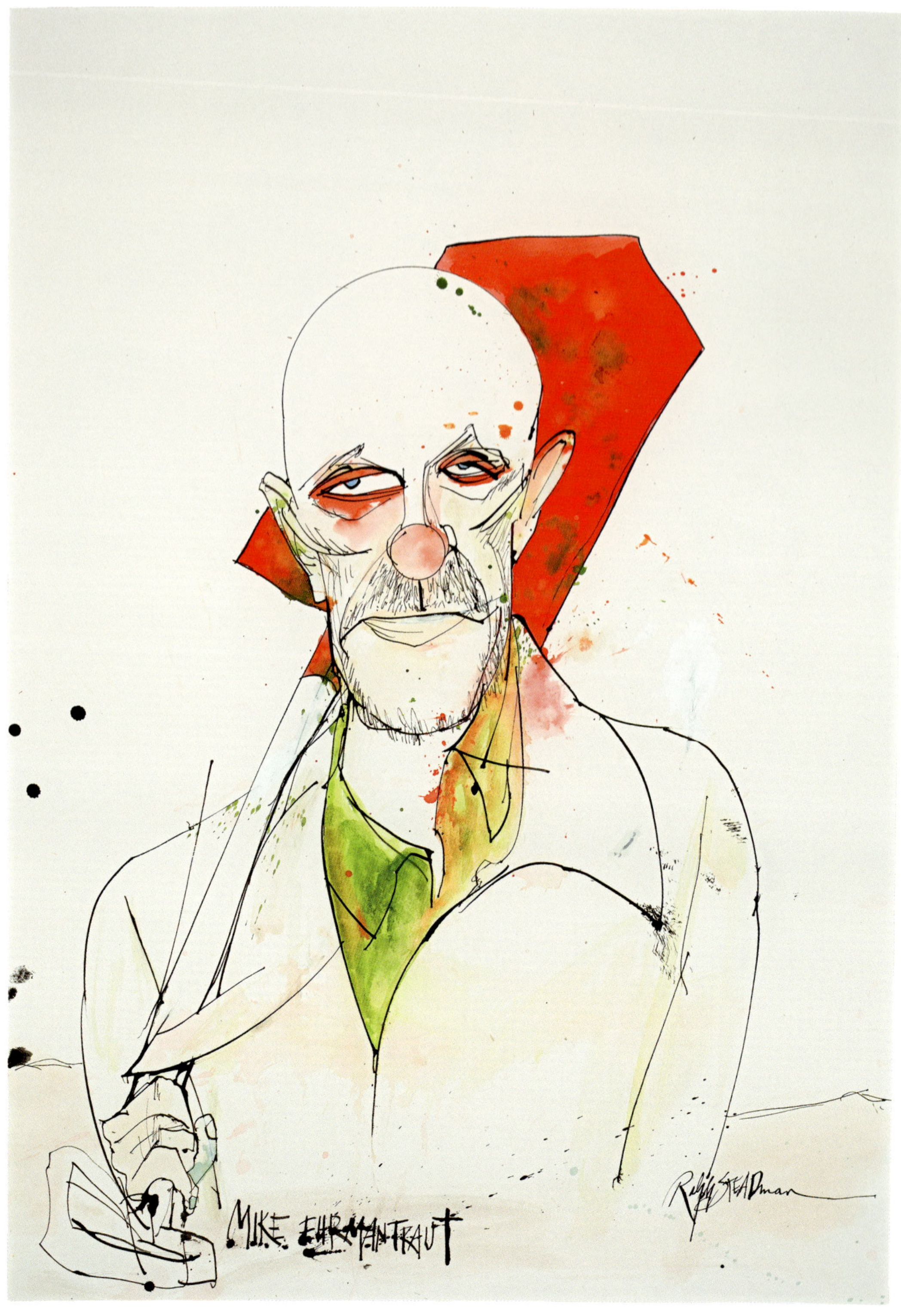

Mike Ehrmantraut, **Breaking Bad Collector's Edition** DVD, Sony, 2014

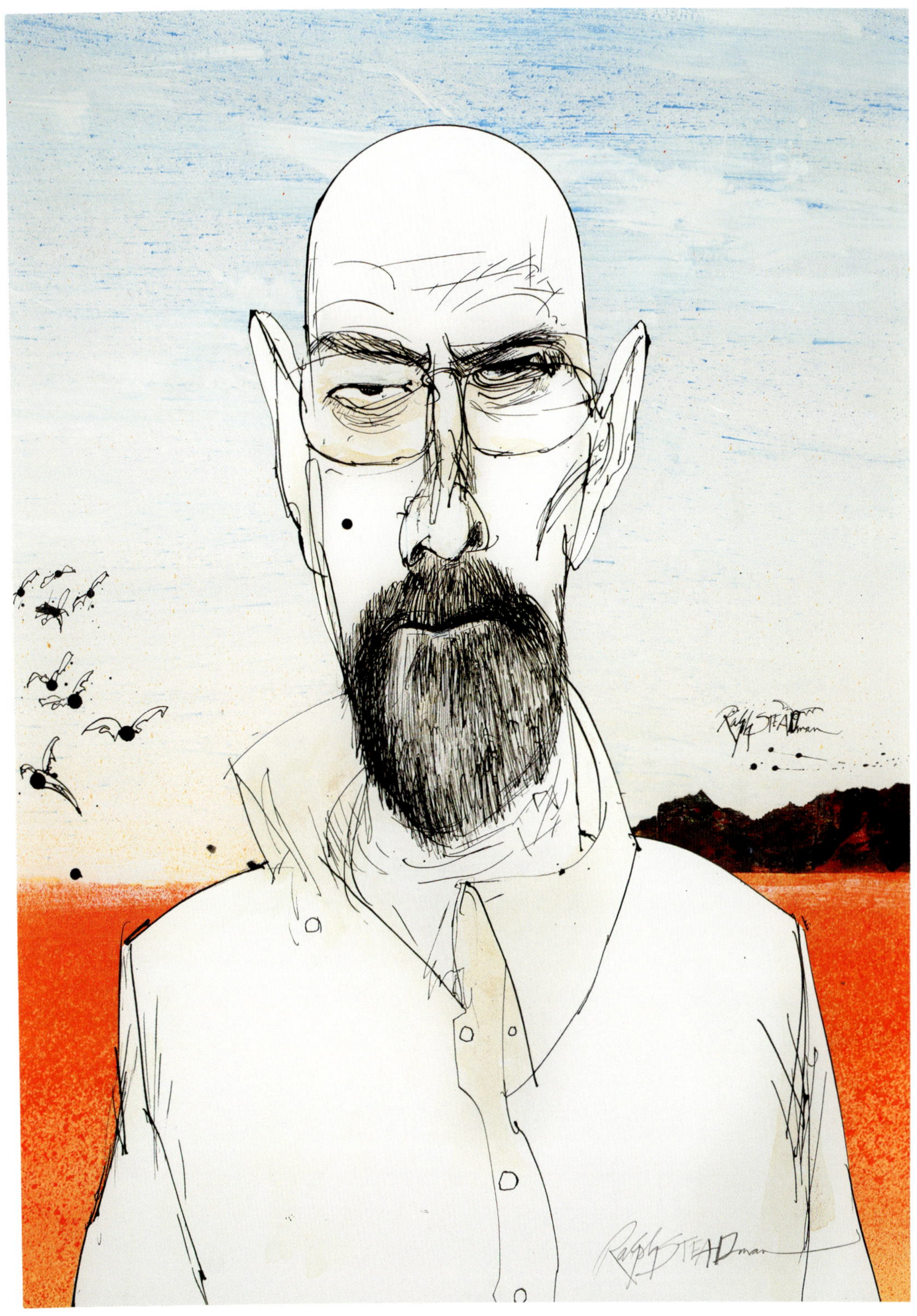

*Walter White, **Breaking Bad Collector's Edition** DVD, Sony, 2014*

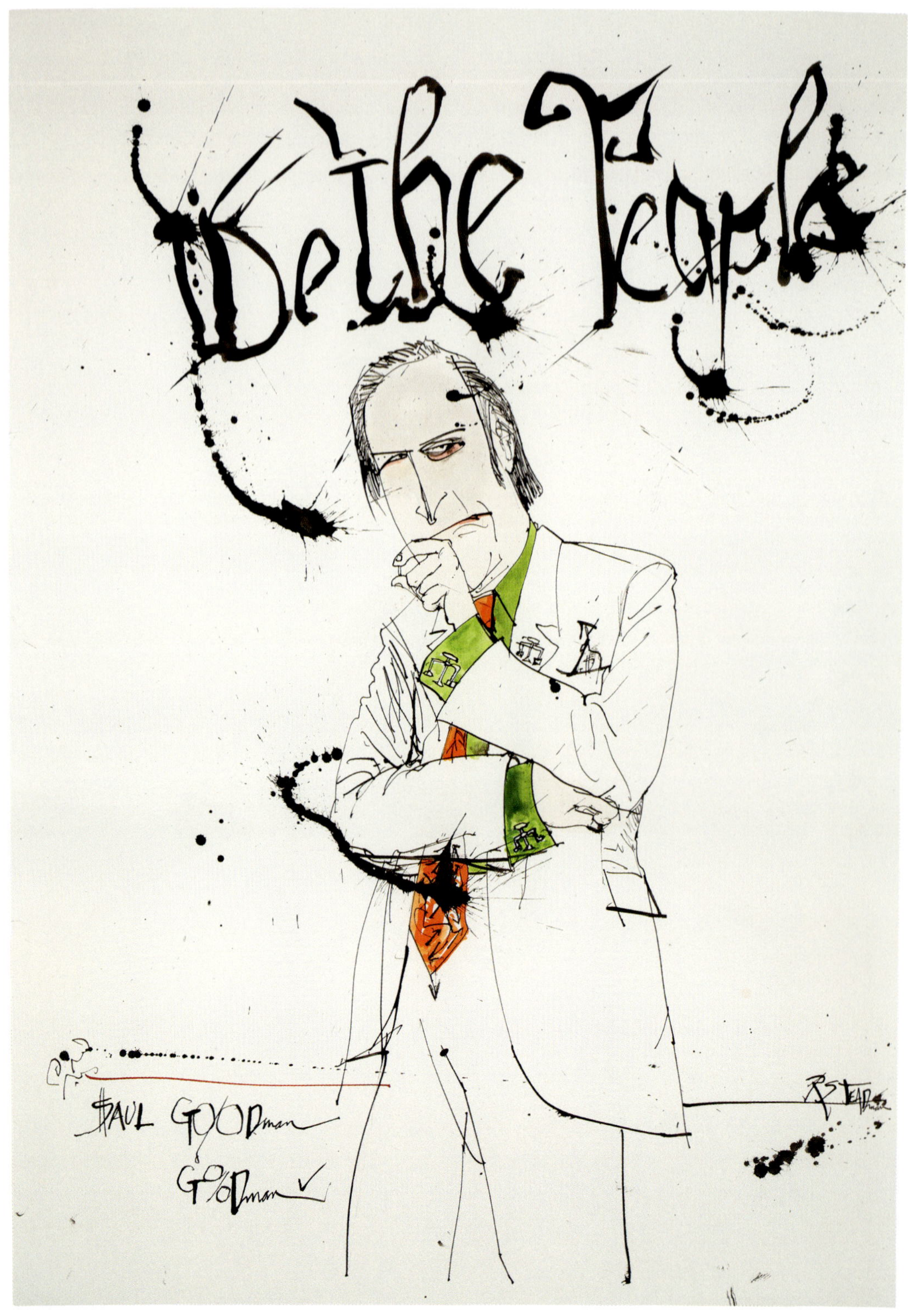

Saul Goodman, *Breaking Bad Collector's Edition* DVD, Sony, 2014

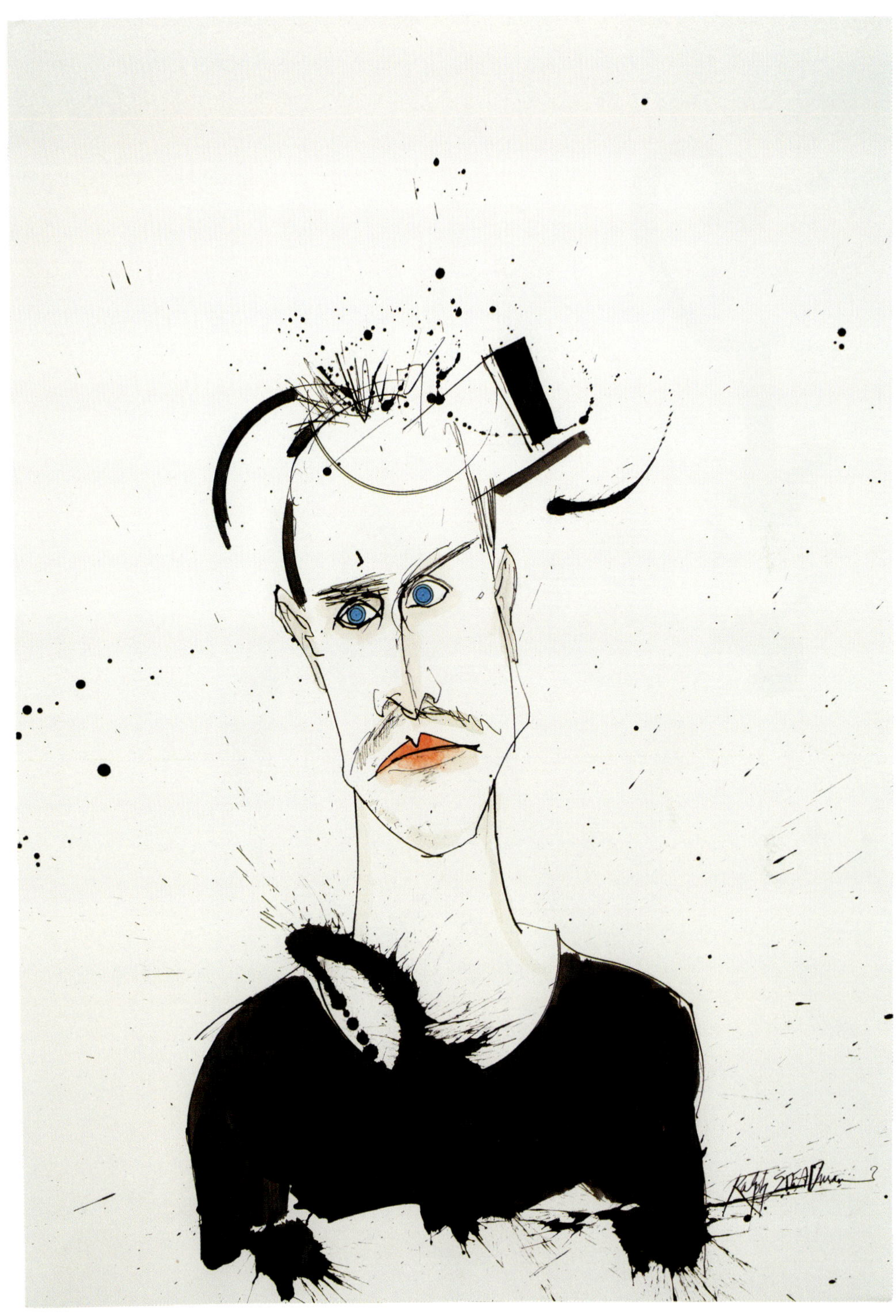

Jesse Pinkman, **Breaking Bad Collector's Edition** *DVD, Sony, 2014* "Anna and I watched three episodes a night to catch up with the series as I had not heard of it until Sony got in touch. My granddaughter Grace was so excited that I had been asked to do these portraits that I said yes. Sony biked the DVDs over the next day, and we started watching. I missed the show when we had finished watching it."

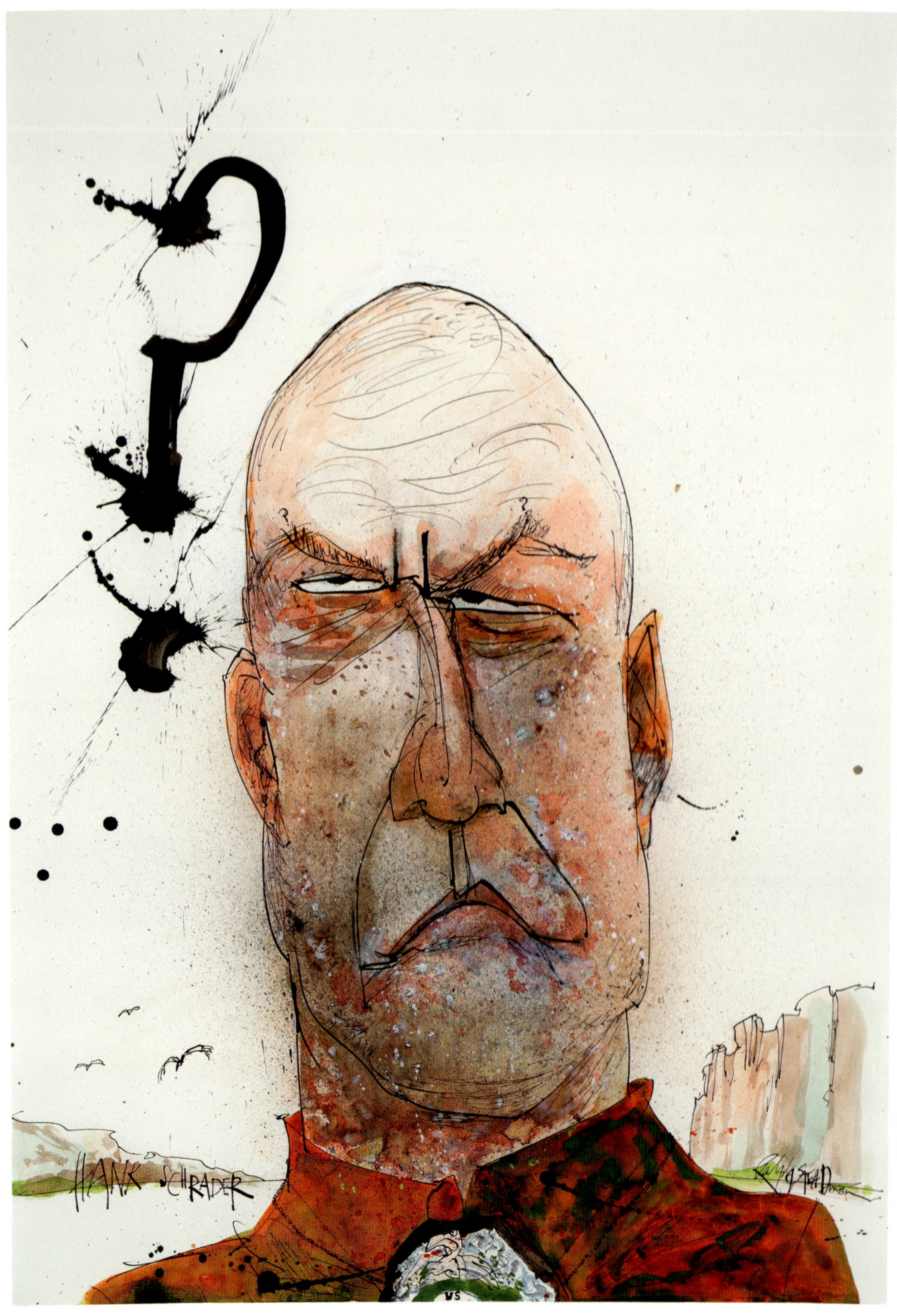

Hank Schrader, **Breaking Bad Collector's Edition** DVD, Sony, 2014

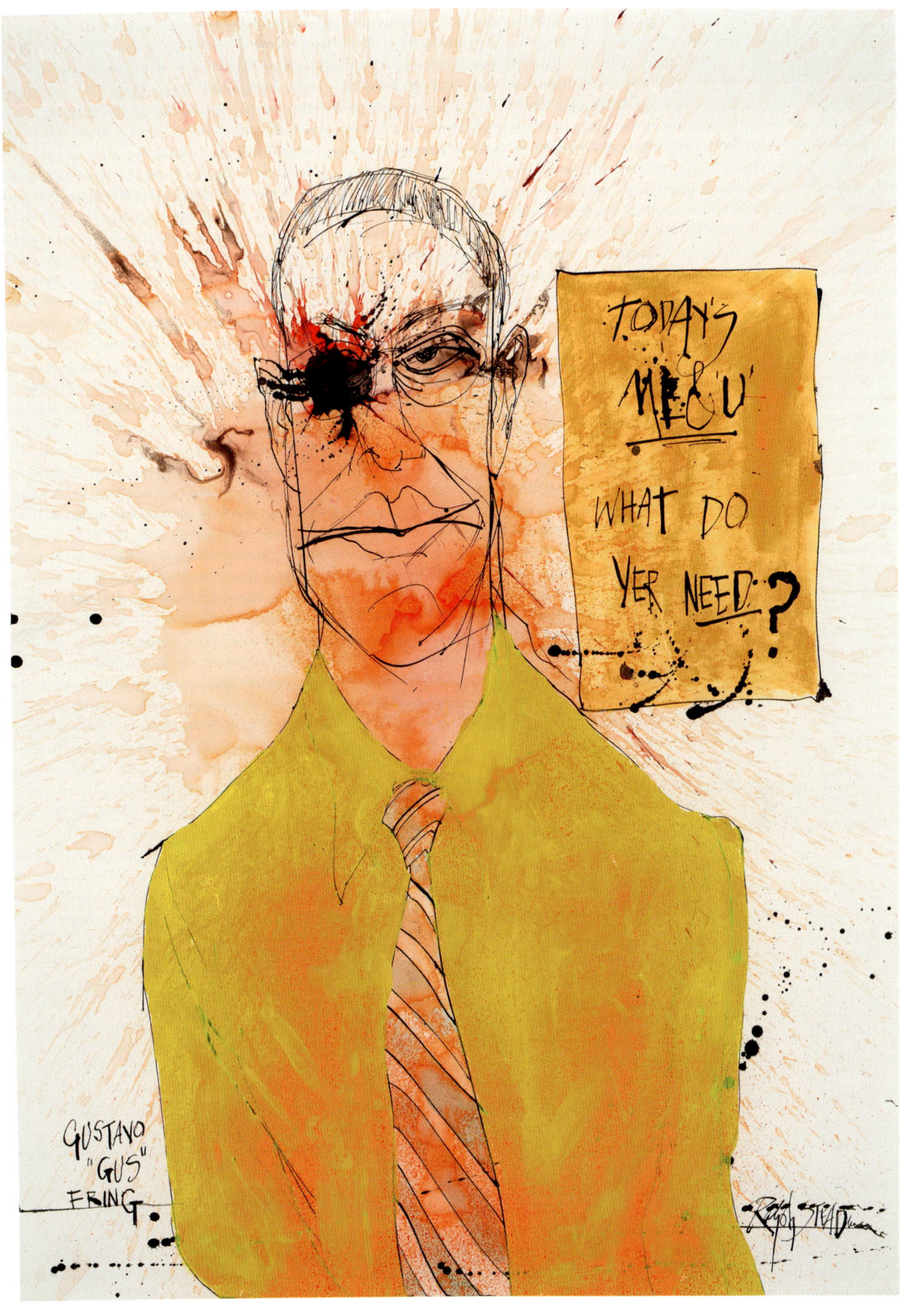

Gus Fring, ***Breaking Bad Collector's Edition*** *DVD, Sony, 2014* "Someone once commented that I had only drawn the male characters in the show. In fact there are two portraits of Skyler White, but they were not cleared for use, and will likely never see the light of day."

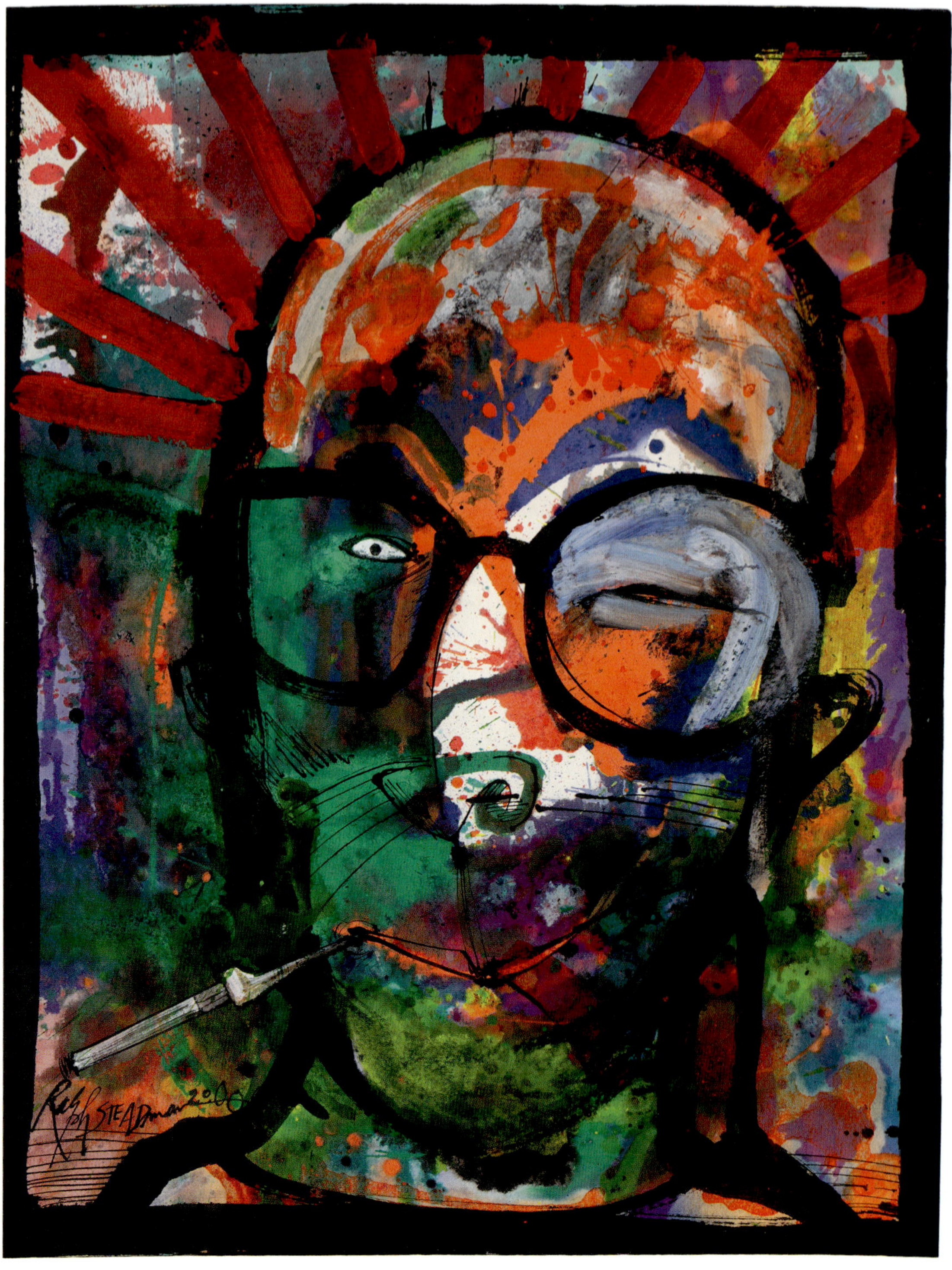

Psychedelic Hunter as the Dalai Lama, 2000

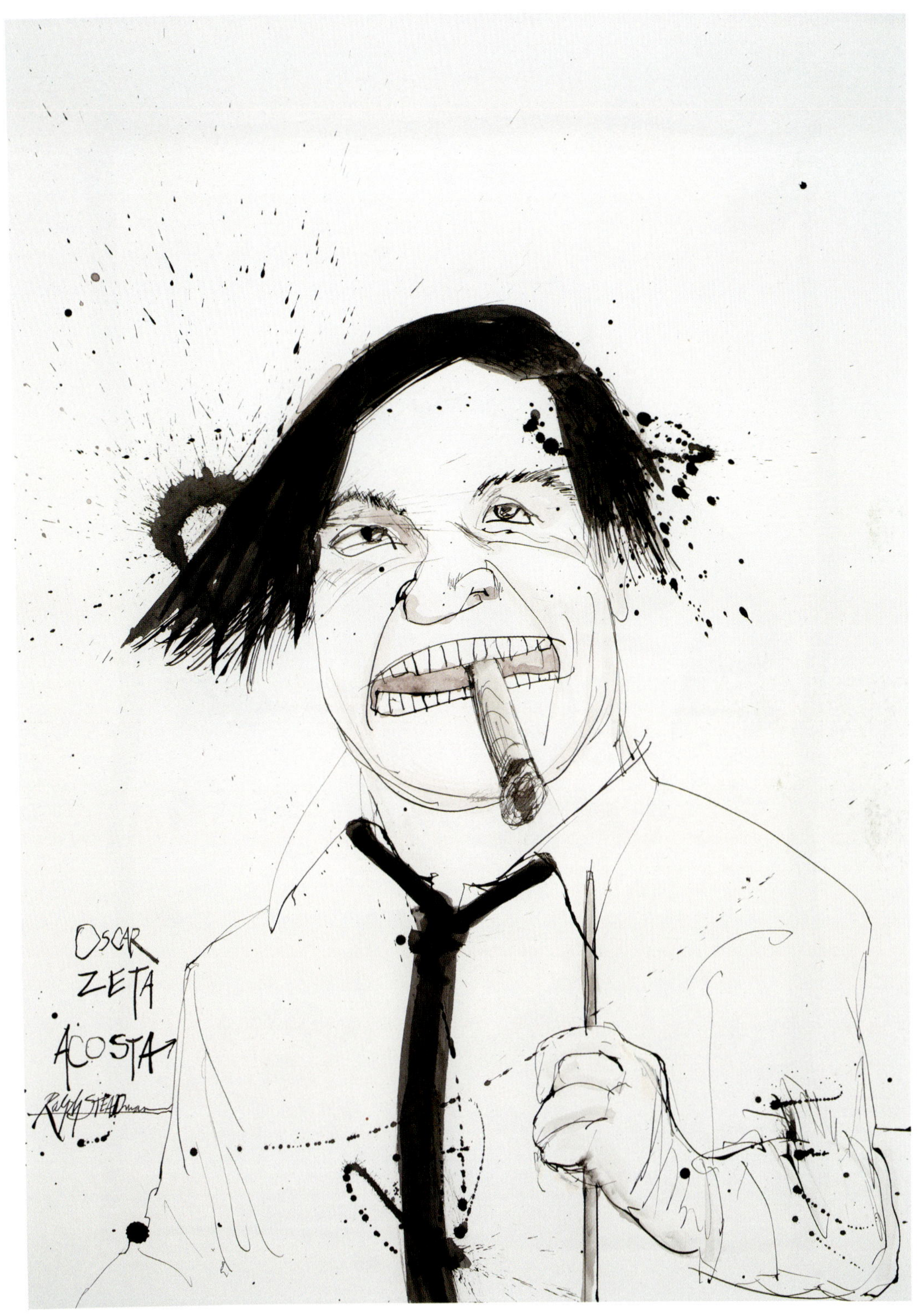

*Oscar Zeta Acosta, who was Hunter's companion in **Fear and Loathing in Las Vegas**—it was not Ralph as many people suppose. 2019*

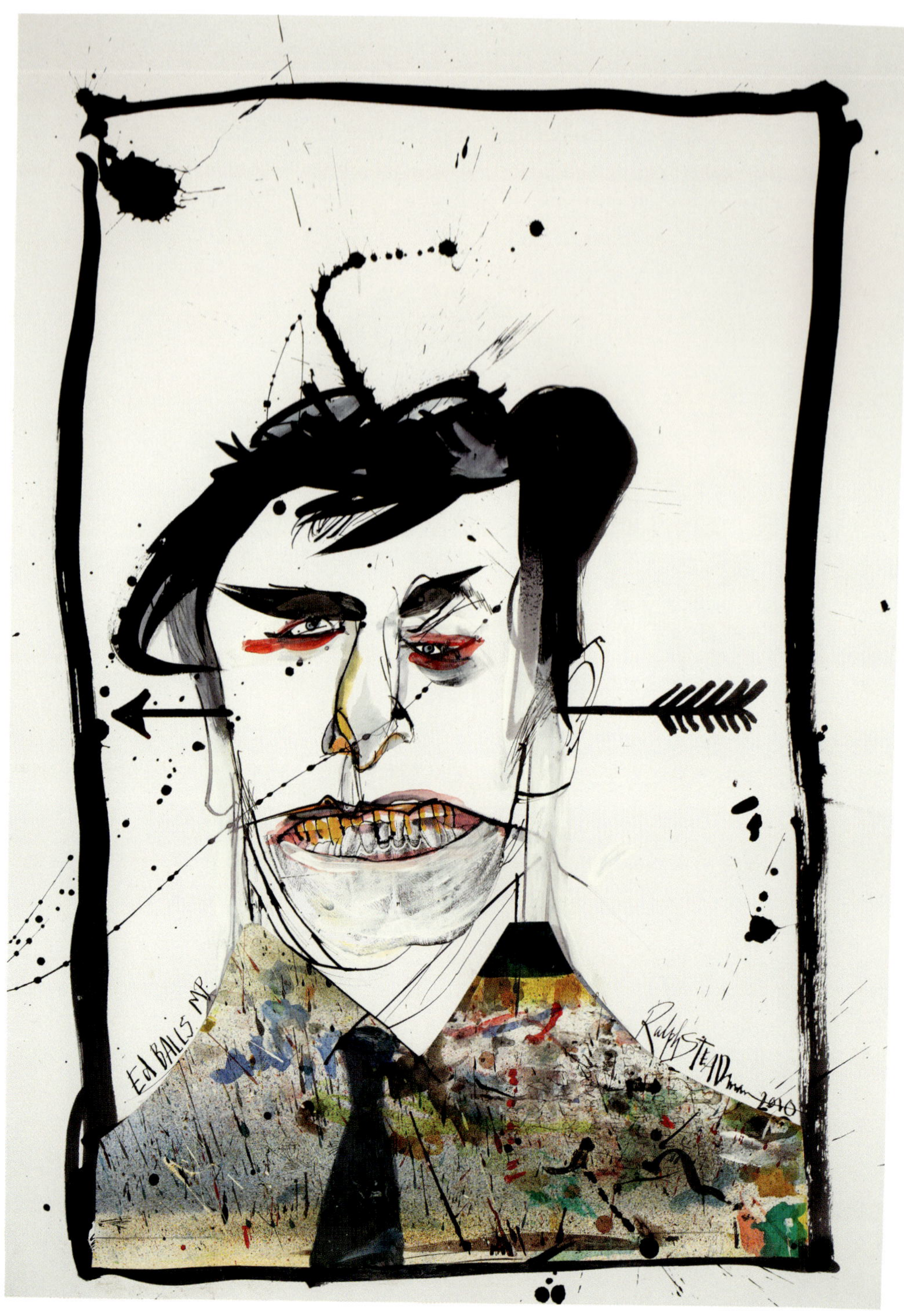

Ed Balls MP, 2010

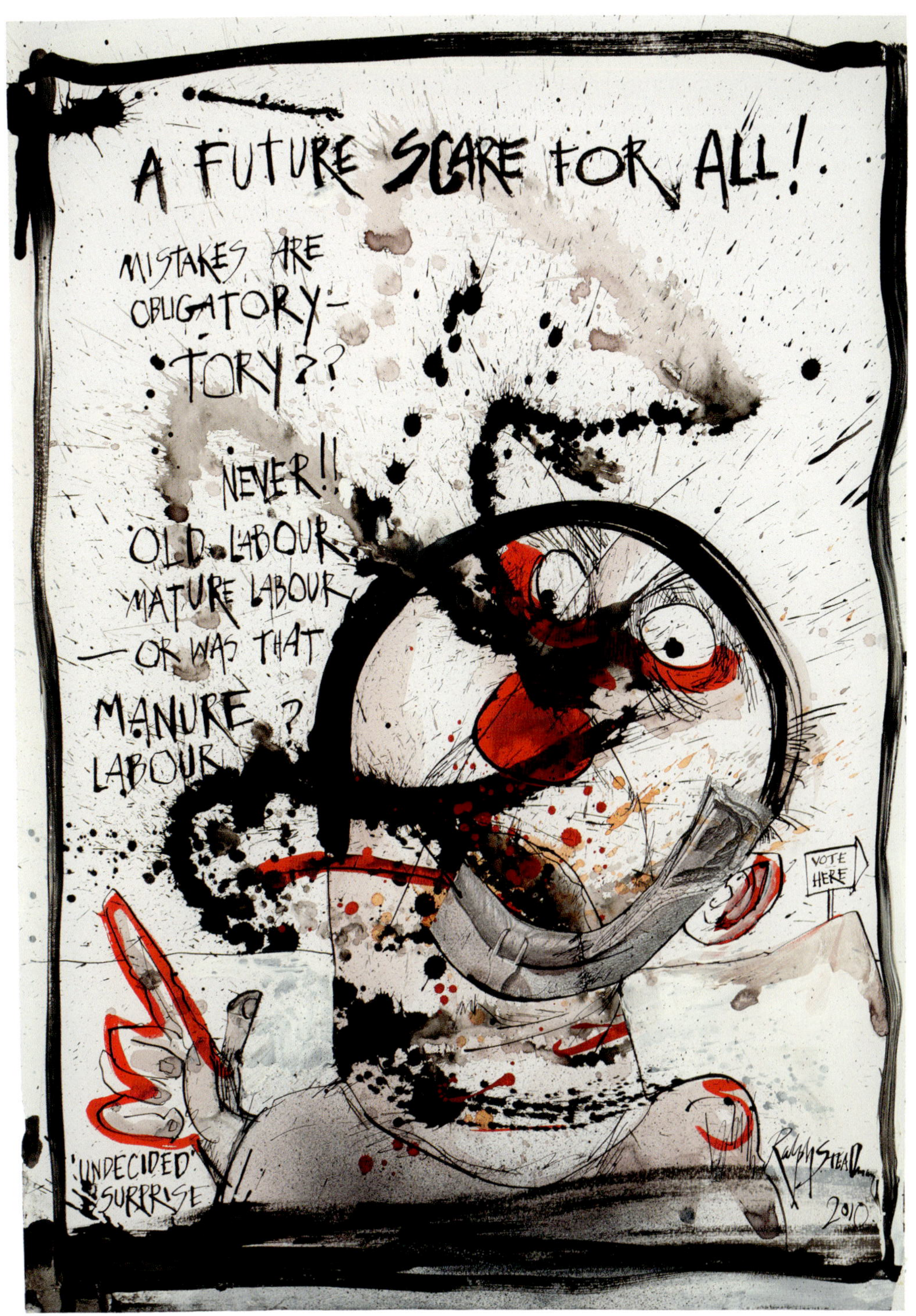

Obligatory Tory, 2010

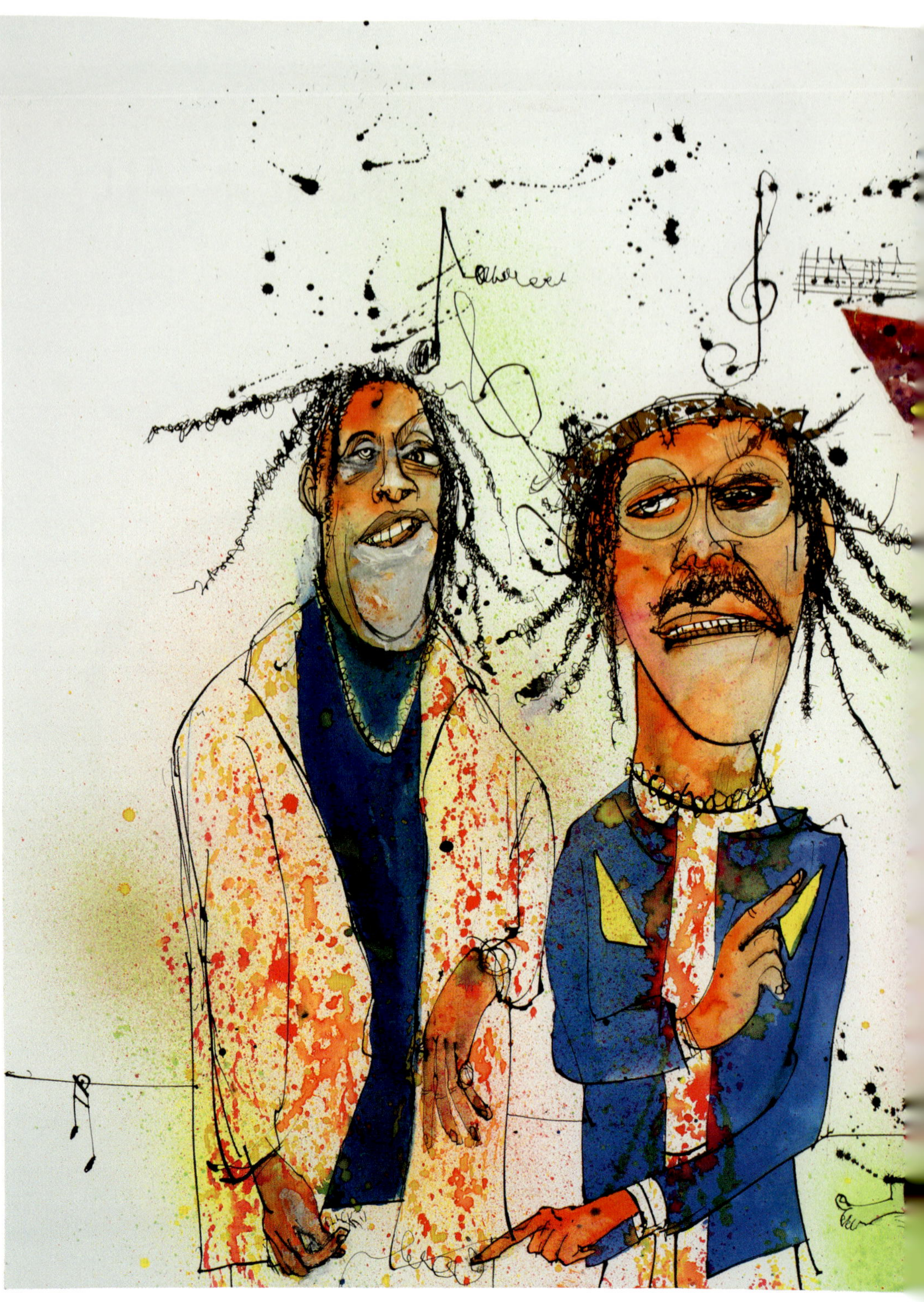

Huncho Jack, Jack Huncho, album cover artwork for Quavo and Travis Scott, 2017 "The artwork they used for the album was the half-completed version of this, which one of the studio elves had decided to photograph and send over so they could see the direction they were going in."

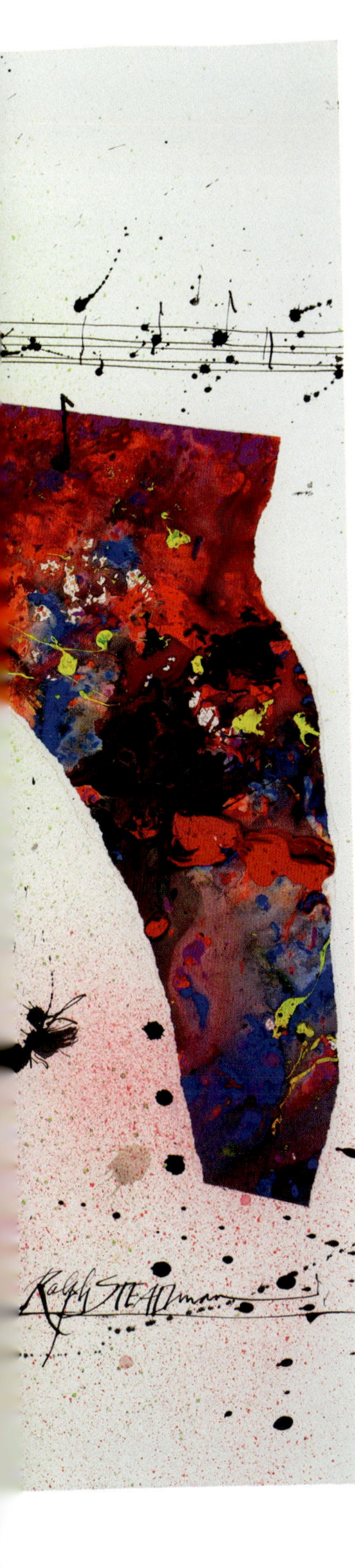

Ralph STEADman

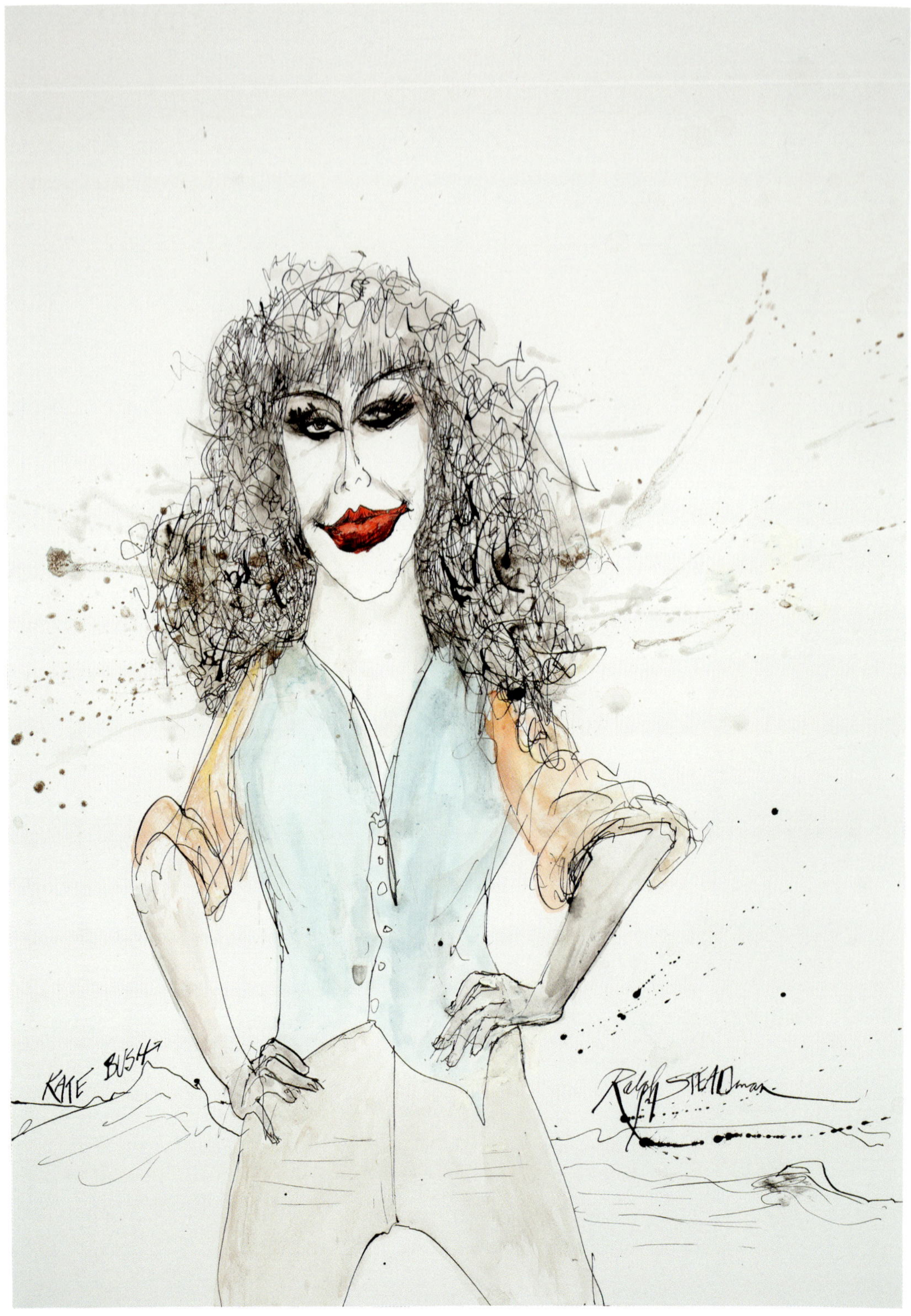

Kate Bush, 2018

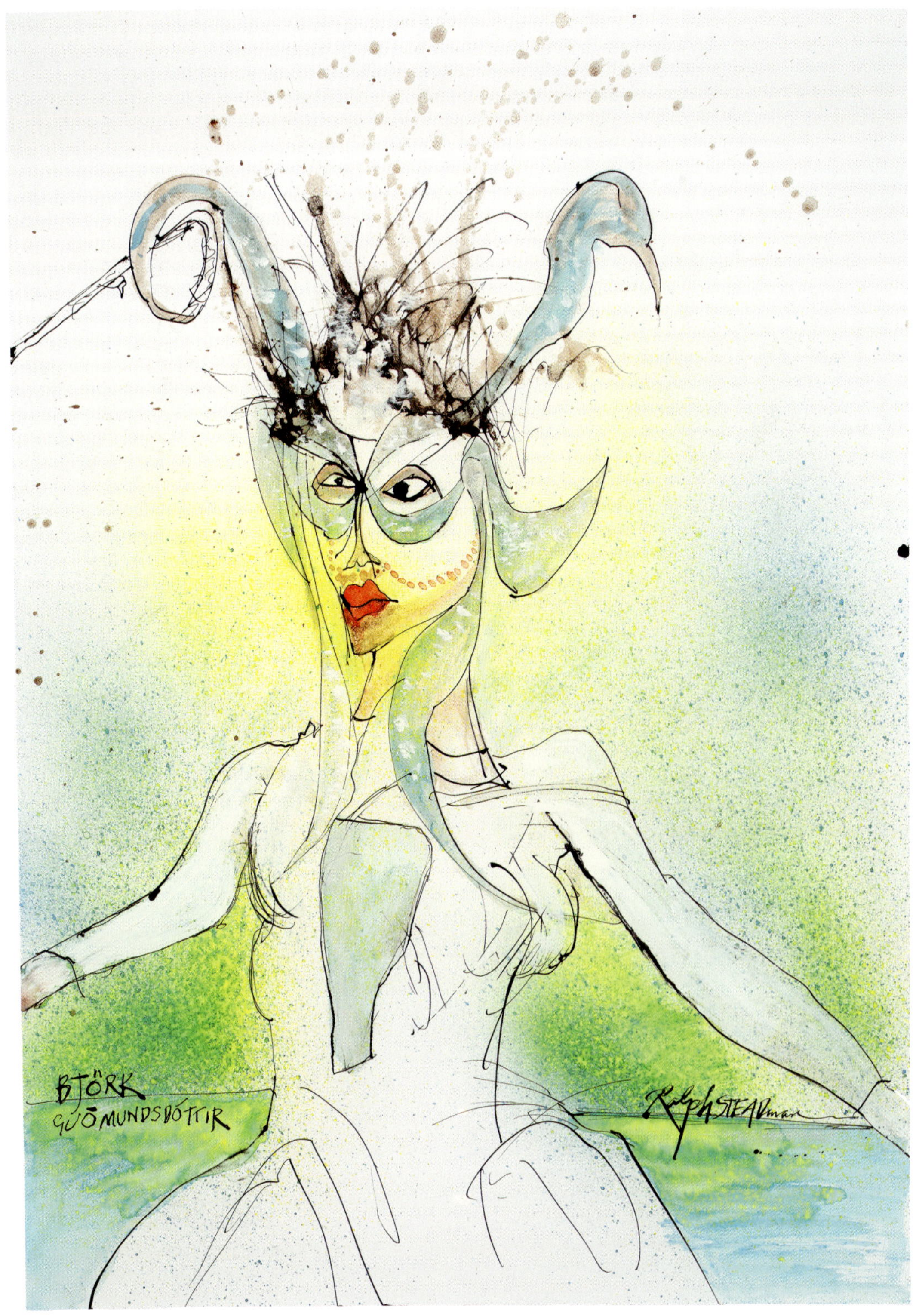

Bjork, created for Sonos for a store exhibition of original artworks, 2018

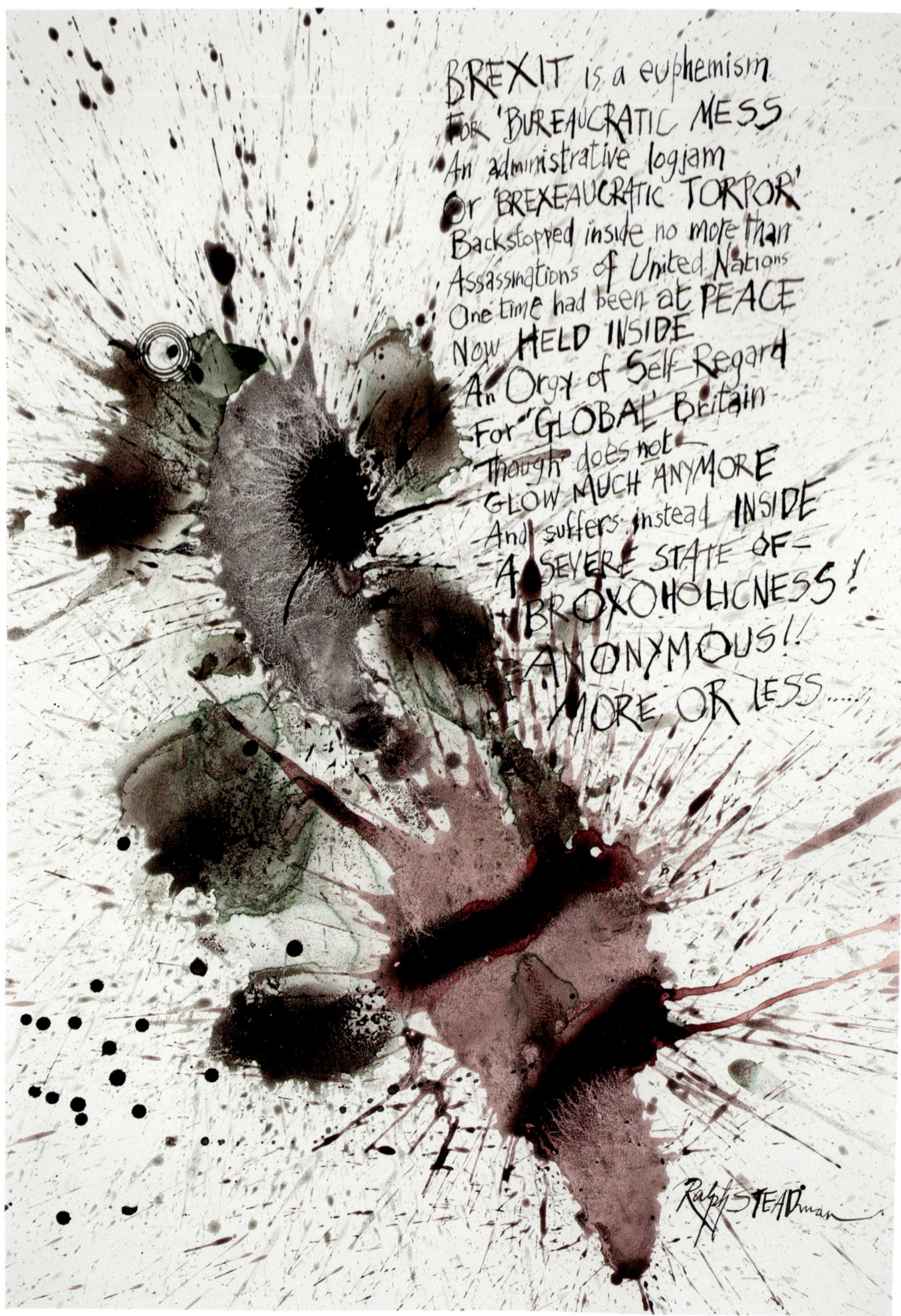

Brexit Poem, Bureaucratic Mess, 2019

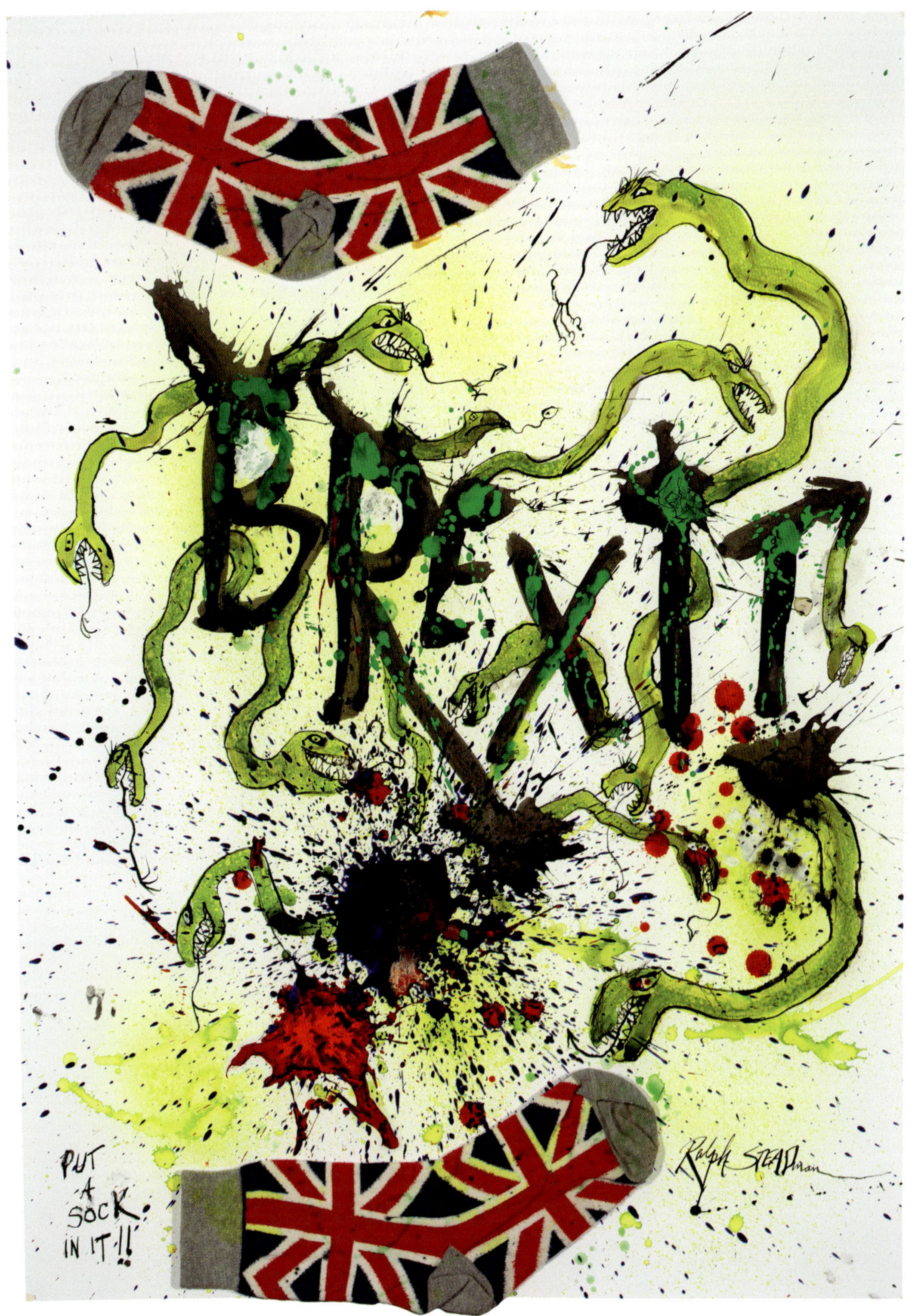

Brexit with Cottage Socks, 2018

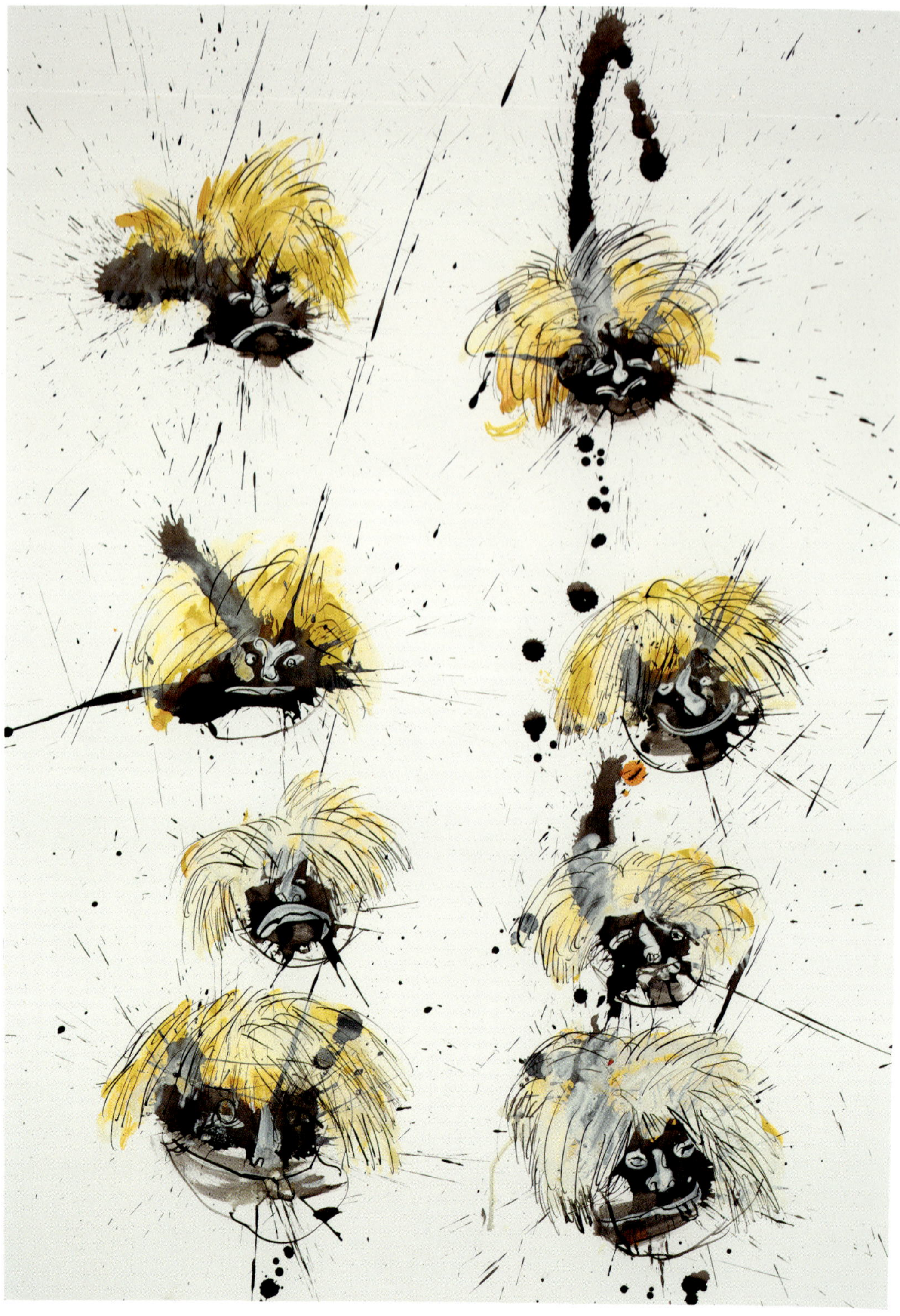

Boris as London Mayor, 2016

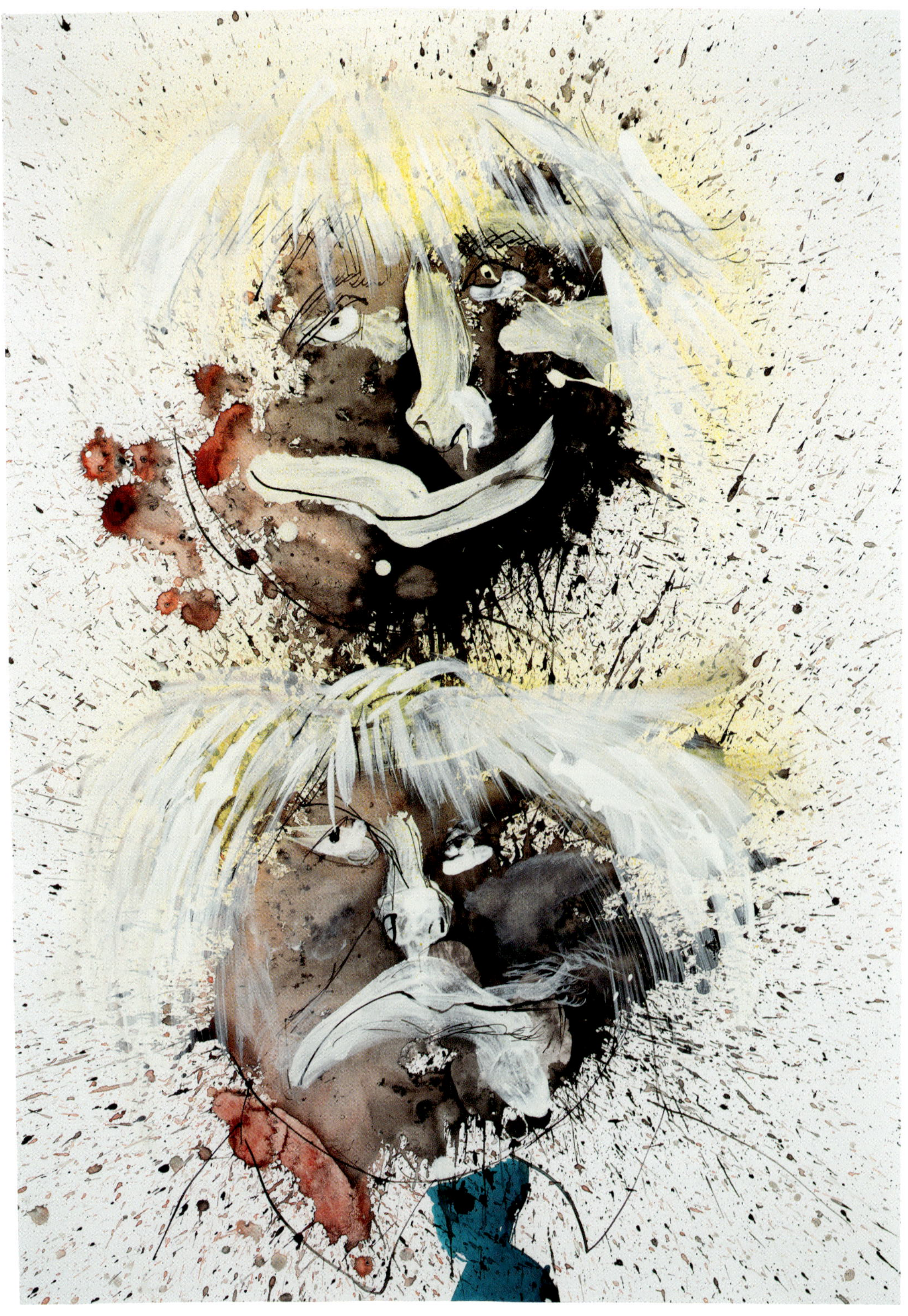

Boris Johnson, 2016

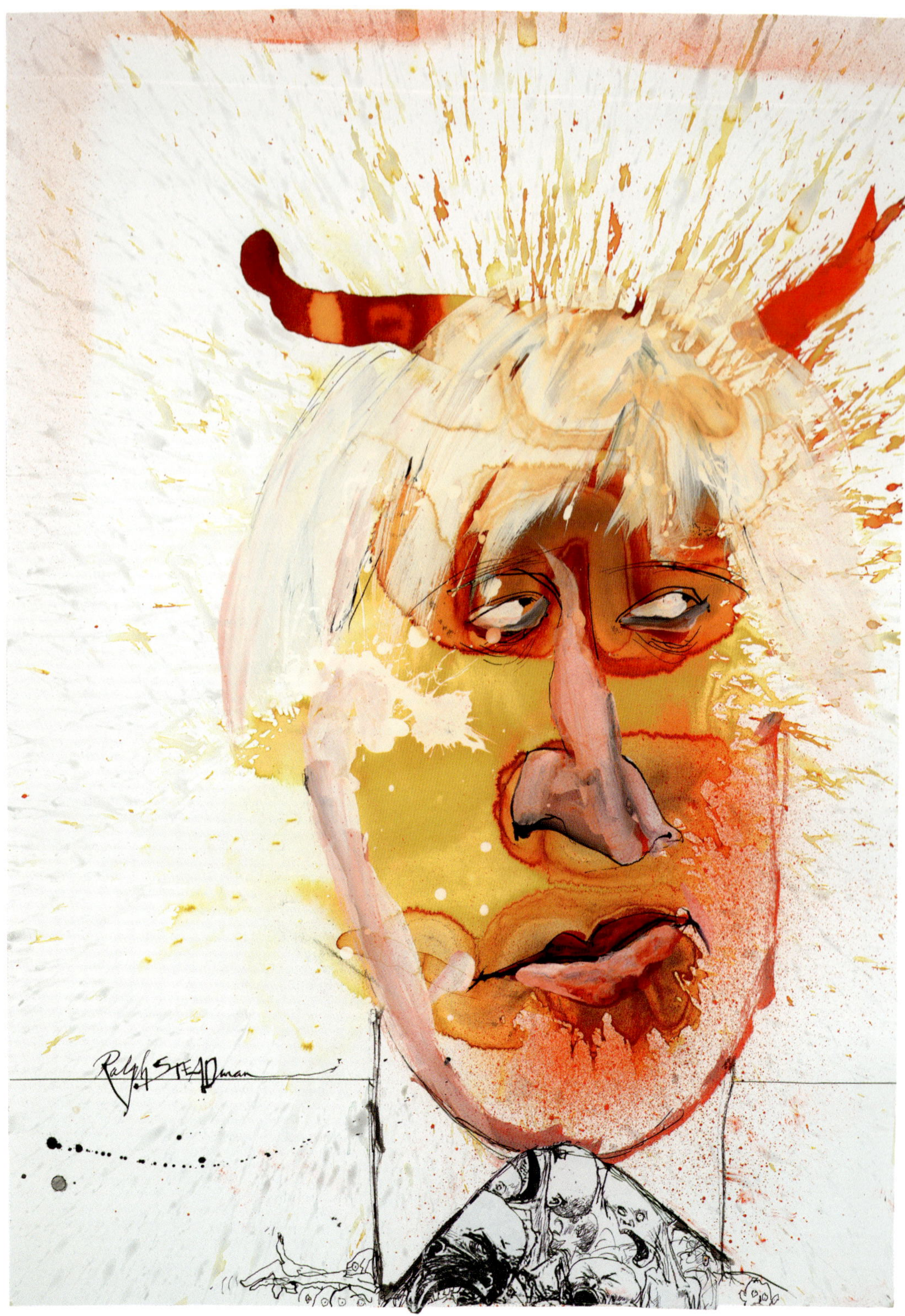

Boris Johnson for the cover of **The Big Issue**, *2019*

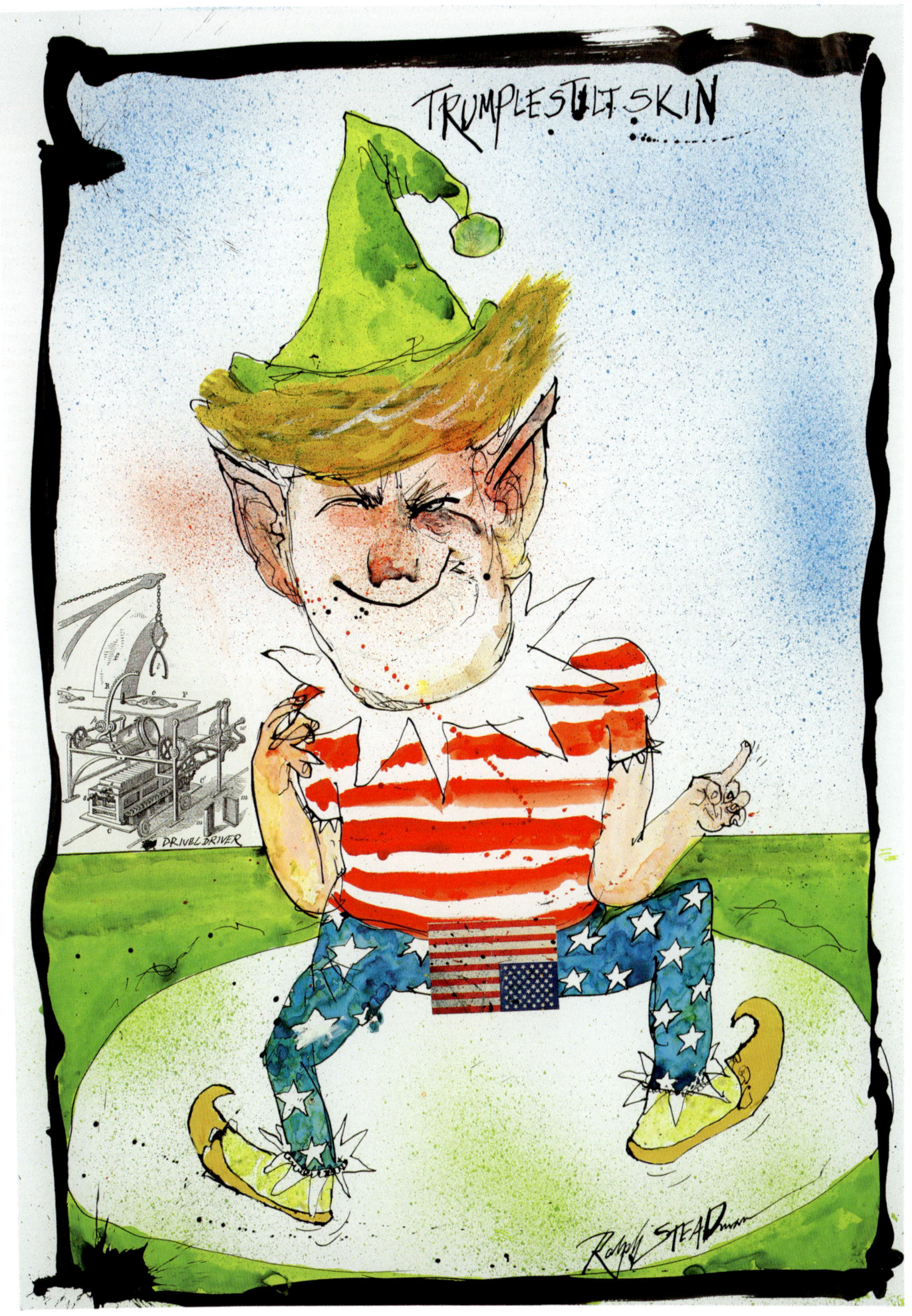

Trumplestiltskin, 2017

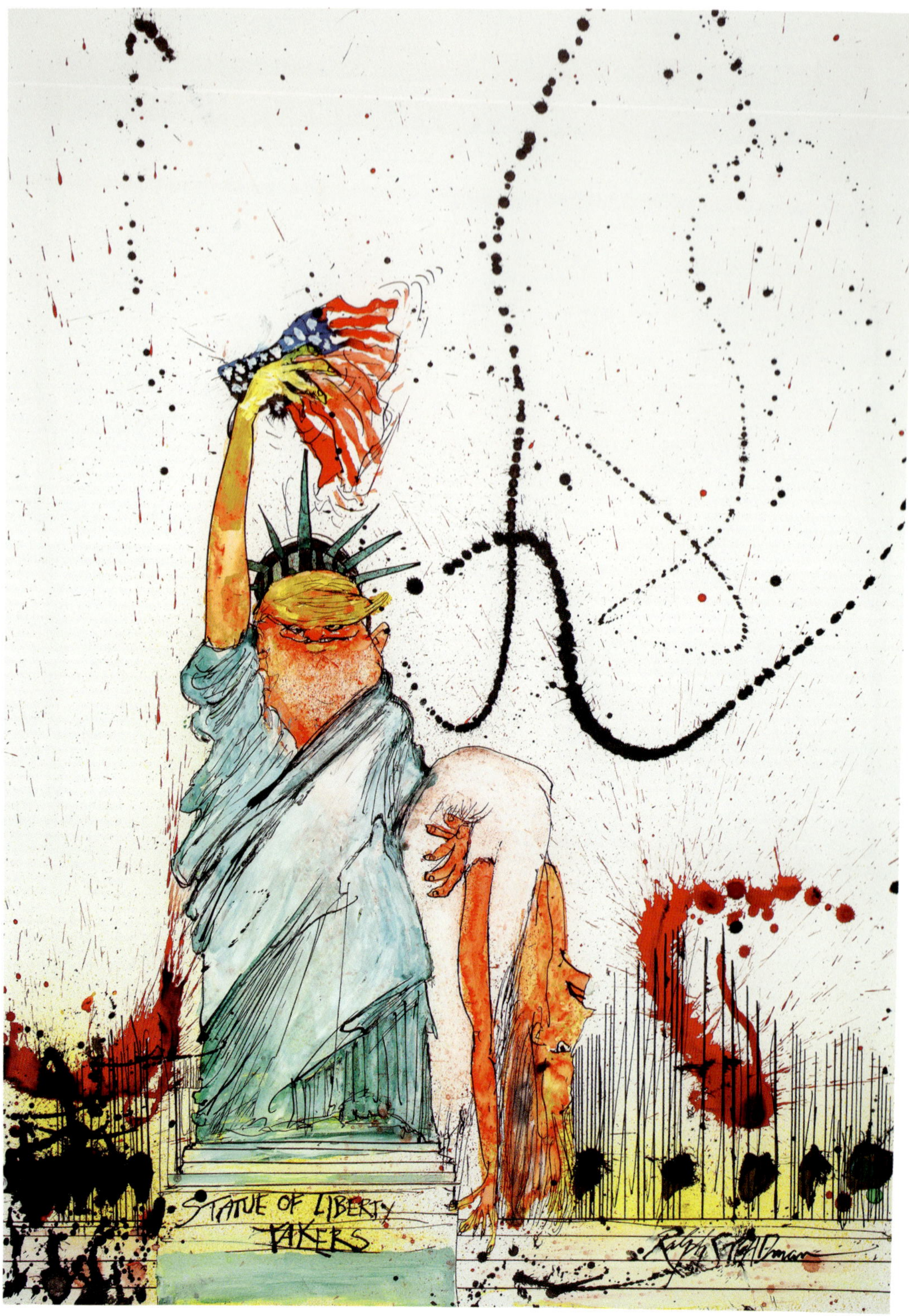

The Statue of Liberty Takers, 2016

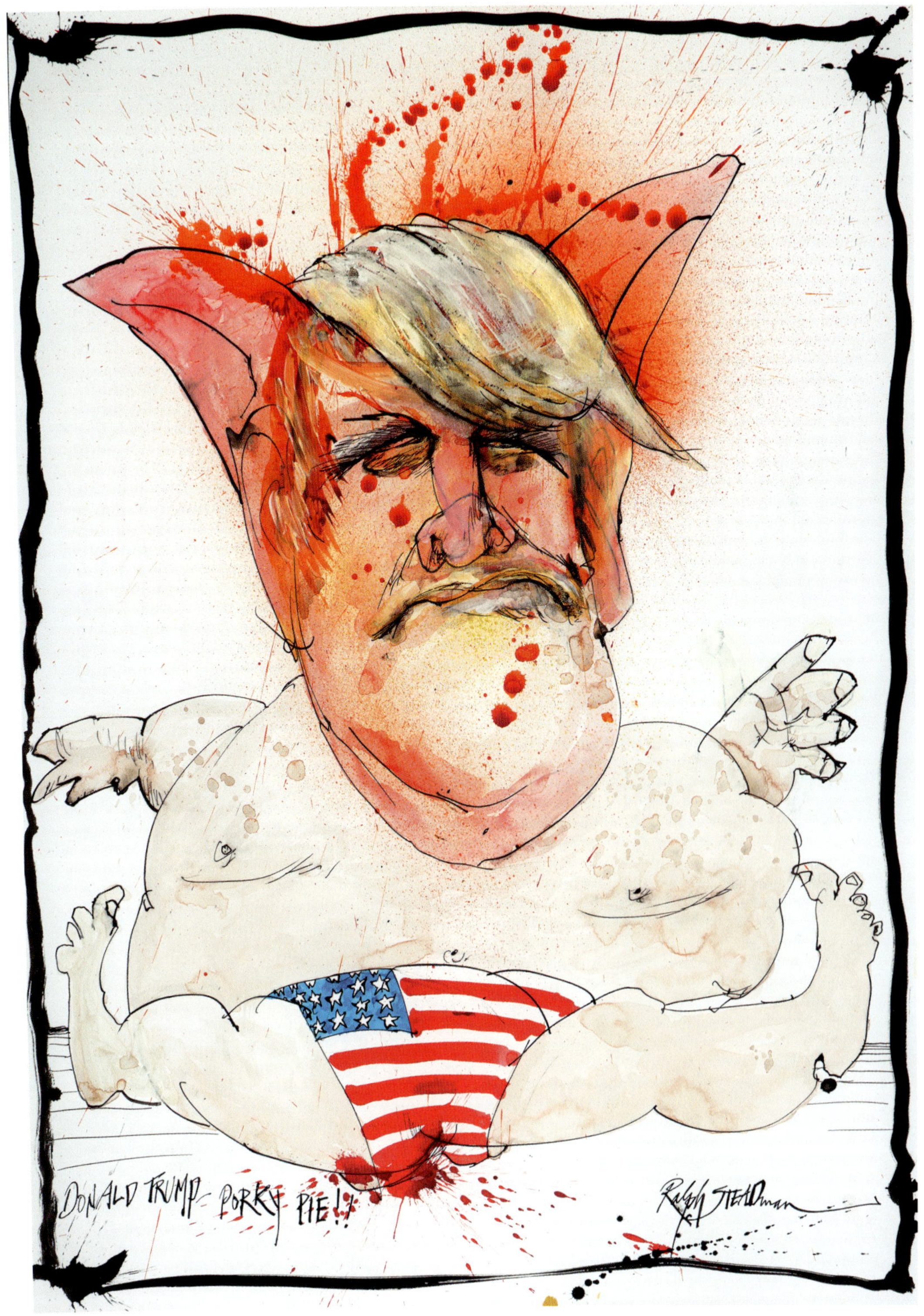

Donald Trump, Porky Pie!!, 2015

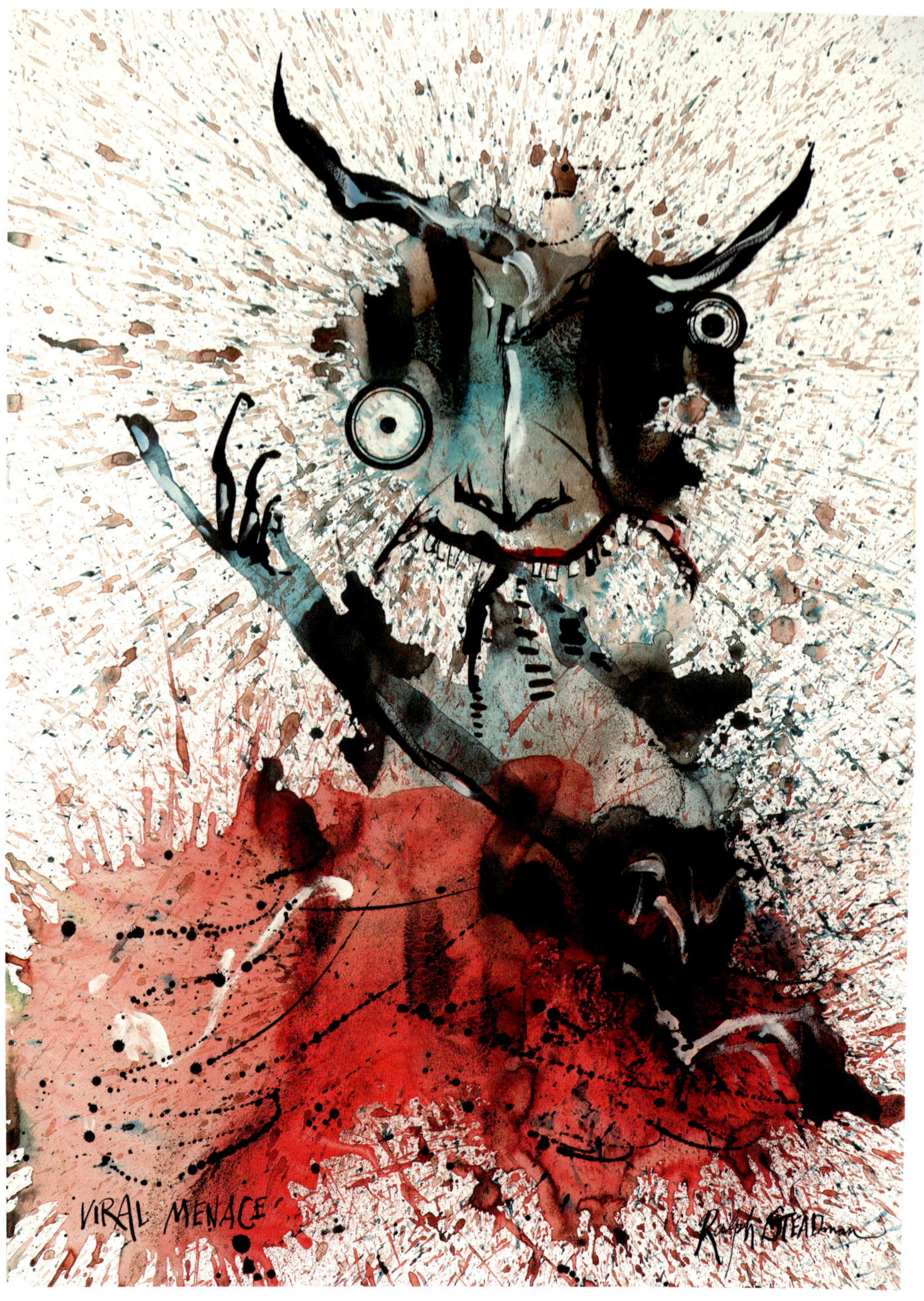

Viral Menace, 2020

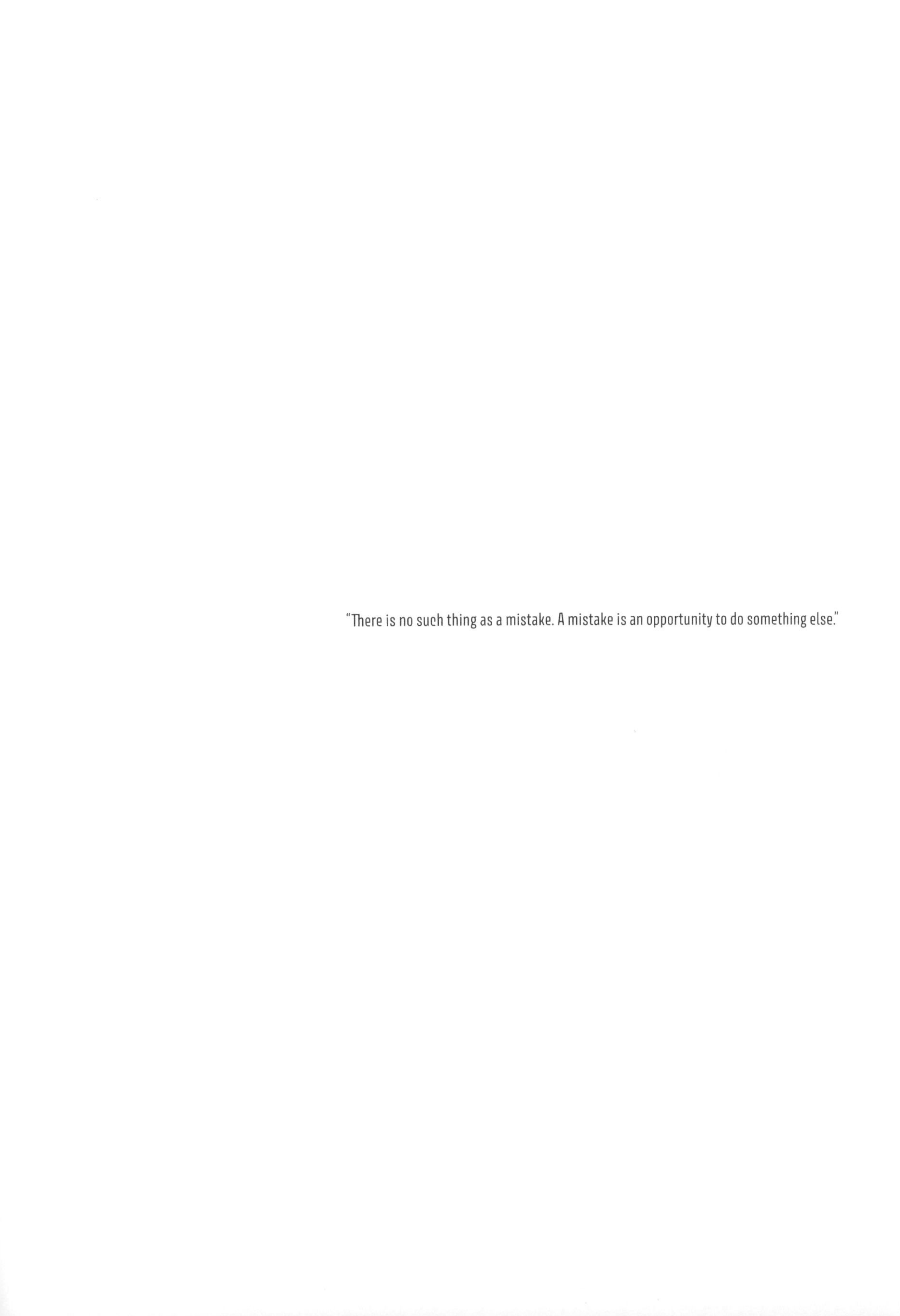

"There is no such thing as a mistake. A mistake is an opportunity to do something else."

It seems I have done a lot of pictures over my lifetime, and pictures explain quite a lot about life that words do not. Right now, we are experiencing one of the worst crises in world history. People are genuinely afraid of consequences they may experience if they haven't already. We have unfortunately talked ourselves into fear, but great kindness and creativity have also come out of this event, and I hope that will carry us through.

What I don't want to do is to stir the animosity, be repetitive, be pessimistic—but rather try to look objectively upon the situation that has received more comment in so many different directions it has almost been talked out of existence, used and misused in every which way possible. I look at my pictures and I consider them my contribution to the thought processes that have gone on since the pandemic began and before.

If we have learnt anything about ourselves during this pandemic, it's that everybody seems to have an opinion.

We can only be positive about this period when somebody actually produces a vaccine.

To finish on a high note, I think we are all seriously doomed. Listen for the blackbird, which has the most beautiful song you can imagine.

As I look back over these pictures, at least they leave me with surprise and the realization that I worked in a way that I always thought was a part of the reason I started—a picture explains so much more than words.

Ralph Idris Steadman
Maidstone, Kent, England
July 22, 2020

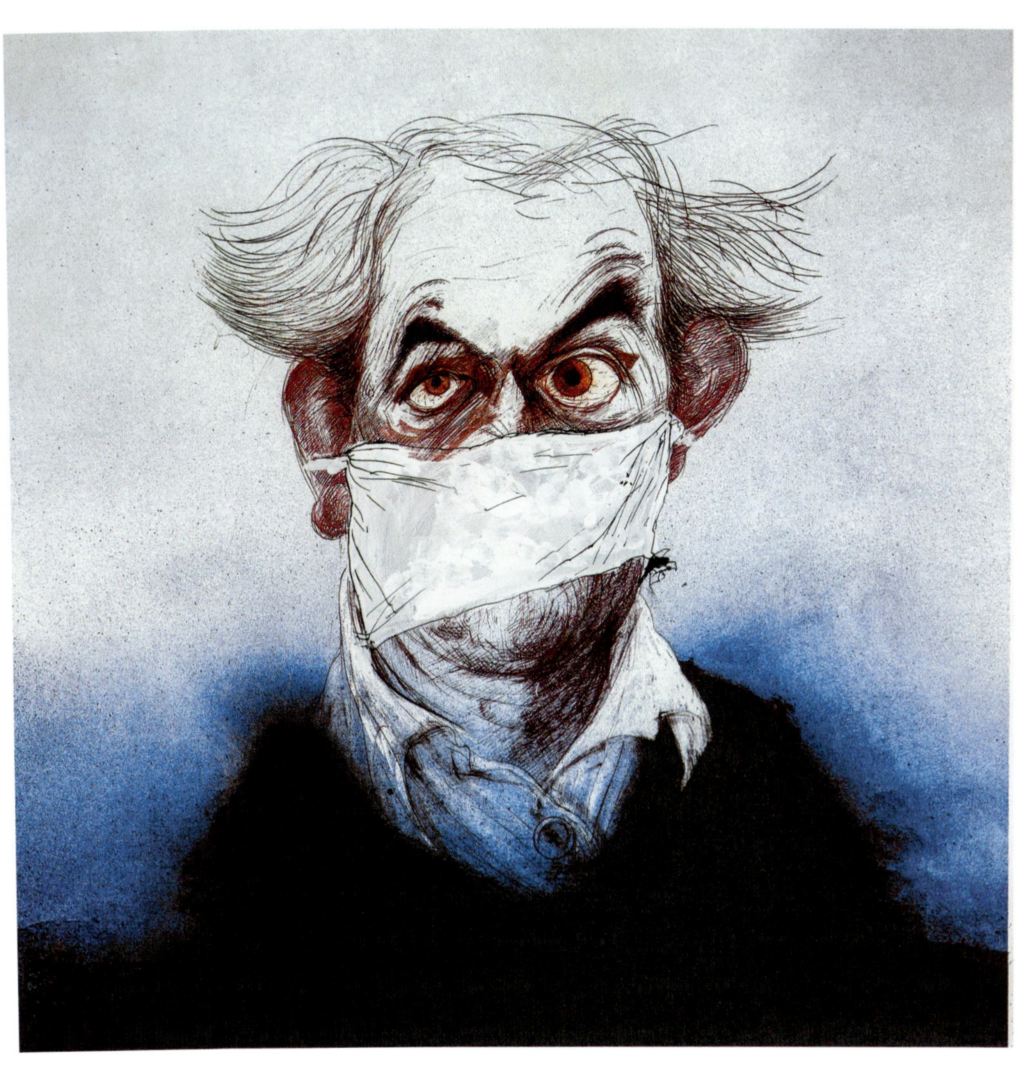

Silk Screen print of the portrait from **Between the Eyes** with hand-drawn surgical mask.
Hand-coloured print in response to Covid 19, 2020

Honour Roll

Charlotte Bellett

Percy V. Bradshaw

Georges Braque

Bob Braudis

William S. Burroughs

Jim Caruso

Bill Cardoso

Robert Chalmers

Sid Cole

Ian Craig

Quentin Crisp

Michael Dempsey

Marcel Duchamp

Raoul Duke

Sigmund Freud

Conrad Frost

Debra Fuller

Giles

Terry Gilliam

Gillray

God

Don Goddard

Gerry and Christine Goldstein

George Grosz

Warren Hinckle

William Hogarth

Leslie Illingworth

Joe Jenkins

Grace Jenkins

Rebecca Jenkins

Suzannah Jenkins

Gordon Kerr

Anita Kunz

Ceri Levy

Lulu the Dog

Adrian Mitchell

Mr "Baggy" Morgan

Laila Nabulsi

Anita O'Brien

Charlie and Lucy Paul

Joe Petro III

Pablo Picasso

Leslie Richardson

Martin Rowson

Ronald Searle

Will Self

Nat Sobel

Ella Steadman

Finn Steadman

Genevive Steadman

Gwen and Lional Steadman

Henry Steadman

Noah Steadman

Theo Steadman

Abner Stein

John Steinberg

"Stella"

Bernard Stone

George Stranahan

Laurie Taylor

Hunter S. Thompson

Gavin Twinge

Vicky

The V&A Museum

Leonardo da Vinci

Kurt Vonnegut

Jann Wenner

Andrew Williams

Oliver Williams

Toby Williams

Terry and Jean Williams

Hal Willner

Winsor & Newton

Ralph Steadman. A Life In Ink.

Published by: Steve Crist and Gloria Fowler

Edited by: Steve Crist and Sadie Steadman Williams

Artwork Photography: Sadie Steadman Williams, Ollie Harrop, and Holly Craven

Design: Carrie Worthen & Ben Pope, Thirdthing

Production: Alexandria Martinez

Copy Editor: Sara Richmond

Ralph Steadman would like to thank:
Steve Crist
Anna Steadman
Holly Craven
Sadie Williams

Steve Crist would like to thank:
Ralph, Anna and Sadie
Adia Wright
Gloria Fowler
Laila Nabulsi
Hunter Stockton Thompson

This Chronicle Chroma edition published in 2025.
Originally published in hardcover in 2020 by Chronicle Chroma.

ISBN: 978-1-7972-3475-5
Library of Congress Cataloging-in-Publication Data available.

The Library of Congress has cataloged the previous edition under
ISBN 978-1-7972-0300-3.

Manufactured in Malaysia

CHRONICLE CHROMA

Chronicle Chroma is an imprint of Chronicle Books
Los Angeles, California

chroniclechroma.com

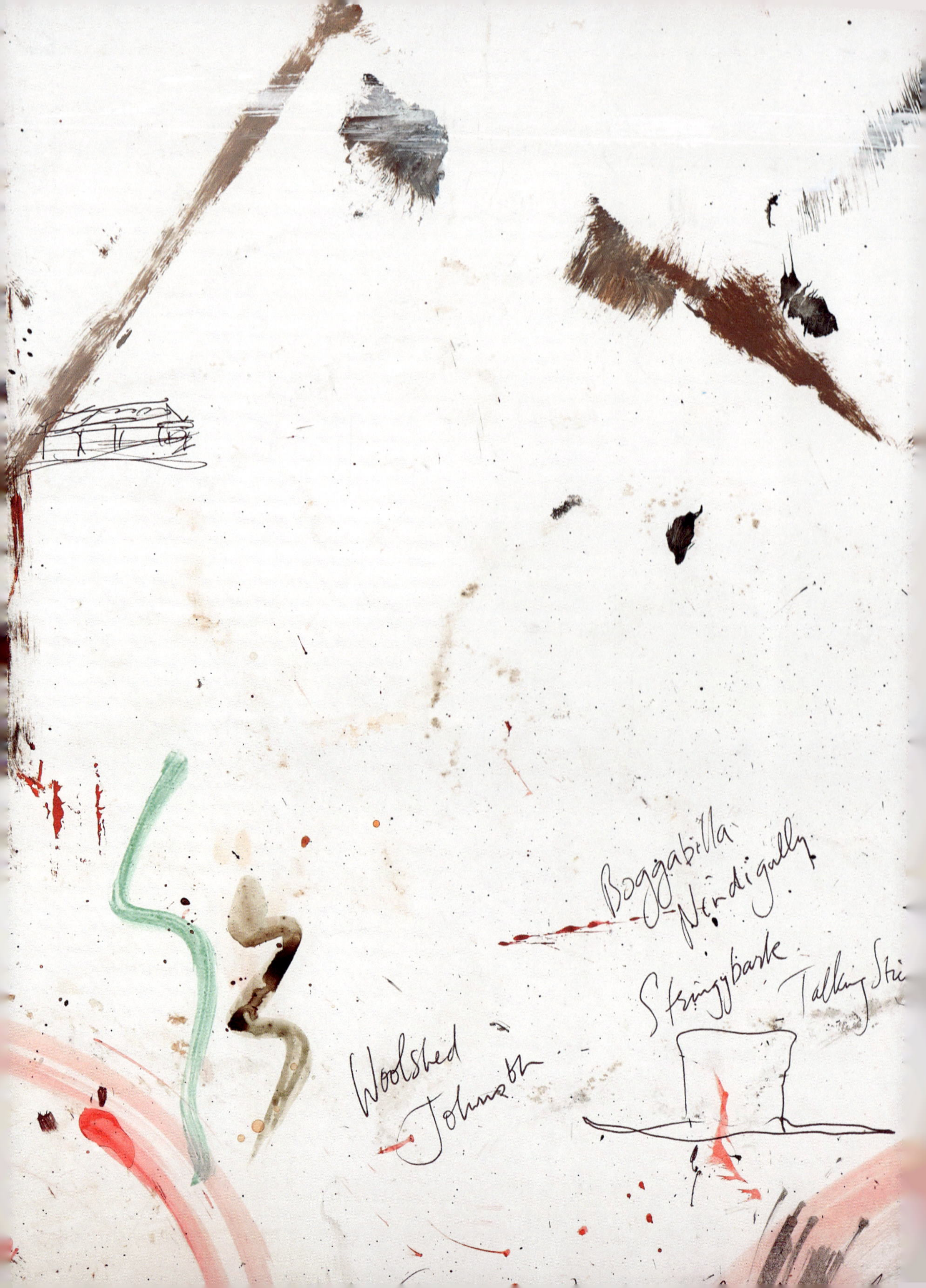

Boggabilla
Nindigully
Stringybark
Talking Sti
Woolshed
Johnson